Strategic Planning for Public Relations

Strategic Planning for Public Relations

Third Edition

Ronald D. Smith, APR

Buffalo State College

Routledge
Taylor & Francis Group
NEW YORK AND LONDON

Senior Commissioning Editor: Linda Bathgate
Textbook Development Editor: Nicole Solano
Editorial Assistant: Katherine Ghezzi
Cover Design: Kathryn Houghtaling
Production Manager: Mhairi Baxter

This edition published 2009
by Routledge
270 Madison Ave, New York, NY 10016

Simultaneously published in the UK
by Routledge
2 Park Square, Milton Park, Abingdon, Oxon OX14 4RN

Routledge is an imprint of the Taylor & Francis Group, an informa business

Typeset in Abode Caslon and Times New Roman by
Florence Production Ltd, Stoodleigh, Devon
Printed and bound in the United States of America on acid-free paper by
Edwards Brothers Inc.

Library of Congress Cataloging in Publication Data
Smith, Ronald D., 1948–.
Strategic planning for public relations/by Ronald D. Smith. – 3rd ed.
p.cm.
1. Public relations. 2. Strategic planning. I. Title.
HM1221.S77 2009
659.2–dc22 2008030593

ISBN10: 0–415–99422–5 (pbk)
ISBN10: 0–203–89118–X (ebk)

ISBN13: 978–0–415–99422–4 (pbk)
ISBN13: 978–0–203–89118–6 (ebk)

Brief Contents

Contents

Preface

Strategic Planning for Public Relations offers college and university students a new way to deepen their understanding of public relations and other kinds of strategic communication. It is intended for people serious about entering a profession that is rapidly changing—a profession that is shedding a past that often involved merely performing tasks managed by others and taking on a newer, more mature role in the management of organizations based on research-driven strategic planning, ethical principles, and programmatic evaluation.

This book provides an in-depth approach to public relations planning, more comprehensive than can be found anywhere else. It is built on a step-by-step unfolding of the planning process most often used in public relations, with explanations, examples, and exercises that combine to guide students toward a contemporary understanding of the profession. It is written in a reader-friendly style designed to appeal both to students and practitioners.

The approach used in *Strategic Planning for Public Relations* is rooted in the author's belief and observation that students learn best through a threefold pattern of being exposed to an idea, seeing it in use, and then applying it themselves. This is the rhythm of this book—its cadence, if you will. This is the design that takes a complex problem-solving and decision-making process and turns it into a series of easy-to-follow steps. These nine steps provide enough flexibility to make the process applicable to all kinds of situations and to organizations with different missions, diverse sizes, varying resources, and differing skill levels among the staff.

This third edition of *Strategic Planning for Public Relations* follows the same format as the previous editions. It updates examples and incorporates recent research. It also adds a few new sections, particularly a section on stereotyping in Step 3 and a section on statistics in Step 6.

Note to Students

Thank you for allowing me to share my ideas and insights into a profession that I have found to be both challenging and rewarding. I wish you much success as you proceed toward a career that I hope you, too, will discover to be exhilarating.

I stumbled into public relations somewhat by accident, at least not by my own conscious design. I began my career as a newspaper reporter, and later as an editor, with some side trips into television writing and producing, freelance magazine writing, and newsletter editing. I then made the transition into public relations—at first building on a familiar base of media relations, publicity, and newsletters, and only later navigating into issues management, crisis response, integrated communication, and a host of related areas. Along the way I incorporated the new technological developments (particularly desktop publishing, e-mail, and the Internet) and now wonder how we once managed without these tools. Frankly, I wish there had been a book like this to guide me toward an understanding of how to undertake public relations, especially the research and planning parts. So I'm pleased to be able to share with you some of the insights I've picked up along the way.

With this book and the practical exercises that go with it, you are proceeding along the road to professional success. I wish you the best of luck.

You should be aware that this book is intended for group development and class activities. While you certainly can use it alone, you will find that it comes more fully alive as a text to guide group projects. Even if you are not a student in a traditional classroom, try to use this book in the context of your own project task force or professional work team.

Note to Public Relations Practitioners

The author is proud to note that the Public Relations Society of America has found *Strategic Planning for Public Relations* to be relevant for practitioners. The PRSA selected the book for its short list of endorsed readings for candidates of the APR professional accrediting exam.

I've heard from many public relations practitioners who have used the previous editions of this book and are looking forward to this edition. Some find it useful in their day-to-day work, particularly those who are working public relations without benefit of an educational background in the discipline. I myself entered the professional with a background in journalism, so I understand the pros and cons of learning public relations on the job. I'm pleased that this book has been helpful to many of my professional colleagues.

The book also has spurred others who have written to me with issues and comments from their vantage as leaders within the field of public relations. It has been particularly rewarding to hear not only from the PRSA and various U.S. chapters, but also from our Canadian counterpart, the Canadian Public Relations Society, as well as public relations people around the world, including the Azerbaijan Public Relations Association.

Note to Instructors

Thank you for choosing this textbook for your students. Thanks especially for the opportunity to share with them some of my thoughts and observations on an exciting profession. I trust that you will find the information contained in this book to be well within the framework of contemporary professional practice and academic principles.

Strategic Planning for Public Relations grew out of my observation that students seem to learn best when they understand concepts, have patterns to follow and adapt, and have the opportunity to work individually and in groups on tasks that gradually unfold to reveal the bigger picture. This is my intention with this book—to provide a structure, yet to give you much flexibility in leading your students through the planning process.

I also can share with you that your colleagues have found this book useful in introductory courses as well as in courses focusing on campaign and case studies. Personally, I use the book for an intensive introductory course, supplemented with some online information on history and other foundational elements such as my website—http://faculty.buffalostate.edu/smithrd—which you are free to use if you find it helpful. We also use the book in our senior-level campaign course as the basis for students developing their own campaign proposals. Additionally, the book serves as a basis for the campaigns that our graduate students develop.

Acknowledgments

John Dunne was right that no one is an island. Neither does an author write alone, but instead reflects in some way the insight of others in the field who write, teach and engage in the practice.

Strategic Planning for Public Relations enjoys the input of many people. As the author of this textbook, I'll take personal responsibility for any errors or omissions, but I'm confident these are fewer because of the advice and assistance of many knowledgeable people who helped along the way.

Collectively, my students have been major contributors to this book. It is in the classroom that I have tested and refined the ideas contained herein. My students have prodded me to articulate my ideas and to bolster them with plenty of real-world examples.

My academic colleagues at Buffalo State College emphasize practical, applied communication, and I have benefited from ongoing professional conversations with them—Marian Deutschman in particular, as well as my newer academic colleague Deborah Silverman, APR. My professional colleagues within the Public Relations Society of America consistently have helped me with their insight and constructive criticism.

In particular, Jeff Paterson, APR; Ann Reynolds Carden, APR and Fellow; Stanton H. Hudson, APR and Fellow, PRSA; and William E. Sledzik, APR and Fellow, PRSA have helped me refine some of my ideas.

The publishing team at Routledge/Taylor & Francis is superb. Linda Bathgate has guided me through the conceptual development of this third edition, steering it to its final form.

Personal Dedication

Like the entirety of my life, *Strategic Planning for Public Relations* is dedicated to my family. Though they don't realize it, my three sons have been an inspiration as I worked on this book.

As he progressed through his teaching job near Kobe, Japan, and now through his doctoral studies at the University of Osaka, my son Josh has challenged me to explain public relations every time I suggest that he consider the insights of the discipline on his own work as a sociologist studying and participating in Japanese culture. My son Aaron graduated with a degree in public relations and after starting his own business in the field joined the Army, continuing to develop his excellent writing skills and his keen strategic sense. My youngest son Matt is still uncertain about his career plans, but I'm confident that his writing talent and artistic sensitivity will serve him well in whatever he does.

My greatest appreciation goes to my wife, Dawn Minier Smith. During the evolution of each edition of this and my other books—indeed, during my entire teaching career—Dawn has been my sounding board. A teacher herself, she has lent her ear as I tested ideas, tried out new ways to present lessons, and attempted to make sense of theories, cases and observations. Since she doesn't see any domestic value in a wife fawning over her husband, Dawn's constructive criticism has been always trustworthy and thus most valuable. I always take her suggestions seriously. Sometimes I've even had the good sense to follow them.

An Invitation

This book is the result of much dialogue with others, particularly feedback from my students. But reader reaction inevitably is useful. I invite all readers—students, teachers, and practitioners—to share your thoughts with me. Give me comments and suggestions for future editions. Share your success stories and your frustrations with this book. I also invite you to use my website, where I have included an expanding number of pages and links related to public relations and other aspects of strategic communication.

—Ron Smith
smithrd@buffalostate.edu
http://faculty.buffalostate.edu/smithrd
http://www.buffalostate.edu/communication

About the Author

Ronald D. Smith, APR is a professor of public communication at Buffalo State College, the largest college within the State University of New York and the only public institution in New York State accredited by the Accrediting Council for Education in Journalism and Mass Communications.

He teaches public relations planning, writing, and related courses to undergraduate and graduate students, and since 2003 has served as chair of the 550-student Communication Department. As time permits, he also is active as a consultant in public relations and strategic communication, assisting businesses and nonprofit organizations with planning, research, communication management, and media training.

In this book, Smith draws on considerable professional experience. In addition to 18 years as an educator, he worked for 10 years as a public relations director and eight years as a newspaper reporter and editor. He also was a Navy journalist in Vietnam.

Smith holds a bachelor's degree in English education from Lock Haven (Pennsylvania) State College (now Lock Haven University) and a master's degree in public relations from Syracuse University. He has presented numerous workshops and seminars and has published research on public relations and persuasive communication.

He is the author of *Becoming a Public Relations Writer* (3rd edition, 2008) and coauthor, with W. Richard Whitaker and Janet E. Ramsey, of *MediaWriting* (3rd edition, 2009), both published by Routledge/Taylor & Francis. He has also written *Introduction to Language and Communication: A Primer on Human and Media Communication* (United Arab Emirates University, 2004) and the chapter "Campaign Design and Management" in *21st Century Communication: A Reference Handbook*, edited by William F. Eadie (Sage, 2009).

Smith also serves as director of the American Indian Policy and Media Initiative at Buffalo State. He has been lead researcher in several studies dealing with media and Native Americans, and is coeditor, with Kara Briggs and José Barreiro, of *Shoot the Indian: Media, Misperception and Native Truth* (AIPMI, 2007). For additional information, see http://www.buffalostate.edu/communication/americanindianinitiative.xml.

Smith is an accredited member of the Public Relations Society of America and has served as president of the PRSA's Buffalo/Niagara chapter and as chair of PRSA's Northeast District. He was named Practitioner of the Year in 1998 by the Buffalo chapter, which has given him several other awards and citations. He also has twice been nominated as PRSA Educator of the Year.

Cases and Examples

Following is an index of actual cases, persons, organizations and events cited in *Strategic Planning for Public Relations* as examples of various principles, strategies, tactics, and techniques.

Introduction

Why write a book on strategic planning for public relations? Because effective and creative planning is at the heart of all public relations and related activity. And because the field is changing. No longer is it enough merely to know *how* to do things. Now the effective communicator needs to know *what* to do, and *why*, and *how to evaluate* the effectiveness of the chosen approach. Public relations professionals used to be called upon mainly for tasks such as writing news releases, making speeches, producing videos, publishing newsletters, organizing displays and so on. Now the profession demands competency in conducting research, making decisions, and solving problems. The call now is for strategic communicators.

To put it another way, **communication technicians** are specialists in public relations and marketing communication. They typically perform entry-level jobs or specialized tasks, often directed by others.

Communication managers, meanwhile, are organizational decision makers. Consider the complementary roles of two categories of communications managers: tactical and strategic.

- **Tactical managers** make day-to-day decisions on many practical and specific issues. Should they send a news release or hold a news conference? Are they better off with a brochure or a webpage? Should they develop a mall exhibit, or would it be more effective to create a computer presentation? Do they need another advertisement, and if so, for which publication or station, and with what message using which strategy?
- **Strategic managers**, on the other hand, are concerned with management, trends, issues, policies, and corporate structure. What problems are likely to face the organization over the next several years, and how might they be addressed? What is the crisis readiness of the organization? Should senior personnel be offered an advanced level of media training? What should the policies be for the webpage?

In the workplace, public relations practitioners often find themselves functioning in both the technician and the managerial roles, but the balance is shifting. Today's environment—and more important, tomorrow's—calls for greater skill on the management side of communication. The job of strategic communication planning calls for four particular skills: (1) understanding research and planning, (2) knowing how to make strategic choices, (3) making selections from an expanding inventory of tactical choices and (4) completing the process by evaluating program effectiveness.

A premise underlying this book is that public relations and marketing communication are becoming more strategic, more scientific. It is this strategic perspective that will differentiate the effective practitioner from the one who simply performs tasks and provides basic services.

Strategic Planning for Public Relations is about making such decisions—not by hunches or instinct but by solid and informed reasoning that draws on the science of communication as well as its various art forms. This book tries to make the complex process of strategic communication easily understandable by taking you through the process step by step. You'll find nine steps, each presented with the following three basic elements:

1. Explanations that are clear and understandable, drawn from contemporary theory and current practice.
2. Examples that help you see the concept in action, drawn from both nonprofit and for-profit organizations.
3. Hands-on exercises in both short form and expanded versions that help you apply the process in your own situation.

Note also that key words, printed in **boldface**, are collected into a glossary at the end of the book.

Experience shows that this hybrid format—part textbook, part workbook—can make it easier to learn about the planning process because it helps you think, see, and do. *Strategic Planning for Public Relations* gives you a solid, proven process that works. It doesn't offer any secrets of the trade, because there really are no secrets. Effective managers in public relations and marketing communication use these kinds of processes every day, and that's not much of a secret. This book makes field-tested procedures available to you in an understandable way so you can apply them yourself.

Relationship Management

A new emphasis is being placed on public relations as a central and essential aspect of organizational management.

In their influential book *Managing Public Relations,* James Grunig and Todd Hunt (1984) identified four now-famous evolutionary models of public relations. The first two—exemplified by press agentry and public information—rely on one-way dissemination of information. The latter models—an asymmetrical one associated with persuasion and advocacy, a symmetrical model dealing with dialogue and relationship-building—feature two-way communication for both dissemination and research/feedback. A close look at this evolution shows a practice becoming a profession, and a useful skill becoming an essential element of management.

Since 1982, the Public Relations Society of America (PRSA; see their website at http://www.prsa.org) has used an official statement identifying public relations as a "management function" that encompasses activities such as opinion tracking and analysis, relationship building, research, planning, objective setting, and evaluation.

Meanwhile, for the last 25 years or so, textbooks have identified public relations as a management function. For example, Scott Cutlip, Allen Center, and Glen Broom's *Effective Public Relations* (2005) define public relations as "the management function that identifies, establishes and maintains mutually beneficial relationships between an organization and the various publics on whom its success or failure depends." All serious textbooks in the field have followed suit with an emphasis on public relations as an element of organizational management. In *Excellence in Public Relations and Communication Management,* Grunig (1992) used the earlier definition by Grunig and Hunt (1984), defining public relations as "management of communication between an organization and its publics" (p. 6).

At the same time, scholarly research has helped pave the way for seating public relations at the management table. Stephen Bruning is a leading researcher in the role of a relationship-management approach to public relations. He has identified relationship management as "a paradigm for public relations scholarship and practice" (Ledingham & Bruning, 2000,

The 1998 appointment of a public relations executive to head Young & Rubicam's international advertising network dispelled some fears within the public relations community about integrated communication. Thomas Bell, former head of Y&R's sister agency, Burson-Marsteller Worldwide, vowed to be "someone who can deliver integrated thinking" so the ad agency will consider "all the persuasive disciplines" in servicing clients (Holmes, 1998).

The State of the Public Relations Profession Opinion Survey by the PRSA and Bacon's Information (2006) reports that top organizational managers and CEOs overwhelmingly believe that public relations enhances an organization's reputation (4.51 on a 5-point scale) and only slightly less that it furthers financial success and sales (3.94) and market share (3.90).

Some people are working mightily to coordinate the complementary fields while maintaining the autonomy and distinctive role of each. Notably, some of these people are outside the formal structures of public relations and marketing. They include chief executive officers who direct their marketing and public relations teams to collaborate in new-product campaigns, and university presidents who enjoin their media relations people to be attentive to recruiting and fund-raising needs. Their ranks also involve professors and other educators who blend public relations and marketing/advertising within a single academic program. The annual survey *Where Shall I Go to Study Advertising and Public Relations* (Ross & Richards, 2008) identifies 128 free-standing public relations programs, 92 advertising programs, and 45 combined advertising/public relations. Thus, the combined programs account for 26% of all undergraduate programs studying public relations.

The integrated link between public relations and marketing is a fact of life, often assumed by people and forces outside the professions more readily than it may be recognized from within. Here are two examples of how outsiders link public relations and marketing. One is the common misunderstanding among laypersons between publicity and advertising. They may ask, for example, how much it costs to get a news release published, or they may talk about sending an ad to a newspaper when they actually mean a news release.

More ominously, some external entities are forcing an unwanted link between public relations and marketing. This was the problem in play in the legal case of *Nike v. Kasky*. Consumer activist Marc Kasky sued Nike under false advertising provisions over its public defense against charges of using child sweatshop labor. The chill was caused when the California Supreme Court upheld Kasky's claim that Nike had engaged in "commercial speech," even though the company had done no advertising but instead had used traditional public relations venues—news releases, its website, speeches, and letters to the editor—to defend against the charges. An out-of-court settlement in 2003 ended the 5-year legal battle but did not settle the legal question of where public relations ends and marketing begins.

Communication integration seems to be happening globally. Philip Kitchen and Don Schultz (1999) report that the concept is gaining momentum not only in the United States but also in the United Kingdom, New Zealand, Australia, and India. The integrated model, they observe, "has become 'acceptable.' But, as we have seen it is *not yet* the 'established norm' . . ." (p. 36; emphasis in the original).

Gronstedt (2000) cites Saturn, Xerox, Motorola, Hewlett-Packard, and Federal Express as examples of companies that have effectively integrated their communication. Companies such as these use integrated communication on three levels: external communication, focusing on customers; vertical internal communication between senior management and frontline workers; and horizontal internal communication across departments, business units, and geographic boundaries (Hiebert, 2000).

Some folks say the concept of integrated communication is wrapped in the history of public relations itself. Porter Novelli vice president Helen Ostrowski (1999) believes that marketing-based public relations lie at the very roots of public relations. After all, public relations founding father Edward Bernays engineered the debutante march in New York City's Easter parade in 1929 to make smoking fashionable among women so Lucky Strike could sell more cigarettes.

Thomas L. Harris is a leading proponent of integrated communication, which he calls an outside-in process that begins with an understanding of the consumer publics, particularly their wants, interests, needs and lifestyles. Harris (2000) points out that public relations is particularly effective in building brand equity, which is based on the organization's reputation. The practical benefit of reputation is seen in the 1992 Los Angeles riots, when none of the 30 McDonald's restaurants in the riot area were touched while more than 2,000 other buildings were destroyed. Harris said that is because McDonald's had long been involved and visible in the community.

Each of the four models that Grunig and Hunt observed in the evolution of public relations—press agentry, public information, persuasion/advocacy, and dialogue/relationship-building—is evident today, often used by the same organization. While the latter two models that build from two-way communication generally find more favor among theorists, none of the approaches is necessarily "the best." Each model has its purpose, and each can be effective in achieving particular organizational objectives.

An interesting tug-of-war exists between the persuasion and relationship models. In subsequent research, Grunig (1992) himself notes that many organizations still primarily practice the persuasion model. With only anecdotal evidence, it seems safe to suggest that most of today's public relations agencies are hired to engage in persuasion on behalf of their clients, who believe their problems can be solved if only they can gain the support of their publics. Persuasion isn't necessarily bad: The same principles and techniques that persuade people to buy this CD or that perfume can be deployed on behalf of responsible sexual behavior or nutritional literacy, volunteerism, or other social virtues. Public relations students are exposed to this persuasion-based model through case studies and campaigns courses, through practicums and senior seminars, and especially through professional internships.

Perhaps we need to envision public relations anew, seeing it as serving the persuasive needs of client organizations as well as fostering more productive and beneficial relationships between organizations and their various publics. Public relations practitioners should be prepared to help organizations engage their publics in both word and deed.

This is the vision that guides *Strategic Planning for Public Relations.* The planning process this book presents can be used for persuasion or dialogue, because each is a strategic activity and each helps practitioners influence behavior and generate consensus. The planning process also can help organizations both overcome obstacles and capitalize on opportunities. Additionally, the process works equally well for businesses and nonprofits, whether they be large or small, international or grassroots, richly endowed or impoverished.

Advertising

From the approach of integrated communication, advertising can be seen as a tool for both public relations and marketing. As organizations set out to create such a cooperative environment, the political task can be dicey, but the potential rewards are huge. Often it is

Attributes of a Strategic Communication Program

An effective communication program includes the following attributes, which apply equally to corporations and nonprofit organizations and to large and small endeavors:

Spurred both by regulation and customer demand, organizations must be *accountable* to their publics. Most publics are increasing their expectations for *quality performance* and *open communication.* Organizations are successful in the long run only to the extent that they have high performance, delivering quality products and services. All organizations operate in a *competitive environment.* Publics besought by rivals will remain loyal to those organizations that earn loyalty consistently and continuously.

Effective communication involves *cooperation* between public relations and marketing. Just as each knight was an equal participant at the round table in King Arthur's court, so too should both disciplines have effective and equal voices.

The consumer philosophy has taken hold of all aspects of society, and organizations must answer with a *customer-driven response,* focusing on benefits for their publics. People support organizations that serve their interests and needs.

Organizational communication adheres to high *ethical standards* of honesty, accuracy, decency, truth, public interest, and mutual good. Growing numbers of organizations have developed clear credos or codes of ethics.

Mergers, downsizing, and restructuring have led both businesses and nonprofits to seek ways to operate with *lean resources,* and the duplication that exists amid the isolation of marketing from public relations often is too great a price for organizations to pay.

Strategic communication is part of an organization's *management function* and decision-making process. It is rooted in the organization's mission as lived out through its bottom line. This bottom line goes beyond money earned or raised; it focuses on the organization's fundamental purpose or mission. Strategists plot courses, set objectives, and measure results.

Many *media changes* are affecting the way organizations communicate. The "mass media" have fragmented to the point that none rules supreme anymore. Lines are blurring between news and entertainment. Meanwhile, increasing advertising costs and tighter promotional budgets have led organizations to look at the more cost-effective communication and promotional tools from the public relations side of the house.

Strategic communication uses *multiple tools,* drawing from all communication-related disciplines to talk with various groups of people. New technologies make it easier to supplement general media with more personal and interactive targeted communication vehicles.

The strategy of choice in a competitive environment is *proactive, two-way communication*, in which organizations plan for and initiate relationships with the people important to their success. This approach emphasizes dialogue over monologue.

Organizations are successful to the extent they enjoy a strong *reputation,* which results from neither accident nor luck. Strategic planning can identify and evaluate an organization's visibility and reputation. No organization can afford to be a "best-kept secret" among a relatively small number of supporters.

All kinds of organizations are realizing more keenly the need for long-term, mutually beneficial *relationships* between the organization and its various publics and market segments. Public relations practitioners long have recognized this, and marketing more recently has been discussing the need for relationship marketing.

enlightened organizational leaders who see the big picture, recognizing the value of a coordinated and strategic approach to communication.

Some of the most successful corporations in North America integrate their communication, blending the traditional disciplines of publicity and advertising to creatively present a clear and consistent message to their various publics. For example, when McDonald's introduced its McLean sandwich, it first used publicity and other public relations tactics to create awareness through the media, followed by advertising messages to reinforce the publicity and promotion. Additionally, it was publicity that enabled Goodyear to sell 150,000 new Aquatred tires before the first advertisements ran. Pfizer used publicity alone to sell $250 million worth of Viagra and gain a 90% market share before any consumer advertising began. And in several cities, when Krispy Kreme Doughnuts announced plans to open a store in a new area, the publicity created such a huge expectation among prospective customers that extra police had to be hired for opening day to handle the traffic jams.

The integrated approach also has been used by nonprofit organizations such as the American Cancer Society in its campaign for sunblock, and has been adopted by more loosely organized social campaigns dealing with bicycle safety, teen smoking, animal rights, birth control, utility deregulation, and AIDS research. One study suggested that nonprofit organizations are particularly open to the coordinated use of public relations and marketing communication techniques (Nemec, 1999).

As a practical matter, an integrated approach to strategic communication often begins with publicity, followed by advertising. Al Ries and Laura Ries note this in *The Fall of Advertising and the Rise of PR:* "The purpose of advertising is not to build a brand, but to defend a brand once the brand has been built by other means, primarily public relations or third-party endorsements . . . . Advertising cannot start a fire. It can only fan a fire after it has been started" (2002). They provide an overview of organizations and products that have achieved success with this format:

- Wal-Mart, which became the world's largest retailer with little advertising.
- Starbucks, which spent less than $10 million in advertising during its first 10 years.
- The Harry Potter book series, which soared to previously unheard of sales without any appreciable advertising, making British author J. K. Rowling literally richer than the queen of England.

Ries and Ries also note some of the differences between public relations (or publicity) and advertising: Advertising uses a "big bang," while public relations uses a slow buildup; advertising is visual, public relations is verbal; advertising reaches a mass audience, public relations reaches a targeted audience; advertising favors new lines and extensions, public relations favors new brands; advertising likes old names, public relations likes new names. The writers also present both an opinion (public relations is more creative than advertising) and a fact (public relations is more credible).

Strategic Public Relations

Most textbooks dealing with public relations encourage a four-phase process. Some use the RACE acronym (research, action, communication, evaluation) articulated by John Marston (1963) in *The Nature of Public Relations.* In *Public Relations Cases,* Jerry Hendrix (2006, and in earlier editions) uses the acronym ROPE (research, objectives, programming, evaluation). In *Public Relations Campaign Strategies,* Robert Kendall (1997) offers another formula—RAISE (research, adaptation, implementation strategy, evaluation). Kathleen Kelly (2001) posits ROPES (research, objectives, program, evaluation, stewardship), and Sheila Crifasi (2000) has come up with ROSIE (research, objectives, strategy, implementation, evaluation). Most public relations textbooks, however, simply refer to a four-stage process without constraining it to an acronym.

Marketing communication books also present a step-by-step process, but with little consistency about the number of steps involved. While acronyms can be useful mnemonic devices, they can be too confining. The four stages of communication planning are sometimes more complex than acronyms indicate, though in their crossover text on social marketing, Philip Kotler, Ned Roberto and Nancy Lee (2002) identify sight steps in four general stages that focus on analysis of the environment, identification of audiences and objectives, development of a strategic approach, and development of the implementation plan.

Strategic Planning for Public Relations offers a model that is meant to be both logical and easy to follow. The steps are grouped into four phases that are both descriptive and accurate, but their names don't lend themselves to an acronym. So without a great deal of fanfare, this model is called, simply, the Nine Steps of Strategic Public Relations.

The process of these steps is deliberate, and they must be taken in sequence. After identifying a problem, our tendency too often is to skip ahead to seeking solutions, leaping over research and analysis. This can result in unwarranted assumptions that later prove to be costly, counterproductive, and embarrassing. Careful planning leads to programs that are proactive and preventive rather than to activities that are reactive and remedial. At the same time, the steps in this process are flexible enough to allow for constant monitoring, testing, and adjusting as needed.

Exhibit Intro.1 Phases

PHASE ONE
FORMATIVE RESEARCH
1. Analyzing the Situation
2. Analyzing the Organization
3. Analyzing the Publics

PHASE TWO
STRATEGY
4. Establishing Goals and Objectives
5. Formulating Action and Response Strategies
6. Developing the Message Strategy

PHASE THREE
TACTICS
7. Selecting Communication Tactics
8. Implementing the Strategic Plan

PHASE FOUR
EVALUATIVE RESEARCH
9. Evaluating the Strategic Plan

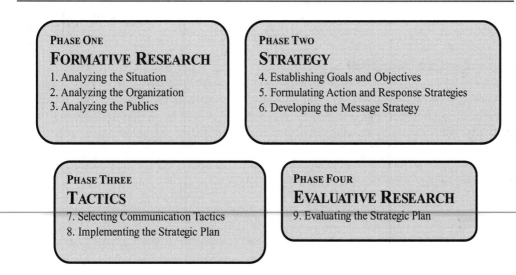

If you ask experienced communication managers you may find that they don't necessarily articulate their planning specifically along the lines of these nine steps. But talk with them about their work and you are likely to find that they go through a process pretty much like the one being presented here, whether they identify "steps" or not.

A few practitioners may admit (somewhat guiltily) that they don't do much planning. If they are being honest, they'll tell you they know they've been lucky so far with their hunches. Perhaps they don't do formal planning because they don't have the time or because the environment is so unstable that all they can do is react. Some practitioners may tell you their bosses and clients want action rather than planning (though such shortsighted bosses and clients often don't remain in business very long).

If you could observe how professionals work, however, you'd probably find that effective communication managers do plan. The good ones have learned how to build the research and planning components into their work and "sell" it to their clients and bosses. Increasingly, public relations organizations are using their websites to set the stage for such a four-stage planning process.

Formative Research

During the first of the four phases, Formative Research, the focus is on the preliminary work of communication planning, which is the need to gather information and analyze the situation. In three steps, the planner draws on existing information available to the organization and, at the same time, creates a research program for gaining additional information needed to drive the decisions that will come later in the planning process.

Step 1: Analyzing the Situation. Your analysis of the situation is the crucial beginning to the process. It is imperative that all involved—planner, clients, supervisors, key colleagues, and the ultimate decision makers—are in solid agreement about the nature of the opportunity or obstacle to be addressed in this program.

Step 2: Analyzing the Organization. This step involves a careful and candid look at three aspects of the organization: (1) its internal environment (mission, performance, and resources), (2) its public perception (reputation), and (3) its external environment (competitors and opponents, as well as supporters).

Step 3: Analyzing the Publics. In this step you identify and analyze your key publics—the various groups of people who interact with your organization on the issue at hand. *Strategic Planning for Public Relations* provides an objective technique for setting priorities among the various publics, helping you select those most important on the particular issue being dealt with. This step includes an analysis of each public in terms of its wants, needs, and expectations about the issue, its relationship to the organization, its involvement in communication and with various media, and a variety of social, economic, political, cultural, and technological trends that may affect it.

Strategy

The second phase of the planning process, Strategy, deals with the heart of planning: making decisions dealing with the expected impact of the communication, as well as the nature of the communication itself.

Step 4: Establishing Goals and Objectives. Step 4 focuses on the ultimate position being sought for the organization and for the product or service. This step helps you develop clear, specific, and measurable objectives that identify the organization's hoped for impact on the awareness, acceptance, and action of each key public. A good deal of attention is given to objectives dealing with acceptance of the message, because this is the most crucial area for public relations and marketing communication strategists.

Step 5: Formulating Action and Response Strategies. A range of actions is available to the organization, and in this step you consider what you might do in various situations. This section includes typologies of public relations initiatives and responses.

Step 6: Developing the Message Strategy. This step deals with the various decisions about the message, such as the sources who will present the message to the key publics, the content of the message, its tone and style, verbal and nonverbal cues, and related issues. Lessons from research about persuasive communication and dialogue will be applied for the ultimate purpose of designing a message that reflects the information gained through Step 3.

Tactics

During the third phase, Tactics, various communication tools are considered and the visible elements of the communication plan are created.

Step 7: Selecting Communication Tactics. This inventory deals with the various communication options. Specifically, the planner considers four categories: (1) face-to-face communication and opportunities for personal involvement, (2) organizational media (sometimes called controlled media), (3) news media (uncontrolled media) and (4) advertising and promotional media (another form of controlled media). While all of these tools can be used by any organization, not every tool is appropriate for each issue. Following the menu review, the planner packages the tactics into a cohesive communication program.

The Jargon of Strategic Public Relations

Consider the following terms that distinguish among various types of public relations activities:

Projects are single and usually short-lived public relations activities designed to meet an objective. Examples: A news release or a few closely related tactics surrounding an open house.

Programs are ongoing public relations activities dealing with several objectives associated with a goal. Programs have a continuing commission within the organization and focus on its relationship with a particular public. Examples: An organization's program in community relations or employee relations.

Campaigns are systematic sets of public relations activities, each with a specific and finite purpose, sustained over a length of time and dealing with objectives associated with a particular issue. Examples: A campaign to reduce accidents associated with drunk driving or a campaign to improve employee morale and productivity.

Step 8: Implementing the Strategic Plan. In this step, planners develop budgets and schedules and otherwise prepare to implement the communication program. This step turns the raw ingredients identified in the previous step into a recipe for successful public relations and marketing communication.

Evaluative Research

The final phase, Evaluative Research, deals with evaluation and assessment, enabling you to determine the degree to which the stated objectives have been met and thus to modify or continue the communication activities.

Step 9: Evaluating the Strategic Plan. This is the final planning element, indicating specific methods for measuring the effectiveness of each recommended tactic in meeting the stated objectives.

Effective Creativity

Before we begin putting a plan together, a word about creativity. Most communications professionals are creative people, visual or verbal artists who bring imaginative ideas to the task at hand. But mere novelty doesn't guarantee success. We all have seen people whose creative ideas seem to flop around without any sense of direction, artists who can't seem to apply their artistic concept. For creativity to be effective, it must have relevance; innovative ideas need to serve a purpose. Too many campaigns never get off the ground because they are built more on novelty than on effectiveness. Some are just too cute for words; others are downright bizarre. An inside joke in the advertising industry is that sometimes agencies win creative awards but lose the account, because their innovative advertising programs didn't sell the product or their imaginative approach didn't achieve the desired results for the client. Not a very funny joke, is it?

In the not-so-distant past, some practitioners worried that strategic planning might interfere with their creativity. But things are changing. In a crowded field of competitors all courting the same audiences, communication professionals have turned to greater use of research as a complement to the creative approach. Practitioners who once flew by the seat of their pants have found that careful planning can raise an organization's messages above the commotion of everyday life.

One thing has become clear: It really is counterproductive to separate creative and research people, because each can help the other. They share the common purpose of helping their client or their organization solve a problem. Research can nurture creative inspiration, help develop ideas, keep things on target, and evaluate the effectiveness of the creative endeavors.

Strategic Planning for Public Relations is built on two notions that can help make you creatively effective. First, a step-by-step system of planning is essential to learning how to develop an effective communication program. Second, effective creativity is more likely to result from careful and insightful planning than from a lightning bolt of inspiration.

This book is for people who appreciate road maps. A map doesn't tell you where you must go; rather, it helps you explore possibilities. You consider options, make choices, select alternatives, and develop contingencies. In short, you plan. Then you implement the plan by getting behind the wheel and beginning the road trip.

So it is with *Strategic Planning for Public Relations.* This book won't tell you what has to be done to develop your communication program, but it will lead you through the various decision points and options. The resulting program will be as unique as each individual student or practitioner and as tailored as each organization needs it to be. It will be a comprehensive, well-thought-out program that is both deliberate and creative. Use this book to nurture your creativity and channel it to make your work more effective.

Every person can be both deliberate and creative, each to a greater or lesser degree. *Strategic Planning for Public Relations* tries to help you cultivate both qualities. It helps creative people become more organized in their planning, and it helps methodical people bring more creative energy to their work. This book gives you a model—one to be considered, adapted to fit your particular circumstances, and used to the extent that it helps you be both effective and creative in your communication planning.

Creativity and Structure

Most people consider themselves at either end of a pole. They are creative people, or they are analytical types. *Strategic Planning for Public Relations* is geared to both types.

Are you easily creative? This book will help transform your artistry, insight, and spontaneity into something more than mere novelty. It will lead you to consider every aspect of a strategic communication plan, helping you be creative within an effective framework.

Are you analytical and well-organized? This book will enhance your innate sense of organization and structure, freeing your creativity to enhance your program effectiveness.

The reality is that we are seldom one or the other, creative or structured. Rather than two ends of a pole, it is more like a continuum. Regardless of where you place yourself on this continuum, *Strategic Planning for Public Relations* can help you work through your strengths and at the same time shore up less dominate aspects of your work style.

Phase One

FORMATIVE RESEARCH

The phrase "shooting in the dark" refers to trying to hit a target without being able to see it. In the context of strategic communication planning, "shooting in the dark" means designing a program without the needed research. In more common language, it means not doing your homework. In any context, it's not a good idea!

Step 1
Analyzing the Situation

Step 2
Analyzing the Organization

Step 3
Analyzing the Publics

Research is the planner's homework. It's the foundation of every effective campaign for public relations and marketing communication. Your communication tactics might be innovative, but they will probably be ineffective if you don't have adequate research. Without research, you will probably end up sending messages of little value to your organization and little interest to your publics (who most likely won't be listening anyway).

How common is research in public relations and marketing communication? In a special issue of his professional newsletter *PR Reporter*, the late Patrick Jackson summarized information from Ketchum Public Relations. The newsletter noted that 75% of practitioners use research to plan new programs, 58% to monitor progress and make midcourse revisions, and 58% to measure outcomes (Jackson, 1994). Even during crises, when reaction time is minimal, 36% do research to get a quick read on public opinion. Virtually all practitioners report that they are doing more research than ever before.

The first of the four phases of the strategic planning process deals specifically with gathering and analyzing **formative research**, which is the data on which you will build your communication program. Fran Matera and Ray Artigue (2000) call this **strategic research**, the systematic gathering of information about issues and publics that affect organizations, particularly as the organization engages in the two-way models of public relations that were outlined in the introduction to this book. In contract, they also note a second category, **tactical research**, which is information obtained to guide the production and dissemination of messages. Whereas tactical research helps public relations practitioners do their job effectively, strategic research more directly impacts on the organization's overall mission.

During this formative research phase, focused as it is on strategy, you will conduct a comprehensive situation analysis to gather the information needed to make wise decisions.

To accomplish this, you will gather information in three key areas: (1) the situation you are facing, (2) your organization or client, and (3) your intended publics. Specifically, you will obtain background information on the issue, assess the organization's performance and reputation and catalogue its resources, and identify and analyze key publics.

Don't let the idea of research scare you. Research begins with informal and often simple methods of gathering relevant information. Often you can look to a three-prong research program for most public relations projects:

Casual Research. Recollect what is already known. Think about the situation. "Pick the brains" of clients, colleagues, and other helpful individuals. Interview other people with experience and expertise. Brainstorm alone or with other planners.

Secondary Research. Look for existing information. Investigate organizational files to learn what already exists on the issue. Search the library for information from books, periodicals, and special reports. Check for similar material on the Internet (but be wary about the validity of what you find out there). Review and analyze how other organizations handled similar situations.

Primary Research. If necessary, conduct your own research. Appendix A: Applied Research Techniques will help with the basic primary research techniques such as surveys, focus groups, and content analysis. This appendix also discusses the ethics of research.

As you conduct formative research, keep one thing in mind: The information you obtain through research will help in planning, but research does not offset the need for common sense. Your professional judgment remains the strongest resource you bring to the planning process. Use research to inform your professional judgment, but make decisions on relevant information as well as on your own reliable experience and professional insight.

This section looks at the three areas in which you will conduct your research, starting with an analysis of the situation.

Step 1

Analyzing the Situation

The first step in any effective public relations plan or marketing communication program is to carefully and accurately identify the situation facing your organization. This seems simple enough. Common sense, right? But sense isn't all that common, and people sometimes have different ideas about what the public relations situation is.

The Public Relations Situation

Put simply, a **situation** is a set of circumstances facing an organization. A situation is similar in meaning to a problem, if by "problem" you use the classic definition of a question needing to be addressed. For example, a situation for an automotive manufacturer might be the availability of side air bags (rather than just front air bags) in its new model-year cars. For a small nonprofit organization dealing with at-risk youth, a situation might be the misunderstanding and fear that some people have of these youth. Without an early and clear statement of the situation to be addressed, you will not be able to conduct efficient research or define the goal of your communication program later in the planning process.

Note that situations are stated as nouns—*availability* of air bags, *fear* of youths. Later when we talk about organizational goals, we will add the verbs to indicate how we want to impact on these situations—*promoting* consumer acceptance of the air bags, *dispelling* the notion that all at-risk youth are dangerous. For now, simply identify the situation without commenting on it. A situation is approached in either a positive or negative vein:

Opportunity. The public relations situation may be identified as an **opportunity** to be embraced because it offers a potential advantage to the organization or its publics (such as side air bags).

Obstacle. On the other hand, the public relations situation may be an **obstacle** to be overcome because it limits the organization in realizing its mission (such as fear of at-risk youth).

Depending on how they assess the situation and its potential impact on the organization, two planners may look differently at the same situation—one calling it an obstacle, the other an opportunity.

Even in crisis situations, obstacles can be approached as opportunities, if the problem has not been self-inflicted. Organizations under attack may use the public attention generated by a crisis to explain their values and demonstrate their quality. Pepsi fought a 1993 hoax in which it was asserted that syringes had been found in cans of the company's products by issuing video news releases showing how its production process made it impossible to contaminate the product before it left the plant. Similarly, Johnson & Johnson used satellite news conferences when it reintroduced Tylenol after several people were killed in 1982 when someone tampered with the over-the-counter medicine. In doing so, the company, which already enjoyed a good reputation, emerged from the crisis with even more consumer respect and confidence.

Gold'n Plump Poultry is the Midwest's largest chicken company, but in 2006 sales had tanked because of consumer fears about industrywide health risks (avian flu, salmonella, arsenic in feed) spurred by ongoing media reports. The company budgeted $150,000 and launched a 6-month "Takin' Names Tour" community relations campaign to shore up its relationship with its consumer base. An old farm truck traveled throughout towns and villages in Minnesota and Wisconsin, asking residents to sign their names on the vehicle. For every signature, the company donated four meals to rural food shelves to help families in danger of losing their small farms. It also distributed "I give a peep about local family farmers" T-shirts. As the campaign ended, the company had donated 190,000 meals, generated media attention throughout the region, reversed its sales decline, and rebuilt brand loyalty, with seven out of 10 consumers saying Gold'n Plump was the chicken they would buy. They even won the support of vegans who don't eat chicken but applauded the company's community commitment.

Unilever is another company that turned a problem into an opportunity. The problem was that traditional marketing of beauty products relied on idealized portrayals of women. The opportunity: to redefine the situation. Unilever, which produces Dove beauty products, commissioned an international study on women's attitudes toward beauty. What resulted was an entirely new approach called the "Campaign for Real Beauty." Dove advertising featured images of ordinary women, not supermodels. The company launched a new product line, Dove Firming, with no television advertising and only limited print ads, but with primary implementation through public relations venues. The campaign produced exposure through 62 national television programs and 200 local news programs, as well as feature coverage in major national print media and more than 700 local newspapers. More than a million visitors logged onto its website (http://www.campaignforrealbeauty.com) in the first year alone. The campaign not only sold beauty products but also sparked an international discussion about women and beauty, drawing praise from psychologists, teachers, parents, media analysts, and real women with curves.

Whether the issue is viewed as an opportunity, as an obstacle, or simply as an unrealized potential, the communication team and the organization's or client's leadership must come to a common understanding of the issue before it can be adequately addressed.

Consider the following example of mixed signals: The executive director of a drug abuse-prevention agency wanted a public relations consultant to focus on communication between the agency and external publics such as the courts, police, and probation personnel. The board of directors, on the other hand, wanted a plan for better communication among the board, staff, and executive director. Significantly different expectations, to say the least! How do you think you might handle this?

In this case, the consultant asked both the director and the board to reach consensus about the central issue and to rethink what they wanted. They asked themselves what the real issues were and concluded that the focus should be on the agency's visibility and reputation with its external publics. Once this was clarified, the consultant developed a strategic plan and

Scandal Reveals the Worst . . . and Brings Out the Best

When St. Bonaventure University, a small Franciscan school in upstate New York, was rocked by a basketball eligibility scandal in 2003, the flap drew the scrutiny of national media. The ensuing scandal eventually toppled administrators up to and including the president and figured in the suicide of a university trustee.

The small public relations staff moved quickly to respond to the sweeping crisis, which in just one week triggered more than 200 media inquiries and hundreds of calls from outraged alumni.

"It's important to note that our Board of Trustees did the right thing. We simply communicated their actions," David Ferguson, then vice president of marketing and public relations told reporters. "But it's also vital that the way we communicated reflected our core values of community and respect for all."

Enlisting the help of expert crisis communications counsel (Ric Wanetik and Chan Cochran of Columbus, Ohio), Ferguson led the team in executing an action plan with four key goals:

1. Repair the damage done to St. Bonaventure's image by the scandal.
2. Recruit a strong class of incoming freshmen.
3. Turn the adversity into a vehicle for learning and personal growth on the part of members of the campus community.
4. Have the university viewed as a values-driven institution whose response to scandal stands as an example of a "best practice" in dealing with problems.

Pledging to deal "forthrightly, transparently, and uncompromisingly" with the scandal, which had erupted over spring break, the trustees first called together the entire campus. At a unity convocation they shared the facts, apologized, announced interim leadership, and established a committee to work with a National Collegiate Athletic Association investigation.

The university sent letters to alumni, parents, and prospective students. It quickly developed a special issue of the alumni magazine and established communications links with key alumni and supporters. Meanwhile, the new campus leaders met with media in cities with large student and alumni populations.

The result? The incoming freshman class was the largest in a decade, and the university received kudos from commentators on several fronts. Perhaps the sweetest compliment of all came from veteran newsman Bob Schieffer in unsolicited comments during his address as commencement speaker, who noted,

> I am proud to be part of a ceremony at an institution that faced a hard choice and did the right thing. I am proud to associate myself with you and St. Bonaventure. Here's the headline: Your school is not going to be remembered because a sports recruiting scandal happened here. There have been recruiting scandals before and I am sorry to say, human nature being what it is, there will be recruiting scandals again. What St. Bonaventure will be remembered for is doing the right thing and doing it quickly and without excuse.

helped the agency implement it. The strategic planning checklist at the end of this chapter will help you clarify the issue at hand for your organization.

Ongoing communication with the research client is imperative. In their book *Applied Research Design,* Terry Hedrick, Leonard Bickman, and Debra Rog (1993) recommend at least four research touch points:

1. An initial meeting with the client to develop a common understanding of the client's research needs, resources and expected uses.
2. A meeting to agree on the scope of the project, particularly its costs and other resources.
3. Following an initial review of literature and other secondary sources, a meeting to refine the research questions and discuss potential approaches and limitations.
4. A meeting for agreement on the proposed study approach.

Your job in this first step of the strategic planning process is to carefully identify the issue at hand. Come to consensus about whether it is seen as an opportunity or an obstacle, and if the latter, how it might be turned into an opportunity.

It is important to take the broad view in this. Fast food chains such as McDonald's, Arby's, and Burger King, for example, could have ignored growing national and international concerns about obesity, particularly their long-term effects on young people. Yet all three of these companies have introduced new menu items that are more healthful and less calorie-laden.

Maybe it's seeing the writing on the wall. Maybe it's a conversion. Maybe not, since these are the companies that gave us supersized meals in the first place, so perhaps the health talk is simply part of the ongoing profit lust. Regardless of motivation, it's clear that fast-food companies are changing their ways in the face of mounting public concern over the issue

The Zen of Public Relations

Sometimes a new paradigm—a different perspective—can enhance our understanding. And what could be farther from the practicality of public relations than spirituality?

To better understand an important public relations concept, consider the principle of interconnectedness—the duality in which everything is related. What appears to be opposite is not separate; it is only the other end of the one pole, the other side of the same lake.

When we think of public relations issues, our tendency often is to identify them as either *obstacles* or *opportunities*. But such words mask an important relationship. The spirituality associated with Zen values harmony. A problem is not necessarily something negative but instead something lacking harmony, a point of yet-unrealized potential. An obstacle puts us at a crossroads, allowing us to go this way or that, with consequences based on the choice we make.

The ultimate public relations problem is a *crisis*. Yet even that word gives us philosophical pause. Interestingly, the Chinese term *wei ji* and the parallel Japanese word *kiki,* both of which translate as "crisis," are made up of two characters—one meaning "danger," the other meaning "opportunity." A crisis is a decision point where choices point to consequences.

The job of public relations, then, is to restore harmony, to re-establish equilibrium.

of obesity. Similarly, tobacco companies are responding to public concern on the issue of smoking, particularly health aspects of secondhand smoke, and health care providers are reacting to issues such as the cost of medical prescriptions.

Issues Management

Issues are situations that present matters of concern to organizations, what Abe Bakhsheshy (2003) of the University of Utah defines as a trend, an event, a development or a matter in dispute that may affect an organization. Issues exist within a changing environment and often are the result of conflicting values (either different values held by the organization and one of its publics, or a different balance among similar values). In their book *Agenda Setting*, John Dearing and Everett Rogers define an issue as "a social problem, often conflictual, that has received media coverage" (1996, p. 4).

Bakhsheshy notes that early anticipation permits an organization to study the issue, to orient itself to deal with the issue, and to better identify and potentially involve itself with its publics. He asks several questions in analyzing issues: Which stakeholders are affected by the issue? Who has an interest? Who is in a position to exert influence? Who ought to care? Who started the ball rolling? Who is now involved?

Issues management is the process by which an organization tries to anticipate emerging issues and respond to them before they get out of hand. It is a process of monitoring and evaluating information. Like many other aspects of public relations, issues management involves potential change. For example, insurance companies, hospitals and health maintenance organizations all are trying to predict trends within the health care industry and to have some kind of impact on the future.

Some organizations use a **best practices** approach as they weigh their options during issues management. This approach to organizational problem solving, also known as **benchmarking**, involves research into how other organizations have handled similar situations, identifying those that handle them well. It is a continuous and systematic process of measuring an organization and its products and services against the best practices of strong competitors and recognized industry leaders, in order to improve the organization's performance. Put more simply, benchmarking is the search for better ways of doing the things you do.

Peter Schwartz and Blair Gibb (1999) note three benefits of benchmarking: (1) organizational initiative that prevents internal inertia from taking over, (2) continual awareness of innovations coming from competitors and (3) introduction of fresh air from outside the organization.

Despite its name, issues management does not focus on control; neither does it involve one-way communication nor manipulation of a public. Rather, it helps the organization interact with its publics. It may help an organization settle the issue early or divert it, or perhaps even prevent its emergence. More likely, however, the organization will have to adjust itself to the issue, trying to maximize the benefits or at least minimize the negative impact. Public relations often drives this early-warning system within an organization.

Risk Management

Strategic communicators often give the name **risk management** to the process of identifying, controlling, and minimizing the impact of uncertain events on an organization. The term is

The Background of Issues Management

F. J. Aguilar (1967) explained **environmental scanning** as a process of seeking "information about events and relationships in a company's outside environment, the knowledge of which would assist top management in its task of charting the company's future course of action" (p. 1).

W. Howard Chase (1977) coined the term **issues management**, though the concept has been around since since the days when Ivy Lee first did the work of what has become known as public relations. But Chase pushed the concept forward, away from a catch-as-catch-can approach and toward a more systematic technique, which he outlined in five steps (Jones & Chase, 1979). Raymond Ewing (1997) expanded this into a seven-step process. Here is a newer, six-stage, synthesis of the process of issues management:

1. Identify future issues that are likely to affect an organization. Develop an early warning scanning system that considers where the organization wants to go and looks at potential roadblocks and other outside economic, political, technological, social, and other kinds of pressures on the organization. Look for forces that could help move the organization along its path.
2. Research and analyze each issue. Carefully gather as many facts as possible about these issues. Consult specialists who are particularly familiar with the issues.
3. Consider options in responding to each issue. Use creative problem-solving techniques to discover as many alternatives as possible to deal with the issue at hand. Establish your standards for success and the criteria that your organization should use to make choices among the various alternatives.
4. Develop an action plan for the best option. Select the most appropriate alternative, usually in terms of cost-effectiveness, practicality, and organizational fit. Then develop a specific plan to address the issue.
5. Implement this plan, giving as much energy and as many resources as it warrants.
6. Evaluate the effectiveness of the response, both during its implementation when there is still time to make appropriate adjustments and when the program is completed.

Archie Boe (1979), then CEO of Allstate Insurance Companies, has explained that "issues management and strategic planning are both born of the dynamic tradition in American business management that rejects the passive approach of hoping to know the future and merely adjusting to it, for an affirmative posture of *creating* the future and *fitting* the corporate enterprise into it" (p. 5; emphasis in the original).

After interviewing 248 public relations managers, Martha Lauzen (1997) found a link between two-way public relations and both the early detection and accurate diagnosis of issues: "The answer lies in the confluence of public relations and issues management as they become true boundary-spanning functions, acting as the eyes and ears of organizations, serving as parts of an early warning system" (p. 79).

For practitioners, the conclusion is that two-way public relations, which inherently involves issues management, leads to more effective outcomes and ultimately will move the practitioner into the "dominant coalition" of managers who wield power and make decisions within organizations.

used in many disciplines—from politics to engineering, business to biology. Public relations people often need to force their organizations and clients to listen to criticism. Many public relations disasters are rooted in the myopic failure to learn from others' mistakes.

One reason for this is what Michael Regester (2005) calls "believing your own PR." The risk management specialist gives as an example Nestlé International, which, he says, saw itself as a nurturing company and thus failed to recognize the intensity of criticism over its marketing of infant formula. Similarly, Dow Corning saw itself as a conscientious company, so it aggressively countered criticism and public concern about the safety of its silicone breast implants.

Exxon was another company that refused to take the critics seriously, and it suffered in the long term for its mishandling of the Alaska oil spill caused by its freighter *Valdez* in 1989. Showing the ramifications of continuing anti-Exxon sentiment, a jury in 2000 ordered the oil company (now called ExxonMobil) to pay $3.5 billion for defrauding Alabama on royalties involving oil wells in the Gulf of Mexico. That verdict was set aside, and in a new trial in November 2003, the jury awarded the state damages of $11.9 billion. Jurors said one reason for the high penalties was that the Alaska situation showed them that Exxon was a company that could not be trusted and deserved to be punished. A state appeals court later reduced the award to $3.5 billion, and in late 2007 the Alabama Supreme Court split on partisan lines (Republicans for ExxonMobil, the lone Democrat siding with the state) to eliminate the punitive damages, assessing the company a mere $52 million—the amount it had failed to pay Alabama in the first place. In 2008, the state came back with another lawsuit seeking $143 million in interest. Meanwhile, the company went to court because it said the state charged it too much in tax.

The case clearly revived public distrust of the corporate giant and underscored the long-term consequences of public opinion turned sour against a company. While ExxonMobil in 2007 posted record profits of $40.61 billion, it also has been probed for its political contributions. Meanwhile, critics also saw the whole Exxon-Alabama affair as another example of the stench of corruption in state politics, calling for ethics charges against the eight Republican justices who, according to media reports, accepted a total of $5.5 million in political contributions from ExxonMobil over the previous five years. Legal cases being what they are, the situation could drag on for years, providing a continuing embarrassment to ExxonMobil.

Risk management involves a careful assessment of the potential impact on both the organization and its publics. Often this means taking into consideration the emotional elements that may be in play. An example of this is the "perfect storm" effect of the Duke University rape case in 2006, what a British newspaper called a "gourmet feast, a deluxe news-hook omelet."

Here are the ingredients in that omelet, destined to catapult the case into a major public relations crisis:

- *Race.* A black woman accused three white members of a university lacrosse team of raping her at a team party.
- *Sex.* In addition to the rape charge itself, the woman was an exotic dancer and escort who had been hired by the team as a stripper. One of the arrested players had an earlier charge of shouting antigay epithets at a man.
- *Class and Privilege.* The woman was a single mother at a small primarily black school, also in Durham. The accused were prep school graduates from wealthy families from Long Island.

- *Credibility.* The ongoing investigation yielded much confusion and many inconsistencies, much of this because the accuser's story kept changing. Additionally a second stripper disputed the rape claim. Evidence showed that the victim appeared to be under the influence of alcohol or drugs when she arrived at the party and that she had had multiple sex partners earlier in the day.
- *Legal Reversals.* Midway through the investigation, the rape charges were dismissed, but kidnapping and sexual offense charges remained. Eventually the state attorney general dismissed all charges.
- *Politics.* The district attorney was running for re-election, and many observers claimed he exploited the media interest to win votes. He later was disbarred for improper actions in the case, the first such penalty in state history.
- *Police Collusion.* The police department violated its own investigation rules in favor of the district attorney and allowed improper photo identification.
- *Media Scrutiny.* The district attorney gave at least 70 media interviews. National print and television media converged on Durham. Even international media covered the case.
- *Cause Advocates.* The case also fed several single-issue advocates: a feminist who said her research shows that women never lie about rape, another who said the case exploits social prejudice against strippers, others allying themselves with the racial themes, still others who decried white victimization.
- *Premature Campus Reaction.* The university tried to balance the seriousness of the issue, compassion for the victim, cooperation with police, and support for its students. In retrospect, campus actions left it open to criticism from all sides. The college forced the coach's resignation, cancelled the remainder of the team's season, and announced the suspension of the following season (later lifted).

With the legal charges dismissed and the resulting lawsuits by the fired coach, the three accused players, and the rest of the team back in practice, the situation settled down. School public relations people recalled that their first priority was to the North Carolina media with which they interacted frequently, the media "we will be dealing with when the rest go home," said one official.

Notably, the one winner may have been the campus bookstore. Sale of Duke lacrosse T-shirts tripled during the months of public scrutiny.

Crisis Management

The purpose of issues management, as previously noted, is to deal with issues before they get out of hand. When that happens, the issue becomes a crisis. **Crisis management** is the name given to the process by which an organization deals with out-of-control issues. But "management" is a bit of a misnomer. It's more about *coping* with crises.

Consider this analogy: Issues management is like steering a sailboat. You run with the wind when it happens to be blowing in the direction you want to go, and you tack to make some progress against the wind. Sometimes you stall when there is no wind. But always, you adapt to an ever-changing environment. In a crisis situation, the analogy is more like trying to ride out a storm. Often the best you can do is drop sail, hang on, and hope the vessel is strong enough to survive without too much damage. A bit of luck helps, too.

One thing to remember about crises: They may be sudden and unpredicted, but they seldom are unpredictable. Crises are more like volcanoes that smolder for awhile before they erupt. Warning signs abound, at least to the trained eye.

A 2006 study by the Institute for Crisis Management (http://www.crisisexperts.com) found that only 34% of companies' crises burst suddenly onto the scene, while 66% had been smoldering situations that eventually ignited. Catastrophes represented only 9% of the cases. The biggest crisis categories were white-collar crime (21%), mismanagement (14%), labor disputes (10%), along with workplace violence (9%) tying with outside catastrophes. Casualty accidents and class-action lawsuits were other significant categories. All of these represent areas in which organizations should be paying attention to the quality of their performance and its impact on their reputation.

Overall, the institute reported that management caused 52% of all crises, with employees causing another 29%. Only 19% were caused by outside influences. Enron, Hewlett-Packard, Microsoft, and Wal-Mart were the most crisis-prone companies. The institute concludes that two-thirds of the crises never need to reach crisis stage and could be prevented by effective risk-management programs that involve an appropriate communication plan and that put a premium on organization reputation—two issues paramount in public relations.

An organization committed to the concept of strategic communication is probably engaged in an ongoing issues management program that identifies crises in their early stages. Less nimble organizations that always seem to be in reactive mode are the ones likely to be caught off guard by a crisis.

Reality sometimes slaps you in the face and forces you to think the unthinkable. It happened at Virginia Polytechnic Institute and State University (Virginia Tech) in Blacksburg, Virginia, and at Columbine High School in Littleton, Colorado; and it happened in New York City with the attack on the World Trade Center.

What happened in Chicago in 1982 remains an example of how companies can be unshakable in facing the unthinkable. Johnson & Johnson woke up in crisis when somebody laced its Tylenol medicine with poisonous cyanide. Seven Chicago-area residents died. That's an unthinkable tragedy for a pharmaceutical company. As the country worried about the safety of its medicines (not only Tylenol, but by extension, all packaged medicine), Johnson & Johnson quickly issued a nationwide warning. It pulled 31 million bottles of Tylenol from store shelves. It then reintroduced the medicine with a triple-seal tamper-resistant package that soon became an industry standard, and it offered customer incentives such as free replacements and discount coupons. The incident also led insurance companies to introduce malicious-product-tampering coverage to companies that cover the cost of a recall, interruption of business, and public relations/marketing costs associated with rehabilitating the product and its brand. Amid predictions that the Tylenol brand was doomed, the company saw a quick recovery of its 35% market share and in the process fostered an ongoing customer loyalty.

Today, more than 20 years later, the legacy of Johnson & Johnson is a case study in good crisis communication and solid public relations, a morality tale that shows the value of a corporate conscientiousness that places its customers first and keeps its promise of safety.

But considering the subsequent scandals associated with corporations such as Blackwater, Enron, WorldCom, and Arthur Andersen, obviously some companies didn't get the point. Nevertheless, those that did take note learned the value of proactive management and quick communication in crisis situations. Those forward-looking companies realized that preparedness is the key to effective issues management, particularly in crisis situations. James

Lukaszewski (1997) focuses on a six-step program of preparedness: (1) early and competent leadership; (2) a prioritized approach; (3) strategies to preserve and/or recover the organization's reputation; (4) implementation of effective plans; (5) preauthorization for the organization to act quickly on its own; and (6) a response based on openness, truthfulness, and empathy.

Some experts have banded together as a kind of self-help group to guide each other in risk and crisis situations. One such coalition is the British-based Crisis Communications Network (CCN), a register of business and communication people with experience in managing crises that is associated with the Institute for Public Relations. The CCN focuses on both external and internal communications, and it offers strong encouragement for engaging in employee communication to prevent potentially hurtful rumors from developing in the first place. Speaking about the network, Morag Cuddeford-Jones (2002) lists several tips for issues management:

- Develop active dialogue with various stakeholders.
- Make sure an issue is worth trying to manage.
- Nurture expert contacts who can provide third-party research and endorsement when necessary.
- Form a coalition with organizations similar to yours.
- Create a risk-management plan and review it regularly, updating and modifying it as necessary.
- Include senior management on this team.

Public Relations and Ethics

Part of your research into the situation should involve an examination of ethical aspects, particularly the basis on which practitioners and their organizations or clients make ethical decisions. You might begin by considering three classic approaches to making such determinations: deontological ethics, teleological ethics, and situational ethics.

Deontological Ethics

The approach to decision making rooted in a standard or moral code is called **deontological ethics**. In essence, the deontological approach says that certain actions are, in and of themselves, good; others, bad.

On the positive side, this is a humanitarian approach in which actions are judged on basic principles of human rights and dignity. On the negative side, it can give way to a fundamentalist application of rules without regard to consequence.

An example of deontological ethics is professional codes, such as the Public Relations Member Code of Ethics (see Appendix B: Ethical Standards), which proclaims the intrinsic and unquestioned value of honesty, integrity, fairness, accuracy, and so on.

Teleological Ethics

On the other hand, **teleological ethics** is an approach focused more on the impact that actions have on people. It is more results-oriented. The teleological approach is rooted in the notion that good actions produce good results. Thus something is judged to be ethical because it generates good consequences.

Strategic Principles for Crisis Management

The strategic approach to crisis management might be encompassed in the following six principles:

1. *The principle of existing relationships.* During a crisis, communicate with employees, volunteers, stockholders, donors, community leaders, customers, government and professional authorities, and other constituent groups, as well as with colleagues. Minimally, keep everyone informed, because their continued support will be important in your rebuilding activities following the crisis. Ideally, enlist the help of some of these publics during the crisis to communicate credibly and effectively.
2. *The principle of media as ally.* Crises invite scrutiny because they have a potential impact on a large number of people. So treat the news media as allies that provide opportunities to communicate with key publics. If the media become intrusive and/or hostile, this often is because an organization has not been forthcoming in providing legitimate information to the media and its other publics. A good preexisting program of media relations can minimize media hostility.
3. *The principle of reputational priorities.* Your top priority after safety issues is to your organization's reputation. Remembering this can help you focus on doing what's best for your customers, employees, and other key publics. Set objectives that deal with maintaining (or if necessary, restoring) your credibility. Use the crisis as an opportunity to enhance your reputation for social responsibility with your various publics.
4. *The principle of quick response.* Be accessible to your publics as quickly as possible. A standard guideline for crises that capture the immediate attention of the news media is the one-hour rule. Within an hour of learning about a crisis, the organization should have its first message available to its publics, particularly the media (which generally is the most compelling public in the early stages of an active crisis). For less attention-getting crises, an organization might be able to prepare for five or six hours before going public.
5. *The principle of full disclosure.* Silence is not an acceptable response during a crisis. Without admitting fault and without speculating about facts not yet known, the organization should provide as much information as possible. The presumption should be that everything the organization knows should be made available. Any decision not to release certain information should be based on careful deliberation with specific justification for the silence. And use of misleading or false information is never an ethical option.
6. *The principle of one voice.* A single, trained spokesperson should represent the organization. If multiple spokespersons are needed, each should be aware of what the others are saying, and all should work together from the same set of facts and the same coordinated message.

Teleological ethics asks the question: What will produce the greater good for the most people? A positive aspect of this approach is that it requires practitioners to consider the consequences of their actions. A negative aspect is that it creates a scenario in which the greater good, always difficult to calculate, sometimes is allowed to reign without account for the harm inflicted on the minority.

An example of the teleological approach also is implied in the Public Relations Society of America code, which connects the need for ethical behavior and conduct with the public interest.

Situational Ethics

A third approach to ethical decision making is **situational ethics** (otherwise called **ethical relativism**), which suggests that actions are ethical to the extent they reflect particular social norms. The situational approach is considered on a case-by-case basis. While an advantage of this approach is respect for cultural diversity and conflicting values, it has the mirrored disadvantage both of dominance of mainstream culture as well as an inability to judge the basic rightness or wrongness of actions.

Communication strategists help themselves and their organizations when they anticipate how they will approach ethical decisions. Without advance thinking, the planner often is left either with no guidelines on determining whether something is ethical or simply with an unexamined personal feeling. Neither of those choices is particularly useful.

Ethics by Committee

Hospitals have their ethics committees, so why not public relations agencies? One such panel is found at Ruder-Finn; the company's ethics committee brings together account executives with outside ethical experts such as rabbis, ministers, priests, theologians, and philosophers. Their goal: to struggle with the ethical dimension of issues and then to advise management.

Ruder-Finn special projects coordinator Emmanuel Tchividjian, who coordinates the committee, says the ethics team has reviewed issues such as whether the agency should continue a lucrative account with a national tourism office after a military coup in that country. After the committee (including an ethics professor at a theological seminary) went to the country to investigate, Ruder-Finn resigned from the account because it did not want to assist a military dictatorship.

The agency also considered whether to accept a book-promotion account involving the Church of Scientology. That account was rejected because the firm did not want to be involved with what it considered a religious cult.

But Ruder-Finn did accept an account with the Swiss government over the issue of money and gold that the Nazis took from Jews during the Holocaust—a particularly sensitive issue for an agency where most of the managers and staff are Jewish. That account, notes Tchividjian, was accepted on the belief that much could be gained by open communication. The committee serves to remind employees that "the bottom line is not the most important thing," he explains. "We do have to make money, but there are values that have a higher priority" (Tchividjian, interview with the author).

Another ethical innovation by Ruder-Finn was borrowed from the legal profession. When the company is approached by a potential client with an issue that raises ethical concerns, the agency conducts discovery research at the client's expense, soliciting information from industry insiders and ethicists about the moral dimension of the issue. Based on the findings, Ruder-Finn may reject the client or, conversely, it may use the information to help frame the client's position on the sensitive issue.

Don't presume that you have to decide ahead of time which of the classic approaches to use. In truth, most organizations—as most individuals—slip back and forth among the three styles of ethical decision making. The value of advance thinking is that you can recognize the different foundations for determining ethical actions and responses and you can consider each approach as you make your decisions.

David Finn of the Ruder-Finn public relations agency in New York City has observed that ethical decision making is not a choice between good and bad but a choice between two conflicting goods. The challenge is first to discern the difference and then to make an appropriate choice. In a column on ethics in *Reputation Management* magazine, Finn (1998) observes that "addressing ethical issues intelligently calls for a probing as well as an open mind."

Planning Example 1: Analyzing the Situation

Because it has received state permission to expand from a two-year to a four-year program, Upstate College wants to develop a strategic communication plan to deal with student enrollment and retention, financial contributions, and community support.

■ ■ ■

In the wake of the highly publicized recall of a defective crib toy, Tiny Tykes Toys needs a strategic communication plan focusing on consumer confidence and the eventual expansion of its customer base.

Checklist 1: The Public Relations Situation

To participate in this exercise, use a class or group project assigned by your instructor, or select an organization that has both your personal interest and of which you have some firsthand knowledge. For example, you might select your current business, nonprofit organization, or client; a volunteer project; or an enterprise in which you were once involved. If you are a student, you might select an issue related to the college or university you attend.

Start with the basic planning questions. Careful consideration of these may satisfy your informational needs. You also may find it useful to address the more complete set of expanded planning questions. Use this checklist to the extent that the items can help you get a better understanding of the situation facing your organization. If some of these questions don't seem to address your specific planning needs, skip over them.

Basic Questions

1. What is the situation facing the organization?
2. What is the background of the situation?
3. What is the significance or importance of the situation?

Expanded Questions

A. EXISTING INFORMATION

Answer the following questions based on what you know directly or what you can learn from your client or from colleagues within your organization.

Background on the Issue

1. Is this the first time your organization has dealt with this situation, or are you setting out to modify an existing communication program? If the latter, is this a minor modification or a major one?
2. What is the cause of this situation?
3. Is there any dispute that this is the cause?
4. What is the history of this situation?
5. What are the important facts related to this situation?
6. Does this situation involve the organization's relationship with another group?
7. If yes, what group(s)?

Consequences of the Situation

1. How important is this situation to the organization's mission?
2. How consistent is this situation with the mission statement or vision statement?
3. How serious a response is warranted to this situation?
4. What is the likely duration of this situation: one time, limited/short term, or ongoing/long term?
5. Who or what is affected by this situation?
6. What predictions or trends are associated with this situation? (These can be organizational, industry related, community relations, nation-related, etc.)
7. What potential impact can this situation make on the organization's mission or bottom line?
8. Do you consider this situation to be an opportunity (positive) or an obstacle (negative) for your organization? Why? If you consider this an obstacle, how might you turn it into an opportunity?

Resolution of the Situation

1. Might information (quality or quantity) affect how this situation is resolved?
2. How can this situation be resolved to the mutual benefit of everyone involved?
3. What priority does this situation hold for the public relations/communications staff and for the organization's top management?
4. How strong is the organization's commitment to resolving this situation?

B. RESEARCH PROGRAM

If there are any significant gaps in the existing information, you may have to conduct research to learn more about the issue. This section will guide you through consideration of that option.

1. What is the basis for the existing information noted above: previous formal research, informal or anecdotal feedback, organizational experience, personal observation, presumption/supposition by planner(s) and/or something else?

2. How accurate is this existing information?
3. How appropriate is it to conduct additional research?
4. What information remains to be obtained?
5. If the existing information is not highly reliable, consider additional research, such as the following:
   - ✓ Interviews with key people within the organization
   - ✓ Review of organizational literature/information
   - ✓ Additional personal observation
   - ✓ Interviews with external experts or opinion leaders
   - ✓ Surveys with representative publics
6. What research methods will you use to obtain the needed information?

C. RESEARCH FINDINGS

After you have conducted formal research, indicate here your findings as they shed light on the issue facing your organization, and write a brief summary of the issue facing your organization.

> *Consensus Check*
>
> Does agreement exist within your organization about the observations and findings about the public relations situation? If "yes," proceed to Step 2, Analyzing the Organization. If "no," consider the value and/or possibility of achieving consensus before proceeding.

Step 2

Analyzing the Organization

The basis of effective communication is self-awareness. As such, strategists must have a thorough and factual understanding of their organization—its performance, its reputation, and its structure—before a successful strategic communication plan can be created. They must also seek to understand any factors that might limit the plan's success.

The second step of the strategic planning process involves a **public relations audit**, an analysis of the strengths and weaknesses of your organization or client. Writing in *Public Relations Tactics*, Rebecca Hart (2006) of the strategic communications/research firm of Hart & Partners, advises that an audit should be performed prior to developing an important new campaign, before rolling out a new product or service, or after management changes within an organization. At the company website (http://www.hartandpartners.com), she further suggests that audits should be conducted every five to seven years, as well as following a crisis situation.

Hart also notes the value of audits for individual public relations practitioners:

> First, you will gain a better understanding of how communications fits into your organization's big picture and how you can help the organization succeed. Senior managers will appreciate your numbers-oriented approach to communications and will be more likely to turn to you for advice on measuring results in the future. Finally, you'll have demonstrated strategic thinking, initiative, and business-savvy through your interactions with upper management, which will give you increased credibility for future situations. (2006)

A traditional method drawn from marketing is called **SWOT analysis**, because it considers the organization's strengths, weaknesses, opportunities, and threats. Typically, a SWOT analysis would look at each of these from two perspectives: internal and external. Such an analysis would consider both internal factors and external forces when focusing on strengths, for example, and not allow an illusion that the organization itself is strong but that all weaknesses come from outside. (Recall the findings of the Institute for Crisis Management, noted in the previous chapter, which found that 81% of corporate and organizational crises began on the inside, most of them because of mismanagement.)

What follows here is a more elaborate analysis focusing on three aspects of the organization: internal environment, public perception, and external environment.

Before moving on to the details of the analysis, it is important to point out that candor is the key to this step. To create an effective communication program, you must take an honest

Exhibit 2.1 The Public Relations Audit

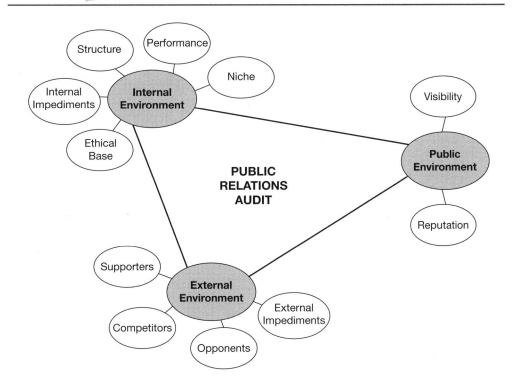

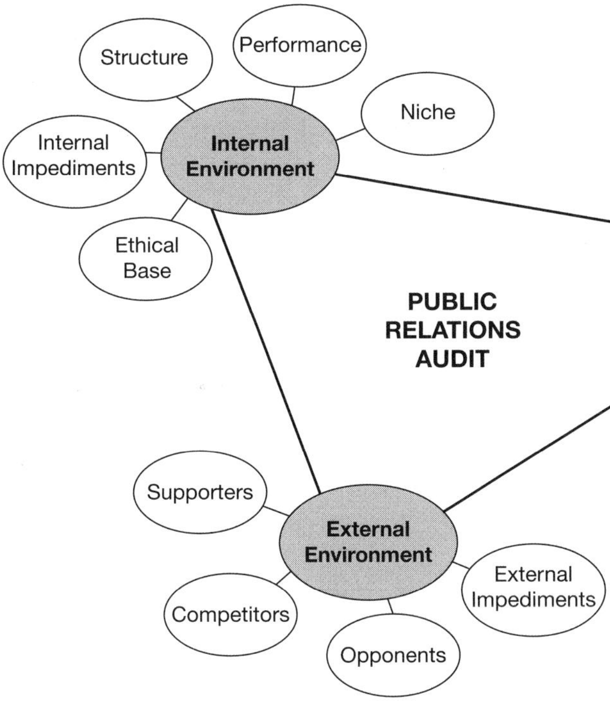

look at your organization, identifying its weaknesses and limitations as well as its strengths. If your organization is second best, admit it and proceed from that basis. Don't delude yourself by pretending that your organization is something that it's not. No successful public relations program has ever been built on fiction, and it does not serve your purposes to overlook flaws or shortcomings within your organization. However, temper your candor with tact. Brutal or indiscriminate honesty may turn off a client or a boss.

Exhibit 2.1 shows the relationship among the various elements of a public relations audit.

Internal Environment

Because public relations involves more than words, begin the audit by looking at the organization's performance and structure and any internal impediments to success. Here is an overview of each.

Performance

The most important aspect of the internal environment is **performance**. This includes the quality of the goods and services provided by the organization as well as the viability of the causes and ideas it espouses. The audit looks at this quality both as it is now and as it was in the past; it also considers the level of satisfaction that the organizational leadership has with this quality. Review the discussion of benchmarking in Step 1, since one of the purposes of benchmarking is to help an organization improve its performance.

Niche

Within the topic of performance, the internal audit also looks at the organization's **niche**—its specialty, the function or role that makes the organization different from other organizations. The word *niche* originally referred to a wall recess or alcove for displaying a vase of flowers, a religious statue, a bust or some other accent piece. In the context of public relations and marketing, a niche retains some of that original notion. It is a viewing point, the nook or cubbyhole that an organization occupies in a position for all to see.

Structure

The audit also considers the **structure** of the public relations operation within the organization. Specifically, it reviews the purpose or mission of the organization as it relates to the situation at hand, as well as the role public relations plays within the organization's administration. One particularly important consideration is whether public relations sits at the management table as part of the organization's decision-making process or whether it merely receives orders after the decisions are made by others.

The audit also inventories organizational resources that can be marshaled for the communication program, such as personnel, equipment, time, and budgets. No decisions or commitments are being made at this point as to what resources to use. During the audit stage, you merely are identifying the organization's available resources as they relate to the situation to be addressed.

Ethical Base

Public relations has been called the conscience of an organization, serving as its ethical base and moral grounding. In analyzing the internal environment of an organization, give thought to this ethical base. Consider whether the organization has a stated ethical ideal, and note if such an ideal is structural to the organization or personal to certain individuals. That is, is it based on how the organization sees itself, or is it merely the concern of an individual currently on the scene? If structural, the ethical base is likely to continue beyond the personal tenure of any individual manager or executive.

Internal Impediments

The final part of this internal audit is a look at **internal impediments**. Here you consider any impediments or obstacles within the organization that might limit the effectiveness of the public relations program. For example, many practitioners have expressed that their college education did not prepare them for the lack of organizational support, the need for continuing vigilance, and the amount of political infighting that goes on within some organizations. Wounded egos, shortsighted executives, company favorites, and other barriers must be considered as you develop the program. The term *impediment* is chosen with care. An impediment is not an insurmountable barrier, such as a road blocked off for repaving. Rather, it is a hindrance, more like a slow-moving truck on a country road. You can allow the truck to set the pace and remain behind it, or you can carefully and safely pass the truck and continue on your way. Or you can find another road.

Public Perception

The second focus for a public relations audit is public perception. What people think about the organization is the key focus for the public relations audit. This perception is based on both visibility and reputation.

Visibility

The extent to which an organization is known is its **visibility**. More subtly, this includes whether people know about an organization, what they know about it, and how accurate this information is. Public relations practitioners can do a great deal to affect the visibility of their organization or client.

Reputation

Based on an organization's visibility is its **reputation**, which deals with how people evaluate the information they have. It is the general prevailing sense that people have of an organization. Reputation is based on both word and deed—on the verbal, visual, and behavioral messages, both planned and unplanned, that come from an organization. Though we speak of reputation as a single perception, it really may be inconsistent, varying from one public to another and from one time to another. Reputation generally lags behind an organization's conscious attempt to affect the way people perceive it.

Generally, the stronger the organization's visibility and the more positive its reputation, the greater the ability it has to build on this positive base. On the other hand, low visibility suggests the need to create more awareness, and a poor reputation calls for efforts to rehabilitate the public perception of the organization, first by making sure the organization is offering quality performance, and then by trying to bring awareness into harmony with that performance.

Writing in *Communication World*, Pamela Klein (1999) notes that psychologically, a company with a solid reputation earns the benefit of the doubt in times of crisis. Supporting her claim, she points to an Ernst & Young study, *Measures That Matter*, which found that 40% of a company's market value is based on nonfinancial assets, including reputation. Klein also cites a Burson-Marsteller study, *Maximizing Corporate Reputations*, which reported that a CEO's reputation accounts for 40% of how a company is viewed by stakeholders and other publics.

A 2006 survey of health-care executives in collaboration with the Public Relations Society of America's Health Academy showed that 64% of CEOs rate reputation as "critical" or "very important" to their organization's success. Two-thirds (66%) say a positive shift in reputation can "significantly" or "dramatically" impact the bottom line, while 86% said a negative shift would hurt the organization. All self-reported that their corporations have "good" or "excellent" reputations. Aside from, perhaps, a bit of self-deception about their own reputations, the CEOs clearly see the importance of a good reputation as a real business asset.

This chapter's strategic planning checklist on analyzing public perception contains an Image Index, a tool developed to help you determine the public perception of an organization.

Where to Get Information for a Public Relations Audit

You can get information for a public relations audit from several different sources. Consider the following steps in gathering the information you will need:

1. See if past research has addressed some of the relevant issues, and obtain that information.
2. Check the public information about your organization, such as your annual reports, past news releases, and clipping files of published stories about your organization.
3. Ask people close to your organization if they can provide some of the necessary information from their own experience. Talk with managers and long-term employees. Talk especially with your front-line staff, such as clerks and sales representatives, and with the key service providers, such as nurses in a hospital or teachers in a school. Ask all of these sources what customers and other people outside the organization are asking and saying.
4. Conduct your own research, beginning with free or low-cost technology for online polling. SurveyMonkey and Zoomerang are probably the best known, but dozens of companies offer similar products.
5. Check out your organization with an Internet search engine. In particular, see what bloggers may be saying about you.

If additional information still is needed, conduct more formal research. Begin by broadening your resources for informal research. Eventually you may find that you require more formal research techniques. (See Appendix A: Applied Research Techniques for more information on secondary and primary research.)

The index is a series of contrasting characteristics or attributes—fun or tedious, expensive or inexpensive, risky or safe—that can be applied to any organization. Obviously there is no right or wrong response to any of these characteristics, and the index does not lead to a numerical answer. Rather, it is meant to stimulate your insight. By considering your organization in relation to these terms, you may come to an inference or a conclusion that perhaps you did not have before. In the planning process, you can use the index twice, first based on what the organization thinks of itself and later based on what its publics think of it.

The related concepts of visibility and reputation play a significant role in crisis communication. Appendix D: Effective Media Engagement is rooted in the premise that, particularly in crisis situations when an organization's visibility is high, an important public relations objective should be to focus on reputation.

External Environment

The analysis of the organization concludes with an examination of its external environment. In particular, this analysis looks at supporters, competitors, opponents, and other external impediments. Here is an overview of each.

Supporters

Every organization has a group of **supporters**—the people and groups who currently or at least potentially are likely to help the organization achieve its objectives. What groups share similar interests and values?

Competitors

Likewise, most organizations have **competitors**, people or groups who are doing the same thing as you in essentially the same arena. Research suggests that in a highly competitive environment, public relations activities often use messages and communication tactics to be persuasive in highlighting differences with competitors, while lower levels of competition may lend themselves less to advocacy and more to relationship building. But an organization's environment also may be uneven; it may be competitive with one public while cooperative with another.

Additionally, the mere fact that an organization is doing essentially the same thing as yours does not make it an opponent. Proximity is important. For example, a candidate for mayor in Seattle may have several competitors, but one of them is not the candidate for mayor in Baltimore. Indeed, organizations doing similar things in different areas might better be considered as colleagues, and as such, valuable resources for sharing information and perhaps assistance.

Opponents

Another important aspect of the external analysis is to consider the nature of any rivalry that may exist. **Opponents** are people or groups who are against your organization, perhaps because of something it says or does, perhaps because of its very existence. They have the potential to damage your organization by limiting its ability to pursue its mission and achieve its goals.

Note that there can be a big difference between a competitor, who provides a similar product or service, and an opponent, who is fighting your organization. Consider a store selling fur coats: A competitor might be the other fur store across town, while an opponent might be an animal rights group. The other stores just want to sell their products, while the activists want to see you go out of business. But even opponents come in different shapes and sizes, and planners have some important questions to ask about the nature of opposition. On the other hand, in some situations—political campaigns come to mind—opponents are competitors, and individuals as well as their political organizations have a primary strategy of besting the opponents.

Consider the various types of opponents and the potential impact of communication when you are analyzing this aspect of your external environment:

- **Advocates** may oppose you because they support something else, and you appear to stand in the way of their goal. Their tactics are mainly vocal. Through public communication, you may be able to find common ground for discussion and perhaps even the creation of an alliance between your organization and the advocates.
- **Dissidents** may oppose you primarily because of the position you hold or the actions you have undertaken. Their opposition is not irrational, and communication that addresses their interests and concerns might soften their opposition.

- **Antis** are dissidents on a global scale, people or groups who seem to oppose everything. Often such opposition is generic toward any kind of change or toward any established institution, so public communication probably would have little impact on them unless it were able to show that the presumed change is only illusional. But realize that the antis are suspicious of your organization in the first place, so they probably won't trust your messages.
- **Activists** are similar to advocates, but they want more than discussion. They generally seek change, so their opposition to your organization may be a by-product of their goal. Communication might reveal and promote a common basis for at least limited cooperation. But realize that activists, by definition, seek something specific and tangible, so talk alone won't move them.
- **Missionaries** are self-righteous activists in support of a cause, often operating under the presumption of moral imperative. Communication would have only limited potential for moderating their opposition, though it could help the organization avoid being an obvious target.
- **Zealots** are single-issue activists with a missionary fervor, so public communication is unlikely to coax them out of their opposition.
- **Fanatics** have been called zealots without the social stabilizers. These are the suicide bombers and terrorist snipers ready to go to any lengths in their opposition. Because of their willingness to undertake a no-holds-barred fight and to suffer personal injury, public communication can have little impact on them, though it may impact less fanatical supporters in the cause.

External Impediments

Additionally, consider any **external impediments** such as social, political, or economic factors outside an organization that might limit the effectiveness of a public relations program.

Planning Example 2: Analyzing the Organization

UPSTATE COLLEGE

Here is the analysis for Upstate College.

Internal Environment

Upstate College is a private liberal-arts college with 2,000 students, primarily commuters and residents from within a 100-mile radius. Most of the students had average grades in high school. They selected Upstate because of its reputation for small classes, reasonable tuition, and practical programs. In the past, about half the graduates went into the workforce and half transferred to four-year colleges and universities. The college has a news bureau and marketing office with a one-person staff assisted by freelancers and alumni volunteers. The office has equipment for desktop publishing, and the college publishes a weekly student newspaper and a quarterly alumni newsletter and oversees a website. It has only a token advertising budget.

Public Perception

Upstate College sees its reputation as being beneficial, relatively inexpensive, practical and an essential ingredient in the educational mix of this part of the state.

External Environment

Higher education has been a relatively noncompetitive environment until recent years, when lower numbers of students, fewer funds, and more alternatives for students have combined to create a climate that is somewhat competitive, though not unfriendly. Competition includes a private four-year college with very high entrance standards and even higher tuition, a large state university with entrance standards similar to Upstate's at about half the tuition, and a community college with only token costs, minimal entrance requirements, and a background (and continuing reputation) as a trade school. Upstate City recently has lost several major employers, and weakening family finances have begun to affect the ability of some Upstate College students to remain full-time students. Research reveals declining numbers of students in most area high schools, indicating a shrinking pool of traditional-age candidates for college. Additionally, general research reveals growing educational opportunities for web-based distance learning.

■ ■ ■

Here is the analysis for Tiny Tykes Toys.

TINY TYKES TOYS

Internal Environment

Tiny Tykes Toys manufactures toys for infants and toddlers. It recently voluntarily recalled one of its crib toys, a plush animal doll with a shiny nose. When babies chewed on the nose, it secreted an indelible green dye into their mouths and on their faces that lasted for several months. The dye was harmless, but the consumer lawsuits (minor) and resulting publicity (major and sensationalized) have caused a decrease in sales of other Tiny Tykes toys. The company has 130 union workers and 27 management staff. It also has a two-person public relations/marketing staff. Unrelated to the recall, but happening around the same time, a small but vocal group of employees began agitating for increased pay and shorter working hours.

Public Perception

The recall endangered the company's reputation for quality among stockholders, consumers, pediatricians, and other interest groups. The defect has been eliminated in new versions of the toy. The company perceives its image as fun, low-tech, inexpensive, beneficial, and safe.

External Environment

The business environment for children's toys is highly competitive, and it has become more so due to increasing international rivals and the expansion into the toy market of domestic companies once associated primarily with children's clothing. Tiny Tykes has several competitors, some of them nationally known companies with huge promotional budgets. Several of these companies have products of similar quality and cost to Tiny Tykes; they currently enjoy a more favorable reputation because of the recall. The overall business environment for toys is a growing and highly competitive market. The dissident employee faction has the potential for contributing to a wider consumer backlash against the company.

Checklist 2A: Internal Environment

Basic Questions

1. What is the quality of your organization's performance?
2. What communication resources, including budget, are available?
3. How supportive is the organization of public relations activity?

Expanded Questions

A. EXISTING INFORMATION

Answer the following questions based on what you know directly or what you can learn from your client or colleagues within your organization.

Performance

1. What service/product do you provide related to the issue identified in the Strategic Planning Exercise in Step 1?
2. What are the criteria for determining its quality?
3. What is its quality?
4. Within the last three years, has the quality improved, remained unchanged, or deteriorated?
5. How satisfied is organizational leadership with this quality?
6. What benefit or advantage does the product/service offer?
7. What problems or disadvantages are associated with this product/service?
8. What is the niche or specialty that sets you apart from competitors?
9. How has the service/product changed within the last three years?
10. How is the service/product likely to change within the next two years?
11. Should changes be introduced to improve the service/product?
12. Are organizational leaders willing to make such changes?

Structure

1. What is the purpose/mission of your organization related to this issue?
2. How does this issue fit into the organizational vision?
3. Is this expressed in a strategic business plan for your organization?
4. What communication resources are available for potential public relations/marketing communication activity: personnel, equipment, time, money, and/or something else?

5. Within the next three years, are these resources likely to increase, remain unchanged, or decrease?
6. How strong is the public relations/communication staff's role in the organization's decision-making process?

Internal Impediments

1. How supportive is the internal environment for public relations activities?
2. Are there any impediments or obstacles to success that come from within your organization:
   Among top management?
   ✓ Are these impediments caused by policy/procedure?
   ✓ Are these impediments deliberate?
   Among public relations/marketing staff?
   ✓ Are these impediments caused by policy/procedure?
   ✓ Are these impediments deliberate?
   Among other internal publics?
   ✓ Are these impediments caused by policy/procedure?
   ✓ Are these impediments deliberate?
3. If you have identified impediments, how can you overcome them?

B. RESEARCH PROGRAM

If there are any significant gaps in the existing information, you may have to conduct research to learn more about the internal environment. This section will guide you through consideration of that option.

1. What is the basis for the existing information noted above: previous formal research, informal or anecdotal feedback, organizational experience, personal observation, presumption/supposition by planner(s) and/or something else?
2. How accurate is this existing information?
3. How appropriate would it be to conduct additional research?
4. What information remains to be obtained?
5. If the existing information is not highly reliable, consider additional research, such as the following:
   ✓ Interviews with key people within the organization
   ✓ Review of organizational literature/information
   ✓ Additional personal observation
   ✓ Interviews with external experts or opinion leaders
   ✓ Surveys with representative publics
6. What research methods will you use to obtain the needed information?

C. RESEARCH FINDINGS

After you have conducted formal research, indicate your findings as they shed light on the internal environment of your organization and write a brief summary of the internal environment.

Checklist 2B: Public Perception

Basic Questions

1. How well known is your organization?
2. What is the reputation of your organization?
3. How do you want to affect this reputation?

Expanded Questions

A. EXISTING INFORMATION

Answer the following questions based on what you know directly or what you can learn from your client or colleagues within your organization.

Reputation

1. How visible is your service/product?
2. How widely used is your service/product?
3. How is the product/service generally perceived?
4. How is your organization generally perceived?
5. Is the public perception about your organization correct?
6. What communication already has been done about this situation?
7. Within the last three years, has your organization's reputation improved, remained unchanged, or deteriorated?
8. How satisfied is organizational leadership with this reputation?

Image Index

Place an "X" at the appropriate location on the continuum of what this key public thinks of your organization's product(s) or service(s):

Contemporary	__ __ __ __ __	Traditional
Fun	__ __ __ __ __	Tedious
High-Tech	__ __ __ __ __	Low-Tech
Ordinary	__ __ __ __ __	Distinguished
Expensive	__ __ __ __ __	Inexpensive
Idealistic	__ __ __ __ __	Practical
Modest	__ __ __ __ __	Pretentious
Scarce	__ __ __ __ __	Abundant
Worthless	__ __ __ __ __	Beneficial
Efficient	__ __ __ __ __	Inefficient
Ordinary	__ __ __ __ __	Innovative
Essential	__ __ __ __ __	Luxury
Risky	__ __ __ __ __	Safe
High-Quality	__ __ __ __ __	Low-Quality

B. RESEARCH PROGRAM

If there are any significant gaps in the existing information, you may have to conduct research to learn more about the public perception of your organization. This section will guide you through consideration of that option.

1. What is the basis for the existing information noted above: previous formal research, informal or anecdotal feedback, organizational experience, personal observation, presumption/supposition by planner(s), and/or something else?
2. How reliable is this existing information?
3. How appropriate would it be to conduct additional research?
4. If the existing information is not highly reliable, consider additional research, such as the following:
   - ✓ Interviews with key people within the organization
   - ✓ Review of organizational literature/information
   - ✓ Additional personal observation
   - ✓ Interviews with external experts or opinion leaders
   - ✓ Surveys with representative publics

C. RESEARCH FINDINGS

After you have conducted formal research, indicate your findings as they shed light on the public perception of your organization and write a brief summary of the public perception.

Checklist 2C: External Environment

Basic Questions

1. What is the major competition for your organization?
2. What significant opposition exists?
3. Is anything happening in the environment that can limit the effectiveness of the public relations program?

Expanded Questions

A. EXISTING INFORMATION

Answer the following questions based on what you know directly or what you can learn from your client or colleagues within your organization.

Competition

1. How competitive is the external environment of your organization?
2. What other organizations compete on this issue?
3. What are their performance levels?
4. What are their reputations?

5. What are their resources?
6. What does the competition offer that you don't?
7. How has the competition changed within the last three years?
8. Within the next three years, is the competition likely to increase, remain unchanged, or decrease?

Opposition

1. What groups exist with a mission to resist or hinder your organization?
2. How effective have these groups been in the past?
3. What is their reputation?
4. What are their resources?
5. How have these groups changed within the last three years?
6. How have their tactics changed?
7. Within the next three years, is the opposition likely to increase, remain unchanged or decrease?

External Impediments

1. Is the environment in which you are operating currently growing, stable, declining, or unpredictable?
2. What changes, if any, are projected for this environment?
3. What impediments deal with customers?
4. What impediments deal with regulators?
5. What impediments have financial or economic origins?
6. What impediments have political origins?
7. What impediments originate in society at large?

B. RESEARCH PROGRAM

If there are any significant gaps in the existing information, you may have to conduct research to learn more about the external environment of your organization. This section will guide you through consideration of that option.

1. What is the basis for the existing information noted above: previous formal research, informal or anecdotal feedback, organizational experience, personal observation, presumption/supposition by planner(s), and/or something else?
2. How reliable is this existing information?
3. How appropriate would it be to conduct additional research?
4. What information remains to be obtained?
5. If the existing information is not highly reliable, consider additional research, such as the following:
   - ✓ Review of organizational literature/information
   - ✓ Review of other published information (books, periodicals, etc.)
   - ✓ Review of electronic information (Internet, CD-ROMs, etc.)
   - ✓ Interviews with key people within the organization
   - ✓ Interviews with external experts or opinion leaders
   - ✓ Focus groups with representative publics

✓ Surveys with representative publics
✓ Content analysis of materials

6. What research methods will you use to obtain the needed information?

C. RESEARCH FINDINGS

After you have conducted formal research, indicate your findings as they shed light on the external environment of your organization and write a brief summary of the external environment. ■

Consensus Check

Does agreement exist within your organization about these observations on the internal and external environment and the public perception of your organization? If "yes," proceed to Step 3, Analyzing the Publics. If "no," consider the value and/or possibility of achieving consensus before proceeding.

Step 3

Analyzing the Publics

The planner's ability to identify and analyze publics is the cornerstone of an effective integrated communication campaign. The two elements of this—identification and analysis—are equally important. First, the planner needs to address the right group of people, so as not to squander organizational resources or miss opportunities to interact with important publics. Second, the planner must carefully examine each public in order to develop a strategy to communicate effectively.

Publics

What do we mean by the term *public*? One definition that still holds true is the classic definition given by social philosopher John Dewey in *The Public and Its Problems* (1927): A **public** is a group of people that shares a common interest vis-à-vis an organization, recognizes its significance, and sets out to do something about it. Publics are homogeneous in that they are similar in their interests and characteristics. They usually are aware of the situation and their relationship with the organization. They think the issue is relevant, and they are at least potentially organized or energized to act on the issue.

Publics, Markets, and Audiences

There are several different strategic groupings of people associated with an organization. The terms can be confusing, and sometimes they are used differently. Here's is an overview of these strategic groupings—publics, markets, audiences, and stakeholders:

Public. Don't confuse publics with other labels for groups of people who may interact with your organization. A **public** is like your family. You don't pick them; they just are—like generous Cousin Ezekiel and crazy Aunt Bertie. Publics may be helpful or annoying, friendly or not, but an organization must deal with them regardless. Publics exist because of their interaction and interdependency with an organization or because both they and the organization face a common issue.

Market. The **market** (and similarly called **market segment**) are more like your friends: you pick them, they pick you. Most people select friends on the basis of shared interests and common values. Markets are particular types of publics, and organizations develop marketing efforts among those publics with whom they intend to conduct business or generate support and participation. As segments of a particular population, markets include people with characteristics (age, income, lifestyle, and so on) that can help the organization achieve its bottom line. For public relations purposes, **bottom line** is a term that identifies an organization's mission or fundamental goal (selling cars, educating students, serving patients, and so on). It has less to do with finance and more with organizational success on the broader scale.

Audience. Don't confuse publics with **audiences**, which are merely people who pay attention to a particular medium of communication and receive messages through it. Both public relations and marketing will deal with audiences. An organization's relationship with an audience is usually brief, such as the length of time it takes to read an article or listen to a speech—much more temporary than its relationship with a public.

Stakeholder. A final category is a **stakeholder**, which some people identify as different from a public. The concept is that a stakeholder relates to an organization through its potential impact on the organization's mission and objectives, whereas a public relates to an organization through its messages (Rawlins, 2006). Others take the position that publics are people who don't necessarily care about an organization, whereas stakeholders are people who are conscious of a mutual relationship with an organization (Sandman, 2003). But because the term *stakeholder* is variously defined and because it generally refers to a group rather than an individual, this text takes the position that stakeholders and publics are the same thing, since the ultimate relationship with a public is based not merely on words but on relationships that involve mutual understanding and support.

Let's consider the various ways of grouping people through the example of a presidential candidate. The audience includes people using a particular medium who hear a speech or watch a television commercial. Some members of these audiences may be part of one of the candidate's wider publics, such as registered party members. Other registered members may not be found within a particular media audience, though they remain part of an important public for the candidate. Additionally, other members of the audiences may be members of a different public, such as voters registered with the opposing political party.

Usually audiences are not homogeneous but more often are **aggregates**—mere assortments of individuals with perhaps nothing in common other than their use of a particular communication medium. However, the more specialized the communication medium is, the more likely its audiences are to have in common both demographic characteristics (such as age and income) and psychographic characteristics (such as lifestyles and values). So the audiences of very specialized media may coincide with your public.

Audiences are relatively unimportant to your planning for strategic communication. Most organizations want to develop mutually beneficial relationships with their various publics, such as a company that hopes to create satisfactory business relationships with its customers. Strategic communicators try to reach those audiences who also happen to include their publics and markets.

Much overlap exists among publics, markets, and audiences. While differences among the three are important, sometimes it is their similarities that shed more light.

Characteristics of Publics

When you begin to identify publics, how do you know what to look for? Here are five important characteristics of a public:

Generation Y as a Public

The so-called Generation Y (teens and 20-somethings born roughly between 1980 and 2000) is of interest from both public relations and marketing perspectives. Consider the following facts and observations about Gen Y-ers. Linda P. Morton (2002b) has drawn some of this information from a variety of sources for her series on segmenting publics for *Public Relations Quarterly*.

Generation Y is the largest teen population in American history. At 60 or 65 million, this group is larger than the celebrated Generation X (about 50 million people born in the 1960s and '70s). It is the largest cohort group since the 75 million baby boomers. Its values and attitudes have been shaped by such formative public events as the 1999 shootings at Columbine High School in Littleton, Colorado; the contested 2000 election and extreme partisan politics ever since; the September 2001 terrorist attacks on the United States and the resultant accusations of government secrecy, torture, and violation of human rights; the subsequent U.S. wars in Afghanistan and Iraq, as well as the international distrust associated with them; and topping off with the election of Barack Obama.

More than one in three U.S. teens is not white, the largest percentage ever. Additionally, teens today have greater experience than previous generations with nontraditional family structures, which has fostered an appreciation for diversity, equality, and tolerance. A concern for privacy and a distrust of both government and mass media also are characteristics of this generation.

Meanwhile, teens have more money to spend than in previous years. They are brand conscious but not necessarily brand loyal. Huge image campaigns mean little when brands simply go out of style. Teens don't like a hard sell, but they trust each other and respond to word-of-mouth endorsements. Celebrity endorsements, not so much. For example, Nike may be losing its grip on Gen Y-ers, who don't find it particularly persuasive that Michael Jordan endorses the brand.

Gen Y people don't read newspapers often. They do listen to a lot of radio, but only to a narrow range of stations; they are more likely to listen to individually tailored music sources. They watch TV but have access to an average of 62 channels.

They use the Internet a lot, but don't necessarily visit websites of even the organizations and brands that they like, and they don't necessarily purchase products or services associated with their favorite websites. And the high-speed action of the Internet also means that trends and fashions can change overnight.

Does this sound like anybody you know?

Distinguishability. A public is a recognizable grouping of individuals, though not necessarily a recognized organization or formal group. For example, a jewelry company might want to promote itself to "everyone who wants to buy expensive jewelry." But that isn't a public, because it does not identify a particular group of people. Rather, the jeweler might identify its public as "people with incomes above $50,000 who are marking life events such as birthdays, anniversaries, graduations, and so on."

Homogeneity. A public's members share common traits and features. They may not know each other, but they have enough in common for you to treat them as a group. For example, all college professors who teach criminal justice courses do not know each other and may not even agree on specific issues within the discipline. But their collective interest in and knowledge of criminal justice warrant their identification as a public by an organization such as the National Association of Chiefs of Police. Consumer publics identified as market segments traditionally have been identified by common traits, such as the baby boomers, ethnics, seniors, Generation X-ers, and so on.

Importance. Not every identifiable group and certainly not every isolated individual is important to your organization's success. Some can prudently be overlooked or deferred. Strategists for public relations and marketing communication are most interested in those publics that can significantly impact on an organization's bottom line and affect its progress toward achieving its mission.

Large Size. Make sure your public is large enough to warrant strategic attention and the possible use of public media. If you are dealing with only a few people, they don't constitute a public and your programming tactics would probably be limited to personal communication tools. Having said that, don't hesitate to treat a small group of individuals as a public if they are vital to the organization. For example, a lobbying effort may be directed at a handful of members of an important senate committee.

Accessibility. A public is a group with which you are able to interact and communicate. For example, it is easy for a community college to reach potential students, because most are concentrated within a small geographic area, often in narrow demographics such as high school students or underemployed 20-somethings. It is more difficult for a university of world renown to reach potential students because they are thinly scattered throughout the world and have many and varied interests.

Key Publics

Good communication planning calls for the identification of an organization's various publics. As pointed out at the beginning of this section, there is no such thing as a general public. Rather, each public is linked with the organization in a unique relationship.

Over the years, sociologists studying organizations have developed the useful concept of linkages, which are the patterns of relationships that exist between an organization and its various publics (see Esman, 1972; Evan, 1976; and Grunig & Hunt, 1984). While various categories of linkages have been suggested, this book presents four useful categories of linkages: customers, producers, enablers, and limiters. If you consider these linkages, you are likely to identify each relevant public for your program. Exhibit 3.1 shows the relationship among the various public relations linkages.

Customers. The most obvious type of public may be **customers** who receive the products or services of an organization, such as current or potential consumers, purchasers, clients, students, patients, fans, patrons, shoppers, parishioners, members, and so on. This category also includes **secondary customers**, who are the customers of your customers, such as the companies and graduate schools to which a college's graduating seniors apply. The category of customers also includes what has been called **shadow constituencies** (Mau & Dennis, 1994), people who may not have a direct link with the organization's products or services but who can affect the perception of an organization. For example, if hard times force a high-tech company known for its philanthropy to cut back on charitable contributions to the arts, members of the arts community (a shadow constituency) may vocally criticize the company, adding to its problems.

Exhibit 3.1 Categories of Publics

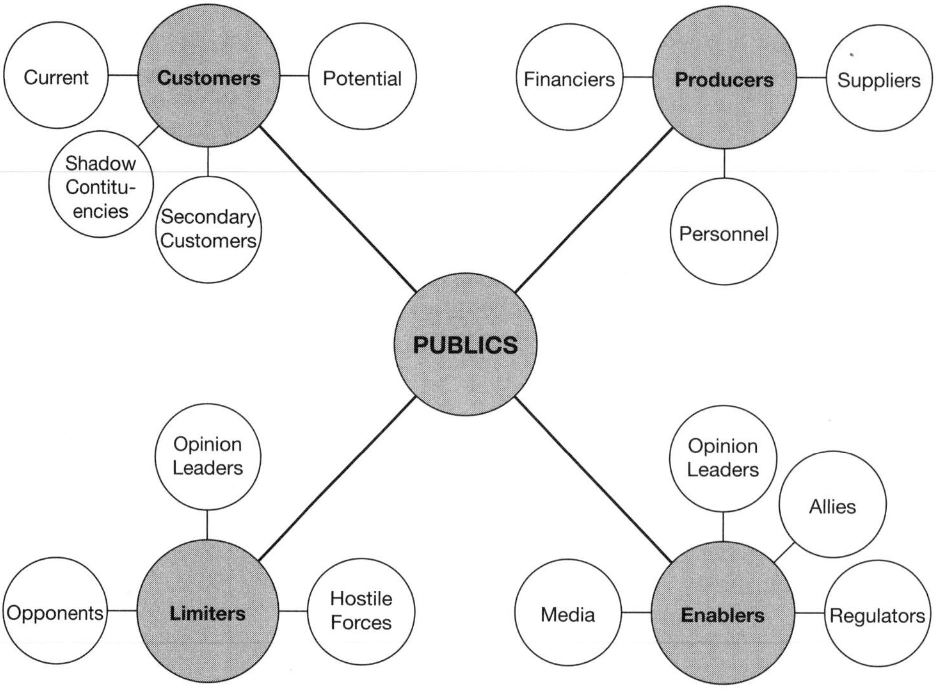

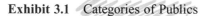

Consider this example of a charity seeking to raise funds for research into amyotrophic lateral sclerosis (ALS), Lou Gehrig's Disease. Obvious stakeholders are the charity itself and people suffering from the fatal disease, but they are not likely to have the resources to support the organization financially. A better strategy might be to expand the concept of stakeholder to other groups: extended families of ALS patients who look on with frustration as their loved ones become paralyzed and die, medical people who treat ALS patients, and the insurance companies responsible for many of the costs associated with treatment.

Producers. Those publics that provide input to the organization are called **producers**. These include personnel such as employees, volunteers and unions; producers of needed materials such as suppliers; and producers of the financial resources such as investors, donors, and stockholders.

Enablers. Another type of public are **enablers**, groups that serve as regulators by setting the norms or standards for the organization (such as professional associations or governmental agencies), opinion leaders with influence over potential customers (such as stockbrokers and analysts), and groups that otherwise help make the organization successful (such as the media). Other groups of publics include allies, which the organization may be able to work with on cooperative projects and to construct parallel interests.

Limiters. Those publics that in some way reduce or undermine the success of an organization (such as competitors, opponents, and hostile forces) are known as **limiters**. The same activist

A Typology of Publics

Here are some examples of the common families of publics appropriate to various public relations or marketing communication situations. Let this list spark your creative thinking about identifying publics relevant to your organization.

Customers
Occasional/regular
Current/potential/former
Competitive/loyal
Age/ethnicity/spending potential/other variables
Members/casual customers
Secondary customers
Shadow constituencies
Stakeholders

Producers
Employees/volunteers
Veteran/novice
Volunteers: leadership/grassroots
Line/staff
Management/nonmanagement
  Management: upper/middle
  Nonmanagement: supervisory/staff/maintenance/production/uniformed
Management/union
Families/retirees
Investors/shareholders
Donors/foundations/grantors
Current/potential/former

Enablers
Community leaders: government/professional/business/union/educational/religious/ethnic
Community organizations: service/professional/religious/social/ethnic/cultural/political/environmental/activist
Industry association/regulatory agencies
Accreditation bodies
Professional experts/consultants/analysts
Government bodies
  town/city/county/state/federal
  elective/appointive
  legislative/executive/judicial
  staff/advisory/committee/department
Diplomatic bodies: embassy/consulate
Military/civilian
Media: local/state/regional/national/international
Specialized media: professional/financial/consumer/religious/ethnic/trade/advocacy/academic
Media availability: general/limited/restricted
Print media: newspaper/magazine/newsletter
Newspapers: daily/nondaily
Electronic media: television/radio/internet
  Television: broadcast/cable
  Radio: AM/FM; commercial/public; satellite
  Internet: newsgroups/websites/blogs

Limiters
Competitors
Opponents
Activists

groups that were cited above as potential enablers can become limiting publics when the organization is unable to walk in step with them. Likewise, an unfriendly newspaper or television station can become a limiting public.

The above four categories are not the only typology for identifying publics. Some practitioners distinguish between internal and external publics (often shorthand for producer and consumer publics). Another approach identifies primary, secondary, and marginal publics, which seems to be rather a listing in order of importance to the task at hand. Another categorization looks at current versus future publics; still another at proponents, opponents, and uncommitted publics.

Some practitioners identify a category of special publics, groups usually outside the organization who are labeled according to age, race, ethnicity, gender, lifestyle, or some other dominant demographic criterion. In the typology of publics presented in this book, we look at each public in its relationship to the organization (customers, producers, enablers, and limiters). Thus, the concept of special publics has little practical value for a student or newcomer to the field of public relations and little to offer beyond the more comprehensive fourfold typology used here.

Additionally, some planners refer to primary publics as the key groups interacting with an organization, secondary publics as the intercessory groups who can influence the primary public, and tertiary publics as those special publics identified according to a relevant demographic.

Amid the confusing verbiage of different categorization styles, the aim remains the same: To identify all the possible publics interacting with an organization, and then to move on to analyzing their relationship(s) with the organization.

Having identified major categories of publics, the next step is to look at each of them in more detail. By more narrowly identifying our publics we can understand them better. For example, a university embarking on a recruiting campaign can't simply identify potential students as a public. That is too broad a category, because there are so many different kinds of potential students. Rather, it might classify its publics as high school students, junior college transfers, returning adult learners, employed people seeking retraining and professional development, underserved minorities, and perhaps even recreational learners. Each of these publics might have very different characteristics, and if the university is to be effective it must deal with each public individually.

We also want to eliminate from consideration groups that are not publics, having no present or impending relationship with an organization and thus no mutual consequences. For example, people getting married and planning a honeymoon would not be a public for a travel agency specializing in senior-citizen bus tours. The best advice in dealing with groups that are not publics is *don't*—don't waste time and money trying to communicate with people who have no reasonable or relevant relationship with your organization or no interest in your products or services.

Intercessory Publics and Opinion Leaders

In everyday situations, it is not uncommon to ask a friend to put in a good word with someone we want to impress. We do this to get dates, jobs, and good deals on stereos. This practice is often called **networking**. But the more appropriate term is **intercession**, which basically means using an influential go-between. Accordingly, an intercessor is a person who presents your case to another, someone who uses her influence to intercede on your behalf to obtain a favor, mediate a dispute, or to speak for you.

What's common in everyday life is also found in public relations activity. An organization often will address itself not only to its key publics but also to groups who already are in contact with that public. Such an **intercessory public** can serve as an influential bridge between an organization and its publics. In many planning situations, some of the publics listed as enablers can function as intercessory publics, because they already have the attention and respect of the ultimate public.

Take the news media, for example. In most public relations activities, the media are not the public you are finally trying to reach. Rather, they are a first point of contact, providing a means to reach another public, such as music lovers whom an opera company might identify as one of its key publics. In this case the media, particularly their music critics, already have the attention of the music lovers, who presumably read and appreciate the reviews. So the public relations practitioner sets out to inform, interest, and impress the critic.

As another example, consider an organization providing job training to high school dropouts in an inner-city area. The organization might find through research that coaches in community centers and ministers in urban churches can be intercessory publics. These people share the organization's interest in helping the young adults who left school early, and they often hold the confidence of the young people. The job-training agency could direct some attention toward coaches and ministers, increasing their knowledge of the program and the benefits it offers the community and the participants. With proper orchestration, coaches and ministers could become vocal supporters and even unofficial recruiters for the job-training program.

In addition to intercessory publics, we sometimes deal with intercessory individuals. Usually we call these people **opinion leaders**, men and women who have a particular influence over an organization's publics. Research provides some guidance into working with people who will carry an organization's messages to others. Paul Lazarsfeld's **two-step flow of communication theory** (Lazarsfeld, Berelson, & Gaudet, 1944), and the multistep flow theory that evolved from it observe that the media influence opinion leaders, who in turn influence other people. Everett Rogers's **diffusion of innovations theory** (1995) notes that people who are quick to try new ideas or products are influential with latecomers to the innovation.

An opinion leader is an influential role model who has the respect and confidence of the public. Members of publics look to opinion leaders as they obtain information, form attitudes and opinions, and determine action. Opinion leaders are particularly useful because they generate **word-of-mouth support**, perhaps the most effective type of communication precisely because opinion leaders are independent. That is, they do not speak under the auspices of the organization, nor do they directly benefit from it. Because of this independence they are often quite believable.

Where can you find an opinion leader? Ask. Look around. Research the publics.

- **Formal opinion leaders** have structured roles, such as elected or appointed officials or people who hold a recognized position of authority.
- **Informal opinion leaders** exert influence simply because they are informed, articulate, and recognized leaders on a particular issue.

For both, their influence is based on existing relationships, real or perceived. Examples of these are family; neighborhoods; political parties; ethnicity; and shared lifestyle, social, or professional interests. Opinion leaders may be global or local.

For example, informal opinion leaders might include talk-show hosts such as Oprah Winfrey, or they might be local people like an opinionated clerk at the corner store or a well-read neighbor. Increasingly, bloggers fit this category.

Some opinion leaders fall into the category of **vocal activists**, people who are linked to particular issues and who are known as advocates for their cause. While some activists can be dismissed as single-issue zealots, most are perceived as both independent and critical, and their support can add credibility to an organization's message. Opinion leaders may have some characteristics different from your publics. Researchers with the Roper Organization have found that people who are identified as opinion leaders prefer reading over television as a source of their information ("Opinion Leaders," 1992). They also initiate action on topics of interest by writing letters to the editor, attending public meetings and rallies, working with activist groups, and the like.

Prioritizing Key Publics

Sometimes the task of selecting publics for a strategic communication program is an easy one. In many situations, the appropriate public is quite evident—a manufacturing plant seeking to increase productivity looks to its employees; a church wanting to increase contributions looks to its congregation; a politician seeking re-election targets voters in her district.

A major element of an effective communication campaign is the identification of appropriate specific publics, called **key publics** or **strategic publics**. (Note that this book uses the term *key publics* for those specific publics that the planner identifies as being most important to the public relations activity. Other books sometimes use the term *target public*, though this seems to suggest that the public is merely a bull's-eye for the organization's darts rather than part of a reciprocal relationship.)

Key publics are the people you want to engage in a communication process. Don't allow yourself to generalize here. The manufacturing plant may not need to address all of its employees. Some already are very productive; others are new and still learning their responsibilities, so an accent on productivity could hinder their progress. Instead, the company may focus on a particular work shift to increase productivity. Likewise, the church may raise funds primarily among its affluent parishioners, and the politician may aim the re-election campaign particularly toward senior citizens who vote proportionately more often than younger residents.

If key publics are not readily obvious to your planning team, the examples and exercises that follow can help you identify them systematically and objectively. After you have identified your many publics, you will select those that are particularly important for the situation you are working on. These key publics often number from two to five, though this could increase considerably with complex issues.

Readers coming from a background in marketing should be forewarned: The tendency in marketing has been to identify objectives before selecting key publics. However, this book uses the publics-before-objectives order for three reasons: (1) the first two steps in the planning process have already helped you identify the focus for your planning; (2) publics exist in a relationship with an organization even prior to any objectives for impacting that relationship; and (3) objectives are relevant only when they link an organization's goals with a particular public.

Based on the issue you identified in Step 1: Analyzing the Situation, as well as the above information and insights about your various publics, select several publics that warrant particular attention. These become your key publics as you address this issue.

While all your publics may be important in various situations, not all warrant your attention as you deal with the situation at hand. For example, the college's recruiting program may not choose to involve its graduates, and the toy company's competitors may not be a significant public in a campaign to regain consumer confidence.

This is the point in your planning process where you weed out the less important publics, concentrating instead on those few that have particular relevance to the issue with which you are dealing.

Planning Example 3A: Identifying Publics

Here is a listing of publics for Upstate College.

- *Customers* include students and, in most cases, parents. Potential customers are academically average high school students or employed people seeking an education. Secondary customers include eventual employers and (with the program expansion) graduate schools.
- *Producers* include the faculty and administration, alumni and other donors, and banks and other financial aid programs.
- *Enablers* include the state education department and the media (both state and local). Opinion leaders include guidance counselors and career counselors.
- *Limiters* include other area colleges and universities as well as banks cutting back on student loans.

After due consideration, three key publics for this campaign are identified:

- Students
- Guidance counselors
- Alumni

■ ■ ■

Here is a listing of publics for Tiny Tykes Toys.

- *Customers* include parents, grandparents and other purchasers of baby toys.
- *Producers* include employees (both union and management), stockholders, and suppliers.
- *Enablers* include other members of the American Toy Institute, financial media, family- and child-oriented media, and consumer protection agencies (which are increasing their regulation of toy manufacturers). Opinion leaders for customers include pediatricians, early childhood educators, child psychologists and consumer groups.
- *Limiters* include other toy companies (especially importers of cheap toys), a consumer activist group threatening a boycott and a faction of disgruntled employees challenging the union and encouraging a walkout.

After due consideration, four key publics for this campaign are identified:

- Employees
- Parents and other purchasers
- Family- and child-oriented media
- Consumer protection agencies.

Checklist 3A: Publics

Basic Questions

1. Who are the major publics for your organization?
2. Who are the key publics for this situation?
3. Who are the intercessory publics or major opinion leaders?

Expanded Questions

A. EXISTING INFORMATION

Answer the following questions based on what you know directly or what you can learn from your client or colleagues within your organization.

Customers

1. Who are your primary customers?
2. Who are your secondary customers—who uses the products or services of your primary customers?
3. How have your customers changed within the last three years?
4. How are your customers likely to change within the next three years?

Producers

1. Who produces your service/product?
2. Who provides your organization with services and materials?
3. Who provides money?
4. How have your producers changed within the last three years?
5. How are your producers likely to change within the next three years?

Enablers

1. Who are opinion leaders among your customers?
2. Who are your colleagues?
3. Who are your regulators?
4. How have regulators helped you within the last three years?
5. With whom do you have contracts or agreements?
6. What media are available to you?
7. How have the media helped you in the last three years?
8. How have your enablers changed within the last three years?
9. How are your enablers likely to change within the next three years?

Limiters

1. Who are your competitors?
2. Who are your opponents?
3. What type of opponents are they: advocates, dissidents, activists, or zealots?
4. Who can stop you or slow you down?
5. How have your limiters changed within the last three years?
6. How are your limiters likely to change within the next three years?

Intercessory Publics and Opinion Leaders

1. What publics are in a position of influence with your key publics?
2. How likely is it that they will speak for your organization's position?
3. Who are formal opinion leaders for this audience—elected government officials, appointed government officials, or someone else?
4. How likely is it that they will speak for your organization's position?
5. Who are informal opinion leaders for this audience—family leaders, neighborhood leaders, occupational leaders, religious leaders, ethnic leaders, and/or community leaders?
6. How likely is it that they will speak for your organization's position?
7. Who are vocal activists on this issue?
8. How close is their position on this issue vis-à-vis the organization's?
9. How likely is it that they will speak for your organization's position?

B. RESEARCH PROGRAM

If there are any significant gaps in the existing information, you may have to conduct research to learn more about your organization's various publics. This section will guide you through consideration of that option.

1. What is the basis for the existing information noted above—previous formal research, informal or anecdotal feedback, organizational experience, personal observation, presumption/supposition by planner(s), and/or something else?
2. How reliable is this existing information?
3. How appropriate would it be to conduct additional research?
4. What information remains to be obtained?
5. If the existing information is not highly reliable, consider additional research, such as the following:
   - ✓ Review of organizational literature/information
   - ✓ Review of other published information (books, periodicals, etc.)
   - ✓ Interviews with key people within the organization
   - ✓ Interviews with external experts or opinion leaders
   - ✓ Focus groups with representative publics
   - ✓ Surveys with representative publics
6. What research methods will you use to obtain the needed information?

C. RESEARCH FINDINGS

After you have conducted formal research, indicate your findings as they shed light on the organization's publics.

Analyzing Key Publics

Here's a maxim that organizational communications can live by: Know your audience. The newspaper advice columnist Miss Manners demonstrates this effectively in some of her columns. Miss Manners is witty, if a bit stodgy, as she writes protocol (which dinner fork to use), politeness (how to say thanks for a gift you don't like), relationships (how to introduce your lesbian lover to your father's former mistress) and other elements of etiquette (how to apologize for getting snockered at your best friend's wedding).

Clearly the know-your-audience counsel was unheeded by this letter writer—a 14-year-old girl whose mother wouldn't let her wear thong underwear and whose friends made fun of her because of it. Miss Manner's response: "Of all the advice columnists in the world, you chose Miss Manners as the most likely one to support the cause of thong underwear? And you wonder why your mother questions your judgment?" (Martin, 2008).

It is most important to understand the publics with which we seek to interact. Careful analysis of each key public is the cornerstone of the research phase. The more information and insight planners can bring to this step, the more effective the overall program.

The idea behind this step is to allow the planner to "get inside the mind" of the organization's key publics. Much of this information can be obtained through informal research such as interviews and brainstorming; some of it may require more formal research techniques such as focus groups and surveys. (See Appendix A: Applied Research Techniques for information on how to conduct these research methods.) Through formal and informal research, as well as good sense, the planner carefully examines each public.

One of the most important ways of analyzing a public is to consider the consequences it has on the organization and, conversely, the consequences the organization has on the public—actively or at least potentially. In a very real way, consequences create publics, and our public relations involvement with publics often is guided by an analysis of how real and obvious those consequences are.

In this section you will reconsider the general information uncovered in Step 2: Analyzing the Organization and apply it to each key public. You'll want to note the public's stage of development and its key characteristics. Each of these topics is discussed below.

Stages of Development

Publics are not fixed in concrete; rather, they are fluid and evolving. Grunig and Hunt (1984) have identified four stages of publics: nonpublics, latent publics, aware publics, and active publics. To this list, a fifth type can be added: apathetic publics. The relationship of each stage can be seen in Exhibit 3.2, where the solid arrow points to the changes that can be encouraged by effective public relations activity and the dotted arrow shows changes that may evolve with or without public relations input. Let's look at each type of public.

Nonpublic. A **nonpublic** is a group that does not share any issues with the organization, and no real consequences exist to or from the organization. At this level and this time, this group simply is of no significance to the organization. For example, a nonpublic for an animal adoption shelter would be people who live in apartments that don't allow pets. The logical public relations response for this public is observation, periodically monitoring the situation to see if it changes; for example, if the restrictions are eased, or if people move to a new building with different rules.

Latent public. A **latent public** shares an issue with the organization but does not yet recognize this situation or its potential. You might call it an embryonic public, because it has potential but as yet no self-awareness. For the animal adoption shelter, senior citizens who might appreciate companionship would be a latent public. An organization's public relations response is to plan communication to enhance its relationship with this public, perhaps by helping the shelter adapt itself to the interests of this group. For example, it may invite apartment dwellers to volunteer a couple hours each week to interact with the animals awaiting adopting from the shelter, giving companionship and exercise to both the animals and the volunteers, creating knowledgeable people who might serve as opinion leaders for others who could adopt a pet, and perhaps fostering future adoptions when the volunteers are in a pet-friendly environment.

Apathetic public. A public that faces an issue, knows it, and simply doesn't care is an **apathetic public**. To this public, the issue is not important enough to warrant its attention, and the consequences are not perceived as being important. This can be frustrating for an organization, but properly identifying an apathetic public may help the organization reframe its message to overcome the apathy. An apathetic public for the animal adoption shelter might be people who don't particularly like pets. The public relations response to such a public is to monitor the situation carefully, for it could change quickly if the issue begins to capture the public imagination. Meanwhile, the organization also should develop plans to communicate with the apathetic public, trying to transform its apathy into interest. But realize that changing negative attitudes and opinions is a difficult task. Public relations is unlikely to be effective in convincing someone who doesn't like animals that she should become a pet lover.

Aware public. An **aware public** recognizes that it shares an issue and perceives the consequences as being relevant, but it is not organized to discuss and act on the issue. An aware public for the animal adoption agency may be people who have learned that psychologists believe the companionship of pets improves the quality of life for senior citizens. The public relations response is to initiate proactive communication, providing information about the issue, stressing its significance to the public and presenting the organization's opinion or intended action. At this stage the organization can control the tone and themes of the message.

Active public. In the final stage of its development, an **active public** has reached the fullness of what we identify as a public. It is discussing and acting on the shared issue. For the animal shelter, an active public might be the local chapter of a senior citizen organization that is actively encouraging senior citizens to adopt pets. In friendly circumstances such as the one described above, this can be an opportunity for building coalitions. In confrontational situations, on the other hand, an organization's response to an active public generally is reactive communication, responding to questions and often to accusations or even active opposition. In this reactive setting, the tone or message themes are no longer controlled by the organization but instead by the active public.

Sometimes, active publics split in their relationship to an organization and issues associated with it. **Single-issue publics** may be active on all of the issues important to the organization, active only on some popular issues, or active on single and often controversial issues. One animal rights group, for example, may confine its activism to local issues involving impounding of stray animals, neutering, credentialing of pet owners, and other issues related to a particular shelter, while a similar group may be active on a wider range of issues, including testing of

Exhibit 3.2 Stages of Publics

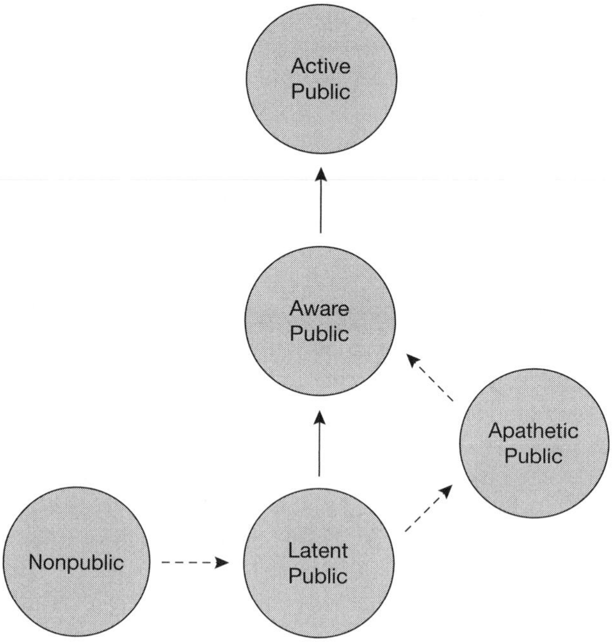

medicines and cosmetics on animals, fur and leather fashion, hunting and fishing, and vegetarianism.

Key Characteristics

After noting the stages of development, look at each public in reference to the following five key characteristics: the public relations situation, the organization, the public's communication behavior, its demographics, and its personality.

- *The Public Relations Situation.* Assess the public's wants, interests, needs, and expectations related to the issue, as well as what it does not want or need. Consider relevant attitudes of the public. The hierarchy of needs (Maslow, 1987) and the hidden needs (Packard, 1964) outlined in this chapter can be useful aids in considering the interests and needs of publics.
- *Organization.* Consider each key public's relationship with the organization—how your organization impacts on the public and vice versa. Also consider the visibility and reputation of your organization with this public.
- *Communication Behavior.* Study the public's communication habits, such as the media or communication channels it uses. Identify people who might be credible message sources for this public and who are its opinion leaders. Also indicate whether the public is seeking information on the issue. This assessment will have major impact later when you choose your communication tools, because information seekers

Maslow's Hierarchy of Needs

Psychologist Abraham Maslow (1987) developed the **drive-motive theory** or the **theory of human motivation**, commonly known as the **hierarchy of needs**. This theory offers an understanding not only of what people need but also of what Maslow called **prepotency**, the ordered internal relationship among needs by which more basic needs must be addressed first. His theory is presented visually as a two-part pyramid of five levels, with the stronger needs at the base.

The base of the pyramid includes four levels of needs:

1. **Basic physiological needs** deal with oxygen, food and water, and sleep, as well as basic sexual urges.
2. **Safety needs** include shelter, employment, economic stability, and other kinds of security.
3. **Love needs** focus on belonging, family, friends, and group identity.
4. **Esteem needs** deal with respect and appreciation.

The top of the pyramid includes the fifth level, **self-actualization needs**. This category deals with achieving potential and with pursuing ideals such as spirituality and perfection, beauty and art, and peace and understanding.

Note that the self-actualization needs are in a category by themselves, separated from the others. Whereas a deficiency in any of the four levels in the base of the pyramid can create tension within a person, the fifth level adds to the person's freedom to explore and achieve his greatest ambitions.

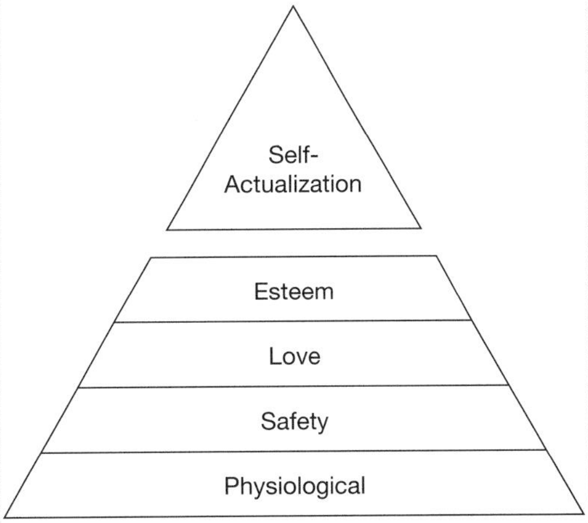

Needs at each level of Maslow's pyramid are interrelated and can be fulfilled in different ways.

Recent research suggests that Maslow's categories of motivation are more appropriate than their particular order. For example, while the sex urge is a basic psychological need, it is an urge that can be controlled. For some people, sex also can have application to a feeling of security; for others, it may be less associated with basic physiological needs and more with a sense of love and belonging, self-esteem, and even spirituality.

Phase One

Step 3

are likely to initiate communication or make use of tactics that require their direct involvement.

- *Demographics.* Identify demographic traits such as age, income, gender, socio-economic status, or other relevant information about this public.
- *Personality Preferences.* Consider the psychological and temperamental preferences of this key public. Appraise the relative merits of logical versus emotional appeals.

Packard's Hidden Persuaders

In his book *The Hidden Persuaders*, Vance Packard (1964) noted that advertising and public relations agencies sometimes turn to psychology to gain insight into why people react to messages in certain ways.

He identified eight motivations that persuaders often tap to sell products, social messages, and political candidates. Here is the list of these eight motivations:

1. Need for emotional security
2. Need for reassurance of worth
3. Need for ego gratification
4. Need for creative outlets
5. Need for love objects
6. Need for a sense of power
7. Need for roots
8. Need for immortality

Knowing something about the personality of the key public and then tailoring messages to fit such psychological preferences can make communication more persuasive and more effective. During this step of the planning process, use the Personality Preferences checklist to look more closely at each of your key publics. Later in the process you will consider ways to craft messages that complement these preferences.

Like other aspects of this research phase, your answers to the questions posed in the planning checklist may be tentative and based on presumptions or common sense. However, insight from the organization's experience can prove useful as you begin to understand the communication preferences of your key publics. Eventually you may decide that formal research is needed; if so, consult Appendix A: Applied Research Techniques for some research suggestions.

Stereotypes

Stereotypes are short cuts in describing groups of people. They are based on common and repeated perceptions of who people are, how they act, and what they think and value. Stereotypes are what Walter Lippman, (1922) called "pictures in our heads," and they are helpful precisely because they can whittle down the complexity of the real world.

Stereotyping has some value use in social interaction. We can identify threatening situations based on our ability to read other people. We are told to anticipate danger, drive defensively, and otherwise use what we know (or presume) about others to our advantage. Parents tell their children not to associate with "a bad crowd" or "the wrong kind of people." Despite the obvious social concerns associated with profiling, law enforcement agencies know how to look at peoples' behaviors and conclude when they are acting suspiciously.

The problem with stereotyping is not that it is a generalization, but rather that it is an overgeneralization. Appropriate stereotyping reflects judgments about people based on things about them over which they have some choice: their actions and behaviors, their choices in occupation, fashion, speech, grooming, and the like. It makes less sense to judge people based on aspects of over which they have little or no control: race, ethnicity, age, skin tone, religious or cultural background, language accent, and so on.

Decisions about who is or is not part of a bad crowd may be made on the basis of the both types of stereotypes—ethnic background or family structure over which the person has little control, or grooming and fashion choices that the person has made.

Stereotype-based decisions also can be dead wrong. For years, stereotyping has led many people to associate drug use with inner-city youth rather than suburban youth, yet studies show that drug abuse, as well as underage drinking and drunk driving, is higher in the suburbs than in inner cities. The stereotype simply is wrong, and as public relations planners, we use such stereotypes to our own detriment.

Consider the following facts, which may challenge some of your own stereotypes about certain groups of people.

A 2003 poll by Zogby International found that 78% of teens associate Italian Americans with mobsters, gang members, or restaurant workers. Another poll found that 74% of adults think most Italian Americans are connected to organized crime, though the U.S. Justice Department reports less than .0025% of Italian Americans (that's one in 40,000) as being involved in organized crime. The U.S. Census Bureau reports that two-thirds of Italian Americans in the workforce are on professional jobs such as teachers, attorneys, executives, and physicians. Nevertheless, the entertainment and advertising industries continue to draw heavily on the unreal stereotype of America's fifth-largest ethnic group ("Italian American Stereotypes in U.S. Advertising," 2003).

Asian Americans are stereotypically thought of as well educated. The Census Bureau reported in 1999 that 26% of Asian Americans have a college degree, compared with 17% of all Americans. That supports the stereotype. On the other hand, the bureau also reported that 8% of Asian American adults over age 25 have less than a ninth-grade education, compared to 7% of all Americans. That fact goes against the stereotype. Maybe the stereotype needs revision.

In analyzing publics, it is important to consider the level of diversity within them. Often, research and close observation reveals that a public is more diverse than it might appear from only a cursory glance. In particular, two groups within American society are subjected to all kinds of inaccurate stereotyping that masks a diversity which is much richer than may first appear. Consider the facts about Arab Americans and Native Americans in light of what you know to be the common stereotypes in the boxed insets.

Why are these issues for us? Because public relations practitioners develop campaigns, craft speeches, prepare scripts, write newsletters, and in so many other ways research and write about people and issues that are affected by stereotyping. Our role is not to change the social structure of our environment but to be accurate with facts and fair to people.

Rethinking Your Publics

Occasionally, this part of the process may point out a problem in your earlier identification of key publics. If you find it difficult to identify traits common to your public, perhaps you have defined the public in terms that are too general.

American Indians: Stereotype vs. Reality

Of the many populations within American society, few are more assaulted by stereotypes than are Native Americans. Consider the following facts in light of the common stereotypes.

The U.S. Census Bureau in 2006 reported 4.5 million American Indians, most of them of mixed ancestry. The collective Native population is the smallest minority group in America based on race. The largest Native nations are Cherokee, Navajo, Choctaw, Sioux, and Chippewa. The comprehensive designation of American Indians, Alaska Natives, and Native Hawaiians sometimes is used.

There are 562 federally recognized tribes in the United States, plus another 250 or so seeking federal recognition. Each tribe is an autonomous and self-governing entity whose sovereignty is recognized by the federal government and whose lands are legally distinct from state lands that encircle them. Thus, in significant ways, tribal laws replace state law. Because tribes are autonomous, it is not appropriate to consider American Indians a single political entity. Official membership and citizenship eligibility varies by tribe.

Culturally, Native peoples of North America are richly diverse. About 200 languages are spoken by half a million people in the U.S. and Canada, many with very different linguistic roots, often with sophisticated grammar.

Here are some additional facts that shatter stereotypes:

- The Native population is growing faster than the general U.S. population (38% between the 1980 and 1990 federal censuses, 43% between 1990 and 2005). Many of these are multiracial people with some Native heritage. Additionally, 7 million Americans claim some Indian ancestry but are not officially counted within the Native population.
- Less than 15% of Indians live on reservations, which concentrate geographically in six states (led by Oklahoma, Arizona, and New Mexico). Only three states east of the Mississippi (New York, North Carolina, and Michigan) have sizable Native populations.
- Prosperity is increasing among American Indians. While 25% live below the poverty level, this is the same as most other ethnic and racial groups in America. Economically, Native Americans are second only to Asian Americans for income through minority-owned businesses. They also show an 84% growth in business ownership, particularly in service, construction, and retail businesses.
- Two-thirds of tribes do not run casinos. For those that do operate reservation-owned casinos, it is a $5 billion industry.
- School dropout rates are higher among Indians than any other population group. Nevertheless, three-fourths of adult Indians have a high school degree. More than half of high school graduates attend college, and 14% hold a bachelor's degree. More than 125,000 have a master's or doctoral degree.
- Contemporary Indians are part of mainstream American life. They operate radio and television stations, run public relations agencies, sponsor colleges, and work in every occupation. New York City and Los Angeles are the two biggest cities for Native-owned businesses.
- Though life expectancy among Native Americans is 10 years less than the national average, health is steadily improving. Suicide rates are decreasing. Alcoholism remains high, and many deaths are accidental and alcohol related.

- Indians pay federal income tax, state income tax except on income earned on reservations, sales tax on off-reservation purchases, and off-reservation property tax. Federal and tribal laws, but not state laws, generally apply on reservations.
- Native Americans have national newspapers and radio programs. They are increasingly exercising a presence in public relations and the media. Most tribes have their own public relations department or functions, as do many Native-related organizations, such as the National Native American Law Students Association, the American Indian Science and Engineering Society, the (Canadian) Assembly of First Nations, and the (Catholic) Tekakwitha Conference.

Public relations strategists will be mindful of such diversity among the Native communities. In particular, communicators should be careful not to adopt icons and images of one Indian group and project it upon all. Many Indians come from the Northeast, Southeast or Southwest, where buffalo never roamed. The stereotype of the Plains Indian with feathered headdresses and teepees simply does not apply to the Navajo and Apache of the Southwest, the Salish and Yakama of the Northwest, nor the Mohegan, Seminole, or Haudenoshaunee (Iroquois) of the eastern states. Additionally, not all Indians hold powwows.

The Public Relations Society of America includes Native Americans in its Multicultural Affairs committee, and several Native-owned public relations agencies exist.

Treaty, taxation, and casino-related issues are leading some Native Americans to get involved with government. Lobbying and the use of news media is increasing, as is activism in some areas. In New York, for example, the six nations of the Haudenoshaunee (Iroquois) are fighting the state's sporadic attempts to collect sales taxes on tribal lands, which they see as a clear violation of federal treaties and law.

What's the value of all this information? It can serve as a reminder that stereotypes are inaccurate. Are there differences between Native Americans and others? Certainly. Some are positive: close families, respect for the environment. Some are negative: higher school dropout rates, higher rates of alcoholism. But the stereotypes often perpetuated through movies, advertising, and other forms of media are outdated at best, and certainly demeaning and hurtful—and thus of little value to a strategic communicator.

Consider the plight of a group of planners developing a program to raise awareness, generate interest, and obtain funds to help save the African elephant from human predators. The planners misidentified as one of their key publics "people with incomes above $50,000." As they analyzed their publics, the planners were having difficulty because they could not identify the mind-set of this public, which was too broad and had no common traits other than income. That's because income wasn't really a public at all but rather a demographic description, and not a very comprehensive one at that.

So the planners redefined their public more specifically as "people with incomes above $50,000 who have a pre-existing interest in issues of conservation and endangered animals." With those criteria, the planning team then could develop a profile of its public: people who want to help animals, expect a workable plan for doing so, want an organization with a proven track record, have an altruistic spirit to make the world a better place, and have the financial

Arab Americans and Muslims

What little most Americans know about Arabs and Muslims they learn through the media, which—whether focused on news or entertainment—tends to continue negative and misleading stereotypes. Islamic and Arab publics are oversimplified by outsiders, but a good public relations strategist will work her contacts within the Arab and Islamic communities to help understand the sometimes subtle differences.

First off, note the double focus of this section. The public generally confuses Arab (member of an ethnic group originating in the Middle East) and Muslim (member of a religious group known as Islam). The two are not the same. Most Arab Americans are not Muslims, and most Muslims are not Arab.

Arab Americans

Here are some relevant facts about Arab Americans:

- Though statistics are a bit unreliable, most reports indicate that the United States is home to about 3.5 million Arab Americans. Most are citizens born here.
- Nearly half of all Arab Americans (47%) trace their ancestry to Lebanon; most of their families came to the United States a century ago. Other Arab Americans are from Arabia (14%), Syria (11%), and Egypt and Palestine (both 6%), with smaller numbers from Jordan, Morocco, the Sudan, Algeria, Libya, Yemen, and other countries in the Middle East and northern Africa.
- Arab Americans are the fastest-growing minority in the United States, with a 30% growth between 1990 and 2000 according to the federal census.
- Politically they are split fairly evenly between Democrats and Republicans.
- About 85% of adult Arab-Americans have a high school degree. More than 40% have a bachelor's degree (compared to about 25% for Americans in general).
- Arab Americans generally have a higher household income than the U.S. average.
- They are more likely to run their own businesses.
- Two-thirds of Arab Americans are Christian. About 35% are Catholic, 18% Orthodox, and 10% Protestant. An estimated 25% are Muslim (according to a Zogby International Survey of 2002). Some Christian religious groups are historically rooted in the Arab community, such as the Catholic Maronites from Lebanon, the Coptic Orthodox Christians from Egypt, and the Chaldean Catholics from Iraq.

American Muslims

Here are some related facts about Americans who are Muslims, adherents to the religion of Islam. Much of the data is drawn from a 2001 study by the Hartford Institute on Religious Research.

- Most reports indicate that the United States is home to about 1.5 or 3 million Muslims, though some internal sources estimate twice that number.
- Two-thirds of Muslims are immigrants or children of immigrants.
- In general, the Islamic community subdivides into four nearly equal segments: Southeast Asians; African Americans; Arabs; and other groups such as Turks, Kurds, Iranian/Persians, Berber/Moroccans, and so on. Muslims percentages are growing six times faster than the general population, and Muslims have a younger population than the country overall.

- Muslims lead national averages in education; 67% of adults have at least a bachelor's degree (compared to 44% of the general population); 32% have a master's degree or doctorate.
- They also have higher incomes than the general population, and often are found in engineering, computing and medicine; they are under-represented in journalism and law and are less likely than others to own their own businesses.
- There is religious diversity within Islamic America. About two million people are affiliated with mosques, and there are more than 1,200 mosques in America; they are represented in every state, with the largest numbers in California, New York, Texas, Pennsylvania, and Ohio. About 30% of mosque members are converts.
- The largest groups in mosque membership were South Asian Americans (33%), African Americans (30%), and Arab Americans (25%).
- Most U.S. mosques are intercultural, with members of various ethnic backgrounds. On average, membership is one-third South Asian, one-third African American, and one-quarter Arab. In general, political and social divisions in the Middle East among Sunni, Shi'ite, Sufi, and Wahabi Muslims and home-grown American sects such as the Nation of Islam have had only minimal affect on most American mosques.
- More than 20% of mosques operate full-time schools, but less than 3% of Islamic children receive religious education outside the home.
- The first Muslim to be elected to the U.S. Congress is Keith Ellison, a Democratic congressman from Minnesota who was elected in 2007. In Texas that year, a Muslim running as a Republican was defeated for a congressional seat. In 2000, Muslim Americans voted overwhelmingly Republican; in 2008, 89% voted for Barack Obama. It's clear that Muslims are becoming more politically active. Nearly 80% are registered to vote, and 85% of those registered say that they vote.

ability to contribute to this cause. This redefinition also helped the planners avoid wasting resources by trying to convert people to a cause in which they had no interest.

Sometimes an analysis of the publics will reveal that you simply need more information to take you beyond the insufficient common knowledge. For example, you may have identified African Americans as a key public for your campaign. Yet in your analysis you are likely to discover that, other than the physical characteristic of race itself, there may be few common elements within this public. For example, there are significant differences between American-born and foreign-born blacks; and in some cities, the foreign-born population is quite large—about a third in New York City, and nearly half in Miami. Likewise, Southern blacks are culturally Southern, which may give them more in common with Southern whites than with Northern blacks.

Meanwhile, just as within Hispanic, Asian American, and Native American communities, there is much diversity among American blacks. Significant cultural differences are to be found among blacks from Haiti, Senegal, Nigeria and Ethiopia (not to mention Newark, San Diego, Seattle, and Baltimore). And a closer look will reveal a population divided by language as well. Additionally, one might suspect that the half-million black Mormons or the 200 million black Catholics worldwide might, at least on some issues, have more in common with their coreligionists than with certain other members of their race.

Once you are satisfied that you have identified your publics appropriately, review the analysis of each and consider whether the information you have generated should lead you to make any changes in the lineup. For example, a public that earlier seemed to be key may now be shown to be too apathetic to justify your action at this time.

Remember: Planning is a flexible process. The conclusion of Step 3 is one point along the way where you should rethink your plans so far, adjusting them based on the information becoming available to you through continuing research.

The Benefit Statement

Conclude your analysis of the publics with a benefit statement that briefly indicates the benefit or advantage your product or service can offer this public, or how you can help satisfy its need or solve its problems. For example, the benefit a community foundation might offer its donors could be stated as follows:

> The Equity Foundation offers donors the opportunity to pool their money with the donations of others, thereby compounding small donations into larger, more effective grants.

In more of a marketing vein, the benefit an online bookstore might offer college and university students could be written as:

> Cyber Booksellers can assure university students that it can provide class textbooks at discount prices with immediate delivery.

This concludes the Formative Research phase of the strategic planning process. Having completed these steps, you now should have some clear insights about your issue, the status of your organization as it relates to this issue, and your various publics and their relationship to your organization. You are probably already beginning to get ideas about how to communicate with these publics. Jot down whatever may come to mind, but don't worry yet about developing specific program tactics. The next phase of the planning process addresses strategic questions, such as the outcomes you want to accomplish and the approach you will take.

Planning Example 3B: Analyzing Key Publics

UPSTATE COLLEGE

Upstate College alumni and other donors are a latent public that can quickly become an active one.

Analysis of Key Characteristics

Issue: The alumni/donor public will appreciate this program expansion; this public needs only basic information to instill appreciation.

Organization: This key public provides continued support for the college, while the college provides this public with a sense of pride and value of the academic degree. This public has high knowledge of the college and thinks favorably about it. It can be called upon for action. It shares the college's self-image as a high-quality institution.

Communication: This public occasionally participates in on-campus activities and has access to general news media as well as the college newsletter. The college has a mailing list of alumni and donors. This public is not actively seeking information because an announcement has not yet been made, but it could be expected to be attentive to information. Credible sources include famous alumni and respected donors.

Personality Preferences: This is a diverse group, with some members having a preference for messages that are factual, logical, and reality based, while others prefer messages focused on ideas, sentiment, and vision.

Demographics: Wide range. Higher than average in education. No particular significance in demographics other than geographic proximity to college.

Benefit Statement

Upstate College can provide information to alumni about the college's successes and strengths, giving alumni a sense of pride in their alma mater and an opportunity to help build on those strengths. (Note: Similar analyses would be made for each individual key public you have identified.)

■ ■ ■

TINY TYKES TOYS

Tiny Tykes Toy Company employees are an active public.

Analysis of Key Characteristics

Issue: The employee public wants to see the company reputation improved and wants to see the employer regarded as a leader in the industry. Morale has been affected negatively by the recall: employee public does not want to feel bad about making an inferior infant product, needs information on quality and safety, and cautiously expects leadership from the company in improving quality and reputation.

Organization: This employee public ultimately affects the quality and productivity of the company, knows the company intimately, and has organized for action through unions and through work teams. The company affects this public through continuing employment. Employees do not share management's self-image of being beneficial and safe.

Communication: The employee public gets its information in an interpersonal setting with management and supervisors, can be reached through direct mailings and newsletters, and also receives information from local news media. This public is actively seeking info on this issue. Credible sources include management officials, veteran employees, and union leaders.

Personality Preferences: Rank-and-file employees are accustomed to receiving messages based on fact, certainty, and logical analysis. Managers may be more disposed to messages that also deal with vision.

Demographics: The employee public spans age groups but has in common lower-middle-class socioeconomic/educational background; there are many ethnic workers. Most members of this public do not personally use company products, but often in the past they have given the products as gifts to family and friends.

Benefit Statement

Tiny Tykes can provide information that will give employees renewed purpose and pride about the quality and safety of its products. (Note: Similar analyses would be made for each individual key public you have identified.)

Checklist 3B: Key Publics

Basic Questions

1. What is the nature and type of each key public?
2. What are the major wants, interests, needs and expectations of each public?
3. What benefits can you offer this public?

Expanded Questions

A. EXISTING INFORMATION

Answer the following questions based on what you know directly or what you can learn from your client or colleagues within your organization.

1. Who is your key public?
2. Indicate the category below that best describes that key public at this time and consider the public relations response indicated.

Category	**Response**
Latent public. Faces an obstacle or opportunity vis-à-vis the organization. Does not yet recognize this situation or its potential.	Monitor the situation, anticipating change toward awareness. Meanwhile, begin to plan a communication process to provide information about the issue, explain its significance to the public and present your organization's opinion or intended action.
Apathetic public. Recognizes an obstacle or opportunity vis-à-vis the organization. Does not perceive this issue as important or interesting.	Monitor the situation, looking for any change toward perceiving the relevance of the issue. Meanwhile, begin to plan a communication process to provide information about the issue, explain its significance to the public, and present your organization's opinion or intended action.
Aware public. Recognizes an obstacle or opportunity vis-à-vis the organization. Not yet organized for action.	Initiate a communication process to present the issue, explain its significance to the public, and present your organization's opinion or intended action.

Active public. Recognizes an obstacle or opportunity vis-à-vis the organization. Preparing to organize or already organized for action.

Because you did not communicate sooner, you must now engage in reactive communication, responding to questions and perhaps to criticism and accusations without being able to control the tone or themes of the messages.

Analysis of Key Characteristics

Issue

1. What does this key public know about this issue?
2. What does this public think about this issue?
3. What does this public want on this issue?
4. What does this public not want on this issue?
5. What does this public need on this issue?
6. What problem(s) does this public have related to this issue?
7. What does this public expect from the organization vis-à-vis this issue?
8. How free does this public see itself to act on this issue?

Organization (including product/service)

1. How does or how might the key public affect your organization?
2. How does or how might your organization affect this public?
3. What does this public know about your organization?
4. How accurate is this information (compared to information in Step 2)?
5. What does this public think about your organization?
6. How satisfied are you with this attitude?
7. What does this public expect from your organization?
8. How much loyalty does this public have for your organization?
9. How organized or ready for action on this issue is this public?
10. How influential does this public see itself as being within the organization?
11. How influential does the organization see this public as being?
12. Place an "X" at the appropriate location on the continuum of what this key public thinks of your organization's product(s) or service(s):

Contemporary	___ ___ ___ ___ ___	Traditional
Fun	___ ___ ___ ___ ___	Tedious
High-Tech	___ ___ ___ ___ ___	Low-Tech
Ordinary	___ ___ ___ ___ ___	Distinguished
Expensive	___ ___ ___ ___ ___	Inexpensive
Idealistic	___ ___ ___ ___ ___	Practical
Modest	___ ___ ___ ___ ___	Pretentious
Scarce	___ ___ ___ ___ ___	Abundant
Worthless	___ ___ ___ ___ ___	Beneficial
Efficient	___ ___ ___ ___ ___	Inefficient
Ordinary	___ ___ ___ ___ ___	Innovative
Essential	___ ___ ___ ___ ___	Luxury
Risky	___ ___ ___ ___ ___	Safe
High Quality	___ ___ ___ ___ ___	Low Quality

13. What are the similarities and the differences between your organization's self-image in the exercise from Step 2 and the image of it held by this public?

Communication

1. What media do this public use among each of the following—personal communication channels, organizational media, news media, and advertising/promotional media?
2. Is this public actively seeking information on this issue?
3. How likely is this public to act on information it receives?
4. Who are credible sources and opinion leaders for this public?

Demographics/Psychographics

1. What is the average age of members of your key public?
2. Where is your key public located geographically?
3. What is the socioeconomic status of your key public?
4. What products or services does your key public commonly use?
5. What are the cultural/ethnic/religious traits of your key public?
6. What is the education level of your key public?
7. What lifestyle traits does your key public have?
8. Is this public likely to be persuaded more by facts, more by emotion, or by a combination?
9. Is this public likely to be motivated more by appeals to the past (experience, success, track record) or by appeals to the future (motivation, inspiration, vision)?
10. Are there other relevant characteristics about your key public?

Benefits

1. What benefit or advantage does your organization offer each public?
2. How does this benefit differ from the benefits available from other organizations?

B. RESEARCH PROGRAM

If there are any significant gaps in the existing information, you may have to conduct research to learn more about your organization's various publics. This section will guide you through consideration of that option.

1. What is the basis for existing information noted above—previous formal research, informal or anecdotal feedback, organizational experience, personal observation, presumption/supposition by planner(s), and/or something else?
2. How reliable is this existing information?
3. How appropriate would it be to conduct additional research?
4. What information remains to be obtained?
5. If the existing information is not highly reliable, consider additional research, such as the following:
   - ✓ Review of organizational literature/information
   - ✓ Review of other published information (books, periodicals, etc.)
   - ✓ Interviews with key people within the organization
   - ✓ Interviews with external experts or opinion leaders

✓ Focus groups with representative publics
✓ Surveys with representative publics

6. What research methods will you use to obtain the needed information?

C. RESEARCH FINDINGS

After you have conducted formal research, indicate your findings as they shed light on the organization's publics. Also, write a benefit statement about how the organization can satisfy the wants and needs, address the interests, and solve the problems of this particular key public.

> *Consensus Check*
>
> Does agreement exist within your organization on the analysis of these key publics? If "yes," proceed to Step 4, Establishing Goals and Objectives. If "no," consider the value and/or possibility of achieving consensus before proceeding.

Phase Two

STRATEGY

Strategy is the heart of planning for public relations, marketing communication, and related areas. All the embodiments of strategic communication are rooted in the research already undertaken in the previous phase and growing toward the eventual choice of communication tactics. Just as rushing through the research phase would have jeopardized the foundation on which to build your public relations or marketing communication plan, so will failing to give adequate attention to strategy result in weak messages and pointless activity.

Step 4
Establishing Goals and Objectives

Step 5
Formulating Action and Response Strategies

Step 6
Developing the Message Strategy

Simply stated, **strategy** is the organization's overall plan. It is the determination of how the organization decides what it wants to achieve and how it wants to achieve it. Strategy has a dual focus: the action of the organization (both proactive and responsive) and the content of its messages (theme, source, content, and tone). Refer to strategy in the singular, because each program should have a single, unifying strategy. Phase Two deals with mapping the course toward your overall destination, deciding both where to go and how to get there. By building on research from Phase One of the planning process, you will anchor your program in the mission or vision of the organization and you will maintain a fixed gaze on your chosen publics.

Specifically, this phase of the planning process leads you to a closer look at your organization: its vision of itself, as well as its hopes for the various publics important to it. These hopes will be fleshed out as goals, positioning statements, and objectives. Then the strategy phase will focus your attention on two key aspects of your planning: what you will do, and what you will say about what you will do. The first of these delves into both action and response, under the notion that actions speak louder than words. First you focus on the things you do; then you turn your attention to how you communicate about those actions.

The entire strategic process is interrelated and interdependent: goals guide the development of objectives, which in turn help drive decisions about what persuasive strategies to use and what tactics to employ to address the problem or opportunity.

Admittedly, there are different approaches to strategic planning, and various practitioners may use different terminology. For example, some planners set goals before they identify and analyze publics. This often is true when the planner comes from a marketing perspective, where the organization starts with its sales or promotional goals, then identifies potential customers who might be or become interested in the organization's products or services. Classic public relations generally builds its strategic plans from an understanding of the ongoing relationships between the organization and its various publics, then looks at how the organization's goals and objectives potentially impact on these publics.

Step 4

Establishing Goals and Objectives

This step is about looking inward and deciding what you want to achieve. To better understand this step, you need to understand the twin concepts of goals and objectives. It should be noted that public relations and marketing strategists generally make the distinction that goals are general and global while objectives are specific. However, some advertisers and other specialists rooted in business disciplines either reverse the meanings of the terms or use them interchangeably. In your actual practice, you may find people applying different definitions to these terms, so make sure you understand what the words mean and how colleagues use them. In *Strategic Planning for Public Relations*, we use the terms as they are outlined below.

Organizational Goals

As you set out to articulate the desired interaction you can have with your publics, first focus on positioning and organizational goals. Having previously identified the relevant public relations situation in Step 1, ask yourself these simple questions: What do we want people to think about us? What position do we seek with our publics?

A successful approach to strategic communication in a competitive environment is to position the organization according to its own particular niche. **Positioning** is the process of managing how an organization distinguishes itself with a unique meaning in the mind of its publics—that is, how it wants to be seen and known by its publics, especially as distinct from its competitors.

The concept of distinctiveness is an important one for all organizations—large and small businesses, educational and charitable organizations, political and human service groups, hospitals, churches, and sports teams. In most settings, organizations are known more by their distinctiveness than by their similarities. For example, in the field of higher education, a dozen or more schools might be located in a particular metropolitan area. Each is likely to be identified by its unique characteristics: the large public university, the small church-affiliated college, the high-priced two-year private school, the community college with an open admissions policy, the midsized public institution that used to be a teachers college, and so on. Problems can occur when the niche is not unique. For example, if your school is one of two small church-affiliated colleges in the area, you will emphasize what distinguishes it from the other, such as lower costs, a suburban campus, graduate degrees, evening/weekend programs, or the particular denomination or religious community that sponsors the college.

Organizations have found that the concept of positioning is fluid, and some organizations have made successful attempts to reposition themselves to keep pace with a changing environment. Consider the "This is not your father's Oldsmobile" campaign, which tried to reposition Oldsmobile from a line of cars popular with middle-aged and senior drivers to one fashionable for a younger generation. The campaign had a lot going for it: a catchy slogan, upbeat music, a sporty new design for its new models. And it achieved high levels of awareness. Unfortunately, sales declined, and in terms of average age, the typical Olds owners became . . . well, older. So much for the value of awareness alone.

How does an organization position itself? First it conducts and analyzes research to determine just how it is perceived by various publics; it also considers the position held by its major competitors. The organization then identifies the position it would like to hold, seeking to distinguish itself from its competition. Having done all this, the organization develops a strategy to modify its current position or perhaps simply to maintain the niche it already holds.

Make sure that your desired position is realistic. Who wouldn't want to be known as "the industry leader" or "the first name in (whatever)"? But there can be only one leader, one first name. A good strategic planner will be wary of pretense and of stretching beyond possibility. At best, it would be an exercise in futility. At worst, chasing an impossible dream wastes valuable organizational resources, invites ridicule, and exposes the organization to risk.

Also, don't confuse the public relations concept of *positioning* with its use in marketing, where the term refers to the competitive approach for a persuasive message (i.e., positioning according to features such as customer focus, competitive advantage, social responsibility, lifestyle, or product attribute). When we talk about positioning in public relations, we refer less to the presentation of the products or services and the messages about these, and more to perception—how we want our organization to be seen by our publics. As Al Ries and Jack Trout explain in *Positioning: The Battle for Your Mind*, "Positioning is not what you do to a product. Positioning is what you do to the mind of the prospect" (2001, p. 2).

A **goal** is a statement rooted in the organization's mission or vision. Using everyday language, a goal acknowledges the issue and sketches out how the organization hopes to see

Examples of Positioning Statements

Here are some examples of how various organizations might try to position themselves. Note how each statement highlights a desired attribute of the organization by implying a distinction from competitors.

- The leader that sets industry standards
- The best value, reflecting low cost and high quality
- The most economical
- The most expensive and most prestigious
- The hospital preferred by women
- The family-friendly restaurant
- The "green" brand

Positioning Ethics

Carefully think through the ethical implications in creating a positioning statement for your organization.

Don't state your desired position merely to brag, particularly if the bragging is based on an inflated view of reality. Wanting to be the first, biggest, cleanest, or fastest is not the same as actually being the first, biggest, or cleanest. Your publics will easily see through boasting and swaggering.

More important, don't use the positioning statement as a putdown for another organization. For example, a candidate for political office might seek to position herself as "a soccer mom who cares about her community." There could be a lot of potential to such an appeal. But it would be unethical if instead she aimed to be seen as "a better parent than the other candidate." While that might be true, it's far better for individual voters to conclude this rather than for the candidate's political organization to explicitly state the theme.

it settled. A goal is stated in general terms and lacks measures; these will come later, in the objectives.

In their classic book *Public Relations Management by Objectives*, Norman Nager and T. Harrell Allen (1984) use the analogy of transportation: Goals provide the direction while objectives pinpoint the destination. In general, communication goals can be categorized as relating to three different types of management situations.

1. **Reputation management goals** deal with the identity and perception of the organization.
2. **Relationship management goals** focus on how the organization connects with its publics.
3. **Task management goals** are concerned with getting certain things done.

The three types of goals together offer a way of laying out the various aims associated with public relations and integrated communication campaigns. However it is unnecessary, even unlikely, that every campaign will have each type of goal. Planners mix and match these as they consider appropriate to their specific campaign.

Who sets an organization's communication goals? Generally, public relations managers do, usually as an implementation of the organization's strategic plans, which ideally the public relations people have had a hand in developing. These overall plans may be identified in global documents, such as the strategic business plan, or they may be found in implementation guidelines, such as an annual strategic plan or a statement of priorities or directions.

Whatever source they use, strategic communication planners first should note how the organization defines what it means to be successful and then develop goals that grow out of this understanding.

Objectives

An **objective** is a statement emerging from the organization's goals. It is a clear and measurable statement, written to point the way toward particular levels of awareness, acceptance or action.

Examples of Public Relations Goals

Here are several examples of the three different types of public relations goals.

Reputation Management Goals

- Improve the company's reputation within the industry
- Enhance the hospital's prestige as the leading center for sports medicine
- Reinforce the organization's image with potential donors or investors
- Strengthen the agency's standing within the environmental movement

Relationship Management Goals

- Promote better appreciation of the firm among potential clients
- Enhance the relationship between the company and its customers
- Maintain a favorable relationship amid social or organizational changes

Task Management Goals

- Increase public support for organizational goals
- Advance social change on a particular issue
- Impact public behavior on matters associated with the organization's mission
- Create a favorable climate for our client among regulatory agencies
- Attract a sell-out crowd to a fund-raising concert

An objective is what Mitchell Friedman of PR Insight calls "a milestone measuring progress toward a goal" (2003).

Objectives often are established by communication managers responding to broader organizational goals. Like goals, objectives deal with intended outcomes rather than procedures for reaching them. A single goal may be the basis for several objectives.

Management by objectives (MBO) is the process by which effective and efficient organizations plan their activities. While the acronym MBO has somewhat gone out of favor, the approach remains useful. From this perspective, organizations don't merely do things because they can be done; rather, they act because managers have determined that they should act in order to further the work of the organization in some strategic and measurable way.

For instance, a reactive and nonstrategic public relations or marketing communication department may decide that because the company has just purchased new desktop publishing software, a scanner, and a color printer, the department should prepare new promotional brochures and flyers. But a proactive and strategic department would first determine what needs to be done, say, to promote more understanding among potential customers. Then it might conclude that it should produce new brochures and buy the equipment with which to do so. This is managing by objectives, not by whim.

As you can see by this example, objectives help direct the organization to act in ways that make sense. Objectives also serve another purpose: They give the planner a reference point for evaluation. When you measure the effectiveness of your strategic communication program in Step 9, you look back to your objectives and ask whether your messages and actions have had the effect you wanted. You then scrutinize each objective to determine if you have been successful.

Standards for Objectives

Eleven specific criteria can be identified for public relations objectives. These will become the elements of effective and practical objectives.

Objectives are rooted in goals. They are based on the organization's goal statements, which themselves grow out of the mission or vision that the organization has defined for itself. Thus, objectives are responsive to a particular issue that the organization has recognized as important to its effectiveness. Public relations objectives often reflect organizational strategic plans and they may parallel financial projections, marketing ambitions, advertising or promotional expectations and objectives associated with other aspects of the organization.

Objectives are public-focused. They are linked firmly to a particular public and are based on the wants, interests, and needs of that public. Objectives for one public may be similar to those for another public, but each must be distinct.

Objectives are oriented toward the impact they can achieve. They define the effect you hope to make on your public, focusing not on the tools but on intended accomplishments. In writing objectives, avoid statements about disseminating news releases, producing brochures, holding open houses, and other activities that belong with an eventual tactical response to the objectives. Such nonobjective language is dangerous; it confuses activity with achievement and can lull you into a false belief that because you are *doing* something you are also *accomplishing* something.

Objectives are linked to research. Good objectives aren't just pulled out of the air; they are tied to research. For example, if research shows that 40% of your key public is familiar with your organization's products or services, your objective might be to increase that to 50%—not because 50% is a magic number, but because it represents a reasonable ambition based on the current situation, as revealed through research.

Objectives are explicit and clearly defined. There is no room for varying interpretations; everyone involved in the public relations activity must share a common understanding of where the objective is leading. Don't use ambiguous verbs such as *educate*, *inform*, *promote*, or *encourage*. Instead, use strong action verbs to state your objective specifically. For example, instead of saying you want "to enhance knowledge of recycling," say your objective is "to increase residents' understanding of the benefits of recycling."

Objectives are measurable. They are precise and quantifiable, with clear measures that state the degree of change being sought. Avoid adjectives such as *appropriate* or *reasonable*. Instead, for example, state that you want "to effect a 20% increase in recycling of paper products."

Objectives are time definite. Objectives include a clear indication of a time frame—"by December 31," "within six months," "during the spring semester," and so on. Avoid ambiguous phrases such as "in the near future" or "as soon as possible." Some objectives may indicate a graduated or multistage approach to the time frame. For example, you might indicate that a certain effect is expected in two stages: a 50% increase within six months, a 75% increase after the first year.

Objectives are singular. They focus on one desired response from one public. Don't state in an objective that you want "to increase awareness *and* generate positive attitudes." You may be successful in the first effort but unsuccessful in the latter, making it difficult to evaluate your effectiveness. Most strategic communication programs will have multiple objectives, but each objective should be stated separately.

Objectives are challenging. They should stretch the organization a bit and inspire people to action. Don't aim at too safe a level of achievement or you might find that you haven't really achieved anything worthwhile. Instead, set your sights high.

Objectives are attainable. Though challenging, objectives also need to be attainable and doable according to the organization's needs and resources, so don't set your sights too high. Seldom is it realistic to aim for 100% of anything, whether you are trying to expand your customer base or reduce opposition. Don't create a recipe for failure by setting objectives that are unattainable.

Objectives are acceptable. They enjoy the understanding and support of the entire organizational team—public relations or communication staff, managers, right up to the CEO. The value of objectives is not that they are written but that they are used. They need the strength of consensus if they are to be useful to both your organization's planners and its decision makers.

Hierarchy of Objectives

An ordered hierarchy exists among communication objectives, growing out of a logical progression through three stages of persuasion: awareness, acceptance, and action. Awareness begins the process, increasing gradually; interest then builds in stages, and attitudes bloom into an acceptable choice; verbal and physical actions are modified in steps. Note how this model parallels the AIDA pattern (attention, interest, desire and action), the hierarchy of effects associated with advertising since the 1920s (Lipstein, 1985). This model also echoes the standard communication effects of cognitive, affective and conative changes (Ray, 1973). Similarly, Philip Kotler, Ned Roberto, and Nancy Lee (2007) focus on objectives for social-marketing campaigns, identifying these as knowledge objectives (information or facts), belief objectives (values or attitudes), and behavior objectives (specific actions).

Whatever formula you use, remember: In your enthusiasm to resolve the issue, don't let your expectations get ahead of themselves. Develop a plan that will take your communication with each of your publics through each of the necessary steps. Make sure your message first will reach your target publics, who will then agree with this message and finally act on it. Here's a closer look at the three levels of objectives:

Awareness objectives deal with information and knowledge.

- Attention
- Comprehension
- Retention

Well-Written Objectives

Here are two examples of well-written objectives in each category.

Awareness Objectives

- To have an effect on the *awareness* of senior citizens in Lake County; specifically *to increase their understanding* of the advantages that Upstate Health Program offers senior patients (60% of senior residents within six months)
- To have an effect on the *awareness* of legislators from the Southern Tier; specifically to *increase their understanding* of the environmental impact that House Bill 311 will have on their constituents (all 15 Republican and seven Democratic members of the House Committee on Environmental Affairs within two months)

Acceptance Objectives

- To have an effect on the *acceptance* of senior citizens in Lake County; specifically to *increase their positive attitudes* toward membership in Upstate Health Program (30% within six months)
- To have an effect on the *acceptance* of legislators from the Southern Tier; specifically *to gain their interest* in the environmental issues addressed by House Bill 311 (10 of the 15 Republican members and six of the seven Democratic members of the House committee within two months)

Action Objectives

- To have an effect on the *action* of senior citizens in Lake County; specifically *to obtain an increase in their membership* in the Upstate Health Program (10% within six months, and an additional 10% within a year)
- To have an effect on the *action* of legislators from the Southern Tier; specifically for them *to vote in favor* of House Bill 311 (six of the 15 Republican members of the House and six of the seven Democratic members of the House committee when the bill comes to a vote next spring)

Acceptance objectives focus on how people react to information.

- Interest
- Attitude

Action objectives address a hoped-for response to information and feelings.

- Opinion
- Behavior

Awareness Objectives. The first level of objectives, **awareness objectives**, focuses on information, providing the **cognitive**, or thinking, component of the message. These objectives specify what information you want your publics first to be exposed to and then to know, understand and remember. Awareness objectives particularly deal with dissemination and message exposure, comprehension and retention.

When would you use awareness objectives? They are appropriate for transmitting purely functional information, for communicating on noncontroversial issues, and for the early stages of any communication campaign. Awareness objectives also are particularly useful for publicity and public information models of public relations. In general, awareness objectives impact on what people know about an organization and its products, services, and ideas.

Acceptance Objectives. The next level, **acceptance objectives**, deals with the **affective**, or feeling, part of the message—how people respond emotionally to information they have received. These objectives indicate the level of interest or the kind of attitude an organization hopes to generate among its publics. Acceptance objectives are useful in several situations: forming interests and attitudes where none existed before, reinforcing existing interests and attitudes, and changing existing positive or negative attitudes.

Acceptance objectives are particularly important amid controversy and in persuasive situations using the advocacy (or asymmetrical) model of public relations. They impact on *how* people feel about the organization and its products, services, and ideas. Notice how the examples of acceptance objectives above differ from the earlier examples of awareness objectives.

Action Objectives. The final level of objectives, **action objectives**, takes aim at expression and conduct, providing the **conative**, or behavioral, element of the message. These objectives offer two types of action: opinion (verbal action) and behavior (physical action). Action objectives may attempt to create new behaviors or change existing ones, positively or negatively. They should be focused on the organization's bottom line, such as customer buying, student enrollment, donor giving, fan attendance, and so on. Remember that action objectives serve not only as persuasive objectives that encourage audiences to act according to the wishes of the organization but also as objectives for building consensus and enhancing the relationship between the organization and its publics. Note how the action objectives shown in the example box differ from the earlier examples of awareness and acceptance objectives. Just as most issues will have more than one goal, so too will each goal have a full set of objectives—at least one in each of the above categories for each of the identified publics. Too often, efforts in public relations and marketing communication fail because they pursue the awareness objectives and then jump quickly to action, forgetting the important bridge step of generating acceptance.

Indeed, acceptance is the key to effective public relations, and its importance has been obvious since 1947 when one of the accepted "fathers" of public relations, Edward Bernays, wrote about "the engineering of consent." This implies more than merely disseminating information; it involves connecting with people's inner desires. We must take time to foster the public's acceptance of both our organization and its messages, through means that are both practical and ethical. For example, in a political campaign, news releases and debates may be useful tools for achieving awareness. But awareness doesn't guarantee acceptance, and through the release or the debate voters may actually learn that they disagree with the candidate on important issues. Thus, successful awareness efforts could actually hinder acceptance of your client—just one of life's little ironies.

Another paradox: As this hierarchy moves along the awareness–acceptance–action path from least important to most important objectives, the impact on the public will inevitably decrease. You might achieve an 80% awareness level among the public, for example, but perhaps only 40% will accept the message favorably, and only 15% or 20% may act on it.

Students often ask, "Where do you get the numbers from?" Good question. Here's an example that might shed some light, based on a real campaign being developed by a student group for a local Alzheimer's association. The goal was task-oriented: increasing volunteers for the local chapter. At first, the students were all over the place, setting unrealistic objectives. They were trying to create awareness in 40% of college students, acceptance in 20%, and action in those same 20%, which, if it were to be accomplished, would have yielded 10,000, an impossible number for the chapter to deal with. Here's how we talked things out.

First we worked backward, focusing on just how many volunteers the organization realistically could use. The number: about 200. Then we considered how many college and university students there were in the region, about 50,000. Then we discussed some realistic expectations. How many of those 50,000 could the campaign reach? The 40% (20,000) seemed realistic, given the fact that students are reachable through a relatively narrow channel of communication vehicles such as campus media, social networking, and perhaps direct mail with fraternities and sororities.

Then came the questions about acceptance and action. How many of those 20,000 students who hear about the organization would think it was a good idea? The planners estimated perhaps one in 10, or 2,000 students; that is, 4% of the original population. And how many of that 2,000 would be likely to volunteer? Perhaps another one in 10, or 200 student volunteers; 0.2% of the original total. Sounds like a small percentage, but that's just what the Alzheimer's association needs.

Adding some complexity to the process, the planners were aware that most of the current volunteers for the chapter were women and the organization needed some male volunteers. So a mix of 70 to 30 for women and men volunteers was factored in. Here are the resulting objectives:

- To create awareness of Alzheimer volunteer opportunities among college students, specifically 40%, or 20,000 of the 50,000 students in area colleges and universities within six months.
- To create acceptance among college students, specifically generating interest among 4% of the student population, or 5,000 students within six months (70% or 1,400 women; 30% or 600 men).
- To generate action among college specifically, specifically to achieve a 0.4% action rate with 200 new volunteers (70% or 140 women; 30% or 60 men).

Writing Public Relations Objectives

In writing objectives, keep your language simple and brief. Avoid jargon. Use everyday language and strong action verbs. As part of the planning for a strategic communication campaign, objectives are not meant to be presented publicly, so don't worry if they begin to sound repetitious and formulaic. The guidelines that follow can help you deal with each important element of a well-stated objective.

Public. Indicate the public to whom the objective is addressed.

Category. Indicate simply the category of the objective: awareness, acceptance, or action.

Direction. Indicate the direction of movement you are seeking—that is, to *create* or *generate* something new that did not exist before; to *increase* or *maximize* a condition; to *maintain*

Writing Public Relations Objectives

Public	Objective for ______________________			
Category	To have an effect on	❑ Awareness ❑ Acceptance ❑ Action		
Direction	Specifically, to	❑ Create, Generate ❑ Increase, Maximize ❑ Maintain, Reinforce ❑ Decrease, Minimize		
Effect	(w/ awareness category)	❑ Attention	or	❑ Comprehension
	(w/ acceptance category)	❑ Interest	or	❑ ± Attitude
	(w/ action category)	❑ Opinion	or	❑ Behavior
Focus	About ______________________			
Performance Measure	______________________			
Time Period	______________________			

effects or *reinforce* current conditions; or to *decrease* or *minimize* something. Notice that *elimination* is not an option because a public relations undertaking is seldom able to completely remove an unwanted effect; the best we can hope to do is minimize it. Another observation: Public relations and other strategic communication programs too often don't pay enough attention to maintaining current support. While generating new support is important, don't overlook those who currently help you and agree with you.

Specific effect. Indicate the specific effect that you will address. If you are writing an awareness objective, the specific effect should deal with receiving the message, understanding it, or perhaps remembering it. If you are focusing on the acceptance level, deal with generating interest, reducing apathy, or fostering attitudes (usually positive attitudes, such as support for wearing a helmet while bicycling; sometimes negative attitudes, such as a sentiment against drinking alcohol during pregnancy). For action objectives, focus on evoking a particular opinion or drawing out a desired action.

Focus. Indicate the focus of the specific effect you hope to achieve. Provide some detail about what you are seeking. However, don't move away from objectives by providing information about either strategy or tactics. That will come later in the planning process.

Performance measure. Indicate the desired level of achievement in measurement terms. Raw numbers or percentages usually do this well. The number itself should reflect baseline research and/or desired outcomes. For example, a university library might calculate that 35% of students use the library facility in any 2-week period. However, guidelines from the Association of College and Research Libraries might suggest that 50% is the desired usage pattern, including both in-person use and Internet connections. Therefore the campus library's public relations campaign might aim for a performance increase to 50% of the students. Stated other ways, the objective might specify a 30% increase over the present usage, or an increase from the present 2,800 students to 4,000 out of a total student population of 8,000. Each variant aims for the same level of usage.

Time period. Indicate the desired time frame, either within a single period or in multiple stages. Here again, you can be specific (a May 15 deadline) or relative (within six weeks, by the end of the fall semester).

Poorly Worded Objectives

Here are three examples of poorly worded objectives. Note how each can be improved.

Poorly Worded Objective 1

- To interest more people in recycling as soon as possible

Critique: No public is indicated, merely a vague reference to "people." "Interest" is a nonspecific term. Recycling is a very broad concept. The focus is on communication activity rather than impact on the public. Measurement is nonexistent. The time frame is imprecise.

Restatement: To have an effect on the *action* of Allen County residents; specifically *to generate telephone inquiries* to the CLEAN-UP help line (100 telephone calls during the first two months of the campaign; 400 telephone calls within six months).

Poorly Worded Objective 2

- To prepare a new brochure about recycling

Critique: No public is indicated. The focus is on communication activity rather than impact on the public. Measurement and time frame are not included.

Restatement: To have an effect on the *awareness* of residents of the Oxford Apartments; specifically *to increase the understanding* of students about the benefits of recycling (45% during the fall semester).

Poorly Worded Objective 3

- To become more student focused

Critique: This is a strategic choice more appropriate for the next step, but it doesn't indicate a desired outcome.

Restatement: To have an effect on the *acceptance* of students at St. Martin's College; specifically *to increase their positive attitudes* toward the student centeredness of the Career Counseling Center (50% increase within two years).

Planning Example 4: Establishing Goals and Objectives

UPSTATE COLLEGE

Here is the first part of strategic planning for Upstate College.

Goals

- To re-create the college's image into that of a four-year institution (reputational goal)
- To recruit more students (task goal)
- To generate new donor support (task goal)

Position

Upstate College wants to be known for its quality education and for its accessibility in terms of both cost and admission standards.

Objectives for High School Students in a Three-County Area

- To have an effect on *awareness*; specifically *to increase their knowledge* that Upstate College is expanding into a four-year college (75% of students during their junior year)
- To have an effect on *acceptance*; specifically *to generate interest* in attending a growing institution (25% of high school students during their junior and senior years)
- To have an effect on *action*; specifically *to obtain inquiries* from an average of 15% of high school students in the college's primary three-county area during their junior or senior years
- To have an effect on *action*; specifically *to obtain applications* from an average of 5% of all high school graduates in the college's primary three-county area during their senior year.

(Note: You also will have objectives for each of your other key publics.)

■ ■ ■

TINY TYKES TOYS

Here is the first part of strategic planning for Tiny Tykes Toys.

Goals

- To regain customer confidence (reputational goal)
- To recapture the company's previous sales rates (task goal)

Position

Tiny Tykes wants to be known as the company that cares about babies more than about its own profitability.

Objectives for Parents

- To have an effect on *awareness*; specifically *to create knowledge* among 75% of parent-customers about the redesign of the baby toy within six weeks.
- To have an effect on *awareness*; specifically *to create understanding* by 65% of the parents about the sacrifices and commitment that the company has made by recalling and redesigning the toys.
- To have an effect on *acceptance*; specifically *to regain trust* among 40% of these parents that the company has acted responsibly in redesigning the toy.
- To have an effect on *acceptance*; specifically *to create interest* among 30% of the parents in buying toys from the company within the next two years.
- To have an effect on *action*; specifically *to foster sales* to 25% of the parents from the company within the next two years.

(Note: You also will have objectives for each of your other key publics.)

Checklist 4: Goals and Objectives

Basic Questions

1. What are the goals?
2. What position do you seek?
3. What are the specific objectives (awareness, acceptance, and action for each public)?

Expanded Questions

A. GOALS

1. What are the organization's reputation goals on this issue?
2. What are the organization's relationship goals on this issue?
3. What are the organization's task goals on this issue?
4. Do any of these goals contradict another goal? If yes, which goal(s) will you eliminate?
5. What is the relative priority among the viable goals?
6. Does the organization have resources (time, personnel, money, etc.) to achieve these goals? If no, can resources be obtained? From where?
7. Does the organization have willingness to work toward these goals? If no, how can willingness be generated?
8. Are there any ethical problems with these goals? If yes, how can you modify the goals to eliminate the problems?

B. POSITION

1. What is a key public for this product/service/concept?
2. What position do you seek for your product/service/concept for this public?

3. Is this desired position appropriate? If no, reconsider the position.
4. What is your current position?
5. What change do you need to make to achieve the desired position?
6. What is the competition?
7. What is its position?

(Note: Replicate the above position questions for each public.)

C. OBJECTIVES

1. Write at least one awareness objective for each key public, such as "To have an effect on awareness; specifically . . ."
2. Write at least one acceptance objective for each key public, such as "To have an effect on acceptance; specifically . . ."
3. Write at least one action objective for each key public, such as "To have an effect on action; specifically . . ."
4. Answer the following questions for each individual objective:
   - ✓ Is this objective linked to the organization's mission or vision statement?
   - ✓ Is this objective responsive to the issue/problem/opportunity/goal?
   - ✓ Is this objective focused on a particular public?
   - ✓ Is this objective clearly measurable?
   - ✓ Does this objective indicate a time frame?
   - ✓ Is this objective challenging to the organization?
   - ✓ Is this objective realistically attainable?

(Note: You should be able to answer yes to each of these questions. If not, revise the objectives.)

Consensus Check

Does agreement exist within your organization about the recommended objectives included within this step of the planning process? If "yes," proceed to Step 5, Formulating Action and Response Strategies. If "no," consider the value and/or possibility of achieving consensus before proceeding.

Step 5

Formulating Action and Response Strategies

Effective public relations involves deeds as well as words, and strong programs can be built only on solid and consistent action. Ideally, action and messages work hand in hand, complementing each other as the organization interacts with its publics. This step of the planning process will focus on your decisions about action strategies as you prepare to achieve your objectives.

Strategic communication planners have many options for what their organization can do and say on any particular issue. These actions can be either proactive or reactive.

Proactive strategies are those approaches that enable an organization to launch a communication program under the conditions and according to the timeline that seem to best fit the organization's interests. Proactive strategies include both action and communication.

Reactive strategies, conversely, are measures that respond to influences and opportunities from an organization's environment. Response strategies include preemptive action, offensive and defensive responses, diversion, commiseration, rectifying behavior, and strategic inaction.

Proactive Public Relations Strategies

Public relations strategies initiated by the organization are called proactive strategies. These can be the most effective strategies because they are implemented according to the planning of the organization, rather than because of a need to respond to outside pressure and expectations from publics. Proactive action strategies include the enhancement of organizational performance, audience participation, and special events; development of alliances and coalitions; sponsorships; and sometimes activism. Key proactive communication strategies include the presentation of newsworthy information and the development of a transparent communication process.

Proactive Strategy 1: Public Relations Action

The first category of proactive public relations strategies involves **action strategies**—tangible deeds undertaken by the organization in an effort to achieve its objectives. Let's look at the six categories.

Organizational performance. The performance of the organization is the first and most important area to consider when weighing various strategic communication initiatives. Ensure

A Typology of Proactive Public Relations Strategies

Proactive Strategy 1: Action
- Organizational performance
- Audience participation
- Special events
- Alliances and coalitions
- Sponsorships
- Strategic philanthropy
- Activism

Proactive Strategy 2: Communication
- Publicity
- Newsworthy information
- Transparent communication

that the organization is working at its highest possible level of quality for its customers. One of the first questions in the formative research phase of this planning process (Step 2, Analyzing the Organization) was designed to identify the quality of the product or service associated with the issue being addressed. Public relations can't be expected to promote the good name of an organization that doesn't give good performance, and products or services should reflect a level of quality that meets the wants, interests, needs, and expectations of key publics.

What do customers want? Quality products. Value. Customer service. Reasonable prices. They also expect the organizations they choose to patronize to be responsible members of society. For example, some companies have been unpleasantly surprised to find that customers won't buy products made by exploiting child laborers or cosmetics developed through animal testing. Consumers also may avoid firms with poor records on safety, pollution, and discrimination. In his book *Building Your Company's Good Name*, Davis Young (1996) notes that a good reputation—an organization's most valuable asset—is built on performance rather than on mere words.

One of the principles of effective public relations is **adaptation**, the willingness and ability of the organization to make changes necessary to create harmony between itself and its key publics. Some organizations use strategic communication to convince their publics to conform to the offerings of the organization; this is the persuasive model of public relations. Another model of public relations aims to enhance the mutual relationship between the organization and its publics, which means that sometimes the organization will need to change.

If a college or university wants to promote registration for its summer program, for example, one of the first activities should be to research key publics (such as currently registered students, incoming freshmen, and people who applied to the school and were accepted but who did not register), identifying the courses they want and the schedules they prefer. In other words, the school would create the summer program around its key publics' needs, rather than building it around the convenience of the faculty and administrators.

Similarly, if a dental office wants to attract a professional clientele, it might schedule office hours on weekends and evenings, perhaps with a couple of nights with appointments as late as 10 or 11 p.m. to accommodate busy executives.

Audience participation. Another important strategy initiative for the public relations planner is audience participation. This involves using strong two-way communication tactics and engaging audiences and publics in your communication activities.

One way to do this is to communicate about the audience's relevant interests rather than the needs of the message source or the sponsoring organization. The formal term for this is **salience** of the information—the degree to which information is perceived as being applicable or useful to the audience. Use examples and applications that address a key question of your public: "What's in it for me?" In a fund-raising letter for AIDS research, for example, tell your readers that they can help make a cure possible rather than merely citing the researchers' need for financial support. When possible, base your message on values shared by the organization and the public.

Audience participation also can be built on activities that bring individual members of your publics into direct contact with the products and services of your organization. For example, police departments in many cities routinely use ride-along programs to give citizens a firsthand look at their communities from inside a patrol car. Cosmetic companies give free samples, health clubs give low-cost trial memberships, and private schools have shadow programs for prospective students.

Several years ago the Union of American Hebrew Congregations (UAHC), the denominational leadership of Reform Judaism in the United States, wanted to strengthen bonds with Reform Jews around the country ("The Lives We Touch," 1992). Invoking the principle of audience participation, UAHC invited its 800 member congregations to participate in a video project by sharing their success stories. More than 200 congregations responded and asked to be included in the documentary, gaining a sense of solidarity with the national association—virtually guaranteeing their use of the eventual video.

Another way to foster audience participation is by generating feedback. Create convenient ways your audience can respond to your message and engage in dialogue. Use techniques such as toll-free phone numbers, surveys, question-and-answer sessions, interactive websites, and similar tools.

A company may look to research in determining whether to establish a consumer complaints hotline as a form of feedback. A complaints department can gauge customer satisfaction, minimize the loss of customers, and perhaps identify ways to prevent problems. Recent studies (Kowalski & Erickson, 1997; Nyer, 1999, 2000) suggest that soliciting complaints can actually help an organization reduce customer dissatisfaction. It seems that people feel better about the source of their complaints when they actually have an opportunity to voice those complaints. After venting, they also feel better about the product or service they had complained about, according to the studies.

You also can build into your program **triggering events**—activities that generate action among key publics. Examples of triggering events are speeches that conclude with an invitation for the audience to sign a petition, or an open house that ends with an opportunity to join. Sometimes the triggering element is built into an event, such as election day as the triggering event for a political campaign.

Experienced public relations practitioners realize that sometimes triggering events may be unplanned, so they are quick to take advantages of opportunities that present themselves. Often the events themselves are tragic, but in their tragedy they focus attention on particular issues. For example, the death of Rock Hudson gave AIDS a face and energized AIDS activists. Likewise, the student killings at Columbine High School in Littleton, Colorado, provided a focus for issues such as teen alienation. The election of the first openly gay Episcopalian bishop in 2005 served as a triggering event both positive and negative for issues such as gay rights and church unity.

Opportunity Born of Tragedy

Suffering in silence may be a virtue, but suffering in public can make money. Public misfortune can make your cause hot.

When First Lady Betty Ford went public with her diagnosis and treatment for breast cancer in 1974, she broke a social taboo against discussing personal issues in the media. Her honesty and candor did more than put the disease on the public agenda; it also provided a lesson for public relations practitioners: Move quickly when injury or disease captures the nation's attention.

Often that attention surrounds celebrity. When track star Florence Griffith Joyner died in 1998 of a seizure, the Epilepsy Foundation mobilized quickly. Its medical expert told ABC's *Good Morning America* audiences about the disease that affects 2.5 million people. It sent news releases urging women to speak out about the discrimination that exists because of epilepsy, and it quickly sent a video news release to every TV station in America. Likewise, the National Parkinson Foundation found that public interest grew when actor Michael J. Fox revealed that he suffered from Parkinson's disease.

With media interest comes money. Donations doubled for the American Paralysis Association after actor Christopher Reeve was paralyzed in a horse-riding accident; the association even changed its name to the Christopher Reeve Paralysis Association. And contributions to the Alzheimer's Association jumped after President Ronald Reagan was diagnosed with the disease.

Assisting the public relations efforts of some organizations, celebrities have helped turn the spotlight on illnesses and diseases afflicting themselves or their loved ones. Awareness of testicular cancer, for example, is the cause of comedian Tom Green, actor Richard Belzer, and athletes such as cyclist Lance Armstrong, Boston Bruins hockey forward Phil Kessel, Boston Red Sox third baseman Mike Lowell, and skater Scott Hamilton, themselves survivors of the disease. Model Christy Turlington became a spokesperson for her own disease, emphysema, and for the lung cancer that killed her father. Sharon Osborne dealt with her diagnosis of colorectal cancer during her reality TV show in 2002, earning praise for increasing public awareness about the disease.

Other celebrities giving publicity to various maladies include actor Jimmy Smits for colon cancer, country singer Toby Keith for childhood cancers, talk show host Montel Williams for multiple sclerosis, basketball star Alonzo Mourning for anemia, basketball star Magic Johnson for HIV/AIDS, R&B singer Tionne T-Boz Watkins for sickle cell disease, and quarterback Doug Flutie for childhood autism. Diabetes awareness is the cause supported by soul singer Gladys Knight and actors Halle Barry and Cuba Gooding Jr. Breast cancer awareness has strong support from entertainers such as Reese Witherspoon, Nicole Kidman, and Vivica A. Fox.

Some celebrities even have created their own foundations, such as Livestrong, the Lance Armstrong Foundation to fight cancer; the (Jane) Fonda Family Foundation, the (Richard) Gere Foundation, and the Calvin Klein Foundation.

Others have created their own charities, such as Sean Combs's Daddy's House Social Programs for inner-city kids, the Whitney Houston Foundation for Children, Oprah Winfrey's Angel Network assisting Boys and Girls Clubs, the Tiger Woods Foundation for children, and Hunter's Hope Foundation founded by former Buffalo Bills quarterback Jim Kelly (named for his infant son, Hunter) to fight Krabbe's disease and to promote newborn screening for it.

Special events. Special events are another useful way to generate audience participation. These are **staged activities** (also called **pseudo-events**), activities that an organization develops or orchestrates to gain the attention and acceptance of key publics. Special events should be legitimate, meaning they are designed primarily as a means of engaging publics and encouraging their interaction with your organization, with the potential for media attention being secondary.

Opposite this type of special event is the **publicity stunt**, a gimmick planned mainly to gain publicity and having little value beyond that. Avoid self-serving publicity stunts, but don't dismiss the news value of legitimate special events. An appropriate event can attract the attention of reporters and generate interest among your publics. To distinguish a legitimate special event from a publicity stunt ask yourself: Even if the news media won't report this activity, will it still be worthwhile? If you can answer "yes" to this question, then it's probably a real special event. Another important requirement for effective special events is that they should be creative, with a spark of originality that sets them apart from the ordinary and the routine. Brainstorming with your colleagues sometimes can suggest an approach that would be distinctive enough so that the special event can become, literally, "the talk of the town." There are many types of special events, which are outlined in the next section on tactics. For now, simply consider the wide range of possibilities:

- Artistic programs, such as recitals and art shows
- Competitions, such as sporting events and essay contests
- Community events, such as parades, festivals and fairs
- Holiday celebrations for civic, cultural, ethnic, religious and other occasions
- Observances, such as anniversaries, birthdays, special days or months
- Progress-oriented activities, such as groundbreaking ceremonies, cornerstone placements and grand openings

A later section on activism deals with special events of a more polemic or confrontational nature.

Ethics: Publicity Stunt

In a campaign titled "Holocaust on Your Plate," People for the Ethical Treatment of Animals compared the slaughtering of chickens to the murder of Jews by Nazis in World War II. Not unexpectedly, PETA drew hostile criticism and a lot of media attention to its cause of animal rights. While attention does not necessarily result in support, the action did seem to further PETA's publicity agenda.

In developing public relations strategies, give thought to the ethical considerations that underlie publicity stunts.

- Does the action have any intrinsic value, or is it mainly for show?
- Will it be offensive? To whom?
- If it is offensive, does this matter to your organization?
- Does the publicity stunt trivialize an otherwise serious topic?

Alliances and coalitions. When two or more organizations join together in a common purpose, the combined energy offers a real opportunity for strategic communication initiatives.

- **Alliances** tend to be informal, loosely structured, and perhaps small working relationships among organizations
- **Coalitions** are similar relationships that are a bit more formal and structured than alliances.

Alliances and coalitions seek to forge relationships—often new ones—with groups that share similar values and concerns. Using this strength-in-numbers approach, organizations try to compound their influence toward meeting objectives and to enhance their ability to break through barriers while trying to relate to their publics.

The nature of alliances is that they generate energy and cooperation around a single and often narrow issue. In 2005, the Coalition of Immokalee Workers ended a four-year boycott of Yum! Brands, the world's largest fast-foot conglomerate (including Taco Bell, Pizza Hut, and KFC, among others). The boycott was sponsored by the Student-Farmer Alliance, a nationwide network of youth, farmers, unions, clergy, and workers. The boycott ended when the company agreed to the alliance's demands: a penny a pound more for tomatoes picked by migrant workers from Haiti, Guatemala, and Mexico working in Immokalee, Florida, improved working conditions, and an end to harassment and threats against workers. The alliance had coordinated a nationwide Boot the Bell campaign that challenged Taco Bell establishments on high school and college campuses, organized a rolling nationwide hunger strike against Taco Bell, and dispatched Taco Bell Truth Tours. The alliance forced Notre Dame University to cancel Taco Bell's $75,000 sponsorship of its football program.

After the Yum! victory, the alliance turned to Burger King, sponsoring a weeklong "Kingdoom Days of Action" with similar demands for a penny a pound more for tomato pickers and promising similar resistance if they didn't. The multibillion-dollar Burger King said the demand would cost $250,000 a year, and it threatened to buy tomatoes directly from Mexico instead of from Florida, where most winter tomatoes are grown for U.S. restaurants.

Alliances sometimes are made with internal publics, such as when a company convenes a task force of its employees to consider workplace concerns. Other alliances focus on external publics. For example, a health care system facing unprofitable duplication of services among several of its hospital sites might hold public hearings to discuss the problem and invite community input toward finding a solution, thus building an alliance with its publics.

Other alliances involve customers. When Lee Jeans joined with the Entertainment Industry Foundation (Hollywood's leading charitable organization) to promote National Denim Day, the company called on people to put on their favorite jeans and donate $5 for breast cancer research. Lee also invited celebrities—country singer Billy Ray Cyrus and actors Mariska Hargitay (*Law and Order*) and Steve Carrel (*The Office*). The annual Denim Day has raised more than $70 million in 12 years, making it one of the largest single-day fund-raising events.

Sometimes organizations seek alliances with influential individuals, particularly with community leaders who are respected among the organization's publics. An organization trying to encourage African Americans to participate in a bone marrow screening, for instance, may look to respected minority leaders in the community or perhaps to influential organizations such as the National Association for the Advancement of Colored People (NAACP) or the Urban League, professional sports teams, black professional fraternities or sororities, or similar groups.

Alliances and Opinion Leaders

A particularly beneficial alliance can exist between an organization and opinion leaders. Having identified opinion leaders in Step 3, public relations planners can find themselves in a good place to develop a strategy for communicating with them.

One piece of advice from the field is to involve opinion leaders early. For example, 39% of pharmaceutical companies communicate with opinion leaders before they launch the public phase of their public relations tactics, according to a survey by Cutting Edge Information, a pharmaceutical research/planning firm in Durham, North Carolina.

Jason Richardson, president of Cutting Edge, explains the value of taking an early lead with opinion leaders: "One of the biggest mistakes pharmaceutical companies make is waiting to contact key opinion leaders—and not involving them enough. Opinion leader relationships are built on activities that begin years before a product reaches the market." Richardson also reports that too few companies allot adequate funds to communicate with opinion leaders, whom he calls "thought leaders."

A campaign to reduce AIDS and other sexually transmitted diseases consciously drew on Everett Rogers's diffusion of innovation theory by targeting bartenders as opinion leaders with influence through the social network of bars (Kelly et al., 1991).

The campaign identified as opinion leaders people who were popular and well-liked and who have frequent interaction with the key publics of the campaign. The campaign then enlisted the involvement of these opinion leaders, providing training on how to encourage behavioral changes to lower the risk of HIV infection. The campaign reported a 25–30% decrease in risky behaviors following the intervention of the opinion leaders (Kelly et al., 1992).

Organizations that recognize they have a poor reputation with their public sometimes seek alliances with organizations having a better standing with the public. For example, several years ago when the U.S. Immigration and Naturalization Service (INS) declared an amnesty for undocumented aliens who met certain residency requirements, in several communities it turned to churches that had an existing credibility within the Hispanic community, on the belief that the aliens' distrust of the INS would be overcome by their greater trust in the churches. The third-party endorsement the churches were able to provide the INS helped many people become legal residents.

At times, coalition building can lead to some unlikely bedfellows. In some communities, for example, coalitions advocating sexual responsibility or access to prenatal and postnatal care bring together pro-life and pro-choice activists who otherwise would have little in common.

Sponsorships. Another proactive step that organizations can take to gain visibility and respect among their key publics is through **sponsorships**. A sponsorship is a significant strategy for programs oriented toward community relations. It involves either providing a program directly or providing financial, personnel, or other resources the program requires.

Make sure there is a logical link between the activity being sponsored and the purpose or mission of your organization. For example, a science museum might sponsor a trip to view a space shuttle launch, a college might host a junior high school science fair, or a bookstore might support a literacy program. Kleenex has done this since the 2004 Olympic Games through a series of "Kleenex Moments" focusing on human emotions in the various athletic events.

It's also a good idea to establish levels or categories for potential sponsors so smaller businesses or individual funders will be able to participate, as well as larger and better-funded sponsors. An organization may seek a single program or "title" sponsor donating $20,000, as well as a dozen or more corporate patrons contributing $1,000 each. Membership organizations such as zoos likewise have varying levels for individual sponsors. Beyond the levels of individual and family memberships, zoos create categories for more involved donors. The Denver Zoo has a whole range of advanced levels for individual memberships: the Curator's Club ($250–$499), the Director's Circle ($500–$999), the President's Club ($1,000–$2,499), the Chairman's Circle ($2,500–$4,999), the Guardian Society ($5,000–$9,000), and the Conservation Society ($10,000 or higher). Some zoos use clever names: the Milwaukee Zoo has its Platypus Society, the St. Louis Zoo has a Safari Circle and a Wildlife Circle, and the Indianapolis Zoo has a Keeper's Circle.

Some sponsorships are based on existing marketing relationships. For example, Lexus sponsors polo championships because polo enthusiasts reflect the luxury car's customer base. So too with Budweiser's sponsorship of the Super Bowl and Snickers' arrangement as the official candy of Little League Baseball and U.S. Youth Soccer. Other sponsorship programs are designed to appeal to new publics. These programs often have a clear marketing connection, paving the way for the company to obtain new customers.

The Boeing Corporation has an eye on its customers and other support bases as it uses strategic philanthropy to generate tangible benefits, create enduring value, reach target publics, and built sustainable long-term relationships. Its corporate beneficiaries include the Kennedy Center for the Performing Arts and sponsorship of the national anthem at all home games of the Chicago Bears (Chicago being its corporate headquarters), as well as signage at the Seattle Mariners baseball field and support for its Museum of Flight near its operations in Seattle. The company, which posts its philanthropic criteria at its website (http://www.boeing.com), reported charitable giving of $51.6 million in 2006.

Sponsorships can stretch a company's promotion dollars much further than media advertising, at the same time creating more intensive relationships between the organization and its publics. For example, during the Gay Games VII in 2006 with 12,500 athletes from 30 countries, many companies actively courted the gay and lesbian community. Sirius Satellite Radio, Absolut Vodka, Walgreens, Orbitz, American Airlines, Best Buy, MetLife, and Nike were among the 350 corporate sponsors, as well as gay-oriented organizations such as the Logo TV network and *Pink* magazine. The PlanetOut (http://www.planetout.com) website alone contributed $1 million for the Chicago-based athletic competition, which raised more than $10 million in sponsorship support. Organizers, sponsors, and consumers alike noted the value of the sponsorships, and many participants and fans reported that they went out of their way to buy from the sponsors. Advertisers and sponsors called it niche marketing intended to shore up its relationship with consumers.

Yet such sponsorships are not without risk. Kraft Foods was heavily criticized by conservative consumers who were spurred on by the well-funded American Family Association, which charged the food corporation with promoting homosexuality.

Strategic philanthropy. Successful sponsor organizations find ways to attract continuing visibility and reputational benefits. This is the notion of **strategic philanthropy**, in which businesses fund or otherwise support community relations gestures with an eye toward their employees and customers. This is more than charity. It is part of the wider approach to corporate social responsibility in which organizations realize that their success depends in part on the goodwill of the community and their perception as being a contributing member of society.

Sometimes this philanthropy takes the form of financial support. Corporations may give money for scholarships, though increasingly they are asking what they get for their money. Recipients of corporate charity would be wise to find ways to publicly recognize their donors and other supporters, not only as a matter of common courtesy but also as a way to foster an ongoing mutually beneficial relationship between the corporate donor and the recipient organization.

David Eisenstadt, partner with the Communications Group based in Toronto, points out that, in the past, some corporate giving was based on whim. The CEO's wife loved figure skating, so the company gave to a skating program, though such a gift didn't serve the corporate interest. Eisenstadt counsels that such philanthropy, part of a program of **corporate social responsibility** (CSR), should be a business decision, not an emotional one. "'Our strategy is kind of back-to-basics,'" he told a reporter from *Strategy*, a Canadian marketing magazine. "'If women are the people who make the buying decisions for our clients' services, then we would be looking at charitable organizations that have a strong female connect. The objective is that everybody should win'" (Minogue, 2003a, p. 18).

The guiding principle of strategic philanthropy is to create a program with a value higher than the cost. Nonprofit organizations seeking corporate contributions should do their homework before approaching the potential donor. Before you ask for funds, anticipate how you might acknowledge the gift, both immediately and in a continuing way. For example, tangible gifts might feature a sign or a plaque recognizing the donor, and other substantial gifts might result in using the corporate name for a program or facility. All gifts can be acknowledged in newsletters and at websites. In short, think about how to add public relations value before seeking any corporate gift.

Increasingly, national causes are going local with a coordinated series of events. One example of this is the Race for the Cure, which in 2007 raised $266 million from more than 1 million runners and walkers in more than 100 local races. Since its founding 25 years ago, the annual 5-kilometer race sponsored by Susan G. Komen for the Cure (http://www.komen.org) has raised more than $1 billion for breast-cancer awareness and research. Komen leaders anticipate adding another $2 billion to the cause over the next decade. In addition to holding its own races throughout the country, the foundation works with affiliated activities such as the Bowl for the Cure, organized with the U.S. Bowling Congress, which raised $7 million over six years. Meanwhile, General Mills will donate $2 million a year through its Pink for the Cure campaign during October (National Breast Cancer Awareness Month) from sales of pink-packaged cereal, soup, cookie mix, and vegetables. Additionally, On Deck for the Cure sponsored by Holland America, Princess, Carnival and several other cruise lines is seeking to raise $1 million over two years through customer-focused events on board their ships.

Some campaigns respond to data pointing toward the need for higher visibility in the public eye. This was the situation in 2007 when FedEx commissioned a national survey of 22,000 consumers and found that only 39% felt the company had a strong commitment to social responsibility. FedEx prized its social commitment and wanted to be recognized for it. The aftermath of Hurricane Katrina presented an opportunity for the transport giant, which created an event to transport 19 penguins back to the New Orleans aquarium from a temporary shelter in California where they had been taken after the hurricane. Drawing on its own prior

Principles of Strategic Philanthropy

The guiding principle of strategic philanthropy is to get the biggest bang for the buck. This can be accomplished in three different ways.

1. *Give something more valuable to others than it is costly to you.* This principle is one of basic economy. A dollar given that generates only a dollar's worth of benefit is not a good sponsorship investment; a more strategic sponsorship is a donation with more value to the recipient than cost to the giver. For example, if a company that makes television sets wants to sponsor an educational program through the county library system, it could give $10,000 to the library for new books, earning a modest amount of visibility and appreciation. A better move, however, might be to donate $10,000 worth of television sets so that the library can expand its use of educational and cultural videos. This donation will be worth far more to the library if it would otherwise have to purchase the sets on the retail market. And the TV sets would be a continuing reminder to library patrons of the company's donation to the community's quality of life.
2. *Give something you already own.* A parallel principle of sponsorship also is one of economy: Give something of value to others that you already own, and thus costs nothing to give away. This is the premise behind Operation Home Free, begun by Trailways Bus Lines and continued when Greyhound bought that company. The program formed an alliance with the International Association of Chiefs of Police and the National Runaway Switchboard to help runaway youths. Over the years it provided free bus rides to about 10,000 runaways returning home. The value? Tickets worth $120,000 in the first year alone. The actual cost? Virtually nothing to Greyhound, since its buses already were running, usually with some empty seats. The benefits? To runaways, a safe return home. To the police and runaway agencies, assistance in getting kids off the streets, into counseling and back home. To Greyhound, a boost in its reputation among employees, customers, police, and other important publics. A real win-win-win situation!
3. *Maximize your investment.* Another sponsorship principle is to make the most of what you donate. Consider giving several small gifts, each with the potential for significant publicity, instead of a single large one. While a large gift might yield one-time publicity, a series of well-timed and strategically placed smaller gifts can generate greater overall attention. Additionally, while personal altruism might be enhanced by giving anonymously, corporate philanthropy relies on the public spotlight. Give items or support projects that can be labeled with your organization's name, out there for all to see.

experience in transporting pandas from China to Washington's National Zoo, FedEx realized that it should create a series of media moments for the "flight" of the flightless penguins.

The first media opportunity was in Oakland, where police escorted the penguins to the airport for a bon voyage send-off. The next media moment came with the landing at the New Orleans airport, where the birds were greeted by a jazz band, a purple carpet for the matriarch penguin, and another police escort. Finally, a large crowd, including 250 "influentials," was waiting at the aquarium as the penguins returned home.

FedEx counted 300 national and international media clips, many of them focused on the 200 local communities that the company had identified in its media plan. The event cost FedEx $36,000 in expenses, along with a $100,000 contribution to the new penguin habitat.

Some sponsorship activities focus more on issues rather than on events. An example of this is the Rock the Vote campaign (http://www.rockthevote.org), which encourages young adults to register to vote. During the 2006 elections, Rock the Vote joined with Facebook to provide online registration for the 9.5 million registered Facebook users. In the earlier off-year election, Rock the Vote had registered 1.4 million new voters, most of them online, and claimed to have sparked a 20% increase in young voter turnout. The organization has built its success on alliances, including promotions cosponsored by malls, sporting events, and college campuses, as well as its interactive website and a toll-free 800 phone number promoted on television—particularly on MTV. Working with LL Cool J's Camp Cool Foundation, Rock the Vote formed the Hip Hop Coalition for Political Change, extending its message into the inner city. It also formed Radio Rocks the Vote, a partnership with urban, alternative, and Top 40 stations.

Does all of this happen because MTV and the radio stations are civic-minded companies? Perhaps they are. But there's also an element of self-service, as there is with every good sponsorship. The purpose behind Rock the Vote, founded in 1990 by recording industry folks concerned about free-speech issues, is to motivate a core of supporters who can use the political process to the advantage of the music industry.

Finally, some sponsorships have involved a strong component of volunteerism. AT&T provides its employees worldwide with paid time off for volunteer work in community activities. In 2005, AT&T employees contributed 11.3 million hours worth more than $204 million in volunteer time, while employees from the company's newly acquired BellSouth gave an additional 3 million hours worth $51 million. This AT&T Pioneers program also had special projects to assist survivors of Hurricane Katrina and to support U.S. troops in Iraq. Pioneers is part of the AT&T Foundation, which *Forbes* magazine ranked in 2006 as among the most generous corporate foundations. Altruism isn't the only motivation for community volunteer programs. AT&T believes the move gives it a better standing in the community and potentially higher profits.

The MTV Network, meanwhile, believes that its generous policy on employee volunteerism helps it attract and keep younger workers. The Points of Light Foundation (http://www.pointsoflight.org) offers similar examples of corporate volunteerism: a law firm that gives an hour a week for each employee to tutor a child in the community, a manufacturer that allows up to 40 hours a year for volunteer work, and a utility that bases 20% of its incentive pay on community involvement.

Such perceived value is not just anecdotal or wishful thinking. A health-care system, for example, tracked the productivity of its workers relative to its 1½-hour-a-week paid-time policy for volunteering. In the billing department, which processes checks, the company found that people who volunteer work faster, process more checks, are better organized, manage their time better, and are more enthusiastic about their job.

Activism. Another initiative planners can use is **activism**, a confrontational strategy focused mainly on persuasive communication and the advocacy model of public relations. A strong strategy to be used only after careful consideration of the pros and cons, activism offers many opportunities for organizations to present their messages and enhance their relationship with key publics, particularly their members and sympathizers.

The Benefits of Employee Volunteer Programs

Employee volunteerism got high marks in a study (Wild, 1993) cosponsored by the Conference Board (http://www.conference-board.org), a private business research group, and the Points of Light Foundation (http://www.pointsoflight.org), an organization that encourages community service. Based on responses by 454 companies representing all sectors of U.S. industry, the study reported the following findings:

Corporate benefits. Employee volunteer programs offer bottom-line benefits to the company by boosting company productivity (agreed to by more than 60% of the executives), increasing employee productivity (75%) and furthering corporate strategic goals (nearly 80%).

Employee benefits. Such programs offer employee benefits, including building teamwork skills and improving morale (both more than 90%), as well as attracting better employees (almost 90%) and keeping valued employees (nearly 80%).

Community benefits. These programs offer indirect community benefits by helping create "healthier" communities and improving corporate public image (more than 90% each) and improving relations with the community and with local government (nearly 85%).

Activism generally deals with causes or movements, such as social issues (crime, capital punishment, or abortion, for example), environmental matters (pollution, suburban sprawl, nuclear waste), political concerns, and so on. A distinction might be made between **advocates**, who essentially are vocal proponents for causes, and **activists**, who are more inclined to act out their support for the cause. Look at the discussion on opponents in Step 3, Analyzing the Publics, for more information about advocates and other types of social activists.

Consider some of the tactics associated with the strategy of activism: strikes, pickets, sit-ins, petitions, boycotts, marches, vigils, rallies, and outright civil disobedience. Activists often make effective use of the news media because their tactics involve physical protests and thus are highly visible. Effective activism often has an element of visual appeal. More than a publicity stunt, activist events involve newsworthy action done as much for the television viewers as for any other public. For example, when demonstrators have marched past governor's mansions and capitols in various states to protest the death penalty, they often have dressed in mourning clothes and carried cardboard coffins and paper tombstones; and news photographers and television crews undoubtedly appreciated their visual creativity.

Sometimes activism involves **civil disobedience**, a nonviolent and nonlegal but generally visual undertaking, often in support of social causes such as civil rights, environmentalism, Native American sovereignty, and similar issues. Often such protests are loaded with symbolism. Julia "Butterfly" Hill set the tree-sitting record in 1999, spending 738 days—more than two years—atop a 1,000-year-old redwood tree in Northern California in a well-orchestrated protest against a logging project. From her perch in the tree that she called "Luna," Hill gave cell-phone interviews to reporters and talked with schoolchildren around the world.

This kind of activism often transforms itself into theater, particularly when protestors are courting TV coverage. The term **street theater** (alternatively called **guerrilla theater**) refers to social and political protests that take the form of dramatizations in public places. In 2007, members of a political activist/environmental group in Madison, Wisconsin, dressed as polar bears and staged a "die-in" at the local electric company to protest its coal-burning power plants, which the protestors said contribute to global warming and threaten polar bears and other species. During a presidential campaign debate in 2004, protestors dubbed themselves Billionaires for Bush and dramatized what they saw as the administration's contempt for the masses. Dressing as big-money contributors with top hats and three-piece suits, they chanted, mockingly, "One-two-three-four. We are rich and you are poor!" and "Four more wars! Four more wars!" while holding signs reading "Privatize Everything" and "No Billionaire Left Behind." And the TV video crews were delighted!

In 2008, Amnesty International coordinated an International Day of Action in 83 cities around the world, mostly near military bases or U.S. embassies. Protestors dressed in orange jumpsuits and black hoods, courting media attention as they protested the lack of due process for 275 prisoners held by the U.S. military at Guantanamo Bay, Cuba, for six years without charges or even access to lawyers. Some activities also took aim at allegations of torture of prisoners by the military.

The author's award for creative activist strategy goes to this well-orchestrated 1999 publicity stunt: Two dozen New York City community activists staged a sit-in on the marble floor of City Hall, singing "We Shall Overcome" accompanied by kazoos and wearing bee outfits and flowered hats. They were protesting the mayor's decision to auction off city-owned lots that neighborhood groups had turned into community gardens. Wait, there's more: Enter the New York Police Department in riot gear, and as the protestors went limp, the police had to carry them to a waiting police van. Now, *that's* entertainment!

But many protests are more serious. The Makah, a Native American tribe in Washington, is the only whaling tribe in the lower 48 states, the right to maintain its 2,000-year-old whaling tradition enshrined in federal treaty. After the tribal whaling commission declared its intention to return to its traditional ways and hold a whale hunt, its first in 70 years, a successful hunt was televised by American and international media, including the ceremonial butchering of the captured whale. Meanwhile the hunt attracted demonstrators including whaling protestors, animal-rights activists, and anti-Indian groups, all of them courting media attention. In 2007, five members of the tribe killed a whale without tribal or federal permission. Three received probation and community service; two received a few months in jail following a federal trial. All five also faced charges in tribal court.

Activists sometimes stretch ethical boundaries, entering an area that public relations practitioners should avoid. Pie throwing has become a tactic-of-choice for some activists, who found they could gain media attention and thus a platform for their messages by pulling their relatively benign stunts on famous people. Targets have included fashion designer Oscar de la Renta, who was pied because of his use of fur; Fred Phelps, pastor of the anti-gay Westboro (Kansas) Baptist Church, which pickets funerals of soldiers killed in Iraq as a protest against what it deems is America's acceptance of homosexuality; Proctor & Gamble chairman John Pepper, over animal rights; Ralph Klein, premiere of the Canadian province of Alberta, for opposing the Kyoto environmental accords; Dutch finance minister Gerrit Zalm, over the Euro currency; Renato Ruggiero, director general of the World Trade Organization, over endangered sea turtles; and Microsoft chairman Bill Gates, just because.

Usually the only consequence of pie throwing is media coverage, but three San Francisco activists who protested the mayor's policies on the homeless by throwing tofu-cream and pumpkin pies in his face were sentenced to six months in prison, and in Europe several anti-Euro protestors who used lemon meringue as their weapon of choice received short jail terms.

The Value of Symbolism

Effective public relations activity usually is more than mere words, which come and go often without staying with the audience. Yet symbolic actions can be powerful tools that not only enhance the message but actually can become the message itself.

Consider some of the classic and more recent examples of symbolic action that support a public relations purpose.

Pope Benedict XVI not only used powerful words on his first visit to the United States in 2008 regarding the sex abuse scandal in the Catholic Church ("I am ashamed") but he met with several abuse survivors. In another instance of symbolic action, his visit to a New York City synagogue highlighted the similarities among the rabbi, a Holocaust survivor, and the pope, who had himself been drafted into Adolf Hitler's army but later deserted.

Because of their high visibility, popes have been particularly able to harness the power of symbolic action, such as the late Pope John Paul II's habit of kissing the ground on his many international trips as a sign of respect for the land and its people, and Pope Paul VI's unexpected embrace of Greek Orthodox Patriarch Athenagoras I in Jerusalem after centuries of animosity between the Roman Catholic and Eastern Orthodox churches.

History also has many examples of powerful symbolic action: the Boston Tea Party, the driving of the Golden Spike that completed the transcontinental railroad, the raising of the U.S. flag over Iwo Jima.

Political and governmental leaders continue to engage in symbolic action because it often strikes a chord with voters. For example, candidates serve sandwiches in soup kitchens and wear hard hats at construction sites to show their concern for the poor and for working people, respectively.

In Tucson, Arizona, two men calling themselves members of "Al Pieda" were arrested for assault and disorderly conduct after they pied conservative pundit Ann Coulter, but charges were reduced and fines suspended. No charges were filed against students at Brown University who pied New York Times columnist Thomas Friedman because they sought to dramatize their opposition to the university sponsoring him as part of 2008 Earth Day events.

If you are planning an activist strategy, keep a clear eye on all your publics. Certainly the news media are important. So too are the targets of your activism, whom you are attempting to persuade toward some kind of action or response. But perhaps most important is your internal public—generally volunteers, often with mixed motivations—who are being asked to give time and perhaps take risks on behalf of the cause. Activist strategy must provide for the "feeding" of these troops with continuing motivation, ongoing communication and, when possible, the attainment of milestone victories that can shore up their dedication.

Proactive Strategy 2: Communication

While the previous proactive strategies focus on the action of the organization, another cluster of strategies deals more with communication. Three such strategies are publicity, newsworthy information, and transparent communication.

Publicity. Most organizations intuitively understand the value of **publicity**, which is the attention given by the news media to an organization, person, event, product, or idea. CEOs, program directors, and other organizational leaders often put much faith in the premise that public attention is good. For this reason, they often press public relations specialists into holding news conferences, distributing news releases, and otherwise inviting the media to report on the activities and concerns of the organization.

What is the value of news reporting about your organization? Corporate executives sometimes believe there is a causal link between publicity and public support. It's not that easy, as we will see later in this section. But the underlying value of publicity is that it provides **third-party endorsement** for the organization's message, referring to the extra credibility that comes with the endorsement of an outside and unbiased agent, such as a reporter, editor, or news director. Audiences assume that the news they obtain from television, radio, and newspapers is more believable than information they obtain directly from the organization through advertising, websites, brochures, and the like. That's because the information reported in the news media has passed the screen of the gatekeepers. Audiences know that not everything gets on the air or in the paper, so intuitively they recognize that the professional journalists have made some choices as to what information is worth presenting as news: a reporter or an editor considered what the organization had to say and decided it was accurate enough to pass along to the audience.

Some media are more believable than others and thus deserve particular attention from the public relations strategist. Specialized newspapers and magazines—in one category, those dealing with business, industry, and the professions; in another, those focused on a specific ethnic, political, religious, cultural, or lifestyle group—have particular credibility with their audiences. Likewise, certain commentators or talk show hosts carry enormous influence among their steady listeners and readers.

An interesting study by Kevin Barnhurst and Diana Mutz observes that newspaper journalism is moving away from simply reporting events to providing news analysis. They note that in 1960, 90% of front-page election stories were about events; 32 years later, 80% of front-page stories were interpretive. Meanwhile, in broadcast reporting, the length of candidate sound bites decreased during the same time period as election coverage became more centered on journalist commentators. "To qualify as news these days, an event also must fit into a larger body of interpretations and themes," the researchers report (1997, p. 51). The lesson for practitioners, then, is to build their events and frame their messages around the larger issues that blip on the media agenda screen.

Sometimes you will find that newsworthy activities are occurring within your organization, and your role becomes that of an in-house journalist reporting on the existing news events. But more often your role will be that of public relations counselor and strategist. Public relations people regularly create or orchestrate newsworthy events within their organizations to carry an important message to the key publics.

There is a saying, "I don't care what they say about me, as long as they spell my name right." (For the record, it wasn't said by P.T. Barnum, despite that recurring miscitation.) But that approach is simplistic and naive, because public relations professionals know that all publicity cannot be treated the same way. Positive publicity obviously helps an organization, but negative publicity can have a devastating impact. When the media reported that the poison cyanide was discovered in Tylenol pain relief tablets, Johnson & Johnson stock dropped by $1 billion, 14%. Exxon stock dropped $3 billion after the Exxon *Valdez* oil spill. Motorola

Ten Ways Organizations Can Generate News

1. Give an award to draw attention to values and issues.
2. Hold a contest to involve others in your values and issues.
3. Select personnel to head a new program or begin a new project.
4. Comment on a local need or problem.
5. Conduct research and issue a report about a local need or problem.
6. Launch a campaign to accomplish something.
7. Give a speech to a significant audience and tell the media about it.
8. Involve a celebrity to visit and/or address your organization on a topic of concern to you.
9. Tie into an issue already high on the public or media agenda or link your organization to the top news of the day.
10. Localize a general report.

Source: Smith, 2008.

stock dropped $6 billion after reports linking cell phones and brain cancer. Those companies recovered, but some companies have gone bankrupt in the wake of negative publicity.

Sometimes, however, even negative publicity can help an organization. Traditionally, Boston was one of the first cities to book a play as it was leaving Broadway and beginning a nationwide tour. Because of Boston's conservative social sensitivities, it sometimes banned plays or books as being too offensive. Producers noted with interest that the very banning of plays in Boston often assured their success in attracting audiences elsewhere, and some theatrical companies deliberately tried to be banned in Boston.

Negative publicity often has had a positive effect on generating interest, particularly among potential audiences. Seldom is this more true than with religiously motivated protests. Former New York City Mayor Rudy Giuliani unwittingly generated valuable publicity and increased audiences for museums when he publicly criticized them—a 2001 exhibit with a photo of Christ depicted as a naked black woman; a 1999 exhibit with a portrait of the Virgin Mary covered with elephant dung. Movies such as Martin Scorsese's *The Last Temptation of Christ* and Mel Gibson's *The Passion of the Christ* have gained attention and audiences as various religious groups lined up in protest. So maybe that old saying might make some sense after all.

To attract the interest of the news media, particularly of television reporters, the news and publicity events must have a strong visual element. Stand-up commentators or talking heads don't make it on most television news reports, other than on occasional local-access cable programs that few people watch. Audiences have become sophisticated—some might say spoiled. Regardless, they demand active, even entertaining, visual presentation of their news. Reporters do their best to comply with the expectations of their audiences, so unless you are able to present newsworthy information with a visual dimension, you are unlikely to find the news media receptive vehicles for your message.

The quest for a strong visual element to news is an opportunity for creative minds, as noted in the previous section on the strategy of activism. Even in nonconfrontational situations, events staged for their publicity value have their place—as long as they are vehicles for news and not simply hollow attention-getters. At one university, a student theater group called Casting Hall wanted to attract attention and new members, so its members went "fishing" in the student union on a very snowy January day. Students in waders carried fishing poles, casting and reeling in new members. It was a visual pun, appropriate for both the name and the theatrical nature of the organization. The gimmick drew attention, generated publicity, raised some interest. and resulted in several new members.

Newsworthy information. Presenting newsworthy information is a must for any organization that hopes to use the news media to carry its message and capture the interest of its publics. For the communication strategist, news is one of the strongest proactive strategies because something truly newsworthy is almost guaranteed to gain the attention of the news media and, through them, the organization's other publics. Even if you are presenting a message through personal or organizational channels, keep in mind that your audiences will be more drawn to a newsworthy message.

What is news? The element of news deals with information that offers the audience a new idea or the latest development. From a journalistic perspective—which is the perspective every public relations practitioner needs to respect and adopt—news is information that involves action, adventure, change, conflict, consequence, contest, controversy, drama, effect, fame, importance, interest, personality, prominence, proximity, and dozens of other attributes often listed in journalism textbooks.

For our purposes, we will define news as significant information relevant to the local area, presented with balance and objectivity and in a timely manner. The value of news is magnified by two more elements: unusualness and fame. Let's "simplify" things with the acronym **SiLoBaTi + UnFa**. This convenient way to remember the main ingredients of news is made up of the first two letters of each of the elements: *si*gnificance, *lo*calness, *ba*lance, and *ti*meliness, plus *un*usualness and *fa*me.

- First, news is information of *significance*. It has meaning to many people, even those beyond the organization; it is information of consequence and magnitude.
- News also deals with information relevant to the *local* area, as defined by the coverage area of the news medium featuring the information.
- News is information with *balance* and objectivity. While the public relations practitioner uses information to promote the organization or client, it should not be presented merely in a promotional manner; rather, it should be presented with an air of detachment and neutrality.
- The final key ingredient in news is that it is *timely*, being connected with current issues, especially those high on public and media agendas.

In addition to these four key elements, newsworthiness is magnified by two other factors.

- News interest is enhanced when the information deals with *unusual* situations. This is what writers call human interest, that hard-to-define quality involving rarity, novelty, uniqueness, milestones, or slightly offbeat occurences.
- News interest also is enhanced when the information involves *fame*. "Names make news" isn't idle chatter. Well-known or important people can add interest to a newsworthy situation. Sometimes their involvement can take an otherwise routine event and elevate it to the status of news.

News judgment is relative. Public relations writers attempt to predict newsworthiness, but the decision to call something news is made only by the media **gatekeepers**, those people who control the flow of information in their various publications, newscasts, or talk shows. Examples of media gatekeepers are editors, columnists, news directors, producers and webmasters.

As a public relations professional, part of your job is to analyze the relationship among three things to establish newsworthiness: (1) your organization's activities and messages; (2) the media agenda; and (3) the interests of a key public. The Venn diagram in Exhibit 5.1 shows this relationship, with circle A indicating the interests of the news media, circle B information about the organization, and circle C the interests of a key public.

The AB area denotes newsworthy information about the organization. This involves activities and messages the organization potentially can publicize through the news media. The ABC area represents information about the organization that is of interest both to the news media and to the key publics. This represents information that is the primary focus of a media relations person, because it is newsworthy information that the public will look for

Exhibit 5.1 Relationship Between Organizational Activities/Messages, Media Agenda and Interests of Key Public

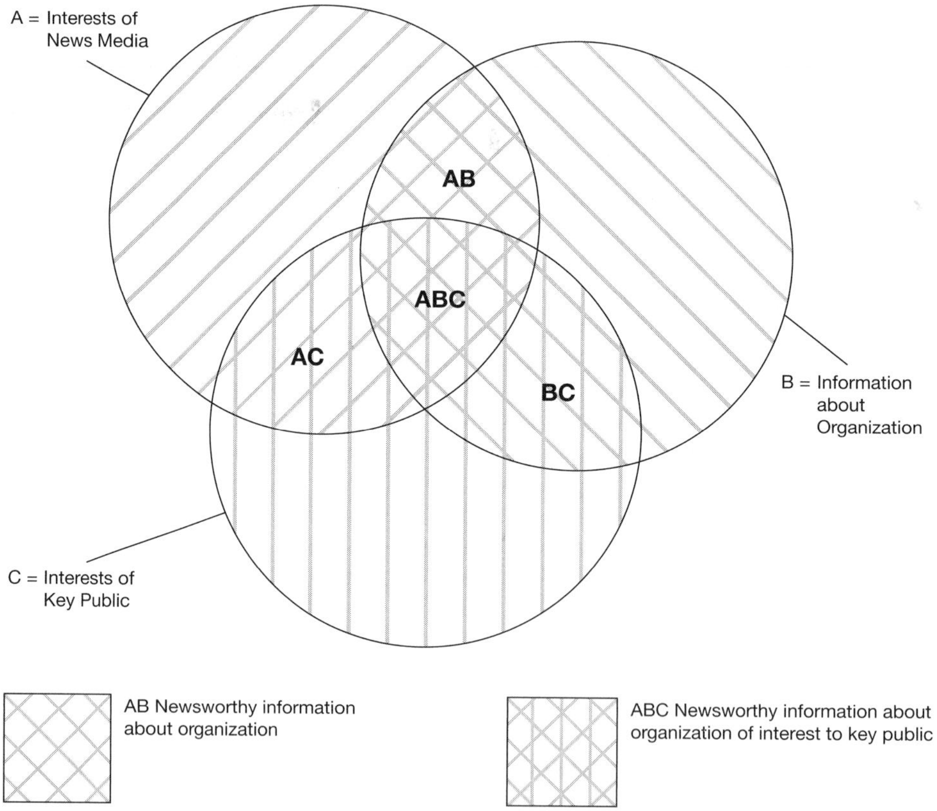

or at least will be attentive to. Often strategic public relations practitioners find that topics associated with all three groups (media, publics, and the organization) result in a **news peg**—that is, an item that the media is already reporting on that also touches, in some way, on the organization. For example, if the media is reporting on a national story involving an international crisis in Asia, a local Asian-based cultural organization may contact the media and offer an informed local perspective on events half a world away. Or if a high-profile celebrity goes public with a diagnosis of depression, a mental-health clinic might move quickly to offer media interviews on how to identify and deal with the illness.

Back at the Venn diagram, the BC area indicates nonnewsworthy information that the organization will have to present to the public through organizational or advertising media unless the public relations practitioner can reshape or enhance the information to make it of more interest to the news media. The AC area indicates information not involving the organization that is of interest both to the media and to the key public, essentially information on the media and public agendas. Strategic communicators look to these agendas for opportunities to insert their organizations into the news of the day.

In some situations, circle A could fully overlap circle C, meaning that topics on the media agenda are of interest to the key public. In such a case, media relations would pay a major role in the organization's strategic communication program. In other situations, circle A might not intersect at all with circle C, leaving the public relations person to develop alternatives to the news media to present the organization's message. It is up to the public relations professional to determine, through both research and experience, the relationships among these three entities.

Transparent communication. A relatively new concept is an important idea in developing a proactive public relations communication strategy. **Transparent communication** is the term given to the notion that open and observable activity by an organization helps publics understand the organization and support its actions. Transparent communication, which deals with the awareness objectives of increasing knowledge and understanding, simply means making your case. Many communication efforts have failed because the publics are aware of facts but not the reasons behind them.

Too often, organizations exhibit a "just trust us" mentality by announcing plans without providing reasons why those plans are necessary, and today's publics aren't inclined to trust blindly. For example, within a four-month period in one midsized city, community opposition was strong in four different situations—a proposed relocation of the zoo, an announcement by a health management organization to drop coverage for half the hospitals in the area, plans by a public radio station to suspend operations, and the decision of a bridge authority to turn away millions of federal dollars for a high-profile "signature" bridge in favor of a less architecturally impressive bridge. In each situation, the organization in question drew criticism because it had failed to provide plausible reasons for its plans. Publics had been left surprised, confused, and only partly informed; facts had been given, but there was no convincing rationale for the decisions and plans.

In an example of doing it right, the CIA's report of the crash of TWA flight 800 off Long Island, New York, not only detailed what the investigators found, but also included a thorough discussion of the investigation process that led to the conclusion. "Report goes beyond being 'open,'" wrote the late Pat Jackson in *PR Reporter*. "Open implies something else is closed, which raises questions. CIA's report is transparent—everything is laid on the line. Its thoroughness leaves no questions" (1997, n.p.).

Advocacy and Celebrity Influence

Public relations planners often try to involve celebrities who not only can attract media attention but who also might impact on key publics.

Because studies show that 88% of Americans get most of their health information from television, the National Cancer Institute's Entertainment Education Program works with Hollywood and with advocacy groups to promote TV story lines. It has tip sheets and other resources for writers and producers. Meanwhile, the NCI teamed with the U.S. Centers for Disease Control and Prevention and the Annenberg Norman Lear Center to recognize television's attention to health issues with the Sentinel for Health Awards.

Results of the cooperation between Hollywood and advocacy groups have been surprising—and documented—as some celebrity-based activities have shown themselves to be strong enough to effect major public response.

For example, journalist Katie Couric became a national spokesperson for awareness about colorectal cancer after her husband, TV commentator Jay Monahan, died from the disease. Hoping to influence viewers of NBC's *Today* show, Couric underwent a colonoscopy live on national television in 2000. The result? Testing for the disease increased 22% nationwide and held steady for nine months. Media analysts dubbed this "The Couric Effect." In 2005 Couric broadcast her own mammogram to similarly influence women to undergo the potentially life-saving exam for breast cancer.

In a similar vein, publicity about celebrities and their illnesses also can cause others to pay closer attention to their own health. A study (Larson et al., 2005) shows that celebrity endorsements led to a 21% increase for mammograms, 31% for prostate exams, and 37% for colonoscopies. Health statisticians documented increased interest in diagnostic exams when Vice President Dick Cheney received a pacemaker for his heart condition in 2001 and when Secretary of State Colin Powell was treated for prostate cancer in 2003.

Other medical researchers pointed to a 2003 story line in the British TV series *Coronation Street* about a woman's death from cervical cancer as the major cause of a 21% increase in testing for that disease.

In 2006, organizers of the New York City Alzheimer's Association said that the presence of actress Jean Smart (*24*) as emcee for a fund-raising dinner resulted in a $400,000 increase in donations from the previous year. The Alzheimer's Association previously had used actor David Hyde Pierce (*Frasier*) as a spokesperson for its appearance at a congressional caucus, resulting not only in publicity for the organization's cause but the increased participation of senators and representatives.

When organizations engage in transparent communication, they provide the kind of communication that identifies the problem, gets people interested in it, airs the various options and otherwise creates a climate of understanding and involvement before plans are announced that affect the publics. If financial pressures are pushing your organization to curtail services, let your publics know about the financial problems and the various options before announcing a service cutback. Nobody likes bad surprises, especially when it is clear that the organization has been hiding information from key publics.

Transparent communication is particularly relevant to the stereotypically secretive world of finance. Harvey Pitt, chairman of the federal Securities and Exchange Commission (SEC), identified one of the top SEC goals as "to ensure that our financial markets are transparent and fair to all investors." Helen Vollmer, CEO of the largest full-service public relations firm in the Southwest, advises her clients that today's marketplace requires transparent communication between corporate leadership and stockholders. Meanwhile, her vice president for investor relations (IR), Jennifer Tweeton, lists transparency second only to credibility as the most important ingredients of an IR program (http://www.vollmerpr.com).

Here's a case in point: Transparency and balancing it with confidentiality issues were uppermost in the mind of leaders of San Diego Children's Hospital who, in 2006, saw two employees arrested on child-abuse charges in unrelated cases.

In March, police notified the hospital that they were investigating a respiratory therapist working with comatose children. A few days later the man was arrested for abusing at least nine victims under his care at the hospital. Police later discovered more than 100,000 child pornography images on his home computer. The hospital's crisis plan went into effect. Letters in English and Spanish were sent to 176 families of his former patients. Another 30,000 letters were sent to people associated with the hospital, including employees, families of patients, donors, and legislators. Adopting a posture of openness and transparency, the hospital gave media interviews, held a news conference, and set up a special telephone inquiry line. The crisis plan called for speed and flexibility; it valued transparency of information while at the same time seeking patient confidentiality. Media and law enforcement generally agreed that the hospital was transparent in this approach to the public.

Then lightning struck twice. Within 5½ weeks, police notified the hospital that another employee was being investigated on similar charges. The hospital suspended the nurse, who a few days later was arrested for molesting a child at the hospital and for possessing child pornography at home. The hospital held a second news conference, with assurances that these were isolated cases. Eventually both men pleaded guilty, the first receiving a 45-year sentence, the second a 14-year prison term.

Later that year, the hospital presented its case study to colleagues attending the Boston convention of the National Association of Children's Hospitals and Related Institutions. It pointed to jarring statistics: An estimated 3–5% of males are sexually interested in prepubescent children, and even a greater number in adolescents. Thus, a hospital with 1,000 male employees might expect 50 who are potential child abusers. More alarmingly, the presenters noted that organizations such as children's hospitals are magnets for people with perverse interests in children and thus may attract an even higher rate of potential abusers. Thus the need for a carefully prepared program to screen employees, minimize risk, and respond responsibly when the crime occurs.

San Diego Children's Hospital offered several lessons to its colleagues: have a crisis plan that balances transparency with patient privacy, involve the CEO visibly, frame the response agenda to emphasize quality improvement, communicate with all patients involved, expect leaks to the media, and visibly cooperate with law enforcement. As with other situations of crisis communication, the public relations potential in such circumstances allows the organization to show its true colors—undue concern for internal privacy or transparent commitment to its many publics and its long-term reputation within the community.

Media Theories and Public Relations

How powerful are the news media? Can they make us care about an issue or act on it in a certain way just because they report it? Or are they simply information sources used at the discretion of their audiences?

Insight into the issue begins with social psychology in general, as well as specific applications to media presentations and news audiences. In particular, three theories are useful in discussing the role of the news media: agenda-setting, priming and framing.

1. *Agenda-setting theory.* Communication researchers and public relations practitioners believe there is a middle ground, explained by the **agenda-setting theory** associated with Maxwell McCombs and Donald Shaw (1972). According to this theory, the news media are not powerful enough to make audiences react in a certain way. Rather, they raise issues that both they and their audiences consider to be newsworthy. In simple terms, the news media tell us what to think about, but they don't tell us what to think.

   Through the issues they choose to cover, the news media can legitimize a story. Conversely, failure to report on issues marginalizes a topic as not being newsworthy. There is still a bit of a debate: Does an issue move into the public interest because the media report it? Or, do the media report an issue because it already is a matter of public interest? Probably a bit of both.

   For the public relations strategist, the important lesson from this theory is to link organizational information with the current news: What is the news of the day and how does my organization fit into it? Sometimes the link is obvious. During a high-profile trial in which child abuse is an issue, a child-services agency easily could become a resource to reporters about the nature and extent of child abuse in the local community.

   At other times the public relations person must be creative in finding the links. In one situation, when control of Hong Kong was reverting from England to China, the local branch of a U.S. bank connected to the international story through its corporate genealogy: It was owned by a British company that also grew out of banking in Hong Kong. In another situation, a hospital was able to be linked to news about genocide in Rwanda because one of its doctors recently had returned from a stint as a medical volunteer there.
2. *Priming theory.* Another theoretical concept is priming, which deals with context of news reports. The observation is that the amount of time and space that media devote to an issue make an audience receptive and perhaps alert the audience to particular themes.

   Shanto Iyengar and Donald Kinder (1987) have identified a priming process in which media attention to or avoidance of various issues creates a framework for relatively uninformed audiences, calling up past information and applying it to present situations. For example, voters may evaluate a political candidate according to themes resurrected from previous media reporting on topics such as taxation, abortion, gay rights, and other topics selected by the media.
3. *Framing theory.* A related and perhaps more useful theory deals with framing. It focuses on the presentation of the story and organizes discourse about the topic. How do the news media frame a story? Is there an inherent "good guy" in the story? Whose version of the

story gets top billing? Which version becomes the standard against which other points of view are measured?

Framing theory was developed by Erving Goffman (1974) and applied to communication studies by Dietram Scheufele (1999). Framing provides a rhetorical context for the text, involving the use of metaphor, storytelling, jargon, word choice, and other narrative elements. For example, a report on repeat drunk driving might be framed in various ways: criminal recidivism, police incompetence, judicial lenience, or the power of addiction. If agenda setting tells audiences what to think about, framing theory suggests that the media influence how the audience thinks about an issue.

Consider each of these three theories in light of an example: news coverage of the 2007 citizenship vote by the Cherokee Nation. In the vote, the tribal government sought to end a 100-year confusion caused when the federal government determined that after the Civil War certain ex-slaves (who came to be known as Freedmen) should be considered members of the tribe because they were living in the Indian territory of what is now Oklahoma. The Cherokees finally were voting on whether to restrict tribal citizenship to people—whether ethnically black, white, or Indian—who actually have Cherokee blood lineage.

In terms of agenda setting, the Cherokee-Freedmen story failed to register in a major way on the national agenda. It received limited national and international coverage, often from media that had previously taken an editorial stand on the topic. But during the first two weeks of March 2007, other news placed higher on the media agenda: the scandal over conditions at Walter Reed Army Medical Center, conviction of I. Lewis "Scooter" Libby in the "outing" of CIA agent Valerie Plame, scandals over politically inspired firing of federal attorneys, killer tornadoes in several states, continuing death in the Iraq War, and new attention on genocide in Darfur.

Priming influenced the story through prior ongoing media coverage of civil rights. Reports of the denial of voting rights in particular may have prepared audiences to see the Cherokee-Freedmen story in that light. Likewise, the storytelling is impacted by the historical context that is known to journalists and audiences alike.

The relevant issue to the Cherokee-Freedmen story in the context of framing theory deals with the manner in which the media reports placed various elements. Such elements include the diversity of the mixed-race Cherokee community and the convoluted history involved. Other issues are racism, tribal sovereignty, and government complicity in creating the problem in the first place, as well as nuances in the voting procedure and the precise language of the ballot question. Framing also entered into which news sources were quoted and which side received top billing.

For a full report of the media analysis on the citizenship vote, see "The Cherokee-Freedmen Story: What the Media Saw" (http://www.buffalostate.edu/communication/documents/Cherokee2007.pdf).

Reactive Public Relations Strategies

When accusations or other criticisms have been made, or when an organization has been visited by difficulties or worse, public relations strategists are thrown into a reactive mode. In responding to outside forces, organizations should develop objectives such as gaining public understanding, maintaining and restoring reputation, and rebuilding trust and support.

The field of crisis communication management is ripe with examples of response strategies that work.

The classical term for a communication response to negative situations is **apologia**, a formal defense that offers a compelling case for an organization's opinions, positions, or actions. Don't confuse *apologia* with **apology**, which is an expression of fault and remorse. An apologia could include an apology, but it is much more. Through an apologia an organization explains its actions and positions with a clear eye toward convincing critics of its rightness. Applying the concept of apologia to corporate crises, Keith Michael Hearit notes that an apologia offers an organization a strategic opportunity to manage its reputation in the wake of accusations of wrongdoing. Hearit suggests a threefold approach: persuasive accounts offering (1) an explanation and, if necessary, a defense; (2) statements of regret; and (3) disassociation tactics to separate the organization from the problem (1994).

Another approach to public relations response strategy considers the **theory of accounts**, which refers to the use of communication to manage relationships in the wake of rebuke or criticism. Accounts can range from defensive to offensive. Some research (Cody & McLaughlin, 1985) has found that the harsher the criticism, the more a strong offensive account is warranted. That was a lesson not learned by political candidates John Kerry and John McCain (in his first bid for the presidency), who lost presidential elections in part because they failed to take seriously vicious political criticism that demeaned their military service as war heroes.

In *Accounts, Excuses, and Apologies,* William Benoit (1995) deals with accounts and apologia, drawing on research from sociology, social psychology, and communication. He presents a **theory of image restoration**, based on the presumption that, in the face of criticism, both people and organizations seek to maintain or rebuild a positive reputation.

Organizations can use a range of verbal and behavioral reactions in managing their response to opposition and their recovery from criticism. The following typology of public relations responses is based on a reflection of contemporary research and consulting practices, as well as the work of the above-mentioned researchers.

Reactive Strategy 1: Pre-emptive Action

One type of strategy actually involves pre-emptive action, which is taken before the opposition launches its first charge against the organization.

Prebuttal. This strategy is called a **prebuttal**. The term itself is a play on the word *rebuttal*, but these are preemptive strikes when bad news is inevitable. It was a prebuttal when the White House countered anticipated charges that begat impeachment for President Bill Clinton even before those charges were made public. It was a prebuttal in 2007, when presidential candidate Rudy Giuliani criticized a video prior to its release, in which the International Association of Fire Fighters claimed that, contrary to Giuliani's self-promotion as a 9/11 hero, his actions on the day of the attacks actually caused the unnecessary death of many firemen.

In today's era of viral messaging in a fast-paced sociopolitical environment, prebuttals are becoming commonplace attempts to deflate opposing arguments even before they are made. The concept of prebuttal is based on the observation that the first one to tell the story sets the tone, against which all alternative versions must compete. It's a lesson you may have learned in elementary school, when your sister or brother beat you home with a story of how you got into trouble on the playground. Following that account, your own version may have

A Typology of Reactive Public Relations Strategies

Reactive Strategy 1: Pre-emptive Action
Prebuttal

Reactive Strategy 2: Offensive Response
Attack
Embarrassment
Shock
Threat

Reactive Strategy 3: Defensive Response
Denial
Excuse
Justification

Reactive Strategy 4: Diversionary Response
Concession
Ingratiation
Disassociation
Relabeling

Reactive Strategy 5: Vocal Commiseration
Concern
Condolence
Regret
Apology

Reactive Strategy 6: Rectifying Behavior
Investigation
Corrective Action
Restitution
Repentance

Reactive Strategy 7: Deliberate Inaction
Strategic Silence
Strategic Ambiguity

been not only second place but somehow second best. The first telling of the story becomes normative, and other versions are considered in light of the first account.

The same thing holds true for organizations. When something bad is about to happen, organizations can do more than merely brace for the aftershock. *Carpe diem!* as the Romans said; *seize the day!*

Consider this real-life situation: A hospital had to deal with a pending report that would list it as having one of the highest patient death rates in the state. Knowing that the report was only days away and that it was statistically accurate, the hospital held a news conference to announce the forthcoming report and to explain why the rate was high: This particular hospital accepted charity patients too poor to have regular health care, specialized in geriatrics, and was the only hospital in the area treating AIDS patients at a time in the not-too-distant past when the disease meant certain death. These were important reasons explaining the high death rate. Local reporters gave the hospital's announcement minimal coverage, and they virtually ignored the state report a few days later as old news.

Consider using the strategy of prebuttal when the public inevitably will hear the accusation or other bad news and when the organization can offer strong evidence to give its publics reasons to disregard the bad news or excuse the organization.

Attacking the news media is particularly risky, because they have the last word. But in 1999 Metabolife did so because it feared biased reporting from ABC News. The ABC program *20/20* had spent 4 months in research and interviews, and Metabolife worried about how its popular but controversial herbal diet pill would be portrayed.

Combining the strategies of prebuttal and attack, Metabolife posted a website with its own videotape of ABC's 70-minute interview with its CEO, along with a full transcript and additional medical information. The posting went up 10 days before the ABC program was scheduled to air. The company also purchased full-page ads in the *New York Times* and the *New York Post*, gained coverage in the *Wall Street Journal*, and ran radio commercials across the country to draw hits to the website—all prior to the story's broadcast. Metabolife also placed a short ad during the program, asking viewers to visit its website.

The website received 1.1 million hits a day, and the company later claimed that its preemptive action caused the *20/20* story to be fairer than it otherwise would have been. ABC denied Metabolife's interpretation, calling the company's action "a not-so-subtle form of intimidation," claiming that it had no effect on the report.

Many crisis communication experts suggest that an organizational interview or news conference should always include at least an audio recording, preferably a videotape, of the media encounter. Make sure the taping is obvious to the media. The presence of your own recording devices will serve notice that everything is on the record, minimizing the chance of being misquoted and providing proof if you are.

Reactive Strategy 2: Offensive Response

Public relations planners sometimes use offensive response strategies such as attack, embarrassment, or threat in response to criticism. These are based on the premise that the organization is operating from a position of strength in the face of opposition. Here is an overview of each of these strategies.

Attack. An **attack** is an offensive response strategy of claiming that an accusation of wrongdoing is an attempt to impugn the organization's reputation by an accuser who is negligent or malicious. Often the objective behind this strategy is to encourage an opponent to retreat or at least to refrain from future criticism. Use this approach only when a strong case can be made that accusers have grossly overstated the organization's involvement in a problem. Let's look at two examples of the attack strategy—one that backfired, one that was successful.

Dow Corning used the attack strategy, to its own misfortune, in handling a lawsuit over its silicone-gel breast implants. Faced with reports filled with unfavorable scientific information, the company's first response was to attack the investigators. This and other strategic missteps led to a $7.3 million judgment against the company and class-action lawsuits of more than $4 billion that put the corporation into Chapter 11 bankruptcy, despite the fact that no reputable scientific evidence showed that the implants caused disease or illness.

On the other hand, Itsy Bitsy Entertainment Company was successful in attacking criticism by the late Reverend Jerry Falwell that its Tinky Winky Teletubby, seen by an estimated 16 million viewers, is a gay character. Company spokesman Steve Rice told reporters, "Falwell was attacking something sweet and innocent to further his conservative political agenda. To out a Teletubby in a preschool show is kind of sad on his part. I really find it absurd and kind of offensive.")

Embarrassment. A related offensive strategy deals with **embarrassment**, in which an organization tries to lessen an opponent's influence by using shame or humiliation. An example of this strategy was the Liberian Women's Peace Movement, which held street demonstrations to embarrass the government into ending a violent civil war. In 2003, the women locked down a conference hall until a peace accord was signed. Soon after the U.N. charged Liberia's president with crimes against humanity. He resigned and was exiled and replaced—by a woman.

Shock. Sometimes, in an effort to make a point, embarrassment may take a turn toward alarm. In public relations and strategic communication, **shock** is the deliberate agitation of the mind or emotions, particularly through the use of surprise, disgust, or some other strong and unexpected stimulus. As such, it seldom offers a long-term positive strategy for any organization unwilling to be seen as out of step with mainstream values of decency and fair play.

People for the Ethical Treatment of Animals (PETA) has built a reputation for outrageous strategies in its animal-rights campaigns. PETA used shock strategy to force McDonald's to agree to more human practices in chicken coops and slaughterhouses under its control. The advocacy group distributed "Son of Ron Unhappy Meal" boxes with a plastic cow in blood-stained hay, a plastic butchered pig, and a Ronald McDonald figure wearing a blood-spattered butcher's apron and wielding a meat cleaver. After McDonald's conceded the fight, PETA turned its attention to how Burger King raised and killed chickens, quickly gaining the compliance of that company as well.

Threat. Making a **threat** is another offensive strategy, involving the promise that harm will come to the accuser or the purveyor of bad news. The threatened harm may be in the form of a lawsuit for defamation, for example. Use public threats only if the information cannot be disputed in another way, and beware of the ethical concerns about misusing this strategy.

Reactive Strategy 3: Defensive Response

Another strategic communication response involves defensive response strategies such as denial, excuse or justification, all of which involve the organization reacting less aggressively to criticism.

Denial. Using the defensive strategy of **denial**, an organization tries not to accept blame, claiming that the reputed problem doesn't exist or didn't occur, or if it did, that it's not related to the organization. In the latter case, the claim generally is either one of **innocence** ("We didn't do it"), **mistaken identity** ("You have us confused with someone else") or **blame shifting** ("So-and-so did it").

A few years ago, a student at a public university was arrested for prostitution. She tried to justify her actions by claiming that she couldn't otherwise afford tuition because of a financial-aid snafu. The university was quick to say "That's absurd!" and shifted responsibility back to the student.

Be careful in shifting blame, however, because the strategy can backfire if the organization is ultimately responsible. An executive who claims that an employee's inappropriate action was against company policy must be prepared for scrutiny of both the company's official policy and its way of doing business. It is best to use the strategy of denial only when the case can be publicly supported and when it can be proven that neither the organization nor anyone in its policy-setting ranks was involved in the wrongdoing.

Excuse. A commonly used defensive strategy is **excuse**, in which an organization tries to minimize its responsibility for the harm or wrongdoing. Excuse can take several forms, including provocation, lack of control, accident, victimization, and mere association.

Faith-Based Shock Strategy

People for the Ethical Treatment of Animals has a strong and consistent anti-meat, pro-vegetarian, pro–animal rights message aimed at "total animal liberation." The organization has also taken up the challenge to convert religious observers of all faiths to its way of thinking, and it often uses a shock strategy that uses religious imagery designed to surprise and even outrage its audiences.

One PETA ad depicts the Holy Shroud of Turin, which many believe to be a remnant from biblical times with an image of Jesus' face, with the caption "Make a lasting impression. Go vegetarian." Another suggests that, despite recorded biblical evidence to the contrary, Jesus was a vegetarian, specifically the "Prince of Peas." Still another provocatively proclaims to Christians that livestock, not Jesus, died for their sins.

A PETA news release announced that it was "enlisting Jesus as its newest spokesperson." In 2000 it used the icon of the Priests of the Sacred Heart, substituting an orange slice for a halo. When the Catholic religious order objected, PETA switched to a version of Jesus from the animated TV show *South Park*—also a copyright violation—that the Comedy Central Network found unfunny and demanded that PETA stop using.

Some PETA ads focus on the Catholic devotion to Mary. In 2002, PETA introduced a billboard of the Virgin Mary breastfeeding the Infant Jesus with the caption "If it was good enough for Jesus . . . Dump Dairy." Reminiscent of many medieval paintings, the ad didn't create much chatter. But an ad introduced the next year did generate a reaction as Catholic groups demanded the removal of a PETA billboard depicting the Virgin Mary cradling a chicken carcass in her arms with the theologically perplexing caption "Go vegetarian. It's an Immaculate Conception."

Meanwhile, PETA campaign director Bruce Friedrich wrote to the pope asking him to tell Catholics to keep lamb off the traditional Easter menu in Italy. The pope didn't respond, perhaps because a few years earlier, during a papal visit to Chicago, PETA had protestors dressed as a nun and a cow with a placard "Eating meat is a bad habit." Friedrich describes himself as a devout Catholic who believes that cruelty to animals is against his faith.

PETA activists wearing Jesus costumes also have protested outside barbecue restaurants in Texas, Alabama, Mississippi, and other Southern states that take both their religion and their barbecues seriously. In 2003, the group held a boisterous rally outside Southeast Christian Church in Louisville, Kentucky, where Greg Dedrick, the president of KFC (formerly Kentucky Fried Chicken), was worshipping on Christmas Eve. And during Holy Week in 2004, PETA placed a 10-foot cow dressed as the pope with a crucified cow on his cross outside Catholic cathedrals in several Eastern cities. In New York, the cow-pope mobile was ticketed for an illegal turn on Fifth Avenue.

PETA spokespeople said such shock tactics are timed to generate the most publicity for their cause. For PETA, negative publicity is not considered . . . well, negative.

If nothing else, PETA is an equal-opportunity instrument of religious shock. In 2003 it unveiled a traveling "Holocaust on Your Plate" campaign claiming that "six million people died in concentration camps, but six billion broiler chickens will die this year in slaughterhouses." The exhibit toured in 70 U.S. cities, three Canadian provinces, and 15 foreign countries during an 18-month period. The public outcry was quick, loud, and widespread, as expected. Responded PETA, "Sometimes people need to be offended."

In its subsequent "Holocaust" campaign, PETA displayed 10-foot-high photos of the Nazi concentration camps interspersed with photos of a livestock farm. One quote from the exhibit states,

"The leather sofa and handbag are the moral equivalent of lampshades made from the skin of people killed in the death camps." The last frame juxtaposes images of dead Jews in the concentration camp with dead pigs in the slaughterhouse. In 2005 on Holocaust Remembrance Day, PETA e-mailed a terse apology to the Jewish press for the hurt it admitted the campaign caused, but the organization's website maintained 200 pages on the Holocaust campaign.

PETA also has taken aim on kosher requirements and has called upon Jews to abandon their ancient dietary laws. Meanwhile, it has erected billboards in Utah that Mormons say misrepresent their scripture to conform to PETA's call for vegetarianism. And the organization has lately taken its campaign to Muslims, challenging their interpretation that the Koran permits meat eating. To date, only the Hindus and the Buddhists seem to have escaped PETA's faith-based shock strategy, though neither religion is strictly vegetarian.

"The world's great religions are under attack by disrespectful PETA activists who twist scripture and history to suit their goals," comments David Martosko, director of research with the Center for Consumer Freedom.

The organization may claim **provocation**, essentially saying that it had no choice. An example of this would be a police department that excuses its elimination of a popular mounted patrol by reporting that the police union insisted that seniority, not horse-riding ability, be the key factor in selecting officers for the patrol, thereby making the mounted patrol inefficient and even dangerous. A variation on the excuse theme is **lack of control**, in which the organization reports that its actions were forced upon it, such as the manager of a local manufacturing plant who blames local employee layoffs on decisions made at national corporate offices.

Another excuse is **accident**, in which the organization suggests that factors beyond anyone's control led to a problem. An example of this is a mayor who excuses his city's slow progress in snow removal on unusually heavy snowfall during a two-week period.

A related but even stronger excuse is **victimization**, in which the organization shows that it was the target of criminals. This was the excuse presented by Pepsi amid claims that syringes were found in its diet drink cans in 1993—an excuse so thoroughly accepted that consumers barely cut back on their consumption, then rebounded to give the company one of its best quarters ever in terms of sales.

A final type of excuse deals with mere **association**, in which the organization claims that it more or less inherited a problem. For example, a newly elected city administration might try to disassociate itself from a $2 million income shortfall by claiming that the financial loss was caused by careless planning by the previous administration.

Justification. Another defensive strategy is **justification**, which admits the organization did the deed but did so for good reason. Like the excuse response, justification has several subcategories.

One type of justification is based on **good intention**, in which an organization attempts to soften the blow of bad results by claiming that it was trying to accomplish something positive. For example, a cab company may justify one of its drivers sideswiping a parked car by claiming the driver was trying to avoid hitting a pedestrian.

Another type of justification is **context**, in which the organization asks its publics to "look at it from our side." Robin Hood seen from the point of view of the sheriff of Nottingham looks much different than from the perspective of the Nottingham peasants. Likewise, investors and environmentalists each may view differently a company that violated technicalities of clean-air regulations.

Idealism is a type of justification based on an appeal to ethical, moral or spiritual values, such as leaders of a church protest against the death penalty who explain that their actions, though perhaps unpopular with some church members, are nevertheless in line with—even commanded by—their religious principles.

Another type of justification involves **mitigation**, with the admission that the problem occurred but that blame is lessened because of a factor such as impairment, illness, coercion, lack of training, and so on. However, if the mitigating factor is the responsibility of the organization, the attempt at justification probably will fail, as the reported drunkenness of the *Valdez* captain did not allow Exxon to escape responsibility for the oil spill in the Alaskan waters of Prince William Sound. Similarly a major, governor, or president who appoints to an important post somebody who turns out to be incompetent is unlikely to escape blame for having made the appointment in the first place.

Reactive Strategy 4: Diversionary Response

Several diversionary response strategies also are open to communication planners. They include concessions, ingratiation, disassociation, and relabeling, all of which are attempts to shift the gaze of the publics from the problem associated with the organization.

Concession. Using the diversionary strategy of **concession**, an organization tries to rebuild its relationship with its publics by giving the public something it wants. The focus here should be on a concession that is mutually valued by both the organization and its public. For example, after objections to a car advertisement parodying Leonardo da Vinci's *The Last Supper* with the caption, "My friends, let us rejoice, because a new Golf is born," Volkswagen France and its advertising agency offered as a concession a major financial contribution to a religious charity whose work was supported by the protestors. The value of the donation by Volkswagen France was recognized by both the company and its offended public.

Public relations strategists should use concession only if the gift will be valued by adversaries and if the organization will remain committed to the concession. Amid criticism of its marketing of infant formula in lesser-developed nations during the 1980s, Nestlé established the International Council on Infant Food Industries and a code of ethics, attempting to offer its critics concession. But the strategy provided only a temporary diversion for critics, who quickly saw evidence that the company was not abiding by its own code of ethics. Subsequent opposition to Nestlé grew in the face of what critics viewed as insincerity and hypocrisy. As recent as 2008, the International Nestlé Boycott Committee was still opposing the Swiss multinational. The committee claims success in 60 countries that have adopted stronger laws monitoring marketing practices, and many European universities still ban the sale of Nestlé products on campus.

Instead of providing gifts to involved publics, some concessions are aimed at generating favorable publicity for an organization under fire. An example of this is found in *Crisis Response: Inside Stories in Managing Image Under Siege* (Gottschalk, 1993), in which crisis counselor James Lukaszewski revealed that he advised Exxon to charter aircraft to carry volunteers from major U.S. cities to Alaska so they could help clean up some of the 11 million gallons of oil spilled in Prince William Sound. Exxon rejected the idea on grounds that the airlift would cost too much, a few hundred thousand dollars. The company eventually spent $2.2 billion in cleanup costs, another $1 billion to settle state and federal lawsuits, and $300 million in lost wages to Alaskan fishermen, plus millions in legal fees fighting lawsuits that ordered punitive damages as high as $11.9 billion, much of it linked to Exxon's poor reputation.

Certainly an environmental airlift would not have eliminated all of Exxon's expenses. But in hindsight, it seems fair to conclude that an airlift would have helped the company's reputation, which in turn could have eased its legal battles as well as its strained relations with stockholders, consumers, government agencies, and the media. *Business Week* magazine later commented that "Exxon could have emerged from the case with a far better image if it had taken a more conciliatory approach . . . . Instead, Exxon took a tough stand. And more than a decade later, the furious debates, and the bitterness, continue" ("Commentary: It's Time to Put the Valdez Behind Us," 1999). As noted in Step 1, the Valdez case also had negative residual effects, such as the continuing and costly legal dispute with the State of Alabama.

Ingratiation. Another diversionary strategy, one of rather questionable ethical standing, is **ingratiation**. Essentially the organization attempts to manage the negative situation by charming its publics or "tossing a bone," giving something of relatively little significance to the organization in an attempt to turn the spotlight away from the accusations and criticisms. Ingratiation differs from concessions in that the latter involves something of real value to the public, while ingratiation is more cosmetic. Examples of ingratiation are seen in the case of state lawmakers who vote against long-term tax reform for homeowners while offering a token and temporary tax reduction.

Disassociation. Another diversionary strategy is **disassociation**, which attempts to distance an organization from the wrongdoing associated with it. This can be effective when a mishap has occurred not because of organizational policy but because policy was not observed, especially when the organization has severed ties with the cause of the problem.

Texaco accomplished disassociation when its corporate chairman quickly and publicly apologized for racist statements made by several top executives, suspended two of the officials, ordered sensitivity training and established a corporate hotline for reporting violations of company antidiscrimination policies. On the political scene, most Republican candidates attempted to similarly distance themselves from the policies of the unpopular presidential administration of George W. Bush during the election seasons in 2006 and 2008.

Think through the implications of disassociation. Justin Timberlake found that his success in distancing himself from Janet Jackson and the Super Bowl halftime controversy in 2004 also alienated many of his black fans.

Relabeling. Another diversionary strategy, **relabeling**, tries to distance the organization from criticism. It involves offering an agreeable name in replacement of a negative label that has been applied by others. Chrysler CEO Lee Iacocca used the strategy—with little success—when he tried to handle charges of odometer fraud. He claimed that Chrysler executives had merely driven new cars with disconnected odometers as part of a "quality test program" that was at worst a mistake in judgment. Chrysler was fined $7.6 million, and the judge said the test program, which he allowed may have been a good idea, went sour when Chrysler sold the cars as new vehicles, even though some had been in accidents.

Much relabeling involves corporate names. For decades, Philip Morris was synonymous with tobacco, but when tobacco became a magnet for social criticism and lawsuits, Philip

Morris Companies changed its name in 2003 to the Altria Group in an attempt to insulate the company from political pressure. The company also bought web domain names such as altria-stinks.org and altriakills.com to prevent rogue sites from having easy dissemination of anti-Altria messages. The name change also allowed Altria subsidiaries such as Kraft Foods to disassociate themselves from the tainted tobacco label and, as one critic said, "to make itself invisible."

Similarly, trying to create a distance from its own record of fraud and bankruptcy, WorldCom in 2003 changed its name to MCI, the name of its more respected subsidiary. Charging that WorldCom had hijacked the name, critics called for a boycott, and the name change did not cause the company's reputation to improve.

Other examples of relabeling reflect a more positive rationale to capitalize on a particular consumer strength. Thus, in 2005, Matsushita Kotobuki Electronics Industries changed its name to that of its most recognized brand and became Panasonic Shikoku Electronics. In 2007, Federated Department Stores changed its name to the Macy's Group in a bow to the drawing power of its most famous brand.

The strategy of relabeling can backfire if an organization's publics conclude that relabeling is deceptive or, worse, if it trivializes the problem. MTV may have created a new phrase with its "wardrobe malfunction" to explain Janet Jackson's exposed breast during the 2004 Super Bowl halftime show it produced, but the FCC was unamused as it fined CBS television a record $550,000 for indecency over the incident. Relabeling is only a short step away from **doublespeak**, which is deliberately misleading language and a highly unethical practice. Don't go too far in your effort to put on the best face.

Reactive Strategy 5: Vocal Commiseration

Another family of strategies deals with vocal commiseration, in which the organization expresses empathy and understanding about the misfortune suffered by its publics. These include concern, condolence, regret, and apology.

Concern. One type of vocal commiseration is **concern**, through which the organization expresses that it is not indifferent to a problem without admitting guilt. The apparent lack of care and concern for women harmed by breast implants was a continuing public relations burden for Dow Corning, which seemed unable to balance lawyerly advice ("admit nothing") with public expectation of compassion for people's suffering. The failure to respond aggravated the eventual legal judgments against the company, which climbed to $3.2 billion.

Condolence. A more formal type of vocal commiseration is **condolence**, in which the organization expresses grief over someone's loss or misfortune, again without admitting guilt. A good example of this strategy is the response of ValuJet president Lewis Jordan to the crash of one of his airplanes in the Florida Everglades, which killed 110 people—a crash later attributed to a shipper who had illegally mislabeled canisters of highly flammable oxygen. "It's Mother's Day weekend—we know that," Jordan said in a news conference the day after the crash. "Words in the English language, at least the ones I know, are inadequate to express the amount of grief and sadness we feel." The company later put action behind its words, sponsoring a memorial service for 46 victims whose remains could not be identified.

Regret. Another vocal strategy, **regret**, involves admitting sorrow and remorse for a situation, a wish that an event had not happened. Like compassion, regret does not necessarily imply fault; in fact, statements of regret may specifically not admit to any wrongdoing. This is an important perspective that public relations advisors bring in crisis situations. By expressing regret, public hostility can be tempered and the number and intensity of lawsuits may be contained.

Be aware, however, that regret without apology sometimes is not enough. Japan's Emperor Akihito learned that lesson on a visit to England. The emperor spoke of his "deep sorrow and pain" over suffering during the Second World War. But former prisoners of war booed the emperor, and one protestor burned a Japanese flag in his presence. A spokesman for the veterans said, "The emperor's speech does not alter the position one jot as far as any expression of an apology to the POWs is concerned." The reluctance of the Japanese government to officially apologize for wartime military atrocities has strained its relations with a number of countries.

Representative Cynthia McKinney (D.-Georgia) learned a similar lesson in 2006 after she punched a police officer who stopped her at a security checkpoint in the U.S. Capitol. She later called it a "misunderstanding" that had escalated. In a nonapology on the House floor, McKinney expressed "sincere regret about the encounter with the Capitol Hill Police" and, using passive voice, said "there should not have been any physical contact in this incident."

Regret sometimes extends to the actions of others. The prime minister of Japan in 2007 called "regrettable" a U.S. House of Representatives resolution demanding that Japan formally apologize for sex slavery in territories occupied by the Japanese military during World War II. But it was the American resolution that was found regrettable by the prime minister, who expressed sympathy but offered no apology to the euphemistically named "comfort women." Congress also incurred the wrath of the Turkish government in 2007 when a House committee passed a similar nonbinding resolution labeling as "genocide" the Turkish massacre of Armenians during World War I. The irony is that Congress has yet to apologize to its own people for black slavery in the American South, nor for the forced removal, massacres, and other patterns of genocide against American Indians.

Apology. The vocal strategy focused most on the public's interests and least on the organization's is **apology**. Issuing an apology involves publicly accepting full responsibility and asking forgiveness. Use the strategy of apology when the organization is clearly at fault and when long-term rebuilding of relationships is more important than short-term stalling or legal posturing.

Make sure the apology is straightforward, such as the statement by Frank Lorenzo, chairman of Continental Airlines, who said in a full-page newspaper ad, "We grew so fast that we made mistakes." Communication strategists can take a lesson from etiquette columnist Judith Martin (1999), who advised in one of her Miss Manners columns that apologizing is a way to diffuse angry responses. A good apology should include an acknowledgment of having done something wrong, a sense of remorse, an attempt to repair the injustice (if possible), and a promise not to commit the offense again.

Also, make sure the apology is timely. When Arnold Schwarzenegger campaigned for governor in the 2003 California recall race, he wasted no time in defusing allegations of groping women and making lewd comments by acknowledging them in a general way, apologizing, and explaining them basically as the indiscretions of his youth.

Michael Vick scored high points for his apology after pleading guilty to illegal dog fighting and being suspended as quarterback with the Atlanta Falcons (and later imprisoned). In a televised apology, Vick accepted personal responsibility, apologized to kids who look up to

Crisis Counsel: Public Relations vs. Legal

Odwalla, a producer of juice products, faced a crisis in 1996 when its apple juice was found to be contaminated with the bacteria *E. coli*. Several people became ill, and one child died.

When faced with media attention during the crisis, Odwalla used classic public relations techniques associated with Johnson & Johnson's handling of the 1983 Tylenol cyanide poisoning crisis, which put the public safety and the common good above the individual interests of the company. Odwalla initiated a voluntary recall in eight Western states and a Canadian province. It sent representatives to meet with the family of the young victim, and it set up a webpage to update its customers.

Odwalla earned some praise for its response. A case study by Kathleen Martinelli and William Briggs (1998) noted that Odwalla relied on advice from both public relations and legal counselors, with strategists from each field taking a collaborative rather than an adversarial approach to the crisis. They found that nearly 47% of the company's statements reflected traditional public relations responses: explaining its policy, investigating allegations, expressing concern for victims, taking steps to prevent a recurrence of the problem. Meanwhile, only 12% reflected the common legal response of denying guilt, minimizing responsibility, and shifting blame to the plaintiffs. The remaining messages were mixed between legal and public relations approaches.

Kathy Fitzpatrick and Maureen Rubin (1995) have pointed out that such collaboration between public relations and legal counsel usually results in more favorable media coverage and thus a more positive public response, serving the organization's long-term interests if the situation ends up in court.

In the Odwalla case, sales actually increased after the recall, a response similar to Pepsi's following its smooth handling of the 1993 syringe hoax. Odwalla eventually was fined $1.5 million—a relatively mild sum, considering that juries have imposed much heavier fines in other cases, even those that didn't involve a death. Continuing its public relations approach, the company responded to the fine with grace. "'We hope the visibility of [the size of the fine] will raise awareness and send a message to consumers about food safety,'" said a company spokesman ("Juice-Poisoning Case Brings Guilty Plea and a Huge Fine," 1998).

Compare Odwalla's experience with that of the 1993 Jack-in-the-Box fast food crisis, in which four people died from *E. coli*. The company's first response was from a legal standpoint: no comment, followed by attempts to shift blame to its supplier. Jack-in-the-Box eventually paid $58.5 million in fines.

athletes as role models, and said he was ashamed of himself for having misled his teammates by his initial statements of innocence.

Corporations also benefit from quick action on the apology front. When it became public that JetBlue—a year earlier—violated its own privacy policy by giving private passenger data to Pentagon researchers attempting to profile high-risk passengers following the 9/11 terrorist attacks, founding CEO of JetBlue David Neeleman issued a quick apology. Public relations observers noted that the quick response shortened the news cycle, reduced speculation, and allowed the story to become yesterday's news. JetBlue weathered the potential crisis well and remained a popular and profitable airline.

When an ice storm grounded hundreds of airplanes and stranded hundreds of thousands of travelers, Neeleman again was quick to apologize: "Words cannot express how truly sorry we are for the anxiety, frustration and inconvenience that you, your family, friends and colleagues experienced." No "if you were inconvenienced"; this was a flat out "I'm sorry" from the top guy, for a problem caused by Mother Nature.

As with the previously discussed concept of regret, nonapologies are worse than no apology. A **nonapology** is an insincere or halfhearted apology, often a statement that blames the person who was offended by the original statement or action: "I'm sorry that you took offense" or "I regret your reaction to what I did." Or this from radio talker Rush Limbaugh: "I regret that you heard me say that." Beware also similar false apologies that lament the effect but not the underlying transgression. Avoid pseudo-apologies such as those by any number of politicians who have felt compelled to apologize "for anything I may have done that offended you" or who add, "but it was only meant as a joke."

After using a double-barreled racist/sexist slur ("nappy-headed hos") against the Rutgers women's basketball team on live radio in 2007, "shock jock" Don Imus came under immediate fire. Despite apologies that critics saw as being too little too late as well as disingenuous (it was just a joke that "went way too far," he said), Imus lost his job with MSNBC-TV and NBC radio. He returned to the airwaves eight months later on CBS radio. The irony is that Imus had built his reputation as a serial offender on race, religion, and gender, and many fans tuned in specifically to eavesdrop on his public insults.

Sometimes an apology needs to be put into context so the public relations impact is not overlooked. That was the case as concern grew about the safety of Mattel toys made in China. A top Mattel official met with China's product-safety official to issue an apology to consumers. Mattel said it was sorry for the recall of millions of toys and that it would do all it could to prevent future problems—at least, that's the version reported in Europe and North America. The Chinese version went more like this: "Mattel is sorry for having to recall Chinese-made toys due to the company's design flaws and for harming the reputation of Chinese manufacturing companies." In fact, it was a design flaw that caused the recall of more than 17 million toys; only 2 million were recalled because the Chinese firms used lead paint, which is prohibited in the United States. China had previously been stung with a series of recalls undermining confidence in its manufactured goods (pet food, toothpaste, packaged seafood, baby cribs). It needed the public apology, and needed for the explanation to be clear that the fault was with Mattel, who, critics agree, deserved the bigger blame because of corporate policies to cut costs and speed up production.

Like all strategies, apology must be considered in light of the particular public involved. Don't assume that the manner in which organizational managers or spokespersons might naturally frame an apology is the best way to do so. Ask yourself how the key public will respond to the apology. Naomi Sugimoto (1997) has reported in a study, for example, that the Japanese are three times more likely than Americans are to ask for forgiveness as part of an apology, and the Japanese request is much more explicit ("Please forgive me") than is the typical American one ("I hope you will understand").

Apologies often are associated with relationship goals and with the symmetrical model of public relations that focuses on the long-term association of an organization with its publics. Michael J. Cody and Margaret L. McLaughlin (1990) point out that apologies are more likely to occur when it is important to save face.

Strategic apologies often are opposed by lawyers who fear they will be used against an organization in a lawsuit. This concern is legitimate, but you also need to look at the opportunities an apology makes possible. An apology can prevent lawsuits or at least limit damages sought by claimants or assessed by judges or juries. It also can be good business with stockholders. Fiona Lee, Christopher Peterson, and Larissa Tiedens (2004) looked at annual stock prices for 14 companies over 21 years and conclude that stocks increased for companies that accepted responsibility for poor financial performances, compared with those that blamed external factors.

Immediate apologies have short-circuited what could have been serious repercussions, such as when the Caldor department store chain in Norwalk, Connecticut, quickly apologized after 11 million copies of an advertising circular placed in 85 newspapers had a picture of two smiling boys playing Scrabble on a board with the word *RAPE* spelled out. Instead of blaming its advertising agency, the company accepted responsibility and apologized. "Obviously, it's a mistake," said company spokeswoman Jennifer Belodeau in an Associated Press report. "It's not something that we would ever have done intentionally" (Associated Press, 1998). It would be difficult to pursue legal or economic sanctions against a company that shows such integrity.

Conversely, lack of prompt apologies have been cited as the reason for lawsuits, such as a $400,000 claim against police in London, Ontario, by a man erroneously accused of drug

Culture-Bound Apologies

An apology can take on differing expectations depending on culture. This was the lesson in 2001 when a U.S. submarine surfaced quickly and collided with a small Japanese high school training boat, killing nine fishermen and students.

In Japan, a person who injures others is expected to personally apologize, like the CEO of Japan Airlines who visited the homes of 24 victims' families after the crash of one of his company's planes, or the owner of the country's largest milk company who visited each of his retail outlets to personally express his regrets after 13,000 people were poisoned by contaminated dairy products.

After the sea tragedy off Hawaii, the U.S. submarine captain issued a statement through his lawyer expressing "sincere regret," but the Japanese rejected it as a proper apology. President George W. Bush apologized to the Japanese people, but they remained unsatisfied. Likewise, apologies from the secretaries of state and defense and from the U.S. ambassador were found insufficient. Instead, the Japanese wanted to hear personally from the man who caused the accident, Commander Scott Waddle.

Three weeks later, Waddle hand wrote nine letters and asked that they be delivered to the families of the victims. Admiral William Fallon, the Navy's second in command, went to a small town in Japan to meet with the fathers of two of the dead students. Bowing deeply in a gesture of profound humility, he personally apologized and promised a full investigation.

A month after the accident, Waddle met personally—against his lawyers' advice—with family members who had been brought to Hawaii to observe the Navy investigation. He, too, bowed deeply and spoke with tears in his eyes about his remorse. And finally, the families accepted his apology.

trafficking; the man explained that he filed the lawsuit mainly because the police would not apologize. Similarly, a Las Vegas man who sued a doctor for keeping him three hours in the waiting room said all he really wanted was an apology. After the trial, which ruled in the man's favor, the doctor retorted that the patient should be the one to apologize for dragging the doctor to court for 2½ days. Finally, six months after the waiting-room wait, the doctor wrote a letter of apology; he also had to pay the patient $250 plus court costs and make a charitable contribution as well.

Ford and Bridgestone/Firestone faced massive lawsuits after their products were linked to 148 rollover deaths. In 2001, three Ford officials went to the bedside of a Texas woman who was paralyzed in one of the accidents. There they apologized, videotaping their action for broadcast on national television.

Defense attorneys often fear corporate apologies, but in personal-injury cases in particular, apologies can save the company money. Some attorneys point out that lawsuits often are brought by clients who seek an admission of corporate guilt, and a public apology can lessen the amount of money sought by an injured party or awarded by a sympathetic jury. Easing the way for corporate apologies, Massachusetts passed a law that "statements, writings or benevolent gestures expressing sympathy . . . relating to the pain, suffering, or death of a person involved in an accident . . . shall be inadmissible as evidence of an admission of liability in a civil action." California, Texas, Florida, and Washington followed with similar laws. Additionally, 29 states have laws preventing expressions of condolence or apology by doctors to patients or their families as being admissible in court as evidence of wrongdoing. These "I'm sorry" laws are meant to promote communication between doctors and their patients. Meanwhile, some states are considering medical apology laws that mitigate malpractice lawsuits when a doctor expresses regret over a patient's death or injury.

Reactive Strategy 6: Rectifying Behavior

A positive response to opposition and criticism involves rectifying behavior strategies, in which the organization does something to repair the damage done to its publics. These include investigation, corrective action, restitution, and repentance.

Investigation. Using the rectifying behavior of **investigation**, the organization promises to examine the situation and then to act as the facts warrant. This is only a short-term strategy, a way of buying time—eventually the organization will have to respond with more substance. Use the investigation strategy only when the facts are uncertain enough to warrant a delay in other strategic response.

Corrective action. A stronger rectifying behavior is **corrective action**, which involves taking steps to contain a problem, repair the damage, and/or prevent its recurrence. This is a strategy that can serve the mutual interests of both the organization and its public. Take corrective action if the organization is in a position to fix a problem, especially if the organization was in some way unprepared or negligent. This was the case with Texaco when, as noted previously, company executives made racist statements. Texaco responded aggressively with rectifying action that included sensitivity training and a procedure to weed out discrimination within the company.

Corrective action generally is expected when the organization has been at fault. But the response is even more powerful and positive when an organization willingly accepts responsibility for fixing a problem it did not cause. An example of this strategy is Johnson & Johnson's handling of the cyanide deaths associated with Tylenol. Though it was clear from the beginning that the company was not even negligently responsible for the product tampering, Johnson & Johnson nevertheless accepted the challenge to contain the damage and prevent any more. It recalled the product and then introduced a new triple-seal safety packaging that soon became the industry standard.

Restitution. Another rectifying behavior, **restitution**, serves the mutual interests of the organization and its publics. It involves making amends by compensating victims or restoring a situation to its earlier condition. Such a response may be forced upon an organization through the legal process, but some organizations have found it beneficial to offer restitution before it is required.

Repentance. The strongest type of rectifying behavior is **repentance**, which involves both a change of heart and a change in action. Repentance signals an organization's full atonement in the classic sense that it turns away from a former position and becomes an advocate for a new way of doing business. Many organizations, caught in a moral or legal embarrassment, promise repentance and a future of right doing, but few achieve such a turnaround.

Often an organization will use several strategies. An apology, for example, may also involve investigation, justification, restitution, and concession. During the Tylenol crisis, Johnson & Johnson used the strategies of investigation, compassion, excuse, relabeling, and corrective action.

One example of an organization that seems to be repenting is the Denny's restaurant chain. Its story is one of transformation from a symbol of corporate racism to a model of workplace diversity.

Denny's faced accusations and lawsuits for racial discrimination at several of its restaurants. One of the most notorious cases involved 21 members of the Secret Service in 1994: while 15 white agents were served quickly, a waitress and manager delayed serving six black agents for nearly an hour, alowing their food to get cold. The ensuing publicity highlighted a series of lawsuits for similar acts of discrimination at other Denny's restaurants: Asian American students at Syracuse University refused service and beaten by customers, Muslim customers in Montana served pork after asking for a vegetarian menu, Hispanic customers in San Jose refused service, a blind woman refused service because she was accompanied by a service dog; men of Middle Eastern descent kicked out of a restaurant in South Florida.

Denny's eventually paid $54 million in legal settlements. Denny's CDO ("chief diversity officer") later looked back on that "historic low point" in the company's history as presenting "huge opportunities. We had no place to go but up."

Dramatically from a public relations perspective, the company seems to have embraced the concept for corporate repentance. It adopted an aggressive antidiscrimination policy that included hiring minority managers, training employees, and firing those who discriminated. Denny's increased minority franchise ownership from one to 109 over a span of five years (later up to 42% of all Denny's franchises—450 minority-run restaurants). The company launched a $2 million antidiscrimination advertising series, and now purchases goods worth more than $100 million a year from minority vendors and gives proceeds from some sales to the King Center in Atlanta. It has worked with the Hispanic Association on Corporate Responsibility and the NAACP. The result of this turnaround is that Denny's and its parent company ranked No. 1 in *Fortune* magazine's listing of best companies for minorities. Some white-nativist organizations now are calling for boycotts because Denny's has become too multicultural.

Denny's certainly isn't the only company with such problems, and with 1,600 franchises throughout the United States incidents are bound to occur. But every time an allegation of discrimination is reported, the news media repeats the litany of past complaints against the company, while commentators and customers weigh the sincerity of Denny's protestations that it has repented of such sins and adopted new policies and training programs to prevent their repetition.

Reactive Strategy 7: Deliberate Inaction

The final category of public relations responses involves deliberate inaction, the considered decision by an organization under siege to offer no substantive comment or to make no overt action (strategic silence) or to respond vaguely and indistinctly (strategic ambiguity).

Strategic silence. Occasionally the decision to remain nonresponsive—that is, **strategic silence**—is an appropriate public relations response, a strategy of patience and composure. By not responding to criticism an organization may be able to shorten the life span of a crisis situation. Strategic silence can work when publics accept that an organization is remaining silent not out of guilt or embarrassment but because it is motivated by higher intentions such as compassion for victims, respect for privacy or other noble considerations, or simply because it is working on the problem and refuses to be sidetracked into talking much about it.

When cancer-causing benzene was discovered in the bottled water produced by Perrier, the upscale European company pulled millions of bottles from store shelves, but the chairman refused to hold a news conference or give interviews. His silence, though frustrating for the media, prevented the company from appearing to be under siege while at the same time it moved publicly to correct the problem, fostering what was considered a successful survival of the crisis.

In some circumstances, the law requires organizations to maintain silence, at least on particulars. If so, this requirement should be explained by the organization as the reason for its silence. This concept of strategic silence sometimes is given the name **purdah** (an Arabic reference to the veil or screen used in the practice of social isolation of women in some Islamic and Hindu societies).

When considering strategic silence, however, remember that the response is likely to be accepted only by those publics that already trust the integrity of the organization; opponents will find plenty of ammunition in the lack of response. Silence also risks allowing negative statements to stand unchallenged, which could hurt the organization in the long run. Additionally, a policy of strategic silence may be difficult to maintain if a strong opponent is able to insist on a public response. Remember that silence can imply indifference not only to an opponent but also to the issue itself. This might be of real interest to some of an organization's key publics. By dismissing the issue, the organization also risks slighting anyone who feels the issue is worthy of response.

Strategic silence is not the same as saying "No comment." Such a statement invariably is interpreted as an acknowledgment of guilt, implying that the organization not only did something wrong but did it so ineptly or so blatantly that it can't think of any explanation that would be accepted by its publics. Avoid "no comment" responses and related disdainful statements such as "we won't dignify that accusation with a reply."

If strategic silence is the chosen response, the organization or its defender nevertheless may need to make a public statement giving the reason it chooses not to address the issue further. That was the situation in late 2003 when President George W. Bush made a state visit to England, where he was hosted by Queen Elizabeth at Buckingham Palace. Bush brought with him five of his own personal chefs, news of which the miffed British monarch greeted with strategic silence. "Her Majesty greeted the news that President Bush was coming with his own chef with absolute silence," said a court source. "That's her general way of expressing disapproval. She's not thought to be thrilled about the visit, anyway, but when you consider that she has excellent cooks herself, you can see why this would be taken as a bit of an insult." Silence, and then the silence explained.

Strategic ambiguity. Similar to the concept of strategic silence is **strategic ambiguity**, the refusal to be pinned down to a particular response. Often this involves the artful dodging of a question.

How to Make Ethical Judgments

In considering various proactive and reactive strategies, it's worth asking one of those sometimes uncomfortable ethical questions, the kind that doesn't have an easy answer and may give rise to more questions than answers. "To whom is moral duty owed?" ask Clifford Christians, Mark Fackler, and Kim Rotzoll in their book *Media Ethics* (2004). In response to this question they suggest that communication strategists—journalists and editors, public relations practitioners, and advertisers—clarify who will be influenced by their decisions and what obligations we have to them. Good advice. Here are five obligations or duties, along with some thoughts on relevant considerations:

1. *Duty to ourselves.* Be careful to distinguish between following your conscience and simply acting on your own careerist self-interest. One way to do this is to pause and reflect on the basis of your own moral values and on the consistency with which you apply them in your own decision making.
2. *Duty to our clients.* Our clients, as well as our publics and audiences, deserve our best efforts, especially when they are paying the bills. But don't just blindly go where a client would send you without giving some thought to the client's motives and moral base and how these intersect with your own.
3. *Duty to our companies or bosses.* Strike a balance between company loyalty and stoogism. Stick to the recurring advice: Consider motivations and the impact that a company's policies and actions are likely to have.
4. *Duty to our professional colleagues.* Consider how your work is enhancing the prestige of your profession and the reputation of your fellow practitioners. Consider especially the commitments implied in the codes of ethics of the various professional organizations. (See Appendix B: Ethical Standards for the text of these codes.)
5. *Duty to society.* This is the ultimate ethical test: What does an action do *for* people? What does it do *to* them?

In an ideal world, ethical decisions would be simple and clear-cut. But the world isn't an ideal place, so be prepared to carefully discern among competing loyalties and differing values.

Politicians use strategic ambiguity frequently so they can avoid taking a public stand or tipping their hand about future potentials. U.S. diplomats, for example, have for decades been deliberately vague about what action might be taken if China moves to forcibly implement its claim that Taiwan is part of China and not an independent nation. Washington and Beijing exchange ambassadors. The State Department uses terms such as "acknowledging" rather than "recognizing" a single Chinese political entity, and diplomats "take note of" rather than "support" Peking's claim to be the legitimate government of China. When President George W. Bush referred to Taiwan as a country, his aides quickly gave behind-the-scenes disclaimers that this was merely an informal designation and did not signal a shift in U.S. foreign policy.

Corporate leaders use the device to avoid negotiating in public and to maintain their options. Much of the literature of crisis communication suggests that companies can minimize fallout by avoiding quick responses to stakeholder demands.

Clearly there is an ethical dimension to the concept of strategic ambiguity. At what point does ambiguity become obfuscation? Under what circumstances, if any, is it ethical to answer a direct question with a deliberately evasive response? In the hierarchy of organizational objectives, does transparency trump ambiguity? How long can credibility be maintained when underlings have to explain away the language of the boss?

Planning Example 5: Formulating Action and Response Strategies

UPSTATE COLLEGE

Upstate College will develop the following strategies:

Proactive Strategy

- Involve student public in celebrations and other special events focused on the academic expansion.
- Enhance alliances with high schools based on new academic opportunities at the college.
- Take advantage of the many newsworthy activities associated with the expansion.

Reactive Strategy

- No responsive strategy is anticipated, because the expansion to a 4-year program is unlikely to generate opposition or criticism.

■ ■ ■

TINY TYKES TOYS

Tiny Tykes will develop the following strategies:

Proactive Strategy

- Place a high priority on research and development as they relate to high-quality standards for toy products.

- Form alliances with customers and consumer advocates focused on the safety of children's toys.
- Initiate news activities focused on toy safety.
- Engage in transparent communication to allow employees and consumer advocates to observe the company's efforts to produce safe and high-quality toys.

Reactive Strategy

- Make a concession to customers and consumer advocates by sponsoring university research on the role of play in child psychological and educational development.
- If necessary, reiterate statement of regret issued prior to the toy recall.
- Display corporate repentance by publicly relaunching the product with a recommitment to quality and excellence.

Checklist 5: Action and Response Strategies

Basic Questions

1. What proactive strategies might you develop?
2. What reactive strategies might you develop?
3. How consistent are these strategies with past practices of your organization?

Expanded Questions

A. PROACTIVE STRATEGY

1. Is it appropriate to use any of the following approaches? If "yes," how?

   Action
   Organizational performance
   Audience participation
   Alliances
   Sponsorships
   Activism

   Communication
   Publicity
   Newsworthy information
   Transparent communication
2. Summarize the proactive strategy of your organization.

B. REACTIVE STRATEGY

1. Is it appropriate to use any of the following approaches? If "yes," how?

   Pre-emptive Action
   Prebuttal

Offensive Response
Attack
Embarrassment
Shock
Threat

Defensive Response
Denial
Excuse
Justification

Diversionary Response
Concession
Ingratiation
Disassociation
Relabeling

Vocal Commiseration
Concern
Condolence
Regret
Apology

Rectifying Behavior
Investigation
Corrective Action
Restitution
Repentance

Deliberate Inaction
Strategic Silence
Strategic Ambiguity

2. Summarize the reactive strategy of your organization.

C. ACTION/RESPONSE CONSISTENCY

1. Is this action/response consistent with past verbal messages of this organization/spokesperson? If "no," explain the inconsistency.
2. Is the action/response consistent with past actions of this organization/spokesperson? If "no," explain the inconsistency.
3. Is the action/response consistent with the mission of this source? If "no," explain the inconsistency.
4. Is the action/response consistent with image of this source? If "no," explain the inconsistency.
5. Is the action/response ethical? If "no," develop a different response.

Consensus Check

Does agreement exist within your organization about the recommended strategies included within this step of the planning process? If "yes," proceed to Step 6, Developing the Message Strategy. If "no," consider the value and/or possibility of achieving consensus before proceeding.

Step 6

Developing the Message Strategy

Having identified your publics and established objectives for what you want to achieve, and having set into motion the way the organization is preparing to act to achieve those objectives, it is time to turn your attention to the best means of communication. Since strategic communication is carefully planned communication, this is an important step.

Remember what we said earlier about publics and audiences: Publics are groups of people in a relationship with your organization; audiences are people who receive messages. At this stage of the planning process, begin treating your publics as the audiences with whom you are communicating, and consider the various elements of effective communication. Who should present the message? What appeals should be made in the message? How should the message be structured? What words should be used? What symbols? How can you create a buzz?

Thousands of public relations and marketing messages bombard people each day—that's more than three different messages every minute of every waking hour—most of them trying to sell something or gain support in some way. Amid all this noise, how can your organization's message stand out? It's not easy, but effective communication can help your message rise above the clamor.

The Communication Process

Several different approaches to communication are used in public relations and related fields. Three particular models are worth particular attention—the information, persuasion, and dialogue models. These align loosely with the classic models of public relations outlined by James Grunig and Todd Hunt (see the introduction to this book). The information model of communication plays out as press agentry and public information. The persuasion model is asymmetric, with a focus on advocacy and attempts to influence. The dialogue model of communication, meanwhile, is a symmetric approach rooted in relationships. Let's look more closely at each process of communication.

Information: The Flow of Communication

The **information model** of communication focuses on the content and channels of communication. It involves a message sent by a source to a receiver, with ideas encoded and interpreted through symbols (words or images) that are transmitted person to person or through some technical connection. Harold Lasswell (1948) offered a simple verbal formula of communication: "Who says what to whom with what effect." Today we might add "how" and perhaps even "why" to this formula.

Exhibit 6.1 provides a visual model of information-based communication. This model is based on the frequently cited work of Claude Shannon and Warren Weaver (1949) and Norbert Wiener (1954), echoed later by David Berlo (1960) and Wilbur Schramm (1971). Shannon and Weaver, scientists with Bell Telephone Laboratories, developed a visual model of what they called the **mathematical theory of communication**. Their approach was linear, with virtually tangible data encoded and transmitted through a channel to a receiver. In essence, theirs was a model for monologue, with the source person or organization talking at an audience, in simplified terms, the press agentry model of public relations. Wiener's **cybernetic model of communication** was more circular in design, involving feedback from the receiver to

Exhibit 6.1 A Model of Information-Based Communication

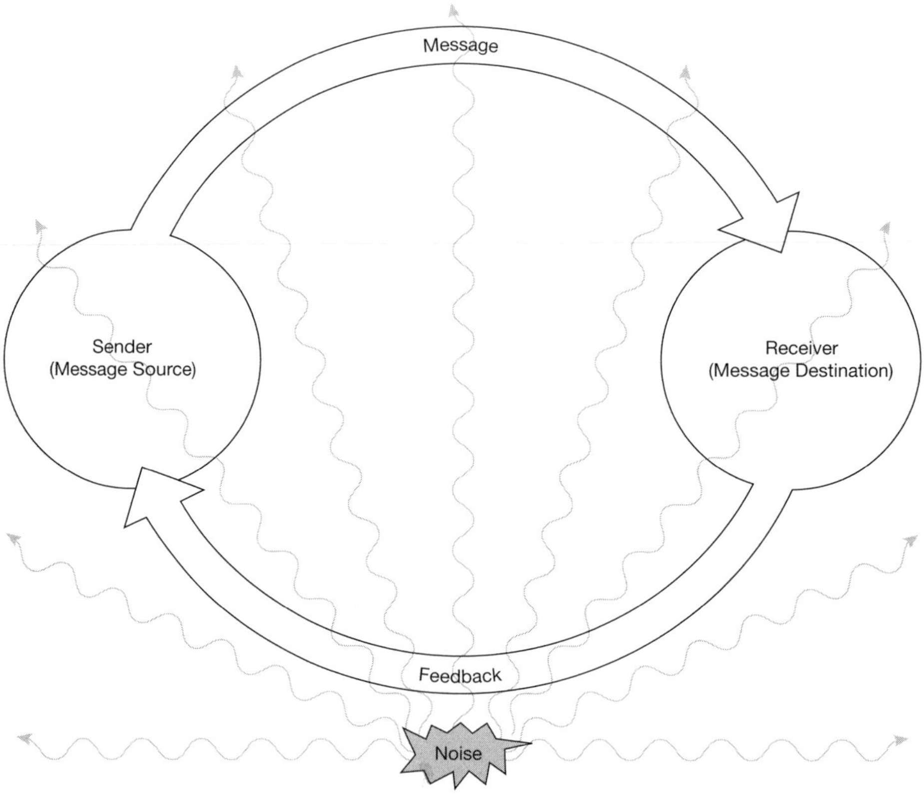

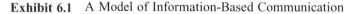

In this model of communication, a sender (which can be a person or an organization) encodes a message (using verbal and/or nonverbal symbols) that is sent through a particular channel (such as a speech, a brochure, a phone call, etc.) to a receiver, who decodes (or interprets) the message. The receiver in turn reacts and responds to the message by encoding feedback that is sent back to the original sender. Any communication context also involves noise, which is any interference that limits the ability of the channel to carry a message faithfully from sender to receiver. Such interference can be in the encoding or decoding of the message or in the channels used to transmit the message.

influence the sender. This model is a bit more focused on two-way communication, talking with an audience (similar to the public information model).

Persuasion: Attempts to Influence

Another process of communication, the **persuasion model**, consciously attempts to influence people, using ethical means that enhance a democratic society. Persuasion is an inherent part of social interaction, something people everywhere do. Persuasion is not deception, which relies on miscommunication. Neither is it coercion, which relies on force rather than on communication. Nor is it **propaganda**, which is a debasement of persuasive communication because it is associated with half-truths and hidden agendas.

Persuasion is particularly associated with the advocacy or asymmetric approach to strategic communication, in which an organization presents its point of view in an attempt to convince its publics to give their agreement and support.

The practice of persuasion is widespread and popular. In marketing, for example, most companies try to convince potential consumers to buy the company's products or services. In public relations, organizations try to convince publics to agree with this concept, support that candidate, or follow those procedures. In public health and safety campaigns, agencies try to

Research Background on Persuasion

Several theories dealing with persuasion are relevant to much public relations and marketing activity. Here are a few of the most common theories.

The **balance theory**, articulated by psychologist Fritz Heider (1946, 1958), is the oldest consistency theory, observing that unbalanced mental stances create tension and force an individual to restore balance. Theodore Newcomb (1953) extended this to groups, calling it the **symmetry theory**. Charles Osgood and Percy Tannenbaum's **congruity theory** (1955) added some measurement in attitude. The lesson of these consistency theories for public relations practitioners is that attitude change can be stimulated by information that causes people to realize that two attitudes are in conflict and that the persuasiveness of the source is a major factor to accomplish this.

Social psychologist Leon Festinger's **cognitive dissonance theory** (1957) explained that the more people experience the psychological discomfort of having contradictory attitudes or beliefs, the more likely they will reduce the discomfort, usually by changing one of their attitudes or beliefs. An important element of this theory is the concept of **selective exposure**, which refers to seeking information that supports a currently held attitude while avoiding information that does not support it.

The **inoculation theory**, proposed by William McGuire and Demetrios Papageorgis (1961), suggests that unchallenged beliefs and attitudes can be swayed with persuasive information, while attitudes that have been tested are more resistant to change. This latter aspect is particularly useful to strategic communicators seeking to create resistance to potentially opposing arguments.

The **social judgment theory**, put forward by Muzafer Sherif and Carl Hovland (1961), observes that individuals accept or reject messages to the extent that they perceive the messages as corresponding to their internal anchors (attitudes and beliefs) and as being ego-involved (affecting the person's self-concept).

persuade young people to stop smoking, motorists to start wearing seat belts, and middle-aged people to get more exercise. In international relations, governments try to convince counterparts in other countries to adopt democratic practices, and nongovernmental organizations try to influence governments to respect human rights or to eliminate gender-based, religious, or racial discrimination.

Dialogue: Quest for Understanding

The **dialogue model** involves the deeply conscious interaction of two parties in communication. It involves a sincere and competent attempt at mutual understanding, paralleling the symmetrical model of public relations. This is the kind of communication described by existentialist philosopher Martin Buber (1947). It is what Evelyn Sieberg has called "confirming communication," which seeks to heal and strengthen relationships. "Confirmation," notes Sieberg, "like existential dialogue, is a mutual experience involving sharing at several levels–sharing of talking, sharing of self, sharing of respect, sharing of trust" (1976). Dialogue involves four goals useful to public relations:

1. To provide for an information exchange between individuals or groups.
2. To help communication partners make responsible and personally acceptable decisions.
3. To help revive the original vitality of a relationship.
4. To foster a deep relationship that continues to unite communication partners ever more closely.

Dialogue also generates two management practices—consensus building and conflict resolution—that help parties consider issues in light of their mutual needs and arrive at solutions that enhance their relationships. **Consensus building** is a process of identifying and then preventing or overcoming barriers between people and/or organizations. The related concept of **conflict resolution** involves making peace and restoring harmony, often with communication as the primary tool. Carl Botan (1997) has observed the relationship between dialogue and ethics. He notes that dialogic communication is characterized by a relationship in which both parties genuinely care about each other rather than merely seek to fulfill their own needs. This kind of relationship is embodied in the symmetrical model of public relations, in which organizations try to adapt and harmonize with their publics. It elevates publics to an equal footing with the organization itself, allowing either party in the interchange to take the initiative. An example of this would be an equal relationship between corporate management and either an external public such as an activist group or an internal public such as an employee union, in which either side could call meetings, propose agenda topics, conduct research, launch a communication program, and so on. Botan also noted that advances in communication technology have made it easier for organizations to engage with their publics in a two-way dialogue. Certainly advances in Internet-based technology are breaking down old hierarchical structures in communication.

In the practice of strategic communication, there is a role for each type of communication model: information, persuasion, and dialogue. Information approaches to communication often focus on the message sender and receiver, while persuasive communication deals with the content of the message. Dialogue, in turn, emphasizes the relationship between the parties in the communication process. Each of these elements is important to public relations, which necessarily deals with the actors in the communication process, the messages shared between them, and their relationship.

Rhetorical Tradition

The use of communication to influence ideas and actions and to strengthen relationships is a basic element of human society. History has handed down to us some ancient examples of the art of effective communication. Much of it comes from the dawn of Western civilization in the lands encircling the Mediterranean Sea. Two of the oldest-known pieces of literature, the *Iliad* and the *Odyssey*, both ascribed to the Greek poet Homer about 2,800 years ago, feature examples of effective persuasive speeches. Consider Odysseus's plea with the Cyclops about why the monster should not eat him, or Paris's entreaty for Helen to leave her husband and go off with him, or the acclaim given to Hector and Achilles for their speeches that stir up their military troops.

Even earlier pieces of literature, though difficult to date precisely—the Pentateuch of the Hebrew Bible, the epic of Gilgamesh—have passages with strong persuasive rhetoric, such as Moses' persuasive skills before pharaoh or his verbal arguments with God. The Egyptian philosopher and court official Ptah-Hotep advised the pharaohs to link their message to the interests of their audience.

The effective use of persuasive communication was a particular interest in classical Greece, with its focus on participatory democracy. In the fifth century BCE, Corax of Syracuse wrote a handbook on **rhetoric**, the art of using words effectively in speaking and writing for the purpose of influencing, persuading, or entertaining. Basically, rhetoric is persuasive communication. Corax noted the relationship between certainty and probability: while physical evidence can prove something true and thus beyond argument, verbal evidence can show only greater or lesser probabilities that something is true.

Later, in Athens, Socrates and his student Plato criticized rhetoric as verbal maneuvering that could make right seem wrong and important appear unimportant. They called for a grounding in truth and taught some of the skills associated with ethical communication, such as logical organization of ideas. Plato outlined the differences between true and false rhetoric.

The first person known to have studied persuasive communication systematically was one of Plato's students, Aristotle, who became the court educator to Alexander the Great. Twenty-five centuries ago, in his treatise called *Rhetoric*, Aristotle identified three central elements that today remain as cornerstones of persuasive communication: ethos, logos, and pathos. Following the don't-mess-with-success principle, *Strategic Planning for Public Relations* uses these elements as the framework for developing a strategic and effective public relations and marketing communication message. Each will be discussed in detail shortly.

From the Greek foundation, the study of communication passed over to classical Rome, where Marcus Tullius Cicero organized rhetoric into five principles (roughly argumentation, organization, style, delivery, and memorization). Marcus Fabius Quintillianus wrote on the education of communicators, advising that they were about more than simply persuasion; they also were in the business of informing, motivating and inspiring.

During the Middle Ages, the Saxon theologian Alcuin, teacher and advisor to the emperor Charlemagne, reinterpreted Roman rhetoric and applied it to practical areas such as public policy, legal and judicial proceedings, and the placement of blame or praise.

Rhetoric also influenced the field of religion, and vice versa. Augustine of Hippo, a Christian bishop in Roman Africa and professor of rhetoric at Milan, became one of the most influential figures in persuasive communication with his study, teaching, and personal examples dealing with preaching. Augustine was influential in developing the practice of **apologetics** (the systematic attempt to explain the reasonableness of religious faith and to refute opposing arguments) and **homiletics** (the study and application of effective communication for preaching). After the fall of Western civilization, the teaching of Aristotle was virtually lost to European society.

During the ninth century, Muslim scholars, Christian Arabs, and Arabic-speaking Jews kept alive the study of Aristotle in the Middle East. The Crusades introduced Arab scholarship to the West, such as the "science of eloquence" associated with Abd al Jurijani. Through Arab scholars, the West also rediscovered Aristotle.

Later the Italian philosopher-monk Thomas Aquinas applied Aristotelian principles of ethos, logos, and pathos to the understanding and explanation of religious belief. During the Enlightenment period of the 16th century, Desiderius Erasmas of Rotterdam influenced a renewed interest in rhetoric with a more secular perspective. John Milton wrote a textbook on rhetoric.

More contemporary figures in the evolution of our understanding of communication include the English philosopher Francis Bacon, credited with formulating the scientific method; philosopher Thomas Hobbes, who also wrote on rhetoric; American language theorist Kenneth Burke, who studied the nature and power of symbols in human interaction; language critic Richard Weaver, who dealt with the cultural role of persuasion; Belgian philosopher Chaim Perelman, who analyzed how communicators can gain "the adherence of minds"; and Canadian theologian and philosopher Bernard Lonergan. Canadian theorist Marshall McLuhan wrote his doctoral theses at Cambridge University on the history of rhetorical thought.

Most of the study of rhetoric has been done from a Western perspective, though increasingly attention is being given to Asian traditions. From a Buddhist perspective, the characteristics of speech are said to be that it is true, real, and useful. The Buddha's description of an effective preacher is a monk who abandons falsehood and is truthful, faithful, and trustworthy. Confucius recognized that sincerity and respectfulness are important elements of effective speaking.

The African and Native American traditions emphasize storytelling, the graceful use of language, the development of consensus, and even the communicative value of silence.

Ethos: Selecting Message Sources

Ethos is communication effectiveness based on the character of the speaker and on the common ground shared by speakers and audiences. Years of research by social scientists have produced a snapshot of an effective message source. This is a person or an organization perceived by an audience as being credible, having charisma, and exercising some kind of control—what we might call the "three C's" of an effective communicator. These are presented visually in Exhibit 6.2. Individually, each of these perceptions is a powerful tool for the practitioner; in combination, they create a compelling factor in effective communication.

It is important to note that each of these elements is based on the audience's perception of the speaker. Aristotle observed that reputation precedes the speaker, setting the stage for the audience to accept or reject the speaker's message. Even before the speaker presents a

Exhibit 6.2 The Three C's of Effective Communication

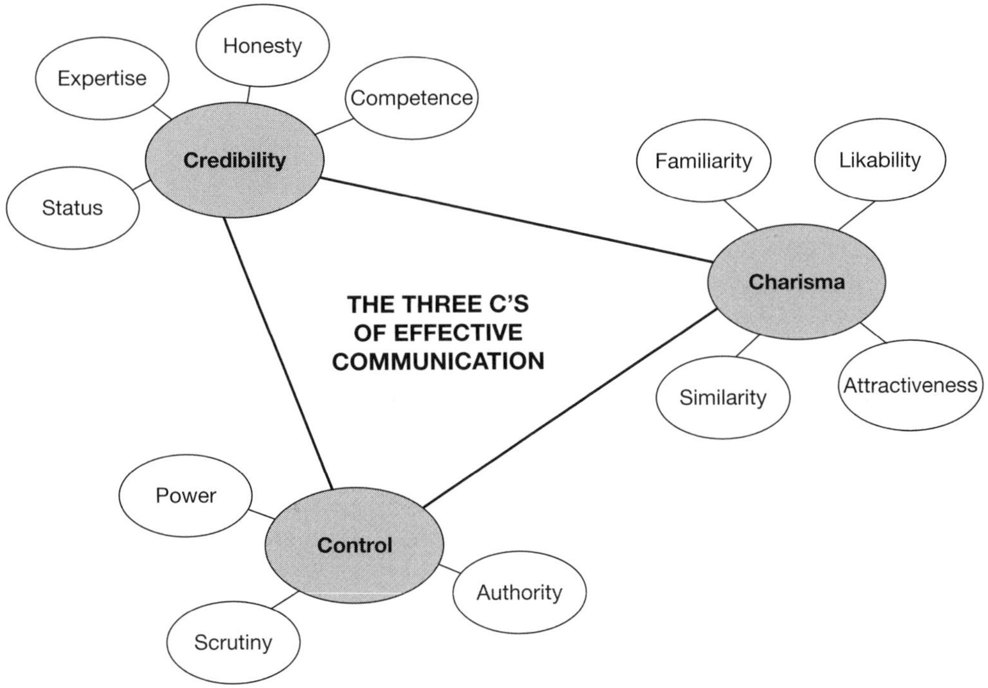

message, the audience makes a judgment based on the speaker's prestige and prominence. Precisely because reputation has such a direct and predictable impact on their ability to influence their publics, organizations pay much attention to what people know and think about them. Let's look at the Three C's in detail.

Credibility: Power to Inspire Trust

A source who has **credibility**—the power to inspire belief—is one who demonstrates the qualities of expertise, status, competence, and honesty. Or rather, one in whom audiences perceive such qualities, real or imagined.

Expertise. The most important factor in making a message source effective is **expertise**, which means that the source knows what he or she is talking about.

Status. Related to expertise is **status**, but this rests more with the audience's deference to the social position or prestige of a message source.

Competence. Another related concept is **competence**, the ability to remain calm under pressure and to be clear and dynamic in presenting the message to others, especially those who may not share the same knowledge or loyalties.

Honesty. Finally, **honesty** means that the source is willing to provide full and accurate information, is operating without bias, and thus is worthy of trust.

Credibility is tremendously important to persuasion. Though we might wish it were different, being a good speaker or writer is more effective than having good physical evidence. Sources perceived as being highly credible are believed on their own merits and whatever evidence they present has little added value. Even audiences that don't understand an issue often will accept a message when the source is believable.

Highly credible sources can appeal to fear and use intense or opinionated language that would be counterproductive coming from sources with lesser credibility. For example, it was his high credibility that allowed President Ronald Reagan to call the Soviet Union "an evil empire" and be effective in such extreme speech. When President George W. Bush revived the idea in reference to an "axis of evil" encompassing Iraq, Iran, and North Korea, his credibility was lower and the phrase was criticized, belittled, and parodied as an "axis of weasles," "axis of feebles" and "asses of evil." As a result of such criticism, the president didn't use the phrase again in a public speech.

As part of the process of strategic planning, you can enhance source credibility by reinforcing each of these characteristics. Remember that perception is the key: The source's expertise and honesty must be apparent to the audience. Some campaigns have faltered because the audience didn't realize the source was an expert or because the source didn't appear trustworthy.

Perceived expertise can be intensified by using a message source who has experience, knowledge, intelligence, occupational or professional background, or the wisdom that comes with age. Likewise, perceived status is enhanced by the use of message sources who have social status and prestige. Of course, both of these must be relevant to the topic being addressed—a physician may be very credible on the issue of health but not particularly so on a political topic. Expertise and status can be borrowed from recognized experts by quoting them.

Communication competence is obviously a matter of perception. The audience perceives (or not) that the speaker is calm, clear, and able to communicate. Perceived competence can be enhanced by two elements associated with effective presentations. One element is physical stature, which includes being tall, sitting or standing erect, maintaining eye contact, and having facial composure. The other element that enhances competence is vocal quality, which involves enunciating clearly, initiating communication, speaking with conviction and authority, exuding energy and enthusiasm, and avoiding language fillers such as *um* and *uh.* Two kinds of skill builders—coaching in public speaking and training for media interviews—can help a speaker strategically develop vocal emphasis, convincing gestures and other aspects of communication competence.

Like the other characteristics of credibility, perceived honesty can be enhanced to help a source appear more trustworthy by emphasizing the objectivity, integrity, and neutrality with which the source approaches the subject. Message sources who advocate positions contrary to their personal interests or who take an unexpected position have a special credibility. For example, a physician who recommends herbal medicine will be particularly believable because the health care establishment traditionally has ignored, even scorned, the medicinal value of herbs. Honesty also is enhanced when the message source shows a consistency between past and present, and between words and deeds.

As a side note, if you are presenting a position that differs from one taken by your organization in the past, signal the change and carefully explain not only the new posture but also the reason for the change. Try not to allow yourself to be labeled as inconsistent or as contradictory of past statements. In the current political and social climate, charges of

Credibility and News Sources

A survey of 545 Americans by Burson-Marsteller Public Relations (1998) probed the relative credibility of different types of news sources on an environmental issue, specifically global warming. The researchers identified several hypothetical news sources and asked respondents to rate the credibility of each. Here are the credibility levels reported:

- 53% Professor of atmospheric science at a well-known university
- 43% Government scientists from the National Oceanographic and Atmospheric Administration
- 29% Spokesperson for an environmental group
- 11% Spokesperson for an oil or natural gas company
- 10% Hollywood celebrity active on environmental issues

What's the lesson to be learned from this research? It deals with expertise. Recognized experts without apparent self-interest are the most credible message sources. The public may admire celebrities and may even pay attention to them without being persuaded in favor of the messages they present.

flip-flopping on issues and changing positions are exploited by opponents as signs of weakness, lack of underlying values, and political pandering. Certainly you may change your mind, but make sure you let your audience know the reason for such a change.

Charisma: Power of Personal Charm

The magnetic appeal or personal charm that some message sources enjoy over an audience is called **charisma**, another important element of persuasion. Like credibility, charisma is a matter of perception, and it varies greatly from one person to another and from one public to another.

Charisma has several specific characteristics: familiarity, likability, similarity, and attractiveness.

Familiarity. One important aspect of charisma is **familiarity**, the extent to which the audience already knows (or thinks it knows) the message source.

Likability. Charisma also involves **likability**, the extent to which the audience admires what it knows about the source or what it sees and hears when the source begins to communicate. This generally means that the message source is neutral on divisive social and political issues and not associated with controversy or partisanship—unless the audience itself is particularly partisan. The principle of likability may suggest that, for a general and mixed audience, you would avoid using a message source who is closely associated with a particular cultural, ethnic or religious group, because the audience may not like someone closely identified with alien characteristics.

Similarity. Charisma also involves **similarity**, the extent to which the source resembles the audience (or the way in which audience members would like to see themselves). This may be a reflection of audience demographics in terms of age, gender, occupation, ethnicity, religion, culture, shared values, or sociopolitical perspectives. Thus the principle of similarity offers a parallel guideline to that of familiarity. You might consider using a message source closely associated with a particular cultural, ethnic, or religious group when the audience also is associated with that group. Similarity is particularly important when a communicator is seeking long-term persuasion, less so for short-term objectives. It also is a major factor in enhancing dialogic communication.

Attractiveness. Finally, charisma is affected by the **attractiveness** of the source, which involves the source's physical looks, demeanor, poise, and presence, as well as both the clothing worn and the setting in which the source is presented. Note, however, that physical attractiveness and beauty are significantly less important than credibility and other aspects of charisma. Despite the Hollywood emphasis on sex appeal and glamour, average-looking people can be highly effective message sources. Indeed, speakers who are very good-looking, especially if they flaunt their looks, may have difficulty being perceived as much more than pretty faces and beautiful bodies.

Control: Power of Command

The third component of an effective message source is **control**, which is rooted in a message source's command over the audience and on the perceived willingness to exercise that control.

Power. One of the most important aspects of control is **power**, the raw and recognized ability to dominate and to reward or punish. Guilt appeals (which we will discuss later) often are associated with powerful message sources.

Authority. Control also may be based on a message source's **authority**, which is the right to rule over or direct the actions of another. Authority implies that the audience more or less willingly has granted the right of control and thus will give obedience. Authority often involves a legal or social prerogative. It also can involve moral leverage, such as by summoning the audience to its stated values or calling it to its accepted duty. Both guilt appeals and virtue appeals (which we will discuss later) may be associated with authority figures.

Scrutiny. Finally, the persuasive element of control suggests **scrutiny**, the ability to examine. Someone who is able to investigate you also is able to pronounce your blame, proclaim your innocence, and perhaps grant forgiveness. As with the previous characteristics of an effective source, control must be perceived by the receiver. Keep in mind that perceptions change. The so-called **halo effect** demonstrates that a source perceived as credible, charismatic, and/or in control can rely on this reputation. Think of the many situations in which a politician—you supply the name, from either side of the aisle—can do no wrong in the eyes of his supporters but can do nothing right in the eyes of those who despise him. The same can be said about some athletes and entertainers who evoke passionate responses of either adoration or condemnation. The halo effect is very useful for the communicator. But halos slip and stars fall, so be careful about where you shine your spotlight. Also, realize that while one person may have a halo effect on some members of an audience, the same person may have an opposite **horns effect** on other members of the audience who dislike the messenger. Haloes and horns often evoke unreasonable passion.

Organizational Spokespeople

The elements of credibility, charisma and control can be maximized as part of strategic planning—for example, by selecting an appropriate spokesperson who is likely to appeal to an organization's publics.

Celebrity spokespersons. Celebrities often are used because they are charismatic and familiar. Entertainers and sports figures frequently are spokespersons for companies and nonprofit organizations as well as for social and political causes. Celebrity endorsement doesn't automatically translate into money or votes, but it does garner media attention. It also encourages audiences to look at websites and to read brochures and letters they otherwise might ignore.

Ethics and Celebrity Endorsements

There is an ethical consideration for nonprofit organizations over the use of celebrity endorsements.

Some charities simply cannot afford the price tag that comes with many celebrities—they don't necessarily donate their time. For some charities, fame is not worth the price. The American Diabetes Association, for example, chooses not to spend donated money on celebrity spokespersons. The ADA says it's not interested in redesigning its campaign to fit the publicity needs of celebrities and their agents.

Additionally, pharmaceutical companies sometimes offer the pick up the tab for celebrity endorsements of a medical charity. But such offers usually come with strings, generally product endorsement by the celebrity. Such an arrangement came to light when actress Lauren Bacall, who generally avoided TV talk shows, started showing up on the circuit talking about friends with macular degeneration and the drug that treated it. The *Today Show* discovered that her appearance was paid for by the Norvatis drug company. And when Lance Armstrong did a series of cancer-awareness ads, they were sponsored by Bristol-Myers Squibb, the company that made the drugs that cured his testicular cancer.

Industry sources report that celebrity endorsers generally receive honorariums as high as $100,000. Not all celebrity spokespersons are paid. WebMD (http://www.webmd.com) reports that the National Parkinson Foundation and the Alzheimer's Association, for example, indicate that their celebrity endorsers donate their time and even pick up their own travel expenses. The Entertainment Industry Foundation, a clearinghouse for many entertainers who become involved with charity work, insists that the celebrity "ambassadors" work for free. Most of the expenses are picked up by sponsoring companies such as Revlon, People Magazine, and Lee Jeans, but this is not so with pharmaceutical companies.

Additionally, some observers question the criteria that some celebrities use in deciding whether to align themselves with charitable causes. Dr. Arthur Caplan, a medical ethicist at the University of Pennsylvania, has noted that some celebrities gravitate toward illnesses they perceive as "media-friendly—less stigmatizing, and less embarrassing" and that "otherwise worthy diseases, some that impact far more people, go unrecognized simply because they have less sex appeal" (Bouchez, n.d., p. 2).

Celebrities are in great demand by charitable causes. Thus we find actors Nicole Kidman, Vivica A. Fox and Reese Witherspoon promoting breast cancer awareness, country singer Toby Keith creating attention for childhood cancers, Jimmy Smits for colon cancer, Halle Barry and Cuba Gooding Jr. for diabetes awareness, and J. J. Redick of the Orlando Magic basketball team for Torch Relay Children's Miracle Network on behalf of children's hospitals across the country. Jennifer Love Hewitt has good things to say on behalf of the Veteran's Administration and various veterans groups, and Kirstie Alley, Tom Cruise, and Isaac Hayes have pitched anti-drug messages.

After newsman Mike Wallace went public with his struggle against depression, the Colorado Behavioral Healthcare Council felt he would be just the famous face to use in its public service campaign on suicide and depression prevention. In 2006, organizers of the New York City Alzheimer's Association credited the presence of actress Jean Smart (*24*) as MC for a fund-raising dinner for a $400,000 increase in donations from the previous year.

Meanwhile, politicians line up celebrity endorsements to translate fame into voter influence. The 2008 election cycle saw traditional Hollywood endorsers such as Tim Robbins, Sean Penn, and Barbra Streisand joined by newcomers to the political-influence arena such as Chuck Norris, Adam Sandler, and Oprah Winfrey. Historians say the practice began in 1920 when Hollywood heavyweights Al Jolson, Lillian Russell, Douglas Fairbanks, and Mary Pickford threw their fame behind presidential candidate Warren G. Harding. He won, and candidates have courted celebrity endorsement ever since. The 2008 campaign also continued the trend popularized by the two George W. Bush campaigns that drew heavily on celebrity religious endorsers.

Sometimes spokespersons actually are likable "spokescharacters," such as Morris the Cat for Nine Lives cat food, McGruff the Crime Dog, or Geico insurance's gecko. Other spokescharacters have included the Budweiser Clydesdales, Elsie the Cow for Borden's Milk, and Charlie the Tuna for StarKist. *Advertising Week's* Walk of Fame on Madison Avenue in New York City honors advertising icons such as Juan Valdez (for Columain Coffee), Colonel Sanders (for KFC), the Aflac duck, Tony the Tiger (for Kellogg's Frosted Flakes), and the Pillsbury Doughboy.

Public relations and marketing people selecting celebrity spokespersons generally look for a connection with their key publics. It's not accidental, for example, that Hurley Hayward is the spokesperson for Porsche. Ninety percent of Porsche's customers are men, and most of them are racing fans. Hayward is one of the world's best race-car drivers, a multiple winner of the LeMans, Sebring, and Daytona races. Likewise, it makes sense for people like tennis great John McEnroe and basketball player Karl Malone to be the pitchmen for Rogaine Extra Strength in an ongoing promotional campaign using sports figures who have had positive results with the hair-growth formula. Or Brazilian soccer legend Pele and conservative talk-radio host Rush Limbaugh doing ads for the erectile-dysfunction drug Viagra. On its website and in ads, Pfizer Pharmaceuticals used Lorraine Bracco, who played a psychiatrist on the *Sopranos* TV series, to promote one of the company's antidepressants; the promotion included her testimony about her own depression and its treatment with the medication Zoloft.

Celebrities are used for more than fundraising. Their star power is a great attraction for media and other attention. The Alzheimer's Association used actor David Hyde Pierce (*Frasier*) as a spokesperson for its appearance at a congressional caucus, resulting not only in publicity for the organization's cause but the increased participation of senators and representatives. Similarly, when film star Julia Roberts went to congress to speak about a rare neurological disorder, Rhett syndrome, influential lawmakers paid attention.

Researchers Alan Miciak and William Shanklin (1994) report that advertisers look for five characteristics in spokespersons: they must be trustworthy, readily recognizable, affordable, at little risk for negative publicity, and appropriately matched to the audience.

Golf icon Tiger Woods currently is among the company's highest-rated celebrities, a fact that helped him land a five-year, $100 million endorsement contract with Nike. In 2008, he was estimated to have earned $105 million in endorsements, in addition to about $23 million in golfing prize money.

Following Woods is fellow golfer Phil Mickelson, who in 2008 had an estimated $63 million in endorsements, many of them golf related; $28 million for basketball star LeBron James; about $25 million for NASCAR winner Dale Earnhardt Jr.; $19.5 million for golfer Michelle Wei; and a $15 million tie for Nascar's Jeff Gordan and basketball's Shaquille O'Neal.

Discretion is needed in identifying celebrity spokespersons. Their fame might draw attention to your cause or company, but celebrities aren't yours alone, and endorsements can bring unwanted attention. A drug-education agency understood this and took great care in selecting a professional sports figure as a spokesperson and board member. The agency signed a football player who had a consistent reputation and a clean record not only on alcohol but also with respect to both recreational and performance-enhancing drugs.

Some organizations have been humiliated by celebrity spokespersons, and endorsements have fallen off, at least temporarily. *Sports Illustrated* reports that pitcher Roger Clemens earned $3.5 million in endorsements in 2007 from companies such as AT&T and promos for the ESPN sports network on TV. After he was named in a steroid scandal, endorsements fell.

Soccer great David Beckham lost some endorsements when the British tabloid press reported that he had cheated on his wife, but after the issue died down he emerged with a $10 million contract with Gillette, followed by a $161 million lifetime deal with Adidas (an estimated $4 million a year). Beckham was later courted by Nike.

L.A. Laker Kobe Bryant lost endorsements because of his 2003 sexual assault charge, but he came back as the second highest-paid celebrity endorser in the National Basketball Association in 2008 with $16 million in endorsements.

After a British newspaper published a photo in 2009 of Michael Phelps smoking from a bong, the Olympic swimming champion salvaged millions in endorsement deals (Speedo, Omega, Mazda, and Visa.) He quickly apologized, attributing his transgression to youthful bad judgment—he was 23 at the time—and promising it wouldn't happen again. But advertising analysts warned that this, following a DUI arrest four years earlier, was Strike 2, Phelps' last chance to maintain his endorsement worth.

In 2007, AirTran, Powerade, Nike, and Kraft Foods each dropped their advertising contracts with Atlanta Falcons quarterback Michael Vick after he pled guilty and was jailed on federal charges for illegal dog fighting, facing additional state charges and more potential prison time. Meanwhile, Reebok dropped his replica jersey from its shelves and Upper Deck pulled his trading card from its National Football League sets. The public shunning was reminiscent of that of O. J. Simpson a decade earlier who was dropped by Hertz Rental Cars and other contracts because of his murder trial.

Endorsement problems are not limited to celebrity athletes. After a British tabloid published photos of Kate Moss snorting cocaine, the model lost her contracts with Chanel and Burberry, though she kept contracts with Yves Saint Laurent and Gucci, companies that themselves have edgier ads that appeal to their target demographics.

Similarly, St. John fashions dropped Angelina Jolie because it felt some customers were put off by her social activism. Pepsi canceled million-dollar advertising commitments involving Madonna, Michael Jackson, Britney Spears, and Mike Tyson after embarrassing personal publicity about each. When the then world's fastest runner Canadian Olympic athlete Ben Johnson was stripped of his gold medal for using steroids, he also was dropped as spokesperson for companies in the United States, Canada, Japan, Finland, and Italy. In 1991, Magic Johnson lost $9 million a year in endorsements when he went public with his HIV status; it wasn't until 2003 that he obtained another endorsement (for Lincoln automobiles).

Some examples of wayward celebrity spokespersons fall into the "What were they thinking?" category. The Beef Industry Council dropped Cybill Shepherd after she told a national magazine that one of her beauty secrets is avoiding red meats. And when Brylcreem sales dropped 25% after its celebrity hairdo guy David Beckham shaved his head, Beckham lost his $7.9 million contract.

Company spokespeople. In identifying organizational spokespersons, don't confine yourself to a single individual if more than one would better serve your communication needs with various publics. Your organization must speak with a single voice, but effective communication may be accomplished with two or more speakers presenting coordinated and complementary messages. The important thing is to make sure that a single, consistent message is being presented in the name of your organization.

Also, give careful thought to who from your organization might be selected as a spokesperson for a particular issue. Some companies used the CEO-as-spokesperson approach, which has worked well with corporate founders while they lived: popcorn king Orville Redenbacher, Wendy's Dave Thomas, Frank Purdue of chicken fame. Redenbacher was authentic, Thomas was likable, and Purdue—well, anybody who can successfully brag about dead chickens must have something going for him.

But don't presume that the CEO is the best person in every case. There are three good reasons not to use the CEO as organizational spokesperson. First, you don't want to overexpose the boss; save him for the big issues. Second, the CEO may not know the level of detail

When the Fur Flies

People for the Ethical Treatment of Animals (PETA) faced its own ethical problem when supermodel Naomi Campbell, a PETA volunteer who had pledged not to wear natural fur, was reported to be modeling in Europe wearing fur. After unsuccessful attempts to reach her, PETA took a public tack: With much fanfare, it fired Ms. Campbell as a spokesmodel.

The firing was a strategic design, a twist to several of the news-making tips, such as involving a celebrity, tying in to a public issue, and appointing personnel as a way to highlight an issue. Instead, PETA "unappointed" a volunteer—not coincidentally, a wayward one who also happened to be a big celebrity. PETA spokesman Michael McGraw described the activist group's plan: Once it got the media's attention by firing Ms. Campbell, PETA would turn the focus back to the issue of the suffering caused to animals in the name of fashion. "We were able to turn something quite negative into something quite positive," said McGraw, "because what it allowed us to do was get the message out that the fur industry hurts animals and kills them and tortures them."

necessary for a news conference or interview; perhaps a project planner, department manager or another hands-on person would be more knowledgeable and credible. Third, the CEO may not have the personality to exhibit in public or especially on camera the calm, credibility, charisma or other characteristics of an effective spokesperson.

Some organizations buffer the CEO by appointing another spokesperson for negative news, saving the CEO for the more positive public and media encounters. In a news conference, the CEO could be put on the spot and expected to indicate what the organization's activity or response might be. Another organizational spokesperson could more easily deflect such forecasts and avoid inappropriate speculation.

Don't presume that the public relations director should automatically become the spokesperson, either. Especially in confrontational or other crisis situations, the director may be busy behind the scenes advising on strategy and message delivery. Also, the media often don't recognize the public relations director as a high-ranking organizational official; instead they see her as a mere mouthpiece for the people they really wish to interview. In a 1999 study by the Public Relations Society of America, public relations specialists ranked low in terms of credibility as corporate spokespersons. Most organizations use their public relations directors not as spokespersons but as preliminary media contacts, conduits for factual information that doesn't require attribution, and sources for other media background information.

Spokespeople and ethos. Celebrity or not, speakers should strive to identify with their audiences. One way is to emphasize similar backgrounds, especially when such common ground may not be evident to the audience. For example, a university professor before a group of entering freshmen may recall her first months in college or an affluent politician may explain to a group of inner-city residents his experience of growing up amid poverty, albeit of a rural variety.

Another way for speakers to emphasize similarity is to avoid language that separates them from their audience. A white speaker cannot use the phrase "you people" before a black audience without emphasizing his differentness and insulting his listeners.

Be careful about uncommon words that people may misunderstand. An aide to the mayor of Washington, D.C., was fired because he used the term *niggardly* (meaning stingy), which one listener mistook for a racial slur (he was later rehired). And the University of Wisconsin killed a proposed speech code after a student ignited a campus controversy because she was offended when a professor used the same term in a literature class. In both situations, the term *niggardly* was used correctly, but from a public relations perspective, it is best to avoid language that may not be properly understood, especially if they are not part of the shared experiences of both the speaker and the audience. After all, people who don't know any better may think *titillate* and *masticate* are nasty words.

Planning Example 6A: Selecting Message Sources

UPSTATE COLLEGE

In its current efforts to expand enrollment and retention, financial contributions and community support, Upstate will use the following three spokespeople:

Dr. Alexandra Jolin, president of Upstate College.
Dr. Jolin will be perceived by most audiences as highly credible because of her position. She is a dynamic speaker who projects an enthusiasm and friendliness that most people appreciate.

In addition, she holds various leadership positions not only with the college but within the local community and within the state's higher education establishment.

Michael McMillan, chair of the Upstate College Board of Trustees, Upstate alumnus, and prominent business leader in Upstate City.
Mr. McMillan will be perceived as a credible source, especially by residents of Upstate City. He has received media training and is articulate and competent in media and other public presentations. He is in a position of leadership.

Inez SantaElana, president of the UC Student Government.
Because of her leadership position with the student government, Ms. SantaElana will be perceived as a credible source, especially with current and potential students. She also is a regional celebrity among area high school students who has developed much poise and confidence as a result of her athletic achievements, including state records in speed skating.

■ ■ ■

TINY TYKES TOYS

In its campaign to increase consumer confidence, Tiny Tykes will use the following two spokespeople:

Michael Beaucheforte, senior vice president for consumer affairs.
Mr. Beaucheforte will be perceived as credible because of his expertise within the company and because he was hired specifically to address consumer issues. He is a persuasive speaker, with a friendliness that exudes trust and disarms skeptics. (Note that company president Theodore Frankelberger should not be used as a spokesperson in media situations because he becomes very nervous when speaking in public; this nervousness is often perceived as insincerity and evasiveness.)

Mary Margaret O'Sullivan, Tiny Tykes Consumer Advisory Council member.
Ms. O'Sullivan is a consumer whose child was stained by the defective toy. She now sits on the Consumer Advisory Council that helped relaunch the product. Because of her personal involvement, Ms. O'Sullivan will be perceived as a trustworthy and expert spokesperson. She is not an accomplished public speaker, but her uneasiness adds to her credibility and charisma.

Checklist 6A: Message Sources

Basic Questions

1. Identify several possible spokespersons who could present your message.
2. What is the level of credibility for each possible spokesperson?
3. What is the level of charisma for each?
4. What is the level of control for each?

Expanded Questions

Answer the following items for each possible message source. Then compare your responses to determine the sources best suited for this communication task. An effective message source will have mainly high and positive rankings in each item.

A. CREDIBILITY

1. How expert on this topic is the message source?
2. How well known are his/her credentials to the audience?
   If expertise is high, should the audience be reminded of this?
   If expertise is not known, can the audience be made informed of this?
3. Does the message source enunciate clearly?
4. Does the source speak with dynamism and authority?
5. Does the source speak calmly and reassuringly on this topic?
6. How trustworthy will the source be perceived as being?
7. Can the source speak truthfully and independently about the topic?
8. Does the source have any associations that compete with the organization?
9. Does the source have any associations that are inconsistent with the organization's image?
10. Is the source available to your organization?

B. CHARISMA

1. How similar is the source to the audience?
2. How familiar is the audience with the source?
3. How attractive is the source to the audience?
4. Can the source be presented in an attractive setting?

C. CONTROL

1. Does the source have any moral leverage with this audience?
2. Does the source have any power over this audience?
3. Does the source have the willingness to use this power?
4. Does the source have the ability to investigate this audience?
5. Does the source have the authority to reward or punish this audience?
6. Does the source have the authority to blame or forgive this audience?

Logos: Appealing to Reason

Having selected the spokesperson for the campaign or project, the strategic planning next focuses on the content of the message. What will be said, and how will the message be framed? Will you appeal to the intellect, or to the emotions—or to both? What facts and arguments will you offer? What examples might you suggest? Let's first consider messages based on logic, then messages on sentiment.

Communication effectiveness based on the rational appeal of the message was known to the ancient Greeks as **logos**. The conscious attempt to persuade by appealing to logos—logic and reason—is an obvious place to start planning your strategic message. Distill your message and resist the temptation to bombard your audience with every bit of information available to you. Clarify and simplify.

The ancient art of rhetoric is kept current with an expanding research base (see Benjamin, 1997; Infante, Rancer, & Womack, 2003; Johnston, 1994; Larson, 2000; Ross, 1994). Following is a summary of recommendations and conclusions from many different research studies into effective communication and persuasion.

The primary idea in a speech, editorial, advertisement, television program, or any other communication vehicle is called a **proposition**, also known as a **claim**. Only one proposition should be presented at a time; more than one can confuse the audience and lessen the impact of the message. There are four kinds of propositions: factual, conjecture, value, and policy.

- A **factual proposition** states that something exists, based on provable (usually physical) evidence. For example, proof of an increase in urban air pollution may be environmental tests. Factual claims often link to communication objectives focused on awareness, which seek to increase attention or build greater understanding.
- A **conjecture proposition** states that something probably exists, based on reasoned conclusion drawn from physical evidence, and asks audiences to agree with the conclusion. An example of this is a conclusion for or against the continuation of affirmative action regulations, in which the conclusion flows logically from the facts as they are presented. Conjecture propositions often relate to communication objectives dealing with acceptance, fostering supportive attitudes.
- A **value proposition** identifies the virtue of something, such as the merits (or folly) of health care reform. Value claims also relate to objectives dealing with acceptance, which try to increase interest or build positive attitudes.
- A **policy proposition** identifies a new course of action and encourages its adoption, such as advocacy for changing the legal drinking age or for beginning a school dress code. Policy claims often reflect objectives associated with opinion and action.

Whatever the type of proposition, it should be supported with strong arguments and clear proof. Such proof varies from person to person and from group to group. To some, an intelligent argument with understandable data and logical conclusions may prove a point; to others, only the strongest and most consistent of physical data may be considered as proof.

Verbal Evidence

About 2,500 years ago, Corax of Syracuse taught that disputes are settled easily when clear physical evidence shows inarguably the truth or falsity of a claim. That remains true today. Most of the time, however, we are not lucky enough to have such unchallenged hard evidence, so we have to rely on other arguments. This verbal evidence can take several different forms, including analogies, comparisons, examples, statistics and testimonials. Here's a brief look at each.

Analogies. As a type of persuasion technique, **analogies** use familiar situations and allusions to help your audience understand new ideas, specifically by making a comparison between two things that are essentially different but nevertheless strikingly alike in an important aspect. For example, cars double-parked on a congested city street can be analogous to the effect of cholesterol in clogging arteries. Analogies usually are presented as the grammatical forms of similes and metaphors.

Comparisons. By highlighting the characteristics or values related to an issue, **comparisons** can liken it to something else the audience might understand. Make positive comparisons to things the audience already acknowledges and admires, and make negative comparisons to things the audience holds in low esteem. Make comparisons that are easy to understand, such as by showing how one issue, product, or theme relates to another. For example, show how a particular tax-reform proposal is more economically feasible than an alternative proposal.

Examples. Another type of verbal evidence, **examples**, provide conclusions drawn from related instances. Such illustrations can be effective, particularly if the case is recent, reliable, and relevant to the situation at hand. Be careful not to argue from far-fetched examples that are easy to dismiss as being not only irrelevant but also deceitful.

Statistics. The use of **statistics** can provide clear and hard-to-dispute facts in order to make the best case. For example, it is easy to argue the superiority of a particular automobile with statistics dealing with safety, cost, and other easily understood data. But be careful, because statistics can be misinterpreted and manipulated, and many people have learned through hard personal experience that comparative statistics are not always as neat and clean as they appear to be. More on this a bit later.

Testimonies and endorsements. Comments by witnesses and people who have used your organization's product or service are called **testimonies**. Comments by people who espouse an idea your organization supports are called **endorsements**. Both can provide effective verbal evidence. Testimonies can take the form of letters or other statements of support from satisfied customers or engaged employees. Similarly, endorsements and recommendations from celebrities can be persuasive, especially if the celebrity is known to have used the product (such as Michael Jordan and Gatorade), participated in the service or program (Kirstie Alley for the Jenny Craig weight-loss program) or espoused the idea being presented (Rosie O'Donnell for gun control, Whoopi Goldberg for abortion rights, Brooke Shields for pro-life issues).

Visual Supporting Evidence

Strong visual presentation can enhance the effectiveness of these writing techniques. Use photographs, charts, graphs, and diagrams as visual aids in presenting statistical and technical information. Also think about ways to include demonstrations and performances in your presentation. Consider too the role that computer-based presentations can make.

Errors of Logic

As you are preparing your rational message, avoid errors in logic. Some common errors result from unfounded presumptions. For example, don't overgeneralize the argument or leap to an **unwarranted conclusion**, which is a deduction that is not supported by evidence. Make sure your facts are indisputable and understood by your audience; building on incorrect or uncertain data will create a case that is easy to refute. Also, be careful not to make a **false assumption**, a conclusion that the audience may not accept, such as by arguing that U.S. schools should adopt a Japanese school calendar on the untested presumption that the audience agrees that the intensity of Japanese education produces better graduates.

Other errors in logic deal with ignoring the issue and instead attacking the person or reacting with an air of pity or disdain. Finally, remember that any appeal to authority or tradition will be effective only if the audience already respects and accepts that authority or tradition.

Misuse of Statistics

The 19th-century British prime minister Benjamin Disraeli once wrote, "There are three kinds of lies: lies, damned lies and statistics." That captures the feeling of many people, who in the face of the supposed statistical evidence have learned that statistics aren't always to be trusted. Actually, inaccurate data can usually be spotted. The problem lies less with the statistics and more in their interpretation. Often it's a matter of arriving at a common definition of terms.

Take the simple concept of "average," for example. In general terms, **average** refers to the usual or ordinary instance. But in dealing with statistics, average can be a real sticking point for understanding, because it can mean different things. Consider the following information about 11 university students who share a dorm suite.

- Alan works in the dean's office and earns $10,000.
- Jere, Jamal, and Monika work for the university police and earn $7,500 each.
- Maria and Tomiko work in the library and earn $5,000 each.
- Tim, Pat, and Lori work in the department office and earn $4,000 each.
- Sylvia and Juan work with food service and earn $4,000 each.

What's the average salary? It could be $5,681 (if you calculate average as the **mean**, total wages divided by the number of wage earners). Or, the average is $5,000 (if you use the **median**, the middle number on the list; in this case, Tomiko). Or you can say the average is $4,000 (if you reference the **mode**, the most common number; that is, the number occurring most frequently). The point is, make sure you are clear in defining your terms.

Often, the problem with statistics is how they are interpreted. Few things in society are more contested and controversial than the issue of abortion, and statistics seem only to muddy the waters. One side says most people support access to abortion services; the other side says most people oppose abortion. Both can't be right, can they? Well, yes, depending on how you interpret the nuance of the data. Consider the following survey results, all presumably accurate statistics.

- Gallup Poll, 2007: 56% of Americans would have abortion legal in certain circumstances; 26%, legal in any circumstance; 18%, illegal. Additionally, 49% call themselves pro-choice, and 45% pro-life.
- Fox News Poll, 2007: 50% would have abortion illegal in all but life-threatening circumstances for the mother; 39%, legal in any circumstance; 10% are not sure.
- Gallup Youth Survey, 2003: 45% would have abortion legal in certain circumstances; 21%, legal in any circumstance; 33%, illegal.
- The Center for the Advancement of Women (a women's advocacy group) in July 2003: 30% would have abortion legal and available on request; 55 legal in some situations (34 in cases of rape or incest or to protect the mother's health; 21 with various limitations); 17%, illegal.

When Facts Lead to "So What?"

Statistics may be completely accurate, but if they are used in a false context or without logical reasoning, they can be meaningless. Consider the following examples; in each, the fact is accurate, but each statement gives a false impression. The casual reader might be misled into presuming that the statement provides some insight. A more careful reader will be left wondering "So what?"

- There are about as many vegetarians in the U.S. as there are Lutherans (about 12.5 million people, 4% of the population).
- Jews and gay people make up about the same proportion of voters (4%).
- The U.S. prison population is the same as the number of German speakers in the United States (2 million, 0.7%).
- There are as many French speakers in the U.S. as Episcopalians (2.3 million, 0.8%).
- There are about as many atheists in the U.S. as there are people who speak Tagalog, or those whose families have immigrated from Wales (1.1 million, 0.4%).

The U.S. population includes about the same number of people of Assyrian ancestry as those whose families came from Cape Verde, Palestine, Slovakia, Albania, and the Basque region. But, so what?

So what do such statistics say? One interpretation is that because 17–21% would ban abortions, the remaining 80% support abortion, right? Well, that's not quite what the data reveals. Another interpretation is that if 10–30% would allow abortions for any reason, the remaining 70–90% must be against abortion. Again, it's not quite that simple. Obviously, numbers can be found to support the bias of a writer, but perhaps the most fair interpretation is that the data show a lot of centrist opinions, not a clear-cut mandate on either side of this public policy discussion.

Here's another example of misleading statistics. Your campus provost's office tracks and reports on cases of plagiarism each year. The current report notes that 150 of the 200 incidents of plagiarism involved the Internet, or 75% of the cases. This compares with 108 of 180 incidents during the previous year, or 60%. What can you say about this increase? You could report a 15-point rise in the percentage of Internet-assisted plagiarism cases. Or is it a 25% increase (the proportional difference from 60 to 75)? Or you might cite a 39% increase in the number of cases (180 compared to 150). All of the figures are mathematically accurate, but—obviously—they leave significantly different impressions. The key to using statistics that do not mislead is to interpret them fairly and honestly and to be clear about what the numbers really mean—in this example, whether you are comparing total plagiarism cases or the annual percentage change.

Sometimes the issue is about how accurately the statistics reflect the population under study. Accurate use of statistics involves what is included as well as what is left out—a matter of context. Consider the scandal of sexual abuse among Catholic priests. "A casual observer relying on the mass media would form the overwhelming impression of a Church institution awash in perversion, conspiracy, and criminality," notes Philip Jenkins (2003, p. 137). Early media reports relied on claims by activist and victims' groups, which counted as many as 10% of priests as pedophiles, about 5,000 of the current 53,000 American priests. Yet more reliable statistics paint a different picture. Studies in some of the largest dioceses indicated that about 3% of priests had been accused, less than 2% with credible evidence. Many of the accusations involved adult women and men as well as adolescents—all, by definition, not pedophilia. A 2004 nationwide study found that 4% of priests had been accused during the

Appealing to Hearts and Minds

Research tells us that it is tremendously important to provide messages that appeal to both the mind and the heart. Three areas of study—two from psychology, one from physiology—shed some light on the question of how we can best frame messages to our audiences:

1. *Psychological Type.* The concept of **psychological type** is based on the work of Carl Jung and the application of his theories by the mother-daughter team of Isabel Myers and Catharine Briggs (see Myers, 1987; Myers & Myers, 1980) and a host of their disciples. This approach observes that people have different natural preferences in how they gather information, make decisions, and act on those decisions. Some people, labeled "thinkers" in Myers-Briggs terminology, tend to rely mainly on logic and data in making decisions. "Feelers," on the other hand, base their decisions more on sentiment and emotion. Seldom will your publics and audiences be so like minded as to uniformly prefer one type of message appeal over the other. Thus, good strategy calls for the use of both types of messages.

   Note that this may not be a natural response for many practitioners, because many of the artistic or creative disciplines—writing, journalism, design, advertising, and public relations—tend to attract people who themselves are feelers rather than thinkers. The disciplines more associated with management, such as research and marketing, attract a higher-than-average percentage of thinkers. In either case, it is undependable to rely simply on your personal preferences.
2. *Temperament.* The concept of **temperament** is an approach related to personality and natural disposition, associated with psychologists David Keirsey and Marilyn Bates (1984) and their followers. From them we learn of four specific temperaments— artisan, idealist, guardian and rationalist—with different innate preferences regarding organization and creativity.
3. *Left Brain/Right Brain Differences.* The working of the human brain—and, in particular, the relationship between the two hemispheres of the brain—have been explored by Roger Sperry (1985) of the California Institute of Technology. He received a Nobel Prize in 1981 for his pioneering work in the field. Evidence suggests that the left side of the brain is responsible for logical and analytical thought, while the right side controls creativity and imagination. Like psychological type and temperament, hemispheric brain studies suggest that most individuals are stronger in one function and weaker in the other.

These three fields have many common bonds. That's not surprising for the first two, because Keirsey and Bates's research is a conscious reworking of the psychological insights of Myers and Briggs. Sperry took a different path that led him through physiology, but he arrived at surprisingly similar patterns. By comparing and blending this research, evidence suggests that some people are innately more deliberate or logical, while others are more spontaneous and imaginative.

previous 50 years. Compare this to estimates by psychologists and law enforcement that 3–5% of the entire male population in North America is linked to child or adolescent sexual abuse. Meanwhile, clergy of other religious groups—Episcopalian, Baptist, Hare Krishna, and Orthodox Jews, among others—had been similarly accused of child sexual abuse. The Boy Scouts reported dismissing hundreds of scoutmasters for alleged sexual abuse. An educational activist group reported that up to 5% of teachers sexually abuse their students, with more than a third of them keeping their jobs. In Step 5 we noted estimates of 5% or more of health workers who are sexually attracted to children, even higher among those working in children's hospitals. So the clergy abuse situation seems no different statistically than the rest of the population, perhaps lower than in some professions. While this doesn't minimize the tragedy of sexual abuse, it serves to point out that statistics of doubtful reliability and/or out of context can mislead.

Pathos: Appealing to Sentiment

Human beings are not mere thinking machines. We see in Mr. Spock of the original *Star Trek* TV series examples of inappropriate responses that are so "logical" they are absurd. As humans, we rely heavily on our feelings, and effective communicators take this into consideration. An important part of the strategy of public relations and marketing communication is to link the message to an emotional appeal, either positive or negative.

Positive Emotional Appeals

Many persuasive appeals seek to generate responses based on a variety of positive emotions. Here is a brief look at positive appeals to love, virtue, humor, and sex.

Love appeals. Love appeals can vary—bittersweet poignancy, family togetherness, nostalgia, pity, compassion, sensitivity, sympathy, or any of the many other sides of love. Pleasant images lead consumers not only to remember the persuasive message but also to be more likely to act on the message. For years, Michelin has built a successful advertising campaign around warm images of cute babies sitting in tires, and the verbal cue "so much is riding on your tires." Maxwell House coffee and Hallmark greeting cards also have been successful with this "warm and fuzzy" approach. Fundraising appeals frequently evoke images of compassion and sympathy.

Virtue appeals. Appeals based on virtue can evoke any of the various values that society or individuals hold in esteem. These are qualities that most people treasure. Recall how patriotic appeals inspired record levels of volunteerism, blood donations, and financial contributions to relief agencies in the wake of the 9/11 attacks on the World Trade Center and the Pentagon.

- *Justice appeals* deal with fairness, human or civil rights, and issues of right or wrong.
- *Altruism appeals* focus on generosity, charity, kindness, and unselfishness.
- *Loyalty appeals* focus on patriotism and fidelity.
- *Bravery appeals* evoke images of boldness, endurance, and courage.
- *Piety appeals* focus on religious faith, spirituality, and prayer.
- *Discretion appeals* relate to restraint, moderation, wisdom, and self-control.

- *Improvement appeals* focus on progress, social advancement, and making the world a better place.
- *Esteem appeals* focus on self-respect, pride, vanity, and self-worth.
- *Social acceptance appeals* focus on the importance of peer support—the "everybody's doing it" theme.

Humor appeals. Appeals based on humor can be powerful because comedy and amusement are strong human instincts. Humor is useful in reinforcing existing attitudes and behaviors, but it generally is not very effective in changing them. Humor can make the speaker more liked by the audience, but seldom does it make the speaker seem more credible. However, the use of humor can reduce the speaker's likability when audiences perceive the humor as excessive or inappropriate. Additionally, humor tends to get old fast, so its use in public relations and advertising limits the effectiveness of the otherwise valuable practice of repeating messages. Finally, if audiences evaluate the message from an entertainment perspective, they can fail to take it as a serious persuasive message. With these cautions in mind, here are some guidelines on using humor in persuasive communication.

1. The humor should complement a clear and consistent message about the organization or the product/service/concept. It should never be used as a substitute for an understandable message.
2. The humor should be relevant to the issue and appropriate for the organization. For instance, it is unlikely that a funeral home could effectively use humor in its brochures.
3. The humor should be tasteful. The *South Park* phenomenon aside, bathroom and bedroom humor generally are counterproductive for most audiences, as is disparaging humor directed against others, particularly groups of people. Self-deprecating humor can be effective in causing an audience to like a speaker.
4. The humor should be funny. This is difficult to achieve, because what is humorous to one person may be droll, too cute, ludicrous, or simply unfunny to others. Make sure the humor does not insult people's intelligence by becoming absurd or pointless. Also, given the choice, prefer the lighthearted and amusing touch over an attempt to present uproarious farce.
5. Humor is more effective with dull topics (which need sparking up) than with topics the audience already finds interesting. With interesting topics, humor can detract from the message.

Sex appeals. Appeals based on sex range from nudity to double entendres to outright shock. These sexual messages can be effective in commanding attention, though audience demographics affect how that attention is received. But the very pulling power of sex appeals has a built-in problem. Tests show that audiences often remember the sexual content of an advertisement but fail to associate it with the brand being promoted or the sponsor presenting the message. Likewise, what one demographic group may find appropriate and positive another may judge unnecessary and negative. For example, women respond to sex appeals less than men do, and younger people are more positively influenced by sex appeals than older audiences.

An even bigger problem with sex-appeal messages is that, for all their high ability to gain attention, they are notoriously weak in leading receivers toward desired action.

One consistent finding from persuasion research is that sex appeal should not be used simply for shock value. It is far more effective when the sexual theme has a legitimate association with the product (such as lingerie, perfume, or condoms) or with the cause (such as birth control or responsible sexual behavior).

Negative Emotional Appeals

Some messages invoke responses based on negative emotions—fear and guilt being the most common. A third type of negative appeal, to hatred, has no ethical use for public relations and thus is not worth considering here.

Fear appeals. Fear is one of the strongest human emotions, and fear appeals are intended to arouse anxiety or worry among receivers, such as advertising that focuses on the fear of body odor or political messages centered on the alleged disasters that await the public if the opposing candidate is elected. Government, particularly in recent years, has stepped up its use of fear appeals to press for quick passage of security-based legislation, often without time for thoughtful consideration of the potential impact.

The key to using fear appeals effectively is to accompany them with a quick fix featuring an easy, reasonable and immediate solution to the problem. Fear appeals to persuade audiences to obtain a one-time vaccination, for example, are more effective than those designed to persuade audiences to floss over a lifetime in the name of dental hygiene.

Beware of offering too much of a good thing. Moderate fear appeals can be effective, but too much fearful content can make people either avoid the message or take a defiant stance against it. Appeals that present harsh consequences may cause audiences to cope with their fear simply by refusing to consider the message or even by denying the underlying issue.

Another problem with fear appeals is that the balance point between effective and ineffective shifts according to various demographic factors such as age, education, and gender. Younger people, for example, have higher resistance to fear appeals, and some research suggests that fear appeals likewise have only a limited effect on audience members with high self-esteem who feel immune to impending doom.

Fear appeals may increase levels of awareness without delivering the desired action. For example, strong fear appeals used in a seat-belt campaign may make drivers aware of the consequences of not wearing seat belts—perhaps even fostering an intention of wearing them—without actually changing the likelihood that they will, indeed, buckle up.

Here is a way to make fear appeals more effective: Include in the message a strong how-to approach. For example, don't just deal with the dangers associated with poor nutrition; give several clear and simple examples of how to prepare or order more nutritional meals.

Source and significance also play a role in the effective use of fear appeals. For example, fear appeals are more effective when they come from highly credible sources who are dissimilar to the audience. Often this dissimilarity can be reinforced by symbols, such as clothing a doctor in a lab coat as she presents moderate fear-based information about disease prevention or using someone in a military uniform to speak about threats to national interests and preparation for war. Fear appeals also can be effective when the issue is significant or important to the audience. In a study related to environmental threats—specifically plutonium contamination from a nuclear weapons plant—Connie Roser and Margaret Thompson (1995) have observed that fear appeals can motivate even latent publics to become active, especially to take action against the fear-producing organization.

Aaron Delwiche of Trinity University in San Antonio, Texas, supervises a propaganda website (http://www.propagandacritic.com) in which he identifies four elements of a successful fear appeal: (1) a threat; (2) a recommendation about how the audience should behave; (3) audience perception that the recommendation can effectively address the threat; and (4) perception that the audience can actually behave as recommended (Delwiche, n.d).

Guilt appeals. Appeals to a personal sense of guilt or shame comprise another negative message strategy, one that is the flip side of the virtue appeal. Consider the "Buy American" theme. Only a fine line separates a positive appeal to patriotism and national pride from one that tries to make people feel guilty. With a positive approach, the message focuses on the common economic good, shared values among citizens, and a healthy respect for the quality of American products. With a negative approach, however, the same appeal can elicit a sense of guilt for having bought foreign-made products. Since nobody wants to feel guilty, a typical reaction against guilt appeals is to justify our actions ("foreign cars are better made") and to lament the alternative ("American cars just don't last as long").

Like fear appeals, the use of guilt strategy can be effective in moderation. In a fund-raising message, for example, a guilt message might try to make readers feel a bit uneasy or apologetic in their relative comfort amid so much misery elsewhere. But try to move guilt appeals away from the negative emotion and toward a positive sentiment such as compassion and justice. If guilt appeals are to be effective, their messages must make people feel part of the solution. "Will you help? Or will you turn the page?" is the kind of modest guilt appeal that can be quite effective. Like the fear appeal, guilt appeals should feature solutions to the problem of conscience that they raise.

Planning Example 6B: Determining Message Appeals

Step 6

UPSTATE COLLEGE

Upstate College will combine rational and emotional message appeals in its message.

Rational Appeal

Upstate College will present two types of appeals:

- A factual proposition based on advantages to students, including current and future academic programs, accreditation, financial aid, and alumni and community commitments for internships and mentoring.
- A value proposition asserting that this expansion is in the best interests of students and this region of the state.

These messages will include statistics, personal endorsements and specific examples of hypothetical students in various academic and economic situations. They also will include visual elements such as photographs, charts and graphs.

Emotional Appeal

UC will present appeals to positive emotions, particularly the virtues of self-improvement and the realization of personal potential. For fund-raising purposes, it will appeal to the virtue of altruism and sharing with students who need an assist in obtaining a college education.

■ ■ ■

Tiny Tykes will present both rational and emotional message appeals.

Rational Appeal
Tiny Tykes will present several rational propositions:

- A factual proposition based on information about the product redesign.
- A value proposition stating a renewed commitment to consumer safety.
- A policy proposition asserting the rightness of continuing to use Tiny Tykes products, which have a long history of being responsive to customer concerns.

These messages will include physical evidence from outside testing agencies about the safety of Tiny Tykes products, a comparison with similar products by competitors, and testimony by consumers and consumer advocacy groups.

Emotional Appeal
Tiny Tykes will present two types of emotional appeals:

- Appeals to positive emotions, such as child development and family fun.
- Appeals to negative emotions such as a mild level of fear appeal about using toys not tested and approved by independent agencies.

Regardless of the type of emotional appeal being made, consider the ethical ramifications. Ask yourself, Is this appeal ethical? Is it the right way to communicate about this issue? Is it fair? Will the organization gain respect by using this approach?

Checklist 6B: Message Appeals

Basic Questions

1. What is the key message that forms the basis of this public relations or marketing communication program?
2. How does this message use a rational appeal?
3. How does this message use an emotional appeal?

Expanded Questions

1. Does your message include a rational appeal and/or an emotional appeal? (Note: Most persuasive messages provide both kinds of appeals.)

A. RATIONAL APPEAL

1. How does your message make a rational appeal?
2. Does the message feature a factual proposition, a value proposition, or a policy proposition?

3. Which of the following provide arguments for your claims: physical evidence, analogy, audience interest, comparison, context, examples, statistics, testimony and endorsements, and/or visual presentation?

B. EMOTIONAL APPEAL

1. How does your message make an emotional appeal?
2. Does the message feature an appeal to positive emotions or negative emotions?
3. What is the emotion?

Love Appeal

1. What kind of love?

Virtue Appeal

1. What virtue?

Humor Appeal

(Note: If you answer "yes" to these questions, the humorous message may be effective.)

1. Will the use of humor make the source more persuasive?
2. Is the humor relevant to the issue?
3. Is the humor funny?
4. Is the humor appropriate for the audience?
5. Is the humor appropriate for the organization?
6. Will the humor enhance the message?
7. Will the humor help meet the objectives?

Sex Appeal

(Note: If you answer "yes" to these questions, the sexual message may be effective.)

1. Will the use of sex appeal make the source more persuasive?
2. Is the sex relevant to the issue?
3. Is the sex appropriate for the audience?
4. Is the sex appropriate for the organization?
5. Will the sex help enhance the message?
6. Will the sex help meet the objectives?

Fear Appeal

(Note: If you answer "yes" to these questions, the fearful message may be effective.)

1. Will the use of fear appeal make the source more persuasive?
2. Is the fear relevant to the issue?
3. Is the fear appropriate for the audience?
4. Is the fear appropriate for the organization?
5. Does the message include a solution to overcome the fear?
6. Will the fear enhance the message?
7. Will the fear help meet the objectives?

Guilt Appeal

(Note: If you answer "yes" to these questions, the guilt appeal may be effective.)

1. Will the use of guilt appeal make the source more persuasive?
2. Is the guilt relevant to the issue?
3. Is the guilt appropriate for the audience?
4. Is the guilt appropriate for the organization?
5. Does the message include a solution to overcome the guilt?
6. Will the guilt enhance the message?
7. Will the guilt help meet the objectives?

Verbal Communication

Both kinds of appeals, logical and emotional, can be communicated either verbally or nonverbally. Let's look first at verbal and then at nonverbal communication as they apply to public relations, marketing, and related disciplines.

Verbal communication occurs through written and spoken words. The right words—and the right use of those words—can effectively present your organization's message to its publics. Several verbal factors combine to create an effective message, among them structure, clarity, saliency, power words, product and program names, strong quotes, and both ethical and legal language. Here is a closer look at each of these.

Message Structure

The structure of the message and the relationship between the arrangement of the message and its effectiveness have been subjects of much research. Several particular elements have been researched: giving one side or multiple sides of an argument, the order of presentation, and the value of drawing conclusions or making recommendations. Should you present only your point of view, or should you address the opposition's argument? The research suggests that it depends upon both the audience and the circumstances.

One-sided arguments present the organization's or speaker's point of view but not opposing views. This kind of argument is useful in reinforcing opinions, because one-sided arguments don't confuse the audience with alternatives. But one-sided arguments are less effective in changing opinions. Four conditions warrant the use of one-sided arguments: (1) the audience is friendly and already agrees with your position; (2) its members have low educational or knowledge levels; (3) your position will be the only one presented; or (4) the objective is immediate opinion change. Presenting only one side of an argument can cause a temporary attitudinal change, but this probably will be eliminated if the audience later hears a convincing argument from the other side.

Two-sided arguments present both the pros and the cons of an issue, though not necessarily objectively. They usually criticize the opposition's position. Two-sided arguments are necessary with better-educated audiences, with audiences that are undecided on an issue or initially opposed to the idea being presented, and with more knowledgeable audiences that are aware that another side of the issue exists or that are likely to be exposed to other sides in the future. Such two-sided arguments can improve your ability to persuade these audiences because you will be perceived as being more honest and more respectful of the audience's intelligence.

If you present each side of the argument, you have a better chance of achieving a greater attitude change that will remain high when the audience hears the opposing argument from another source.

Order of presentation refers to the way the argument unfolds. Should you present arguments in order of least to most important, or vice versa? It generally doesn't seem to matter, as long as you are consistent. In developing your persuasive message, you may have reason to choose one form over the other. For example, do you think your audience will be more attentive at the beginning of the message? If so, then use your strongest arguments there. The final word is also very important, and plenty of research points out that the last point made is the one best remembered. This is especially true with less-sophisticated audiences, as well as for audiences that are less knowledgeable or less personally involved in the issue. Comic Paula Poundstone said it well in a stand-up routine referring to a political campaign that dealt with the economy: "I don't know anything about the economy. I tend to agree with the last guy who spoke."

In your two-sided arguments, sandwich the information. That is, first present your side—the first argument often is perceived as the strongest. Then present and refute the opposing arguments. Finally restate your position, because of the power of the last word.

Drawing conclusions—that is, presenting the evidence and then explicitly telling the audience how to interpret it—has been the subject of much research. To date, most of the findings suggest that making a recommendation or drawing a conclusion usually is more

Barriers to Effective Communication

Several factors can limit the effectiveness of communication. Each of these is a type of "noise" within the communication process. By knowing what they are, communication planners may be able to eliminate these noise types or at least minimize their impact. Here are some of the common barriers:

- **Physical noise**, such as ineffective communication channels that do not transmit the message from sender to receiver or distracting sounds within the communication process that interfere with the receiver's reception of the message.
- **Psychological noise**, such as emotional distractions by the receiver.
- **Semantic noise**, such as the use of jargon that is not understood by the receiver or other language that carries different meaning for the sender and the receiver, often because of different backgrounds and experiences.
- **Demographic noise**, such as differences between sender and receiver in terms of age, ethnicity, social status, and the like.

With all the barriers that can interfere with effective communication, it's a wonder people and organizations are able to communicate at all. But the noise can be turned down and the barriers overcome. Senders who understand the potential communication pitfalls can find ways to avoid them; receivers can be particularly attentive to the message and engage in active listening to overcome communication noise.

Persuasive Arguments

A classic pattern for persuasive arguments comes from Hugh Rank (1976), a researcher with the National Council of Teachers of English who outlined a model that considered both positive and negative arguments.

In what has become known as **Rank's model of persuasion**, he observed that persuaders generally choose between two different strategies when comparing their own and their opponent's positions. One approach is to magnify both their own good points and their opponents' bad points. The other is to downplay their own bad points as well as their opponents' good points.

Rank believes that message receivers can make themselves resistant to persuasive manipulation by recognizing the intensifying/downplaying strategies of advertisers and other would-be persuaders and then by downplaying the messages the persuader emphasized and intensifying those that were minimized. Rank's model also can give strategic communicators insight into how they can more effectively present a persuasive argument.

effective than leaving it to the audience to draw its own conclusion. However, some evidence suggests that if audience members—especially educated ones—do draw their own conclusion, both the conclusion and the attitude on which it rests are more resistant to change than if the conclusion is presented by the source. Some studies have indicated that when the purpose of a message is to reduce criticism or opposition it may be better not to draw conclusions for the audience. However, can you risk not having the audience draw the "right" conclusion?

Reiteration, the final area to consider for effective message structure, refers to internal repetition of the main ideas within a persuasive message. This is not the kind of redundancy that involves superfluous turns of phrase, such as "puppy dog," "totally destroyed," or "small village." Rather, reiteration means presenting the same message in different forms, with different words and different examples, each reinforcing the other. For example, an effective fund-raising letter will ask for a donation frequently throughout the letter, each time making the request with different words and phrases and perhaps based on different types of appeals. Such internal repetition can make messages more memorable and, over time, more acceptable. Reiteration often means using synonyms—different words with similar meanings—as a way of restating the main point. Another technique is to develop parallel structure within sentences and paragraphs to make your information easier to recognize and remember. For example, use a "B" list: "Be alert. Be prepared. Be resourceful." Alliteration, using words that have the same beginning sounds, is another memory enhancer.

Message Content

The content of the message contributes significantly to the effectiveness of the message strategy. Whether positive or negative, the importance of content cannot be overstressed.

Clarity. A message first and foremost must be understood. **Clarity** helps the audience quickly and easily understand your message. To accomplish this, use words precisely, with an eye to their exact and commonly understood meaning. Use simple language—*try* instead of *endeavor*, *use* rather than *utilize*, *say* instead of *articulate*. Avoid jargon unless the language is shared by your listeners, readers or viewers. In all cases, use a vocabulary appropriate to your audience. Consider the differences in language fitting for teens, senior citizens, or business executives. Consider also the setting for your verbal message, such as the differences in language appropriate for boardrooms, locker rooms, and dining rooms.

The **Fog Index** (also called the **Gunning Readability Formula**) is an easy-to-use tool that helps writers measure the level of reading difficulty for any piece of writing and then adjust the writing according to the skills of their audience. Some computer programs also can calculate grade-level readability measures. In addition to clear writing, communication strategists should ensure that their messages use correct and simple English, avoid redundancies, generally use an active voice, and observe other guidelines for good writing. Consult a good textbook on public relations writing to brush up on your writing skills.

Salience. In advertising, planners focus on the **unique selling proposition**, that special something that their product or service offers that is different from all the competition. It is a kind of niche statement that positions the product for the intended market segment. We can use the product also in public relations planning. We call it **salience**, the ability to stand out from the crowd. Specifically, salient information is that which speaks directly to the intended public by letting people know just how a product, service or idea will help them.

Power words. The use of strong language can play a significant role in communication effectiveness. **Power words**, also called **grabbers**, refer to terminology and definitions that are so influential that they often can determine public relations success for a movement or campaign. Edward Bernays, the public relations pioneer who rooted the profession in social psychology, said he had achieved "semantic tyranny" with his name for the anniversary campaign to commemorate Thomas Edison's invention of the electric light. Light's Golden Jubilee was the title Bernays devised, linking three words that he believed guaranteed interest and support.

Bernays's advice to choose words carefully is particularly valid today, when media are overflowing with messages that compete for attention and interest. Descriptions such as "low-

How to Use the Fog Index

1. Select a 100-word passage of writing.
2. Count the number of sentences. If the passage ends within a sentence, estimate a percentage of the final sentence. Round this to a single decimal space.
3. Determine the average sentence length by dividing 100 by the number of sentences in the passage.
4. Count the number of long words in the passage. Long words are those with three or more syllables. But don't count words in which *-es*, *-er*, or *-ed* form the third and final syllable, hyphenated terms such as *state-of-the-art* or compound words such as *newspaper*.
5. Add the average sentence length and the number of long words (totals from steps 3 and 4).
6. Multiply this total by 0.4. The resulting number indicates the approximate grade level of the passage.

fat," "environment-friendly" and "Bible-believing," and labels such as "family values," "flip-flopper," "the right to bear arms," and "tax-and-spend liberal" are terms that have been carefully orchestrated to present a particular emotional connotation. The same gunmen who robbed, raped and mutilated villagers in Central America were called "freedom fighters" by their political supporters and "terrorists" by opponents. Instead of referring to "political prisoners," Amnesty International uses the ennobling term "prisoners of conscience" while the administration of George W. Bush called suspected terrorists held in military prisons "detainees" who, by definition, were not entitled to legal protections of prisoners of war under international law.

Sometimes the grabber is a full paragraph. Consider the following statement that could be used by any of the 560 or so American Indian nations to explain their historic relationship with their lands: "My people lived on this land when Moses was crossing the desert. We have fished these rivers since Cleopatra was queen. We have hunted these mountains since before Genghis Khan. This land is as much a part of me as the color of my eyes."

Rhetorical warfare is associated with some of society's most divisive issues. For example, "pro-choice" activists generally disavow the label "pro-abortion" foisted upon them by the other side (which calls itself "pro-life," and which in turn is called "anti-choice" by opponents). One side speaks of a "fetus," the other side of an "unborn baby"—a differentiation in terminology on which hinges the entire controversy. When obstetrician-gynecologist Barnett Slepian was killed by a sniper in 1998, most initial news reports called him an "abortion doctor," rhetorically bolstering abortion opponents and ignoring the bulk of his medical practice.

Consider the strategy of language. The news media first called the Watergate break-in a "caper," a minimizing and rather frolicsome term that might have saved President Richard Nixon's job had the media not switched to a more momentous term, "scandal." Likewise, consider the strategic value of trying to minimize the controversy of the 2004 Super Bowl halftime show with talk of a mere "wardrobe malfunction."

Southern border states are dealing with problems associated with what some call "illegal immigrants," the same people who others call "undocumented workers." The latter term avoids the stigma of lawbreaking, which is precisely the issue for some people. So definitely consider the strategy of language, but consider, too, your potential role in what U.S. News and World Report columnist John Leo calls "compassionate incoherency." Check back to the previous chapter about "strategic ambiguity."

If rhetorical warfare is part of society's divisiveness, then rhetorical peacemaking can lead to more beneficial relationships when organizations and their publics engage in shared language, and the path of consensus building and conflict resolution is made smoother by sensitivity to the words used to communicate.

Product and Program Names. What we call things can greatly affect how others perceive them. **Product names** receive much attention in commercial enterprises. The California Prune Board went to court to gain permission to market prunes under the name "diced plums." Exxon changed the name of the tanker *Valdez* to *SeaRiver Mediterranean*. Meanwhile we find luxury automobiles with names such as Imperial, Coupe de Ville, and Continental, while sport utility vehicles are named Explorer, Blazer, and Pathfinder. If you aren't convinced of the power of names, try thinking up a promotional campaign for the all-wheel-drive Chevrolet Petunia, the luxury Ford Cockroach, the hybrid Toyota Slug or the sporty GM Aardvark. Perhaps one reason New Jersey–based Kiwi Airlines went bankrupt in 1996 was because it has the name of a bird that cannot fly.

The naming game can be a lucrative and mutually beneficial endeavor, with sports serving as the primary stage. From the Virginia Slims Legends Tour for professional women's tennis to the FedEx Orange Bowl, companies are spending millions of dollars to keep their names on the tongues of their publics. San Francisco's historic Candlestick Park became a pawn in the corporate naming game when it became 3COM Park and later Monster Park, but voters decided to return to the historic Candlestick name with the end of the Monster naming lease in 2008.

Even naming programs can become controversial. After John DuPont of the wealthy Philadelphia family was convicted of murdering an Olympic athlete and found to be mentally ill, Villanova University changed the name of its basketball arena, the DuPont Pavilion, to simply The Pavilion. And with the Enron crisis in 2002, the Houston Astros bought back the naming rights to Enron Field and rechristened it the following year as Minute Maid Field.

Program names in the nonprofit sector traditionally receive less attention than product names. Organizations sometimes attempt to devise memorable acronyms, though these often end up being somewhat less effective than hoped. In the same locality, the acronym CASA might stand for Central American Scientific Association, Clean Air Strategic Alliance, Council on Alcoholism and Substance Abuse, Christian Associates in South America, Catholic Appeal for Saint Anthony, Center for the Advancement of Saudi Arabia, and Coalition to Annex South Alexandria. A title like CASA might look nice on the letterhead, but it doesn't communicate much about an organization.

Be careful that the program name does not deliberately mislead people; serious ethical issues arise from names of front organizations or programs that fail to reflect their partisan or sectarian sponsors. **Front organizations** are set up to appear to operate independently, when in fact they are controlled by another organization that wants to remain anonymous in the relationship. The Cult Awareness Network, World Literacy Crusade, and Citizens Commission for Human Rights have been exposed as front organizations for the Church of Scientology. The Physicians Committee for Responsible Medicine, which advocates vegetarianism, has been accused of being a front group for People for the Ethical Treatment of Animals. John Kerry supporters labeled as a front group for the George W. Bush campaign the Swift Board Veterans for Truth that denigrated Kerry's military service in Vietnam. The controversy lead to a new political term, "swiftboating," referring to smear campaigns that question without evidence a candidate's patriotism and credibility.

Many front groups adopt misleading names. The oil-company-funded Global Climate Coalition opposes climate controls. The National Wetlands Coalition funded by utilities and industrial companies actually opposes government efforts to protect wetlands. The Greening Earth Society was created by coal companies to present a message that coal burning is good for the environment. And Farmers for Clean Air and Water was founded to lobby congress to exempt large agricultural corporations from environmental regulations. Meanwhile, a number of organizations have sprung up, purportedly over the issue of casino gaming, that adopt innocuous sounding names dealing with equity and fairness but act on a consistent anti–American Indian agenda.

Related to front organizations are **Astroturf organizations**, which pretend to be grassroots efforts when they are in fact established and funded by corporations—hence the name suggesting artificial grass. The grassroots-sounding Coalition for Responsible Healthcare Reform was created in 2007 by Blue Cross to fight the very thing that its name suggests.

Unfortunately, some Astroturf organizations have been created by public relations agencies to help their clients avoid the glare of publicity, a rather unethical approach for a profession that values honesty, openness, and transparency. One of the most notorious of these was Citizens for a Free Kuwait, created by the Hill & Knowlton public relations agency to promote the 1991 war in the Persian Gulf. Working Families for Wal-Mart is funded by—surprise!—Wal-Mart. It also is directed by the corporation's public relations agency, Edelman Public Relations. Another agency, Manning Selvage and Lee, created the Center for Medicine in the Public Interest that furthers the interests of its many pharmaceutical clients.

Strong quotes. The statements that people make, **quotes**, are an important aspect of verbal communication. Such quotes should be memorable and meaty. Public relations writers should use strong quotes in their news releases, news conference statements, and interviews and on other occasions for interacting with the media.

Here is an example of a reallly pithy quote. In 1998 Oliver Stone directed a television special that promoted the theory that TWA Flight 800, which had exploded two years earlier, killing all 230 passengers and crew, was downed by a missile. FBI investigators had specifically ruled out that possibility. Consider the passion in this response by James Kallstrom, who headed the FBI investigation: "The real facts are glossed over by the likes of Mr. Stone and others who spend their life bottom-feeding in those small, dark crevices of doubt and hypocrisy." Wow! That is so much better than a dreary bureaucratic statement such as "The FBI stands by its original report" or "We disagree with Mr. Stone's missile theory." This is a quote with attitude. It both sings and stings.

Another way to be memorable is to use colorful language. Consider the statement by attorney Johnny Cochran who, during O. J. Simpson's criminal trial, rhymed a key message meant not only for the jury but also for the viewing public: "If the glove doesn't fit, you must acquit." The sentence is still quoted, years after the trial.

A more formalized kind of quote is a **slogan**, the catchphrase in a communication program. This sometimes is called a **verbal logo** that complements an organization's graphic logo. Increasingly the term **tagline**, once associated mainly with marketing, is being used in reference to slogans used for public relations and other promotional purposes. Serving more or less as a battle cry, a tagline can be quite effective, especially during the awareness phase of a strategic communication campaign. But make sure the slogan is relevant. In 1995, Los Angeles County launched the tagline "Together, We're the Best. Los Angeles." But this begs the questions: Who is together? Best at what? On the other hand, state tourism slogans and taglines such as "Virginia is for Lovers" and "I ❤ New York" have been quite effective because they are both clear and open to having various interpretations laid upon them.

In recent years, corporations and nonprofit organizations have tried to brand themselves with memorable taglines, such as Greenpeace's "Take action for the climate," Nokia's "Connecting people," DeBeers's "A diamond is forever," and Barak Obama's "Yes we can."

Many effective taglines are associated with social movements or organizations. They service the purpose of what anthropologists call **symbolic consensus**, a rallying cry for supporters. Consider these taglines of longstanding use associated with social causes: "Guns don't kill people; people kill people." "Only you can prevent forest fires." "A mind is a terrible thing to waste."

The Seneca Nation of Indians developed a strong verbal logo amid an ongoing public controversy over state attempts to levy taxes on Indian lands. The Western New York–based tribe has a unique treaty with the federal government that business conducted in its territory is immune from state taxes. Using the slogan "Break a treaty, break the law," the campaign has been effective in forcing three successive New York governors to back away from plans to push for taxation.

Closely related to slogans and taglines are **service marks**, words and phrases that marketing and public relations people develop to be closely associated with organizations. Essentially, these are taglines that have been registered, much as trademarks are, and corporate lawyers go to great lengths to protect them.

Examples of service marks are the Army's "Be all you can be," Budweiser's "This Bud's for you" and Nike's "Just do it." Burger King is the only restaurant that can legally claim to be the "Home of the Whopper" and the *New York Times* is the only paper that can claim to have "All the news that's fit to print."

Ethical language. Using ethical language is a must for every public relations practitioner. In considering the verbal formulation of your message, pay attention to the implication of language. Certainly you will want to use language with pizzazz. Power words can lead audiences to perceive an image instantly and to take on an immediate mood—"beautiful people," "cutting edge," "right wing," "workaholic." But be careful with the stereotypes on which power words are built and make sure that reality underlies these images.

Pretentious language is words or phrases that imply more than is warranted. Avoid them, because they can mislead readers. Examples of pretentious language are "experienced vehicles" for used cars or "follically impaired" for bald. Such words can have a backlash if they are perceived as either silly or too crafty. Sometimes pretentious language raises confusing questions. For example, if pets are "companion animals," then should pet owners be called "human associates of companion animals"?

Doublespeak is outright dishonest language meant to obscure the real meaning behind the words. Don't use such language. Besides being unethical, it invites the obvious criticism that the organization is trying to hide the facts. Examples of doublespeak include military terms such as calling civilian wartime deaths "collateral damage" or genocide "ethnic cleansing" and business references to employee layoffs as "downsizing," "rightsizing," "employee repositioning," "workforce readjustment," or "retirement for personal reasons." Bureaucratic reports have called drunkenness a "nonsober condition" and suicide on a train track "pedestrian involvement."

Unfortunately, many examples of doublespeak are associated with governmental agencies and officials who, through such language, betray an appalling lack of commitment to the honest communication necessary in a democratic society. For example, the Secret Service under the administration of George W. Bush had local police set up "free speech zones" for protesters far removed from the visiting president or vice president—and the television cameras. Business and other organizational leaders, too, have demonstrated far too much creativity in concocting language that clouds, rather than illuminates, deceitful language that fails the transparency test.

The task for practitioners of strategic communication is to avoid dishonest language for themselves and to counsel their organizations and clients to avoid it as well, not only for ethical reasons but for the practical benefit that honest and clear language provides the best means to communicate effectively and thus to generate understanding and continuing support.

Legal language. Strategic communicators also are familiar with laws affecting their choice of language, and they respect both the letter and the spirit of such laws.

Defamation is a legal condition to be avoided at all costs. Defamatory language meets a fivefold test: It is (1) false information, (2) published or communicated to a third party, (3) that identifies a person (4) and holds that person up to public hatred, contempt, or ridicule, while (5) involving some measure of negligence and/or malice on the part of the communicator. **Defamation** is classified either as **libel**, which is written or broadcast defamation, or **slander**, which is spoken defamation.

A related area of problematic language is information that intrudes on someone's **privacy**, which is the legal right to be left alone.

These language indiscretions generally can be avoided if you pay attention to ethical principles, such as those found in the professional conduct codes of such organizations as the Public Relations Society of America and the Canadian Public Relations Society. Such codes call upon practitioners to adhere to high standards of accuracy, honesty, fairness, truth, and concern for the public interest. (See Appendix B: Ethical Standards.)

Nonverbal Communication

Nonverbal communication occurs through actions and cues other than words that carry meaning. Images and ambience create the most powerful and enduring aspects of communication. For example, when the words say "I'm happy to be here" but the facial expression shows boredom, we tend to believe our eyes. Likewise, corporate spokespersons who use facial or other body language associated with hedging and lying limit their effectiveness in gaining audience trust. Twenty-four-hour news and talk TV networks have begun hiring "body-language experts" to dissect nonverbal cues of politicians and other newsmakers.

Most communication relies not on mere words but on the images, symbols, setting, mood, music, clothing, and so on that carry messages. Here is an overview of some of the most common types of nonverbal communication.

Symbols. As visual representations of realities beyond themselves, **symbols** are among the most effective ways to communicate. Good symbols have a complex and rich psychological impact on people who see and use them. Baby harp seals and red AIDS ribbons have generated widespread public acceptance for the causes associated with them; armbands associated with the Holocaust or classic news photos of the Vietnam War and antiwar protests evoke emotions decades after those events; and personal keepsakes from weddings, proms, and special vacations summon up emotions over a lifetime.

Some of the most enduring symbols are rooted in religion (such as the crescent, cross, Star of David, and the Madonna figure) and country (for Americans, for example, the Capitol dome, the Statue of Liberty, and especially the flag). A nation's flag is more than a piece of cloth; to many people it is the symbol of family, country, patriotism, duty, and honor, which many have been willing both to die for or kill for. As such, it has the power to inspire both devotion and disrespect, and much energy has been spent in nations around the world on the issue of the appropriate role the national flag plays in both patriotism and social protest.

Meanwhile, in other countries, the national flag may symbolize less about reverence and patriotism and more about social cohesiveness and cultural exuberance.

Logos. Corporate **logos** are special kinds of symbols that visually identify businesses, nonprofit organizations and other groups. Contemporary or traditional? Elegant or casual? Much attention goes into the development of a corporate logo, which needs to present the right image and send the proper message. Consider the promotional value and enduring impact of the Nike "swoosh" or the Dodge star. For an organizational symbol to be effective, it must be both memorable and appropriate for the organization. It also must be unique to the organization, one reason that much legal energy is spent protecting registered trademarks.

Music. Music has a special symbolic value. Songs such as "Auld Lang Syne," "God Bless America," and "Pomp and Circumstance" have special meanings related to New Year's Eve, patriotic holidays, and graduation, respectively. The next time you go to the movies, pay attention to the power of the background music in setting the right mood for romance, happiness, impending doom, and so on.

Music also can stir negative passions. The singing of the national anthem at sporting events sometimes results in perceived disrespect by players or fans or disapproval of the musical style or behavior of the singers themselves. A small controversy was sparked by the Winter Classic (aka Ice Bowl) on New Year's Day in 2008 with the Pittsburgh Penguins at the Buffalo Sabers, the first regular-season outdoor game of the National Hockey League in the U.S. (and the highest-rated game in 12 years). Irish tenor/Sabres fan Ronan Tynan opened the game with "God Bless America" instead of the national anthem. Then the Sabre's regular anthem singer, Doug Allen, sang the Canadian national anthem, a song common at NHL matches in many Northern states in recognition of the Canadian connection of the many hockey players and fans. For days, critics complained about the appropriateness of the musical selections.

Passions were stirred in 1999 when Japan's parliament approved a law making the traditional "Kimigayo" the official national anthem. The vote over the imperial hymn, Japan's unofficial anthem since before World War II, revived bitter memories and renewed the controversy over nationalism and war guilt. Much of the debate centered on schools, particularly on how children should be educated about the war and on the role of national symbols such as the anthem and the flag in school ceremonies.

Language. In some contexts, language itself can be symbolic. Consider the cultural symbolism of Hebrew, Latin, Arabic, Hindi, and other languages associated with religious traditions, as well as the recurring English-as-official-language debate that appeals to populist feelings within American politics. Consider also how some of the "in" language used by groups of teenagers, for example, has a symbolism for its users that is neither appreciated nor understood—nor meant to be—by outsiders.

Physical artifacts. Symbolic value is sometimes attached to physical artifacts, such as the gavel used by a presiding judge or the badge worn by a police officer. Over the years, cigarettes have been variously presented as symbols of independence, youth, rebellion, ruggedness, and adventure. Automobiles are presented as symbolic mirrors of the people who drive them. And it was the symbolic power of the Pentagon and the World Trade Center as icons of America that led terrorists to target those buildings on 9/11.

Clothing. A particular type of physical artifact, clothing, often takes on symbolic proportions. This is why much attention often is paid to military uniforms, academic attire, religious vestments, ethnic apparel or royal garb, where each design element often has a special meaning. When President George W. Bush wore a Navy flight suit on an aircraft carrier to proclaim the end of the war in Iraq, his choice of clothing got a strong reaction—both pro and con.

Small controversies sometimes arise over the symbolism of clothing, particularly for women, such as the appropriate dress for nurses, Catholic nuns, or Muslim women. Attention is also given to less formal but nonetheless powerful symbols such as designer clothing or trendy brand-name eyeglasses. For persuasive purposes, a spokesperson might wear clothing related to a particular profession or occupation as a way of suggesting expertise.

People. Even people can function as symbols—especially royalty such as a king or queen, religious figures such as the Dalai Lama or the pope, and other important and well-known characters. As symbols, they stand as more than human beings; they represent the dignity and prestige of the office they hold. Media attention given to scandals involving princes, presidents, and prime ministers, however, has weakened the symbolic value of such figures.

Offense Given and Offense Taken

Here's a real-life example from one university. The school's theater department was performing *Hair*, the controversial and artistically significant 40-year-old musical. Directors generally face an early decision on whether to be authentic to the original production or update it for contemporary audiences. This production chose historical authenticity, complete with the famous nude scene.

In preshow publicity shots, cast members dressed in stage costumes. Two photos were used at the university's website to promote the upcoming play. Both photos included cast members in hippie dress, most of them imitating American Indians—fringe, beads, feathers, and loin cloths.

Native Americans on the faculty and the organization of Indian students objected to the depiction—not so much to the theatrical decision but rather to the posting of the photos on the Web. They found the depiction of American Indians degrading, presenting stereotypes no longer acceptable.

If you were editor of the university website, what would you do? Consider the various alternatives:

- Leave the story posting alone (because it was not meant to be offensive, or because you believe the audience was being overly sensitive).
- Pull the story.
- Change the photos to something inoffensive (the famous nude scene is not an option).
- Run the story without photos.
- Continue using the story and photos along with information about the protest, or with a commentary from those who felt offended.

At play here are issues of artistic freedom, editorial judgment, sensitivity to minority concerns, historical authenticity, and censorship. There is no single best response. But there are strategic approaches to help you make the best possible decision. Consider the various publics. Weigh the conflicting values. Assess the options.

From a communication perspective, it's important to remember that audiences will interpret information and images from their own perspective. Editors, journalists, public relations practitioners, and other media gatekeepers do not have the prerogative of telling audiences they should not be offended. In this situation, offense was not intended. But offense was given and offense was taken. How would you respond to such offense?

Mascots and promotional characters. Another kind of symbol is the mascot. From Smokey Bear to the San Diego Chicken, mascots embody much of the spirit of an organization. Meanwhile, many companies and organizations also use promotional characters such as Ronald McDonald, the U.S. Postal Service eagle, the Aflac duck, and the Geico gecko.

The symbolic significance of such fictional personifications can change. Betty Crocker and Aunt Jemima have gotten younger and more professional looking each decade as their company's customers have changed. Sports teams are under increasing pressure to retire their Native American mascots, which many people find offensive and archaic.

Colors. Colors also can be symbolic or emblematic—green for environmental issues, pink for Owens-Corning fiberglass insulation and so on. But the symbolic value of colors is socially defined. For example, the Western identification of white for happy occasions such as weddings and black for funerals is not universally shared, something that communicators in international or multicultural settings need to consider.

Setting. The setting or environment also has strong symbolic value, and much meaning can be created by putting a speaker in, say, a cemetery, laboratory, or library.

This concludes the Strategy phase of the planning process for public relations and marketing communication. Having completed these steps, which have built on those of the Formative Research phase, you now should have a clear sense of direction for your program. Before going any farther, present your planning thus far to the decision makers, such as your client or boss. Gain the buy-in from the key decision makers in your organization, who must agree with the direction you suggest, with the objectives and with the resulting strategy recommendations.

In the next phase of planning, you will turn your attention to preparing and implementing specific communication tools to carry the strategic message you have just devised.

Step 6

Planning Example 6C: Verbal and Nonverbal Communication

UPSTATE COLLEGE

Here is an outline of the verbal and nonverbal communication strategies for Upstate College.

Verbal Communication

- One point of view will be presented: Expansion is beneficial for students, the community, and the college.
- A conclusion will be drawn: students should consider Upstate College.
- Message clarity will be enhanced by a Fog Index level of 10th grade.
- Messages will include power words such as "benefit to community" and "quality education."
- Messages will avoid any exaggeration.
- Messages will rely on facts and documentation rather than empty claims.

Nonverbal Communication

- The college logo will be featured in messages.
- Upbeat music popular with teens and young adults will be featured in messages.

- The college mascot, salamander "Upstate Eddie," will be featured.

■ ■ ■

Here is an outline of the verbal and nonverbal communication strategies for Tiny Tykes Toys.

TINY TYKES TOYS

Verbal Communication

- Opposing points of view will be included in messages: Tiny Tykes is committed to toy safety; the company had a problem in the past but has learned from mistakes and now is recommitted to toy safety.
- A conclusion will be drawn: The company now makes high-quality, safe toys and deserves consumer support.
- Message clarity will be enhanced by a Fog Index level of ninth grade.
- Messages will include power words such as "commitment to excellence" and "baby safe."
- Messages will avoid any exaggeration.
- Messages will rely on facts and documentation rather than empty claims.

Nonverbal Communication

- Messages will be enhanced by happy music.
- Corporate spokespersons will be shown wearing research and professional clothing, reinforcing the message of research and high standards.
- Clinical settings will be used for presentations by corporate spokespersons, reinforcing the message of research and high standards.

Checklist 6C: Verbal and Nonverbal Communication

Basic Questions

1. How does your message use verbal communication?
2. How does your message use nonverbal communication?
3. How can either be made stronger?

Expanded Questions

A. VERBAL COMMUNICATION

Message Structure

1. Does your message present only one point of view or more than one (opposing) point of view? If more than one point of view is presented, is your message sandwiched (stating your argument, noting the opposing argument, and finally restating your argument and refuting the opposing argument)?

2. Does your message present a conclusion?
3. Does your message reiterate its main idea?

Clarity

1. Will your publics find your message clear, simple, and understandable?
2. What is the education level of your target public?
3. How does this compare with the Fog Index for your written message?

Power Words

1. Have you used powerful language in your message?
2. Does your product/program have a descriptive and memorable name?
3. Does your product/program have a descriptive and memorable slogan?

Ethical Language

1. Does your message use pretentious or exaggerated language?
2. Does your message use dishonest or misleading language?
3. Does your message use defamatory language?
4. How could any of these verbal elements be made stronger?

B. NONVERBAL COMMUNICATION

1. Does the presentation of your message include a symbol, a logo, music, symbolic language, symbolic physical artifacts, symbolic clothing, symbolic people, a mascot, symbolic use of color and/or a symbolic setting?
2. How could any of these nonverbal elements be made stronger?

Consensus Check

Does agreement exist within your organization about the recommended strategies for effective communication included within this step of the planning process? If "yes," proceed to Step 7, Selecting Communication Tactics. If "no," consider the value and/or possibility of achieving consensus before proceeding.

Branding the Strategic Message

A concept drawn from marketing that should be part of strategic communication planning is **branding**, which is the creation of a clear and consistent message for an organization. A brand is the articulation of an organization's purpose and the way it is presented to customers, employees, and other publics. If one traditional description of public relations is valid—that public relations is doing good and receiving credit for it—then it can be said that branding is seeing that the truth is well told.

Branding has been associated with advertising because of its marketing base. But it is more than a logo or a look, though these are important. Nonetheless, their importance lies in their ability to convey a message and to associate the corporate name with a favorable concept in the mind of the consumer or other public.

Branding belongs more in the realm of public relations, because it is rooted so much in an organization's strategic communication plan, a messaging strategy to express its purpose and character so that audiences will understand it and differentiate it from other organizations. The goal of branding is to foster understanding and goodwill and to encourage participation and support. Presentation is important, but message content is more important. Strong brands come from what people say about you, not on what you say about yourself, and that's the difference between public relations and advertising.

Corporations have used the concept of branding for years. Nonprofit organizations and other non-business entities are finding that the concept has value for them as well. It fits particularly well with such organizations, for whom the creation of an emotional perception is a natural thing to do. There are many ways in which branding fits smoothly with groups focused on educating young people, promoting safety, finding cures, celebrating the arts, or addressing human needs.

Because it evolved in the corporate world, economic competition sometimes has taken the form of warfare. A car dealership has "the greatest deals in town," this toothpaste cleans "better than all the rest." There are good guys and bad; heroes and villains; us and them, the enemy.

It might be unseemly for a university to proclaim itself the best in the state, or for a hospital to slam the competition. Nevertheless, nonprofit organizations can work with this concept. The enemy probably won't be another organization, but it might easily be an intangible foe. The American Heart Association declares war on obesity, the Anti-Defamation League of B'Nai Brith sees religious bigotry as the enemy, People for the Ethical Treatment of Animals (PETA) demonizes furriers and elements of the fashion industry. Even wholesome organizations and uplifting causes have foes to address.

Consider some of the ideas presented by the National Mentoring Center and the U.S. Department of Education as part of a marketing panel for a program seeking male mentors for inner-city children.

- "We're looking for a few good MENtors."
- "Mentor one child. Change two lives."
- "See a man. Become a man."
- "Been there? Done that? Pass it on. Become a mentor."

In addition to the message strategy, branding also has a practical component. Logo, color, type font, and other elements of the visual look of the organization's name and branded tagline are important. Consult artists and designers, and give careful thought to the visual design that offers the best possibility for versatile and long-term use.

Lessons About Branding

Good branding can help your organization (1) by defining and differentiating you in the minds of your publics (particularly customers) and (2) by providing a structure to convey a consistent message.

Consider some of the branding strategies associated with businesses. Volvo brands itself as the car for safety. Maytag presents a message of dependability. Starbucks takes premium coffee as a given and brands itself as for community-mindedness. Holiday Inn boasts about "Pleasing people the world over" and Timex highlights durability with its slogan "Takes a licking and keeps on ticking." DeBeers' advertising line appeals to the sentiment of couples who see their relationship as permanent: "A diamond is forever."

Successful branding efforts have given rise to some lessons for public relations planners and writers. In particular, much attention has been given to the development of effective taglines or slogans. A **tagline** is a succinct phrase that, associated with the organization's logo, presents a comprehensive message that identifies the organization and seeks to position it in the minds of consumers and other publics. Because of this intended impact, some have given taglines the status of verbal logos.

The entertainment media use taglines aimed at potential audiences. Thus the film *Alien* promoted its sci-fi horror genre ("In space, no one can hear you scream"), the movie sequel *Jaws II* drew on earlier success with the slogan "Just when you thought it was safe to go back in the water," and the *X-Files* TV series built on its UFO/conspiracy theme ("The truth is out there"). Fox News wants viewers to see it as "fair and balanced" even though many media analysts see it as neither.

ESPN opted for a serial tagline with a humorous twist for the sports network: "Without sports, weekends would be weekdays." "Without sports, what would bring a family together?" "Without sports, would you know how to spell J-E-T-S?"

Nonprofits also use branding successfully. The University of Texas at Austin uses the tagline "What starts here changes the world." The March of Dimes reminds supporters that they are "Saving babies, together." The Sierra Club enjoins people to "Explore, enjoy and protect the planet." Catholic Charities focuses on "Providing help. Creating hope." Camp Fire USA touts "Today's kids. Tomorrow's leaders." Meanwhile, "Only kids. Only Phoenix Children's Hospital" is a tagline for the only hospital in Arizona focused on children.

Here are a few suggestions about taglines:

1. Don't mistake a tagline for a proverb or a maxim, and don't think it's merely a mission statement, though that may suggest key phrases that can be developed into a branding message.
2. Make the tagline memorable. Cadence, rhythm, and rhyme can enhance this.
3. Keep the tagline short and succinct. Some suggest that seven or eight words should be the maximum.
4. Look at the organizational goals, and allow the tagline to energize them, as in the Salvation Army's "Doing the most good."
5. Use a branding tagline to highlight your unique situation and to distinguish you from competitors and colleagues alike, as in Altoids' "Curiously strong peppermints."
6. Focus on a benefit, as in the American Society for the Prevention of Cruelty to Animals' "We are their voice."
7. Focus on a potential, as in St. Jude's Children's Hospital's "Finding cures. Saving children."
8. Offer a challenge, as in "The few. The proud. The Marines" and "The Marines are looking for a few good men" (a slogan first used in a U.S. Navy recruiting ad in 1779).
9. Draw on a positive association with your product or service, as in Hershey chocolates' website, "The sweetest site on the net."

10. Address the wants and needs of your audience, as in "Wheaties, the Breakfast of Champions."
11. Turn a disadvantage into an opportunity, as in No. 2 car rental company Avis's "We try harder."
12. Look for the inspiration, as in United Negro College Fund's "A mind is a terrible thing to waste."
13. Go with a pun. The public radio station at Morehouse State College in Atlanta turned the tables with a health program called "A Waist Is a Terrible Thing to Mind."
14. Focus on a characteristics or quality, as in Chevy trucks' "Like a rock."
15. Focus on an attitude, as in Nike's "Just do it."

Note that, from a legal perspective, taglines are service marks, which enjoy protection similar to trademarks.

Creating Creativity

So how do people come up with ideas for branding messages? The process isn't magical; it doesn't require genius, and it isn't necessarily rooted in lightning-bolt inspiration. An easy-to-apply group-creativity technique called **brainstorming** is a useful tool in this part of the strategic planning process. Brainstorming is associated with the effective creativity addressed in the introduction to this book.

The first step in brainstorming is **divergence**, in which the group surfaces a large number of ideas on how to solve a problem or answer a question. Here's how it can work. Assemble a small team of people to consider questions such as the following:

1. What do we want people to remember about our organization? Pepsi wants you to make "The choice of a new generation."
2. What do we want them to do? The Yellow Pages people distilled this question into "Let your fingers do the walking."
3. What feeling do we want to evoke, or what attitude do we want to bring to mind? United Cerebral Palsy suggests "Life without limits for people with disabilities."
4. What is our niche, or how are we different or unique? M&Ms candies set themselves apart from other candy with "Melts in your mouth, not in your hands."

Do you have any artifacts associated with your organization? These might be personal items such as clothing and grooming, or cultural elements such as music, art, and architecture. Disney draws on images of its theme parks with the slogan "The happiest place on earth."

Here are a few rules for effective brainstorming: Write down every idea. Don't edit yourself. Put criticism on hold, because nothing is too "far out" at this point. Work with your colleagues on the brainstorming team, tossing around ideas and building on each others' contributions. The idea is to get as many different ideas on the table. Consider each one, and see how many variations you can come up with.

Next comes the **convergence** part, as you pare the list, selecting those few that are worth further consideration. With all of the ideas on the table, consider each one. It's best to have each member of the team rank each idea individually. Then compare results and hold on to those that seem most useful to the group. At this point, you might want to get the input from others beyond the brainstorming team. Take the top three or four ideas to a wider group, perhaps a formal focus group.

Phase Three

TACTICS

If the strategy phase of the planning process provided the skeleton and muscles for your communication programming, then Phase Three is the flesh. This section deals specifically with communication tactics, which are the things we see—the visible elements of a public relations or marketing communication plan.

Step 7
Selecting Communication Tactics

Step 8
Implementing the Strategic Plan

In the introduction to this book you encountered the concept of integrated communication, the conscious blending of the instruments of both public relations and marketing communication. Integrated communication creates a comprehensive and cohesive program aimed at implementing the best possible mix of communication tools. It is here in Phase Three that this integrated approach will become most visible, as you consider the various communication tools that can be used to achieve your objectives. The menu of tactics outlined in this phase feature communication tools drawn from the full range of disciplines and specialties. For example, you consider interpersonal communication opportunities that involve speeches and special events, and organizational media such as newsletters and websites. Also on the menu is a full plate of tactics involving the journalistic side of the news media, as well as tactics associated with advertising and promotion appropriate for issues and situations associated with strategic communication.

The activities in Phase Three will also lead you to select an effective mix of tactics, packaging your creative and strategic ideas into a comprehensive program. To accomplish this, you need to tap into your creative side. Your goal here is to boost your plan well above the level of a mere laundry list of tactics. Instead you attempt to create a compelling and resourceful action plan that can help your client organization achieve its goals and objectives.

You also will deal with the administrative details of budgeting and scheduling that are so important for the smooth implementation of your plan. This tactics phase calls for the twin skills of creativity and attention to detail. All aspects of implementation involve many components, and the person who can manage simultaneous tasks skillfully should find success in the field of strategic communication.

The need for micromanagement might seem overwhelming, but by remaining focused on your plan you will avoid unnecessary side trips that sap your time and resources without advancing you toward your goal.

At the same time, effective tactics call for a measure of creativity and innovation—that certain spark that separates the ordinary from the unusual, replacing the commonplace with the memorable or exceptional.

Step 7

Selecting Communication Tactics

Communication tactics are the visible elements of a strategic plan. They are what people see and do—websites and news releases, tours and billboards, blogs and special events, and so much more. Tactics are also the elements of the plan that can carry a hefty price tag, so planning and coordination are particularly important. The range of communication tactics is extensive, and it is continually growing because of technological advances. Step 7 offers you a convenient menu of the various tactics. These tactics should be considered in light of your goals and objectives, evaluated in relationship to each other, matched to the taste of the organization and the publics, and chosen with an eye toward time and budget constraints. At a restaurant, you wouldn't order every item on the menu. Likewise, don't try every tactic you can think of. Instead, review this menu of public relations tactics carefully, then select a full plate of items appropriate to the situation you are addressing.

Before we review the menu, let's look at some of the conventional categories of communication tactics, along with a description of the distinctions this book uses.

Conventional Communication Tactics

Media and media tactics are often divided into categories based on distinguishing features. Here are several frequently used pairs that describe types of media: controlled versus uncontrolled, internal versus external, mass versus targeted, popular versus trade, public versus nonpublic, and print versus electronic. Each categorization can be useful, but as we will see, these conventional communication categories have some limitations as well.

One category of media is based on the organization's ability to control the content of its messages. **Controlled media** allow the organization to determine various attributes of the message—most notably its content, but also its timing, presentation, packaging, tone, and distribution. Examples of controlled media are newsletters, brochures, corporate videos, and websites. Conversely, **uncontrolled media** are those in which someone unrelated to the organization, such as a media gatekeeper, determines those message attributes. Examples of uncontrolled media tactics include news conferences and interviews.

Another category of media describes the relationship of the media to the organization. **Internal media** exist within the organization and thus parallel the previous definition of controlled media. **External media**, which exist outside the organization, may be controlled (such as advertising media) or uncontrolled (such as news media). Specific examples include billboards, newspapers, and television news broadcasts.

Still another category is defined by the size and breadth of the intended audience. **Mass media** are those that are accessible to most people; thus they are media that enjoy vast audiences, such as television networks and the mainstream daily newspaper establishment. On the other hand, **targeted media** have not only much narrower but also more homogeneous audiences. Examples of targeted media are special-interest publications (such as a magazine for people who live aboard sailboats) and broadcast programs that appeal to a particular narrow audience (such as a program on retirement finances).

Media also can be categorized by audience type. **Popular media** focus on information of interest to people in their personal lives, including fashion, grooming, relationships, hobbies, and self-help, as well as news and current events. These are the publications found at the supermarket or the bookstore. Examples of popular media include *Maxim*, *USA Today*, and top-of-the-hour radio news broadcasts. **Trade media**, on the other hand, generally are distributed via subscription and are read for professional or business purposes. They are a main focus for many public relations writers. Examples of trade media include *Auto Glass Journal* and *Wine Business Monthly*.

Another categorization defined by the audience, mainly in terms of availability and access, is public versus nonpublic media. **Public media** generally are accessible to everybody. Examples of public media are local newspapers and both commercial and public radio and television stations. **Nonpublic media** are more restricted in their coverage and their availability. They often choose to limit access and circulation to audiences drawn from specific occupations, professions, or associations. Examples of nonpublic media are company newsletters, e-mail newsgroups, and magazines and other trade publications that circulate mainly to members of a particular industry or profession.

A final categorization of media is based on the technical production methods of the medium. **Print media** are those that involve the printed word, such as newsletters, newspapers, and magazines. **Electronic media** are based on newer technologies. Examples of electronic media include television (both broadcast and cable), radio, and computer-based media such as e-mail and websites.

Strategic Communication Tactics

Don't look for any single categorization style to suit every purpose. For one thing, there is a significant amount of overlap in the conventional category systems. For another, no single classification is necessarily superior to the others. Rather, use these various categories to help you analyze the pros and cons of each communication tool you might consider as you put together your tactical plan.

Strategic Planning for Public Relations looks at the various media and communication tactics in their complexity. In doing so, this book tries to avoid oversimplification, so you won't find media grouped according to any of the conventional categories described in the section above. This is not a rejection of the conventional approach but rather an attempt to go beyond the inherent limitations.

A better way to categorize communication media and tactics is to consider their distinctiveness as they relate to the organization using them. Thus, this book presents a menu of communication tactics in four categories.

- **Interpersonal communication** offers face-to-face opportunities for personal involvement and interaction.

- **Organizational media** are published or produced by the organization, which controls the message content as well as its timing, packaging, distribution, and audience access.
- **News media** provide opportunities for the credible presentation of organizational messages to large audiences.
- **Advertising and promotional media** are controlled media, either internal or external to the organization, that also can offer access to large audiences.

Together, these four categories offer hundreds of different communication tactics. Each can be used by organizations to communicate with their publics, though not every tool is appropriate for each issue. Remember to be selective in choosing your communication tools.

These four categories of communication tactics complement each other. In Exhibit 7.1, notice how they fit within a reversed pyramid pattern that reflects the relationship between the size of the audience that each type of media can reach and the impact it can have on that audience. Interpersonal tactics may reach only a few people, but they have a stronger impact on their audiences than any other form of communication. The reverse is true of advertising and promotional media: They can reach people in great numbers, but with less impact. Don't forget that impact often is the bottom line for a strategic communication program, whether it uses the persuasion or the dialogue model of communication.

With insight into the strengths and limitations of various kinds of media, communication planners try to create a tactical mix, using several types of communication activities to engage key publics in different ways that, blended together, will effectively achieve the organization's public relations or marketing objectives.

Technological advancements are offering even more tools for communicators, but the new technology isn't squeezing out the old. In a study of 480 marketing and communication executives (Corder, Deasy, & Thompson, 1999a), Ketchum Public Relations (http://www.ketchum.com) found that the use of Internet home pages is on the rise. Eighty-eight percent

Exhibit 7.1 The Relationship between Audience Reach and Persuasive Impact

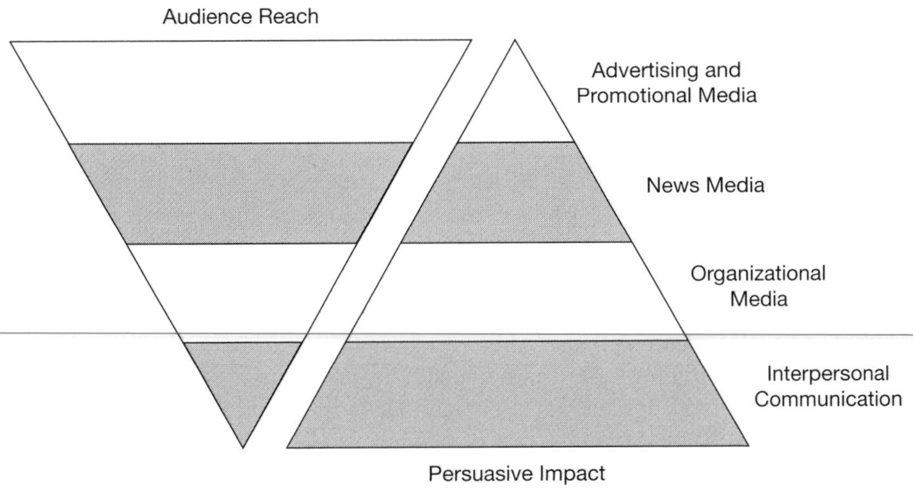

of respondents reported having a home page, compared with 65% a year earlier. More significantly, 84% expected to increase their Internet activities within the next three to five years. Meanwhile, 95% reported using news releases, and 40% of those expected to increase use of this tactic. Likewise, trade shows and special events were expected to be up 25%, direct mail up 48%, and brochures up 31%. Clearly the traditional tools are going to be around for a long time, even as new media are added to the mix. Let's look first at interpersonal communication tactics.

Interpersonal Communication Techniques

In the disciplines of public relations and marketing communication, both the academic experts who are proficient in concepts and theories and the professional experts with applied training and practical experience agree on a crucial point: Interpersonal communication is the most persuasive and engaging of all the communication tactics. Don't think this statement demeans other forms of communication. To the contrary, newspaper and television news reports can extend an organization's message to vast audiences.

Direct mail can be a cost-effective way to reach great numbers of the key public. Advertising can present messages to large numbers of people with great precision. But in terms of influential communication, the effectiveness of other types of communication pales beside the vigor of direct, face-to-face, interpersonal communication. Interpersonal communication channels can serve the needs of both businesses and nonprofit organizations. In your consideration of the various tools of communication, then, interpersonal methods should get your first attention. Let's consider the strategy of using interpersonal tactics and then we'll look at the various types of face-to-face communication that can be used for public relations purposes: personal involvement, information exchange, and special events.

Strategy for Interpersonal Communication

Interpersonal communication tactics offer several strategic advantages to organizations. For one thing, they are controlled tactics through which the organization can oversee its message and the way that message is delivered. Remember, however, that audience response to the message can't be controlled.

Like all public relations tactics, interpersonal ones can be misused if they are applied too generally. But with careful planning, they can be tailored for specific publics, both internal and external.

In terms of organizational resources, interpersonal tactics generally are inexpensive or cost only a moderate amount, though some types of special events can become quite expensive projects if the budget permits. Interpersonal tactics as a group will claim more staff time to plan and implement than some of the other categories of tactics that we will consider.

Interpersonal tactics can work with either internal or external publics, but the organization should have some relationship with the publics for these tactics to be successful. Interpersonal tactics have the potential to make a strong impact. They are particularly useful in achieving acceptance objectives, which is the most difficult category of objective to reach. Through interpersonal tactics, the organization can communicate with its publics in ways that can have a major effect not only on what they know but especially on how they feel about that

Interpersonal Communication Tactics

Personal Involvement

- Organizational site involvement (plant tour, open house, test drive, trial membership, free class, shadow program, ride along, sneak preview, premiere performance)
- Audience site involvement (door-to-door canvassing, in-home demonstration)

Information Exchange

- Educational gathering (convention, council, convocation, synod, conclave, conference, seminar, symposium, colloquium, class, workshop, training session)
- Product exhibition (trade show)
- Meeting (annual stockholder meeting, lobbying exchange, public affairs meeting)
- Demonstration (rally, march, picket, boycott)
- Speech (oration, talk, guest lecture, address, keynote speech, sermon, homily, panel, debate, forum, town meeting, speaker's bureau)

Special Events

- Civic event (fair, festival, carnival, circus, parade, flotilla)
- Sporting event (tournament, marathon, triathlon, outdoor spectator event, track meet, field days, rodeo, games, match, meet)
- Contest (science fair, spelling bee, beauty pageant, talent contest, dance-a-thon)
- Holiday event
- Progress-oriented event (launching, procession, motorcade, ground-breaking ceremony, cornerstone ceremony, dedication, ribbon-cutting, tour, grand opening)
- Historic commemoration (founders' days, anniversary, centennial, play, pageant, caravan)
- Social event (luncheon, banquet, roast, awards dinner, recognition lunch, party, dance, fashion show, tea)
- Artistic event (concert, concert tour, recital, play, film festival, arts show, photo exhibit)
- Fund-raising event (antique show, auction, haunted house, pony ride, murder mystery dinner theater, fashion show, house or garden tour, tasting party)

information. Thus interpersonal tactics are useful for both the persuasion and dialogue models of communication.

Similarly, interpersonal tactics generally involve **information-seeking publics**—people who have gone somewhat out of their way to interact with the organization. These people presumably are already interested in the issue, perhaps have some knowledge of the relevant facts and are at least open to (perhaps even leaning toward) the organization's message.

The downside? Interpersonal tactics reach only a small number of people, compared to tactics in other categories. So if numbers are important, these tactics won't be heavy producers.

Like all the categories of tactics presented in this book, interpersonal ones should never be considered in isolation from those in other categories. These are the first ones to consider precisely because they can make such an impact, but they are not necessarily the first ones that will be used in your general order of tactics.

Let's look at three different types of interpersonal communication tactics: personal involvement, information exchange, and special events.

Personal Involvement

Personal involvement is a powerful element of communication, whether for purposes of information, education, persuasion, or dialogue. When the organization actively involves its publics and creates an environment rooted in two-way communication, the mutual interests of both the organization and its publics are likely to be addressed. This category of tactics includes organizational-site involvement and audience-site involvement.

Organizational-site involvement. A growing number of audience-involvement activities are bringing members of the audience to the organization, as more and more organizations realize the importance of public interaction. "Keep out" signs are being replaced by welcome mats. Examples of this type of audience interaction include plant tours and open houses. For example, Hershey Foods Corporation sponsors Chocolate World, a free plant tour that feels like a theme park. Such tactics offer for-profit and nonprofit organizations alike an opportunity to "show off" for the various publics of the organization: employees and volunteers, both current and prospective; current and would be customers; investors, donors, and other funding sources; community or governmental supporters.

Some interpersonal tactics involve more hands-on activities. Auto dealers, for example, routinely give test drives. Fitness clubs, dance studios, and other activity centers may offer trial memberships to allow potential members to personally experience the facility and its atmosphere. Educational activities such as martial-arts programs and cooking schools may offer a limited number of free classes to give potential recruits a sample of their offerings.

Private schools have shadow programs in which potential students are invited to spend a day accompanying a current student on the daily round of classes. Police, fire, and emergency crews offer ride-alongs so local residents can see firsthand how various situations are handled. Sneak previews and premiere performances of movies and plays also are effective in generating future audiences.

Audience-site involvement. Instead of inviting the public in, sometimes the organization goes to its publics, a real convenience for the audience. For example, door-to-door canvassing offers an opportunity for organizations with a political, social, or religious cause to take their message or charitable solicitation directly to people who might be interested. Petition drives seek to get signatures of voters and other constituents. Meanwhile, in-home demonstrations can help people to see how various products or services will work and personally evaluate their effectiveness.

Information Exchange

Another significant category of interpersonal communication tactics, **information exchange**, centers on opportunities for organizations and their publics to meet face to face and thus to exchange information, ask questions, and clarify understandings. This category includes educational gatherings, product exhibitions, meetings, demonstrations, and speeches.

Educational gatherings. Various types of meetings provide an opportunity for both commercial and nonprofit organizations to educate large numbers of information-seeking people.

Be aware that the following terms sometimes may be used somewhat interchangeably. But here is a definition of the difference among the various types of educational gatherings. Conventions are gatherings that generally involve the transaction of organizational business such as the election of officers; many conventions also have a component of education or professional development. Likewise, councils are meetings with a policy-setting agenda. Convocations, synods, and conclaves are formal conventions, often with a religious or academic purpose. Conferences are similar to conventions, though the former term transfers the focus away from organizational business and toward professional development and education.

Seminars are educational meetings, often ones that bring together peers who discuss issues among themselves. Symposiums also are educational meetings in which specialists deliver short papers, whereas colloquiums are educational meetings in which specialists deliver formal addresses and then conduct a public discussion of the topic. Workshops and training sessions have a more practical, applied focus, often with an interactive presentation style.

Product exhibitions. Companies often seek opportunities to display their products to sales people and potential customers. The special feature of these trade shows is that they bring together information-seeking publics—often people who attend trade shows specifically to find out about new products—as well as companies and their competitors. Because competitors are displaying their wares at the same show, each company is challenged to provide a bigger and better presentation than others with a similar product line. For this reason, trade shows generally feature elaborate displays and state-of-the-art interactive technology, often with colorful and attention-getting entertainment and refreshments.

Trade shows often are held as part of conferences and conventions that bring together potential customers. Indeed one of the reasons people attend conferences is to view the latest products associated with their industry or profession. When the National Rifle Association scaled down its annual convention in Denver just days following the massacre at Columbine High School in suburban Littleton, the absence of the usual trade show featuring the latest in weapons disappointed many conventioneers.

Meetings. Meetings provide an excellent opportunity for organizations to set up positive information interchanges with their publics. Some of these settings are formal occasions. For example, annual stockholder meetings are required of companies that issue stock. While many such meetings are pretty dull, a growing number of companies are turning the required annual event into a sort of internal trade show with elaborate luncheons and colorful displays about the company's current and future products as well as its financial success.

Often meetings are businesslike occasions that involve only a limited number of participants. Lobbying exchanges and public affairs meetings, for example, may involve just one or two representatives of an organization and a few staff members to an elected official.

Rallies. Some activities focus on advocacy or opposition. Rallies and other types of public demonstrations can bring together hundreds—even thousands—of people in support of a particular cause, often with speakers. Similarly, marches are public processions, often for the purpose of making a political or social statement. Consider, for example, the numerous rallies for social or political causes that are staged in Washington, D.C., or in state capitals.

Other public gatherings may be confrontational or negative in nature. Demonstrations, for example, with an element of protest, are opportunities for information exchange, often through speakers as well as by the distribution of printed literature.

Pickets are demonstrations against an organization. Often they involve an element of disruption, such as encouraging or trying to prevent people from doing business with the organization. Usually they include vocal and visual messages criticizing the organization.

Boycotts, meanwhile, are public protests, sometimes accompanied by picketing, in which customers refrain from using the products or services of the organization being opposed, often accompanied by public education endeavors.

All of these types of rallies and demonstrations also tend to generate news coverage, which we discuss later. Additionally, they can galvanize existing support.

Speeches. Speeches are public discourses in which the speaker controls the presentation and intends to impact the awareness, acceptance or action of an audience. As such, speeches are excellent vehicles for face-to-face communication, especially when question-and-answer sessions are part of the speech presentation.

Consider the different varieties of speeches. Orations are very formal and dignified presentations with a high and eloquent rhetorical style. Talks, on the other hand, are informal, off-the-cuff speeches, usually on a professional subject. Lectures are carefully prepared speeches associated with classrooms and the presentation of academic information; guest lectures are often more practical educational presentations given by an expert in a particular area. Addresses are formal speeches that require significant preparation, and keynote speeches are major addresses at conferences and other meetings. Two kinds of speeches are associated with the field of religion: sermons, which are moral exhortations, based on religious teaching, and homilies, which are explanations of the practical application of a scriptural passage.

In some speechlike situations, the speaker gives up much of the control of the communication.

Consider, for example, panels, in which a moderator guides the discussion of several speakers. Panels often involve a short, formal opening statement followed by questions offered by the moderator or by other panelists. Debates are formal, adversarial speaking occasions in which one side (an individual or a team) argues with an opponent using a set of formal rules. Forums and town meetings are speeches with questions and generally lively discussion, usually on topics of civic or public interest. Speaker's bureaus are programs within organizations to promote the availability of knowledgeable and trained employees or volunteers to give presentations, usually free, to organizations within the community on topics related to the organization's interests. For example, a fuel-gas company may make speakers available to community associations, tenants groups, and homeowners clubs, as well as to business and professional organizations that often have the ear of various opinion leaders. Topics for such a company might include energy saving, high-efficiency heating and cooling equipment, and energy tax matters.

Special Events

The most common category of interpersonal communication tactics is **special events**, activities that are created by an organization mainly to provide a venue to interact with members of its publics. The list of special events is bounded only by the imagination of the planners, but some of the more common types of special events are civic events, sporting events, contests, holiday events, progress-oriented events, historic commemorations, social events, artistic events, and fundraising events.

Civic events. Public activities can bring a community together in celebration and fun. Some of the popular civic activities are fairs, which feature food and entertainment, and festivals, which sometimes offer games and are often organized around a theme, such as ethnic heritage, flowers, or music. Carnivals with an atmosphere of public merriment and circuses with performing animals can also be important civic events.

Parades on land and flotillas on water are other forms of popular civic celebration, as are themed events, such as those associated with community history.

Sporting events. Many special events are created around a sports theme. Tournaments are often held for such activities as skiing, fishing, and golf that have several levels of difficulty and thus can attract a wide range of participants. Marathons are races of all sorts, and triathlons that typically combine running, cycling, and swimming are events that are increasingly popular athletic events. Also popular are outdoor spectator events, such as rodeos, lumberjack roundups, and Highland games. Other athletic activities, such as track meets and field days, provide opportunities to turn sporting events into larger community activities. Many sporting events are designed both for participant interaction and as spectator activities.

Contests. Competitive engagements offer another type of special event, allowing participants to display their knowledge, skills, or other assets. By their nature, contests create winners, and this also leads to increased visibility because of the built-in news value. Science fairs, spelling bees, and other types of academically oriented contests are popular, as are those that mimic various television quiz shows or reality shows. These and similar events, such as beauty pageants and talent contests, can attract wide audiences of both participants and spectators.

Often grand openings and similar events feature purely fun contests—for pizza tossing, pie eating, dancing, and the like—in which every participant is a winner.

Holiday events. Some special events are based on popular and widespread observances. Many of these are civic celebrations, such as Memorial Day, Independence Day, Labor Day, and Thanksgiving. Some holiday activities are rooted within a particular cultural group, such as the Kwanzaa and Juneteenth celebrations in the African American community, or Chinese New Year. Some of the most popular holidays, such as Hanukkah and Easter, have religious roots; others are hybrids of popular religion and cultural celebrations, such as St. Patrick's Day, observed by the Irish and Irish-at-heart, or the pre-Lenten Mardi Gras and Carnival festivities. Be careful not to give offense by trivializing an event that some of your publics consider sacred in nature.

Holidays sometimes become occasions for social comment and action, such as American Indian protests around Columbus Day activities, highlighting the devastating effects of European contact.

Progress-oriented events. Several different kinds of events celebrate the growth and development of an organization or community. Ships and boats traditionally are launched by smashing a champagne bottle on the ship's bow, or now by the more environmentally friendly pouring of champagne over the bow. Progress-oriented events often are marked by musical entertainment, fireworks and other celebratory activities.

When a school or religious congregation moves into a new building nearby, the transition often is marked by a procession from the old building to the new. For example, students might carry symbols such as textbooks, globes, and other artifacts of school life to the new school site. Similarly, a motorcade might be arranged to inaugurate the opening of a new bridge.

A single project might lend itself to a series of progress-oriented special events. Consider, for example, the building of a new community center. You might schedule a groundbreaking ceremony for the turning of the first shovelful of dirt, a cornerstone ceremony when construction begins, and a dedication ceremony including a ribbon cutting to mark the completion of the center, and then follow these with tours and grand opening events.

Historic commemorations. The history of an organization or community provides the background for another kind of special event. Towns observe founders' days; companies mark the anniversary of their incorporation. Sometimes historic events are observed by re-creating the sights and sounds of an earlier era, such as a centennial celebration that features costumes, buggies, or antique cars, and music and food of the bygone era.

Some historic commemorations include plays, dramatic reenactments of historical events, and pageants, and historical plays with a certain amount of music and pomp. Additionally, caravans reenact historic travels.

Social events. Social events comprise a major type of special event. Luncheons and dinners are events sponsored by all kinds of organizations. These social events involve entertainment activities. Receptions with beverages and hors d'oeuvres or snacks are a similar kind of event. Among the various special types of ceremonial meals are tributes that honor people or organizations and banquets that offer more sumptuous menus and entertainment. Roasts use sarcastic humor to recognize a person's achievements and contributions.

Many social events are aimed at employees and volunteers, and their purpose is to thank or recognize members of an important public. The purpose of awards dinners and recognition lunches is to enhance the camaraderie among people who work together, a potential boost to worker productivity. In other cases, luncheons and banquets often may have educational or fund-raising objectives and involve a variety of publics.

Social events often occur at elegant or unusual locations, including cruise ships, museums and private mansions. Budget limitations can be offset by an extra dash of creativity, and many social events have been successful because they have had an interesting theme, such as an imitation Caribbean island getaway complete with appropriate music, food, and dancing, or historical themes related to the Old West, medieval knights, the flapper era, or the antebellum South. Futuristic themes also can be popular. Other social events include fashion shows and teas.

Artistic events. Another area of special events deals with art and culture. Consider events such as concerts or concert tours, recitals, plays, film festivals, arts shows, photo exhibits, and related activities.

Fundraising events. Activities in which nonprofit organizations interact with their key publics, especially individual donors, for the purpose of generating support can be important public relations opportunities. Americans donated more than $306 billion to charitable organizations (Giving USA, 2008). Nearly 75% of this amount was given by individuals, the remainder through bequests and by foundations (13%), bequests (8%), and corporations (5%). Religious organizations received a more than third of the total, followed by education (14%), human-service organizations (10%), health agencies (8%), the arts (5%), international affairs (4%), environment and animals (2%), and the remainder in miscellaneous categories. In addition, the presidential primaries raised $580 million (which is less than ¼ of a percent of all charitable giving).

Donor Bill of Rights

Philanthropy is based on voluntary action for the common good. It is a tradition of giving and sharing that is primary to the quality of life. To assure that philanthropy merits the respect and trust of the general public, and that donors and prospective donors can have full confidence in the not-for-profit organizations and causes they are asked to support, we declare that all donors have these rights:

1. To be informed of the organization's mission, of the way the organization intends to use donated resources and of its capacity to use donations effectively and for their intended purposes.
2. To be informed of the identity of those serving on the organization's governing board, and to expect the board to exercise prudent judgment in its stewardship responsibilities.
3. To have access to the organization's most recent financial statements.
4. To be assured that their gifts will be used for the purposes for which they were given.
5. To receive appropriate acknowledgment and recognition.
6. To be assured the information about their donations is handled with respect and with confidentiality to the extent provided by law.
7. To expect that all relationships with individuals representing organizations of interest to the donor will be professional in nature.
8. To be informed whether those seeking donations are volunteers, employees of the organization, or hired solicitors.
9. To have the opportunity for their names to be deleted from mailing lists that an organization may intend to share.
10. To feel free to ask questions when making a donation and to receive prompt, truthful, and forthright answers.

This statement was developed by the American Association of Fund-Raising Counsel, now known as the Giving Institute (http://www.aafrc.org), the Association of Fundraising Professionals (http://www.afpnet.org), the Association for Healthcare Philanthropy (http://www.ahp.org), and the Council for the Advancement and Support of Education (http://www.case.org).

It has been officially endorsed by numerous other organizations such as the Independent Sector (http://www.indepsec.org), the National Catholic Development Conference (http://www.ncdc.org), the National Committee on Planned Giving (http://www.ncpg.org), the Council for Resource Development (http://www.crdnet.org), the American Indian College Fund (http://www.collegefund.org) and United Way of America (http://www.unitedway.org), as well as hundreds of individual hospitals, colleges, and nonprofit charitable, religious, educational, medical, and human-service organizations in both the United States and Canada.

The variety of fund-raising events is limitless. Consider the following ideas: an antique show, an auction, a haunted house, pony rides, murder mystery dinner theater, a fashion show, a house or garden tour, or a tasting party (see Amos, 1995; Williams, 1994). All of these require careful planning and an eye for detail.

The ethics of both public relations and fund-raising require honest and forthright disclosure of organizational information to donors and to the media.

Special events and most of the other tactics noted in this section require a tremendous amount of careful planning; attention to detail is a must during the preparation stages. Organizations sometimes handle these details internally; other times, they hire events-management companies to help plan and execute the activities. Either way, consider some of the following practical questions that can arise around a special event:

- Is the date appropriate for everyone? Does it conflict with holidays (particularly cultural or religious holidays that may not be familiar to the planners)? Does it conflict with other major happenings, such as sporting or social activities—not only local events but larger events such as the Kentucky Derby, the Super Bowl, or the opening of the fishing season? Any such competition can limit attendance at your event.
- What is the appropriate length of an event? If it is too long, participants will become bored or restless and may leave early. If it is too short, they may decide it's not worth attending in the first place.
- Is the theme appropriate? Will it offend anyone, or will anyone feel excluded because of it?
- Is the site appropriate and accessible? Is climate a factor? If it is an outdoor event, is there an indoor location to serve as a backup in the event of bad weather? Does the location of a conference or meeting offer too many pleasant diversions that might tempt participants away from the conference itself?
- Are speakers and entertainers appropriate to the participants of the special event or meeting?
- Is planning assistance available through a convention/visitors' bureau in the host city of the meeting? If so, the agency may be able to simplify local contacts.

All special events call for careful planning, staffing, and financing, and they need creative promotion. Use the planning process presented throughout this book to identify and analyze key publics, establish objectives, and develop a strategy for the special event or other type of interpersonal communication tactic. Also make sure you evaluate its effectiveness, showing in measurable terms how well the activity achieved its objectives.

Step 7

Planning Example 7A: Selecting Interpersonal Communication Tactics

UPSTATE COLLEGE

Upstate College will develop interpersonal communication tactics to publicize its expanded program:

Interpersonal Tactic 1: Open house for recruiting
Key publics, hands-on, low cost, audience feedback

Interpersonal Tactic 2: Rededication ceremony
Low cost, news value, reaffirming existing support

Interpersonal Tactic 3: Existing event
Little additional cost, news value, power of ritualization

Interpersonal Tactic 4: Musical events
Key student publics, moderate cost, serving acceptance objectives

Interpersonal Tactic 5: Festival
Key student publics, high visibility, moderate cost

Interpersonal Tactic 6: Banquet
Key publics (community leaders, donors), high cost, high impact

■ ■ ■

Tiny Tykes will develop the following interpersonal communication tactics for an employee-oriented public relations program:

Interpersonal Tactic 1: Customer satisfaction workshops
Key external publics, high impact

Interpersonal Tactic 2: Work-group meeting
Key internal public, interaction and feedback

Interpersonal Tactic 3: Product safety and quality session
Key publics, direct benefit to employees and training management, indirect benefits to customers

Interpersonal Tactic 4: Motivational speech by CEO about safety and quality
Key employee public, low cost, moderate impact

Interpersonal Tactic 5: Samples of reintroduced products
Maintain credibility with employees (and family/friends of employees) as customers, moderate cost

Checklist 7A: Interpersonal Communication Tactics

Basic Questions

1. What interpersonal communication tactics will you use?
2. How will these tactics help the organization achieve its objectives?
3. What resources will these tactics require?

Expanded Questions

A. SELECTION OF TACTICS

From the following categories of interpersonal tactics, identify several that you would consider using:

Personal Involvement

- Organizational-site involvement (plant tour, open house, test drive, trial membership, free class, sample, shadow program, ride-along, premiere)
- Audience-site involvement
- Door-to-door canvassing, in-home demonstration, petition drive

Information Exchange

- Educational gathering (convention, council, convocation, synod, conclave, conference, seminar, symposium, colloquium, workshop, training session)
- Product exhibition
- Trade show
- Meeting (annual stockholder meeting, lobbying exchange, public affairs meeting)
- Demonstration (rally, march, demonstration, picket, boycott)
- Speech (question-and-answer session, oration, talk, lecture, guest lecture, address, keynote, sermon, homily, panel, debate, speaker's bureau, forum, town meeting)
- Special event
- Civic event (fair, festival, carnival, circus, parade, theme event)
- Sporting event (tournament, marathon, triathlon, outdoor spectator event, meet, field day)
- Contest (science fair, spelling bee, beauty pageant, talent contest)
- Holiday event (civic, cultural, religious)
- Progress-oriented event (procession, motorcade, grand opening, groundbreaking, cornerstone, dedication, ribbon cutting)
- Historic event (founders' day, anniversary, centennial, play, pageant, caravan)
- Social event (luncheon, dinner, reception, tribute, banquet, roast, awards, recognition, fashion show, tea)
- Artistic event (concert, concert tour, recital, play, film festival, art show, photo exhibit)
- Fundraising event

B. STRATEGIC IMPLICATIONS

For each item identified, answer the following questions:

1. Will this tactic help the organization to interact with the appropriate public?
2. What level of impact will this tactic make on the key public?
3. Will this tactic advance the organization toward its awareness objectives?
4. Will this tactic advance the organization toward its acceptance objectives?
5. Will this tactic advance the organization toward its action objectives?
6. What is the main advantage to this tactic?

7. What advantages does this tactic offer that other tactics do not?
8. Are there any disadvantages to this tactic? If so, what are they?

C. IMPLEMENTATION ITEMS

For each item identified, answer the following questions:

1. How much will it cost to implement this tactic? Is the cost justified? Is the cost practical, based on the organization's resources?
2. How much staff time will it take to implement this tactic? Is the time practical, based on the organization's resources?
3. What level of skill, equipment, and expertise is needed to implement this tactic? Is the needed level available within the organization? Is it available from outside sources?

Organizational Media Tactics

A host of communication vehicles are managed by each organization and are used at its discretion. These media generally are controlled, internal, nonpublic media that we can look at in four categories: general publications, direct mail, miscellaneous print media, and audiovisual/digital media. Let's consider the overall strategy and then look at each category of organizational media.

Strategy for Organizational Media

When should you select organizational media tactics? When your publics are too widespread or too large to interact with on a more personal level, but when you yet want to keep control of the content of your organization's message as well as its timing and distribution.

Conversely, when would you not use organizational media? When the audience is too small to warrant it, or so scattered that dissemination would be next to impossible. Or when you need the higher credibility that might be associated with other news tactics or the greater visibility that might be possible through advertising.

One of the benefits of organizational media tactics is that they provide a middle ground between high-impact, small-audience interpersonal tactics and lower-impact, large-audience news and advertising tactics. Organizational media can reasonably be addressed to both internal and external publics that fall in the midsized range. Because tactics in this category can be tailored to specific publics, they are more likely than news or advertising tactics to achieve success with acceptance and action objectives.

Another significant benefit of organizational media is that they are likely to be used by **information-seeking publics**, those who are actively searching for information on a particular topic. These are the people who will access a website, read a brochure, or watch a video.

Organizational media can be expensive to use, but because they can be targeted to specific publics and individuals, they usually are cost-effective. For example, the tactic of direct mail can involve high postage costs. But the impact of direct mail—if done properly—is higher than most other media, and thus the results should be greater.

Organizational Media Tactics

General Publications

- Serial publication (newsletter, bulletin)
- Stand-alone publication (brochure, flyer, booklet, folder, pamphlet, tract, circular, fact sheet, FAQ)
- Progress report (annual report, quarterly report)
- User kit
- Research report
- Miscellaneous print media

Direct Mail

- Memo
- Letter (appeal letter, marketing letter)
- Postcard
- Invitation
- Catalog (retail, full-line, specialty, business-to-business)

Electronic Media

- Audio media (telephone, dial-a-message, recorded information, voice mail, toll-free line, demo tape, demo CD, podcast)
- Video media (nonbroadcast video, videoconference, teleconference, videotape, slide show)
- Digital media (presentations software, e-mail, listserv, Internet, newsgroup, websites, web home page, web-based television, web-based radio, touch-sensitive computer, cell phone)
- Electronic publishing

Social Media

- Wiki
- Blog
- Social networking

Remember that organizational media are only one set of tools for public relations and marketing communication. Consider them carefully, but always with the intention of combining them with other kinds of communication tactics.

Publications

General publications include a variety of materials published and printed by an organization. Their distribution generally is handled by the organization as well. This category includes serial publications, stand-alone publications, reprints, progress reports, user kits, and research reports.

Serial publications. Most organizations make heavy use of serial publications, which may be issued weekly, monthly, or quarterly. The most common serial publication is a **newsletter**, an organizational publication that combines the informative approach of newspapers and magazines with the relationship-building features of mail. It's hard to tell just how many organizational newsletters exist. Guesses range from 100,000 to more than a million. But some figures are available. For example, more than 50,000 in-house corporate newsletters in the United States have a combined readership of about 500 million. The 19th edition of *Newsletters in Print* (2005) lists more than 12,000 newsletters in the United States and Canada that are national or regional in their outlook and are available to the public; many of these are available in online versions as well. Additionally, there are untold numbers of private publications and house organs, which are newsletters published by companies and organizations, with distribution to members, employees and other groups of readers.

Whatever the total, an estimated two-thirds of newsletters are internal publications directed toward employees, volunteers, alumni, members, customers, patients, and so on. The remaining third are external publications, a category that includes advocacy newsletters aimed at persuading readers, such as that published by a waste management company as part of a campaign to minimize opposition among local residents, and special-interest newsletters dealing with a particular industry, profession, or pursuit (such as financial investments, stamp collecting, or white-water canoeing), or with a particular group of people (such as economists, breast-cancer survivors, or former nuns). Another type of external newsletter is the subscription newsletter, which is often a high-cost publication providing insider information on a particular profession or industry; two such newsletters popular with public relations and marketing practitioners are *Media Relations Report* (http://www.ragan.com) and *Communication Briefings* (http://www.business-magazines.com).

Many public relations and marketing communication campaigns publish one or more newsletters as a convenient way to communicate with an organization's publics. If you plan to use the tactic of newsletters, having an appropriate mailing list is a must. When writing newsletters, follow the principles of newsworthiness and audience self-interest. Make sure the articles provide information of interest to the readers, and not just data that the organization wishes to present to the readers.

Bulletins, meanwhile, are a different kind of serial publication. Typographically, bulletins often feature only headlines and body text, with little or no graphic content. They generally include official organizational information and are most often circulated to internal audiences.

Stand-alone publications. Another commonly used tactic in public relations is the stand-alone publication, which differs from a newsletter or bulletin in that it usually is issued only once rather than periodically (though stand-alone publications may occasionally be updated). This category of publications includes brochures, flyers, and fact sheets.

A **brochure** is a common stand-alone organizational publication, dealing with a particular topic or issue. Organizational brochures focus on recruiting, product/service lines, membership services, organizational history, or some other aspect of a particular organization. Advocacy brochures attempt to educate or generate support on a particular issue important to the sponsoring organization. Additionally, some brochures are action-oriented publications with a definite sales pitch, though these are more likely to be associated with marketing efforts than with public relations activities.

A **flyer** is similar to a brochure in that it is a stand-alone piece. Whereas a brochure is meant to be read in panels, a flyer is meant to be read as a single unit.

Note that *brochure* and *flyer* are commonly accepted terms for stand-alone organizational publications, but other names also may be used. Some names deal with the size of the publication. In addition to *flyers*, other terms for single-sheet publications include *leaflets* or *folders*. Alternative terms for *brochures* are *pamphlets* or *booklets*. Other name distinctions grow out of the purpose of the publication. Persuasive brochures called *tracts* deal with political or religious topics, and marketing-oriented stand-alone publications are often called *circulars*.

A **fact sheet** that presents information in bullet form is another common stand-alone piece, as is an **FAQ**, a presentation of frequently asked questions about a particular issue or organization.

Reprints. Copies of published articles about an organization or an issue significant to it can be useful in meeting public relations objectives. Reprints are articles previously published in newspapers, magazines, or newsletters. By issuing a reprint, the organization is able to extend the reach and impact of the original publication, particularly by giving it to the organization's publics, who may not have had access to the original article.

Fair-use provisions in copyright law allow an organization to circulate a limited number of copies of a published article for educational, research, or news purposes. But make sure to obtain permission from the original publisher before disseminating a reprinted article or photograph to a wide group for promotional purposes. This may involve a fee and the permission granted is generally for one-time use only.

A similar tactic is to reprint speeches, especially formal presentations such as keynote addresses or testimony before state, provincial, or federal legislative bodies. These often are shared with key publics, such as boards of directors, major donors or stockholders, community and civic leaders, and other opinion leaders.

Related to reprints is the distribution of news releases to internal audiences. News releases will be discussed more in the section News Media Tactics later in this chapter. While releases are meant primarily for distribution to journalists, some public relations practitioners also selectively send them to key internal publics, such as senior executives, major donors, and stockholders.

Progress reports. Several different types of progress reports focus on the continuing development of an organization, particularly its activity within a recent period of time.

The **annual report** is a special kind of progress report. Annual reports are required by the federal Securities and Exchange Commission (SEC) for American companies that issue stock. These can be simple statements with required information, such as the identification of corporate officials, the salaries and benefits of the top executives, financial statements, and the auditor's certification of accuracy. Often, however, they feature much more. Many annual reports are glossy, magazinelike publications designed not only to provide required information but also to affirm investors' loyalty to the company, attract new investors, and enhance the company's reputation with financial analysts and the financial media.

Some companies also produce quarterly reports, though these are not required by the SEC. Quarterly reports usually are not as elaborate as annual reports.

Though nonprofit organizations and private (non–stock issuing) companies are not required to issue annual reports, many do so. These often provide financial and organizational information of interest to donors and other supporters. Businesses often find that annual and quarterly reports are convenient vehicles for attracting new customers by demonstrating the work they have previously done.

User kits. Several print tactics, generically called user kits, are associated with the people who use a product or service. These kits or manuals often include background and how-to information as well as implementation ideas. For example, teacher kits provide a variety of information and materials that can be used in the classroom; these often include sample lesson plans, suggestions for activities, posters, student handouts, and even test items. To produce these, the public relations person will often team up with teachers so the information is most useful to the intended public.

Research reports. Sometimes, when organizations conduct or sponsor formal research on an issue related to their interests, they consider the information proprietary—that is, private and confidential. After all, they paid for the research, and they may not want to share it with competitors.

Other times, however, they may choose to share the research findings. In issuing a research report, the organization has an ethical requirement to be clear as to its involvement in the research study. The report also should include background information, a description of the research methods and how any samples were drawn, presentation and analysis of the research findings, a discussion of the significance of the findings, and sometimes some recommendations based on the findings. The report may be distributed like other organizational media—to organizational managers, employees, stockholders or donors, regulators, and others.

The report also may be shared with the news media. It is never a good idea to conduct research simply so it can be used for publicity. That would be more like a publicity stunt, and it raises ethical questions about the appropriate use of research and thus about the organization's professionalism. But if the organization believes that a legitimate research report contains some positive news, it may decide to publicize its findings. Often this involves providing reporters with the research report as well as a news release.

In the release, emphasize the validity and objectivity of the study while acknowledging the organization's involvement. Don't use the organization's name too many times in the release.

Miscellaneous print media. A whole range of other tactics offer several opportunities for the public relations planner. Consider the following tactics. Posters are visual materials, often approximately three by five feet in size, that can be displayed prominently. Companies often use window displays to give visibility to their products or services; nonprofit organizations sometimes use commercial storefront space made available to them, often when there is a temporary vacancy in a store in a mall or on a downtown street.

Employees and customers alike can benefit from well-maintained bulletin boards, and suggestion boxes are excellent opportunities for organizations to solicit feedback and input from their publics. Other traditional tactics that still have value are pay stuffers or bill inserts, which are messages placed within pay envelopes or bills, respectively. Door hangers that advocate a cause or promote a product or service also can be useful.

Business cards remain another effective tactic for organizations to keep their names before potential customers and associates.

Some miscellaneous tactics involve recognition programs. For example, certificates are used to acknowledge achievement or participation. Formal proclamations are issued by governmental and sometimes by organizational leaders to draw public attention to a particular cause or theme.

Direct Mail

Direct mail is a category of organizational print media that, though perhaps general in nature, can be addressed to individual recipients. Direct mail pieces can include memos, letters, postcards, invitations, and catalogs.

Memos. A memorandum or **memo** is a brief written message addressed to an individual or to a group of people. Memos generally are internal messages; when issued externally, they usually are directed to persons known to the sender. Memos begin with a format that clearly identifies the sender, recipient, date, and subject. In writing style, memos are informal, crisp, and usually action-oriented. Memos are a good public relations vehicle when you are writing to colleagues, media gatekeepers, or members of key publics, such as when you attach a memo to a reprint you are sending to a major benefactor or stockholder.

Letters. In the category of direct mail, the most common vehicle is the business letter, which generally is a form letter addressed to individuals. Often these will carry the actual name of the reader, such as "Dear Mary Jones" or "Dear Ms. Jones." Sometimes for very large mailings the letters will be addressed more generically, such as "Dear Friend of the Environment" or "Dear Fellow Stamp Collector." Appeal letters are direct-mail pieces sent to potential donors by nonprofit organizations engaged in fund-raising campaigns. Marketing letters are direct-mail pieces sent by businesses for advertising purposes.

With both types of direct-mail letters, response rates generally are very low, often less than 1%. But the response rate increases considerably when the letters are sent to people who in the past have made contributions or done business with the sending organization. The best advice regarding direct mail, as with every other form of public relations or marketing communication, is to target the mail to each public and address the reader's self-interest.

Direct-mail packages generally contain more than a marketing or appeal letter. They often also include a brochure about the company or organization, a response device, such as a donor card or order form, and a return device, such as a payment envelope, usually with return-postage paid.

Postcards. Similar to letters, postcards generally are addressed to individuals, usually by name. Postcards, which include brief messages, are not placed in envelopes, and thus their content should never be of a personal or confidential nature. Postcards often are used as announcements or reminders, and they often complement messages presented through news or advertising media. In some cases, postcards may replace other such tactics, especially when it is possible to obtain a mailing list of members of the key public. Organizations sometimes use postcards to drive traffic to their websites.

Invitations. Organizations sponsoring events, whether public or private, often send formal, personalized invitations to prospective participants.

Catalogs. Catalogs are books or brochures aimed at consumer publics, generally with an inventory of items available for purchase, though nonprofit organizations can use the catalog approach to list available services or programs. Several types of catalogs can be developed. Retail catalogs, with merchandise available in the sponsors' stores, seeks to generate in-store consumer traffic. Full-line catalogs feature the entire range of items in a department store. Specialty catalogs feature products of very narrow consumer interest, such as a catalog of weaving supplies. Business-to-business catalogs contain information on products of specific interest to businesses.

In recent years, some companies have developed catalogs along the lines of lifestyle-oriented magazines, turning a traditional marketing tool into a public relations vehicle as well. For example, the Patagonia Company (http://www.patagonia.com) enhances its clothing catalog with pictures by award-winning outdoor photographers, commentaries on the environment, and field reports about outdoor activities around the world.

Abercrombie & Fitch (http://www.abercrombie.com) sparked calls for a boycott of the clothing store over what critics called racy photos and soft porn in its catalog. The company defended its quarterly publication as being not only a sales tool but also a magazine aimed at the college market.

Electronic Media

Technology has added new choices to the menu of tactics that can be used for public relations and marketing communication. Most of these electronic technologies in some way enhance the audio and/or visual aspects of communication. This category includes audio media and video media.

Audio media. An expanding inventory of audio media is available to public relations planners. Telephone media involve new opportunities for information on demand, such as dial-a-message tactics that allow people to obtain information on topics such as weather or sports scores or to access self-help information and advice on a variety of categories. Dial-a-message services also offer prayers, jokes, and so on.

Technology makes it possible to disseminate recorded messages to thousands of phone users, a development often used by political candidates around election time.

Telephone media also can involve the use of recorded information or persuasive messages to help people wile away the time spent waiting on a telephone. Some organizations add a public relations dimension to their voice mail, such as a community college where the president has recorded a brief welcome message as part of the routing of all incoming phone calls.

Additionally, organizations make frequent use of toll-free lines that give customers and other publics free telephone access to the organization; similar 900 lines, in which callers are charged for the phone call, can generate income for organizations. Some organizations also have found that demo tapes or demo CDs can be useful audio tools.

Podcasts (a portmanteau for *iPod* and *broadcast*) essentially are Internet-based audio feeds that allow users to listen to postings. For example, the University of California–Berkeley began podcasting lectures in 2006. Princeton University podcasts guest lectures, and Georgetown University podcasts a weekly interview with faculty experts on various topics. General Motors sponsors blogs and podcasts on its various auto lines. Police departments, museums, churches, and advocacy groups also are using podcasts to present their messages to interested audiences. Many public relations agencies now include podcasts and other social media among the professional services they offer.

Video media. Video media offer opportunities in nonbroadcast video that use television technology to produce programs that are then disseminated through organizational rather than public channels. For example, organizations may use **nonbroadcast video** in conjunction with a stockholders' meeting, open house, or some other type of interpersonal tactic. Business report using nonbroadcast video (also called **corporate video** and **internal video**) for training, fundraising, employee information, product information for customers, annual meetings, education, and internal marketing.

A particular use of nonbroadcast video is as direct-mail video to promote products or causes. *Advertising Age* has reported the effectiveness of direct-mail video (Kim, 1995). In one case, 94% of people viewed the video they received from a gubernatorial candidate in New Jersey. In another study, a direct-mail video that inaugurated a campaign to encourage landowners in the Connecticut River Tidelands region to develop long-term conservation plans was evaluated as being both educational and persuasive, with increases in six key indicators of environmental behavior (Tyson & Snyder, 1999).

Nonbroadcast video sometimes occurs live—as in **videoconferences**, also called **teleconferences**. Videoconferences use television technology to produce live informational or educational programs for remote audiences. These events are made interactive through the use of satellite or fiber-optic video transmission, sometimes with long-distance telephone connections to link the remote sites to the originating studio.

It is more common that nonbroadcast video is provided on CDs and DVDs, which have replaced videotapes as the vehicles for presenting information of interest to donors and stockholders as well as potential customers. Such video also can be useful for employee training. Increasingly, organizations are turning to the Internet to post their nonbroadcast video products. This **web video** or **streaming video** is also becoming a common feature on multipurpose cell phones that provide not only voice transmission but text messaging, Internet access, and a range of video options.

Slide shows are informational or educational presentations using 35mm photographic slides. Newer technologies enhance this tactic by making possible interactive multiple-slide presentations.

Electronic publishing. A new category of electronic media is emerging in the form of electronic publishing. Newspapers and magazines have developed online versions—at first, mere **shovelware**, a term for the posting of already-published articles in their original print version. Most online publications now provide more sophisticated multimedia adaptations that go beyond the original print text to include additional information, links, continual updates, and interactive features.

Many organizations have shifted to online newsletters replacing print versions. One valuable aspect of online newsletters is that they can be archived so readers can peruse past issues. Another benefit is that online newsletters can be evolutionary, with new daily or weekly postings as newsworthy information becomes available. Public relations practitioners often herald newsletters or updates with e-mail alerts to potential readers. However, be aware that inbox congestion is a growing concern; it is best to direct online newsletters to only those readers who have signed up to receive them.

Digital Media

The growing field of computer-based **digital media** provide even newer strategic communication opportunities. For example, versatile presentations software such as PowerPoint often are used instead of the more traditional slide presentations or overhead transparencies.

Technology is translating many elements of video media into digital. For example, video is now usually recorded digitally rather than onto videocassettes, and editing is now done digitally as well. Video footage is stored and transmitted using computer technology as well.

A mushrooming group of these tactics is associated with electronic mail, or **e-mail**, which has become an accessible means of instantaneous communication between two persons or among large groups. Using electronic mailing lists called **listservs**, public relations practitioners can communicate with information-seeking publics. Meanwhile, electronic newsgroups bring together people interested in discussing a particular topic.

The **Internet** has made it possible for virtually every organization and many individuals to develop home pages on the World Wide Web, an interactive network with growing capabilities, such as the use of web-based television and web radio.

Websites are standard fare for organizations of every kind. From corporations to colleges, social advocates to political groups, everyone is using an Internet home page to communicate with people who are actively seeking their information. For example, as the Makah people were planning to revive a dormant practice of hunting whales in the Pacific Northwest, the tribe used a website (http://www.makah.org) to provide a detailed question-and-answer page about its controversial plan. Animal rights protestors retaliated with a counterfeit rogue site (http://www.makah.com) that mocked the tribal site. When he was campaigning for the presidency, Senator Barack Obama established a website dedicated to countering personal and political rumors about him and viral attacks.

Websites also give organizations access to online tactics associated with news media and promotional/advertising media. These will be discussed in subsequent sections of this chapter.

Additionally, **touch-sensitive computers** make it possible to apply an information-on-demand approach to several situations in which customers can use the computer to interact with the organization, both gaining and giving information.

Cell phones are another form of digital media increasingly being used for public relations and marketing purposes. Newer versions of cell phones feature much more than regular telephone service. Most now include built-in cameras, some with sophisticated features rivaling digital cameras. Other features include camcorders, wireless connection to a personal computer, short-message service associated with text messaging, Internet browsing, music playback, games, radio reception, recording, video calling, downloading for audio and video streaming, calculators, and personal-organizer functions.

The field of **electronic publishing** offers public relations practitioners many potential advantages. Some such publishing involves the translation of printed books into electronic formats. But the field also offers some interesting innovations. For example, e-books are the digital equivalents of printed books that can be used either on personal computers or on e-book readers that feature page-for-page presentations of books, along with search and hyperlink features. Some features even convert text into audio books.

Social Media

A new phenomenon is the emergence of social media, an umbrella term for various types of interactive media in which the audience is an active participant in the development and presentation of the messages.

A 2007 study funded in part by the Institute for Public Relations and Wieck Media ("New Media, New Influences and Implications for the PR Profession") has found that 57% of public relations and marketing communications professionals find social media becoming more important to their programs; 27% said social media are the core of their communication strategy (Gillin, 2007, p. 3).

Another study by Edelman Change and Employee Engagement in partnership with PeopleMetrics (2006) reports a burgeoning field of new technologies: 57 million blogs worldwide, more podcasts than there are radio stations, 10 times more entries in the online Wikipedia than in Encyclopedia Britannica. The study also reports public relations interest in the social media. The respondents were communicators from 75 Fortune 500 companies and dozens of international organizations. Here are some findings:

- Three-fourths of communication executives understand podcasting; one-third produce podcasts.
- Fewer than half knew what a wiki is; 10% use wikis; 13% monitor employee blogging activity.
- Fewer corporate communicators read blogs than most adult Internet users; one-third host a blog.
- Nearly all use an Intranet.

Wikis. A collaborative community website is known as a **wiki**. At a wiki site, any user can edit the content of the website, adding material, modifying it, even deleting it if they wish. One of the most-used wikis is Wikipedia (http://www.wikipedia/org). Some companies and organizations use wikis as an active substitute for the more static Intranet (which essentially is an officewide version of the Internet that users can view but not edit).

Some wikis draw on popular culture, such as a wiki about the television series *Lost* (http://www.lostpedia.com) with reader-provided character sketches, episode synopses, and commentary, insight, and speculation about show's cryptic story line. For six weeks in 2007, more than 1,500 anonymous writers around the world participated in writing an online novel, *A Million Penguins*, but critics said the result was a confusing and unstructured verification of the too-many-cooks-in-the-kitchen adage.

One problem with wikis is online vandalism in which users add false information, thus calling into question the credibility of all wiki information and fueling the criticism that wikis by nature favor consensus over credentials. Many college professors, for example, ban material from Wikipedia from being cited in academic research papers.

What are the implications for public relations practitioners? For one thing, don't be surprised to see information about your company or organization at a wiki site. Realize, however, that the rules of engagement on public relations use of social media are still evolving. Wikipedia, for example, allows anyone except public relations people to edit postings. Company policy specifically bans public relations practitioners from modifying entries on behalf of their organizations or clients. Instead, founder Jimmy Wales has said that public relations practitioners may merely post comments in the discussion section of the entry. Regardless of any such internal controls, the PRSA Code of Ethics (see Appendix B: Ethical Standards) calls for public relations practitioners to disclose any financial or other connections to subjects they write about.

Blogs. Another type of social media is the **blog** (short for **web log**), an open-to-all website maintained usually by an individual. Blogs feature postings of commentary, news, photos and graphics, and links to other blogs or sites. Users are invited to react with additional questions, comments, and responses. Blogs generally focus on a particular topic, and the topics run the gamut—politics, travel, ethics, business, religion, environment, education, lifestyle, art, sports, and the like. Adaptations of blogs include **vlogs** (blogs that contain primarily videos), **MP3 blogs** (music) and **photoblogs**.

Bloggers, like blogs, are a diverse group. Blogging is done by singers and athletes, senators and CEOs. Newspapers and television news stations have their own blogs in which reporters interact with audience members, and audience members with each other.

Blogs also are merging with more traditional forms of news media. Some bloggers consider themselves journalists, and some have broken stories that later are taken up by mainstream newspapers and television. In other situations, journalists publish their own blogs to provide additional commentary and insight into the stories they are reporting.

Blogs also are gaining influence in the political arena. During the 2008 presidential primary season, eight of nine Democratic candidates went to Chicago to address the "Net roots" YearlyKos blogosphere convention (named for its sponsor, the Daily Kos blog, at http://www.dailykos.com) instead of the Democratic Leadership Council, which was meeting at the same time. The Republican-oriented RedState blog (http://www.redstate.com) made news of its own by banning blog talk about candidate Ron Paul, whom the blog owners considered to be not Republican enough.

Bloggers also create third-party endorsement, those independent and influential voices that have the ear of an organization's publics. Because of their independence, they also have potential high credibility. That's why Wal-Mart enlisted bloggers in its campaign to counter media-reported criticism of its efforts to open new stores against rising consumer opposition. That's also why companies such as Cingular Wireless, Microsoft, and General Electric have met with bloggers before going public with new products.

The rules about blogging vis-à-vis public relations are still emerging. Blog readers expect to find only firsthand accounts posted online, and most bloggers resent blatant public relations use of their medium. While the standard public relations consultation services remain appropriate, "ghost-blogging" in someone else's name crosses the ethical line. Transparency is the key. On the other hand, some bloggers have lost credibility for themselves by willingly publishing verbatim "plants" from government or corporate sources without identifying them as handouts.

Blogs generally are search-engine friendly, and with now more than 57 million blogs (and the number doubling every five or six months) it's not surprising that many organizations are eyeing the use of blogs to promote their products, services, and causes. Some organizations even have people assigned to the post of **blogger relations**.

Many people in public relations and marketing communications make it part of their daily research to monitor blogs dealing with topics of interest to their organizations or clients. Blogs can provide a look at the competition and an insight into the interests of customers, donors, fans, and other publics. As an advance glimpse into what could grow into widespread public opinion, they also provide an early warning system into potential problems with your own organization.

How should you pitch a story to bloggers? Alice Marshall of Presto Vivace Communications in Fairfax, Virginia, reminds people attending her workshops that, unlike reporters who work for editors, bloggers work for themselves (or, figuratively, for their audiences). She offers the following tips to pitching to bloggers ("Rules of Engagement," 2005).

1. Remember that it's a conversation, not a confrontation. Reader feedback is a highly prized premium.
2. Introduce yourself to lower-profile bloggers, the people who have links with the top bloggers in your field. A posting there often may attract attention up the line.
3. Be familiar with the blog, and make sure that your topic is appropriate to the audience.
4. Be up front about who you are, and don't hide behind a false identity. Let readers know that you are a public relations person with a vested interest in the conversation.

5. Remember that bloggers are much more likely than journalists to pounce on poorly written or overly pushy news releases, and they may use their blog to rant against you and your organization or client.
6. Try to be known within your organization for your work in blog relations.

Social networking. Posted information, responses, photos, and videos are common elements of social network sites such as Facebook (http://www.facebook.com) and MySpace (http://www.myspace.com), as well as photo- and video-sharing sites such as Flickr (http://www.flickr.com) and YouTube (http://www.youtube.com). Some sites are specialized for particular audiences: ethnic-oriented sites such as BlackPlanet.com (http://www.blackplanet.com) for African Americans and MiGente.com (http://www.migente.com) for the Hispanic community; religion-focused sites such as Muxlim (http://www.muxlim.com) for young Muslims and MyChurch.org (http://www.mychurch.org) for Christian networkers; and nationally oriented sites such as Chirundu.com (http://www.chirundu.com) for social networking among people from Zimbabwe and LunarStorm (http://www.lunarstorm.se) for Swedish teens.

Blogger Relations

Steve Rubel of Edelman Public Relations, in a Marketing Voices podcast posted in 2006 at http://www.podtech.net, recommends that public relations practitioners should focus on how they can help bloggers rather than how bloggers can help the practitioners' client or organization. Practitioners are accepting social media, but not necessarily embracing it, he comments. Rubel advocates a strategy of blending both traditional media and bloggers in an effort to extend the reach and impact of an organization's message.

The NewPR/Wiki website (http://www.thenewpr.com/wiki/pmwiki.php) lists corporate and organizational blogs, as well as tips on developing **blogger relations** (a new form of public relations focused on the key public of bloggers). The site includes information pieces such as "Top Ten Things You Can Do to Get Blogged" and "7 Habits of Highly Effective Blog PR."

Many bloggers see themselves involved in **participatory journalism**, a phenomenon also known as **citizen journalism** or **grassroots journalism**. The principle at work here is that such bloggers self-identify as playing an active role in gathering, reporting, and commenting on news. A few news bloggers have a growing credibility with mainstream news media, in part because, as mavericks who are not constrained by some of the corporate or ethical boundaries of professional journalists, they have occasionally broken important news stories. But some bloggers are seen merely as digital hacks unrestrained by ethical or other journalistic standards.

The 2006 State of the News Media report by the Project for Excellence in Journalism, which is affiliated with the Columbia University Graduate School of Journalism, found that only 5% of bloggers report original news research (Project for Excellence in Journalism, 2006).

Nevertheless, bloggers are making their presence felt. It was bloggers who fueled the debunking of military documents that newscaster Dan Rather and CBS News used in questioning President George W. Bush's military service. In 2007, the Associated Press partnered with the Media Bloggers Association to carry blog-generated news reports in its coverage of I. Lewis "Scooter" Libby's trial for "outing" CIA agent Valerie Plame for political purposes on behalf of the White House.

MySpace (http://www.myspace.com) reports more than 300 million members worldwide posting profiles, personal interests, music, video, and audio. In the 2008 presidential elections, candidates created their own MySpace accounts in an attempt to reach younger voters. Also in 2008, MySpace agreed to provide greater privacy for teen users and to cooperate with police in investigations of sex offenders.

Facebook (http://www.facebook.com) began among students who had university e-mail addresses, expanded into high schools, and later was opened to anyone over age 13. An estimated 70 million members worldwide post personal information, résumés, diaries, photos, videos, and music. Facebook Causes (http://apps.facebook.com/causes/about), a site for nonprofit fund-raising, reported more than 33,000 donations totaling nearly $600,000 in 2008.

Facebook has been called the most used site among American youth, and students use it to get to know future college roommates. But Facebook has other viewers, among them

Viral Philanthropy

The global relief agency Oxfam had no advertising budget for its program to raise $35 million to address the famine in East Africa. So Oxfam turned to YouTube and Facebook. The agency parlayed the donation of a Vera Wang dress worn to the Academy Awards presentation ceremony by actress Keira Knightley into a 9-day eBay auction that raised $8,000—enough to feed 5,000 children in Tanzania for a month.

More important for Oxfam's long-term visibility with a new and younger audience, the auction attracted 2,500 online observers for the final bidding.

The Oxfam project is one example of nonprofit organizations' using social media to raise awareness of a social issue and to raise funds to address the problem. It's called **viral philanthropy**, an emerging aspect of fund-raising that lies with many people being asked to give a little bit to the cause and to encourage their friends to do likewise.

With little or no advertising budget, viral philanthropy turns its attention to social media such as bloggers and social networking media such as MySpace and Facebook, which have embraced the concept of charitable giving among participants. Facebook Causes, for example, claims to have raised $2.5 million for about 20,000 different charities. MySpace's Impact has similar claims of success in online philanthropy among young people.

The Knightley gift to Oxfam was part of a campaign by the Clothes off Our Back celebrity auction program founded by husband-and-wife actors Bradley Whitford (*The West Wing*) and Jane Kaczmarek (*Malcolm in the Middle*). Knightley also gave another charity the gown she wore in the movie *Atonement*. That dress was auctioned on eBay for the benefit of the Children's Charity of Southern California. From an opening bid of $1,000, bidding reached $46,000.

Other organizations also have turned to social networking media to support humanitarian causes. Following the Asian tsunami in 2004, the Yarn Harlot, a blog about knitting, asked readers to give $1 each to Doctors Without Borders, an international medical aid agency. The project, called Knitters Without Borders, raised more than $435,000 in two years and continues to receive donations for the medical charity.

Meanwhile, People for the Ethical Treatment of Animals created a MySpace profile and recruited 120,000 new supporters interested in animal rights.

employers using it to learn what applicants say about themselves and police using the site to conduct investigation of suspected criminals.

YouTube (http://www.youtube.com) began as a video sharing website, and Flickr (http://www.flickr.com) as a photograph sharing site. Public relations practitioners have found use for both, such as the many political ads and videos posted by candidates during the 2008 presidential election cycle. YouTube also includes many video news clips and clips from films, though many such postings have raised copyright concerns on the part of mainstream news and entertainment media.

The Associate Press and Reuters news agencies are posting videos to YouTube, and other businesses and organizations are using the various video media to strategically present their messages to younger audiences.

A study by the Pew Research Center for the People and the Press reported in 2008 that 22% of Americans use social networking sites. The age breakdown varies significantly: 67% of people ages 18–29, 21% of those ages 30–39, and only 6% of Americans over age 40 (Pew Research Center for the People and the Press, 2008).

Meanwhile, the growing availability of user-generated **viral video** is playing an increasing role in strategic communication efforts. The term refers to the widespread dissemination and popularity of a video clip, generally circulated via e-mail or text messaging and posted on Internet blogs or other websites. Some videos are news-based, such as Kanye West discussing Hurricane Katrina and Senator Larry Craig's news conference insisting that he isn't gay and never was. Some feature footage originally captured on cell phones, such as the "Don't Tase Me, Bro" clip from a demonstration at the University of Florida.

The two-minute "Leave Britney Alone!" posting generated 18 million downloads, leading the way as the top viral video of 2007. Runners-up included the inarticulate Miss Teen North Carolina, an anti–Hillary Rodham Clinton ad reminiscent of an old Apple computer ad, and orange-jumpsuited Filipino inmates doing a dance homage to Michael Jackson's *Thriller* choreography.

Viral video has played a notable role in marketing of bands and movies. Super Bowl ads often get similar attention, as do celebrity shenanigans involving people such as Britney Spears and Tom Cruise.

Planning Example 7B: Selecting Organizational Media Tactics

Step 7

UPSTATE COLLEGE

Upstate College will develop the following tactics using organizational media to publicize its expanded program:

- College viewbook—key publics, high visual impact
- Transfer brochure—key publics, high impact, low cost
- Letter to former applicants—targeted, low cost
- Poster—moderate cost, high visual impact
- Video—targeting key publics, high cost
- Home page at upstatecoll.edu—information-seeking publics, low cost, for potential transfer students, interactive

■ ■ ■

TINY TYKES TOYS

Tiny Tykes will develop the following tactics using organizational media for an employee-oriented public relations program:

- Newsletter articles in employee publication about safety, quality, and customer satisfaction—key public, low cost
- Memo about product reintroduction—key public, low cost
- Employee bulletin with updates on customer response to product reintroduction (pro and con)—key public, low cost
- Brochures about safety, quality, and customer satisfaction—moderate cost
- Letter to families of employees thanking them for supporting employees and company during difficult reintroduction period—key public, low cost
- Suggestion box soliciting employee input about safety and quality, with feedback via employee—key public, low cost
- Newsletter—low cost, interactive

Checklist 7B: Organizational Media Tactics

Basic Questions

1. What organizational media tactics will you use?
2. How will these tactics help the organization achieve its objectives?
3. What resources will these tactics require?

Expanded Questions

A. SELECTION OF TACTICS

From the following categories of organizational media tactics, identify several that you would consider using:

Publications

- Serial publications (newsletter, house organ, bulletin)
- Stand-alone publications (brochure, leaflet, folder, pamphlet, booklet, tract, circular)
- Reprints (internal news release)
- Progress reports (annual report, quarterly report)
- User kits, teacher kits
- Research reports
- Miscellaneous print media

Direct Mail

- Memos
- Letters (appeal letter, marketing letter, postcard, invitation, catalog)

- Postcards
- Invitations
- Catalogs

Electronic Media

- Audio (telephone, dial-a-message, recorded information, demo tape, demo CD, podcast)
- Video (nonbroadcast video, corporate video, internal video, video conference, teleconference, slide show)
- Electronic publishing

Digital Media

- E-mail
- Listservs
- Websites
- Cell phones

Social Media

- Wikis
- Blogs
- Social networking websites

B. STRATEGIC IMPLICATIONS

For each item identified, answer the following questions:

1. Will this tactic help the organization to interact with the appropriate public?
2. What level of impact will this tactic make on the key public?
3. Will this tactic advance the organization toward its awareness objectives?
4. Will this tactic advance the organization toward its acceptance objectives?
5. Will this tactic advance the organization toward its action objectives?
6. What is the main advantage to this tactic?
7. What advantages does this tactic offer that other tactics do not?
8. Are there any disadvantages with this tactic? If so, what are they?

C. IMPLEMENTATION ITEMS

For each item identified, answer the following questions:

1. How much will it cost to implement this tactic? Is the cost justified? Is the cost practical, based on the organization's resources?
2. How much staff time will it take to implement this tactic? Is the time practical, based on the organization's resources?
3. What skill level, equipment, and expertise are needed to implement this tactic? Is the needed level available within the organization? Is it available from outside sources?

News Media Tactics

The **news media** are communication vehicles that exist primarily to present newsworthy information to various audiences. There is much variety among news media. Consider the possibilities: print media, such as newspapers and magazines; broadcast media, including radio and television; and interactive news tactics, including interviews and conferences. Though all of these media are focused on news, each provides a somewhat different opportunity for public relations and marketing communication.

Strategy for News Media

The news media offer public relations and marketing practitioners several benefits not usually associated with tactics in the other categories.

First, the news media generally reach large audiences—certainly larger than most audiences associated with interpersonal communication tactics, and usually larger than those for organizational media. News media audiences may encompass most residents of a particular community, most members of a certain profession, or most people who are seriously interested in a given topic. Thus, news media tactics can further an organization's pursuit of awareness objectives.

Second, the publicity that can be generated through these media is free. Unlike the built-in cost of organizational media and the fees associated with advertising, no price tag is associated with publicity. Obviously the organization will have overhead costs, such as staff or agency/contractor time in researching and writing materials such as news releases, as well as the cost associated with printing and distributing such releases or producing electronic versions, but most these are internal administrative costs and incidental expenses.

The news media are considered uncontrolled media, creating the environment for the third, and perhaps most important, benefit they offer: they can add credibility to an organization's message. They have the power of what's called **third-party endorsement**, meaning that someone outside the organization preparing the message—in this case, reporters, editors, or news directors—is in some way attesting to the significance and validity of the information being presented. Unlike a newsletter, website, or advertisement, in which the organization can say pretty much anything it likes, the news media demand a certain level of accuracy. Reporters can evaluate the accuracy of information presented and check the claims being made before the story is presented to readers, listeners, or viewers. This added credibility can go a long way toward achieving the acceptance objectives of the organization.

Traditionally, it is the concept of third-party endorsement that has given the news media high marks as credible disseminators of messages. However, some generational shifts are taking place that may mean significant changes in the future. In the Harris Poll "Generation 2001: The Second Study" (2001), commissioned by Northwestern Mutual, 80% of college seniors rated the Internet as their most important news source, followed by 57% for radio, 55% for television, 39% for magazines, and 37% for newspapers; this compares with television as the top news source for all Americans, at 75%. It is interesting to note that college-age Americans were more likely to trust their grandparents' generation (82%) than their own generation (31%). Their leading social concerns are education (63%), environment (51%), crime and violence (48%), health care (45%), and political leadership (44%).

A 2008 Harris Poll reported a low trust level for all media. Specifically, the poll found that 44% of adults tend to trust radio news (the rest tend not to trust or are unsure); 41%

Internet news sources, 36% television, and 30% the press. Among Republicans, trust in television and print news is well below the norm.

Most materials prepared for news media are written using Associated Press style guidelines. The Dallas chapter of the International Association of Business Communicators in 2006 reported the results of an online survey indicating that 43% of public relations communicators feel it is extremely important to use AP style, and a total of 88% said the style was important, very important, or extremely important.

State of the News Media

The Project for Excellence in Journalism is a nonpartisan project associated with the Pew Research Center, which has published several extensive audits on the state of the health and status of American news media, including its annual State of the News Media Report, which can be found at the project's website (http://www.stateofthenewsmedia.com). The 2007 report indicated findings for U.S. media such as these:

Daily newspapers. The 50 largest newspapers lost circulation, but still about 124 million readers picked up one of the 1,452 daily newspapers every day.

Weekly newspapers. Audiences also dropped for alternative weeklies to about 7.5 million.

Newsweeklies. Circulation was flat, but niche publications found growing audiences; newsweeklies moved more toward digital outlets.

Internet news. An integrated audience using both print and online news sources grew, with 34% of adults (68 million) using the Internet daily for news; 37% of adults (57 million) said they at least occasionally read blogs.

TV network news. The audience is dropping about 1 million a year, at 26 million in 2007; the credibility of network news fell from 31% to 22% over a 10-year period.

Cable news. Audiences for cable news fell to about 2.5 million, led by a 16% drop in Fox News Channel viewers (though corporate profitability was increasing).

Alternative cable news. Program sources increased, but with limited audience access; Al Jazeera, for example, could be viewed only over the Internet; Comedy Central's satirical *Daily Show with Jon Stewart* and *The Colbert Report* increased to 1.6 million and 1.2 million viewers, respectively.

Local TV news. Audiences decreased in every time slot in virtually every market.

Radio news. Audiences for radio news and talk remained steady at 16% (32 million).

Alternative audio. New program sources proliferated, with podcasts, cell phone news, and PDA news, but audiences were slow to adopt them.

Ethnic media. Audiences grew as the number of non-English speaking households increased, led by 18 million readers of Spanish-language publications; African American newspaper audiences were flat or declining; ethnic media in general was slow to move toward digital outlets.

Whereas interpersonal tactics and organizational media generally involve information-seeking publics, the news media more often carry the organization's message to people who are not actively seeking it. Readers intend to catch up on the day's events when they sit down in the evening with the newspaper or when they log on to an Internet news source, but they aren't especially looking for information about a particular organization. They more or less stumble over it and, if it seems to suit their interests and needs, they will read the information and perhaps act on it.

The impact of messages presented by the news media can be looked at from two perspectives. On the one hand, there is the added credibility associated with news reporting.

News Media Tactics

Direct News Material

- News fact sheet
- Event listing
- Interview notes
- News release (announcement, response, hometowner, news brief)
- Feature release (biography, history, backgrounder, question-and-answer piece, service article)
- Actuality
- Audio news release
- Video B-roll
- Video news release
- Social media release
- Photo and caption
- Media kit

Indirect News Material

- Media advisor
- Story idea memo
- Query letter

Opinion Material

- Position statement (position paper, white paper, position paragraph, contingency statement)
- Letter to the editor
- Guest editorial

Interactive News Opportunities

- News interview
- News conference
- Studio interview
- Satellite media tour
- Editorial conference

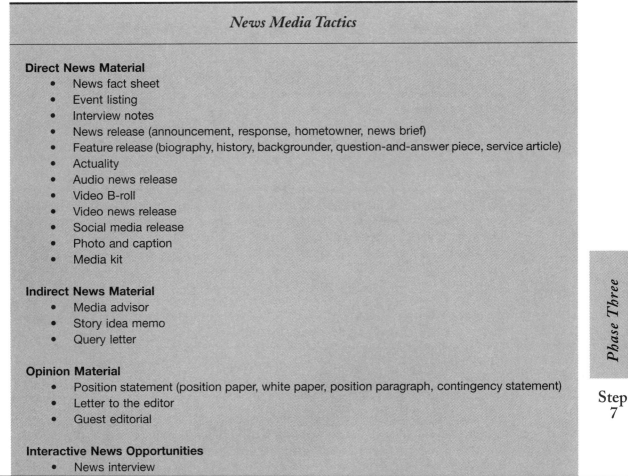

On the other hand, individual news reports seldom affect people who were not previously interested in the topic or in the organization associated with the story. The lesson for public relations: Strive for good publicity, but don't expect it to work miracles. Remember that the news media offer only one set of items on the menu of communication tactics.

Newspapers

Newspapers are publications that boast of up-to-date printed information—reports of what happened the previous day or even earlier on the same day of their distribution. They may be published daily or nondaily (usually weekly, some with more or less frequency). Media directories list more than 12,000 newspapers in the United States and Canada—1,550 daily newspapers, 900 Sunday papers, 700 bi- or triweekly, 8,000 weekly, and 1,100 less often than weekly.

Circulation for daily newspapers can be high. In the United States, *USA Today* and the *Wall Street Journal* are the two largest newspapers, circulating more than 2.6 million and 2.1 million copies, respectively. Internationally, the *Yomiuri Shimbun* in Tokyo circulates more than 14 million copies daily and counts a reading audience of more than 26 million. The world's five largest newspapers are published in Japan. Ten Japanese papers have larger circulations than any in the United States.

At the other end of the spectrum, two-thirds of daily newspapers in North America circulate in towns and cities of less than 50,000 residents, according to *Editor & Publisher International Year Book* (Maddux, 2008). Many weekly newspapers circulate only a few hundred to a few thousand copies.

The number of newspapers has been declining in recent decades as the cost of publishing, corporate mergers and the pressures of competition have forced financially weaker publications out of business. Simultaneously, the newspaper audience is declining: Audiences are getting older, and younger information consumers are more likely to get their news from radio or television than from newspapers. Nevertheless, most opinion leaders—business people, educators, politicians, clergy, and others in positions of influence—are staunch newspaper readers, and many "average citizens" make newspaper reading a part of their daily information-gathering habit.

The Newspaper Association of America's audience profile (http://www.naa.org/TrendsandNumbers/Audience-Profiles.asp) reports the following profile of U.S. newspaper readers for 2006: female-to-male ratio of 53:47; 64% age 45 or older; 89% white; 63% married; 65% with incomes of $40,000 or more; 53% college graduates. This profile could affect the future practice of public relations, with low newspaper readership among growing demographic groups within the population, particularly youth and minorities.

General-interest newspapers. General-interest newspapers are the most common types of newspapers, appealing to the diverse interests of a wide spectrum of readers. Most of these are local newspapers published for the residents of a particular town, city, or metropolitan area. They cover topics such as current events, including crimes, accidents, births and deaths; political and business news; sports and entertainment reports and reviews; information about the arts and leisure pursuits such as cooking and gardening; announcements of upcoming meetings and activities; and specialized information relating to issues such as education and health. Most local newspapers also include opinion sections with editorials and letters from readers.

General-interest newspapers can be further divided into three major subcategories: national newspapers such as *USA Today,* city or metropolitan newspapers such as the *Atlanta Constitution*, and community newspapers such as the weekly *Idaho Enterprise* (circulation 1,500) in rural Malad City, Idaho.

Trade newspapers. Newspapers that are focused on a particular industry or profession are called trade newspapers. Unlike organizational newspapers that are published by a particular company or nonprofit organization, trade newspapers are usually published by professional organizations or trade associations that serve the needs of several different companies and nonprofit groups linked to a particular industry or profession. Some trade newspapers are independently published, such as *Overdrive,* a biweekly newspaper for truckers. Others are published by industry associations for people working in that field, such as *Carolina Cattle Connection,* the official newspaper for members of both the North Carolina and South Carolina Cattlemen's Associations.

Special-interest newspapers. Special-interest newspapers are devoted to markets such as the arts, business, sports, entertainment, or other specific sectors. Though the topic for each publication is narrow, information in such newspapers is intended for a wide audience. *The Hockey News* and *Indian Country Today* are examples of special-interest newspapers.

Special-audience newspapers. Special-audience newspapers are similar to the special-interest newspapers, but they are written for particular audiences, such as gay and lesbian readers, the military, African Americans, Jewish readers, or Hispanic readers, as well as about 40 other ethnic or special-interest groups, according to media directories such as *Editor & Publisher's International Year Book* (http://www.editorandpublisher.com) and the *Gale Directory of Publications and Broadcast Media* (http://www.gale.com). Information in these newspapers is often diverse, though the appeal is clearly linked to a specific audience. Often such newspapers are printed in languages other than English.

Organizational newspapers. Organizational newspapers, also called house organs, are published by political, ethnic, religious, educational, and other groups. Information in them generally deals with those organizations and their members. *Public Relations Tactics* is an example of an organizational newspaper, published for members of the Public Relations Society of America. As a category, this sometimes overlaps special interest and special audience papers. For example, the *Navajo Times* is the official newspaper of the Navajo Nation that is primarily read—not surprisingly—by Navajos (special audience) and by others who are particularly interested in the Navajo people (special interest).

Magazines

Magazines are publications with less frequency and less immediacy than newspapers; prepublication time may include several days, even several weeks, from when a story is written until the time that magazine is distributed to readers. Some magazines are local or regional and thus focused on a particular geographic area, but most are of more general interest and their content is more feature-based than most newspapers.

Like newspapers, magazines based in the United States and Canada are published in many different languages—about 50 in all. These include the three most common languages in North America—English, French, and Spanish—as well as several Native American or

Media Directories

Media directories are useful resource documents or online resources that provide much valuable information about newspapers and magazines, radio and television stations, broadcast networks, blogs, and related media. Here are some of the widely used directories:

Bacon's Directories (http:// us.cision/com/products_services). Newspaper/magazine directories for daily and weekly publications, news services, syndicates, publishers, columnists, Sunday supplements, ethnic publications, and magazines. Radio/television/cable directory with stations, broadcast and cable networks, satellite systems, and syndicates. Internet directory with information on media-related websites.

BurrellesLuce (http:/www.burrellesluce.com): State-by-state listings for media outlets including daily and nondaily newspapers, news services, syndicates, magazines (trade, professional, and consumer), newsletters, radio and television stations, cable services, and networks.

Editor and Publisher International Yearbook (http://www.editorandpublisher.com/eandp/resources/yearbook.jsp): One-volume directory of daily U.S. and Canadian newspapers; weekly, ethnic, special-interest papers; foreign newspapers; and news syndicates.

Gale Directory of Publications and Broadcast Media (http://www.gale.cengage.com/servlet/BrowseSeriesServlet?region=9&imprint=000&titleCode=DOP): State-by-state listings for daily, weekly, special-interest newspapers; periodicals; radio; television; cable; networks; and news syndicates.

Gebbie Press All-in-One Media Directory (http://www.gebbieinc.com/aio.htm): One-volume directory of business, trade, financial, and consumer publications; news syndicates; daily and weekly newspapers; ethnic newspapers; television networks; television and radio stations.

Matthews Media Directories (http://www.marketwire.com/mw/include.do?module=MEDIA&pageid=502): Directories specializing in Canadian print and electronic media.

Media Contacts Pro (http://www.mediacontactspro.com). Listing of print and electronic media including blogs worldwide.

Newsletters in Print (http://www.marketresearch.com/product/display.asp?productid=1270307&g=1). Directory of newsletters in United States and Canada.

Television and Cable Factbook (http://www.warren-news.com/factbook.htm). Directory of commercial and public television stations, cable systems, instructional systems, low-power stations, foreign-language programming, media organizations, networks, satellite services, communication attorneys and engineers in the United States, Canada, Mexico and international markets.

WritersMarket.com (http://www.writersmarket.com). Freelance-oriented information on consumer, trade, and professional magazines.

Additionally, Internet search engines list directories of specialized media such as blogs and social media.

Native Canadian languages, and also less-common languages such as Welsh, Urdu, Latin, and Icelandic.

Writer's Market, a comprehensive annual listing of magazines published in North America, lists thousands of popular or consumer magazines, the kind found on newsstands and through subscription services. These are published in several different categories—general circulation, college, health, foreign language, ethnic, music, men's interest, women's interest, sports, and so on.

Additionally, there are an untold number of house organs, which are magazines produced within a particular company or organization. These usually focus on organizational issues and are intended for employees, volunteers, stockholders, donors, and other interested audiences. Examples of house organs are *Women Police,* a quarterly magazine published by the International Association of Women Police, and *Handball,* the official magazine of the U.S. Handball Association.

Sometimes the categories can overlap. Some magazines are published for special audiences, such as *Essence* for black women, *Seventeen* for teenage girls, and *Sisters Today* for nuns. Meanwhile, trade magazines are published by and/or for particular businesses, professions, and industries. Some of these are published by organizations, such as the *Canadian Guernsey Journal* published by the Canadian Guernsey Association. Others are independently published, such as *Sheep!* a magazine for sheep farmers.

Especially in the trade press, distinctions often blur among newspapers, magazines, and newsletters, because the distinguishing features related to physical format are offset by a similar content and readership. Consider the financial media, for example. It includes daily business-oriented newspapers such as the *Wall Street Journal,* weekly newspapers such as the *Business Journal of Central New York*, regional magazines such as *Colorado Business*, the business sections of most metropolitan daily newspapers, business magazines such as *Barron's* and *Business Week*, consumer magazines such as *Money* and *Fortune,* financial newsletters such as the *Kiplinger Report*, company newsletters published by brokerage firms and investment companies, and financial columnists such as Jane Bryant Quinn. And that's just the print media.

The actual number of magazines is impossible to calculate accurately, but it is vast. In just the area of religion, for example, *Religious Periodicals of the United States: Academic and Scholarly Journals* has estimated that there are more than 2,500 religious magazines, many of them associated with a particular denomination, diocese, or religious order (Lippy, 1986).

E-zines, e-mail based magazines, are a new addition to the publishing field. The trend toward e-zines began in the mid-1990s, when magazine publishers began placing editorial content, stories and photographs at their magazine websites. Now many online magazines also feature interactive opportunities for readers, much of this involving catalog sections of the magazines where readers can order products from a variety of companies. Examples are Stylehog.com (http://www. stylehog.com) about fashion on a budget; WeirdMusic.net (http://www.weirdmusic.net) about creative indie music; and The Dive Site (http://www.thedivesite.com) for scuba divers.

Radio

Radio provides opportunities in the traditional terrestrial or over-the-air radio as well as emerging satellite/Internet radio alternatives.

Terrestrial radio. The category of terrestrial radio includes both the AM and FM formats. Generally AM is more oriented toward news, sports, or talk, whereas FM often includes more all-music formats. The stations may be commercial or public. Experts count about 44,000 radio stations worldwide. The United States and Canada together have about 14,500 radio stations: about 5,100 AM stations and 9,400 FM stations. Most of these are commercial stations, but about 1,260 are public, plus about 2,500 educational stations. Many radio news opportunities exist at the local level, others through about 115 national networks. These include large networks such as ABC Radio or the UPI Radio Network, and smaller, specialized networks such as the Beethoven Satellite Network of classical music; Tobacco Radio Network, with agricultural information; and Kidwaves Radio Network, with children's programming.

Internet radio. The new forms of radio are making inroads in the audiences. **Internet radio** carries web-based stations as well as radiolike collections of music in categories tailored to the individual listener's interests. As of 2006, Internet radio became a meaningful competitor to traditional AM and FM stations, and claimed about 12% of listeners in 2008.

Satellite radio. Another category, satellite radio (sometimes called **subscription radio** or **digital radio**), offers clear digital signals to audience members who subscribe to the service. The signal is transmitted via satellite, so it covers thousands of miles, compared to the limited listening area of terrestrial stations. Satellite radio has advantages of being free from U.S. Federal Comunications Commission content restrictions and of being relatively devoid of commercials. It is growing, while struggling for a wider audience.

Whether in traditional or new configurations, radio is found virtually everywhere. Audiences are large, with 19 out of 20 people listening to radio at some time during a typical week. Combination news, talk, and information stations have the most listeners, followed by stations with a country-music format, according to Arbitron ratings (http://www.arbitron.com). One of the benefits of radio is its mobility—a positive quality in that it can travel with people, but also a negative one from a public relations standpoint because people listen passively to radio while doing other things (such as driving, working, and reading).

Indeed, many people who turn on radios can hardly be called listeners—they use radio mainly to overcome silence, without really listening to it. Because of this, research shows that audience recall of radio commercials is less than that for television commercials; however, the relatively low cost of radio advertising allows for heavier repetition than many organizations generally can afford via television. On the other hand, radio generally attracts individuals alone (unlike television, which often is watched by people in groups). So when radio audiences do really listen, they focus on what is being said.

Because radio formats are specific, audiences tend to be very different from one station to another. National Public Radio, for example, is popular with people who are identified as opinion leaders in many different environments. Classic rock stations, meanwhile, find that two-thirds of their listeners are between the ages of 18 and 34; they are particularly strong with young men under age 25. News and talk stations draw an audience heavy with men and women 55 and older, with the total audience better educated than Americans in general. It also found that stations focused on contemporary hits attract women under 30 and teenagers. Thus it is important to know your key publics before making decisions about particular stations.

What are the strategic implications of all this? Let's say you are operating a restaurant or a retail store. If you want to attract younger customers, pipe classic rock or progressive rock over the sound system. On the other hand, if you want more senior citizens, use easy listening (favored by 51% of radio listeners aged 50 or older) or nostalgic music (72% of listeners), according to Simmons Market Research Bureau (Piirto 1994). Want to appeal more to women customers? Simmons reports that country music listeners tend to be women ages 25 to 54, with lower incomes than women in the Top 40 audience. This kind of demographic information has implications for public relations strategists—for example, in the kind of music-related events they might sponsor or possible topics for articles in a newsletter or website for consumer or employee publics.

Television

Like radio, television may be commercial or public, with opportunities to reach audiences through both local stations and national or regional networks. Other television opportunities include cable programming, both through national networks and local production facilities.

Lead Time

The amount of time it takes reporters and other media professionals to gather and present their news is called *lead time*. This varies with both the type of medium and the kind of presentation that will be given.

The best way to know the lead time required by various media is to ask. Contact the city editor of a newspaper, the news director or assignment editor of a radio or television station, or the acquisitions editor or news editor of a magazine. Or ask an individual reporter or columnist.

Here is an outline of typical lead times needed for various news media tactics:

Daily newspapers. Give about a week's notice for routine information, a day or several hours for important news, and less than an hour for major on-deadline news. Information for special sections such as travel, food, and social events may have a longer lead time. News releases can be submitted at any time, but Sunday and Monday often find less competition for space because weekends traditionally are slow news days, are lightly staffed by most newspapers, and have more pages because of increased advertising.

Nondaily newspapers. Plan to provide information three publication dates before the relevant date of the information. For example, allow three weeks for a weekly newspaper, or a week and a half for a twice-weekly newspaper.

Magazines. Most monthly magazines require at least a two-month lead time for information to be published. Weekly news magazines have a much shorter lead time but seldom take information from public relations sources.

Radio. Give about a week's notice for routine information and for upcoming events that reporters might cover, with important news being handled up to news time. Breaking news may be covered live. Other live coverage may be planned with a lead time of a week or longer. Talk shows and other programs with guests may require several weeks to schedule.

Television. Provide up to a week's notice for routine information and for events that reporters might cover, with important news being handled up to news time. Breaking news may be covered live. Talk shows and programs with guests may require several weeks to schedule.

Nearly 2,300 television stations operate throughout the United States and Canada. Most stations are affiliated with a major network. In the United States, the largest commercial networks are ABC, NBC, CBS and Fox, with PBS as the public network; in Canada, CBC and CTV are nationwide English-language television networks, and Radio-Canada is the French-language public TV network. More than 80 over-the-air television networks operate in the United States and Canada, including many specialized networks such as Inuit Television of Canada, Newfoundland Television, the Univision Spanish-language network, several state-based PBS affiliates such as the Pennsylvania Public Television Network, and nearly 30 religious networks.

About 55% of U.S. households receive cable TV service. About 325 cable television networks are in business, including CNBC, Discovery Channel, MTV, and Nickelodeon. Major categories include arts, entertainment, foreign, Hispanic programming, children's programming, sports, shopping, religion, music, and pay-per-view.

When public relations is able to gain the attention of television reporters, organizations find themselves facing potentially vast audiences. Obviously, however, not every public relations activity is newsworthy, nor should it be. To help you determine what is or is not newsworthy, review the definition of news and the characteristics of newsworthiness in Phase Two, Strategy.

Media Information Needs

The relationship between a public relations practitioner and a journalist is symbiotic; that is, it is a relationship in which each side needs the other and benefits from the other.

Public relations people need journalists and information programmers, who can provide a vehicle to present the organization's messages. Reporters need public relations practitioners to help them identify newsworthy stories and report on them.

Most newspapers are private commercial enterprises. About 70% of their income derives from advertising and 30% from circulation; news and commentary are the products these companies are selling. As businesses protected by the First Amendment of the U.S. Constitution, American newspapers are not required to publish any particular material, including news releases and other information originating from public relations practitioners. Not even government agencies can command news coverage.

Television and radio stations generally are private businesses as well. While they must meet certain government regulations (because they have, in effect, a franchise to operate on a particular channel frequency), they nevertheless have much discretion over what news to cover. An exception to this private ownership, of course, is the system of public radio and television networks.

Editors and news directors usually are receptive to public relations information when they believe it will satisfy the interests of their readers. An estimated one-half to two-thirds of the information in daily newspapers originates from public relations practitioners, either through vehicles initiated by practitioners, such as news releases, news conferences and media alerts, or because practitioners have responded to journalists with interviews or background information. The rate for radio and television news broadcasts is slightly lower, because these media proportionally give more coverage to accidents, crime, and other breaking news. As rising corporate costs lead to news-gathering teams becoming smaller at many publications and broadcast stations, news-oriented public relations practitioners can be of increasing assistance to the remaining reporters, and thus more effective in service to their organizations.

The most common way for public relations practitioners to provide newspeople with information is to give it to them in writing. News releases and other written information traditionally has been distributed through the mail, sometimes through news wires; increasingly, fax and e-mail are become accepted distribution tools, and some organizations service reporters through websites. For breaking news and sometimes for story ideas, some public relations practitioners make telephone contact with reporters.

Virtually all journalists now use the Internet. The Survey of Media in the Wired World (Middleberg & Ross, 2001) reports that 98% of journalists go online at least daily to check for e-mail. Other findings in this seventh national survey: 92% use the Internet to research their articles, 76% of reporters use the Internet to find news sources and experts, 73% look for news releases online, and 53% receive story pitches via e-mail. Digital photography is gaining support, with 46% of magazine journalists and 61% of newspaper reporters preferring digital photography for receiving images, as compared to slides and prints. The study also found that e-mail matches the telephone as the preferred methods for interviewing news sources.

What's a public relations person to do with such information? For starters, use it to develop a media-friendly website. Make the information easy for journalists to find, generally as a well-placed link from the organization's home page. Include the kind of information a journalist might need: basic facts, history, downloadable photos, stats, and so on. Include an easy-to-navigate link to a public relations staff person. Invite reporters to sign up for customized e-mails that will alert them to topics of interest. Make sure you keep the site updated as frequently as possible.

Let's look at some of the ways in which public relations practitioners can provide the news media with newsworthy information and thus disseminate their messages to the vast media audiences. There are four general ways to present information through the news media: direct news material, indirect news material, opinion material and interactive news opportunities.

Direct News Material

One of the most frequently used categories of news media tactics is **direct news material**—information that is presented to the media more or less ready for use. These tactics include news fact sheets, event listings, interview notes, news releases, feature releases, actualities, audio news releases, video B-rolls, video news releases, photos and captions, and media kits. Here's a brief overview of each.

News fact sheets. Brief, generally one-page outlines of information about a newsworthy event or activity are called **news fact sheets**. These often are presented as bulleted items; the format makes it easy for reporters in both print and electronic media to use the information as they write their own stories. Fact sheets also can be used by people other than reporters, such as speechwriters, tour guides, employees, and customers.

Fact sheets are easy to prepare. Simply gather the relevant information and present it along the traditional journalistic lines of who, what, when, where, why and how. It also may be useful to add sections on background, history, significance, and benefits. Additionally, it may be appropriate to include a brief direct quote.

Event listings. Another information format for print media are **event listings**, also called **community calendars**. These are simple notices that most newspapers and many magazines print about upcoming activities such as benefits, meetings, entertainment events, public lectures, and the like. Many publications also offer online postings of community events.

Interview notes. Another useful tactic is **interview notes**, which are verbatim transcripts presented in a question-and-answer format, based on an interview that a public relations writer has done with an organizational news source. For example, a university news bureau might interview a geology professor about breakthrough work involving earthquake prediction, then provide the transcript of that interview for science writers. Interview notes usually begin with a brief narrative paragraph to set the stage. They often include a biographical sketch of the person being interviewed.

Interview notes allow reporters to build their stories as they see fit. Even if they decide to do their own interviews, the interview notes can save them time and give them information to build on.

News releases. Most organizations find that **news releases** are a mainstay of media relations. These are news stories written by public relations practitioners and given to media gatekeepers for use in their news publications, programs and online information sites. Submit them to newspaper city editors or to editors or beat reporters of special interest such as sports, business, or entertainment sections. Special-interest magazines also may use news releases, especially for brief items.

Public Relations Helps Write the News

The news media owe a lot to public relations. Estimates vary on how much information carried in the news media comes from public relations practitioners—one-half, two-thirds, three-fourths. Whatever the actual number, it's evident that most editors and reporters get a lot of their information from public relations sources.

A classic 1981 study in the *Columbia Journalism Review* counted 45% of the 188 news stories in one edition of the *Wall Street Journal* as originating with public relations practitioners. A press secretary to a former New York City mayor estimated that public relations generates 50% of stories in that city's newspapers (Wilcox, Cameron, Ault, & Agee, 2005). Another academic journal reported that 78% of journalists surveyed said they use news releases, at least to spark story ideas, more than half of the time (Curtain, 1999). In that survey, many said they have strict guidelines for using public relations materials, such as using only those from nonprofit organizations promoting social causes but not from businesses seeking economic gain.

The term for such assistance is **information subsidy**—that is, information from public relations sources that increasingly short-staffed editors use to help underwrite the costs of gathering news. In his book *Market-Driven Journalism: Let the Citizen Beware?* John McManus (1994) has predicted that newsrooms will turn more frequently to low-cost public relations information subsidies.

That could be good for public relations practitioners. But there is a downside to the trend. If the media lower their journalistic standards to the point that they lose credibility with their audiences, public relations people will find less value in news media coverage. Thus, despite easier entrée to the news columns and broadcasts, media coverage would be worth less. Something to think about.

For broadcast media, submit news releases to news directors or assignment editors. Also, consider taking the time to rewrite the standard (that is, print-oriented) releases when you intend to send them to radio or television stations.

In the past, news releases were distributed through the mail or were hand delivered, either by the public relations practitioners or by a courier. Some practitioners still try to maintain face-to-face interaction with reporters by delivering their releases. Most media outlets report that many news releases continue to arrive through the mail or via fax.

Increasingly, however, organizations are disseminating news releases via e-mail to individual journalists, or they are posting releases on websites where reporters can retrieve the information. Some practitioners notify reporters via an e-mail distribution list when they post news releases on their websites.

News releases also may be submitted to wire services such as the Associated Press, though most wire-service stories are obtained from local bureaus and member newspapers. Radio stations often obtain information from specialized radio wire services such as the North American Network or the News/Broadcast Network. In addition to submitting information directly to broadcast stations, some organizations provide frequently updated recorded news releases and sound bites that reporters can dial up on a telephone system or download from a website and record for their broadcast news reports. Additionally, news releases can be disseminated through commercial public relations wire services like PR Newswire.

If you are considering preparing a news release, note that there are several different kinds. **Announcement releases**, for example, often are subcategorized as dealing with events, personnel, progress, bad news, programs or products. **Response releases** deal with new or updated information, comments, public interest tie-ins, and speeches. **Hometowner releases** are sent to newspapers serving the permanent residential areas of employees, students, members of the military, and so on.

Whereas a news release involves a page or more of information, a **news brief** is likely to be only a two- or three-paragraph story that provides the basic information of the summary lead as well as a clear indication of the benefit. Some public relations writers try to write each news release so the first couple of paragraphs can be pulled out to serve as a news brief. Written this way, the news-brief portion also can serve as part of an online menu of articles, linking to the longer version for readers seeking more in-depth information.

Note that the news media are not obligated to use news releases. In fact, most releases are rejected, usually because they are either more self-promoting than news reporting or because they are weak in local interest.

Feature releases. In addition to releases that present solid news, other releases focus on some kind of background on the news. Known as **feature releases**, they fall into several categories: biographies, histories, backgrounders, question-and-answer pieces, and service articles.

Biographies provide the personal background on news makers and other people significant to an organization. They can be written in chronological style or as personality profiles. **Histories**, meanwhile, provide a similar focus on the organization itself, usually providing a chronological narrative or an outline of the development of the organization since its founding. Histories generally deal not only with milestones but also with issues facing the organization. Both histories and biographies are written so they can be updated easily when new developments warrant.

Narrative articles providing objective information on an issue are called **backgrounders**. They usually deal with the cause of the problem or issue, a chronological history of how the

Wire Services

Here is a brief overview of the most commonly used news wire services, along with their Internet addresses:

The Associated Press (http://www.ap.org) has 243 bureaus in 97 countries, serving 1,700 U.S. newspapers, and 5,000 radio or television outlets in the United States and thousands more worldwide.

The Canadian Press (http://www.canadianpress.com) provides news for print, broadcast, and multimedia outlets.

Reuters (http://www.reuters.com) provides news in 17 international editions.

United Press International (http://www.upi.com) has bureaus around the world.

Many smaller and more specialized wire services serve the particular needs of their client newspaper and broadcast stations. Examples of these include Cox News (http://www.coxnews.com/html/info/cns.html), the Environment News Service (http://www.ens-news.com) and the Catholic News Service (http://www.catholicnews.com).

Additionally, there are several public relations and business wire services. Most carry news releases, photos, media alerts, and audio or video transmissions and offer broadcast fax and fax-on-demand services. These include PR Newswire (http://www.prnewswire.com); the CNW Group (http://www.newswire.ca), an affiliate of PR Newswire; Business Wire (http://www.businesswire.com); Bloomberg.com (http://www.bloomberg.com) which handles business and financial news and columns, and Dow Jones Newswires (http://www.djnewswires.com), which handles financial news.

issue has progressed, its current status, and perhaps clear projections of its direction and likely future. Backgrounders also provide information on the significance or impact of the issue. The key element for a backgrounder is that it should remain neutral—objective and free of opinion or unsupported speculation; indeed, all sides in an issue should be able to agree on the facts within a well-written backgrounder.

Other categories of feature articles are labeled according to the writing format used in the release. Some releases are presented as a **question-and-answer piece** (also called a **Q&A**). Others are written in the step-by-step format of a **service article** or **how-to piece**, which provides readers with an instructional approach to solving a problem.

Actualities. When public relations writers want to quote someone in a news release going to print journalists, they include a sentence or phrase in quotation marks. When they want to provide radio reports with similar quoted material, they use an **actuality** (sometimes called a **sound bite**), because radio stations need to present quoted information in the voice of the news source. An actuality is a recording—sometimes on cassette, sometimes digitized and made accessible by computer. It involves a couple of highlight quotes from a speech or statement by an organizational spokesperson.

Audio news releases. Whereas actualities are audio sound bites, **audio news releases** (ANRs) are edited story packages that public relations writers offer to radio journalists. ANRs are news stories complete with announcer and sound bite. Most U.S. radio stations use audio news releases in some ways, particularly if the ANR has a local angle. The ANRs that get on the air are most commonly 60-second spots plugged into the morning drive-time reports. Nonprofit organizations, corporations, and government agencies produce audio news releases. For example, the U.S. Department of Labor posts ANRs with other materials at its media website (http://www. dol.gov/dol/media).

Video B-rolls. Quoted statements and other visual information can be made available to television stations through **video B-rolls**, which are tapes providing a series of unedited video shots and sound bites related to the news story. A written news release or other background material often accompanies B-rolls to give television reporters an idea of what the story is all about. B-rolls are becoming increasingly popular with television stations. One video news release production company, The NewsMarket, reported 30,000 media requests for B-rolls for the first 3 months of 2005, compared to 70,000 requests for all of 2004.

Video news releases. A packaged video bite edited into a complete story package is the **video news release**, or VNR. VNRs, which are given to television journalists by public relations people, usually run 30 to 90 seconds long, complete with narration, interviews, and background video, even names titled at the bottom of the screen. B-rolls are sometimes used with VNRs to provide for easier editing of newsworthy material. VNRs generally are one of two types: a **timely release** focusing on a current news event, or an **evergreen release**, often taking a human-interest approach, that has a longer potential time frame for use.

Television stations use about 5,000 VNRs each year. Nielsen Media Research has reported that three out of four television stations use VNRs weekly, and WestGlen Communications has found that 85% of television stations in the United States use outside-produced video for some newscasts. The Project for Excellence in Journalism reported that the amount of VNRs and video B-rolls doubled between 1998 and 2002 ("West Glen Communications Releases New PSA Survey," 2002). Morning and early evening are the two news slots when VNRs and B-rolls are most likely to be used. However, many VNRs are not used because television news directors judge them to be lacking in local news value or some other important criterion. Another reason some VNRs are rejected is that they are overly commercial, lacking what the reporters consider strong news judgment. Still, when they are used, the impact can be huge. For example, Pepsi-Cola reached an estimated 365 million viewers with four VNRs in 1993, when a hoax was perpetrated that claimed syringes had been found in cans of Pepsi products.

Because of the production costs involved, most video news releases are developed by organizations with widespread publics rather than for single-market use. VNRs and B-rolls may be distributed nationally or regionally. National distribution can cost from $25,000 to more than $100,000. Local or regional distribution, especially of B-rolls, can involve only a nominal expense for an organization that has its own video production setup or the assistance of a video production studio.

VNRs have sparked some controversy. The watchdog group Center for Media and Democracy (http://www.prwatch.org), which is critical of many public relations practices, campaigns against VNRs as "fake news." The administration of President George W. Bush used tax money to produce and distribute VNRs promoting its version of a Medicare reform bill, sparking congressional criticism and an investigation by the Federal Communications Commission and the Government Accountability Office into illegal use of federal funds. The GAO ruled that the VNRs were illegal forms of "covert propaganda," but the Justice Department told federal agencies to ignore the ruling, and the administration continued to produce VNRs at taxpayers' expense.

Both the Public Relations Society of America and the Radio-Television News Directors Association have ethical guidelines calling for TV stations to indicate the source of VNR material used in newscasts. A 2005 study by Harris Interactive found that 71% of adult consumers believe that TV news sources should be required to indicate the sources of stories generated by companies, government, or other outside organizations.

Social media releases. A new communication tactics is the **social media release** (SMR), a type of news release intended for blogs, websites, and other online uses. It is the result of new technology and changing information patterns.

The SMR includes many elements not found in a standard news release: liberal use of subheads as well as headlines to help move the reader along; summary statements, as in a news brief; and bulleted facts (similar to those in the news fact sheet previously noted). A social media release also include many kinds of links and feeds: links to photos, MP3 files, podcasts, and other audio clips; graphics; logos; various types of video; downloads of related information and background materials; links to other coverage of the topic; links to additional commentary and quotes from organizational news sources; and links to additional background

Trusted News Sources

A report for the Public Relations Society of America by Harris Interactive (2005) focused in part on the trust level for various information sources by a cross-section of American civil society: adult consumers, corporate executives, and bipartisan congressional staffers. The study found that National Public Radio (NPR) and TV's Public Broadcasting Service (PBS) are the most trusted news sources, and advertising the least trusted.

Here's a synopsis of the findings. The three numbers indicate the positive percentage of adult consumers, executives, and congressional staffers, respectively.

- Belief that most of the news is accurate and unbiased (43, 38, 33).
- Reliance on independent news sources such as Internet chat rooms, blogs, or other alternative media (42, 21, 30).
- Trust levels regarding news via NPR or PBS (61, 75, 70).
- Trust levels regarding news in national newspapers (56, 78, 78).
- Trust levels regarding television and radio network news (53, 59, 62).
- Trust levels regarding advocacy organizations such as the National Rifle Association, the American Association of Retired Persons, and the American Civil Liberties Union (44, 18, 39).
- Trust levels regarding public relations sources (37, 29, 29).
- Trust levels regarding celebrity spokespersons (30, 8, 13).
- Trust levels regarding advertising sources (25, 24, 20).
- Public relations people presenting misleading information (85, 67, 85).
- Public relations people raising public awareness on important issues (71, 84, 84).

information, finances, history, and products or services of the organization, as well as a link to a traditional news release.

The social news release also generally includes a time-date stamp to indicate when the information was last updated.

Photos and captions. Photographs and written captions that explain the people and action in the photos also are of interest to newspaper and magazine editors. Stand-alone captions are complete stories based on a news-related event, written instead of a news release with an accompanying photo. For most newspapers, photos are provided in black-and-white formats, though increasingly newspapers are using color, especially in feature sections such as those devoted to travel, entertainment, gardening, decorating, and similar pursuits. Most magazines use only color slides.

Digital photos can be made available for journalists to download from an organization's website. Generally, these should be made available in JPEG format with at least 333 dpi (dots per inch) for photos in a 5x7 or 8x10 format. Note that this is significantly greater than the standard 72 ppi (pixels per inch, the on-screen equivalent of dpi) that are used for most website photos.

Media kits. Most of the above-described direct news materials can be gathered together in a **media kit**, sometimes called a **press packet**. These are presented to the journalists who attend news conferences and often are delivered to invited reporters who fail to attend. Media kits generally include one or more news releases along with fact sheets, feature releases, photos and other graphics.

Indirect News Material

In addition to the direct materials noted earlier, public relations practitioners also can use several indirect news materials to communicate with reporters, editors, and news directors. These are messages that are not meant to be published but are intended to interest or inform media gatekeepers. Consider the following in your tactical program: media advisories, story idea memos, and query letters.

Media advisories. Brief notes given to media gatekeepers are called **media advisories** or **media alerts**. These memos inform the gatekeepers of upcoming news opportunities. For example, a public relations practitioner might use a media advisory to announce a news conference, to invite photographers to a newsworthy event, or to inform editors and news directors about a newsworthy activity involving the organization. Media advisories differ from news releases in that the advisory is not meant to be published but is intended as useful information for a journalist. Realize, however, that information in a media advisory is not off the record, and enterprising journalists may use the memo to craft a news report preempting the announced news conference or special event. Therefore, be careful not to provide too much information in an advisory.

Story idea memos. Another useful news-oriented tactic is the **story idea memo** or **tip sheet**. These are informal idea memos submitted to the gatekeepers of newspapers, magazines, and electronic news media. The intention is to spark a reporter's interest in developing a feature article. The public relations practitioners suggest available interview subjects or topics for articles that can be developed by the publication's own writers.

Query letters. Letters written to editors or broadcasters proposing a story and inquiring about their interest in it are called **query letters**. These are more commonly used by freelance writers than by public relations practitioners, and they often are directed to magazines or feature supplements to Sunday newspapers. However, some practitioners find it useful to query magazines and then prepare feature articles if an editor expresses interest. Additionally, some practitioners work with freelance writers who prepare stories on assignment for magazines.

Opinion Material

Another category of tactics rooted in the news media involves several opportunities for using newspapers, magazines, and radio and television stations to present an organization's opinion rather than simply the factual information that is the focus of most of the preceding news tactics. Both in proactive situations in which the organization wishes to advocate for a particular position, or when it reactively seeks to explain or defend its position, an organization often realizes several benefits by producing this opinion material.

Consider the following vehicles through which organizations can present their formal opinions about various issues: position statements, letters to the editor, and guest editorials.

Position statements. Going a step beyond backgrounders (which were discussed earlier, in the section Direct News Material), **position statements** add an organization's official and carefully considered opinion on an issue. Position statements can be used in a variety of ways, not only as materials for journalists but also as the basis for editorials in organizational publications, source material for speeches and organizational letters, and documents to be provided directly to employees, donors or stockholders, supporters, legislators, and other influential publics. Position statements often are published as stand-alone organizational publications.

Position statements can vary in their depth and intensity. A position paper, sometimes called a **white paper**, may be a detailed and lengthy discussion of a major issue of long-term significance. A **position paragraph** is a much shorter statement, often providing an organization's comments on a local or short-lived issue. A **contingency statement** or **standby statement** is a prepared comment written so an organization may express its voice in various potential situations. For example, a company nearing the resolution of a lawsuit may prepare several contingency statements to cover the possible outcomes—winning the case, losing it, being convicted of lesser charges, having the charge dismissed, and so on. Obviously, contingency statements should be kept in strict confidence until one of them is needed.

Letters to the editor. Opinion letters written to newspapers and magazines offer many opportunities for public relations practitioners to communicate through the news media even when the gatekeepers have overlooked the organization. Use letters to the editor as publicity vehicles to announce things that don't make it into the news columns. Also, use letters to advocate a cause that likewise hasn't caught the attention of journalists. Occasionally letters can be used to correct errors, though most organizations find it better to ignore all but the most serious factual misstatements in published reports.

Guest editorials. Some commentaries can go beyond the length and impact of letters to the editor. **Guest editorials** generally are placed opposite the editorial page of a newspaper, hence their alternative name, **op-ed pieces**. A guest editorial is a grander version of a letter to the editor. It is a signed essay that, because of its length and placement, has higher prestige and credibility than a letter. Usually it's necessary to contact the publication before submitting an essay to be considered as a guest editorial. In many cases, guest editorials are written by public relations people but carry the signature of an organizational executive, thereby giving the piece additional credibility because of a high-ranking message source.

Interactive News Opportunities

A final category of news activities is interactive news opportunities—that is, those communication opportunities in which public relations practitioners and journalists interact with each other. These include news interviews, news conferences, studio interviews, satellite media tours, and editorial conferences.

News interviews. Sessions in which journalists ask questions and public relations practitioners or organizational spokespersons respond are a mainstay of the interaction between an organization and the news media. **News interviews** usually are one-on-one question-and-answer sessions. Public relations practitioners prepare for interviews by anticipating questions reporters may ask and gathering relevant information to answer the questions. They also help organizational spokespersons frame appropriate responses to reporters' questions. Often this coaching includes mock interviews prior to the actual encounter between the spokesperson and the reporters.

Most interviews are face-to-face encounters. Sometimes, however, when a reporter is seeking mainly factual information, especially from a news source the reporter has worked with in the past, the interview may take place over the telephone or via e-mail. See Appendix D, Effective Media Engagement, for tips on good interviewing.

News conferences. Essentially a group interview, a **news conference** is a contrived media happening in which an organizational spokesperson makes a newsworthy statement. Generally this is followed by a question-and-answer session with reporters.

Journalists do not particularly like news conferences because the format puts them in the awkward position of doing their news gathering—always a highly competitive endeavor—in the presence of their competitors. Only a few circumstances justify holding a news conference: (1) to announce news or give a response of major importance (in the eyes of the media, not simply the hopes of the organization), such as a new product or policy initiative, response to an attack, update in a crisis situation, or comment on a breaking news story; (2) to serve the media's interests when a prominent spokesperson or news maker is available for only a short period of time, such as the whirlwind visit or sandwiched-in interview of a celebrity, official, candidate, or some other important person; and (3) to avoid accusations of playing favorites among reporters, such as by disseminating information to one medium ahead of another.

As an alternative to a news conference, consider making the announcement through a news release, or invite reporters to a coordinated series of interviews with an organizational spokesperson. Another option is to invite reporters to a participatory activity, such as a media preview of the opening of a new roller coaster by an amusement park.

If you do judge it appropriate to invite reporters to a news conference, consider the following guidelines:

- Invite all media that may be interested, even those you don't like. Notify the wire services, which in turn may announce the news conference as part of their advisories to member media.

- In a major market with a variety of media outlets, schedule the news conference mid- to late morning, if possible. Because normal business is slow on weekends, also consider Sunday or early Monday news conferences. In a smaller market with few print reporters and television reporters from stations miles away, you'll have to accommodate the schedule of the reporters. In either case, ask key reporters about convenient times and conflicting news events.
- Hold the news conference in a meeting room rather than in an office. Or if possible, hold the conference at an appropriate on-site location relevant to the information. For example, if you are announcing a new public housing project, hold the news conference at the building site.

Most news conferences are open to all reporters. Generally the word goes out, often posted on media events listings, and interested news media will send reporters. Increasingly, however, invitation-only news conferences are being held, often open only to journalists credentialed by a government or corporate press overseer. As an attempt to control the media or show favorites, these invitation-only events can damage an organization's overall media-relations program.

Remember that journalists seek different outcomes from news conferences. Television reporters need visuals, so try to overcome the talking heads with some creative graphics or locations. Newspaper reporters needs facts and a lot of them; media kits can provide many supplemental materials for them. Bloggers and other alternative journalists may be interested in only a narrow area; some organizations have scheduled separate news conferences for them.

Studio interviews. Another tactic is the **studio interview**, which is a hybrid between the regular interview and the news conference. Like regular interviews, studio interviews involve a reporter/questioner and generally a single interviewee. Sometimes they are set up as a questioner moderating an interview panel. Like a news conference, they often are televised, so everything is presented in "real time" with all the spontaneity of a live interview (even if it is taped for later broadcasting). The growth in popularity of talk radio and, increasingly, talk television offer opportunities to public relations and marketing people promoting new ideas, products, books, and the like. At-home interviews generally include feature or personality profiles for celebrities and other news makers. They can be useful in helping to humanize organizational leaders.

Satellite media tours. A related development in interviewing style is the **satellite media tour** (SMT), a kind of in-studio interview or news conference with a widely dispersed audience. The unique feature of the SMT is that a news source is interviewed by reporters who are in different locations, linked via special television signal or computer link transmitted through satellite technology from the interviewee's location to many reporters throughout the nation, even around the world. Usually these are individual one-on-one interviews, packaged in segments of five minutes or less. SMTs have a role both in political campaigning and in crisis communications.

Editorial conferences. Public relations representatives sometimes meet in **editorial conferences**, meetings with editors and editorial boards of newspapers to present them with background information on important issues. Generally such conferences are arranged on the invitation of the editors, though public relations people often try to solicit such invitations. Such conferences may generate news reports, feature stories, and editorial comment on the issue.

Survey on Media Relations Practices

A national survey of more than 2,000 journalists reported some interesting findings. The Journalist Survey on Media Relations Practices conducted by Bulldog Reporter and TEKgroup International (2007) sought to establish benchmarks for journalists who use the Internet to research and report on the news. Here are some of the findings:

Internet research. On the biggest change in journalistic practices, nearly 79% of journalists identified their ability to use the Internet to conduct their research 24 hours a day; 68% identified access to media contact info online; 46% access to electronic press kits online; 43% identified the ability to search corporate news archives online.

Corporate websites. More than 85% of journalists visit a corporate website at least once a month; more than half do so at least weekly.

Obscured information. Reporters complain that corporate websites often obscure contact information for media relations representatives of the organization.

Blogs. Nearly 70% say they follow at least one blog regularly; more than 28% say they visit a social media site at least weekly as part of their reporting.

Audio and video feeds. Nearly half of reporters say they use audio or video material from corporate websites at least occasionally; 51% said they never seek such information.

Understanding the media. Half of reporters say public relations people don't understand the media.

Phone calls. More than 48% say phone calls from public relations people are a waste of time.

Quick response. More than 54% of journalists disagreed with the notion that public relations people do not respond quickly enough.

Truthfulness. More than 52% disagreed with the notion that public relations practitioners do not tell the truth.

Preferences. Nearly 78% said they prefer to receive news releases via e-mail; less than 2% sought releases via postal mail.

Planning Example 7C: Selecting News Media Tactics

Upstate College will develop the following news media tactics to publicize its expanded program:

UPSTATE COLLEGE

- News release—low cost, accessible, target to potential students, parents, donors, and community leaders
- Fact sheet for media—low cost, directed toward media publics
- Fact sheet for students—low cost, directed toward potential students

- Media alert—low cost
- Social media release—low cost, information-on-demand for key publics
- Photo and caption of preparation for ceremony—low cost, interests community about expanded program
- Letter to the editor—low cost, aimed at key publics (parents, donors, community leaders)
- Editorial conference—low cost, interactive with media, potential to generate support for recruitment and fundraising
- News interview with reporters—low cost, high visibility

■ ■ ■

Tiny Tykes will develop the following news media tactics to publicize its dedication to consumer safety and demonstrate its improved crib toy:

- Letters to the editor—low cost, directed toward key publics
- Story idea memo to reporters—low cost, possibly high visibility
- News release—low cost, accessible, aimed at key publics
- Video news release—high cost, possibly high visibility
- Social media release—low cost, targeted for parents

Checklist 7C: News Media Tactics

Basic Questions

1. What news media tactics will you use?
2. How will these tactics help the organization achieve its objectives?
3. What resources will these tactics require?

Expanded Questions

A. SELECTION OF TACTICS

From the following categories of news media tactics, identify several that you would consider using:

Direct News Material

News fact sheet
Event listing
Community calendar
Interview notes
News release
Feature release
Actuality
Video B-roll

Video news release
Photo and caption
Media kit

Indirect News Material

Media advisory
Story idea memo
Query letter

Opinion Material

Position statement
White paper
Contingency statement
Standby statement
Letter to the editor
Guest editorial
Op-ed piece

Interactive News Opportunity

Interview
News conference
Studio interview
Satellite media tour
Editorial conference

B. STRATEGIC IMPLICATIONS

For each item identified, answer the following questions:

1. Will this tactic help the organization to interact with the appropriate public?
2. What level of impact will this tactic make on the key public?
3. Will this tactic advance the organization toward its awareness objectives?
4. Will this tactic advance the organization toward its acceptance objectives?
5. Will this tactic advance the organization toward its action objectives?
6. What is the main advantage to this tactic?
7. What advantages does this tactic offer that other tactics do not?
8. Are there any disadvantages to this tactic?

C. IMPLEMENTATION ITEMS

For each item identified, answer the following questions:

1. How much will it cost to implement this tactic? Is the cost justified? Is the cost practical, based on the organization's resources?
2. How much staff time will it take to implement this tactic? Is the time practical, based on the organization's resources?
3. What skill level, equipment, and expertise is needed to implement this tactic? Is the needed level available within the organization? Is it available from outside sources?

Advertising and Promotional Media Tactics

The final category of communication tactics involves media associated with advertising and promotion. The list in this category includes four major sections: print advertising media, electronic advertising media, out-of-home advertising media, and promotional items.

Strategy for Advertising and Promotional Media

Most advertising is used for marketing purposes, to sell a particular product or service, or to position a particular brand in the minds of its customers. As noted earlier, however, the tools and techniques of advertising can serve the public relations goals of an organization as well.

Advertising can combine the strengths of two other important categories of tactics: organizational media and news media. Like organizational media, advertising is a form of controlled media that provides another opportunity for the organization to oversee all the details of its messages: content, tone, presentation style, and timing. Advertising also can reach vast audiences, a characteristic shared with the news media.

At the same time, advertising has the combined weaknesses of these tactics. Like organizational media, advertising lacks the credibility of third-party endorsement found in the news media. And like the news media, advertising tends not to be able to address itself to information-seeking publics but instead can simply be available when people stumble upon the message, such as while they are reading a magazine or watching television.

Advertising is more of a public medium than a personal one, and it is used most often with external publics, mainly because many forms of interpersonal and organizational medium are better suited for internal publics.

A major negative for advertising is the cost. It is the most expensive of all the categories of communication tactics discussed so far. A midsized daily newspaper, for example, might charge $185 per column inch (PCI) for an ad, meaning that one full-page ad (PCI cost times 157 column inches) would cost more than $29,000. National magazines may charge $150,000 per page. One 30-second spot on the local TV evening news might cost $5,000 in a midsized market. Compare this with the cost of other tactics, and it is easy to see why advertising often is used as a tactic of last resort.

At one time, advertising was thought of only as a mass medium, but increasingly it is able to target its audiences. This is so largely because advertising can piggyback on more and better targeted media, both print and electronic.

Print Advertising

Because it can reach both local and more widespread audiences, and because it is less expensive than broadcasting alternatives, print advertising is used by many organizations. There are various opportunities available in the category of print advertising: magazine advertising, newspaper advertising, directory advertising, and house ads.

Magazine advertising. Ads in magazines tend to focus on national brands rather than local retail outlets and individual products, because of the diverse and widespread readership of most magazines and because of the high advertising cost.

Magazine advertising generally is sold on the basis of full or partial pages. Most advertising is placed as **run of book** (ROB), which means the ad can be placed anywhere within the

Advertising and Promotional Tactics

Print Advertising Media
- Magazine advertising (center spread, advertisorial, breakout ad)
- Newspaper advertising (display ad, classified ad)
- Directory advertising
- House advertising

Electronic Media Advertising
- Television commercial (network placement, spot, infomercial)
- Cable TV advertising (cable crawl)
- Radio commercial (network radio, spot)
- Digital media advertising (interstitial ad, superstitial ad, virtual ad)

Out-of-Home Advertising
- Outdoor poster (billboard, paint, rotary paint, spectacular, extra, wallscape)
- Arena poster
- Signage
- Out-of-home video
- Transit advertising (bus sign, car card, station poster, diorama, shelter poster, mobile billboard)
- Aerial advertising (blimp, airplane tow, skywriting)
- Inflatable

Promotional Items
- Clothing
- Costume
- Office accessory
- Home accessory

magazine. Trade magazines sometimes place ads with an eye toward the articles that are on the same or facing pages.

Special placements usually entail extra costs, with the highest costs going to advertising on the inside or outside covers. Extra costs are also charged for **bleed ads**, which eliminate the white border and carry the advertising image to the edge of the page, and for **center spreads**, which feature two facing pages. Some magazines also feature **advertising inserts** such as coupons or postcards. Occasionally magazines will publish an advertising section, sometimes called an **advertisorial**, a series of consecutive pages dealing with a single theme or product/service line.

Increasingly, advertisers can place **breakout ads** in national publications for distribution to particular groups of readers. Breakout ads run only in specific geographic editions, those copies of a magazine that are distributed within a particular region, perhaps a metropolitan area or a single state. Magazines also offer demographic editions aimed at subscribers with particular interests or backgrounds. For example, *Sports Illustrated* has special advertising packages for editions that are distributed to golf enthusiasts, homeowners, residents of particular regions, and residents of high-income zip code areas. *Newsweek* has an advertising package that can be directed to high-income and/or managerial subscribers.

Information on advertising rates is published in most media directories. A particularly comprehensive information source is the Standard Rate & Data Service (http://www.srds.com).

Newspaper advertising. Newspaper ads offer several different opportunities for promoting goods, services, and ideas. The two different kinds of newspaper advertising are display ads and classified ads.

Display ads are common newspaper advertisements located anywhere throughout the newspaper except the front pages of various sections and the editorial pages. Display ads feature illustrations, headlines, and copy blocks. Most are marketing-oriented ads placed by local retailers selling various products and promoting sales.

Some display ads, however, are placed for public relations purposes, such as to promote events, support political candidates, or present position statements on public issues. For example, a hospital that has come under public scrutiny because of accusations of sexual or racial discrimination may choose to address those charges in a full-page newspaper ad where it can control the entire message—its content, packaging, and timing. Likewise, a health maintenance organization that feels reporters have not adequately explained its new coverage policy may use a full-page ad; the HMO may use such an ad even if it likes what reporters have written, simply as a way to increase awareness of its new policy.

Most newspaper advertising is purchased to run anywhere within the newspaper, called **run of press** (ROP), as compared to special placement on a particular page as in a specific section.

Classified ads are brief, all-text messages. In most newspapers, the three largest categories of classified ads deal with employment, real estate, and automotive sales, but they also are used to find roommates, sell used vacuum cleaners, find homes for puppies, promote social causes, and so on. Classified ads may be used for some public relations purposes, such as to invite participants to job-training programs, college courses, and similar activities.

Directory advertising. Directory advertising uses the Yellow Pages and professional directories to place business promotional announcements. Some organizational directories, like the *Public Relations Tactics Green Book*, published by the Public Relations Society of America, are focused on particular professions and industries. Others are more geographic, such as the Yellow Pages directories, published both by telephone companies themselves and by independent publishers who may target a particular public, such as business-to-business markets. Increasingly, directories are putting both their information listings and their advertising onto CD-ROM and on the Internet.

House ads. Some organizations place house ads or program advertising—honorary or congratulatory announcements in the organization's name that are placed in programs and publications associated with special events or in publications such as school yearbooks and member directories. Opportunities for this type of advertising include a variety of programs for sporting events, banquets, anniversaries, graduations, and other occasions. This kind of advertising may involve full-page or partial-page display ads similar to those used in newspapers and directories, or they may be business-card ads.

Electronic Media Advertising

Advertising on radio, television, and related media is a high-cost promotional expense that also can generate vast audiences. Consider the following possibilities: television commercials, cable television advertising, radio commercials, and computer media.

Television commercials. Commercial and public relations advertising messages are placed on television in one of two ways. First, **network placement** puts the advertisement on all of the stations affiliated with the network. For some of the largest of the 115 television networks in North America, that could mean hundreds of different local stations. Alternatively, organizations can use **spot advertising** to place messages on individual local stations.

Most television commercials are 30 seconds long, though stations are opening up shorter slots for 10-, 15-, and 20-second advertisements. Less-competitive time slots sometimes carry 60-second advertisements. In addition to regular commercials, most stations provide times of 30 minutes or more for **infomercials**, program-length advertisements that often are packaged as interviews, talk shows, game shows, or educational programs, sometimes masking their true identity as paid advertisements. Certainly there is nothing wrong with combining promotion and entertainment, but an organization raises serious ethical questions if it hides behind artificial news or entertainment programs when in reality it is presenting a sales pitch.

When placing television advertising, consider the specific time of day the ad will run. Television programming is broken into several **dayparts**, time periods that reflect different viewing patterns and thus have different costs associated with buying advertising and different opportunities for the public relations or marketing communications practitioner.

Local advertising tends to focus on specific stores or venues for purchasing products (for example, the Uptown Dodge dealership on North Main Street). National television advertising is more associated with marketing of companies (the Dodge brand) or specific company products (the Dodge Dakota pickup truck).

Television advertising also provides some public relations opportunities. One such opportunity is associated with campaigns aimed at building awareness, acceptance, and supportive action toward an organization or an industry group (such as the Got Milk? campaign for the National Fluid Milk Processor Promotion Board). Additionally, public service advertising takes on even more public relations functions when it becomes an advocate, such as television spots encouraging the use of seat belts or early detection of breast cancer or discouraging drug abuse.

Nonprofit organizations sometimes find that limited budgets require them to be creative, but this also can produce some very effective campaigns. Additionally, many spots for nonprofit organizations are based on contributed services through the Advertising Council, a cooperative venture of the American Association of Advertising Agencies, the Association of National Advertisers, and various media. The Ad Council estimates that its annual campaigns are worth $1.1 billion of donated media. It has produced many memorable campaigns, such as a series for the United Negro College Fund showcasing poet Maya Angelou, the McGruff the Crime Dog "Take a Bite Out of Crime" series for the National Crime Prevention Council, and the "Friends Don't Let Friends Drive Drunk" campaign for the U.S. Department of Transportation.

Because of the appeal of many nonprofit causes, some high-profile organizations are able to attract top talent. For example, when the U.S. Navy fell 7,000 recruits short of its goal several years ago, it turned to the BBDO advertising agency, which hired director Spike Lee

Dayparts

The broadcast day is divided into what the industry calls **dayparts**, which are blocks of time based on different audience patterns. Here are the common designations for dayparts for both television and radio:

Television Dayparts

Here are the standard time periods within a typical broadcast day for television stations. Times reflect Eastern Standard Time; there may be some variations with network programs in other time zones.

Early morning—6 a.m. to 9 a.m.
Daytime—9 a.m. to 4:30 p.m.
Early fringe—4:30 p.m. to 7 p.m.
Prime access—7 p.m. to 8 p.m.
Prime time—8 p.m. to 11 p.m.
Late news time—11 p.m. to 11:30 p.m.
Late night—11:30 p.m. to 1 a.m.
Overnight—1 a.m. to 6 a.m.
Weekend morning—8 a.m. to 1 p.m.
Weekend afternoon—1 p.m. to 7 p.m.

Radio Dayparts

Here are the standard time periods within a typical broadcast day for radio stations. Times are for Eastern Standard Time; there may be some variations with network programs in other time zones.

Morning drive time—6 a.m. to 10 a.m.
Midday or daytime—10 a.m. to 3 p.m.
Afternoon drive time—3 p.m. to 7 p.m.
Evening—7 p.m. to midnight
Late night—midnight to 6 a.m.

to produce a series of recruiting commercials. Lee used a documentary style that focused on Navy SEALS, travel opportunities, sailors in a rock band, and related high-interest topics. The Navy ended the following years with more recruits than expected, while the Air Force, Army, and Marines fell short of their recruitment goals, despite an increase in marketing budgets for all branches of the armed forces. Similarly, after New York City budgeted $10 million for an advertising campaign to help recruit minority people for its police department and to enhance the overall reputation of the department, Arnell Group Brand Consulting volunteered to develop the campaign, freeing the budget for the purchase of newspaper ads, TV commercials, and subway and bus posters.

Another type of television advertisement is the **stealth ad**, also called **product placement**. PQ Media, which tracks product placement on television, estimates that in 2005 the major networks featured 100,000 product placements valued at nearly $2.2 billion, with a growth trend suggesting nearly $7 billion by 2009. Product placement in films is another $1 billion annually. That's why you see Simon Cowell and his fellow judges on *American Idol* with their ever-visible Coke cups. Marg Helgenberger's character Catherine drinks a Pepsi on *CSI* and William Patterson's Gil drives a Ford, because those companies paid to make it so.

Closely related is **product integration**, in which a commercial product is woven into the story line. For example, Sony, Verizon, Visa, and other advertisers pay $1 million an episode to be the featured company in *The Apprentice*. Soap operas have been doing this for decades (the very name comes from both sponsorship by soap companies and product integration into the story line). Recently product integration has become commonplace in prime-time television as well. The film producers of *Memoirs of a Geisha* paid for a triple plug to be mentioned positively within the story line of TV's *The Medium*. *Desperate Housewives* incorporated the Buick LaCrosse, a major sponsor, into its story line.

Stealth advertising is even making inroads into news reporting. Jim Upshaw, journalism professor at the University of Oregon, reported a study that found that 90% of 294 monitored newscasts had at least one example of stealth advertising in each newscast. The average was 2.5 instances. The study also reported a bank executive in Washington, D.C., who meets regularly with television producers to plan new coverage for his bank, and a San Francisco news producer who has established a "product integration fee."

Cable television advertising. Cable networks offer much the same opportunities for advertising as do broadcast networks and local television stations. Additionally, cable television also offers the opportunity to feature **cable crawls**, messages that scroll out across the bottom of the TV screen, often on channels focused on weather, news, or television program listings.

In many areas, advertising contacts with cable companies are handled not by the individual cable system but by a cable broker that places advertising on a variety of cable systems.

Radio commercials. In placing commercials with radio stations, consider the audience you are aiming for and the time of day the spot will run. Media buyers and radio sales people can provide information on several aspects of a radio audience that you can use in comparing stations to make the proper placement choices.

Radio advertising spots generally run for 10, 30, or 60 seconds. Like television advertising placement, radio placement can be made through **network radio**, which includes about 115 national or regional networks providing advertising to perhaps several hundred network-affiliated stations, or as **spot radio**, which means placement on individual local radio stations. Radio commercials can be designated for a specific daypart, or they can be given to the station for use at any time, called **run of station** (ROS) placement.

Digital media. The newest communication channel for electronic advertising is in the rapidly expanding field of computer-based **digital media**. Internet websites offer a growing number of advertising and promotional opportunities.

For example, companies such as Volvo, Norelco, and Ford have created **web-only commercials**, video advertisements that are used only on the Internet. In 2006, Foster's beer dropped all television advertising in favor of web dissemination. Not only are such promotional strategies less expensive than television-based ads, but they also can appeal to generally younger audiences with an edgier message or presentation than might be appropriate for broadcast television. Nielsen Online estimated in 2007 that about 7% of video advertising is for web-only use.

Much creativity goes into Internet promotion. For example, some beer sites on the Internet don't simply advertise beer, they have games, music downloads and contests so the sites can reinforce one of the perceived benefits of the beverage: fun and excitement. Likewise, websites for investment companies feature interactive financial and retirement planning. Provide the asked-for data about your income, lifestyle, work plans, and financial obligations and the program will tell you how much money to invest for the eventual savings you desire.

Several new forms of computer-based advertising have potential for public relations messages. Some websites feature **pop-ups** or **interstitial ads** that insinuate themselves onto the screen as a person is using the Internet. At other times while the user is waiting for a linked connection to load, pages called **superstitial ads** can appear to fill in the time.

Meanwhile, in a blend of computer and television technology, some companies are using **virtual ads** such as product billboards that appear in the background during a televised sporting event—except that the signs don't really exist on the field; they are digitally inserted for the TV audience. Thus they can be used in sequence to promote more than one sponsor during the program, or they can be tailored for viewers in different geographic areas.

Electronic catalogs are not merely electronic versions of printed catalogs. Instead they are interactive versions designed to engage the customers. For example, a web-based clothing catalog or a similar site for a furniture store can let users select among a range of styles, fabric, and colors and then see the result of this custom design.

Long-form television and radio. An emerging area of advertising focuses on long-form television and radio, generally defined as anything longer than two minutes (as compared to the traditional 30-second advertising spots).

One form is **sponsored news** or **sponsored public affairs programming**, in which organizations use their expertise to present objective and credible information to their publics. Strategically, this fits into their overall mix of media tactics, generally in support of information-based objectives. One such example is *The Good Health Radio Hour*, a weekly 60-minute medical discussion program sponsored by Akron (Ohio) General Medical Center on local AM radio. The program is hosted by an obstetrician and a member of the hospital leadership team. Production costs are low and are handled through the hospital's public relations staff working with an outside production company. Guests are booked from the hospital staff and other local experts. The program ranks 7 out of 20 in its Saturday time slot. The sponsored radio program costs only one-third of what the hospital would spend on magazine advertising to pursue similar objectives. (For a full report, see James Armstrong's article in Public Relations Tactics, October 2007.)

The prospect of long-form sponsored programs raises ethical concerns. One is that the sponsor of such programming be clearly identified. Another cause for anxiety is in the potential for further muddling the already blurred line between news and advertising. For decades, nonprofit concerns such as schools, hospitals, religious groups, and environmental organizations have provided television and radio programming in the format of news or public affairs. But when corporations get into the act, it raises some new fears. Many observers are paying attention to the hybrid "PhillyInc," a sponsored column in the *Philadelphia Inquirer* written by staff reporters and sponsored by Citizens Bank.

Long-form advertising sometimes is presented as an **infomercial** (a portmanteau of he words *information* and *commercial*). The term is properly reserved for those advertisements that frequently push a product toward the audience. Infomercials usually are full of demonstrations and testimonials. They also often employ direct-response marketing techniques, such as inviting viewers or listeners to call 800 numbers, log into websites, or similarly interact

Pushing the Envelope a Bit Too Far

Imagine that you are a public relations director for a company or nonprofit organization, and you receive the following offer via fax and a follow-up phone call from a local television station:

> We plan to produce a series of news segments highlighting prominent businesses in the area, and we want you to be part of this series. Specifically we will produce three news segments in 1 week about your organization, along with several promotional spots. Remember that our newscast is the most credible programming for the image of your company. This will cost you $15,000.

That's the offer made a few years ago by WDSI Fox-61 television in Chattanooga, Tennessee.

The offer surprised and shocked several area public relations practitioners, who criticized the TV station for "putting a price on its newscast." One called it "grossly unethical." Another said his organization wanted "to earn any good publicity we receive."

The TV station quickly backed away from its controversial offer, saying it had been considered but should not have been made. The offer was attributed to the naive but nevertheless good intentions of the advertising department. Let's consider the ethical questions raised:

- Is it ever appropriate for a television news team to offer (or appear to be offering) favorable news coverage for a price?
- Is it ever appropriate for a public relations or marketing communication practitioner to accept such an offer?
- Is this offer substantively different from the practice of some television stations in which advertising sales people try to solicit ads from companies that, independent of the advertising department, are being featured in news stories?
- Is it substantively different from the common practice among newspapers of publishing topical advertising sections or progress editions in which stories and photos from the advertisers are prominently featured?
- Is it substantively different from the common practice within the trade press of linking advertisements with news or feature stories?

with the company making the pitch for the product (which often is "not available in stores"). Anybody with insomnia or late-night viewing habits is likely to be familiar with infomercials for products such as the Bowflex home gym, TempurPedic mattresses, Rosetta Stone language systems, Billy Blanks Tae Bo workout program, Ginsu knives, and other assorted products "not available in stores." Some feature temporarily washed-up entertainers, such as Cher pitching hair-care products, Chuck Norris for home gyms, and Suzanne Somers for thigh and ab tighteners.

Out-of-Home Advertising

Out-of-home advertising focuses on several different opportunities to take a persuasive message to a public that is on the move, making it possible to reach people subtly. Sometimes the advertising itself can become an attractive diversion. For example, people waiting for a bus, riding on the subway, or sitting in the stands at a sporting event often pay attention to outside advertising.

This kind of advertising offers several advantages over print and electronic advertising. For example, outdoor ads have 24-hour-a-day visibility to a wide variety of people. They also offer repeat exposure to the advertising message. On the down side, out-of-home advertisements are expensive, and they are limited to short, simple messages.

Categories of out-of-home advertising include outdoor posters, arena posters, signage, out-of-home videos, transit advertising, aerial advertising, and inflatables.

Outdoor posters. In the realm of advertising media, **poster** is a generic name for several different kinds of outdoor stationary ad venues: billboards, paints, and spectaculars.

Billboards are huge signs placed along highways or on the sides of buildings, where they most often are intended to be seen by motorists. Sheets of paper or vinyl are glued onto the billboards, usually for one-month periods. Many billboards are lighted so they can be easily seen day or night. Advertisers have found ways to enhance the basic posters, often with the help of computer-produced images. Some advertisers add **snipes** to their billboards—strips pasted over part of an existing billboard so its message can be updated without the poster being completely changed.

Painted bulletins or **paints** are another type of outdoor sign. They are larger than posters, usually 14 by 48 feet, and because they actually are painted signs they generally are more permanent than billboard posters. Most paints are sold on an annual basis. Permanent paints are displayed in a single location, most often along highways, where they advertise motels, restaurants, and tourist attractions. **Rotary paints** can be physically moved from one location to another.

Spectaculars are another type of outdoor poster involving some kind of extra elements, creatively called **extras**, to the basic flat rectangular surface of the poster. For example, some billboards feature thtree-dimensional elements, such as one for an auto dealer with blinking "headlights" or another for a golf course featuring a giant 3-D golf ball. On one billboard, Mothers Against Drunk Drivers (MADD) hung the actual wreck of a car in which a family had been killed. Extras also may be sections added on a poster to alter its basic rectangular shape. Some spectaculars use computers to add a continuously changing message to billboards, such as a state lottery billboard with the amount of the current week's payout.

Another outdoor venue is the **wall mural** or **wallscape**, the painted exterior of a building leased for advertising purposes.

Arena posters. Billboardlike advertisements placed on walls and fences of arenas such as sports stadiums and ball parks are called **arena posters**. Smaller posters are located inside arenas, often hanging in front of the various levels of seating. Some of these posters are computer generated, allowing for message crawls. In many sports venues, computer-generated posters are rotated every few minutes to provide a sequence of showing during a single public event.

Signage. Visible and appropriate signs can be important aspects in an organization's promotional program. **Signage** includes a variety of stationary outdoor signs, including signs enhanced by a variety of lighting techniques.

Out-of-home video. The category of **out-of-home video advertising** is one of the newest additions to the inventory of promotional vehicles. Out-of-home video includes the giant video screens on which some sports arenas and concert halls present posterlike or full-video images. Another example of this tactic is the **video wall** that features an ever-moving series of computer-generated images.

Advertisements in movie theaters that precede the showing of feature films also fall into the category of out-of-home videos. Because of the variety in films, such advertising can be targeted to specific audience demographics.

Transit advertising. Mobile ads placed on and inside of public commuter vehicles such as buses and trains are known collectively as **transit advertising**. The term also includes stationary ads located on bus shelters and at locations such as subway stationss and airport terminals.

Bus signs are available in several common sizes for different areas of busses: streetside, curbside, front or back. Each can target different audiences. **Car cards** are signs placed above the windows inside buses and trains. **Station posters** or **dioramas** often are small vertical panels located in subway, train, and bus stations, as well as in airport terminals. **Shelter posters** are located in bus shelters.

An advantage to transit advertising is that it can be very specific, focusing on local organizations and addressed to people who live in a particular neighborhood. In large cities, for example, shelter and subway signs may be in a language other than English that is used by a majority of the residents, or they may feature highly specific ethnic images or cultural symbols.

The category of transit advertising also includes **mobile billboards**, the painted sides of tractor-trailer or delivery trucks that increasingly are being rented out as advertising venues.

Aerial advertising. **Aerial advertising** includes various vehicles: blimps with signs or computer-generated scroll messages, airplane tows featuring planes pulling banners over beaches and ballparks, and skywriting airplanes that trail smoke and write messages in the sky. These techniques can be particularly effective if a large number of your target audience is assembled in a single location, such as a resort restaurant might use above a popular beach.

Inflatables. Air-filled objects called **inflatables** are sometimes used as attention-getters. Inflatables range from giant outdoor balloons with a corporate logo to air-filled promotional items such as an ice-cream cone for the grand opening of a dairy bar. Some rooftop inflatables are 20 feet high or larger.

Promotional Items

Many organizations augment their advertising program with promotional items—giveaways for customers that the organization hopes will be a continuing reminder of its cause, product, or service.

Branded clothing includes designer labels such as Tommy Hilfiger or the Gap, which, because they are trendy, are particularly sought out by young people. Not all advertisers, however, are lucky enough to find that their logo is a popular status symbol. On the contrary, it is usually the advertiser that pays to place the logo on T-shirts, athletic and leisure clothing, and other garments. Uniforms for sports teams and individual athletes often carry the name and logo of the corporate sponsor. Likewise, companies increasingly are applying their name, with strong visual reminders, to everything from sports cars and golf tournaments to sports arenas and hospital waiting rooms.

Costumes are another type of promotional clothing, such as the flamboyant chicken suits that might be worn by promoters for the opening of a new fried-chicken restaurant.

Some organizations place promotional logos or messages on office accessories such as calendars, pens, and note pads. Others promote themselves through home accessories such as coffee mugs, bottle openers, matches, napkins, and related goods.

Direct-mail gimmicks are another type of promotional item. Small or miniaturized samples of company products, for example, can be mailed to potential clients. Symbolic items also can be quite effective.

Be careful, however, about what you send through the mail. When one California law firm wanted to let potential clients know that it had the ammunition to fight their legal battles, it mailed out hundreds of fake hand grenades. The come-ons looked so real that some recipients evacuated buildings and called the bomb squads and postal inspectors. In another what-were-they-thinking case, a dot-com company wanted to warn prospects not to be unprepared for computer viruses. Its message strategy: Don't shoot yourself in the foot. So the company mailed out empty bullet shells on a postcard without a return address—just to build suspense—asking, "Who's been shooting [your] readers?" Again the police and FBI were called in.

Planning Example 7D: Selecting Advertising and Promotional Tactics

UPSTATE COLLEGE

Upstate College will develop the following advertising and promotional tactics to publicize its expanded program:

- Display ad in local newspaper—moderate to high cost, focus on key publics
- Display ad in campus newspapers at other colleges—low cost, highlight directed toward transfer students
- Cable TV crawl—low cost, low impact
- Radio commercial—moderate to high cost, directed toward potential students
- Promotional T-shirt—moderate cost

(Note: No television advertising will be used because of the expense involved.)

■ ■ ■

TINY TYKES TOYS

Tiny Tykes will develop the following tactics for an employee-oriented public relations program:

- T-shirts with safety logo—low cost
- Display ads in trade magazine featuring employees with theme of customer safety—moderate cost, directed toward industry leaders
- Display ads in consumer magazines featuring employees with theme of customer safety—high cost, directed toward parents
- Sponsorship of public television series about raising infants and toddlers—moderate to high cost, directed toward parents

Checklist 7D: Advertising and Promotional Tactics

Basic Questions

1. What advertising media and promotional tactics will you use?
2. How will these tactics help the organization achieve its objectives?
3. What resources will these tactics require?

Expanded Questions

A. SELECTION OF TACTICS

From the following categories of advertising and promotional tactics, identify several that you would consider using:

Print Advertising Media

Magazine advertising, advertisorial
Newspaper advertising: display, classified, personal classified
Directory advertising
House ads
Program advertising

Electronic Advertising Media

Television: commercial, spot, infomercial
Radio: commercial, network radio, spot radio
Cable television: advertising, cable crawl
Computer media: e-zine, electronic catalog

Out-of-Home Advertising

Outdoor poster: billboard, paint, spectacular, wall mural
Arena poster
Signage
Out-of-home video, video wall
Transit advertising: bus sign, car card, station poster, diorama, shelter poster, mobile billboard
Aerial advertising: blimp, airplane tows, skywriting, inflatable promotional item
Clothing, costume, office accessory, home accessory

B. STRATEGIC IMPLICATIONS

For each item identified, answer the following questions:

1. Will this tactic help the organization to interact with the appropriate public?
2. What level of impact will this tactic make on the key public?
3. Will this tactic advance the organization toward its awareness objectives?
4. Will this tactic advance the organization toward its acceptance objectives?
5. Will this tactic advance the organization toward its action objectives?

6. What is the main advantage to this tactic?
7. What advantages does this tactic offer that other tactics do not?
8. Are there any disadvantages to this tactic?

C. IMPLEMENTATION ITEMS

For each item identified, answer the following questions:

1. How much will it cost to implement this tactic? Is the cost justified? Is the cost practical, based on the organization's resources?
2. How much staff time will it take to implement this tactic? Is the time practical, based on the organization's resources?
3. What skill level, equipment, and expertise is needed to implement this tactic? Is the needed skill level available within the organization? Is it available from outside sources?

Packaging Communication Tactics

The various communication tactics have been likened to items on a menu, so let's take the analogy a step further. Menu items can be grouped into categories: appetizers, salads, main courses, desserts, beverages, and the like. When you order a meal, you'll probably cover the whole range of menu categories. Additionally, when you review the restaurant menu, you often make your selections based on a particular culinary focus—Japanese, Tex-Mex, Southern, and so on. It's unlikely you would start with tuna sashimi as an appetizer, add a dollop of cole slaw on a bed of lettuce, feature jalapeño chili as main course with sides of grits and ravioli, and end with a flaming cherries jubilee for dessert. Rather, you'd probably develop a culinary theme, creatively packaging your choices to concoct a special dining experience appropriate to the occasion and suitable to your resources, needs, and interests.

The same is true with strategic planning for communication. Now that you have considered items in each of the menu categories, you need to package them into an effective set of tactics to help you achieve your objectives. This should be much more than a "to do" list. Consider how various tactics can be woven together; group some around the themes associated with your strategic planning from Steps 5 and 6.

Remember: You don't need to be tied into a chronological implementation scheme just because you selected interpersonal items before those in the other categories. Let the natural relationship among tactics determine how they fit into your plan. Consider what you learned in Phase Two, Strategy. For example, the diffusion of innovations theory tells us that information presented through the news media can pave the way for personal interaction between opinion leaders and the ultimate public. Or think about the example of some companies, which have preceded an advertising schedule with a publicity program, thus allowing for a smaller advertising budget with higher-than-usual results.

Thinking Creatively

What's the best way to present your plan? You decide. Look for the simplest and most logical way to present the tactics that grow out of your planning. Later on we'll look at some suggestions to help you get started, but first let's consider the importance of creative thinking. As you decide how to package your tactics, try to leap ahead of the crowd with an innovative approach to the problem or opportunity you are dealing with.

For example, if you have a new organizational logo to unveil, consider making it a real unveiling, perhaps with a ceremonial removal of a sequined cloth covering the logo. Or maybe you could have the logo painted large on the outside of the company's building, temporarily draped. One nonprofit organization introduced a new logo by involving five local political and media celebrities who each gave a short testimonial about the organization and then, one by one, placed together cut-out pieces of a giant jigsaw puzzle to create the new logo.

Consider another scenario. Your organization has an announcement to make—usually a routine matter. But you want to have it stand out. One corporation engineered an interactive announcement in two cities at different ends of New York State, with a teleconference hookup. The president of the corporation was in one city, a congressman who actively supported the organization in the other. The two together announced a significant multimillion-dollar project that the corporation was developing. And just in case the technology failed, the public relations planner had prepared a script and a videotape that could be used at each location.

An Indiana group used a symbolic protest as part of its announcement strategy. Hogs Opposed to Government Waste and Silly Highways (HOGWASH) sent Arnold the Pig to deliver a ham to the governor's press secretary, announcing its opposition to the extension of Highway I-69 through southern Indiana. The protesters said the road project was an example of pork-barrel politics, so it was only fitting for Arnold to be their spokespig.

Some organizations have specially designed vehicles used for promotion and other public relations objectives. For example, Rural/Metro Ambulance Service has a three-foot high talking, winking, lighted ambulance called Amby that EMTs take into classrooms during safety presentations. United Parcel Service has a miniature delivery truck that it uses in athletic arenas to deliver a coin for the ceremonial coin toss such as at the start of football games. Notice that each of these vehicles relates to the primary mission of the organization.

Putting the Program Together

When the time comes to begin putting your public relations or marketing communication program together, first review the information gathered during the research phase of the program (Steps 1, 2, and 3). Reconsider the issue and review pertinent information about the organization, its environment and perceptions about it. Next examine the various publics and your analysis of them.

Following this review, consider several different ways to package the tactics you have chosen. No particular format is best for every issue, so let common sense be your guide. Consider the most distinctive element of your program. Your purpose is to select the format that most readily allows you to present your analysis and recommendations to your colleagues, boss, or client.

Among the various ways of packaging your tactics is by tactical category, public, goal, objective, and department. Look at each of these with an open mind; perhaps you'll be able to devise a better way to package the tactical recommendations in your program.

Packaging by tactical category. Using this approach, you move from the research phase to an overview of the goals, objectives, and strategy associated with Steps 4, 5, and 6. Next, list each tactic according to the outline of media categories provided in the Step 7 inventory. That is, list each tactic in order of interpersonal communication, organizational media, news media, and advertising media. With each tactic, indicate the relevant publics and objectives.

This presentation by media type can guide you to draw tactics from each category, though the presentation can appear a bit disjointed because it may overlook a more logical grouping of tactics. Nevertheless, it is a good starting point, or at least an effective preliminary checklist before using one of the following presentation formats. The presentation by tactics is followed by evaluation methods (Step 9), which will come a bit later in this book.

Packaging by public. The research phase moves to an outline of each key public and, for each, an overview of the relevant goals and objectives (Step 4); then the strategy phase focuses on interacting and communicating with each public (Steps 5 and 6). This approach to packaging should include tactics associated with each strategy (Step 7) and evaluation methods (Step 9).

Use this format if the internal cohesion of your plan centers on the differences among several publics. For example, if you are planning a program that identifies three categories of publics—customers, employees, and community—you may decide that you can present your analysis and ideas best by focusing separately on each public.

Packaging by goal. Using this approach, the plan begins with the common research phase and provides an overview of goals associated with the issue. It then identifies a series of initiatives based on each goal and focuses the rest of the plan serially on each initiative.

In your presentation of each initiative, identify relevant research and background information, key publics (Step 3), objectives (Step 4), strategy with key messages (Steps 5 and 6), tactics (Step 7) and evaluation methods (Step 9).

Use this format when goals are sufficiently distinct to allow you to treat each one independently. For example, a public relations and marketing communication program for a university might identify several goal-based initiatives, such as enhancing its reputation among students in high school and community colleges, increasing support from the business and civic community, recruiting more students to professional development programs, and enhancing knowledge and pride among students, faculty, staff, and alumni. Campaign tactics could be associated with each of the four goals, a kind of subcampaign for each component.

Packaging by objective. Presentation by objective begins, like the previous approach, with the common research phase of Steps 1, 2, and 3 and provides an overview of the goals and objectives from Step 4. Then it selects each objective as the focus for the remainder of the presentation, identifying key publics (Step 3), strategy with key messages (Steps 5 and 6), tactics (Step 7) and evaluation methods (Step 9) for each objective.

Use this approach when it is the objectives rather than the goals or publics that are the most significant distinction within the plan. For example, a plan that has only a single goal might be presented according to the objectives associated with awareness, acceptance, and action.

Packaging by department. Similar to presentation by goals or objectives, presentation by department acknowledges that the distinctive segments of the strategic communication plan parallel existing organizational structures, such as departments, divisions, and programs.

Use this approach when the structure of the client's organization coincides with program areas in your strategic plan.

Planning Example 7E: Packaging the Communication Tactics

The following initiative is packaged according to one of the four task goals identified in Planning Example 4: Establishing Goals and Objectives.

UPSTATE COLLEGE

Initiative on Transfer Students
(Transcribe research, goal, key public, objectives and strategy information.)

Upstate College will sponsor the weekend-long "Celebration! UC" (Friday evening, Saturday afternoon and evening, and Sunday afternoon), celebrating the expansion of UC to a four-year institution. Entertainment during this event will include a picnic with two bands, a formal banquet and strolling entertainers. The event will include:

- a rededication ceremony with public officials, leaders of neighboring colleges and universities, and UC students, faculty, and alumni
- a fall festival for current students and alumni
- an open house for prospective transfer students

Support materials for the festival will include a revision of the college viewbook, a new transfer brochure and a poster, as well as production of a video. A special page will be added to the UC website home page.

Students who applied to UC within the last two years and were accepted but did not attend will be sent a letter inviting them to the festival events, along with a fact sheet about Upstate College.

More generally, the festival will be promoted with media fact sheets and news releases, a photo with caption, and a cable TV crawl. Students attending the event will be given an Upstate College T-shirt designed by UC art students. A media advisory will be sent to the news media, inviting them to cover the event, and news interviews will be offered with the UC president, provost, and student government president. Additionally, the media relations office will seek out an editorial conference with the local newspaper to elicit editorial support for the expansion; failing that, a letter to the editor will be sent by a UC official noting the benefits of the program expansion for the community.

The festival also will be promoted with a newspaper advertisement in campus newspapers at other colleges and with radio commercials. Additionally, a display ad in the local newspaper will be aimed at parents as well as community leaders, alumni, and donors.

(Note that each of the other goals would be developed in a similar manner.)

■ ■ ■

The following initiative is packaged according to the four key publics identified in Planning Example 3A: Identifying Publics.

TINY TYKES TOYS

Public Relations Program for Tiny Tykes Employees
(Transcribe research, goal, objectives and strategy information.)

The internal component of a training program for employees will include workshops on customer satisfaction as well as a training session on product safety and quality; brochures about safety and quality issues will be available. Several work-group meetings will be held, at least one involving a motivational speech by the CEO. Similar motivational themes will be presented in newsletter articles and in the employee bulletin.

The program will have an external component to provide employee support. Elements of this component will include letters sent to families of employees, letters to the editors of local newspapers about employee dedication to customer safety, and print advertisements in trade magazines and in the local newspaper. A news release will announce the new safety and quality initiatives, and a story idea memo will be given to reporters about employee dedication to customer safety.

(Note that each of the other publics would be developed in a similar manner.)

Checklist 7E: Packaging Communication Tactics

Basic Questions

1. What specific initiatives or sections make up this plan?
2. What tactics are associated with this plan?
3. What public and objective does each tactic serve?

Expanded Questions

A. SELECTING THE APPROACH

1. From the following categories, indicate which one offers the greatest likelihood of a package of program tactics that is cohesive and logical: by public, by goal, by objective, by department, or by tactic.
2. List specific initiatives or sections in your plan.

B. STRATEGIC IMPLICATIONS

1. Will this approach help the organization to interact with the appropriate public?
2. What is the main advantage to this approach?
3. What advantages does this approach offer that other approaches do not?
4. Are there any disadvantages to this approach?

Step 8

Implementing the Strategic Plan

Now that you have put together a full plate of ways to present your message, turn your attention to implementing these tactics. In this step, you will consider some of the specifics of implementation, especially turning your inventory of tactics into a logical and cohesive program. You also will deal with specific topics dealing with scheduling and budgeting for the program.

Campaign Plan

The campaign plan book—or, more simply, the program plan—is the formal written presentation of your research findings and program recommendations for strategy, tactics, and evaluation. This report should be concise in writing, professional in style, and confident in tone. Here are some of the elements the plan book should include:

- *Title page.* List a program name as well as the names of the client organization, consultant or team members, and date.
- *Executive summary.* Prepare a one- or two-page synopsis of the plan written as an overview for busy executives and for readers who are not directly involved in the program.
- *Table of contents.* Outline the major segments of the program.
- *Statement of principles or philosophy statement* (optional). Lay out the planner's approach to strategic communication campaigns (particularly whether it is rooted in public relations, marketing communication or integrated communication). Also included are definitions of key concepts used in the book.
- *Situation analysis.* Outline your research and synthesis of the issue (Step 1), organization (Step 2), and publics (Step 3). Some program plans present the research data and summaries on paper of a different color from the rest of the report.
- *Recommendations.* Present your strategic and tactical recommendations in whatever format you think works best (such as by public, by goal, by objective, by program, or by tactic) to show your plans and to address the issue.
- *Schedule.* Outline the time and calendar considerations for implementing the various tactics.
- *Budget.* Outline resources needed for the program. Include in this figure the cost of personnel time, money, and equipment, as well as any income to be generated.

- *Evaluation plan.* Provide information on the methods to be used to measure the program's effectiveness.
- *Consultant background* (optional). Indicate the resources the consultant or agency can offer. This element of the plan is especially useful in competitive situations in which more than one consultant or agency prepares program recommendations. A complete strategic campaign is located in Appendix C, Sample Campaigns.

Sometimes you may decide not to use a particular tactic, perhaps not even a particular category of communication tactics. For example, an employee relations project may not lend itself to involving the news media, or an investor relations project may not include advertising. When you deliberately choose not to use what might seem to be an obvious tactic, offer your reasoning in your plan. Especially if you are developing a proposal on competitive-bid basis, it is good to let the potential client know why you recommend against using what others might suggest.

Regardless of the way you package your tactics, it is important to show the internal logic within your planning program. Make it clear to your client or boss how the various elements work together for a common purpose.

A good way to show this internal harmony is to note for each tactic the specific public, goal, and objective to which it is linked. In this way, planners can make sure that each public is adequately served by the various tactics. Likewise, planners can be certain that each goal and objective is played out through a variety of tactics.

Consider the following example outlining one tactic, an open house as part of a campaign proposal for a new graduate program. This tactic shows the internal linkage between a single tactic, previously identified publics, already determined objectives and strategy, administrative details such as budgeting, and subsequent evaluation methods.

Example: Tactics for Open House

- *Public:* Professional architects (specifically, a minimum of 45 practicing architects within a three-county area).
- *Objective:* To increase the understanding of professional architects about the new program (50% of the professional community prior to beginning the academic program).
- *Strategy:* Attract attention of the professional community and create a core of opinion leaders; give specific attention to leading architects, particularly those who have received recognition from the Midstate Association of Professional Architects.
- *Budget:* $1,500.
- *Evaluation Methods:* Attendance figures; follow-up minisurvey conducted as part of a telephone thank-you for attending.

In a complete proposal, each tactic would receive similar treatment. Even individual tactics might have multiple components. For example, the open house noted earlier might have additional publics, perhaps donors or potential students. Each of these would require its own statement of objectives and strategies, though the budget and evaluation methods may remain constant.

Another useful element within the tactical plan is to note the name of the person or department charged with implementing the tactic. Sometimes this is a moot point, because one person will handle the entire project. However, for more complex programs and campaigns, several different people may be involved, each managing different tactics. Either within the plan itself, or in an implementation guide to be worked out later, be clear about who is responsible for each tactic.

Campaign Schedule

You already addressed one aspect of scheduling when you built into your objectives in Step 4 an indication of when you planned to achieve each. This provided the deadline upon which you will measure your effectiveness in reaching the objectives.

Now that Step 7 has generated an outline of tactics, you can establish specific time requirements. This involves two considerations: (1) the pattern and frequency of your communication tactics and (2) the actual timeline of tasks to be accomplished as the tactics are implemented.

Frequency of Tactics

As noted in Step 6, the average person is exposed to thousands of public relations and marketing messages each day, yet most fall on deaf ears. Clearly, mere exposure to a message is insufficient to move someone to action. However, the frequency of exposure is an important factor in whether the message takes root in a person's consciousness.

Repetition increases awareness and leads to greater acceptance. Research has been done both on **message frequency** (the number and pattern of messages presented to a particular public in a given period of time) and on **message reach** (the number of different people who are exposed to a single message). Most of the research on frequency has been focused either on advertising or on the learning process.

However, it is possible to generalize a bit about applications for public relations. It is known, for example, that one exposure to a message has little or no effect unless the audience is particularly attentive. Rather, a minimum of three exposures seems to be needed to make an impact. Much more than this, and effectiveness wanes. This concept has enjoyed general support within the advertising trade since it was articulated by ad manager and theoretician Herbert Krugman (1972). Gerard Tellis (1998) has noted that studies in laboratory settings confirmed Krugman's three-exposure formula, although in natural settings in which consumers are distracted by competing messages, three presentations of the message may not be enough to generate three exposures to the intended audience.

The lessons for the public relations manager? Don't rely on just one presentation of your message to key publics. Don't think that even three exposures guarantee success. Find ways to repeat and reinforce your message, especially through various media. This will not only increase retention among your key publics but also add to the credibility of the message because it will have the third-party endorsement of several different media gatekeepers.

Another lesson gleaned from research is the value of repetition over a period of time. For example, most audiences remember a message they have seen daily for several days more than one presented several times in a single day. Too-frequent presentation of the message seems unnecessarily redundant and can lead to wear-out—which, by the way, comes faster with a humorous message than with a neutral or serious one.

A message presented may not be a message heard, and there is no specific number for how many repetitions is best. Sometimes, even your best efforts won't gain complete success, especially with audiences who are not particularly interested in the issue. For example, for several years one of the most consistent television advertising campaigns featured a pink rabbit beating the drum for a battery company. Yet 40% of viewers in a national survey identified the wrong company as the sponsor of the ad, despite the company's best effort to promote the Energizer Bunny.

Bruce Vanden Bergh and Helen Katz (1999) point out that most organizations with limited budgets must find a balance between reach and frequency. A basic guideline for advertising seems to hold true for other aspects of marketing communication and public relations: Rather than trying to reach a greater number of people, try instead to reach a targeted number of key people more frequently.

Timeline of Tasks

At this point in your planning, you know three things about your tactics: (1) which ones you want to use, (2) how you will package them, and (3) how often to run them. Now turn your attention to carefully considering each significant task needed for these tactics. One of the

Four Patterns of Message Repetition

An insight drawn from advertising is that the pattern of communication can be of crucial importance. If you know that a one-time message is inappropriate, the question becomes when and how you should plan for repetition of the message. Consider four concepts: continuity, flighting, pulsing, and massing.

Continuity is an approach to scheduling that presents a message at a consistent level throughout a particular period of time. Use this approach if you need to maintain a consistent presence over a given period of time. But realize that it is expensive to use a continuous approach with enough intensity to generate an effective reach and frequency. The continuity approach may mean integrating several tactics such as direct mail, publicity, and advertising for external audiences; for internal audiences, the tactics also could include posters, meetings, and brochures.

Flighting (also called **bursting**) refers to the presentation of messages in waves, with periods of intense communication interspersed with dark periods of communication inactivity. A variety of media can be used during the peak communication periods. This approach is useful when organizational activity falls into predictable and discrete periods.

Pulsing is a combination of the two approaches, with a continuous base augmented by intermittent bursts of communication activity.

Massing is the bunching of various presentations of a message into a short period of time.

easiest ways to schedule tasks is to work backward from the final tactic date. For example, if you want a brochure to be received in the readers' homes by May 15, work backward to develop the following hypothetical schedule:

May 12	Deliver to the post office
May 11	Attach address labels
May 10	Receive from printer
May 5	Deliver to printer
April 28	Finalize copy and design, and obtain approvals
April 21	Complete draft, including copy, artwork, and layout
April 14	Begin writing, develop artwork
April 7	Assign writer and designer
April 6	Obtain approval for objectives, determine budget
April 2	Begin planning for brochure

Total time required: 41 days

This plan is your **timeline** or implementation schedule. Timelines are essential when you are dealing with a variety of tactics and managing different programs at the same time. Having a written plan makes it easier to train others and delegate responsibilities. Additionally, having a written timeline makes it easier to keep work records that may be needed for billing purposes.

A good way to manage the scheduling process is to chart out each of the tasks you have identified. You could use a large calendar or a timetable narrative with sections for time periods and bulleted task items to be accomplished during each time period.

However, flow charts are particularly helpful in tracking public relations tactics because they provide a visual representation of the tasks to be completed. A common type of flow chart is the **Gantt chart**, developed by engineer Henry Gantt during the First World War to track shipbuilding projects. The Gantt chart lists each tactic and the various associated tasks, then indicates the time needed for each task. Times can be indicated in days, weeks, or months, depending on the type of project.

Exhibit 8.1 Gantt Chart for Brochure

	April															May						
	2	4	6	8	10	12	14	16	18	20	22	24	26	28	30	2	4	6	8	10	12	14
Brochure																						
Planning (myself)	xxxxxxx																					
Objectives (supervisor)			x																			
Assign writer (myself)				x																		
Writing (freelancer)							xxxxxxxxx															
Complete draft (freelancer)										x												
Final copy (myself)													xxxxxx									
To printer (myself)																		x				
From printer (printer)																				x		
Labels (staff)																				x		
To Post Office (staff)																					x	
Deliver (Post Office)																						xxx

Exhibit 8.2 PERT Chart for Brochure

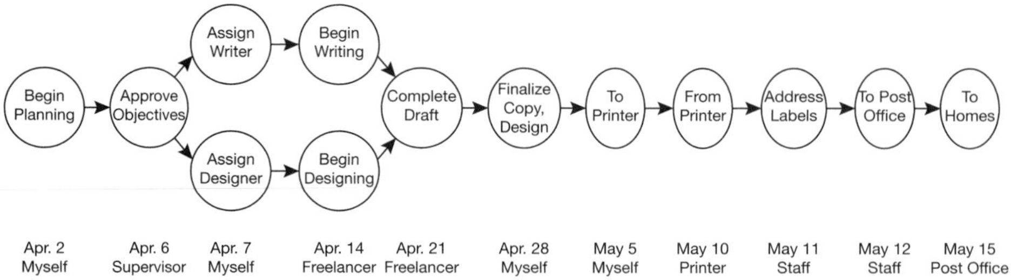

The advantage of the Gantt Chart is that it provides a map of the work that needs to be done. These charts can be kept on computer, written on paper charts, or displayed as wall charts. Exhibit 8.1 shows a Gantt chart for an activity that has not yet been implemented. As the various tasks are completed, underline the Xs or replace them with solid lines.

Because the Gantt chart shows every task associated with the various tactics, planners can spread out activity according to a convenient schedule. For example, under normal conditions preparation of a brochure may take about six weeks. But the Gantt chart may show that several other important and time-consuming activities will be taking place within the same 6-week period. Thus you may need to begin work on the brochure earlier.

Another commonly used flow chart is the **PERT chart**, a process first developed for the Polaris missile system in the 1950s. This chart, shown in Exhibit 8.2, lists tasks within circles, with arrows indicating how one task flows into another. PERT (Program Evaluation and Review Technique) charts generally include dates and assignment to particular individuals, though they lack the calendaring aspect of the Gantt chart.

An effective implementation schedule of public relations tactics generally includes more than dates. Include the name of the person or group responsible for the task. In addition to the deadline date, some charts indicate the latest date by which the tactic can be implemented and still remain useful.

Campaign Budget

Budgeting, the development of resources needed to achieve objectives, is a topic that has been "on the table" since the beginning of this planning process. In Step 1 you considered the importance of the issue and its potential impact on the bottom line of the organization. In Step 2 you analyzed the organization itself, with some consideration going to the level of resources available to address various aspects of public relations and marketing communications. These resources included personnel, equipment, time, and budgeted money.

Throughout the strategic development in Steps 4, 5, and 6 you were advised to be realistic in setting forth on a course of action appropriate to the organization. One measure of propriety is based on the organization's resources. At every turn in a planning process, you must be practical. Consider budget constraints and limitations—and no organization is free of these—so your recommendations will be realistic, practical, and doable.

Budget Item Categories

Remember that budgeting is about more than money. It deals with all the needed resources to implement a tactic. Thus budgets for public relations and marketing communications should consider five elements: personnel, material, media costs, equipment and facilities, and administrative costs.

Personnel. Personnel items in a budget include the number of people and the amount of time needed to achieve the results expected of the tactic. This may include both organizational personnel and outside people, such as consultants, agency staff, subcontracted specialists, and freelance workers. Specifically, personnel costs may be associated with research, analysis, planning, writing, editing, design, photography, events management, and the like. Personnel costs can be expressed either in terms of time (hours or days) needed to complete the task or in labor dollars. In some billing situations, public relations agencies present personnel items in the form of billable hours. Some agencies have a general and average hourly rate; others make distinctions among strategic planning, research, account management, and administrative and support activities. Remember to account for the time of salaried public relations staff within an organization.

Material. Material items in a budget include the "things" associated with the tactics: paper for brochures, banners for an open house, media kits for a news conference, uniforms for the softball team your company is sponsoring, and so on. Additionally, material items may be associated with research activities, such as the cost of questionnaires or materials for focus groups. Each of these items carries a price tag, and it is very important to know exactly the cost of each recommended tactic. If you simply guess or work from old figures, you may find that you cannot implement the tactic for the amount that has been budgeted.

Media costs. Money generally is needed for communication activities, particularly the purchase of time and space associated with advertising tactics. Budgets often identify commissionable media—advertising in newspapers and magazines or commercials on radio and television. When working with an advertising agency, you may find that a commission or agency fee of about 15% has been added as a surcharge to the cost of the final art, production charges for audio and video and talent or model fees, as well as the cost of buying advertising time or space. Meanwhile, public relations agencies sometimes bill all out-of-pocket expenses (perhaps with the exception of travel expenses) at cost plus 15%. In the face of growing competition among agencies, however, commissions increasingly are being replaced with flat fees.

Equipment and facilities. This category includes the capital cost of equipment that must be purchased to implement a tactic, such as a computer, scanner, printer, or desktop publishing software needed to publish a newsletter. Also included here are the capital costs of obtaining a needed facility, such as modifying a storage area into an in-house television studio. Note that items in this category often are one-time expenditures, though a forward-looking budget process would amortize such expenses over the expected life of the equipment or facility and would be prepared for the time when replacements would be needed.

Administrative items. A budget also should include the cost of telephone charges, delivery costs, photocopying, and other office activities, as well as travel costs associated with the project. Some organizations assess a surcharge, often 15%, to offset the cost of overhead expenses such as rent, maintenance, utilities, taxes, and so on.

Fee Structures for Public Relations Agencies

Several different approaches to billing are common with public relations consultants and agencies, as well as with the growing number of public relations departments that are being reorganized into an in-house agency model within organizations.

Hourly rates plus expenses are based on the actual amount of time spent on a project, plus the amount of money spent on materials, production costs, and media. Some agencies lower the hourly rate as the actual number of hours increases. Examples of hourly rates are $45 an hour for copyediting, $150 an hour for research analysis, or $200 an hour for account supervision.

Project fees or **fixed fees** are flat charges for projects, such as $250 for a news release or $1,000 for preparing a brochure for printing.

Retainer fees are fixed monthly base charges paid in advance for a predetermined level of agency availability. The benefit to the agency is that a minimum income is guaranteed; the client benefit is that the retaining charge is calculated lower than regular hourly rates.

Performance fees are a new and somewhat controversial way of obtaining compensation from a client. Under this system, the agency bills based on its success in achieving stated objectives, such as placement of news releases, generation of telephone calls or web hits, and so on.

Approaches to Budgeting

A recurring problem with public relations budgeting is that public relations often is not seen as strategic management but rather as the mere production and distribution of messages.

Additionally, public relations often may be thought to deal with hard-to-measure intangibles such as goodwill or visibility. Because of this mind-set, public relations budgets sometimes are set according to a formula based on last year's budget, or worse, as an arbitrary percentage of the wider administration or marketing program of an organization.

If you have followed the guidelines in *Strategic Planning for Public Relations*, you should find that you can overcome these difficulties. You have learned to conduct public relations and marketing communication as a management activity, and you have learned to work with precise objectives that bring an element of measurement to concepts such as goodwill and support.

Still, the question often comes up: How much should an organization spend on public relations and marketing communications? People asking this are often looking for a simple, accepted formula. But there is no simple answer to that question, because so much depends on variables—the nature of the issue being addressed, the objectives sought, the tactics employed, and so on. Some nonprofit organizations can operate impressive and successful campaigns for only a few hundred dollars. On the other hand, some major motion pictures, which easily run into the hundreds of millions of dollars to produce, may spend even more on promotions, most of that for paid advertising. Every organization and every issue is different. Each requires careful attention and insightful management.

Establishing an appropriate budget can be a difficult task. Often you will find that a client simply has no notion what the appropriate budget should be. Every organization wants to prevent unnecessary spending, but most also are willing to spend the necessary amount to get the job done. Let's consider some of the many different ways to approach budgeting: competitive parity, same-as-before, percentage-of-sales, unit-of-sales, all-you-can-afford, cost-benefit analysis, what-if-not-funded, zero-based, stage-of-life-cycle, and objective-based methods.

Competitive parity. The **competitive parity** approach bases an organization's budget for various activities on the level of similar activity by major competitors. For example, University A may base its budget for recruiting new students on the apparent budget of University B, its biggest competitor. A drawback of this approach is that University A will have to guess what University B is spending, and much of what University B is doing may not be apparent. Additionally, the two universities may have significantly different situations, such as the amount of informal recruiting being done by alumni, the reputation of the two institutions and the amount of their financial endowment.

Same-as-before budgeting. A budget developed on the **same-as-before** approach looks at how much the organization spent on a similar recent project and allows the same budget for this project. But such an approach presumes that two projects are sufficiently similar that one can serve as a benchmark for the other; it also presumes that the first project was successful and deserves to be imitated. A related approach is same-as-before-but-more budgeting, which adds an inflationary increase to a same-as-before budget.

Percentage-of-sales budgeting. The **percentage-of-sales** approach to budgeting is drawn from the field of marketing, where some companies base their advertising budget on the previous year's profits. This approach may give a generous marketing budget following a good year but only a meager budget after a lean year—perhaps just the opposite of what is needed to overcome a sales slump. In the university recruiting scenario above, the budget for public relations might be based on the amount of money obtained through tuition fees. For example, 2% of each tuition payment may be earmarked for the recruiting public relations program. However, because much public relations activity is difficult to quantify on a short-term basis, the percentage-of-sales method generally is a weak approach in this field.

Unit-of-sales budgeting. Similar to percentage-of-sales budgeting, the **unit-of-sales** approach is based not on dollars but on prior outcomes. In the university recruiting situation, the budget might be pegged to the number of students who register as students. For example, for every student recruited, the university might earmark $75 for the public relations program. This approach has a similar drawback to the percentage-of-sales approach in that it pegs future budgets on past prosperity rather than current needs.

All-you-can-afford budgeting. The **all-you-can-afford** approach to budgeting works better in good times than in bad. It provides for public relations funding when the organization's financial condition is sound, but limits funding during lean times. While this is not a good approach, in reality it is the way too many organizations approach public relations, as an optional luxury that can be dispensed with when money is tight. Actually, the hard times are when even more public relations activity may be needed.

Cost-benefit analysis. A budget based on the **cost-benefit analysis** approach identifies the cost of implementing a tactic, then compares this cost to the estimated value of the expected results. Ideally, the cost will be significantly less than the probable benefit. For example, the cost of holding an open house for a day-care center for seniors with Alzheimer's disease might be $1,500, while the benefit of this tactic, if the projected registration goal is met, might be $10,000 from new donors to the program.

What-if-not-funded analysis. Consequences of inaction and their effect on the organization's mission is the concept underlying the **what-if-not-funded budget**. This approach forces a planner to consider expected outcomes. For example, the what-if-not-funded scenario for the tactic of producing a video would have you indicate the expenses necessary to achieve the objective without the video. This might mean more workshops involving additional time from the CEO, or perhaps more brochures with fewer benefits than with the video. Implicitly or explicitly, the recommended tactic is compared with the alternatives.

Zero-based budgeting. A technique known as **zero-based budgeting** is based on current needs rather than past expenditures. It is common for ongoing organizational budgets, such as those associated with annual community relations or investor relations programs; however, the zero-based approach can work with one-time campaigns as well. In this approach, various tactics are ranked according to their importance. The cumulative cost of each tactic is then calculated. The "cut-off line" of the predetermined budget indicates in effect when the client has run out of money and therefore must reject the remaining tactics. This is not really an effective method for public relations planning, because it allows a financial formula and a calculator to determine what tactics will be implemented.

Stage-of-life-cycle budgeting. The **stage-of-life-cycle** approach to budgeting looks closely at the phase of development of the issue, knowing that start-up programs generally require more financial resources than maintenance programs. Consider, for example, the needs of a university communication department in transition. Let's say the university is well known for its "academic" approach to communication, with a focus on research, theory, and critical analysis. Let's further presume that the university decides to extend itself into more applied communication areas such as public relations, advertising, and electronic journalism. The financial resources needed to recruit students for the new program will be greater than what is needed to maintain applications to the current program focus.

Objective-based budgeting. A more enlightened approach is **objective-based budgeting** because, by focusing on objectives, it deals with already identified needs and goals. The underlying premise of this approach is that the organization will provide the resources necessary to achieve its objectives, which already have been approved by organizational decision makers. The consensus check that concludes Step 4 is perhaps the most important part of this approach to budgeting, as it is at this point that agreement is reached on what must be accomplished. The tactics simply provide ways to achieve what already has been adopted as the objective.

Even with the objective-based approach to budgeting, however, financial reality and common sense must rule. The wise strategic planner will develop tactics that are within the reach of the organization. The ability to create effective programs suitable to almost any budget is one of the real advantages of an integrated approach to public relations and marketing communication.

Managing the Budget

In Step 8, you are developing the actual budget for your public relations program. The best way to do this is to list each of the tactics you recommended in Step 7, then indicate the various costs associated with each tactic.

For example, if you have recommended the creation of a brochure, indicate the various costs associated with this tactic. Include one-time costs such as copywriting, artwork, and design. Include costs based on the number of brochures needed, such as paper, printing, folding, and mailing. Add in the value of personnel time, such as hourly figures based on annual salaries of organizational employees or the hourly fees for outside consultants, agency personnel, or freelance workers. Then add these various costs to obtain a total for the brochure tactic. Notice how each of these budget elements is included in Exhibit 8.3.

By breaking down each of the various costs associated with the tactic, you are able to more precisely predict the total cost associated with the program. Additionally, this breakdown allows you to adjust the total budget more easily. Say, for example, that all of your recommended tactics add up to $12,500, but your overall budget is supposed to be only $11,000. You need to shave $1,500 from your recommendations.

One way would be to find a tactic that costs $1,500 and eliminate it, but then you probably would have a hole in your plan—after all, the tactic was recommended to achieve a particular objective. However, by knowing the cost of each aspect of every tactic, you can make minor revisions in several areas. Perhaps you could use spot color rather than four-color printing and save a few hundred dollars on the brochure, or perhaps mail fewer brochures and find an alternative distribution method that would cost less. By modifying enough tactics but not eliminating any of them, you can keep your original plan intact and still meet the budget.

How closely should you stick with the overall budget that your boss or client originally indicated? That probably depends on the boss or client, and how you read his budget projection. If you think the budget was meant merely as a guideline, then going a bit over probably won't

Exhibit 8.3 Fixed Budget for Brochure

Administrative Costs (in-house)	**$ 125**
Hourly Rate: $25	
# hours: 5	
Setup Costs (outsourced)	**$ 900**
Copywriting	500
Artwork	200
Design	200
Production Costs x 2,500 Copies	**$ 775**
Paper	125
Printing (2-color @ $.24)	600
Folding	50
Distribution Costs	**$ 500**
TOTAL	**$2,300**

hurt. If you know him to be the type of manager who routinely cuts a percentage of every budget request, then you may be tempted to pad your budget request a bit, knowing that it will be cut back to the point where you really want it to be. But if you sense that the budget figure was firm, you should make sure your recommendations fall within the projected budget.

One way to deal with a budget that doesn't seem to stretch quite far enough for your ideas is to offer the client a range of costs—low-end and high-end tactics, perhaps with a preferred or optimal level of funding. Take another look at the brochure budget. As Exhibit 8.4 shows, a variable budget could be presented. The $2,300 total for brochure costs is based on printing with spot color. But the final cost actually could range from a low of $1,675 by printing in one color only and not using the mail for distribution, to a high of $2,900 for four-color printing and mail distribution.

Another way to stretch a budget is to provide a basic set of recommendations that fits within the projected budget, then offer an add-on list of optional tactics that the client may wish to fund because of the added expected benefit.

Budgets also have a way of inching upward. Perhaps a supplier charges a bit more than when you first called for an estimate. Or some of your expense items were based on a similar project six months ago, but those items now have increased in price. Most organizations are aware that budget creep can occur, and agencies or consultants often build into their contracts provisions for such changes. A common technique is to assure the client that, for any increase of more than 10%, the cost overrun will be submitted for the client's prior approval.

Once the budget has been approved, it should be used as a tool to help manage the implementation of the project. The budget can offer guidance in scheduling activities, monitoring their progress, and assessing their results. Additionally, the budget should be treated as part of a living document. The strategic plan is not set in stone once it is approved.

Exhibit 8.4 Variable Budget for Brochure

Administrative Costs (in-house)	**$ 125**
Hourly Rate: $25	
# hours: 5	
Setup Costs (outsourced)	**$ 900**
Copywriting	500
Artwork	200
Design	200
Production Costs x 2,500 Copies	**$ 550–1,375**
Paper	125
Printing (1-color @$.15; 2-color @$.24; 4-color @$.48)	375–1,200
Folding	50
Distribution Costs	**$ 100–500**
Non-mail/bulk-mail distribution	100
Mail distribution (optional)	0–500
TOTAL	**$1,675–2,900**

Rather, it must have the flexibility to respond to a changing environment and differing organizational needs.

Full-Cost Budgets

In presenting the budget to your boss or client, include the full cost of all the tactics in the program. Some tactics may not have a specific price tag, but if they are of value to the organization they should be noted, along with equivalent costs if the tactics were to be purchased.

Note the value of donated or contributed services. In particular, include the value of volunteer time as you calculate the full cost of the budget items. For example, a human-services agency might get help from a college public relations class in developing a brochure for new clients. The students may not charge for their services, but the project budget should include a dollar estimate of what those services would cost if the agency had to hire professionals such as a freelance copywriter or a design firm.

Communication plans usually don't feature income items, but don't overlook implicit revenues. For example, corporate sponsorship may have a specific dollar value, which should be presented in the budget as an offset to expenses. It also is appropriate to include projected revenues if you have built a fund-raising tactic into your program recommendations.

Likewise, it may be appropriate to include both the actual expense and real value of that expense item. For example, the full value of discounted consulting fees or free airtime for a public service advertisement can be listed to show the difference between the total value and the actual cost to the organization. A word of caution: Don't be tempted to set a dollar value on publicity by calculating how much the same space would cost for advertising. This is discussed in more detail in Step 9; for now let's just agree that publicity should not be confused with advertising.

By including all of this information, you are presenting a full view of the real value of the campaign, even though the organization's actual cost may be considerably less.

How Much Success Is Necessary?

It sometimes can be useful to determine how much success is necessary. This break-even point is the level of achievement needed simply to cover the cost of the program.

Calculate the **break-even point** (BEP) in three steps: Identify the total project cost (c); determine the outcome value (v), the dollar value for each unit of the desired outcome, especially those associated with the action objectives. Then divide the total project cost by the value of the desired outcome. Thus the formula is: BEP = c/v (cost divided by value).

Let's say a private college will spend $100,000 in recruiting costs this year to develop brochures and booklets, produce and distribute an informational video, and place paid radio commercials and billboards. Let's add another $80,000 in salaries associated with this particular project. Add another $10,000 for expenses such as postage, travel, and phone calls. That's $190,000 in all, the total project cost. Now let's presume that tuition at this college is $10,000. Apply the formula: cost $190,000 divided by outcome value $10,000 equals 19. That's the break-even point, the number of students who must be recruited before the communication program has paid for itself. (Note that this is an oversimplified example that doesn't take into account that the real cost of education is borne not only by tuition but also by donations, endowments, and state aid.)

Another useful budgetary calculation is the **per-capita cost**, the cost associated with the number of people needed to cover the cost. Calculate the per-capita cost (PCC) by dividing the total project cost (c) by the number of people (p) who perform the desired outcome. The formula is: PCC = v/p. Returning to the college scenario, divide the cost by the number of new recruits (let's say that's 1,800). Apply the formula: $190,000 divided by 1,800, which equals $105.56. This is how much the college is spending to recruit each new student. In percentage terms, that is about 1.05% of tuition income, or about a penny for every dollar paid in tuition.

Break-even points and per-capita costs also can be calculated for other public relations objectives, as long as the objectives themselves have been stated in precise and measurable terms.

Planning Example 8: Implementing the Strategic Plan

The following schedule shows one of several events within the four initiatives of the plan to publicize Upstate College's expanding program. It shows the event and its component tactics, along with a cost, an assigned manager, and a start date for each tactic.

Event: Rededication Ceremony

Tactic 1: Print and mail 1,000 invitations
Cost: $800 Manager: Publications Office Begin Work: 12 weeks

Tactic 2: Print 500 programs
Cost: $0 Manager: Publications Office Begin Work: 10 weeks

Tactic 3: Keynote speaker honorarium
Cost: $1,000 Manager: President's Office Begin Work: 12 weeks

Tactic 4: Musicians
Cost: $200 Manager: Music Dept Chair Begin Work: 6 weeks

Tactic 5: Academic processional/ritual
Cost: $200 Manager: Provost Begin Work: 6 weeks

Tactic 6: Video about UC expansion
Cost: $4,000 Manager: Video Task Force Begin work: 20 weeks

Tactic 7: Viewing equipment
Cost $300 Manager: Facilities Office Begin work: 4 weeks

Tactic 8: Plaque engraving
Cost: $400 Manager: Facilities Office Begin work: 4 weeks

■ ■ ■

TINY TYKES TOYS

The following schedule shows one of the several events outlined for the employee publics of the strategic communication plan focusing on consumer confidence.

Tactic: Newsletter articles in employee publication about safety, quality, and customer satisfaction.

Implementation Schedule: With publication slated for the first Wednesday of each month, relevant articles will be written for each publication date, according to the following schedule:

Safety Issues

- January: Industrywide safety standards and government safety regulations.
- April: Product safety record of Tiny Tykes Toys for the last 15 years.
- July: External—marketing consequences of product safety.
- October: Internal—employee consequences of product safety.

Quality Issues

- February: Industrywide quality issues in the toy industry.
- May: Quality comparison between Tiny Tykes Toys and major competitors.
- August: Quality-control and quality-goal programs at Tiny Tykes Toys.
- November: Involvement of employees in quality issues at Tiny Tykes Toys.

Customer Satisfaction Issues

- March: Industrywide importance of customer satisfaction to company's bottom line.
- June: Importance of customer satisfaction to Tiny Tykes Toys' reputation.
- September: Empowering employees to achieve customer satisfaction.
- December: Employee training/motivation for customer satisfaction.

Staffing: The communication director in the public relations office will notify appropriate interviewees two months prior to publication date. A communication specialist will arrange interviews three to four weeks prior to publication and will give completed article to the communication director two weeks prior to publication date.

Budget: There is no significant operating cost to research or write articles. Staff time is already provided, but approximately five hours will be allocated for each article for preparation, research, interviewing, and writing.

Checklist 8: Implementing the Strategic Plan

Basic Questions

1. What is the schedule for this project?
2. What is the budget for this project?
3. Who is responsible for this project?

Expanded Questions

A. SCHEDULING

1. What is the message repetition?
2. What is the message frequency?
3. What is the scheduling pattern (optional): continuous, flighting, pulsing, or massing?
4. What is the timeline for each tactic?
5. Who is the assigned manager for each tactic?

B. BUDGET

1. Identify the following budget line items:
   Personnel
   Materials
   Media costs
   Equipment and facilities
   Miscellaneous expenses
2. What is the full-cost budget?
3. What administrative cost items are associated with this tactic?
4. What is the break-even point?
5. What is the per-capita cost?

Phase Four

EVALUATIVE RESEARCH

Step 9
Evaluating the Strategic Plan

The strategic planning that began with research in Phase One comes full circle in this final phase of the process. Here you turn once again to research techniques, preparing to evaluate the effectiveness of your tactics in achieving your objectives.

Perform well in this phase and you may be able to soar above the competition, because public relations practitioners too often are weak in evaluative research. And they're the first to concede this fault. Professional workshops in evaluation and measurement always seem to draw large audiences. Surveys of public relations practitioners in all kinds of settings—agencies, for-profit corporations, and nonprofit organizations—indicate that, while they may talk a lot about doing evaluative research, often their actions don't quite match their words.

A good baseline for considering the prevalence of evaluative research may be a study by Ketchum Public Relations ("Evaluation Research on the Rise," 1994). When he was Ketchum research director, Walter K. Lindenmann found that 48% of public relations practitioners wanted a systematic and scientific assessment of the impact of their programs on awareness, attitudes, opinions, and behaviors. You might consider that a low percentage—less than half the practitioners. Still, that figure had increased from 30% in a previous study.

Similarly, Rick Fischer (1995) of Memphis State University noted that only a minority of Silver Anvil winners (somewhere between 30 and 48%) measured how well their campaigns had met predetermined goals. (The Silver Anvil awards are sponsored by the Public Relations Society of America, and indicate, presumably, the best of the best in terms of public relations programs and projects.)

In a corporate survey by Edelman Public Relations, Opinion Research Corporation, and Northwestern University (1997), 75% of respondents agreed that measurement of communication efforts on the achievement of corporate goals is an important trend. Yet only 27% said their own communication programs actually have evaluation components.

Meanwhile, even marketing executives—who are generally more comfortable with quantifiable evaluation criteria than are public relations executives—give "greater focus on doing the marketing than on proving it works" (Corder, Deasy, & Thompson, 1999, p. 12).

Why so much talk, with so little action? Several reasons. For one, it is sometimes difficult to know just what to evaluate and how to do so. Research is a specialty many practitioners have not mastered, perhaps not even studied. Another reason is that public relations measures may not be as precise as those used in areas such as finance, operations, and safety. Still another difficulty in measuring public relations is that everything is in motion, clouding the possibility of an accurate count; it's like going into a tropical fish store and trying to count the number of neons in a tank.

Additionally, some public relations measures are negatives—to what extent something bad did *not* happen, or how many negative opinions were minimized. Finally, research takes time, money, and creative energy, three things public relations practitioners guard as precious commodities to be used in only the most important situations.

Perhaps after all the explanations and excuses, it comes down to this: Evaluation is infrequent because public relations practitioners—or their bosses or clients—simply don't recognize its importance. But as you will discover in this section, good evaluative research does not have to be costly or time consuming, nor is it beyond the means of an adequately prepared practitioner.

Properly built into the overall strategic plan, evaluative research can increase the effectiveness of public relations and marketing communication. Additionally, it can save time and money in future endeavors. These advantages should appeal to bosses and clients everywhere.

Finally, proper evaluation can enhance the prestige and role of public relations within an organization. That's an even bigger advantage—one that every practitioner surely can recognize.

Step 9

Evaluating the Strategic Plan

Program evaluation is the systematic measurement of the outcomes of a project, program, or campaign based on the extent to which stated objectives are achieved. As part of the strategic planning process, establishing appropriate and practical evaluation methods wraps up all the previous plans, ideas, and recommendations.

In this section, we will look at various aspects of evaluative research: what, when, and—most important—how to evaluate.

What to Evaluate

You've heard the phrase "starting off on the right foot." In precision marching, the first step is the most important, because it sets up the pattern for the rest of the cadence. The same is true in putting together an effective research program. Starting on the right foot means setting out to answer the appropriate questions.

The overall plan for program evaluation outlines the criteria for judging what is effective. This research plan considers several issues: the criteria to be used to gauge success, timing of the evaluation, and specific ways to measure each of the levels of objectives (awareness, acceptance, and action). It may prescribe the various evaluation tools, and it also should indicate how the evaluation would be used.

Note that this planning happens before any tactics are implemented. Although the design of evaluative research focuses on the results of the program, it is developed as part of the initial planning. It points to how evaluation will be conducted at the appropriate times.

Design Questions

As you design an effective program for evaluation research, ask yourself the following questions:

- On what criteria should the program be judged?
- What information is needed to make the assessment?
- What standards of accuracy and reliability are needed for this assessment?

Next, focus some attention on the source of the information needed:

- Who has this information?
- How can this information be obtained from them?

Finally, consider how the information will be used:

- Who will receive the final evaluation, and what will be done with the information?
- How willing and able are decision makers to receive less-than-fully-positive evaluations?
- Besides decision makers, who else would have an interest in the evaluation?

Remember that research design is always a trade-off between the perfect and the practical. Strategic planners must make choices about the importance of the program, the accuracy and reliability of the information to be received, and the needed resources (time, personnel, financial and so on).

Evaluation Criteria

Before you develop specific evaluation techniques, consider first the criteria on which you will judge something to be effective. What yardsticks should you use? The appropriate standards vary with the objectives and the tactics, but here are a few general guidelines. Evaluation criteria should be (1) useful to the organization by being clearly linked with the established objectives; (2) realistic, feasible, and appropriate as to cost, time, or other resources; (3) ethical and socially responsible; (4) credible because it is supported by accurate data; and (5) presented in a timely manner.

Consider various criteria that might be evaluated in a public relations campaign. The best structure for this is to draw on the earlier-stated objectives. Here are some categories of evaluation criteria for each of the three types of objectives:

- *Evaluation of awareness objectives.* Media coverage and calculation of media impressions. Postcampaign awareness survey.
- *Evaluation of acceptance objectives.* Tabulation of requests for information. Postcampaign attitude/opinion survey. Tabulation of letters, e-mail, and phone calls expressing interest or support. Postevent audience evaluation.
- *Evaluation of action objectives.* Measures of results (such as ticket sales, attendance, memberships, donations, and so on). Measures of improvement. Organizational or environmental change.

Additionally, be prepared to identify and evaluate unplanned results of a campaign. Sometimes a campaign generates reaction beyond what was anticipated. This reaction may be positive or negative in the eyes of the organization, but it is worth considering unplanned results and unintended consequences, if for no other reason than they might be built into subsequent similar campaigns.

Here is an example of how one organization established criteria to judge the effectiveness of its website:

- Ability to navigate easily throughout the site (a measure of awareness objectives)
- Breadth of content (awareness objectives)
- Ability to convey key messages (awareness objectives)
- Stats tracking the number of web visitors (awareness objectives)

- Number and tenor of questions and comments by site visitors (acceptance objectives)
- Interactivity (action objectives)
- Number of visitor names that are captured for organizational response or follow-up (action objectives)
- Number of web visitors who take online surveys or respond to online offers (awareness or action objectives)

Notice that measures of message production and exposure are not included as significant. For example, what matters is not so much the number of hits but the number and content of comments by visitors to the site and the number of retrievable names so the organization can engage the visitor in two-way communication. With appropriate evaluation criteria in mind, the public relations strategist can turn to the task of developing evaluation measures that can rate the website on those criteria.

Notice, too, that all of the criteria should be developed before any implementation of the website, because the particular criteria you identify as necessary will determine some of what you do in putting the website together.

Linda Childers Hon (1997) has compared a study by MediaLink (Weiner, 1995) with a survey conducted by the Detroit chapter of the Public Relations Society of America. MediaLink found that 98% of public relations practitioners felt that the number of positive stories in the media was most important; less than 60% measured awareness or attitudes. The Detroit survey, however, found that most CEOs felt awareness and attitude were most important, and they rated media clippings as the least important indicators of effectiveness. So the question is

A Ray of Hope?

Through a series of interviews with public relations practitioners and corporate executives, one researcher has identified what may be a hopeful trend in public relations evaluation research. Linda Childers Hon (1998) has reported several interesting findings:

1. Practitioners seem to be moving toward more systematic public relations programming.
2. Both practitioners and CEOs have long-range plans to build more formal evaluation into their public relations efforts.
3. Practitioners are trying to educate CEOs and others in their organizations of the importance of public relations measurement.
4. Understanding is growing among both practitioners and executives of how public relations feeds into the strategic goals of organizations.
5. Junior practitioners, who are relatively new to the field of public relations, are more likely than veteran practitioners to be integrating evaluation into their public relations programming.

Is this the beginning of a trend? It's too early to make the call. So far the research has been based only on small samples. But it may signal a time to come when evaluation research routinely plays a more prominent role in the public relations planning and programming.

worth asking: Just what should we be measuring? Or, more pointedly, Why should we continue to focus on awareness when our bosses and clients want to influence attitude and action?

Ken Gofton (1999) has noted the difference between advertising and public relations measurement. He observes that advertising often focuses evaluative research on audience exposure. Public relations evaluation, meanwhile, may measure exposure, but it goes further: profiling audiences, tracking attitude change and assessing impact in terms of behavioral outcomes.

When to Evaluate

There are three stages in the process or program evaluation related to timing: implementation reports, progress reports, and final evaluation. Each is different; each is important.

Implementation Reports

The first potential point for evaluation is in tracking the implementation of each tactic, making sure that it is proceeding according to plan. This **implementation report** documents how the program tactics were carried out. In it, include a schedule of progress to date toward implementing each tactic, as well as any work remaining. Identify any gaps, defects, or potential delays that could hurt the plan. Note any difficulties encountered and how they were (or might be) resolved. Discuss the efficiency with which the tactics were set in motion.

Additionally, note the name of the person or group responsible for each tactic, as well as other personnel resources such as staff, freelancers, consultants, and so on. It might also be useful to include budgetary information, such as how much money has been spent or committed thus far.

Progress Reports

It is important to monitor progress at various key points as the tactics are being implemented. **Progress reports** are preliminary evaluations, on which planners can make strategic modifications as they further implement the program. Such midcourse corrections can keep the project functioning at peak efficiency. In this way, the plan is used as a written guideline rather than a rigid rulebook.

Consider this analogy of an interactive computer travel map for a cross-country road trip. This mapping program receives hourly weather updates and daily progress reports on highway construction projects. It also monitors traffic jams around congested urban areas and newspaper reports of tourism-related events. Before you leave on the road trip, you map out a tentative plan, indicating your goal (traveling cross country) and your objectives (stopping at various points of interest along the way to the destination). A rigid use of your plan would be to follow the map with no deviation—after all, you've planned this trip for a long time, and you shouldn't be distracted by unscheduled changes. However, a more effective use of the map would allow the computerized mapping program to alert you to an interesting community festival only a few miles off the scheduled route or to travel delays resulting from snow buildup on a mountain pass.

The mapping program demonstrates the value of feedback: You can use information gathered during the course of the project to update strategy, modify objectives, and adjust

Twelve Reminders about Evaluative Research

Here are a dozen suggestions for planning and implementing an effective evaluative research program. Most of these tips are based on common-sense principles that you probably already know. But reminders are meant to be remembered, so review these tips and consider them as you prepare your evaluation program.

1. *Don't wait for the program's completion before you evaluate.* Evaluation begins with the planning process, before you actually "do" anything. Effective planning means you determine in advance what you will evaluate and how you will measure.
2. *Guesses aren't good enough.* Evaluation must rely on facts, not estimates. Hunches and gut feelings can point the way, but hard facts are needed to accurately assess impact.
3. *Friends may be telling you what they think you want to hear.* Get beyond the limitations of information volunteered by people who already look kindly on your organization. Also, be cautious of relying too heavily on information solicited from friends and other supporters in situations that don't encourage candor.
4. *Employees have a stake in the program's success.* Realize that they may be seeing what they want to see, for the programs they evaluate affect their own job security and economic future, as well as their day-to-day social relationships on the job.
5. *Samples must reflect the population.* Formal evaluative research draws on a sample that represents the publics addressed in the public relations activity. This kind of research is likely to generate information that is accurate.
6. *Hard work and cost aren't measures of effectiveness.* Be careful not to equate activity with achievement. Your campaign may have claimed many resources in time, energy and budgets, but these are not the measure of program effectiveness.
7. *Creativity is not a gauge of effectiveness.* "Everybody thinks it's a neat idea" may indicate innovation, and a professional award may attest to your ingenuity. But neither is the mark of a successful program.
8. *Dissemination doesn't equal communication.* A mainstay principle of public relations is that distribution of a message does not guarantee that real communication is achieved. Every piece of unopened junk mail, every commercial zapped through or TiVo'd, and every half-time show missed by spectators heading for the rest room is an example of failed communication.
9. *Knowledge doesn't always lead to acceptance.* Better informed publics are more supportive ones, says the common wisdom. Not necessarily. Knowledge is important on the road to support, but this road has an off-ramp as well. Sometimes the more people know about an organization or the issues it faces, the less supportive they may be.
10. *Behavior is the ultimate measure.* Awareness and acceptance objectives are important, and many public relations activities seek to increase knowledge, generate favorable attitudes or foster supportive opinions. But knowledge that doesn't lead to action is pretty weak, and attitudes or opinions that don't have an outcome in behavior are like books sitting unread on the shelf. Missed opportunities. Unrealized potential.
11. *Evaluation doesn't have to be expensive or time-consuming.* Like other aspects of public relations planning, evaluation research—done appropriately—is linked to the organization's resources. Proper evaluation requires insight and creative thinking, not necessarily a lot of time or money.
12. *Evaluative research enables action.* It allows organizations to modify programs, analyze and justify the current program, or make decisions about similar future programs.

tactics. This type of in-process evaluation is important for both public relations and marketing communication programs. After a pilot project and following each significant phase within a program, evaluate whether the program is unfolding as it was planned to do. Ask questions: Are the messages being disseminated as expected? Are they being understood? Are people responding as expected? If the answers turn out to be "no," there is still time to make adjustments before the rest of the program is implemented.

This kind of evaluation allows a public relations plan to be a living document that enhances the atmosphere of open communication. It allows the planning organization to be impacted by its environment and by its publics.

Final Reports

Final reports, sometimes called **summative reports**, review the whole of the program. They measure impact and outcome for the various tactics. The final evaluation gauges how well the tactics achieved what they set out to achieve—namely, the various objectives.

Research Design

The question of when to evaluate leads to a related aspect of research design: How to structure the evaluation in relation to the measurement standards. There are several possibilities, the most common being after-only studies and various approaches to before-and-after models.

After-only studies. The simplest research design is the **after-only study**, which is common in public relations precisely because of its simplicity. Implement a tactic, measure its impact, and presume that the tactic caused the impact. This approach can be appropriate for action objectives that measure audience response, such as attendance, contributions, purchase, and other easily measured reactions. For example, a political candidate running for office would need no preliminary baseline. She simply would be interested in the numbers of votes received in the election.

However, the after-only approach is not appropriate for every situation. Its weakness is its very simplicity, because this design presumes a cause-and-effect relationship that may not be accurate. The after-only approach does not prove that the tactic caused the observed level of awareness or acceptance, only that the result occurred after the tactic. Perhaps the levels were there all along but simply not noticed.

Before-and-after studies. Another format for evaluation research is the **before-and-after study**, also called a **pretest/post-test study**. This model involves an observation before any public relations programming is implemented. The initial observation provides a benchmark or baseline for comparing studies that will be conducted later.

For example, if the candidate noted above wanted to gauge the effectiveness of a new type of campaign message, she would need to measure her support before the message was presented and measure it again following the presentation. The difference would indicate the change—positive or negative—created by the new campaign message. In another example, a public transit system might compare ridership figures before and after a promotional campaign. Note that a before-and-after study is integrated into both the formative research and evaluative research phases of the planning process.

The simplest before-and-after study involves three stages: (1) observe and measure a public, (2) expose the public to a public relations tactic, and (3) measure the public again. Any change in the public's awareness, acceptance, or action can likely be attributed to the tactic.

Remember, however, that public relations activities generally don't take place in a vacuum or in a pure environment. Be aware of extraneous factors. Not every change in your key public may appropriately be linked, cause-and-effect fashion, to your programming. One of the challenges for evaluative research is to sort out the effective public relations tactics from unrelated outside forces.

Controlled before-and-after studies. A more sophisticated type of evaluative research takes into account those unrelated outside forces. A **controlled before-and-after study** involves two sample groups drawn from the same key public. One sample is the group to receive the message; the other is a control group that does not receive the message. This process has four elements: (1) observe and measure each group; (2) expose one group to a tactic, but do not expose the control group; (3) measure each group again; and (4) compare the results of each group. The control group is likely to have remained unchanged, while any change noted in the exposed group presumably can be linked to exposure to the public relations tactic—the key difference between the two groups. For example, the transit system noted above might also compare before-and-after ridership figures with those of a transit system in a similar city in another state (the control group), where riders were not exposed to the promotional campaign.

Remember that research design is always a trade-off. Strategic planners must make choices that consider the importance of the program, the accuracy and reliability of the information to be received, and the needed resources (time, personnel, financial, and the like). They also should look at the whole picture, focusing not on each tactic in isolation but on how the various tactics together have achieved their objectives.

Also be aware of extraneous factors that can mask your evaluation efforts. Not every change in a public's awareness, acceptance, or action may be caused by your public relations programming. Try to account for other activities and influences that the publics have been exposed to.

Let's return to the example of the transit system. If a few days after the ridership campaign begins an international political crisis sends oil prices up 30%, you probably would notice a lot more riders on the trains and buses. But you shouldn't attribute this to your public relations campaign. It's more likely that motorists are reacting to the higher cost of gasoline at the pumps, and your research report must note this.

A benefit of most evaluative research is that it is a form of **unobtrusive research**—the subjects in the study do not know they are being observed, at least not until after the fact, when their awareness of being observed can't affect what they have already done.

An exception to this is the before-and-after study. When conducting a before-and-after study, be aware of the **Hawthorne effect**, also called the **placebo effect**. In the 1930s, researchers at Hawthorne Works, an electric power company near Chicago, were trying to find out how the intensity of lighting affected factory workers. The researchers increased the lighting, and productivity increased. Then they decreased the lighting, and productivity increased again. At first, the researchers believed the changes were the result of teamwork among the employees. Similar studies manipulated other aspects of the work environment: pay incentives, shorter hours, longer hours, more breaks, fewer breaks—in each case, productivity increased for a short time.

Cybernetics and Public Relations

Norbert Wiener's cybernetic model of communication (1954) was noted in Phase Two, Strategy.

Cybernetics deals with the feedback mechanisms of goal-seeking systems, in which goals are established, action and output is monitored, and feedback mechanisms implement corrective action to keep the system on the target of its goal. Furnace thermostats, heat-seeking missiles and cruise-control devices on cars are examples of cybernetics.

In public relations and marketing communication, examples of cybernetics include crisis planning and issues management that feature a radarlike early warning system of monitoring the environment in which the organization operates. An example is the kind of in-process evaluative research being presented in this book.

Cybernetics in public relations operates most effectively in an open-systems approach. In this approach, public relations functions as the liaison between the organization and its publics, with responsibilities to each and to the mutual benefits of both.

Two-way communication between the organization and the environment keeps the organization moving toward its goal, with this approach continuously adjusted through the feedback provided by the publics.

In 1955, Henry Landsberger re-analyzed the older studies. He concluded that the boost in productivity was not caused at all by the amount of lighting but simply because the subjects knew they were being observed and knew that the company was concerned about worker productivity. Landsberger coined the term "Hawthorne effect," which since has been broadened to explain any impact, usually short-term, through which employees are made to feel important or are aware that they are being observed.

How to Evaluate

A question was posed at the beginning of Step 9: What information is needed in order to evaluate a program's effectiveness? Answer this question wisely, and you'll have a strong final phase to your strategic planning. Answer blindly, and you could end up measuring the wrong thing. Consider five levels of evaluation: judgmental assessments, and evaluation of communication outputs, awareness, acceptance, and action.

Judgmental Assessments

An evaluation made on hunches and experience is called a **judgmental assessment**. This type of informal feedback is common in public relations and marketing communication. It is the kind of research that everybody seems to do, because it comes naturally. Judgmental assessment relies on personal and subjective observations such as the following: "The boss liked it," "The client asked us to continue the project," "Everybody said this was a success," "The customers seem happy," and "Hey, we won an award for this project."

Judgmental assessments are based on personal observation, which can be both a strength and a limitation. Some judgmental evaluations, though informal, can be helpful to an

Methods of Evaluative Research

Like formative research, evaluative research involves techniques that can be either quantitative or qualitative.

Quantitative research methods used frequently for evaluation include surveys, content analyses, cost-effectiveness studies, readership studies, head counts and tracking of feedback, as well as direct observation and monitoring of specific results.

Qualitative research techniques commonly used for evaluation include interviews, focus groups, and case studies.

Don't let the availability of so many different research methods hide the fact that direct observation of outcomes can be the simplest way to evaluate the effectiveness of public relations programs. For more information on research techniques, see Appendix A, Applied Research Techniques.

organization. For example, assessment by outside experts, perhaps public relations colleagues in another organization, might offer an excellent analysis of the program.

So too with judgmental assessments based on a formal review of an organization's program by a panel of outside experts. An example is the review teams fielded by the Accrediting Council for Education in Journalism and Mass Communications that assess various aspects of a college or university communication program seeking professional accreditation. Another example is an evaluation based on a program that received an award through a competition sponsored by a professional organization, such as the Silver Anvil, sponsored by the Public Relations Society of America; the Gold Quill Award, sponsored by the International Association of Business Communicators, or local professional competitions.

Additionally, senior practitioners often draw on their experience to make informal judgments about program effectiveness.

However, such informal research has its limitations. For one thing, the informal assessments often are made by program managers, who are never disinterested and seldom impartial. For another, their personal observations are often imprecise and arbitrary, sometimes downright fickle. Granted, the anecdotes on which this feedback is based can provide much insight into the success or failure of a program, but because informal research and gut feelings don't involve representative samples and standard measures they can't confirm the effectiveness of public relations activity.

Another problem with judgmental assessment is that it often gives undue emphasis to apparent creativity and to the expenditure of energy and resources. Throughout this entire planning process you have put in a great deal of effort and energy. In doing so you have articulated a strategy and produced a range of tactics. These, of course, are important, but they are not what you should be measuring. Rather, the evaluation phase should focus on your objectives at each of their three levels: awareness, acceptance and action. Just like objectives, evaluation research should deal with the impact your program has made on your various publics.

Judgmental assessment also can lull you into taking for granted what you should be analyzing. Consider tax-free shopping weeks. Increasingly, state lawmakers are periodically waiving sales tax to encourage spending and help consumers save money. One popular time is the back-to-school shopping time in late August. It's oh-so-obvious that consumers win;

they save money when buying clothing and school supplies. Politicians benefit from the gratitude of their constituents. And merchants like it because buyers flock into their stores. On the surface, tax-free shopping weeks are both popular and successful.

Yet is popularity a valid standard? Stores that used to discount merchandise 15 or 20% no longer have sales because they know the consumers will flock in to save—what? 8½% (the average sales tax)? Meanwhile, states lose important tax revenues, threatening services or leading to increases in other kinds of taxes and fees to make up the difference. So customer satisfaction, if it is based on whim rather than fact, isn't a useful measure.

The lesson is this: Effective evaluation requires careful analysis. Don't rely only on the obvious—because what obviously seems true sometimes isn't. Let's look at a complementary approach to evaluation, this one based on the results of communication tactics.

Evaluation of Communication Outputs

Measuring communication products and their distribution is the focus of **outputs evaluation**, a method that concentrates on the development and presentation of a message. As an evaluation method it is not particularly effective. Outputs may be necessary tasks to do, but they really are not effective measurement tools. Yet current researchers report that many practitioners still rely primarily on output measures (Rice & Atkin, 2002; Xavier, Johnston, Patel, Watson, & Simmons, 2005). Various methods of measuring communication outputs include message production, message dissemination, message cost, and advertising equivalency. Let's look at each.

Message production. Several techniques of evaluation research deal simply with whether the message is produced. For example, count the number of news releases written, brochures printed or pages formatted for a website. Or note the creation of special message vehicles, such as a company float for the Fourth of July parade. Measurement of message production simply quantifies the work output of a public relations office. While it may be useful for a measure of individual job performance, don't be deluded into thinking that it is a measure of program effectiveness.

Message distribution. Another approach to awareness evaluation focuses not merely on the production of messages but also on their distribution. In this category, the evaluator focuses on media contacts and asks how many news releases were mailed, faxed, or uploaded to the website. Measuring message dissemination tells what an organization did to spread the message, but it doesn't measure the message's effectiveness or its impact.

Message cost. Another type of measurement deals with the cost of messages. This approach analyzes how much money an organization spends to present its message. For paid media such as brochures or advertisements, the organization simply divides the cost of the communication vehicle by the number of times the message has been reproduced. For example, if it costs $150 to produce 2,500 copies of a flier, then each piece costs 6 cents.

When dealing with electronic media, the common standard is **cost per thousand**, identified as CPM (from the Latin word *mille,* meaning "thousand"). For example, if a radio station with 75,000 listeners during a particular time period charges $150 for a 30-second commercial, it would cost $2 for each thousand listeners—a mere one-fifth of a penny per listener. Cost per thousand is an effective way to compare costs among various media, even print vehicles. Consider the following:

- A national magazine with a regional edition circulating 17,000 copies charges $9,000 for a full-page color ad; CPM = $529 (nearly 53 cents per each local subscriber).
- A city newspaper with a circulation of 338,000 charges $22,000 for a full-page ad; CPM = $65 (about 6½ cents per reader).
- A local radio station with an estimated 10,000 listeners charges $35 for a 30-second commercial; CPM = $3.50.
- A transit system of bus and light rail service in a metropolitan area charges $290 for each transit poster, with 40 needed to saturate coverage in what is called "100 showing" (100% of the audience—3 million—is likely to see the poster within a 30-day period). The cost for 40 posters is $11,600; CPM = $3.87.
- A cable advertising service charges $150 for a 30-second commercial on a cable network providing 25 channels to 520,000 subscriber households (average per-channel subscriber base of 20,800); CPM = $7.21 (less than a penny per subscriber).

When comparing media costs, however, remember that the elements you are comparing may not be similar. The impact of various media and the amount of repeat presentation for messages to have an impact must be considered, as well as how closely a particular media audience coincides with an organization's key public.

Consider this example of a newspaper ad and a brochure. A 50,000-circulation newspaper charges $5,500 for a half-page ad; CPM = $110. A printer charges $600 for 10,000 copies of a direct-mail letter; CPM = $60. Additionally, it will cost $1,900 to distribute the letters; now the CPM cost to the organization is $250 for the direct-mail letter.

Purely based on production and distribution costs, the newspaper ad is a better deal. But most newspaper readers skip over the ads because they are not particularly interested in the topic. Chances are you don't need to communicate with 50,000 newspaper readers because most of them are not even in the key public you identified in your planning. Meanwhile, people who receive brochures are often more likely to read them, especially if the organization did a good job identifying its public and designed the brochure to be of obvious interest to the readers. So the $2,500 brochure could well be the more cost-effective way to communicate with members of the key publics: less total expense and—more important—more effective message delivery. On the other hand, if your public is widespread and difficult to reach individually, then the newspaper cost would be the better way to communicate with them.

Advertising equivalency. A common but generally inappropriate evaluation technique is related to the message cost. **Advertising equivalency** means treating a nonadvertising item as if it were an ad. For example, a news report about your organization is published in a local newspaper, involving a space totaling 21 column inches including headline, story and photo. How can you evaluate this report? Using the advertising equivalency method, you would look up the advertising cost for a 21-inch ad in that newspaper. At $165 per column inch, for example, that story would have cost $3,465 if it were an advertisement.

That's a neat way to put a dollar figure on a news story, costing it out as if it were an ad. But that "as if" causes a big problem. A news story isn't an advertisement, so the dollar figure is meaningless. Why? Audiences know the difference between news and advertising, and they treat the two information vehicles differently. Generally news stories are far more credible than are advertisements. So how much extra should you add for credibility?

On the other hand, news stories don't necessarily have only positive information about an organization. So how much should you deduct because the news report wasn't glowingly positive? But wait. People read news stories more than they do ads. Perhaps you should add value because of higher audience attention? Back and forth it goes, and in the end any dollar value you give to the news story is simply a fiction, and bad fiction at that—worse than worthless because it gives a false impression that a meaningful assessment has been made.

Despite the obvious misconception that underlies advertising equivalency, it's a myth that doesn't want to go away. Some public relations agencies even have devised formulas to impress their clients. For example, they calculate the value of publicity as being four times the cost of advertising; or ten times. But remember that such arbitrary weighting schemes are all smoke and mirrors.

Evaluation of Awareness Objectives

The methods associated with outputs evaluation focus on documenting communication activity. Perhaps that's a worthwhile exercise, but it doesn't give a solid basis for measuring effectiveness. Rather, it is more important to demonstrate the value that communication tactics offer an organization, specifically their effectiveness in achieving awareness, attitude, and action objectives that already have been established.

The first level of public relations objectives, awareness, provides an important category of evaluation research. **Awareness evaluation** focuses on the content of the message. It considers how many people were exposed to the message, how easy the message is to understand, and how much of the message is remembered. Some of the common measures for awareness evaluation include message exposure, message content, readability measures, and message recall.

Message exposure. Measurement of message exposure, which focuses on the number of people in key publics who were exposed to the message, is a bit more sophisticated than the previous evaluation methodologies. That's because these objectives-based measures look more closely at communication tactics, evaluating not only distribution but also audience attention.

For example, the evaluator may ask how many hits were registered at a website or the actual number of people in the audience who heard a speech or saw a performance. Instead of counting the number of news releases distributed, the evaluator would ask how many newspaper stories or broadcast reports resulted from the release or, more important, how many people actually read those newspaper stories, heard the broadcast reports or read the online posting of the news release.

This can be a difficult number to obtain. Some public relations offices track this on their own; others hire **clipping services**, companies that track publications and/or broadcasts on a regional, national or even international basis. A variety of services and software exists to track traffic at an organization's website, which might include a media room where reporters can download releases and other visitors can read releases. The software can measure not only the number of visitors but where they came from, how long they stay at the site, what pages they visit, what they download, and so on.

Some measures of message exposure count actual audiences, such as the number of people who attend an open house or some other public relations event. Unfortunately, some other measures deal with inferred or potential audiences, weakening the value of this measure by linking it to mere estimates.

Some concepts associated with message exposure are drawn from advertising people who could have been exposed to the message presented in various media, from interpersonal settings to viewers of a television newscast to motorists who pass by a billboard. Sometimes these calculations can be quite impressive, even seductive, such as the 1.1 billion impressions counted by MasterCard for its sponsorship of the 1994 World Cup Soccer Championship through public relations tactics such as news conferences, news releases, interviews, and bylined columns. More recently, the Epilepsy Foundation recorded 140 million impressions in 2002 through a public service radio advertisement and a news release. The following year, the foundation made 121 million teen and adult impressions, including a rate of 75% on its key public of African Americans.

Remember, however, that media impressions and other counts of message exposure may simply estimate audience size. Even if the count is an actual one, such measures indicate only how many people saw or heard the message. They don't indicate whether the audiences understood it, accepted it, or acted on it in any way.

Still, despite little evidence that impression counts are an effective evaluation tool, many respectable public relations and marketing executives continue to use them. The Ketchum study (see Corder et al., 1999) reported that 53% of respondents, all business-to-business marketing executives, track media impressions as their main approach to evaluation, though only 11% said they are happy with this.

Message content. An important type of evaluation focuses on the content of the message. Was it positive or did it provide erroneous data? Unwarranted conclusions? Outdated information?

Outputs and Outcomes

It is important to make a clear distinction between outputs and outcomes.

James Bissland (1990) identifies communication **outputs** as the work done in a public relations activity. He likens this work to the who-says-what-in-which-channel part of Harold Lasswell's classic verbal formula for communication.

Walter K. Lindenmann (1997a, 1997b) has described outputs as short-term, immediate results of a public relations program. Examples of outputs are the number of times a company official is quoted, the number of people who participated in a special event, the number of webpages viewed, and the number of placements that appear in the media.

Outcomes, meanwhile, are far more important. Bissland calles them "terminal goals"—what this book has defined not as general goals but as more specific and measurable action objectives. Examples of outcomes are the number of new recruits, the amount of money raised, or the passage of desired legislation.

The Institute said outcomes "measure whether target audience groups actually received the messages directed at them, paid attention to them, understood them, and retained them. [Outcomes also measure] possible opinion, attitude and/or behavior change, resulting from the communication effort" (Lindenmann, 1997a, p. 392).

So, measure outputs if you wish. They can provide useful assessment of what has been done. But don't stop there. Far more important is to measure program outcomes, specifically as they relate to your objectives.

It is far more important to analyze the content of a message than merely to count the number of newspaper clippings. Appendix A, Applied Research Techniques, provides specific information on how to conduct a content analysis. For now, don't forget to include it prominently in your evaluation program.

Readability measures. Another way to evaluate awareness deals with comprehension—how easy a message is to understand. One of the first steps in developing a public relations plan is to identify and analyze the publics to be addressed. Part of that analysis involves an assessment of their reading level, usually translated into the level of education achieved by members of the public.

For example, most newspapers are written at about a ninth-grade reading level so everybody with that level of education or more—the vast majority of readers—should be able to understand the articles, columns, and editorials. They may not necessarily agree with them or even be interested in them, but they are able to understand the writing. If you are preparing a news release or guest editorial for such a publication, plan on writing for readers with a ninth-grade reading ability. On the other hand, if you are writing a fund-raising letter aimed at health care professionals, it would be safe to presume that all your readers will have completed some level of higher education. Whatever you estimate to be the appropriate reading level, test your writing against that estimate.

Robert Gunning's **Fog Index**, which measures reading ease or difficulty, is one of the easiest readability measures to use; review the directions in the discussion of verbal communication in Phase Two, Strategy. Other commonly used readability instruments include Rudolf Flesch's Readability Score, which is more complicated than the Fog Index but which measures human interest; the associated Flesch-Kincaid readability grade level, Edward Fry's readability graph, which relies on a chart to calculate reading ease; the Dale-Chall formula, based on sentence length and the number of infrequently used words; the Cloze Procedure, which measures comprehension of spoken and visual messages; and Irving Fang's Easy Listening Formula, which provides a comparable way to calculate the comprehension of broadcast copy.

Many computer word-processing programs feature one or more of these readership aids in the program's tools section. For example, Microsoft Word counts 17.2 words per sentence in this chapter and calculates a 12.3 grade-level readability score, based on the Flesch-Kincaid score.

Message recall. This approach involves techniques drawn from advertising research, where day-after recall studies are commonplace. Using this method, participants in interviews, surveys, or focus groups are exposed to a news story, television program, or the like. Then they are interviewed to determine what they remember from the message. A staple of research drawn from advertising is the Starch Readership Reports (http://www.starchresearch.com/services.html). These indicate three levels of reader study: "noted" readers who remember having previously seen an advertisement; "associated" readers who can link the advertisement with a particular brand or advertiser; and "read most" readers who are able to describe most of the written material in the ad.

Here are two examples of how to measure awareness objectives:

- *Awareness objective:* To increase clients' understanding of changes in insurance policy coverage

What Should Be Measured?

Knowing what to measure is sometimes the key to effective evaluation research. The answer often can be found in the objectives. But sometimes the objectives themselves are in conflict, with one of them measuring positively and another barely moving the dial.

That was the case with the Got Milk? campaign by the National Fluid Milk Processor Promotion Board, which presumably sought—as a range of objectives—awareness, acceptance, and action.

The advertising series, which began in 1993, features celebrity photographer Annie Liebovitz's popular photos of celebrities with milk mustaches. Visibility is high, and everybody seems to be familiar with the campaign and the ads. The Promotion Board claims a 90% awareness rate.

Acceptance also runs high. The Promotion Board's research shows that attitudes toward milk have improved. The ads themselves have become collector items and have earned praise from creative designers. They found appeal with a diverse audience largely because of their use of many different celebrities and characters: Batman, David Beckham, Jackie Chan, Cirque de Soleil, Tony Hawk, Kermit the Frog, Marilyn Manson, Nelly, Conan O'Brien, Rihanna, Pete Sampras, Bart and Lisa Simpson, Britney Spears—the list goes on and on.

There's just one problem: It costs $110 million a year, and there's no evidence that the campaign has increased milk consumption. Oops! Milk sales have, in fact dropped. The U.S. Department of Agriculture's inspector general reported that milk usage was up 0.85% one year, down 0.42% the next. Milk usage is an overall downward spiral, as Americans consume only about half the amount of milk recommended by the government's dietary guidelines.

So the question is posed, How effective is a campaign that generates high awareness, measurable acceptance, and even improved attitudes but doesn't effect action?

- *Possible evaluation technique:* Note exposure patterns; do content analysis to gauge how consistent the messages are with the facts; ask a focus group to discuss message recall.
- *Awareness objective:* To increase awareness of a new consumer product being manufactured by a client.
- *Possible evaluation technique:* Track dissemination of messages, noting the size of the potential audience; analyze the message content, noting its accuracy and the use of the client's telephone number and/or website address; survey customers in the company data base regarding message recall.

Evaluation of Acceptance Objectives

A major shortcoming of all the message-based evaluation techniques noted earlier is that they do not address the consequence of the public relations tactics. Instead, they simply gauge the existence of the tactics. At best, message-based evaluation techniques can deal with the level of awareness surrounding a public relations message. However, a more effective area of evaluation is based on levels of acceptance and action. Objectives in Phase Two, Strategy, note the desired impact on interest and attitudes (acceptance) and on opinion and behavior (action). Take steps now to evaluate how well each of those objectives has been achieved. Two common approaches to measuring acceptance objectives are audience feedback and benchmark studies:

Audience feedback. Some evaluation measures count and analyze the voluntary reaction of the audience, such as the number of hits on a webpage, the number of telephone calls and letters, or the number of requests for additional information. This can be an effective measure of the level of the audience's information and interest.

Benchmark study. Another type of research, **benchmark studies** (also called **baseline studies**), provides a basis for comparing program outcomes against a standard. Actually, benchmark studies can be based on any of several different standards: the starting levels of interest or positive attitudes, outcomes of similar programs by other organizations, outcomes of the same program during a previous year or cycle, outcomes of industry or professional models, or the hypothetical outcomes of an "ideal" program.

Here are a couple of examples of how to evaluate acceptance-level objectives:

- *Acceptance objective:* To enhance favorable employee attitudes toward a client's company.
- *Possible evaluation techniques:* Compare retention figures from before and after the tactic was implemented; record oral and written comments given to the human resource department of the company; solicit anecdotal input from managers and supervisors; survey employees about their attitudes and try to learn what they have been telling family and friends about working for the company.
- *Acceptance objective:* To increase employee affirmation of the company's need to change employee benefits.
- *Possible evaluation techniques:* Record immediate anecdotal feedback after the announcement is made; conduct a survey within two days of the announcement; after two weeks, invite employee feedback through response cards provided in pay envelopes.

Evaluation of Action Objectives

The ultimate objectives for most public relations activities should focus on bottom-line issues for an organization, primarily the action sought from the key publics. In this evaluation phase of the planning process, careful consideration should be given to ways to measure these action objectives. Three approaches to action-focused evaluation research involve audience participation, direct observation, and relative media effectiveness.

Audience participation. Figures on the number of people who actively responded to the message generally are easy to obtain. Attendance figures are effective measures when attendance itself is the desired objective, as may be the case with concerts and exhibitions, athletic competitions, benefit fundraising events, and the like. Implicit in these attendance figures also is a measure of the effectiveness of publicity and promotion that preceded the events.

However, attendance figures can be misused if the presumption is made that attendance at some information-sharing session necessarily equates with action impact. For example, attendance at an event in which a political candidate gives a major speech can't be used as a reliable indicator of either audience acceptance or eventual action in the voting booth. People

Real-World Research Practices

Ketchum Public Relations surveyed 480 marketing executives (Corder et al., 1999) to learn how they evaluate their communication activities. Here are some highlights from this study; the percentage number indicates the positive response on using each item as an indicator of evaluation research:

61%	Increase in sales volume
59%	Number of news releases, direct mail, and other tactics distributed
53%	Number of impressions generated
45%	Content analysis of key messages in reported stories
37%	Advertising equivalency
33%	Opinion change based on before-and-after surveys

heard the speech, and the message was presented, but desired action is not guaranteed. Therefore, be careful how attendance figures are interpreted and what value is placed on them.

Direct observation. Sometimes the simplest way to measure the effectiveness of action objectives is to look around. Let's say the objective sought an outcome of enough voter support to win an election. If your candidate won, your objective was achieved. If you sought financial contributions of $2.2 million, count the total of donations and pledges; anything above the target amount means you were that much more successful than planned. Other easy-to-quantify objectives deal with capacity attendance for sporting and artistic events, sales figures, academic scores, membership expectations, and so on.

In some instances, the action objective deals with the general outcome rather than with any quantification. For example, passage (or defeat) of a particular piece of legislation may fully satisfy an action objective. Some evaluation research calls for strategic and creative thinking. Individual behaviors that may not be easily observable are more difficult to measure than the preceding examples.

Here are two examples of how to deal with difficult-to-evaluate action objectives:

- *Action objective:* To increase the use of seat belts.
- *Possible evaluation technique:* Place observers in highway toll booths, and have them record the number of drivers and driver-side passengers wearing seat belts as they pass through the booths.
- *Action objective:* To have elementary, secondary, and college teachers become more active in lobbying state government for increased support of education.
- *Possible evaluation techniques:* In a tactic that encourages the sending of e-mail letters to state officials, attach instructions for sending a copy to your organization. Then simply count the number of copies received. To take this to a higher level of sophistication, work with several sympathetic state legislators; compare the number of e-mail messages sent to their office with the number of copies you received. From the difference, extrapolate the number of messages sent by teachers to all legislators.

How to Measure Publicity Effects

Measuring the effects of media relations takes a bit of creativity, but it's not impossible. Consider the following possibilities:

Set clear objectives in advance and establish the criteria that will form the basis for success.

Do a pretest such as an awareness survey to identify the beginning point.

Do a posttest to measure changes in awareness in comparison with results of the pretest.

Use a focus group to probe the relationships among awareness, acceptance, and action.

Track media placement with clippings and logs. Evaluate these not only in terms of distribution, use, and other measures of audience exposure but also conduct some form of content analysis to evaluate the effectiveness of the message itself.

Measure action in some way, such as by noting changes in attendance, traffic, purchase or other behaviors associated with the campaign.

Some of the benchmark techniques for evaluating acceptance objectives, noted earlier, can be equally useful for evaluating action objectives.

Relative media effectiveness. A final method of evaluating action objectives deals with the behavior generated by a particular medium compared to others. For example, did people vote for a candidate because of a newspaper editorial or because of the candidate's advertising? Often it is difficult to sort out the impact of a specific medium or tactic. But here's an example of how one organization managed to make the comparison.

In 2007, SeaWorld San Antonio introduced a new roller-coaster ride, Journey to Atlantis. The theme park invited members of the media to try out the new ride. The park's public relations–marketing team decided to include social media in the mix. Twenty-two blogs and media forums were identified for their focus on roller coasters; eventually 12 covered the ride. The result was that SeaWorld San Antonio received 50 links from coaster-oriented websites. Media posted on YouTube, Flickr, and other social media sites generated hundreds of thousands of downloads, along with many positive comments.

Over two weekends two months later, a standard exit interview for SeaWorld visitors asked a typical question: Where did you hear about Journey to Atlantis? Forty-seven percent of respondents indicated social media as the source of their information. The research team looked at the various media used to promote the new ride (television commercial, newspaper ad, social media, radio spot, billboard, and so on) and concluded that the cost per impression for social media was 22 cents, compared with $1 for television impressions.

Data Analysis and Reports

Having gathered the data through a variety of means, it is now time to analyze it carefully. Match the observed and reported results with the expectations outlined in your statement of objectives. If the program failed to meet its objectives, do some further analysis. Try to learn if the shortfall was because of a flawed strategy that under girded the program or because the tactics were not implemented as effectively as they might have been. Consider also if there might be a flaw in the evaluation techniques used to gather the data.

If evaluation of the program is particularly important, ask an outside auditor to review the data. For some formal presentations of research findings, in order to enhance credibility, an organization may ask an outside expert or a panel of stakeholders to attest to the validity of the tools used in the evaluation research.

Evaluation Reports

After the evaluation is completed and the information gathered and analyzed, make sure it is presented in a form that is understandable and accessible to decision makers within the

Measuring the Impact of Social Media

As public relations practitioners increasingly use social media as part of their media mix, the question eventually turns to the question of methodology: How can we evaluate the impact of social media? It isn't easy, but it is necessary to measure its effectiveness. One approach focuses on the engagement that web users display.

At her website (http://www.themeasurementstandard.com) Katie Delahaye Paine suggests that *engagement* is a synonym for *relationship*, something public relations practitioners are continually trying to nurture, though less often attempting to measure.

Likewise, Robert Scoble suggests that engagement is an appropriate measurement of the effectiveness of blogging. To what extent does the reader become engaged in the piece? To what extent is dialogue taking place among readers who add comments? For example, Scoble suggests that people engaged in a corporate blog are likely eventually to buy the product (Scoble, 2006).

Meanwhile, Eric Peterson defines engagement as "an estimate of the degree and depth of visitor interaction on the site against a clearly defined set of goals" (2007). He has developed a matrix for calculating engagement, using concepts such as click-depth, recency, duration, brand, feedback, interaction, loyalty and subscription. The matrix counts, for example, the percentage of visitors who give their e-mail addresses, the number of sessions that include visits to more than five pages, the number of visitors who return more than five times, and so on.

Paine lists several no-cost steps that an organization can take to measure the effectiveness of its website and other social media. Here are some of her suggestions:

- Use Google Analyzer or another visitor-tracking device.
- Post a poll at your website and see how many readers respond.
- Track your website or blog at a site such as http://www.xinureturns.com or http://www.typepad.com.
- Review the ratings and comments of your posts on sights such as YouTube and or Flickr.

See how many people have joined sites such as Facebook. Post a question there and count replies.

organization. They usually are busy executives and managers with global but not necessarily specific understandings of the issue. They may not have a high level of insight or information about the program, so be careful not to obscure evaluation findings in the final report. Instead, be very clear, draw obvious conclusions, and highlight the most important data.

If the decision makers have been involved in establishing the objectives of the program, they probably will be disposed to using the evaluation findings. Another way to increase the likelihood that the evaluation will be used is to concentrate on elements that can be changed in subsequent programs.

There is much variety within evaluation reports, which can be of several types. These may be presented separately or merged into a single report. The report itself can take the form of a formal document, an oral presentation, or a meeting agenda item. Whether written or verbal, evaluation reports should be carefully crafted to clearly link the expectations outlined in the objectives with the outcomes.

When writing a report, note how the outcomes were measured, discuss the degree to which they achieved the objectives, and note the significance of this achievement (or lack of it). Finally, make clear recommendations closely linked with the data. For reports of major significance, visual elements such as photographs, tables, and charts can enhance the understanding of readers and listeners.

Evaluation reports sometimes become the basis of a news release or even a news conference if the topic under review is one that is particularly newsworthy. For example, the final evaluation of public relations programs on popular and highly visible social issues such as campaigns to reduce drug abuse or teen pregnancy may warrant a news report.

Any evaluation report longer than five pages should be preceded by an executive summary that provides an overview of the findings and a simplified set of recommendations. An executive summary serves the needs of those decision makers—sometimes the most important ones—who may not have the time to digest the longer document.

Ultimate Evaluation: Value-Added Public Relations

Most evaluation of public relations and other strategic communication programs focus on objectives and tactics: What did we do? What did we accomplish by doing it? How effectively did this achieve what we set out to do? These questions are very important. But there is another, equally important, question to be answered: What did public relations do for the organization as a whole?

Once again, a reminder: The premise underlying *Strategic Planning for Public Relations* is that strategic communication is about more than mere tactics and activities. Rather, it deals with the overall planned program of both proactive and reactive communication that enhances the relationship between an organization and its various publics, a relationship that needs to be linked to the bottom-line concerns of the organization. You might call it value-added public relations, the notion that public relations adds value and benefit to the organization as a whole.

Based on qualitative interview research with both public relations practitioners and their CEOs, Linda Childers Hon (1997) has reported six such values that effective public relations brings to organizations or to the clients of a consultant or agency. Keep these in mind as you complete your evaluation and present it to your client or organization:

1. Effective public relations helps organizations *survive* by reversing negative opinions, promoting awareness of organizational benefits to the community, and effecting balanced media coverage.
2. Effective public relations helps organizations *make money* by generating publicity about products and services as well as the organization's plans and accomplishments; attracting new customers, volunteers, donors, and stockholders; and improving employee performance and productivity.
3. Effective public relations helps other organizational functions *make money* by creating an environment of understanding and goodwill, influencing supportive legislation, and enhancing fundraising efforts.
4. Effective public relations helps organizations *save money* by inducing favorable legislation, retaining members, and minimizing negative publicity during crisis incidents.
5. Effective public relations helps organizations *weaken opposition* by generating favorable public opinion and obtaining cooperation from governmental and other organizations.
6. Effective public relations helps organizations *save lives* through social goals such as advancing highway safety, medical care and research, and the like.

Evaluative Research: Who Uses What?

The various types of evaluative research used in this book loosely parallel the categories identified by D. M. Dozier (1984):

- *Seat-of-the-pants evaluation:* what this book calls judgmental assessment.
- *Scientific dissemination:* evaluation of awareness objectives.
- *Scientific impact:* evaluation of acceptance and action objectives.

Dozier studied public relations practitioners and noted the kind of research they used to evaluate programs and projects. He found that most practitioners he identified as communication technicians (that is, practitioners generally in entry-level jobs with few decision-making responsibilities) showed no patterns as to the type of research they did. The exception to this was media relations specialists, who favored the scientific dissemination type that measured awareness objectives such as distribution, placement, media impressions, and readability.

Dozier also found that communication managers supplemented the seat-of-the-pants evaluation that relied heavily on their professional experience with the scientific impact type of evaluation, the kind of evaluation that used quantitative research methods to measure the more advanced objectives, such as those dealing with acceptance and action.

Planning Example 9: Evaluating the Strategic Plan

UPSTATE COLLEGE

Upstate College will evaluate its Initiative on Transfer Students according to the following plan:

1. Placement report tracking distribution and media use of news releases and other materials disseminated by its public relations department.
2. Telephone survey among people who applied to UC two, three, and four years ago but did not attend. The purpose of this survey will be to assess awareness about the expansion and attitudes toward it.
3. Focus group of new applicants to UC, discussing the source of their information about the expansion and their reasons for applying.
4. Content analysis of newspaper articles, radio and television news reports, and newspaper letters to the editor and editorials, studying the positive/negative nature of the reports about UC's expansion.
5. Brief survey as part of the application process, asking applicants the source of their information about the UC expansion.

The evaluation report will be provided to the college president and provost, who prefer a well-documented and candid report. This report will become the basis for future recruitment and development activities.

(Note: You will develop similar evaluation plans for the other initiatives.)

■ ■ ■

TINY TYKES TOYS

Tiny Tykes Toys will evaluate the employee-oriented phase of its public relations program according to the following plan:

1. Before-and-after surveys of both employees and employee family members, dealing with employee morale, job satisfaction, pride in company, and knowledge of recall, safety, and quality issues. The results of these surveys will be compared to ascertain any change in knowledge, attitudes, and behavior associated with the public relations program.
2. Employee-initiated feedback, such as copies of comments and suggestions in the suggestion box, notes to company managers, letters to the editor of the company newsletter or other publications, and other messages regarding the reintroduction program. These messages will be summarized and analyzed.
3. Analysis of media coverage by tracking placement, measuring employee awareness of coverage, and doing basic content analysis on articles and news reports as to their positive or negative reflection of Tiny Tykes employees.

A written final evaluation will be presented to company managers and then will be shared with employees.

Checklist 9: Evaluation Plan

Basic Questions

1. How will you measure awareness objectives?
2. How will you measure acceptance objectives?
3. How will you measure action objectives?

Expanded Questions

A. METHODOLOGY

1. How and when can this information be obtained: via after-only study or before-and-after study?
2. Which research methodologies would be most effective?
   Judgmental assessment: personal experience or outside experts.
   Interviews with key people. Which people?
   Focus groups with representative publics. Which publics?
   Survey of representative publics. Which publics? Control group?
   Content analysis of representative artifacts. Which artifacts?
   Readership study
   Media tracking

B. EVALUATION CATEGORIES

1. Indicate how each of the methodologies below might be used to evaluate each individual tactic.
2. What standards of accuracy and reliability are needed for the evaluation?
3. Who can provide information for evaluation?

Evaluation of Outputs

Message production
Message dissemination
Message cost analysis
Advertising equivalency

Evaluation of Awareness Objectives

Message exposure
Message content analysis
Readability measures
Message recall

Evaluation of Acceptance Objectives

Audience feedback
Benchmark (baseline) study

Evaluation of Action Objectives

Audience participation
Direct observation of results

C. AUDIENCE

1. Who will receive the final evaluation?
2. How will it be used?
3. What level of candor are decision makers willing to receive?

D. EVALUATION SCHEDULE

1. Timeline for implementation report
2. Timeline for progress report
3. Timeline for final evaluation

E. EVALUATION PROGRAM CHECKLIST

For this evaluation program:

- Is it useful to the organization?
- Is it clearly linked to established objectives?
- Is it appropriate as to cost?
- Is it appropriate as to time?
- Is it appropriate as to other resources?
- Is it ethical and socially responsible?
- Is it credible, with accurate data?
- Is it doable?

Appendix A

Applied Research Techniques

Academic Research and Applied Research

As a student, you probably are already familiar with academic research from journals and textbooks. Academic research generates theory, explores new interests, and focuses on universal knowledge. This is knowledge for its own sake, also called **theoretical research**, **basic research**, or **pure research**.

In your professional life beyond the classroom, however, you are more likely to deal in **applied research** (sometimes called **market research** or **administrative research**), which delves into the practical problems faced by an organization and guides effective resolution of those problems. Your bosses and clients will ask you to get information as quickly and inexpensively as possible to help solve their very real problems. Your applied research may contribute to the theory base of your profession, but that is a side benefit; its primary role is to deal with practical matters for your client.

This appendix gives you a how-to guide to several techniques for doing applied research. In addition to discussing the ethics of research, we'll also look at sampling techniques, secondary research, interviews, focus groups, case studies, surveys, and content analysis.

Each research technique in this section takes you through a four-phase process of (1) defining the research problem, (2) designing a way to obtain information, (3) actually gathering the information, and (4) analyzing your findings and applying them.

Appropriate Research Topics

Applied research is especially important when program planning brings together a specialist (you) working for an expert (your boss or client), because the research can help prevent problems by putting both the specialists and the experts more in touch with their publics.

Take, for example, the experience of a senior campaigns class in which university students developed a comprehensive public relations and advertising program for a new space exhibit at a science museum. The museum had a wealth of marketing research, but as part of the course assignment the four student teams tried out several different strategic concepts on a sampling of their target public: schoolchildren and their parents. This research paid off.

One team considered three different themes: a digitized close-up of a man in a spacesuit with the slogan "Put Your Face in Space"; a rocket being fired from its launch pad with the slogan "Blast Off! Explore the Infinite Possibilities"; and a close-up of a footprint on the moon with the slogan "Space. Touch it!" When they presented the three possible approaches to the museum CEO and his marketing and public relations directors, the clients were enthusiastic and unanimous. They really liked the footprint, because it so poignantly reflected the Apollo 11 lunar landing. But the students cautioned, "Don't jump to conclusions. Our research supports the second option; it shows that the children you want to attract like the action of the space launch much more. For them, the footprint from the first moon landing in 1969 is part of history, not something that excites their imagination." Applied research prevented a false start with a misguided theme.

Do-It-Yourself Research

Many research experts offer a simple warning: Don't try this at home! Research methodologies can be incredibly complex, and many pitfalls exist for the novice who plunges headlong into research using inappropriate techniques that result in inaccurate data and unwarranted conclusions. Clearly some issues are so critical and the needed research so important that you really should get professional research assistance. Nevertheless, the research techniques explained here are not impossible for the do-it-yourselfer. The key is knowing when you should do it yourself and when to call in an expert.

Consider the following generalization: You might do your own research when you have the time, interest, patience, and self-confidence; when you don't need highly accurate statistics and other data; when the decisions riding on the study are relatively minor in terms of your organization's overall mission; or when your budget is such that the choice is between doing your own research or doing none at all.

Academic versus Applied Research Topics

Most of the studies published in the *Journal of Public Relations Research* deal with **academic research**, which by its nature is public and meant to be shared, challenged, and continuously developed.

Here are some topics from the last few years: attribution theory and crisis communication; contingency theory of accommodation; the Internet and litigation; ethics; the rhetorical-organizational approach to organizational identity; knowledge predictors; the integrated symmetrical model of crisis communication; self-efficacy theory; image and symbolic leadership; and information processing and situational theory. Several other journals also publish academic research focused on public relations.

Applied research more often than not remains unpublished because it is proprietary, meaning that it is conducted for and owned by a particular client.

A review of the websites of several major public relations agencies indicates they have conducted the following research topics for specific clients and companies: media content analysis; a survey of residents to identify a location for a chemical plant; monitoring legislation and conducting legislative research; corporate reputation; the impact of public relations and advertising programs; Internet monitoring; audience surveys; surveys of the impact of congressional hearings; and audience analysis of sports organizations to increase both fan and corporate support.

Should You Do Your Own Research?

1. Do you need objective data?
2. Can you be objective in your study even though it involves your own organization?
3. Do you have the ability to conduct the study?
4. Do you have the time and other resources to conduct the study?
5. Does your organization, boss or client have enough confidence in you to respect and use your findings?
6. Can you tolerate less precise statistics than a professional researcher might generate?

If you answered "yes" to each question, you can probably conduct your own research project. If you answered "no" to any question, following the first one, find a professional researcher.

Research Ethics

Ethics deals with the rightness or wrongness of behavior, especially professional or organizational behavior (as compared with personal morality). Social science research involves several areas that can pose ethical risks and temptations.

The Principles of Disclosure of the National Council on Public Polls (http://www.ncpp.org) pledges the commitment of member organizations "to standards of disclosure designed to insure that consumers of survey results that enter the public domain have an adequate basis for judging the reliability and validity of the results reported."

Most colleges and universities have clearly defined policies related to research ethics. So do many companies and public relations counseling agencies. Specific standards may vary, but some common ground can be found in many ethical guidelines. Broadly speaking, the areas of common ground deal with the treatment of the people involved in the research study and the use of information.

Ethical Treatment of People

Below are eight guidelines for dealing ethically with people involved in research programs or projects. These principles apply to the kind of applied research that is common in public relations and marketing research, such as interviews, focus groups, and surveys. These principles do not apply to content analysis, because no active participants are involved in that kind of research.

1. *Respect the dignity of participants in every study.* This is the umbrella that covers all the other principles. It is rooted in common sense and decent interaction with people. Most colleges and universities, as well as other research organizations, have formal requirements for research involving human subjects, so make sure your research is in compliance with these regulations.
2. *Respect the privacy of participants.* Abide fully by any privacy commitments that are made. Note the difference between anonymity and confidentiality. **Anonymity**

means the participant's identity will not be known to anybody, including the researcher, and cannot be linked to a particular response. **Confidentiality** means the researcher will not disclose the participant's identity nor allow it to be linked to a particular response. Anonymity is difficult for most public relations research: interviews and focus groups obviously can't be anonymous, and it is difficult to maintain anonymity for surveys that require more than one mailing. Confidentiality is the more likely protection for participants. Remember that any privacy guarantees extend beyond the time of the research study; questionnaires and notes should be stored in a nonpublic place and should be discarded when they are no longer needed.

3. *Seek only voluntary participation by respondents.* Would-be participants in interviews, focus groups, and surveys should be told explicitly that they may choose not to participate. They must be allowed to decline at the beginning of the research activity or to end their participation at any point. The voluntariness of participation is less of an issue with mail or phone surveys, where respondents can easily ignore the questionnaire or hang up on the researcher.
4. *Obtain informed consent.* Participants should be told enough about the research project so they clearly know what they are being asked to do. When a person agrees to participate in an interview, survey, or focus group, informed consent can logically be presumed, and asking participants to sign consent statements could negate a guarantee of anonymity that might be part of the project. Increasingly, however, researchers are asking participants in studies involving sensitive matters to sign a consent form; the confidentiality issue can be handled by having the consent form separate from any questionnaire that is part of the research tool. Consent forms are generally used for experiments, and they are becoming more common with other types of public relations or marketing research. Informed consent extends to practical matters, such as telling respondents how much time will be expected for their participation.
5. *Disclose the purpose of the research to the participants.* In some cases, the researcher does not want to indicate the full purpose of the study up front, because this might contaminate the results by causing the respondents to provide less-than-truthful information. Even if the respondents try to be truthful, knowing too much about the project could bias their responses. However, respondents or participants have the right to know at least the general purpose of the study. Participants usually can be told the purpose of the research when their role is ended.
6. *Disclose the identity of the researcher.* Active participants should know who you are and that you are conducting research. This often can enhance the credibility of the study.
7. *Disclose the identity of the research sponsor.* Would-be respondents and other participants have the right to know the name of the organization sponsoring and benefiting from the research. As with item 5 about the purpose of the research, the identity of the research sponsor may be withheld until the conclusion of the study, so participants can act and provide information without bias.
8. *Inform participants of the research results.* By debriefing participants, the researcher can explain the study and allow participants to see themselves in relation to the total sample. Especially if the researcher concealed information about the purpose or sponsor to ensure candid responses by participants, explaining to them afterward can make up for the deception.

Ethical Use of Research Data

Three ethical considerations are paramount related to the use of research data for public relations and marketing research of the kind considered in this book. Different ethical principles would apply to more experimental or laboratory-based social research.

1. *Develop a fair research process.* Draw samples with care so that they are likely to represent the target population, and don't yield to the temptation to obtain simply an easy or quick sample. In reporting your research, acknowledge any shortcoming in the sampling process.
2. *Develop fair measurement tools.* Questions and response items should be designed to elicit honest responses, and research participants should not be tricked into giving information they don't believe in. Manipulation and coercion have no place in research.
3. *Analyze and report data ethically.* Treat each piece of data with great respect; never fudge or falsify any data. Discard any data that is unclear, indecipherable, or otherwise contaminated. In analyzing the data, draw only those conclusions justified by the information obtained; never discount or misinterpret data in favor of your own bias or your client's wishes. Fully report the circumstances of the research project: its geography and time frame, sampling techniques, and methodology. Include copies of questionnaires and other data-gathering tools.

Sampling

The purpose of research is to describe various characteristics (such as the level of information, the existence of attitudes or opinions, or the extent of certain behaviors) of a **population**, which is defined as a large group of subjects that are of interest to the researcher. For example, depending on the interests of the researcher, the residents of Kansas could be a population; so too Hispanic athletes at all Kansas colleges and universities, or restaurants with vegetarian menus in the Sunflower State.

Individual **elements** of the population (also called **units of analysis**) are usually people. However, they also could be organizations, products, media artifacts such as news reports or editorials, public relations artifacts such as news releases or brochures, or advertising artifacts such as television commercials or print ads. Each research activity also has a particular time period (usually defined in weeks, months, or years) and an extent (a geographic location such as a region, state, or neighborhood).

Sometimes we conduct a **census**, which is a comprehensive study that includes every member of the population in our study, such as a small business that polls every employee about an issue of companywide interest. Other times, however, it is impractical to survey every member of a very large or scattered population. In such cases, a good alternative is **sampling**, the identification of a subset of the population of individuals (or objects) who reflect and represent the larger body. This subset is known as a **sample**. The value of sampling is that it saves time and money, allowing researchers to study a small group and then use those findings to make predictions for a much larger population.

Depending on how a sample is pulled together, it may or may not be based on the concept of **probability**, which means that every element in the population has an equal chance of being selected for the sample. To help you understand sampling, consider the analogy of cooking stew. A cook mixes a variety of vegetables and herbs in a pot, then stirs—that's the key. Presumably, the stirring has mixed all the ingredients evenly. The cook then dips the ladle and takes a taste. No need to eat the entire pot to determine if more seasoning is needed; one ladle from a well-stirred pot provides a true sampling of the entire stew.

Over the years, the accuracy of polling has improved tremendously. Consider three national presidential polls. In 1936 the influential *Literary Digest* forecast that Alf Landon would beat Franklin Roosevelt 57 to 43%. Instead, Roosevelt easily won re-election with a landslide 61% of the vote. In 1948, the Roper Poll predicted that Thomas Dewey would beat Harry Truman by a 5-point margin in the presidential election. Instead, Truman won by 5 points. In contrast, in the 2004 presidential election, most major poll predictions were accurate within a 3% margin of error.

The evolution of polling accuracy lies in the improved sampling techniques. *Literary Digest* polled two million people using a volunteer sampling frame including telephone listings (in 1936, phones were for the well-to-do) and country club memberships, favoring the wealthy and excluding the poor. The 1948 poll was a cluster sample of 20,000, weighted toward rural Republican voters rather than urban Democratic voters.

By 2004 sampling was down to an average size of about 1,000 respondents for the estimated 200 million voting-age Americans. These respondents were scientifically selected on age, income, ethnicity, location, occupation, religion, education, and many other factors that, taken together, present an accurate picture of the American electorate. Progressively smaller but more representative samples have yielded greater accuracy, on average less than a 1% margin of error, which is particularly striking because George W. Bush beat John Kerry by a margin of only 2.4%, the closest in history for any incumbent president.

Polling has become refined as it focuses on "likely voters," particularly for surveys that take place within a few days prior to an election. Surveys earlier in the election cycle often still rely on registered voters who also are uncommitted at that stage. The increasing incidence of Internet polling is hampered by greater likelihood of error than more traditional polling techniques.

Sampling can be largely divided into nonprobability and probability techniques. Let's look at each type.

Nonprobability Sampling

A variety of techniques are identified as **nonprobability sampling** because every person or artifact in the population does not have an equal chance of being selected for the study. However, they offer several advantages. Nonprobability samples can be chosen simply, quickly, and inexpensively. This technique allows subjects to be selected even if they cannot be identified ahead of time. But because subjects are chosen with no great care as to their makeup, nonprobability sampling has limited credibility. Here are five types of nonprobability samples: convenience, volunteer, purposive, snowball, and quota.

1. *Convenience sampling*. A frequently used technique is **convenience sampling**, which draws subjects because they are readily available to the researcher, such as people

Probability and Nonprobability Sampling

Probability sampling involves the selection of a sample in a manner through which every member of the population has an equal chance statistically of being selected for the sample.

- Simple random sampling
- Systematic sampling
- Stratified sampling
- Cluster sampling

Nonprobability sampling involves the selection of a sample in a manner through which each member of the population has an unequal chance statistically of being selected.

- Convenience sampling
- Volunteer sampling
- Purposive sampling
- Snowball sampling
- Quota sampling

walking through a shopping mall, students enrolled in a particular college course, or participants in so-called (but not really) random street-corner interviews by reporters. This type of sampling generally is an unreliable indicator of a larger population, unless that population is, for example, shoppers at a particular mall.

2. *Volunteer sampling*. Another sampling technique, **volunteer sampling**, uses subjects who ask to be included in the research study. One example of self-selected samples is magazines that invite readers to respond to a printed questionnaire; another is talk show hosts who invite their radio listeners to phone in with comments. The problem with volunteer sampling is that it sometimes is interpreted as being representative when it really isn't. What should we think about the situation in which the talk show's callers overwhelmingly support a political candidate who nevertheless is soundly defeated at the polls? We should remember that such programs attract people with certain preconceptions and biases. Thus the callers are not representative of the voters, perhaps not even of all the program's listeners. They merely are those listeners who felt strongly enough about the issue and took the time to express their opinion.
3. *Purposive sampling*. A technique in which research subjects are chosen because they have certain demographic characteristics is called **purposive sampling** (also known as **judgment sampling**). For example, they may be people who were patients in a particular hospital, or they may be individuals who drive a particular brand of automobile. Remember that they are not representative of the entire population of hospital patients or motorists.
4. *Snowball sampling.* The technique of **snowball sampling** (also called **sociosamples**) begins with a small group of individuals with a certain characteristic who are asked

to identify others to participate in the research. This technique often is used for populations where member lists do not exist and whose members are hard to identify, at least by outsiders.

5. *Quota sampling.* A sampling technique that attempts to be more representative of the population is **quota sampling**. This involves the selection of subjects to fit a predetermined percentage. For example, if 40% of a company's employees have college degrees, then 40% of the company's sample in a study of employee attitudes also should have college degrees. Appropriate quota categories include age, gender, ethnicity, religion, occupation, geography, and other demographic factors. But like the purposive sampling, quota sampling is haphazard because it is not representative of the entire population under study; instead it reflects only one characteristic (or a couple of characteristics) that the researcher considers most important.

ADVANTAGES AND DISADVANTAGES OF NONPROBABILITY SAMPLING

The limitation of any type of nonprobability sample is that it gives no reasonable certainty that findings will be representative of the larger population. To be useful, most sampling research must be applicable to the entire population rather than to only the relatively few people sampled. Still, nonprobability sampling is not without its good side. These techniques do have a legitimate role for public relations and marketing research. You should consider using nonprobability sampling in the following situations:

- When the purpose of the study is to gain general, nonspecific insight into a particular group.
- When a high margin of error is not a major concern.
- When the budget does not allow for more costly probability sampling.
- When the schedule does not allow for more time-consuming probability sampling.

Remember, avoid using a nonprobability sample when you want to be able to project the findings of your research onto a larger population.

Probability Sampling

The other category of sampling techniques, **probability sampling**, follows the guidelines of mathematical probability, generally earning higher respect among researchers. When the research study seeks to learn the attitudes, opinions, or behaviors of a large number of people, probability sampling ensures that every element within the population has an equal and known chance of being selected. Thus, some researchers refer to probability sampling techniques as **EPSEM** (equal probability of selection method) **samples**. By using probability sampling, the researcher can legitimately calculate how accurately the sampled findings reflect the entire population.

Probability sampling requires that the researcher is able to identify every **sampling unit**, which is the individual element to be analyzed. Sampling units reflect the range noted earlier for population elements; they usually are people but also may be organizations, products, and artifacts. The actual listing of sampling units is called the **sampling frame**. Often these are membership rosters or other comprehensive directories.

Some random samples have been based on telephone directories, though phone books generally are bad choices for general populations because they screen out people without phone service and those with unlisted numbers. This is an example of **sampling bias**, when the sampling technique itself introduces an element of weakness into the process.

Sampling bias also may be related to the timing of the data gathering. Consider, for example, a restaurant that has a busy professional lunch crowd, an early-bird dinner special that caters to college students and senior citizens, a formal and relatively upscale dinner crowd, and a trendy after-theater clientele. A study that draws its sample from only the early-bird group would yield significantly different results than one drawing from each of the four customer groups.

Following are four types of probability sampling: simple random, systematic, stratified and cluster.

1. *Simple random sampling.* The basic type of probability sampling is **simple random sampling**, exemplified by lottery-style drawings such as pulling names from a hat. Anybody who has ever played Bingo knows the pure randomness of such sampling.

   Researchers often use a table of random numbers to select the subjects for their study. For example, if you are researching the behavior of 5,000 college students, you might work with a list from the registrar's office and assign every student a number, 0001 through 5000. Let's say you decide to have 250 respondents. Simply generate a list of 250 random four-digit numbers, match them up to the numbered names, and interview the students.

   The major advantage of random sampling is that it produces a sampling in which everyone in the population has an equal chance of being selected. This provides a generally unbiased group of respondents, which, in turn, is good for a research study seeking to project findings for the entire group. Random sampling is particularly good when a population is homogenous, with no significant divisions within it.

   However, simple random sampling has two major disadvantages. First, it requires a sampling frame, which may not be available for all target populations. Second, while random sampling gives every element within the population an equal chance of being selected, it does not necessarily produce a representative sampling if significant subsets exist within the population. For example, a sample of 250 students identified randomly out of a population of 5,000 could produce no students majoring in a foreign language. That could be a limitation, especially if the study dealt with something like international exchange programs, language requirements for graduation or student fees for language labs.
2. *Systematic sampling.* Another common technique is **systematic sampling** (also called **systematic interval sampling**). This involves the selection of subjects spaced at equal intervals, such as every 20th name on a membership roster. Let's stay with the example of the survey of college students. If you do the simple math and divide 5,000 by 250, then you would select every 20th name from your sampling frame. To make the systematic sampling truly unbiased, use a systematic sampling with a random start. This involves a random selection of the starting number (in this case, a number from 1 to 20). Don't use systematic sampling if a particular order or recurring pattern exists within the ranking. For example, if a listing of sororities always begins with the names of officers, then a systematic sampling of every 15th name with a starting number of 2 would result in a sampling top-heavy with sorority vice presidents—not very random after all.

3. *Stratified sampling*. A modification of random and systematic techniques is **stratified sampling**. This sampling technique involves a ranking of elements on a list, such as four subset lists (freshmen, sophomores, juniors, and seniors) for your study of college students. Other relevant demographic categories for research might include age, gender, income, religion, media use, academic major, and product use. By stratifying the list by important characteristics, the researcher is able to ensure a greater likelihood that the sample will be representative of the population. One problem with stratified sampling is that the subsets may indicate more than they appear to. For example, subsets related to residency in different parts of a city may reflect not only geography but also different ethnic, occupational or socioeconomic patterns.

   Stratified sampling may be **proportionate**, with research sizes based on their proportion in the population, such as a research project with a sample of 45% men and 55% women used for a college with a student population of the same gender proportions. Or it may be **disproportionate** (also called a **weighted sample**) if particular attention is given to underrepresented members of a population. Using the college scenario, if the student population is 10% Hispanic, the researcher may want to have a sample of more than 10% Hispanic people so they provide a stronger representation among the respondents than might be expected with a random 25.
4. *Cluster sampling*. A technique known as **cluster sampling** (also called **multistage sampling**) is used when the researcher can't readily generate a list of the entire population but can obtain listings of particular groups within the population. For example, if your research population was all college and university students within your state, you would have a difficult time putting together a complete sampling frame listing every student in the state from which to draw a random, systematic, or stratified sample. But using the cluster sampling technique, you first would identify several schools (either randomly or through a stratified technique based on criteria such as size or location), then select individual students (randomly, systematically or through stratified techniques) using separate sampling frames, such as enrollment lists obtained from each school identified in the first stage.

Sample Error and Size

In textbooks dedicated to research methodologies, you can find sophisticated information about research statistics. To simplify things here, let's consider a few key terms that deal with the inevitable limitations of sampling.

The **sampling error** (sometimes called the **margin of error**) is the extent to which the sample does not perfectly correspond with the target population. Sampling error is usually reported as a percentage. For example, a finding of 62% with a sampling error of 3% indicates that the finding actually could fall between 59% and 65%. The statistic used to describe sampling error is called the **standard error** (more correctly, the **standard error of the mean**). Since sampling is an imperfect reflection of the population, researchers always expect some potential sampling error.

What is the ideal number of subjects for a research study? There is no single answer to this question, because so much depends upon what the researcher needs to accomplish. Focus groups use only a few people, generally 5 to 12 for each session. Surveys for pretest studies may use a sample of 15 to 30 subjects.

Two concepts about sample size often are difficult for nonresearchers to grasp. First, a bigger sample doesn't necessarily mean better results. Second, the appropriate size of the sample is not based in any way on a percentage or fraction of the population. In general, samples of 200 to 400 are commonplace.

Roger Wimmer and Joseph Dominick (2005) note that researchers often use a sample of 100 subjects for each relevant demographic group likely to have distinctive characteristics (for example, 100 men and 100 women; or 100 each of undergraduates, graduate students, and alumni). Here are commonly used guidelines for samples with a 5% margin of error: 217 for a population or demographic breakout group of 500; 278 for 1,000; 322 for 2,000; 357 for 5,000; 370 for 10,000; 381 for 50,000, and 384 for an infinite number. Fewer could be used if you can tolerate a higher margin of error; more if you need a lower margin.

One thing is certain: more doesn't necessarily mean better. Very good research can be based on modest sample sizes. The idea underlying sampling is to use the smallest number of research subjects that can accurately predict characteristics of the population. A small but appropriate sample is better than a larger but haphazard one. Remember also that the smaller the sample size, the less expensive the study will be, the less time it will take and the easier it will be to calculate, analyze, and report.

A common way of determining sample size is first to decide what margin of error you can tolerate in your sample. If the answer is zero, you are headed for a census of the entire population rather than a sampling. But think again, because research seldom requires perfect data. Even if your client or boss wants that, there probably isn't enough money in the budget to achieve it, unless the target population is very small.

Do a simple online search for "margin of error calculator" and you'll find several easy-to-use Internet sites for your research.

Secondary Research

One of the first steps in conducting research is to conduct **secondary research**—that is, research conducted to find out what information already is available through existing sources. This is distinguished from **primary research**, which generates new data collected specifically for this investigation.

Advantages and Disadvantages of Secondary Information

Why use existing information? Because it's there. And because it is less expensive to analyze than if you gather new data. Secondary research also is helpful in refining the research topic, building files of previous findings, keeping current with new developments in the field, and providing a launch point for your own additional research.

When using secondary information, evaluate it carefully. Consider the circumstances surrounding the data, such as when and how it was gathered, for what purpose, by what researcher, and with what sample. Most especially, consider the objectivity and professionalism with which it was gathered. All these factors can affect the usefulness of the information to your situation. However, if the data is relevant, it can save you much time and money.

Even if you have to purchase the data from a commercial information service, it still may be more cost effective than mounting your own primary research activity. Remember that even though you are interested in applied research for a particular client, you still can learn a lot from academic research. Because it is seeking insights into topics more than solutions to specific problems, academic research can provide valuable background information.

Types of Secondary Information

Secondary information is available in many different sources, including organizational files, trade and professional associations, public and academic libraries, government records, commercial information companies, and computer-assisted or online research sources. Let's look briefly at each: organizational files, trade and professional associations, public and academic libraries, government records, and commercial information services.

Organizational files. Information in the organizational files of your employer or client can provide a wealth of information for researchers and practitioners. Many public relations offices include extensive files of news releases, brochures, annual reports, and internal documents, as well as information files about relevant issues. Some organizations also have extensive archives with historical data and artifacts.

Trade and professional associations. Industry groups may offer much useful information for public relations and marketing researchers. For example, the Public Relations Society of America (PRSA) has extensive files about various aspects of public relations that it makes available to members. The *Encyclopedia of Associations* lists thousands of professional groups that can be very helpful in obtaining information about a specific industry.

Public and academic libraries. Public libraries in towns and cities as well as academic libraries on college and university campuses provide an accessible source of information. Information also may be available in specialized libraries such as those operated by companies, museums, industries, hospitals, professional organizations, and so on. Materials available in libraries can be categorized as **one-step resources** that provide information directly (such as encyclopedias and textbooks) and **two-step resources** that direct the researcher to information in other sources (such as indexes and directories).

Government records. Information gathered by governmental agencies is available both in public and academic libraries and directly from the agencies themselves. Vast amounts of information are generated by the U.S. Census Bureau, which actually produces 11 different censuses (population, governments, agriculture, housing, transportation, manufacturing, mineral industries, selected construction industries, selected service industries, retail trade, and wholesale trade). Other information is available from individual federal agencies dealing with commerce, education, labor, justice, and the like. A useful guide to information available through the federal government is the monthly *American Statistics Index* compiled by the Congressional Information Service or the annual *Statistical Abstract of the United States*; both publications are available in most libraries.

Much information is available from state, county, and local governments. Additionally, individual foreign nations have information available to varying degrees, and the United Nations provides information about countries and about various global issues.

Commercial information services. Commercial sources of information include polling firms such as the Gallup Organization, Harris Polls, and Zogby International. Other polling centers are associated with higher education, such as the National Opinion Research Center at the

University of Chicago or the Quinnipiac University Polling Institute. Meanwhile, the Roper Center for Public Opinion Research at the University of Connecticut conducts no research of its own but instead serves as an archive (updated daily) for research from more than 125 research organizations. Trade and professional associations also are sources of syndicated data. Media-ratings companies such as Arbitron and A. C. Nielsen also have useful demographic data. Stanford Research Institute pioneered the VALS (values and lifestyles) system of **psychographics**, which combines demographic and lifestyle data. Other companies have begun offering census-based marketing services using a technique called **geodemography**, which

Research Websites

Research Companies

Arbitron Company (http://www.arbitron.com)
Claritas/PRIZM (http://www.claritas.com)
Gallup Organization (http://www.gallup.com)
Harris Poll (http://www.harrisinteractive.com)
A. C. Nielsen Corporation (acnielsen.com)
Pew Research Center (http://www.people-press.org)
Princeton Survey Research Associates (http://www.psra.com)
Public Agenda (http://www.publicagenda.org)
Survey USA (http://www.surveyuse.com)
Yankelovich Partners (http://www.yankelovich.com)
Zogby International (http://www.Zogby.com)

Media-Related Polling Organizations

ABC News Polling Unit (http://www.abcnews.go.com)
CBS News Poll (http://www.cbsnews.com)
FOX News Poll (http://www.foxnews.com)
NBC News Poll (http://www.msnbc.msn.com)
New York Times Poll (http://www.nytimes.com)
Los Angeles Times Poll (nytimes.com latimes.com)
Washington Post (nytimes.com washingtonpost.com)

University-Related Polling Organizations

Marist College, Marist Institute for Public Polling (http://www.maristpoll.marist.edu)
Quinnipiac University, Polling Institute (http://www.quinnipiac.edu)
Rutgers University, Eagleton Poll (http://www.eagletonpoll.rutgers.edu)
University of Chicago, National Opinion Research Center (http://www.norc.uchicago.edu)
University of Connecticut, Roper Center for Public Opinion Research
(http://www.ropercenter.uconn.edu)
University of Pennsylvania, Annenburg Public Policy Center
(http://www.annenburgpublicpolicycenter.org)

combines census and other demographic information with zip codes, census tracts, and other data to describe the characteristics of particular neighborhoods and the people who live in them. Geodemography has proved very useful for marketing and fund-raising purposes. Sources of this information include PRIZM (Potential Rating Index Zip Markets), created by the Claritas Corporation, Strategic Mapping's ClusterPLUS, Equifax's MicroVision, and ACORN (A Classification of Residential Neighborhoods) by CACI.

Online research. Information searches conducted via computer are becoming increasingly common. CD-ROM and online sources can provide data direct from sources such as the Census Bureau or through commercial databases. Sources for online information can be identified through directories such as the *Directory of On-Line Databases* and the *Directory of On-Line Portable Databases,* both published by Gale Research. The Cambridge Information Group publishes *FINDEX: The Directory of Market Research Reports, Studies, and Surveys*, and the British Overseas Trade Board prepares *Marketsearch: International Directory of Published Market Research*. Some online resources helpful to public relations and marketing practitioners include AMI (Advertising and Marketing Intelligence), LEXIS/NEXIS, the Foundation Directory, the National Newspapers Index, the Wilson Index, and the Dow Jones News/Retrieval, as well as Psychological Abstracts and Sociological Abstracts.

With its ability to connect you directly with the home pages of many businesses, nonprofit organizations, and other organizations, the Internet is a powerful research tool. However, there is also plenty of garbage and gossip on the Web. In judging the quality of information you find on the Internet, ask yourself the following questions:

- Is the source or sponsor of the information indicated?
- Is the information source respected?
- Is the information source knowledgeable about the subject?
- Is the information source free from bias on the subject?
- Is the information presented in an objective manner?
- Is the information documented and verifiable?
- Is the information current?
- Is the information consistent with information from other sources?
- Does the website present links to other sources of unbiased information?

If you can answer "yes" to the above questions, it is probably safe to assume that the information is trustworthy and accurate. However, let common sense prevail. Trust your instincts, which may suggest that some information may not be fully reliable. And remember always to attribute the source of information obtained from the Internet, just as you would any other information obtained from books, periodicals, or other sources.

Interviews

Whatever you need to know, someone probably already knows it. Thus, as public relations and marketing research needs move beyond the information available through secondary research, interviews become a commonly used research tool. Researchers can obtain information by phone, e-mail, or videoconferencing, and even by letter, though in-person interviews generally are the best. These have the added benefit of allowing the interviewer to "read" the body language of the person providing the information.

How to Speak Boolean

Many computer-assisted information searches use the principles of **Boolean logic**, named for the 19th-century British mathematics teacher George Boole. This simply is a method of describing the relationship among several items. The basic Boolean operators are AND, OR, and NOT. Your search for citations will be more effective if you communicate with the computer in terms it understands.

Use common terms. Remember that computers are very literally minded. You may think *college* means about the same as *university*, but the computer doesn't know this. Be prepared to modify your searches using different variations of your topic. Here are the common Boolean operators used in searches:

- OR statements yield citations that include either term within a text. For example, "research OR survey" will give you a long list of items that include either but not necessarily both terms. Thus, OR is the operator that yields the largest number of citations. Another use for the Boolean OR is when words have more than one spelling, such as "online OR on-line OR on line," or when a term has synonyms, such as "survey OR poll."
- AND statements yield citations that include both terms. "Research AND survey" will give you a shorter list of items that feature both terms together.
- NOT statements will yield citations that include the first terms but exclude the second. "Research NOT survey" will give a list of items about research that do not mention surveys.
- NEAR statements are available with some search engines. They are like AND but more restrictive. NEAR locates items that appear within a certain proximity, but this varies up to about 20 words apart. With some search engines, you can indicate the distance between the two words. For example, "research NEAR survey" would locate phrases such as "survey research," "research using telephone surveys," and "survey techniques for professional research projects."
- Most search engines have a way to keep two or more words together, such as "public relations" or "Edward Bernays." For some, single or double quotation marks or parentheses around the terms will keep them together. For most search engines, Boolean AND is a default so you don't need any special notations.
- You can combine the various features in Boolean searches. "Research AND survey AND sampling" will generate citations that feature all three terms but not those with only one or two terms.
- You can force the order of a search by using parentheses around items you want cited before another operation occurs. The process is called **nesting**. Example: "(Public relations OR marketing) NOT advertising" will yield all citations dealing with either public relations or marketing but excluding anything dealing with advertising. The parentheses force the computer to generate the OR list first, then to extract from it any citations mentioning advertising. "Public relations OR (marketing NOT advertising)" would generate marketing listings, extract advertising mentions from this, then add all public relations listings, even those that mention advertising.
- Some search programs allow you to seek a root word and various endings, called a **wildcard**. For example, "alum?" or "alum*" or "alum$"—the feature differs among search engines—might generate the various forms of alumnus, alumni, alumna, and alumnae. But it also would give you unrelated words such as aluminum and alumroot, so you'd be better off using the root *alumn* in your search.

All interviews have a common purpose: to obtain information. Some are general and open-ended, allowing the interview to unfold according to the interaction of the participants and as the information rolls out. Others are more focused and in-depth, with the interviewer sticking to a prepared list of questions. The latter approach is especially good for comparative studies when you ask each interviewee more or less the same set of questions.

Asking Questions During an Interview

Interviews are a good way to get a lot of information quickly and easily. Good interviews need competence and cooperation by both parties. The quality of the information they yield can be limited by several factors, including poor rapport between the interviewer and the interviewee; an interviewer who does not understand the significance of the information; or an interviewee who is unable, unwilling, or uncomfortable about providing information. Still, when interviews are done professionally, they can be excellent research tools. Here are several suggestions for effective interviewing:

1. *Plan the interview.* Identify the topic of your research, noting specifically what information you need to obtain and where you might obtain it.
2. *Decide whom to interview.* Ask yourself who is likely to have the information you need. Perhaps people within your own or your client's organization would be good information sources. Librarians, government or industry officials, regulators, and professionals in the field also may have the information you need. Consider reporters or other public relations practitioners familiar with your topic of interest. Witnesses to events can be particularly helpful.
3. *Build on what you already know about the subject.* Make notes on the information already available to you. If you cannot identify specific sources of information, try to identify knowledgeable people who could refer you to these information sources.
4. *Learn as much as you can before the actual interview.* Study the topic by doing secondary research.
5. *Write out questions before the interview.* Make sure these cover all the areas in which you need information. Be prepared to use these questions as a guide, but remain flexible to allow the discussion to move along its own natural course.
6. *Take good notes.* For lengthy interviews, consider tape-recording the information, so you are freer to interact with the interviewee. Make certain the interviewee knows you are recording the conversation and has no objections to this.
7. *Build a rapport with the interviewee at the beginning of the interview.* Show an interest in this person and the topic under discussion. Note what you might have in common with the interviewee. Explain the purpose of your interview, and briefly summarize the background information you have already obtained.
8. *Build on information you already have.* Instead of asking vaguely, "What do you think about the location for the zoo?" show that you have done your homework by saying, for example, "The planning commission is expected to recommend moving the zoo to the waterfront redevelopment area. What do you think of such a move?"
9. *Look for a window if the interviewee closes a door.* For example, if the head coach of a professional football team refuses to tell you why the contract has not been renewed for an assistant coach, ask what qualities the coach is looking for in a replacement. That might give you some insight into the firing.

10. *Distinguish between knowledge and opinion questions.* You will need some facts. You might ask for explanations: "What happened?" "How does this work?" "What do you know about X?" Or you might ask for examples or anecdotes to clarify abstract points: "Can you give me an example of . . . ?" "Can you tell me about a specific case in which . . . ?" But go beyond the basics, and probe for additional information by asking opinion questions that take you beyond the facts. "Why did this happen?" "How is this useful?"
11. *Consider the relevance of attitudinal questions.* More than simple opinion items, affective or feeling questions seek to elicit how someone responds emotionally. "How does this make you feel?" may yield a different response than "What do you think about this?"
12. *Distinguish between experience-based and hypothetical questions.* For example, it may be important to know both what an interview subject did in a certain situation and what he or she might do in a speculative setting.
13. *Don't rush into sensitive areas.* Tread gently if you wish to guide the interview into topics dealing with touchy areas, especially if they may be illegal, immoral, or otherwise antisocial, or if they could impact negatively on the interviewee. Unless the interviewee clearly wishes to discuss such topics, build up to them gradually. When you have established a level of trust, such issues will be easier to discuss. One technique is to frame a question as a hypothetical: "If someone you trust asked how to buy some cocaine, what would you tell her?
14. *Don't argue with your interviewee.* Ask for clarification of anything you don't understand, and point it out if what you are hearing seems to run counter to other information you have.
15. *Remain neutral and nonjudgmental about the information you receive.* Your role as an interviewer is somewhat akin to that of a psychologist. If the interviewee says something offensive or outrageous, don't yell, "You did *what*?" or "Are you *insane*? I can't report that!" Refrain from commenting on what your interviewee says to you. Even positive feedback can be a problem. "That's good" or "I like what you are saying" could prompt the interviewee to focus on certain topics and avoid others.
16. *Nudge additional information.* Use probing or follow-up questions to elicit additional information from your subject. For example, use questions such as "Who else was involved?" "How did that come about?" and "What else was happening?" Use sentences such as "Tell me more about that" and "Give me an example."
17. *Conclude by inviting the interviewee to provide any additional information that seems relevant to the topic.* Ask if there is anything important that you didn't discuss. Review your notes and verify dates, spellings, and other important details. Try to arrange a time when you can contact the interviewee to clear up any questions that may arise later.

Listening During an Interview

Good interviewing requires good listening skills. Consider the difference between merely hearing and actually listening. **Hearing** is the physiological process of sound waves making the eardrums vibrate, which in turn stimulate nerve impulses to the brain. Hearing is the result of something that happens to us. **Listening**, on the other hand, is something we *choose* to do.

Listening is an interpersonal process in which you not only hear words but also interpret them, attempting to obtain essentially the same meaning in the words as the sender intended.

As the questioner during an interview, focus on what is being said. Avoid distractions, whether they are worries about your recording equipment or plans for your next question. Effective listening also involves understanding the speaker; try to achieve this, to the extent that one person can appreciate the background and experiences of another. As listening involves the interpretation of messages, try to obtain information with your senses beyond hearing. For example, listen with your eyes by observing the interviewee's body language and perhaps the surroundings as well.

Effective listening involves more than concentration. A person may pay close attention when someone speaks in a foreign language she has studied, though she still may not be able to understand the speaker very well.

Communicators talk about **active listening** or **strategic listening**, which goes beyond simply paying attention. Raymond Zeuschner (2002) identifies four steps for active listening:

1. Getting physically and mentally prepared to listen.
2. Staying involved physically and mentally with the communication.
3. Keeping an open mind while listening.
4. Reviewing and evaluating the information after it has been received.

In addition to one-on-one interviews, researchers sometimes obtain information from **intensive interviews** (also called **in-depth interviews**). These are lengthy and detailed interviews on a particular topic that are conducted individually with several respondents. Intensive interviewers often present a set of carefully designed parallel questions for each respondent, so that information more easily can be compared or blended together. Use this type of research technique when it is important both to give the research subject the opportunity to provide personal opinion and insight, but also to keep the subject on a narrow course. Another benefit of intensive interviews is that they reduce variation among different interviewers, since each is working from the same set of questions; follow-up questions probe more deeply along the prearranged line of questioning.

Focus Groups

A particular type of small-group discussion is a **focus group** (or less formally, a **group interview**), in which a researcher guides a conversation about an issue under study and, in doing so, enables group members to stimulate each other with their comments. The result is a more interactive and complete discussion than would be possible through individual interviews. These controlled group discussions are recorded and later analyzed by the researcher.

Focus groups generate ideas, comments and anecdotes. These can help you gain insight into and understanding about an issue. Focus groups are good techniques for clients who want to know "why," "how," and "what if." Specifically, they are used by public relations and marketing practitioners to test concepts, copy, and campaigns, or to evaluate potential logo designs, advertisements, or even program and product names. But focus groups are inappropriate if you need statistical data. If your client wants to know "how much" or "how many," conduct a survey instead. Remember also that focus groups are not decision-making or problem-solving sessions; don't expect the group participants to resolve the issue you are researching.

In some cases, focus groups are the primary research technique used. Other times, researchers use them to complement surveys, either as preliminary tools to gain a better understanding of the issue to be surveyed, or as follow-ups to shed light on the survey findings.

Advantages and Disadvantages of Focus Groups

Focus groups have the advantage of being quick, inexpensive, flexible, and very practical. On the other hand, they can become expensive and more complex if the client requires videotaping and a special viewing room with one-way mirrors. Such a video setup is particularly associated with marketing research, which has been criticized as being somewhat of a show for clients who, unseen behind their mirrors, believe that they are privy to consumer revelations (see Merton, 1987; Rubenstein, 1995). Still, it can be a useful tool in the right research situation.

How a Focus Group Works

Here's how to create an effective focus group. Assemble a small group of people who, as closely as possible, reflect your target population or a specific segment within the population. The group typically consists of between 8 and 12 people, though some researchers find they get better interaction from groups as small as 5.

The **moderator** (sometimes called a **facilitator**) generally introduces the topic, explains a few ground rules, then invites comments on the topic, often with an icebreaking question. For example, in a focus group with college-bound high school students, the moderator might begin by asking each participant his name, areas of academic interest, and future career plans. After the introductions, the real research begins—gently, often wandering through the discussion topic. The session generally lasts 60 to 90 minutes.

Focus groups are meant to be flexible. The moderator has an agenda of topics and themes to present to the group, though not necessarily a specific list of questions. A good moderator is agile, allowing the discussion to flow gracefully through group interaction and keeping obvious control of the discussion to a minimum. In some focus sessions, the moderator will give a high degree of direction; in others, the moderator will manage the group with so much flexibility that it does not feel manipulated.

Consider the following real-life situation: A researcher conducted a pair of focus groups for post–masters degree students (all of them midcareer educational professionals), discussing the ideal learning environment as part of a study commissioned by a university vice president for renovating classrooms. When the findings were shared with participants in a follow-up session, several said they were pleased to have felt unrestrained in their discussions. They confided that they had expected the focus groups merely to seek justification for foregone conclusions by the university. They were even more surprised when the researcher showed them a discussion outline, which included nearly every topic they had discussed. But instead of keeping a tight rein on their interaction, the moderator had allowed the discussion to meander through various aspects of the topic so gently that they felt they were involved more in a casual conversation than a research study. The research goals were accomplished without a feeling of manipulation or control. Mission accomplished.

Who's Who in a Focus Group?

The **research leader** is the person who articulates the topic, conducts appropriate secondary research, selects the participants, and—most important—develops the discussion guide with its questions and agenda topics. After the session, the research leader prepares the formal written report.

The **moderator**, who often is also the research leader, is responsible for the flow of the discussion, especially keeping it on point. The moderator will use open-ended questions such as "What do you think about . . . ," "Tell me more about . . . ," and "Let's now talk about . . . ." The moderator encourages discussion by reserved participants and tempers the involvement of those who may be overly talkative or aggressive. The moderator must be emotionally detached from the issue under study; don't ask the public relations director to moderate a group about the effectiveness of the newsletter or her own staff's edits.

The **assistant moderator** or **host** greets and seats participants, offers refreshments if these are available, prepares nametags if this is appropriate, and escorts any latecomers to their seats. The host is a liaison between the moderator and any viewers who might be present, sometimes delivering to the moderator questions that a viewer-client might wish to have discussed.

The **recorder** takes notes throughout the discussion, producing a log of the discussion and making it easier to obtain quotes from the transcript later on. Special sheets can be prepared for recording key words and phrases of participants; who said what; significant nonverbal activity such as body language, excitement, nods, and so on; and personal observations or insights. The recorder also prepares the typed transcript that the researcher will use in preparing a final report. In some situations, the recorder may be out of view, but in most focus group settings the participants easily ignore a recorder sitting off to the side.

The **technician** is in charge of audio- or videotaping. This person should be as unobtrusive as possible. It is possible to combine these roles. Many setups involve two people: a research leader/moderator and an assistant moderator/recorder/technician. For very simple situations, the moderator might handle all the roles.

Conducting a Focus Group

Various researchers may have slightly different approaches for preparing and conducting a focus group. Edmunds (2000), for example, identifies several variations on the standard focus group. These include a **telefocus group**, which are conducted via a telephone conference call; a **minifocus group**, with only five or six participants; **triads** with only three participants; **Internet focus groups**; and **video focus groups**, conducted via teleconference. Regardless of the variations, most researchers would find their personal techniques reflected in the following 11-step outline for conducting focus groups:

1. *Identify the topic of your research.* Do enough secondary research to gain a good understanding of the topic. Redefine or narrow the topic if you are not convinced the information generated by the focus group will have practical significance for your organization or client or try a different research technique.

2. *Select the moderator.* Professional focus group moderators are available through marketing research firms and some public relations agencies, as well as through some colleges and universities. Look for someone who is unbiased about the issue under study, who has good communication skills (both listening and speaking), a strong ability to probe and analyze, a good memory, and an engaging personality. The moderator must also be able to quickly learn new concepts. Usually a professional moderator can handle almost any topic, but in some sensitive areas, consider carefully who should be selected as moderator. For example, female participants in a focus group dealing with reconstructive surgery following breast cancer may be more comfortable with a moderator of their own gender, as might a group of men discussing products such as condoms. Should you facilitate your own focus group? It can save time and money, and you probably have more knowledge of the issue than an outside moderator. But the problem of bias, even an unconscious bias, can be difficult to overcome. Internal moderators may be tempted to explain and defend rather than merely elicit comments from participants. Meanwhile, participants may be less than candid with a focus group moderator who is professionally involved with the topic under discussion.
3. *Select the sample*, remembering that the small size of focus groups makes a truly representative sample unlikely. A focus group studying attitudes toward a proposed new chain of coffee bars might include veteran coffee drinkers, young professionals, and retired persons. Some researchers find it useful to separate participants by age, gender, or other important characteristics, especially if such homogeneity would enhance interaction within the group. To obtain a group that is as unbiased as possible, avoid populating it with friends, colleagues, or people associated with the client, such as donors, employees, customers, and so on.
4. *Determine the number of groups needed* to obtain an adequate range of opinions. Because focus groups are so easily swayed by intragroup dynamics, it is wise to plan for at least a couple of groups; some researchers prefer as many as five similar groups for a true reading.
5. *Select the participants you will need*, with perhaps a few extra to compensate for the inevitable no-shows. Some researchers recruit 20% more than they actually need. When the research is done for commercial marketing purposes, it is customary to pay participants a participation fee. The rate varies, but currently $25 to $50 is common, with more for doctors, lawyers, and others with professional degrees.
6. *Select the site for the research sessions.* These sometimes are held in special research labs equipped with video cameras, built-in microphones, and a viewing room behind a one-way mirror. A cost-effective alternative is a professionally furnished conference room with a circular or rectangular table and comfortable chairs. Focus groups also can be conducted in classrooms or in a living room or around a kitchen table. Make sure the site is conveniently accessible to your participants and that it is comfortable for them.
7. *Arrange to record the session with either audio- or videotaping*, whichever is more appropriate. Though marketing-oriented focus groups often are videotaped, some researchers find the practice intrusive and instead prefer audiotaping (Morgan, 1997). Remember that the primary reason for taping focus groups is to generate a written transcript of the discussion, which means videotaping probably isn't necessary. Some

focus group work done for public relations purposes can be accomplished with audiotaping; an omnidirectional zone-type microphone can be set inconspicuously in the middle of a conference table, and a tape recorder on a side table will scarcely be noticed by participants. It is a good idea to make a back-up recording or at least to have a microcassette recorder available. Videotaping, meanwhile, allows a more careful review of body language and other nonverbal cues. It also allows researchers to edit the tape for presentations to clients, which can be more powerful than transcripts or quotes presented in a written report.

Sample Focus Group Discussion Guide

Client: Central University recruiting marketing program
Participants: Six to ten high school honor students (seniors)

1. Introduction
   a. Identify moderator, assistant moderator
   b. Explain focus group
      1. Purpose (marketing decisions)
      2. Ground rules (confidentiality, candor, mutual respect, equal participation)

2. Perceptions of Central University
   a. What would your family/friends say if you decided to attend Central University?
   b. What do you know about Central University? How much?
   c. From what you do know, what does Central University do well?
   d. From what you do know, what does Central University not do well?

3. College/University Selection
   a. What are students looking for in a college/university? (location, cost, courses, reputation, jobs, parties)
   b. What do your parents ask you to consider in choosing a college?
   c. What role do guidebooks (Peterson's, Barron's, etc.) play in your college/university choice?

4. Comparisons
   a. What colleges/universities are you seriously considering attending? Why?
   b. How does Central University compare to these colleges/universities? (pros, cons)
   c. In one sentence, what is your impression of Central University?

5. Marketing Critique
   a. Discuss logos (hand out samples)
   b. Discuss newspaper/magazine ads (hand out samples)
   c. Discuss billboard ads (hand out samples)
   d. Discuss messages

8. *Prepare the discussion guide* with an outline of the questions to be used, and organize any participant materials such as samples, brochures, photographs, advertising sketches, slides, and the like.
9. *Conduct the focus group session.* Note the various distinct roles for the research team conducting the session.
10. *Review and analyze the data.* Immediately after the session, review the tape. If any parts of it were not recorded properly, write down everything you can remember. Even if the tape is complete, listen to it and review your notes. Add any additional observations or insights that you didn't have time to note during the session. Transcribe the tape.
11. *Report the data for your client or your boss.* The research report generally is prepared by the moderator. It should include a statement of the purpose of the research, an overview of the selection process for participants and a copy of the discussion guide. The body of the report generally includes both selected comments made by participants and recommendations gleaned by the researcher.

In the comment section both direct quotes and paraphrases are drawn from the discussion, often divided into subtopics. Researchers sometimes present participant comments in a cumulative fashion, simply by noting remarks and suggestions, or they may highlight those comments that were echoed by several different participants. For example, the research report may separate comments that enjoyed general endorsement from those that were mentioned by only one or two persons.

Some focus group reports end with a summary, others with observations by the researcher, still others with specific recommendations that the researcher feels flow from the comments and observations. The decision about including recommendations is based on the expectations and needs of the client, as well as the agreed-upon role of the researcher.

Case Studies

A type of research useful for public relations and marketing communication is the **case study** (sometimes called a **case history** or, more generally, **field research**). A case study investigates a single event, product or situation, looking at how an organization has handled it. The purpose of this investigation is to understand and learn from a real-life example.

The underlying idea is a simple one: Let's see what we can learn from someone who has been there. A public relations director in Virginia might contact a colleague in Iowa about a crisis situation she had successfully managed a year or so earlier. That is a case study, learning from someone else's success. Case studies don't necessarily have to present successful cases. When Sisters Hospital in Buffalo, New York, faced so much community opposition that it had to cancel its plan to open a methadone clinic in a residential neighborhood, the failure became a good case study for other hospitals around the country planning to open similar off-site drug-treatment centers. Public relations practitioners could learn what not to do as well as what to do to avoid such community opposition.

Case studies often are labeled as qualitative research, meaning that they rely more on the researcher's insight than on hard facts. However, Robert Yin (1994) notes that both contemporary and historical case studies can rely on quantitative evidence.

Advantages and Disadvantages of Case Studies

Like any other research technique, case studies feature both advantages and disadvantages. On the plus side, they can suggest why something happened and can deal with a wide spectrum of evidence, such as documents, interviews, even surveys (Babbie, 2006). On the other hand, case studies can't easily be generalized, making it risky to presume that what happened in the observed case will necessarily predict what could happen in other situations.

Though case studies have some limitations, they nevertheless can be very useful. Many university professors have found that both graduate and undergraduate students appreciate the practical value of case studies. Practitioners and students alike can learn a lot about crisis communication by looking at the classic cases: Three Mile Island and the Nestlé boycott in the late 1970s, Tylenol and Exxon in the 1980s, Dow Corning's breast-implant imbroglio and TWA's downed Flight 800 in the 1990s, plus a host of perhaps lesser-known crisis cases dealing with embezzlement (United Way of America), scandal (Covenant House), consumer fraud (Sears Auto Centers), product tampering (the Pepsi syringe hoax), product credibility (Intel Pentium), customer injury (McDonald's) and employee behavior (U.S. Navy "Tailhook" scandal). And that's just a few cases dealing with crises. We can learn from thousands more dealing with employee communication, community relations, investor relations and so on.

Conducting a Case Study

As a research method, case studies offer much flexibility to the researcher. However, some common approaches are helpful. Here are 10 steps for conducting a case study:

1. *Identify the problem* within your organization that generates your research. Make sure the problem is one that can be addressed by making a comparison to another organization.
2. *Select a relevant case to investigate.* Make sure the organization associated with the case is at least somewhat comparable to your own or your client's organization, so that the comparison is a meaningful one.
3. *Identify the information you need.* A case study can yield a wide range of information, but you can make your study more efficient by first noting the parameters of what you need to find out. Remember that you are not seeking merely a journalistic report of events but an insightful analysis of causes and effects, strategies and tactics.
4. *Identify the data sources*, which generally are personal observation, interviews, or documentation such as news releases, press clippings, and other published information as well as internal documents such as letters, organizational files, agendas, reports, and surveys.
5. *Articulate the questions* that you will use with the data sources to obtain the information you seek.
6. *Develop a study protocol* for formal case studies to be reported in writing (optional). Create a document that identifies the study's purpose and procedures, definitions, data sources, questions, and plan for analysis and reporting.
7. *Conduct a pilot study* to pretest and perhaps refine the questions for the eventual investigation.
8. *Gather the information*, using your skills as both an interviewer and a secondary researcher.

9. *Analyze the information*, looking not only at the individual facts but also at their relationship and potential interaction. Apply the information to your own organization.
10. *Report the information*, based on the appropriate audience (you only, professional colleagues, bosses, or clients). This reporting may be verbal and informal, even conversational if you have conducted the case study for your own company, or it may be written as part of a formal series of research and recommendations for a client or as part of a major campaign.

Sampling for case studies usually involves nonprobability methods, particularly convenience, purposive, and snowball sampling (discussed earlier in the section Nonprobability Sampling).

Also important to case studies are the roles of the observer and the informant. The observer is you, the person doing the research, and you are neither unobtrusive nor disinterested. Your informant, meanwhile, is the person you are interviewing to obtain information about the case. This informant also is not disinterested. Good research calls for both the observer and the informant to be objective, fair, and as unbiased as possible. Questions should not be slanted to elicit hoped-for answers, and responses should tell all relevant aspects of the story as they really happened, without reinterpretation or reshaping.

Survey Research

One of the oldest and most common research techniques is the **survey**, which involves asking standard questions of many respondents and then comparing their responses. Surveys, also known as **polls**, have many advantages. They are appropriate for description, analysis, and prediction—three major research needs. They are among the least expensive and quickest types of research. They can be applied to both large and small groups of people. They can be very accurate, and their findings are easy to compare. On the down side, surveys are subject to both the bias and limitations of the researcher, particularly through inadequate samples or poorly worded questions.

Surveys can be administered in a number of ways, each with certain built-in benefits and disadvantages.

- **Telephone surveys** are quick to administer but limited to easy-to-understand questions. With the ubiquity of telemarketing, caller ID, and answering machines or voice mail, it is becoming increasingly difficult to conduct phone surveys.
- The most common type of surveys, **mail surveys** (also called **self-administered surveys**), are convenient for respondents but the response rate generally is lower than for more expensive telephone surveys.
- **Personal interview surveys** are most expensive of all because they are time-consuming, and they are subject to interpersonal variables not found in most other types of surveys.
- Meanwhile, **group-administered surveys** are easy to execute, but there often is a concern about the appropriateness of the group.
- An emerging technique, **computer-based surveys**, offers some benefits of mail surveys, but they often are focused on a volunteer sample, which may not be the most appropriate for the research needs.

Response rates vary considerably with surveys. Some research is reported on the basis of a response rate of 5% or less. The Hite Report on female sexual behavior, a 1976 popular best-seller, was based on a 3% response rate to a mail survey. Such low response rates raise serious doubts about findings. Earl Babbie (2006) considers a response rate of 50% as adequate, 60% as good, and 70% as very good. You'll have to decide what an acceptable rate is for your research, realizing that higher response rates generally are more reliable.

Some researchers use payments or other incentives to increase the response rate. Sometimes the payment is merely a token amount, perhaps a dollar, even a couple of pennies ("We want your two cents' worth"). Incentives may be pens, calendars, tickets, or simple items associated with the sponsor. Some surveys offer a more elaborate gift through a raffle held among participants who return the questionnaires.

Most questionnaires are accompanied by a stamped, self-addressed return envelope to make it easier for the respondent to return the questionnaire. Fax response may be appropriate for questionnaires sent to professionals and dealing with nonpersonal topics. Likewise, e-mail surveys are becoming increasingly popular.

Much depends on how carefully you select the sample and how well you groom your chosen respondents. A general rule applies: The more involved the respondents are with the sponsoring organization or the more concerned they are with the issue, the higher the response rate. Some researchers have the head of the organization send a letter to respondents asking them to complete the questionnaire they will soon receive and noting the importance of the information to the organization.

Follow-up mailings can greatly improve the response rate, as well. The least expensive way is to send a reminder postcard or letter. More effective, however, is to send another copy of the questionnaire. If your client or boss is serious about wanting responses, the price of second or even third mailings is money well spent. Thomas Mangione (1995) reports that a second mailing usually generates half the percentage of response as the first mailing generated, and the third mailing half that of the second. Babbie (2006) recommends two or three follow-up mailings for the best response. He cites the experience of the Survey Research Office at the University of Hawaii, which found a consistent pattern of returns. It generally obtains a 40% response from its initial questionnaire mailing. A second mailing two weeks later brings in another 20%, and a third mailing yields an additional 10%.

Another way to ensure adequate numbers of responses is to use a larger-than-desired sample, on the notion that not everyone in the selected sample will respond. Though this adds to the mailing cost, it may be a legitimate way to obtain responses, especially if it reduces the need for follow-up mailings.

Conducting a Survey

Here is a simple step-by-step formula for conducting a survey. The format is general, though steps 7 through 10 deal specifically with mail surveys; modify these steps for surveys administered over the phone or in person. Following these general steps, we'll talk more specifically about questionnaires.

1. *Identify the topic of your research.* Do enough secondary research to gain a good understanding of the topic. Redefine or narrow the topic if you are not convinced the information generated by the survey will have practical significance for your organization or client, or abandon the survey and use a different research technique.

2. *Select a sample that is appropriate for your organization* in terms of reliability as well as time and cost.
3. *Write the items to be included in the questionnaire*, the written document that presents questions or statements to respondents. (We'll talk more about questionnaires shortly.) Review the wording for each item. Keep the questionnaire as brief as possible, because the more concise it is, the higher response rate you can expect.
4. *Print the questionnaire on letterhead or with the logo of the sponsoring organization.* Visually the questionnaire should be neat and user-friendly, with clear instructions, readable type and easy response formats. Try not to split items over pages or columns.
5. *Test the questionnaire*, preferably with a small group of people reflecting the characteristics of your sample.
6. *Modify the questionnaire*, based on what you learn from your pretest group.
7. For mail surveys: *Write and send a cover letter that introduces the survey to respondents.* Identify the sponsoring organization, explain its purpose, note the level of confidentiality, and encourage their participation. Some researchers prefer to use an advance letter in addition to the cover letter. This can be particularly useful when the questionnaires are going to people associated with the sponsoring organization, such as an advance letter from the director of a nonprofit organization announcing an upcoming questionnaire and encouraging participation. In the cover letter include a telephone number where respondents can contact the research office with questions or simply to verify the legitimacy of the survey.
8. For mail surveys: *Mail the surveys to participants.* Always use first-class postage. Include a return envelope with first-class postage, or use envelopes with a postage-paid business reply imprint. The latter costs more per piece when returned, but you pay for only those envelopes that are returned. On the other hand, there is a

Basic Skills for a Case Study Researcher

Here are five basic research skills necessary for people involved in preparing case studies. The case study preparer should:

1. Be able to ask good questions, and to interpret the answers.
2. Be a good "listener" and not be trapped by his own ideologies or preconceptions.
3. Be adaptive and flexible, so that newly encountered situations can be seen as opportunities, not threats.
4. Have a firm grasp on the issues being studied, whether this is a theoretical or policy orientation, even if in an exploratory mode. Such a grasp focuses the relevant events and information to be sought to manageable proportions.
5. Be unbiased by preconceived notions, including those derived from theory. Thus, a person should be sensitive and responsive to contradictory evidence.

Source: Yin (1994).

psychological advantage in using a postage stamp that respondents will know they are wasting if they don't use it in returning a completed questionnaire. Alternatively, e-mail the questionnaire if you know that your intended respondents are comfortable with using e-mail.

9. For mail surveys: *Monitor the returns.* Keep a daily count of the number of returns received.
10. For mail surveys: *Send a follow-up mailing after about 10 days.* If necessary and appropriate, send a second follow-up mailing after another two weeks.
11. *Analyze and report the data.* Survey results usually are reported with a degree of formality because they are serious research. Generally the written report will include a statement of the purpose of the research, an outline of the methods used to obtain and contact the sample, a copy of the questionnaire, a report on the number of responses received, and a notation of any limitations or weaknesses in the survey. The heart of the survey report is an item-by-item account of what the respondents said; sometimes researcher comments are included within the item reporting, pointing to interesting correlations with other questions. Usually the researcher includes a set of recommendations flowing logically from the findings.

Increasingly, surveys are being administered online, and a growing array of software is making the task easier. Some companies offer free or low-cost basic packages with limits on the number of questions and the number of surveys that may be conducted, graduating to monthly costs for more sophisticated and larger packages. These include Survey Methods (http://www.surveymethods.com), SurveyMonkey (http://www.surveymonkey.com) and Micropoll (http://www.micropoll.com). Other companies specialize in more professional, and thus more expensive, products such as WebSurveyor (http://www.websurveyor.com), Zoomerang (http://www.zoomerang.com) and Opinio (http://www.objectplanet.com).

Questionnaires

A **questionnaire** is the tool used for surveys. It is a written document that features a series of items such as questions or statements that call for a response.

Whether the questionnaire is delivered in person, over the telephone, or in print, the introductory statement sets the stage. This introduction should identify the researcher and the sponsoring organization, indicate the topic, explain why the respondent was selected, guarantee confidentiality, and note the approximate time required of the respondent. Don't ask the respondent to participate, because this provides an opportunity for the respondent to decline. Instead provide the preliminary information and ask the first question.

Data in questionnaires fits into several categories. The main content items generally follow the same hierarchy as do public relations objectives: awareness (knowledge, understanding or retention of information); acceptance (interest or attitude); and action (opinion or behavior). Additionally, demographic items deal with the respondent's background or environment, which is useful information for analyzing the data gathered.

GENERAL TIPS

Asking the right questions in the right way is basic to conducting a good survey. Following are some general tips for questionnaire items, whether they are framed as statements or questions:

- Keep the items short. Using several short, specific items is better than using fewer items that are complex and confusing.
- Use clear and simple words and phrases familiar to the respondents. Avoid jargon unless the respondents share the language. Avoid all but the most commonly used abbreviations.
- Be specific; avoid ambiguous words and phrases. For example, the seemingly simple question "Where do you live?" could actually generate a range of responses. Is the desired answer "United States"? Or is it "Cleveland," "23 Oriole Road," "In an apartment building" or "With my parents"? Likewise, a question such as "What do you think about the mayor's tax proposal?" is unclear. One respondent may focus on the timing, another on the amount of money to be collected, still another on the method of collection or the eventual use of the money raised.
- Don't let your curiosity run amok. Ask only questions that are relevant to the research topic.
- Place items in a logical order, usually easy to difficult. Group items dealing with a similar topic together. Demographic items about the respondents should be kept together; mail surveys often place these items at the end, while telephone surveys may lead with these because they are easy for respondents to answer. Arrange sentences in positive constructions. For example, ask "Do you participate in group exercise or fitness programs?" instead of the more negative "Do you avoid group exercise or fitness programs?" Especially avoid double negatives, such as the awkward "Do you disagree that lack of exercise is unhealthful?" (Presuming you have an opinion on the issue, try figuring out how to respond to the last question.)
- Use words with clear meanings, because every respondent must understand and interpret the questionnaire items exactly the same way. For example, "Have you ever considered having an affair?" begs the question of what "consider" means in this context. And what is an "affair"? Instead, try asking: "While you were married, did you ever engage in sexual activity with someone other than your spouse?"
- Avoid "double-barreled" items, ones that include two different thoughts. For example, the question "Do you think Portland is a friendly and progressive community?" is difficult for respondents to answer if they think Portland is friendly but not very progressive. The relationship between the two modifiers is unclear; they don't belong in the same question.

LEVEL OF INFORMATION

Items dealing with the respondent's level of information may offer a particular challenge to questionnaire writers.

- If necessary, include a brief definition of key terms.
- Make sure the topic is within the competence of average respondents. Don't ask a sample of people without a strong scientific background if fusion or fission is a better process for nuclear energy. Any response would be little more than an uninformed guess.
- Carefully explain when you are testing the knowledge of respondents. Example: "A main purpose of this survey is to find out how much residents know about the bridge proposal. The following six items present multiple-choice items about the proposal. Circle the answers you think are correct."

Timing and Wording Affect Poll Results

The timing of polls and the way questions are worded can have a big impact on how people answer them. Here is an example related by Adam Clymer, a columnist with the *New York Times*, who reflected on the fact that several conflicting surveys were being reported about supposed public support for federal funding of human embryonic stem cell research.

As the issue was heating up during the summer of 2001, an NBC News/*Wall Street Journal* poll said that 69% of Americans favor the research. A Gallup Poll for CNN and *USA Today* reported 54% in favor. A poll by ABC News and Beliefnet (a religious website) found 58% in favor. These three news-related polls had significant differences.

Meanwhile, two less-than-disinterested parties had reported even more disparate results. A poll by the Juvenile Diabetes Foundation, which favors stem cell research, said 70% of Americans favor the research. But the U.S. Conference of Catholic Bishops, which opposes the research on human embryos, reported a survey that said only 24% of Americans approve.

Clymer noted that some of the variations in the polling could be traced to how the questions were phrased. The NBC/*Journal* poll used the phrase "potentially viable human embryos," while the bishops' poll said "the live embryos would be destroyed in their first week of development." The bishop's poll also referred to "experiments," while the others alluded to the goals of the research.

Perhaps more important, the polls were so dissimilar because many respondents were unfamiliar with the topic. All the polls asked long, involved questions. Only the Gallup Poll allowed respondents to answer that they did not know enough about the issue to have an opinion, and 57% chose that response category.

Clymer quoted research experts that the polls were measuring "nonattitudes." One survey expert focused on the newness and complexity of the issue: "Americans are acquiescent so they'll give you an answer. [But] the mere fact that you've got to offer a lengthy summary implies that it's too early to sort it out."

The insightful columnist concluded with a warning for all of us: "Sometimes, the pollsters are measuring phantoms, and the politicians are calling on them for support."

Source: Clymer (2001).

OPINION/ATTITUDE

Some special guidelines apply to questionnaire items that seek to elicit the respondent's opinion or attitude.

- Don't ask for opinions on questions that are matters of fact. For example, don't ask "Do boys get higher grades in mathematics than girls do?" because that question doesn't call for an opinion. You can easily research the facts on math grades. But a legitimate opinion question might be "Why do you think boys get higher grades in mathematics than girls do?" especially if your questionnaire is being answered by teachers, parents, psychologists, or others whose opinions might be relevant.

- Avoid speculative or hypothetical questions. Example: "Would you prefer to move to a colony under the sea or in outer space?" An exception to this is if the item deals with a potential activity of the sponsoring organization. Example: "Given the opportunity, would you consider purchasing a vacuum cleaner that also served as an air purifier?"
- Avoid terms that call for subjective judgment, which can vary from person to person. Example: "Is the current tax structure reasonable?" The word *reasonable* may be interpreted differently by various respondents. Instead ask more specifically, "Is the current tax structure affordable?" (or "equitable," or whatever else you really want to know).
- Be careful about mixing fact and opinion. If a national magazine has just ranked Austin as one of the top 10 progressive cities in the United States, don't ask, "Is Austin a progressive city?" It's unclear if you are asking about the respondent's awareness or opinion. Instead ask, "Do you agree with a magazine ranking that Austin is progressive?"

ACTION/BEHAVIOR

Items dealing with actions and behaviors, whether current or past, also can be particularly difficult for the questionnaire writer.

- Make sure you are asking for relevant behaviors. Example: "Do you ever shop at GreenGrocers?" *Ever?*
- Make sure the questions can reasonably be answered. Avoid asking for highly detailed information, such as, "In the last six months, how many hours of television have you watched?" Instead, use a time frame easier for the respondent, such as, "On an average weekday, how many hours of television do you usually watch?" or, "On an average weekend, how many hours of television do you usually watch?" Then you do the math.
- Make sure the topic is within the respondent's relevant experience. Asking women about how frequently they practice self-examination techniques for testicular cancer isn't a useful question. Either limit it to male respondents or replace it with a question dealing with the frequency of self-examination techniques for two easily detectable cancers (breast cancer or testicular cancer).
- Don't word the questions so that they presume a particular answer, particularly with sensitive issues. Example: "How often do you smoke marijuana?" This wording presumes that one smokes it at least sometimes. This might be better handled with a primary and a contingency question, "Do you smoke marijuana?" and then the contingency, "If yes, how often?"
- Be careful with intrusive or potentially embarrassing questions, especially those that deal with legal, social, or moral transgressions. "Are you always truthful on your income tax returns?" may result in a less-than-truthful answer, in part because the respondent may be concerned about the confidentiality of the study, and in part because the respondent may simply be unwilling to confess a crime, even to himself.

IMPARTIALITY

In general, researchers want questionnaires to be unbiased. Following are a few pointers in writing impartial questions.

- Keep your wording neutral, and avoid leading items that indicate to the respondent what the researcher apparently sees as the "correct" answer. Example: "Do you agree with most Americans that more violent criminals should receive the death penalty?" Telling the respondent that most Americans agree with this statement is biasing the response.
- Make sure the wording doesn't signal your own bias, such as, "Do you prefer reading good literature or just popular novels?" Good literature? Just novels? No doubt about the preferred answer here.
- Take particular care with socially or politically charged words. Kenneth Rasinski (1989) analyzed the wording in several national surveys. He found, for example, that 63% of respondents said too little money was being spent on "assistance to the poor," but only 23% said too little was being spent on "welfare." The difference is mainly in the wording.
- Realize that commonly used social and political terms sometimes have different meanings. Example: "Are you pro-abortion?" Respondents may consider themselves pro-choice but not pro-abortion, or they might be disinclined to answer such a complex question with a simple "yes" or "no." Whenever respondents feel a need to explain their interpretation of a questionnaire item, it is poorly worded.
- Avoid a prestige bias by making associations with respected authorities or well-known figures. Example: "Do you agree with the mayor that property taxes are too high?" The same is true with disrespected figures. If the mayor has just been indicted for embezzlement and tax fraud, respondents may hedge on stating any agreement with a disgraced public official.
- Use leading questions if you are dealing with a potentially embarrassing or controversial issue or if you feel a need to "give permission" to respondents to be truthful. For example: "Recently, several political leaders have admitted to adultery . . . ."

DEMOGRAPHICS

Demographic items also require careful attention by the questionnaire writer.

- Rather than ask a respondent's age or income, group such sensitive questions into ranges. Example: "Which of the following best describes your family income last year? Less than $40,000; $40,001 to $80,000; more than $80,000."
- Tailor educational levels to your target population, and consider asking for the highest grade or degree completed. Example: "How much education have you completed? Less than high school; high school; some college but no degree; associate's degree; bachelor's degree; graduate degree." If this was directed to academic professionals, the response choices might be "Bachelor's degree; academic master's degree; terminal master's degree (MFA, MSW); academic doctorate (PhD); professional doctorate (JD, MD, DDS); postdoctoral study."
- Be careful when asking about racial or ethnic background, and make sure all options are included. Also consider the wording of the question. The U.S. Census Bureau asks people to indicate the race they consider themselves to be, a subtle difference over the strictly matter-of-fact question, "What is your race?" Also, because a growing number of people identify themselves as biracial or multiracial, consider allowing respondents to indicate more than one category.

Guidelines for Open-Ended Versus Closed-Ended Items

Here are some guidelines for when to use open-ended questions and when closed-ended questions are more appropriate. Remember that both can be used within the same questionnaire.

Use closed-ended items if you . . .
prefer that respondents use predetermined choices
want to make it easier for respondents by using predetermined choices
can anticipate the range of response choices
want to directly compare and correlate responses

Use open-ended items if you . . .
prefer that respondents answer in their own words
want to make it easier for respondents by answering in own words
don't know the range of response choices
are willing to consider dissimilar comments from respondents

- Tailor the demographic information to the research needs. For example, for surveys conducted near the northern U.S. border, demographic items might include the name of the specific province for someone who indicates a Canadian background. Likewise, in the Southwest, items might include the names of specific Central or Latin American countries or perhaps Mexican states, if that information is relevant to the researcher.

Questionnaire design also must give attention to the response categories for the various items. First of all, make the options visually simple and consistent. Use checkmarks, circles, boxes, or other simple marks. One of the first considerations is the type of response categories. **Open-ended items** allow respondents to answer in their own words; **closed-ended items** provide for check-offs to predetermined response categories.

Types of Responses

Researchers have devised several different types of items that can be used for responses in questionnaires. Some of the more common types are multiple-choice items, checklist items, forced-choice items, and rating scales. A questionnaire may include more than one type of item, though it's generally a good idea to group similar items.

MULTIPLE-CHOICE ITEMS

Questions or statements with a limited number of responses are called **multiple-choice items**. These allow respondents to choose from a predetermined set of choices. For example: "Indicate your favorite major television news network: ABC, CBS, NBC, CNN, FOX, MSNBC." Often multiple-choice items include an "other" category. Response categories for choice items must be both **comprehensive** and **mutually exclusive**. That is, each response category must provide a full range of potential responses so there is an appropriate response for each respondent (a comprehensive set of responses), and there must be only one possible response (each response being mutually exclusive from the other choices).

For example, on a demographic question asking the income of respondents, the response categories might be "$20,000 or less"; "$20,000 to $40,000"; "$40,000 to $60,000"; and "$60,000 or more." The categories are comprehensive, covering all the bases. But they are not mutually exclusive because they overlap—both the second and third choices are appropriate for someone earning exactly $40,000 a year. A better way to write response categories might be "less than $20,000"; "$20,000 to $39,999"; "$40,000 to $59,999"; and "$60,000 or more."

CHECKLIST ITEMS

Sometimes it is more effective to allow respondents to indicate more than one response through a **checklist**. Example: "What kind of country music do you listen to most often? Check all that apply: classic country, new country, alternative country, honky-tonk, bluegrass, rockabilly, cowboy, country rock, western swing, outlaw country, progressive country."

FORCED-CHOICE ITEMS

Another type of response category is **forced-choice items** that feature two or more statements, with directions for respondents to select the one that most closely reflects their opinion. Example: "Of the following statements, select the one that comes closer to your own belief: Voting is a privilege and thus should be optional. Voting is a responsibility and thus should be required."

RATING SCALES

Some items have the advantage of focusing on the intensity of the respondent's feelings rather than eliciting a simple "yes" or "no" response. These are **rating scales**, in which respondents are asked to rate the degree of their feeling or certainty about an item. Some rating scales are bipolar instruments because they move in both directions from a neutral center point to either positive or negative points. Others are unipolar instruments that range from low to high points.

The popular **Likert scale** (pronounced LICK-ert) is a bipolar scale that asks the intensity of respondents' agreement to a statement along a range of response negative and positive categories, such as "strongly disagree"; "disagree"; "agree"; and "strongly agree." The wording for the Likert scale can be modified, such as by asking "approve," "believe," "interested," and so forth. In some versions, the Likert scale includes a central or neutral option ("neither agree nor disagree"), and sometimes a "no opinion" item. For some issues, researchers use the neutral option; for others they would rather eliminate the midpoint and force the respondent to indicate a preference one way or the other.

Define response options carefully. Rating scales sometimes offer choices such as "excellent"; "very good"; "average"; "fair"; "poor"; and so on. A problem with such scales is that too many response categories can leave respondents confused about the differences among the categories—for example, between "average" and "fair" or between "excellent" and "very good."

To avoid this ambiguity, some rating scales are presented numerically, as in the following example: "Indicate your preference for various flavors of ice cream (1 being dislike, 5 being like): Vanilla 1–2–3–4–5. Chocolate 1–2–3–4–5. Strawberry 1–2–3–4–5" (and so on). When rating scales are used numerically, it is logical to arrange them so that a low or negative response translates into low numbers. Example: "Rate the following on a scale of 1 to 5 (1

How Am I Doing?

With any survey, especially one that seeks to gauge the level of satisfaction by customers, readers, employees, and other key publics, it is important to ask the right question. Howard Waddell (1995) notes that most customer-satisfaction surveys ask variations on "How am I doing?" Several different scales address this question:

- *Performance scale:* poor, fair, good, excellent, superior
- *Expectation scale:* much more than expected, better than expected, as much as expected, less than expected, much less than expected
- *Requirement scale:* exceeded my requirements, met requirements, nearly met requirements, did not meet requirements
- *Satisfaction scale:* very satisfied, satisfied, neither satisfied nor dissatisfied, dissatisfied, very dissatisfied

Waddell suggests a better approach—an improvement scale (none, some, considerable) that presumes there is generally room for better performance.

being low priority, 5 being high priority)." Reversing this, to rank low priority items with a five and high priority items with a one, would be confusing to respondents.

Rating scales can even be presented visually, such as with smiley face caricatures for children's surveys, ranging from very sad through very happy. Writing about questionnaires in a series of books on survey research, Arlene Fink (2002a) recommends five types of response options for rating scales:

- Endorsement: definitely true, true, don't know, false, definitely false.
- Frequency: always, very often, fairly often, sometimes, almost never, never.
- Intensity: none, very mild, mild, moderate, severe.
- Influence: big problem, moderate problem, small problem, very small problem, no problem.
- Comparison: much more than others, somewhat more than others, about the same as others, somewhat less than others, much less than others.

The **semantic differential scale** asks respondents to select a point on a continuum between two opposing positions. The scale generally uses opposing adjectives, usually with a five-point or seven-point scale. Example: "What are your perceptions about professional football? Interesting/uninteresting. Enjoyable/unenjoyable." This scale also can be presented numerically. For example:

Uninteresting	1	2	3	4	5	Interesting
Unenjoyable	1	2	3	4	5	Enjoyable

Content Analysis

Some problems are inherent in focus groups and surveys. When you directly ask people their opinion, their response may not be genuine; it may be shaped by the fact that you asked in the first place, or it may be colored by their desire to give you what they think is an acceptable answer.

For example, ask an acquaintance if he likes you and the answer may be "Yes, of course." But is he saying that just because you asked, because he'd be embarrassed to answer "no" or because he doesn't want to hurt your feelings? Instead of asking outright, you could observe what he says and does without being asked. List all the significant interactions the two of you have had in the last several weeks—conversations, shared experiences, and so on. Then evaluate each activity as being either friendly or unfriendly. If the friendly activities far outweigh the unfriendly ones, you can conclude that he likes you. If the negative interactions predominate, he doesn't like you, no matter what he might say.

That's the idea behind the research methodology known as **content analysis**—the objective, systematic, and quantitative investigation of something that has been written down (or at least something that can be written down for research purposes). Content analysis implements the maxim that actions speak louder than words. As a formal research methodology, content analysis has been used for years to study mass media. This research technique can be used to shed light on the messages of communication, assess the image of a group or organization, and make comparisons between media and reality.

Using Content Analysis

Researchers involved in public relations and marketing communication have found that content analysis can be useful in several different ways. Here are a couple of examples of how content analysis can be used to study various practical issues that could be important to your organization or client.

Let's say your client, an insurance agency, has a new policy covering sports cars. You want to reach your public—sports car drivers—on radio, using both public relations and advertising techniques. As you plan your campaign, you determine that you need to identify the most popular radio stations among people who drive sports cars. You could survey the drivers, but that might be unwieldy, because obtaining a sampling frame would be difficult. You could ask the radio stations about audience demographics, but they probably don't know the kind of cars their listeners drive. Instead, you might take a different tack. Ask mechanics at several maintenance and repair shops specializing in sports cars to keep a list of which stations the radios are tuned to when the cars are brought in. That's content analysis.

Or perhaps you are researching consumer issues for your company, a garment manufacturer. Specifically, you want to know what people think about the new line of lightweight, high-insulating winter coats. You could conduct a survey or a focus group if you had the time. Instead, you might check the letters and phone calls received by the consumer affairs department and compare these with customer comments about other products. This, too, is an example of content analysis.

Remember that the various research methods we're dealing with in this appendix don't have to stand alone. Content analysis can be used to complement other types of research. Researchers in public relations and marketing communication sometimes compare the results of their content analysis with the information they are able to obtain from surveys or focus groups.

For instance, if you are evaluating the effectiveness of your internal newsletter as part of an overall program review of your employee relations program, you might begin with a content analysis of the last three years' issues to identify topics that have been covered. Then you could conduct a focus group or readership survey to find out what topics your employees want to read about. Finally, you might compare the results of the content analysis with the results of your questioning, and from that comparison create a more popular employee publication.

Let's look at one final example. You are a media relations manager for a large public utility. You know that many of your news releases have been ignored by the newspapers and broadcast media in your service area. At a "meet the editors" forum sponsored by the local PRSA chapter, you hear from editors and news directors that they prefer stories with a strong local flavor. You realize you should evaluate the content of your releases as they focus on information of apparent significance to each locality within your service area. So you decide to do a content analysis of your releases of the last two years. Specifically, you evaluate four aspects of each release: the extent of the local significance of the issue or activity (1) as you know it to be, (2) as evident in the body of the release, (3) as identified in the lead sentence or paragraph, and (4) as specifically featured in the headline or title on the release. By combining the information you received from the media gatekeepers and your own analysis of local content, you can gain some helpful insight for both topics and effective writing techniques for your future releases.

Advantages and Disadvantages of Content Analysis

Content analysis has several advantages, including a low investment of time and money. It can be done by a person working alone with little equipment beyond a simple calculator or a computer with relatively inexpensive software. Content analysis is unobtrusive research done "after the fact," without any effect on the people or issues being studied. It also has the advantage of allowing you to look at the facts without being caught up by the heat of the moment, free of the passion and enthusiasm that often surrounds surveys or focus groups. Content analysis also has the advantage of allowing you to go back in time to examine past messages. It can be used to compare an organization with industry norms or with wider trends. Finally, it helps the researcher separate the routine from the unusual.

Another aspect of content analysis is the notion of **intercoder reliability**—the degree to which several coders agree on how to label the content being studied.

Among the disadvantages of content analysis are its limitation to recorded (or recordable) information and its susceptibility to coder influence and bias, in part because content analysis deals with what researchers call manifest content, the obvious and apparent meanings and interpretations that, unfortunately, are not always equally obvious and apparent to everyone. Also, while content analysis can point to coincidences and concurrences, it doesn't establish cause-and-effect relationships.

Conducting a Content Analysis Study

Following is a step-by-step explanation of how to conduct a research study via content analysis. Included with the explanations is a running example of how a health-care company might use content analysis.

SELECT AN APPROPRIATE TOPIC

Content analysis has many applications for all the social sciences. For academic research, it has been used in studies dealing with media content such as sex and violence. As a tool of applied research in public relations and marketing communication, content analysis can be used by planners who want to know what people are saying about their organizations, or how what they are saying coincides with how they are acting. Consider the following possibilities for public relations/marketing applications of content analysis:

- News coverage (topics, balance, frequency)
- Media artifacts (video news releases, radio actualities, photographs)
- Organizational reputation among various media or particular publics
- Letters to the editor (opinions, topics)
- Customer comments (letters, telephone calls)
- Competitors (claims, offerings, positioning, advertising themes)
- Trends in graphic design or publishing techniques
- Effectiveness of various persuasive appeals
- Public issues affecting an organization
- Preferences of various media (story type, political bias, editorial coverage)

Topics appropriate for your organization are those that deal with the content of artifacts that have already been written (reports, releases, publications, scripts, etc.) or that can be put into writing for research purposes (lists of characteristics, conversations, speeches, etc.). The text may originate within your organization, or it may be rooted in the communication or activity of one of your significant publics. Ask yourself how accessible the texts will be for you. Also consider how the information will be useful to your organization, especially because content analysis can help you learn facts about the content but not reasons behind those facts.

SELECT A POPULATION FOR YOUR STUDY

This may be people such as all your employees or just the employees with less than two years' experience on the job. Or the population may center on artifacts such as news releases, company publications, advertisements, and the like. After you identify the population, decide on a census or a representative sample.

DETERMINE THE UNIT OF ANALYSIS

Carefully define the terms related to what you want to study. For purposes of public relations and marketing communication, the unit of analysis may relate to one of the following aspects of communication. Many research studies would involve several of the following approaches mixed together to provide a general view of the whole issue:

- Subject: sorted by themes and topics.
- Communication element: headline, lead, news article, photo caption, letter to the editor, advertising illustration, and the like.
- Incoming communication: sorted by various channels, such as newspapers, magazines, television, radio, direct mail, telephone calls, letters, coupons, and e-mail.
- Outgoing communication: sorted by various tactics such as newsletter, e-mail, brochure, advertising spot, and webpage.

- Source of communication: sorted broadly by various publics or more narrowly by specific individuals or organizations or by subdivisions such as department, work site, and so on.
- Destination: sorted broadly or narrowly; the same as for the source of communication (above).
- Results: sorted by outcome, effect, and consequence.

Develop categories for coding your tallies of these units of analysis. These categories must meet the same two major criteria as response categories for surveys—that is, they need to be comprehensive (by including all the possible responses) and mutually exclusive (by not duplicating other possible responses).

Incoming telephone calls, for example, may be categorized as being "positive," "negative," "neutral," or "other." Too many responses in the "other" category indicate faulty categories. Newspaper articles may be studied to count the number of references to your organization, by both name and implication, and then to assess these references as to how positive they are or how accurately they portray your organization and its products or services. It might also record the message source and the paragraph number in which the source was first identified.

DEVELOP THE MECHANICS OF THE STUDY

This is a simple follow-up step to the previous one. Create a standardized coding form that allows you to record the numbers in each category. Usually this involves simple forms with space for tick marks (////). If you will have other people work on this project with you—it's always a good idea to minimize **coder bias**—you will need to train these coders. Essentially this means writing out and explaining all your definitions so each coder approaches the item in the same way. Because some of the category selection is subjective, there may be some differences here: a positive reference to one person may be neutral to another. That's one of the shortcomings of content analysis. One way around this is to have three coders do each item and then record the majority response. At this stage you also should pretest the coding instrument before actually doing the research. Go through a dozen or so items and see if the coding instrument works well. If not, go back and rethink your categories. When all of these tasks are completed, you are ready to actually measure the information and record it for later analysis.

ANALYZE THE DATA

Data analysis may generate formal reports to your client organization or employer, or it simply may remain as scribbling on your notepad for your own perusal and pondering. That's up to you. Either way, you will want to keep the numbers simple so you can more easily draw insight from them. As you might guess, researchers have developed some sophisticated statistical techniques for use with content analysis. If you want intricate statistics, contact a professional researcher or refer to a statistics textbook. But you don't have to deal heavily with statistics. Many excellent content analyses rely on simple percentages, which are more useful than raw numbers. You don't know much, for example, if you are told that 25 employees have made money-saving suggestions via the company suggestion box. Twenty-five out of 50 workers? Out of 5,000? But if you are told that those 25 employees represent one-third of the night shift, and that 75% of them work in the computer department, you have learned something very interesting and potentially very useful about the quality of ideas originating

Example of Content Analysis Steps

Step 1. You are public education manager for MetroHealth, a large statewide health maintenance organization. One of your job responsibilities is to promote a series of patient workshops on topics such as weight loss, nutrition, exercise and general fitness.

You want to get an accurate picture of how the largest daily newspapers in the state deal with these issues. Your purpose for gaining this information is to arm yourself for an eventual public-education campaign that will look to the newspapers for support. Before asking for this support, you decide that it will be helpful to know something about the newspapers' current and recent coverage of these topics.

Step 2. You identify the six largest newspapers in your state. Let's say you decide to limit your study to their news sections (local and national/international), as well as to relevant specialized sections such as lifestyle and science/health. Because it would be impractical to study every newspaper for every day over the last few years, you select a sample that includes each of the six newspapers for the following varied schedule throughout the last 12 months; one daily edition each month—

Monday, first week of January
Tuesday, second week of February
Wednesday, third week of March
Thursday, fourth week of April
Friday, first week of May
Saturday, second week of June
Monday, third week of July
Tuesday, fourth week of August
Wednesday, first week of September
Thursday, second week of October
Friday, third week of November
Saturday, fourth week of December

—and seven to nine Sunday editions each quarter, every sixth week following the beginning week, indicated by a throw of a dice.

Step 3. You search each sampled newspaper, and count the number of articles and news briefs that deal with one of the topics of your interest (weight loss, nutrition, exercise, general fitness, and so on), as you have defined them. These numbers will be compared to the total number of articles and briefs in the publication.

You then analyze each mention of these topics according to the following criteria:

- *Type of article:* Code each published story as an article or a news brief. Define these terms clearly. For example, you might define the difference in terms of length—a brief is up to three paragraphs and an article is longer, or a brief is less than 150 words while an article is longer.
- *Attitude:* Each article related to fitness will be coded as "positive," "negative" or "neutral," depending on how its tone relates to MetroHealth's message of encouraging fitness.

- *Accuracy:* Each article will be coded as "very accurate," "moderately accurate" or "inaccurate," based on how well it presents information that is currently accepted by medical and fitness professionals. Or you might count the number of factual inaccuracies and unwarranted conclusions within the brief or article.
- *Prominence:* Each article will be rated for a "prominent position" (any location on Page One of a section, or top-of-page placement on an inside page) or "nonprominent position" (placement elsewhere on a page).
- *Demographics:* Each article will be coded as to its evident appeal based on gender (men, women or both genders) and age (young, middle, older readers or all ages). This may be determined through criteria such as placement in a particular section (such as women's page, youth tab, etc.) or by the people shown in accompanying photographs or cited as examples within the article.

Step 4. Let's say that in coding your categories you arrive at the following results for three different newspapers A, B, and C:

News Articles

Newspaper	Articles	Fitness Articles	% Fitness
A	1,000	60	6%
B	940	54	5.7%
C	1,060	25	2.4%

News Briefs

Newspaper	Articles	Fitness Articles	% Fitness
A	400	40	10%
B	640	50	7.8%
C	800	70	8.8%

Articles and News Briefs re: Fitness

Newspaper	Positive	Negative
A	80%	20%
B	82%	18%
C	53%	47%

Articles and News Briefs re: Fitness

Newspaper	Accurate	Inaccurate
A	95%	5%
B	88%	12%
C	62%	38%

(Additional data would follow.)

Step 5. The research shows that newspapers A and B provide similar amounts of coverage to fitness-related information, both as news stories and as news briefs. Newspaper C, however, offers significantly less coverage to fitness information in the form of news articles, though it devotes slightly more space than the other newspapers do to fitness-related news briefs. Newspaper C has a higher number of negative articles and briefs, as this relates to MetroHealth's conclusion about how the articles are likely to promote an appreciation for fitness. This newspaper also has a higher percentage of inaccurate articles and briefs, based on MetroHealth's understanding of up-to-date reliable information. Based on the data from newspaper C, you might want to review your public relations procedures. (Other findings would reflect additional data.)

Recommend Follow-Up. A logical follow-up step to this content analysis would be to contact the editorial staff of newspaper C and arrange a meeting between you as MetroHealth public education manager and editors of the various news and lifestyle sections.

At this meeting, you might noncritically present your findings that indicate the newspaper's relative disinterest in fitness-related articles. Admitting that you are an advocate for fitness information, you might point to surveys indicating a growing interest within the general population (and thus newspaper readers), offering possible ways in which your organization could assist the newspaper in increasing its coverage of this topic. Perhaps you will learn that you could foster more articles by suggesting strong local angles to general fitness information or by offering experts from your organization as interview subjects.

Additionally, you might contact newspapers A and B and share your findings concerning their performance, encouraging their continued attention to fitness matters. For future research you might conduct a similar study in one or two years to note any changes in the media trends.

with night-time computer workers. If you do choose to prepare a formal report, include an explanation of the reason for your research, information about your sample, and a copy of the coding form. Report the results in raw numbers, percentages, or—usually—both. Discuss generalities and insights that you glean from those findings. Many reports conclude with recommendations based on the findings and insights.

Appendix B

Ethical Standards

Public Relations Society of America (PRSA)

Member Code of Ethics

Approved by the PRSA Assembly. October, 2000
Reprinted with permission of Public Relations Society of America (http://www.prsa.org).

PREAMBLE

- Professional Values
- Principles of Conduct
- Commitment and Compliance

This Code applies to Public Relations Society of America (PRSA) members. The Code is designed to be a useful guide for PRSA members as they carry out their ethical responsibilities. This document is designed to anticipate and accommodate, by precedent, ethical challenges that may arise. The scenarios outlined in the Code provision are actual examples of misconduct. More will be added as experience with the Code occurs.

The Public Relations Society of America is committed to ethical practices. The level of public trust PRSA members seek, as we serve the public good, means we have taken on a special obligation to operate ethically.

The value of member reputation depends upon the ethical conduct of everyone affiliated with the Public Relations Society of America. Each of us sets an example for each other—as well as other professionals—by our pursuit of excellence with powerful standards of performance, professionalism, and ethical conduct.

Emphasis on enforcement of the Code has been eliminated. But, the PRSA Board of Directors retains the right to bar from membership or expel from the Society any individual who has been or is sanctioned by a government agency or convicted in a court of law of an action that is in violation of this Code.

Ethical practice is the most important obligation of a PRSA member. We view the Member Code of Ethics as a model for other professions, organizations, and professionals.

PRSA Member Statement of Professional Values

This statement presents the core values of PRSA members and, more broadly, of the public relations profession. These values provide the foundation for the Member Code of Ethics and set the industry standard for the professional practice of public relations. These values are the fundamental beliefs that guide our behaviors and decision-making process. We believe our professional values are vital to the integrity of the profession as a whole.

ADVOCACY

- We serve the public interest by acting as responsible advocates for those we represent.
- We provide a voice in the marketplace of ideas, facts, and viewpoints to aid informed public debate.

HONESTY

- We adhere to the highest standards of accuracy and truth in advancing the interests of those we represent and in communicating with the public.

EXPERTISE

- We acquire and responsibly use specialized knowledge and experience.
- We advance the profession through continued professional development, research, and education.
- We build mutual understanding, credibility, and relationships among a wide array of institutions and audiences.

INDEPENDENCE

- We provide objective counsel to those we represent.
- We are accountable for our actions.

LOYALTY

- We are faithful to those we represent, while honoring our obligation to serve the public interest.

FAIRNESS

- We deal fairly with clients, employers, competitors, peers, vendors, the media, and the general public.
- We respect all opinions and support the right of free expression.

PRSA CODE PROVISIONS

Free Flow of Information.

Core Principle: Protecting and advancing the free flow of accurate and truthful information is essential to serving the public interest and contributing to informed decision making in a democratic society.

Intent:

- To maintain the integrity of relationships with the media, government officials, and the public
- To aid informed decision making

Guidelines:

A member shall:

- Preserve the integrity of the process of communication
- Be honest and accurate in all communications
- Act promptly to correct erroneous communications for which the practitioner is responsible
- Preserve the free flow of unprejudiced information when giving or receiving gifts by ensuring that gifts are nominal, legal, and infrequent

Examples of Improper Conduct under This Provision:

- A member representing a ski manufacturer gives a pair of expensive racing skis to a sports magazine columnist, to influence the columnist to write favorable articles about the product.
- A member entertains a government official beyond legal limits and/or in violation of government reporting requirements.

COMPETITION

Core Principle: Promoting healthy and fair competition among professionals preserves an ethical climate while fostering a robust business environment.

Intent:

- To promote respect and fair competition among public relations professionals
- To serve the public interest by providing the widest choice of practitioner options

Guidelines:

A member shall:

- Follow ethical hiring practices designed to respect free and open competition without deliberately undermining a competitor
- Preserve intellectual property rights in the marketplace

Examples of Improper Conduct under This Provision:

- A member employed by a "client organization" shares helpful information with a counseling firm that is competing with others for the organization's business.
- A member spreads malicious and unfounded rumors about a competitor in order to alienate the competitor's clients and employees in a ploy to recruit people and business.

DISCLOSURE OF INFORMATION

Core Principle: Open communication fosters informed decision making in a democratic society.

Intent:

- To build trust with the public by revealing all information needed for responsible decision making

Guidelines:

A member shall:

- Be honest and accurate in all communications
- Act promptly to correct erroneous communications for which the member is responsible
- Investigate the truthfulness and accuracy of information released on behalf of those represented
- Reveal the sponsors for causes and interests represented
- Disclose financial interest (such as stock ownership) in a client's organization
- Avoid deceptive practices

Examples of Improper Conduct under This Provision:

- Front groups: A member implements "grass roots" campaigns or letter-writing campaigns to legislators on behalf of undisclosed interest groups.
- Lying by omission: A practitioner for a corporation knowingly fails to release financial information, giving a misleading impression of the corporation's performance.
- A member discovers inaccurate information disseminated via a website or media kit and does not correct the information.
- A member deceives the public by employing people to pose as volunteers to speak at public hearings and participate in "grass roots" campaigns.

SAFEGUARDING CONFIDENCES

Core Principle: Client trust requires appropriate protection of confidential and private information.

Intent:

- To protect the privacy rights of clients, organizations, and individuals by safeguarding confidential information

Guidelines:

A member shall:

- Safeguard the confidences and privacy rights of present, former, and prospective clients and employees
- Protect privileged, confidential, or insider information gained from a client or organization
- Immediately advise an appropriate authority if a member discovers that confidential information is being divulged by an employee of a client company or organization

Examples of Improper Conduct under This Provision:

- A member changes jobs, takes confidential information, and uses that information in the new position to the detriment of the former employer.
- A member intentionally leaks proprietary information to the detriment of some other party.

CONFLICTS OF INTEREST

Core Principle: Avoiding real, potential or perceived conflicts of interest builds the trust of clients, employers, and the publics.

Intent:

- To earn trust and mutual respect with clients or employers
- To build trust with the public by avoiding or ending situations that put one's personal or professional interests in conflict with society's interests

Guidelines:

A member shall:

- Act in the best interests of the client or employer, even subordinating the member's personal interests
- Avoid actions and circumstances that may appear to compromise good business judgment or create a conflict between personal and professional interests
- Disclose promptly any existing or potential conflict of interest to affected clients or organizations
- Encourage clients and customers to determine if a conflict exists after notifying all affected parties

Examples of Improper Conduct under This Provision:

- The member fails to disclose that he or she has a strong financial interest in a client's chief competitor.
- The member represents a "competitor company" or a "conflicting interest" without informing a prospective client.

ENHANCING THE PROFESSION

Core Principle: Public relations professionals work constantly to strengthen the public's trust in the profession.

Intent:

- To build respect and credibility with the public for the profession of public relations
- To improve, adapt and expand professional practices

Guidelines:

A member shall:

- Acknowledge that there is an obligation to protect and enhance the profession
- Keep informed and educated about practices in the profession to ensure ethical conduct
- Actively pursue personal professional development
- Decline representation of clients or organizations that urge or require actions contrary to this Code
- Accurately define what public relations activities can accomplish
- Counsel subordinates in proper ethical decision making
- Require that subordinates adhere to the ethical requirements of the Code

- Report ethical violations, whether committed by PRSA members or not, to the appropriate authority

Examples of Improper Conduct under This Provision:

- A PRSA member declares publicly that a product the client sells is safe, without disclosing evidence to the contrary.
- A member initially assigns some questionable client work to a non-member practitioner to avoid the ethical obligation of PRSA membership.

PRSA MEMBER CODE OF ETHICS PLEDGE

I pledge:

- To conduct myself professionally, with truth, accuracy, fairness, and responsibility to the public;
- To improve my individual competence and advance the knowledge and proficiency of the profession through continuing research and education;
- And to adhere to the articles of the Member Code of Ethics 2000 for the practice of public relations as adopted by the governing Assembly of the Public Relations Society of America.

I understand and accept that there is a consequence for misconduct, up to and including membership revocation.

And, I understand that those who have been or are sanctioned by a government agency or convicted in a court of law of an action that is in violation of this Code may be barred from membership or expelled from the Society.

Canadian Public Relations Society

Declaration of Principles

Reprinted with permission of Canadian Public Relations Society (http://www.cprs.ca).

Members of the Canadian Public Relations Society are pledged to maintain the spirit and ideals of the following stated principles of conduct, and to consider these essential to the practice of public relations.

1. **A member shall practice public relations according to the highest professional standards.** Members shall conduct their professional lives in a manner that does not conflict with the public interest and the dignity of the individual, with respect for the rights of the public as contained in the Constitution of Canada and the Charter of Rights and Freedoms.
2. **A member shall deal fairly and honestly with the communications media and the public.** Members shall neither propose nor act to improperly influence the communications media, government bodies or the legislative process. Improper influence may include conferring gifts, privileges or benefits to influence decisions.

3. **A member shall practice the highest standards of honesty, accuracy, integrity and truth, and shall not knowingly disseminate false or misleading information.** Members shall not make extravagant claims or unfair comparisons, nor assume credit for ideas and words not their own. Members shall not engage in professional or personal conduct that will bring discredit to themselves, the Society or the practice of public relations.
4. **A member shall deal fairly with past or present employers/clients, fellow practitioners and members of other professions.** Members shall not intentionally damage another practitioner's practice or professional reputation. Members shall understand, respect and abide by the ethical codes of other professions with whose members they may work from time to time.
5. **Members shall be prepared to disclose the names of their employers or clients for whom public communications are made and refrain from associating themselves with anyone who would not respect such policy.** Members shall be prepared to disclose publicly the names of their employers or clients on whose behalf public communications are made. Members shall not associate themselves with anyone claiming to represent one interest, or professing to be independent or unbiased, but who actually serves another or an undisclosed interest.
6. **A member shall protect the confidences of present, former and prospective employers/clients.** Members shall not use or disclose confidential information obtained from past or present employers/clients without the expressed permission of the employers/clients or an order of a court of law.
7. **A member shall not represent conflicting or competing interests without the expressed consent of those concerned, given after a full disclosure of the facts.** Members shall not permit personal or other professional interests to conflict with those of an employer/client without fully disclosing such interests to everyone involved.
8. **A member shall not guarantee specified results beyond the member's capacity to achieve.**
9. **Members shall personally accept no fees, commissions, gifts or any other considerations for professional services from anyone except employers or clients for whom the services were specifically performed.**

International Public Relations Association

Code of Conduct for the Ethical Practice of Public Affairs—Code of Brussels

Adopted 2006, building on the Codes of Venice and Athens.
Reprinted with permission of International Public Relations Association (http://www.ipra.org).

RECALLING the Code of Venice 1961 and the Code of Athens 1965, of the International Public Relations Association, which together specify an undertaking of ethical conduct by public relations practitioners worldwide;

RECALLING that the Code of Athens binds public relations practitioners to respect the Charter of the United Nations which reaffirms "its faith in fundamental human rights, in the dignity and worth of the human person";

RECALLING that the Code of Athens binds public relations practitioners to observe the moral principles and rules of the "Universal Declaration of Human Rights";

RECALLING that public affairs is one discipline undertaken by public relations practitioners;

RECALLING that the conduct of public affairs provides essential democratic representation to public authorities;

This Code of Brussels is a code of ethical conduct applying to public relations practitioners worldwide as they conduct public affairs and interact with public authorities including staff and public representatives.

In the conduct of public affairs, practitioners shall:

1. **Integrity.**
   Act with honesty and integrity at all times so as to secure the confidence of those with whom the practitioner comes into contact;
2. **Transparency.**
   Be open and transparent in declaring their name, organisation and the interest they represent;
3. **Dialogue.**
   Establish the moral, psychological and intellectual conditions for dialogue, and recognise the rights of all parties involved to state their case and express their views;
4. **Accuracy.**
   Take all reasonable steps to ensure the truth and accuracy of all information provided to public authorities;
5. **Falsehood.**
   Not intentionally disseminate false or misleading information, and shall exercise proper care to avoid doing so unintentionally and correct any such act promptly;
6. **Deception.**
   Not obtain information from public authorities by deceptive or dishonest means;
7. **Confidentiality.**
   Honour confidential information provided to them;
8. **Influence.**
   Neither propose nor undertake any action which would constitute an improper influence on public authorities;
9. **Inducement.**
   Neither directly nor indirectly offer nor give any financial or other inducement to members of public authorities or public representatives;
10. **Conflict.**
    Avoid any professional conflicts of interest and to disclose such conflicts to affected parties when they occur;
11. **Profit.**
    Not sell for profit to third parties copies of documents obtained from public authorities;
12. **Employment.**
    Only employ personnel from public authorities subject to the rules and confidentiality requirements of those authorities.

13. **Sanctions.**
    Practitioners shall co-operate with fellow members in upholding this Code and agree to abide by and help enforce the disciplinary procedures of the International Public Relations Association in regard to any breaching of this Code.

International Code of Ethics—Code of Athens

Adopted May 1965; modified April 1968.
Reprinted with permission of International Public Relations Association.

CONSIDERING that all Member countries of the United National Organisation have agreed to abide by its Charter which reaffirms "its faith in fundamental human rights, in the dignity and worth of the human person" and that having regard to the very nature of the profession, Public Relations practitioners in these countries should undertake to ascertain and observe the principles set out in this Charter;

CONSIDERING that, apart from "rights," human beings have not only physical or material needs but also intellectual, moral and social needs, and that their rights are of real benefit to them only in-so-far as these needs are essentially met;

CONSIDERING that, in the course of their professional duties and depending on how these duties are performed, Public Relations practitioners can substantially help to meet these intellectual, moral and social needs;

And lastly, CONSIDERING that the use of the techniques enabling them to come simultaneously into contact with millions of people gives Public Relations practitioners a power that has to be restrained by the observance of a strict moral code.

On all these grounds, all members of the International Public Relations Association agree to abide by this International Code of Ethics, and that if, in the light of evidence submitted to the Council, a member should be found to have infringed this Code in the course of his/her professional duties, he/she will be deemed to be guilty of serious misconduct calling for an appropriate penalty.

Accordingly, each member:

SHALL ENDEAVOUR

1. To contribute to the achievement of the moral and cultural conditions enabling human beings to reach their full stature and enjoy the indefeasible rights to which they are entitled under the "Universal Declaration of Human Rights";
2. To establish communications patterns and channels which, by fostering the free flow of essential information, will make each member of the group feel that he/she is being kept informed, and also give him/her an awareness of his/her own personal involvement and responsibility, and of his/her solidarity with other members;
3. To conduct himself/herself always and in all circumstances in such a manner as to deserve and secure the confidence of those with whom he/she comes into contact;
4. To bear in mind that, because of the relationship between his/her profession and the public, his/her conduct—even in private—will have an impact on the way in which the profession as a whole is appraised;

SHALL UNDERTAKE

1. To observe, in the course of his/her professional duties, the moral principles and rules of the "Universal Declaration of Human Rights";
2. To pay due regard to, and uphold, human dignity, and to recognise the right of each individual to judge for himself/herself;
3. To establish the moral, psychological and intellectual conditions for dialogue in its true sense, and to recognise the right of these parties involved to state their case and express their views;
4. To act, in all circumstances, in such a manner as to take account of the respective interests of the parties involved: both the interests of the organization which he/she serves and the interests of the publics concerned;
5. To carry out his/her undertakings and commitments which shall always be so worded as to avoid any misunderstanding, and to show loyalty and integrity in all circumstances so as to keep the confidence of his/her clients or employers, past or present, and of all the publics that are affected by his/her actions;

SHALL REFRAIN FROM

1. Subordinating the truth to other requirements;
2. Circulating information which is not based on established and ascertainable facts;
3. Taking part in any venture or undertaking which is unethical or dishonest or capable of impairing human dignity and integrity;
4. Using any "manipulative" methods or techniques designed to create subconscious motivations which the individual cannot control of his/her own free will and so cannot be held accountable for the action taken on them.

Code of Conduct—Code of Venice

Adopted May 1961.
Reprinted with permission of International Public Relations Association.

A. PERSONAL AND PROFESSIONAL INTEGRITY

It is understood that by personal integrity is meant the maintenance of both high moral standards and a sound reputation. By professional integrity is meant observance of the Constitution rules and, particularly the Code as adopted by IPRA.

B. CONDUCT TOWARDS CLIENTS AND EMPLOYERS

1. A member has a general duty of fair dealing towards his/her clients or employers, past and present.
2. A member shall not represent conflicting or competing interests without the express consent of those concerned.
3. A member shall safeguard the confidences of both present and former clients or employers.
4. A member shall not employ methods tending to be derogatory of another member's client or employer.
5. In performing services for a client or employer a member shall not accept fees, commission or any other valuable consideration in connection with those services

from anyone other than his/her client or employer without the express consent of his/her client or employee, given after a full disclosure of the facts.

6. A member shall not propose to a prospective client or employer that his/her fee or other compensation be contingent on the achievement of certain results; nor shall he/she enter into any fee agreement to the same effect.

C. CONDUCT TOWARDS THE PUBLIC AND THE MEDIA

1. A member shall conduct his/her professional activities with respect to the public interest and for the dignity of the individual.
2. A member shall not engage in practice which tends to corrupt the integrity of channels of public communication.
3. A member shall not intentionally disseminate false or misleading information.
4. A member shall at all times seek to give a faithful representation of the organization which he/she serves.
5. A member shall not create any organization to serve some announced cause but actually to serve an undisclosed special or private interest of a member or his/her client or employer, nor shall he/she make use of it or any such existing organization.

D. CONDUCT TOWARDS COLLEAGUES

1. A member shall not intentionally injure the professional reputation or practice of another member. However, if a member has evidence that another member has been guilty of unethical, illegal or unfair practices, including practices in violation of this Code, he should present the information to the Council of IPRA.
2. A member shall not seek to supplant another member with his employer or client.
3. A member shall co-operate with fellow members in upholding and enforcing this Code.

American Marketing Association

Code of Ethics

Revised July 2003.
Reprinted with permission of the American Marketing Association (http://www.marketing power.com).

Members of the American Marketing Association are committed to ethical professional conduct. They have joined together in subscribing to this Code of Ethics embracing the following topics:

RESPONSIBILITIES OF THE MARKETER

Marketers must accept responsibility for the consequences of their activities and make every effort to ensure that their decisions, recommendations and actions function to identify, serve and satisfy all relevant publics: customers, organizations and society. Marketers' Professional Conduct must be guided by:

1. The basic rule of professional ethics: not knowingly to do harm;
2. The adherence to all applicable laws and regulations;

3. The accurate representation of their education, training and experience; and
4. The active support, practice and promotion of this Code of Ethics.

HONESTY AND FAIRNESS

Marketers shall uphold and advance the integrity, honor and dignity of the marketing profession by:

1. Being honest in serving consumers, clients, employees, suppliers, distributors and the public;
2. Not knowingly participating in conflict of interest without prior notice to all parties involved; and
3. Establishing equitable fee schedules including the payment or receipt of usual, customary and/or legal compensation for marketing exchanges.

RIGHTS AND DUTIES OF PARTIES IN THE MARKETING EXCHANGE PROCESS

Participants in the marketing exchange process should be able to expect that:

1. Products and services offered are safe and fit for their intended uses;
2. Communications about offered products and services are not deceptive;
3. All parties intend to discharge their obligations, financial and otherwise, in good faith; and
4. Appropriate internal methods exist for equitable adjustment and/or redress of grievances concerning purchases.

It is understood that the above would include, but is not limited to, the following responsibilities of the marketer:

IN THE AREA OF PRODUCT DEVELOPMENT AND MANAGEMENT:

- Disclosure of all substantial risks associated with product or service usage;
- Identification of any product component substitution that might materially change the product or impact on the buyer's purchase decision;
- Identification of extra cost-added features.

IN THE AREA OF PROMOTIONS:

- Avoidance of false and misleading advertising;
- Rejection of high-pressure manipulations, or misleading sales tactics;
- Avoidance of sales promotions that use deception or manipulation.

IN THE AREA OF DISTRIBUTION:

- Not manipulating the availability of a product for the purpose of exploitation;
- Not using coercion in the marketing channel;
- Not exerting undue influence over the reseller's choice to handle a product.

IN THE AREA OF PRICING:

- Not engaging in price fixing;

- Not practicing predatory pricing;
- Disclosing the full price associated with any purchase.

IN THE AREA OF MARKETING RESEARCH:

- Prohibiting selling or fund-raising under the guise of conducting research;
- Maintaining research integrity by avoiding misrepresentation and omission of pertinent research data;
- Treating outside clients and suppliers fairly.

ORGANIZATIONAL RELATIONSHIP

Marketers should be aware of how their behavior may influence or impact the behavior of others in organizational relationships. They should not demand, encourage, or apply coercion to obtain unethical behavior in their relationships with others, such as employees, suppliers, or customers.

1. Apply confidentiality and anonymity in professional relationships with regard to privileged information;
2. Meet their obligations and responsibilities in contracts and mutual agreements in a timely manner;
3. Avoid taking the work of others, in whole, or in part, and representing this work as their own or directly benefiting from it without compensation or consent of the originator or owner; and
4. Avoid manipulation to take advantage of situations to maximize personal welfare in a way that unfairly deprives or damages the organization of others.

Any AMA member found to be in violation of any provision of this Code of Ethics may have his or her Association membership suspended or revoked.

Code of Ethics for Marketing on the Internet

PREAMBLE

The Internet, including online computer communications, has become increasingly important to marketers' activities, as they provide exchanges and access to markets worldwide. The ability to interact with stakeholders has created new marketing opportunities and risks that are not currently specifically addressed in the American Marketing Association Code of Ethics. The American Marketing Association Code of Ethics for Internet marketing provides additional guidance and direction for ethical responsibility in this dynamic area of marketing. The American Marketing Association is committed to ethical professional conduct and has adopted these principles for using the Internet, including on-line marketing activities utilizing network computers.

GENERAL RESPONSIBILITIES

Internet marketers must assess the risks and take responsibility for the consequences of their activities. Internet marketers' professional conduct must be guided by:

1. Support of professional ethics to avoid harm by protecting the rights of privacy, ownership and access.
2. Adherence to all applicable laws and regulations with no use of Internet marketing that would be illegal, if conducted by mail, telephone, fax or other media.
3. Awareness of changes in regulations related to Internet marketing.
4. Effective communication to organizational members on risks and policies related to Internet marketing, when appropriate.
5. Organizational commitment to ethical Internet practices communicated to employees, customers and relevant stakeholders.

PRIVACY

Information collected from customers should be confidential and used only for expressed purposes. All data, especially confidential customer data, should be safeguarded against unauthorized access. The expressed wishes of others should be respected with regard to the receipt of unsolicited e-mail messages.

OWNERSHIP

Information obtained from the Internet sources should be properly authorized and documented. Information ownership should be safeguarded and respected. Marketers should respect the integrity and ownership of computer and network systems.

ACCESS

Marketers should treat access to accounts, passwords, and other information as confidential, and only examine or disclose content when authorized by a responsible party.

The integrity of others' information systems should be respected with regard to placement of information, advertising or messages.

Appendix C

Sample Campaigns

Following are four examples of public relations and integrated marketing campaigns. Each of these campaigns recently won a Silver Anvil award from the Public Relations Society of America.

As presented here, these are not the fully articulated campaigns but the summaries and overviews provided to the PRSA in the awards competition. According to PRSA competition guidelines, each Silver Anvil entry is limited to two pages of information, which it breaks down into the following categories:

- *Research:* Quality of original or secondary research used to identify the problem or opportunity and the approaches likely to be successful.
- *Planning:* Objectives, originality, and judgment in selecting strategy and techniques, accuracy of budget, and difficulties encountered.
- *Execution:* How the plan was implemented; materials used; in-progress adjustments to the plan; techniques in winning management's support; other techniques; difficulties encountered; and effectiveness of the program's employment dollar, personnel, and other resources.
- *Evaluation:* Efforts made to identify, analyze, and quantify results and to what degree a program has met its objectives.

Check out the PRSA Silver Anvil website (http://www.prsa.org/awards/index.html) for outlines on all the competition winners since 1968. The annual Silver Anvil competition represents the best of the best, at least as represented by the entries in the national contest.

The following examples from the many 2007 Silver Anvil winners have been selected to give you a model of a particularly effective use of at least one phase of the planning process.

Notice, however, that even the best are inexact in how they use some of the elements of a good campaign that have been presented in this book. For example, some Silver Anvil winners have fuzzy approaches to goals and objectives, others mislabel or blend strategy and tactics, and some use inappropriate evaluation criteria such as advertising equivalency. So when you review the Silver Anvil winners, take each one with a grain of salt. Determine for yourself what particular elements of the campaign are good models for you to follow.

Characteristics of Winning Campaigns

A study of recent recipients of Silver Anvil awards noted some characteristics of award winners. The study was conducted by Catherine Ayles and Courtney Bosworth (2002), both of Florida International University.

A key factor to excellent campaigns is that they begin with solid research. The most common research techniques were interviews with key contacts within a public (65%), telephone interviews (57%), focus groups (38%), and mail surveys (12%).

Secondary research consisted of literature searches (44%), comparative analysis (42%), archival research (25%), media audits (22%), and sales and market-share data (22%). General online research was used in 19% of campaigns. In terms of experimental research, 37% tested messages and 18% tested specific communication tactics.

Ayles and Bosworth note that only 45% benchmarked awareness prior to the campaign. They find this surprising, because 79% set awareness objectives. Silver Anvil judges told the researchers that objectives are the most important aspect of an effective campaign. However, only 43% indicated a time frame in the objectives, and only 35% indicated the amount of change desired. That, in turn, led to weak evaluations.

Common evaluation techniques included message exposure via media placement (73%), audience participation (52%), and positive message content (50%)—leading one judge to caution against "thinly veiled attempts" to equate campaign success with mere news clips.

Additionally, 87% of winning campaigns document behavior change. But only 18% of winning campaigns cite opinion change and 24% note attitude change, suggesting a need for greater attention to evaluating awareness and acceptance objectives that, by necessity, must precede action objectives.

So what indicates a great campaign? Creative execution and measured results, one judge told Ayles and Bosworth. A strategic campaign with clear objectives, targeted messages, and obvious results, said another. Still another said the key to success is careful application of the four-phase process.

The Research Phase

Author's commentary: *The campaign that follows, by TheWadeGroup for Oceana, an environmental organization, features extensive research into various aspects of the topic: science, education, politics, and audience analysis. This research led to a targeted advocacy strategy guiding a comprehensive and multiyear series of tactics that, when implemented, achieved success—an environmental victory on behalf of sea mammals amid the anti-environmental mind-set of a Republican-led U.S. Congress.*

Save Flipper: Don't Kill the Dolphin Deadline

Oceana; TheWadeGroup, Inc., 2007.
Silver Anvil Award of Excellence
Category: Public Affairs, Associations/Nonprofit Organizations

SITUATION OVERVIEW AND SUMMARY

More than 30 years ago, Congress enacted the Marine Mammal Protection Act to protect dolphins, whales and other ocean animals from harm by human activities, such as commercial fishing. Most important is a requirement that commercial fisheries reduce the killing and injury of marine mammals to insignificant levels. Congress set a reasonable timeline for this to occur, but the deadline expired without reaching this goal. Instead of working harder to enforce it, some powerful members of Congress were trying to do away with the Dolphin Deadline altogether. In the last three years, repeated attempts were made by Congress to eliminate the Dolphin Deadline, including proposals by House Resources Committee Chairman Richard Pombo (R–CA) and Rep. Wayne Gilchrest (R–MD), Chairman of the House Subcommittee of Fisheries, Wildlife and Oceans. In 2004 and 2005, Oceana was successful in preventing these bills from coming up for floor action, but 2006 promised to be the real battle to save the Dolphin Deadline. Prospects of achieving any environmental victory in a Republican-controlled Congress were daunting, but Oceana—unlike other environmental organizations—took on the challenge and was prepared with a sophisticated political strategy and a highly targeted PR and advocacy program to Save Flipper.

RESEARCH

Research was conducted initially to substantiate the need for the Dolphin Deadline and was employed strategically during the campaign to refine the program in its aim to change legislative and political environments. Research initiatives included:

Political Analysis

Review of voting records and lobbying history on similar issues to determine key targets; online research of targeted Congressional members; opposition research on Reps. Pombo and Gilchrest; campaign analysis to identify districts with tough Republican races to include in additional targeting; and review of Congressional activity to assess the issue "competition."

Constituent/Voter Targeting

Research by Yale University and Case Western Reserve University in conjunction with phone banks to test and refine advocacy messages.

Polling

Selected Ohio for special polling because of the following:

- It was the home state for key Republican leaders.
- Other key targets were in neighboring states and the poll results could be used in those states.
- Ohio represents "America"—a bellwether state for testing everything from toothpaste to elections.
- Commissioned a prominent Republican pollster to conduct a survey of Ohio Republican voters to quantitatively confirm what campaign activities and other research suggested: Republican voters support the Dolphin Deadline and do not want to kill Flipper.

Science

Primary research was conducted to assess the impacts on marine mammals of not enforcing the Dolphin Deadline, which provided important scientific information in support of Oceana's advocacy messages.

STRATEGY

The campaign's ultimate goal was to prevent any legislation that eliminated the Dolphin Deadline from passing the U.S. House of Representatives. Initially, Rep. Wayne Gilchrest was the primary target. When the bill became poised to move to the House floor, a two-part political strategy was initiated: (1) maintain solid Democratic support, and (2) generate broad Republican support by showing that "protecting Flipper" made good political and policy sense, particularly in a difficult election year (2006). Based on the research, the following PR strategies were implemented to support the legislative objectives:

- Increase the visibility of the Dolphin Deadline issue and differentiate it from the "clutter."
- Show strong voter/constituent support for protecting the Dolphin Deadline ("A vote for the bill is a vote to Kill Flipper").
- Demonstrate that protecting the Dolphin Deadline has important policy implications.

A $135,000 budget provided the resources for the 21-month campaign, the bulk of which occurred between September 2005 and July 2006.

TACTICS

Oceana implemented a broad range of tactics and activities to gain and maintain support for protecting the Dolphin Deadline:

- Developed Dolphin Deadline brochure and outreach kit.
- Placed billboards and newspaper ads in Rep. Gilchrest's district, and displayed ads on the Washington, D.C. metro subway trains and in the Capitol Hill station to brand and "create" the issue.
- Conducted media outreach to key outlets in Washington, D.C. and selected Congressional districts.
- Brought the "Dolphin Brigade," a band of dolphin-costumed lobbyists, to Capitol Hill to ask Congress to Protect the Dolphin Deadline; the Dolphin Brigade commuted to Capitol Hill on the Metro, stopped for coffee at Starbucks, read the newspaper and then got to work—holding a news conference and educating new Hill staff friends about the Dolphin Deadline.
- Organized phone banks in Rep. Gilchrest's and 13 other congressional districts to target and cultivate support from key voters.
- Initiated outreach to opinion leaders in Rep. Gilchrest's district to enlist their support.
- Issued a report, "Pointless Peril: Deadlines and Death Counts," on the results of Oceana's scientific work, which found that nearly 10,000 marine mammals would have been saved in the last five years if the Dolphin Deadline had been enforced; the report was used to demonstrate the consequences of removing the Dolphin Deadline and to provide additional credibility to the key messages.

EVALUATION

Despite widespread skepticism from many, including the environmental community, in July 2006, the U.S. House of Representatives passed legislation (H.R. 4075, Pombo) amending the Marine Mammal Protection Act, but only after it took out language that would have eliminated the Dolphin Deadline. Ultimately, more than 20 environmental groups, which had not been previously engaged in this battle because they believed the legislation could not be beaten in the House and were content to "fix the bill" in the Senate, joined Oceana's efforts.

Additional outcomes included:

- Media coverage in publications important to Capitol Hill and political leadership including the *Washington Times*, *Roll Call*, *Political Hotline*, *Washington Post Express* and *Cleveland Plain Dealer*.
- Successful creation and branding of the Dolphin Deadline concept, which has become the regularly used term by Capitol Hill staff and media when referring to these provisions of the Marine Mammal Protection Act.
- Recruitment of more than 4,000 Republican voters in the target districts to call, e-mail, record a message, or post a yard sign telling their Representative to Save Flipper.
- Recruitment of more than 20 local opinion leaders to sign on to a letter to Rep. Gilchrest urging him to protect the Dolphin Deadline.

The Strategy Phase

Author's commentary: *The following campaign, by Philips Norelco, is an interesting example of strategy directed heavily by psychological insight into the mind of its key public. The company focused on what it calls "innuendo terms" to create a positive impression for male body grooming. Focused as it was on young adult males, the campaign featured edgy humor and online activities. The introduction of a new product was one of the most successful launches in Philips's history.*

Creating Buzzzzzz for Philips Norelco Bodygroom

Philips Norelco; Manning Selvage & Lee, 2007
Silver Anvil Award Winner
Category: Marketing Consumer Products

SITUATION OVERVIEW AND SUMMARY

"Trimming the hedges," "taking a little off the top" and "manscaping"—all innuendo terms for describing the act of a man grooming his body hair. In early Q2, 2006, Philips Norelco was introducing a revolutionary new product to the market, Bodygroom—a total body groomer specifically designed to shave and trim, well . . . everywhere. The program would attract men and deliver the Bodygroom benefits through innuendo humor, online activities and enough conversation around the topic of a "hair-free back, well-groomed shoulders and an extra optical inch" to make Bodygroom one of the most successful launches in Philips's history.

RESEARCH

Philips conducted extensive market research through focus groups and MRI data to better understand the Bodygroom target audience, how they thought about and engaged in the act of grooming down under, and how their purchase decisions were influenced.

The research showed that these were men who:

- Already shaved and trimmed their body hair.
- Tended to be sexually active and are shaving/trimming their body hair to look sexier as opposed to maintenance.
- Whether they are single or in a relationship, they first started trimming or shaving at the advice of their mate.
- Wanted to look their best without looking like they made an effort doing so.
- Experimented and used different tools to body groom, but it's not something they brag about.
- There is a fine line when it comes to their grooming—they are conscious about their appearance, their diet, and their grooming, but not at the expense of their masculinity.

To garner additional insights and build a stronger case for media, MS&L conducted an omnibus survey to delve deeper into men's opinions on body grooming and identify specific behavioral habits. Five hundred men between the ages of 24–45 participated in the national telephone survey which revealed that looking good for a mate/potential mate remains the primary motivation for his body grooming habits. Additionally, the survey results supported the relevance and need for a product like Bodygroom and the overall importance men place on their personal appearance.

STRATEGY

MS&L's challenge was to launch a product designed specifically for shaving below the chin and take it mainstream by sparking dialogue about the art of "manscaping" among a target audience at various levels of grooming maturity; then, use this dialogue to fuel a full-scale media debate over the state of the metrosexual. MS&L aimed to create a fully-integrated campaign that would garner buzz for the Bodygroom product, its functionality and performance benefits, by tapping into the ongoing discussion of male grooming, specifically the "death of the metrosexual," and his return to masculinity. The program was designed to create broad exposure for the Philips Norelco brand, reaching the full-age spectrum of the consumer target, with the end goal of moving product off the shelves.

Specifically, our objectives were:

- Help drive sales of at least 150,000 Bodygroom units before the end of the calendar year.
- Attract 100,000 unique visitors to shaveeverywhere.com during the first eight weeks of launch.
- Generate at least 100 million media impressions surrounding the product and website launch in top-tier long lead consumer media, online, short-lead print dailies, broadcast and blogs.
- Establish Philips Norelco as the brand for body grooming by securing product benefit messages in 90% of long lead coverage.

Our strategic approach to the campaign included reaching men via the channels that are most influential to them—peers, personalities and online—and encourage dialogue among like-minded individuals through targeted communications. We also leveraged men's desire to look their best (yes, down there) by elevating the conversation and raising acceptance levels of body grooming. To achieve these, we executed a multi-faceted media relations campaign using various media—broadcast, online, print and radio—and a range of approaches, such as product-centric, trend and advertising/marketing—to deliver maximum coverage.

TACTICS

Talking Taboo: Capitalizing on Influential Channels ("Shave Beetle Juice": Howard Stern Sirius Radio/OnDemand Segment)

Leveraging the "Howard Effect" to appeal to the brand's target demographic, MS&L decided to officially launch Bodygroom and shaveeverywhere.com through a strategic partnership with the King of All Media, Howard Stern. Understanding the medium was integral to landing a coveted segment on one of the most influential shows for our core consumer. The team spent several weeks researching and understanding the show and identifying topics and trends regularly discussed. Staying true to Stern's format, we enticed producers by enlisting a relevant spokesperson, entertainer Jodie Moore, to demonstrate the merits of Bodygroom on-air. Howard's producers responded by offering one of the show's most well-known characters, Beetle Juice, to serve as our guinea pig and be groomed on air. On May 2, 2006, Bodygroom debuted on a 35-minute branded segment during the *Howard Stern Show* on Sirius Satellite Radio.

The segment, which also aired on *Howard Stern on Demand*, helped generate more than three million immediate media impressions, 300,000 visitors to shaveeverywhere.com, and put Bodygroom on the path to becoming the number one selling product on Amazon.com's Health and Personal Care section. And that was only the first week!

Launching Shaveeverywhere.com

Shaveeverywhere.com was designed to leverage humor and "innuendo" when talking about the taboo act of body grooming. Upon entering the site, guys are greeted by the unabashed "Innuendo Guy," an actor who takes them on a journey of life pre and post Bodygroom. Using "provocative" objects (i.e., kiwis, peaches, carrots,) he demonstrates how the Bodygroom can help men obtain that extra "optical inch" or, at the very least, a renewed level of confidence. Throughout the campaign, the "innuendo" theme was brought to life through branding, special events (see tactics below), media outreach, and a strong online/viral effort. Shaveeverywhere.com became a focal point of our communications outreach, sparking great discussions about manscaping and an interest in the marketing efforts behind the campaign.

Shave Your Kiwis: The Sundance Film Festival

What better way to generate buzz for a new product than to debut it to the most influential celebrities in Hollywood? Months before Bodygroom hit the shelves, MS&L previewed it at the Philips Simplicity Lounge at the Sundance Film Festival. To generate buzz for the product in an otherwise cluttered celebrity freebie environment, we challenged celebrities to defuzz kiwis (a nod to one of the more sensitive body parts that Bodygroom handles with ease) and, in doing so, earn a donation for the American Cinematheque, a non-profit that supports the independent film industry. This relevant cause captured the attention of more than 20 celebrities including Adrian Grenier, Shannon Elizabeth and Kristen Bell, who tackled the task with aplomb.

Shave the Brave: International Home and Housewares Show
Drawing attention to your brand on a crowded trade show floor is no easy task, unless you enlist the help of six burly firemen who are willing to bare it all for charity.

MS&L ignited word-of-mouth buzz for Bodygroom among media and key retailers during its largest retail trade show by creating the "Shave the Brave" charity shave-off between the Chicago Fire Department and the FDNY. The match featured three "hairy" firefighters from each city using Bodygroom to take it all off. The event became the topic of discussion around the trade show floor, resulted in a two-minute segment on the local CBS station in Chicago, and heightened awareness and interest among key retailers such as Amazon.com.

The Optical Inch: Leveraging Man's Desire to Look His Best (The Bare Truth: Local Radio Promotions)
MS&L extended Bodygroom's momentum by creating listener-interactive radio promotions with alternative, rock and sports/talk radio stations in 14 key metropolitan markets, including New York, Los Angeles and Chicago. Utilizing the station DJs to spark chatter and buzz about male body grooming and deliver key product messages, Bodygroom was positioned as the ultimate solution for helping men look their best and assuring them about the confidence of an extra "optical inch"—something very important for those men who are out and about town. Bodygrooms were given away to call-in listeners who confessed to be folically challenged.

Smooth Operator: Awards, Awards, Awards
Recognizing that Bodygroom delivered on its claims of being the best system for male grooming (yes, MS&L staff tested the product), MS&L submitted the product for several category awards, and the results speak for themselves: *Men's Health*: 1st Place in Best in Grooming; *FHM* Grooming Awards: 3rd Place in Best Grooming Innovation. Shaveevery where.com also cleaned up, earning several distinguished awards including Advertising Age's Digital Campaign of the Year, a Gold Lion at Cannes, and two Golds at the New York Festivals [an annual advertising event].

Keeping It Within Reach—Media Relations (Hands-on Media Outreach)
Prior to launch, MS&L conducted one-on-one meetings with target long-lead media to highlight the significant benefits of Bodygroom over other "below the chin" grooming options and engaged them on the overall trend of body grooming. The meetings resulted in an influx of coverage in top-rated magazines including *Men's Health*, *FHM*, *Vibe* and *Complex*. The results of the omnibus survey on men's body grooming habits were released in conjunction with the product "launch" release and were featured in short-lead outlets including *USA Today*, *The New York Times*, *Newsday* and the *Miami Herald*.

Staying Smoooooth: Opportunistic Media
Post launch, MS&L continued to identify media opportunities, including heightened interest in the marketing strategy that enabled us to keep the body grooming trend, shaveeverywhere.com and, most importantly, Philips Norelco Bodygroom top-of-mind among media and consumers. By continuing to identify new story angles and channels, we were able to secure

additional coverage for Bodygroom in national outlets including CNBC's *On the Money*, *Geraldo at Large*, *TV Guide*, *Attack of the Show*, NPR and others.

EVALUATION

Objectives

MS&L aimed to create a fully-integrated campaign that would garner buzz for the Bodygroom product, its functionality and performance benefits by tapping into the ongoing discussion of male grooming, specifically the "death of the metrosexual" and his return to masculinity. The program was designed to create broad exposure for the Philips Norelco brand, reaching the full-age spectrum of the consumer target, with the end goal of moving product off the shelves.

Specifically our objectives were:

- Help drive sales of at least 150,000 Bodygroom units before the end of the calendar year.
- Attract 100,000 unique visitors to shaveeverywhere.com during the first eight weeks of launch.
- Generate at least 100 million media impressions surrounding the product and website launch in top-tier long lead consumer media, online, short-lead print dailies, broadcast and blogs.
- Establish Philips Norelco as the brand for body grooming by securing product benefit messages in 90% of long lead coverage.

MS&L successfully over-delivered a public relations campaign that not only raised awareness and interest in the Philips Norelco Bodygroom, but also helped the brand meet its important and aggressive business objectives. A strategic PR approach helped push the topic of body grooming into the mainstream with consumers and media, and, as a result, this previously taboo topic has become the fodder for water cooler discussions across the U.S.

Exceeding Campaign Objectives

- In only six months, Bodygroom became Philips Norelco's second best-selling SKU [stock-keeping unit], representing 25% of grooming sales for 2006.
- Bodygroom has contributed to a 33% increase in Philips Norelco grooming sales from 2005–2006.
- Philips Norelco went from 0% to 70% share of the electric body grooming category.
- Bodygroom exceeded annual projected sales in the first month of availability.
- Philips Norelco Bodygroom became the number-one ranked product sold on Amazon.com's Health and Personal Care section within two days of the *Howard Stern* segment and remained there for more than eight weeks, earning it the distinction of being one of the most successful personal care product launches in Amazon.com history.
- Shaveeverywhere.com has become an Internet success, attracting more than one million unique visitors within the first month alone. The site continues to entice new and repeat visitors each day, and to date had attracted more than 2 million unique visitors.
- To date, MS&L has nearly doubled the media impressions goal by generating more than 195 million consumer impressions through a range of broadcast, radio, online

> and print media. Highlight placements include: The *New York Times*, *Wall Street Journal*, *USA Today*, *Newsday*, *New York Post*, *Los Angeles Times*, *Business Week*, *Variety*, *Men's Health*, *FHM*, *Advertising Age*, *The Howard Stern Show*, NPR, CNBC's *On the Money*, HBO's *Real Time with Bill Maher*, *Geraldo at Large*, Stuff.com, Adrants.com and many, many more.

Shaveeverywhere.com has been written about on more than 1,500 blogs and received more than 103 positive consumer reviews on Amazon.com. The site currently has more than 13,000 links pointing to it.

The Tactics Phase

Author's commentary: *The following campaign, by Ketchum for FedEx and the Audubon Nature Institute, is a good example of using a variety of tactics, many of them drawn from the inventory of interpersonal communication tactics. Notice that this is a community service campaign that was motivated initially by a desire by the FedEx corporation for more positive media and public attention to what it considered its strong record of social responsibility.*

Flight of the Penguins—A Homecoming Celebration to New Orleans

FedEx Corp. and Audubon Nature Institute; Ketchum, 2007
Silver Anvil Award Winner
Category: Events and Observances

SITUATION OVERVIEW AND SUMMARY

When Hurricane Katrina hit, FedEx leapt to the rescue—providing free logistical support to the Red Cross and FEMA and contributing free shipping services for months after the disaster. Government agencies and the media applauded FedEx's response, with *Fortune* declaring on its cover, "How Wal-Mart, FedEx, and Home Depot got the job done after Katrina." But despite such kudos, the story of FedEx's good work was not resonating with the larger public. In a survey of more than 22,000 U.S. consumers in the fall of 2005, only 39 percent perceived FedEx positively when it came to "supporting good causes." FedEx needed to tell its social responsibility story in a way that would capture the public imagination.

FedEx saw just such an opportunity when the New Orleans Audubon Aquarium of the Americas sought help transporting its 19 penguins and two sea otters back home from their temporary shelter in California for the reopening of the Aquarium in May 2006. The penguins had been the biggest draw at the Aquarium, Louisiana's largest tourist attraction before Katrina, and these "stars" had to be there to make the grand reopening complete.

Working with Ketchum, FedEx created a plan to make the penguins' journey a day-long homecoming that would spotlight FedEx's citizenship while symbolizing the return of life to New Orleans. Capitalizing on the "flight" of these flightless birds, the team broke the journey into three media moments—takeoff, landing and arrival—and surrounded the birds at each stage with the symbolism of traveling dignitaries. The choreographed images of penguins waddling on and off planes and onto purple carpets proved irresistible, with stories and photos of the journey appearing in hundreds of outlets from CNN to YouTube. Attendance at the Aquarium's grand reopening soared over 150% above projected levels, and by the fall of 2006 the FedEx's social responsibility numbers had taken off as well, with those viewing FedEx positively in terms of supporting good causes jumping six percentage points to 45 percent.

RESEARCH

FedEx Social Responsibility

From Harris Interactive, an annual assessment of consumer valuation of 60 companies on corporate reputation, the team learned that the general public did not fully recognize FedEx's corporate social responsibility work, despite its disaster relief efforts and its active support of numerous charitable organizations. In a fall 2005 survey of more than 22,000 U.S. consumers, only 39 percent of those polled perceived FedEx positively when it came to "supporting good causes" and 36 percent of those responded that they were "not sure" if FedEx supports good causes at all. Insight: The team needed to find a compelling narrative that would showcase the corporate citizenship of FedEx.

Audubon Aquarium of the Americas

Research showed that Katrina's impact on the aquarium was devastating. Before the hurricane, it had been Louisiana's most popular tourist destination with more than 900,000 annual visitors, and the penguins were the Aquarium's #1 attraction. In the hurricane's aftermath, most of the 10,000 fish and animals in the facility perished. Insight: Helping the Aquarium reopen with a splash would be a high-profile way to draw attention to all of FedEx's disaster relief work.

Media/Consumer Research

Following the hurricane, some of the most popular media stories focused on the plight of the region's wildlife, including the aquarium's penguins and sea otters. Animal rescue organizations also received widespread public support. In the months after Katrina there had not yet been a standout animal "homecoming" story. Insight: A well-crafted homecoming story about the famous "flightless" birds would captivate the public and symbolize a return to life in New Orleans.

Transporting the Pandas

From FedEx's work bringing the pandas from China to the National Zoo in Washington, D.C., the team learned that the media wanted to tell the whole journey story and that airports were the perfect place to showcase FedEx's work—with branded trucks, planes and equipment. Insight: Break up the homecoming journey into its component parts, creating a day-long narrative arc from takeoff to landing to arrival at the Aquarium—creating media moments at the airports in Oakland and New Orleans.

STRATEGY

Objectives

1. Secure traditional and new media coverage in the 20 target FedEx local markets.
2. Increase awareness among consumers of FedEx community responsibility and Gulf Coast recovery efforts.
3. Improve consumer perception of FedEx as a socially responsible company and a "supporter of good causes," as measured by the Harris Interactive Reputation Quotient Survey.

Specific strategies included:

- Make the homecoming of the flightless stars of the Aquarium symbolize a return to life in New Orleans.
- Script a day-long narrative from takeoff to landing to Aquarium arrival, with key media moments at the Oakland and New Orleans airports.

Audience Analysis

- Consumer audience of men and women aged 18—54, with an emphasis on 20 FedEx local markets.
- New Orleans community influencers.

TACTICS

The Flight of the Flightless Stars

Create three distinct, localized, and highly visual media opportunities over the 20-hour journey.

- Takeoff: The special delivery began at 2 a.m., when the penguins and sea otters received a police escort to the Oakland International Airport and were given a royal send-off by local media and FedEx employees. The animals said "Bon Voyage" to California as they boarded the FedEx plane.
- Landing: After four hours in flight, the animals arrived at Louis Armstrong International Airport in New Orleans and were greeted by a local jazz band, aquarium employees and media. Patience, the penguins' matriarch, walked down the purple carpet and paused for media shots before she and the other animals traveled in a motorcade of specially branded FedEx Special Delivery vehicles and a police escort.
- Arrival: At 3 p.m., aquarium handlers carried the animals home as a large crowd of New Orleans residents cheered them on during the "Homecoming Celebration" event. The transport culminated with an event at the aquarium for more than 250 key New Orleans influencers. FedEx made a check presentation of $100,000 for the ongoing care of the penguin habitat and thanked the local influencers for their continued rebuilding efforts, reinforcing the FedEx commitment to the community. Attendees received toy penguins, a lasting reminder of the "Flight of the Penguins."
- Interactive/Visual Elements: The team developed interactive elements for new media and compelling visuals of the adorable animals. A unique website was created to showcase animated videos that illustrated the penguins boarding a plane, flying cross country and even enjoying tasty fish snacks.
- Workplace Elements: FedEx utilized the shipment as an opportunity to increase awareness of the company's community relations activities among its workforce. In addition, FedEx thanked employees based in the Gulf Coast for their continued dedication by providing complimentary tickets to the aquarium.

Budget: $100,000; OOP's [out-of-pocket expenses]: $36,000, Donations: $100,000 for the penguin habitat.

EVALUATION

Secure traditional and new media coverage in the 20 target FedEx local markets. The "Flight of the Penguins" captured the attention of the world with more than 300 clips on national and international network, cable and local television affiliates, 150 print articles and interactive and on-line coverage. Coverage ran in 211 U.S. media markets, including all 20 of the FedEx target local markets. In addition to traditional media, FedEx leveraged unique outlets like Youtube.com, where a "Flight of the Penguins" segment was viewed more than 500 times. Also, a photograph of Patience, the penguin, on the purple carpet was voted the most popular image on Yahoo! the day of the shipment.

1. Increase awareness among consumers of FedEx social responsibility and commitment to ongoing efforts in the Gulf Coast. The unique website created for fedex.com was accessed by more than 12,000 users, three percent of the overall traffic to the site, on the day after the shipment, a compelling number considering most visitors utilize the site for business and tracking purposes. In addition, with the success of the event, aquarium attendance soared as more than 17,000 people visited during its opening weekend—157 percent above projected figures. Visitors were reminded of the FedEx delivery through a specially branded plaque next to the penguin's habitat.
2. Improve consumer perception of FedEx as a socially responsible company and a "supporter of good causes," as measured by the Harris Interactive Reputation Quotient Survey. In 2006, 45 percent of those polled in this year's Harris RQ [Reputation Quotient] survey positively perceived FedEx as "supporting good causes" marking a statistically significant increase of six percent year-over-year. In addition, the number of those responding "not sure" about the causes supported by FedEx decreased by two percentage points, also a statistically significant shift given the size of the overall sample.

Evaluation Phase

Author's commentary: *This international campaign, by Burson-Marsteller and Sagepath for Coca-Cola, has an evaluation phase worthy of its scope. Focused as it was on Coca-Cola's employees and their understanding of the company's values and culture, the campaign generated much excitement throughout its global locations. The evaluation research included both content analysis of thousands of employee-posted blogs and a comparative employee attitude and opinion survey, as well as an environmental analysis based on product sales.*

Walking the Talk to Sustainable Growth: Blog Blast '06

Coca-Cola Company; Burson-Marsteller, Sagepath, 2007
Silver Anvil Award of Excellence Winner
Category: Internal Communications for Businesses with More than 10,000 Employees

SITUATION OVERVIEW AND SUMMARY

The Coca-Cola Company (TCCC) had been experiencing declining market share and slowed growth in recent years, attributed to declining carbonated soft drink sales, increasing health and wellness trends, a series of leadership changes and increasing competition in the industry. The Company's 2005 "Manifesto for Growth" sought to address these and other concerns by outlining a plan to reinvent itself as a sustainable growth company.

As a part of this new commitment, TCCC realized it needed to make fundamental changes to its culture and work environment. To kick off this effort and set a tone for the future, the Company designed a global campaign to help accelerate its transformation into a high-performance culture by inspiring employee commitment to its values: leadership, passion, integrity, accountability, collaboration, innovation and quality.

"Blog Blast '06" was a seven-day worldwide blog discussion about the Company's values. The event engaged TCCC's more than 50,000 employees in over 200 countries to define what it means to "live the values" at the Company and describe how specific behaviors and actions could drive better business results.

RESEARCH

Using secondary research, TCCC built a sound case for the campaign by citing the profound impact high-performance cultures can have on a company's performance. For example, according to the Corporate Leadership Council, over a ten year period, companies who leverage their cultures well experience increases in average revenues of 516% more than companies with weaker cultures. Ernst & Young estimates that strength of corporate culture, among other non-financial criteria, is a key factor that constitutes on average 25% of an investor's decision on where to invest.

TCCC leveraged the results of its global Employee Insights Survey—a tool used to measure factors that contribute to and drive engagement—to provide a benchmark for the campaign's success and to track how well it is "moving the needle." As a basis for measuring success (with 100% being the highest score), the Company wanted to improve scores in Employee Engagement (74%), Diversity and Fairness (69%), Communication and Awareness (65%), Performance Management (68%), and Leadership (54%). Tracking these categories over time would ultimately help TCCC measure the effectiveness of its culture-building efforts and their impact on the growth and success of its business.

STRATEGY

The overall strategy for the campaign was to define, communicate, embed and measure the behaviors associated with the Company's values. "Blog Blast '06" engaged employees worldwide to better define its values, how the Company "gets things done," and how those actions drive business results. The objectives of the campaign were to:

- Accelerate the transformation of TCCC's work environment and culture by inspiring employees' passion and commitment to the values;
- Re-engage employees in the business strategy and increase awareness of each employee's important role in driving business results; and
- Engage employees in a collaborative manner to define what it means to live the values, to describe what makes the company unique, competitive and engaging, and how those actions drive business results.

The team had only four months to fully develop and execute the campaign and to summarize the results of "Blog Blast '06" within a tight project budget of $455,655. Important milestones in the planning process included obtaining support from Executive Committee members and engaging global corporate leadership.

After "Blog Blast '06" concluded, the campaign team would identify the top behaviors for each value, obtain senior management approval, and broadly communicate and reinforce these behaviors within the organization. Later, the behaviors would be embedded into key business policies and procedures.

TACTICS

TCCC worked with Burson-Marsteller (B-M) and Sagepath to quickly develop and execute an extensive, high-profile internal marketing campaign to drive awareness, build excitement and encourage participation. Important components included educating the workforce on how to use the technology, and overcoming challenges such as cultural sensitivities to offering constructive feedback to senior management. Pre-event marketing activity included the creation of both digital and print promotional pieces that were used at Coca-Cola offices around the world. A "Global Activation Team" of internal communications professionals was established to build regional interest and translate and customize promotional items to adequately reach local employees. In addition, extensive correspondence with various internal audiences was maintained in the months leading up to the event, including memos, presentations, intranet articles, email invitations, plasma screen advertisements and a video blog tutorial. Pre-event outreach culminated in a video message from CEO Neville Isdell talking about this important time in the Company's history and personally inviting employees to participate in "Blog Blast '06."

On each day of the event, at 7:00pm ET, an email was distributed to all TCCC employees announcing the start of a new values discussion and inviting employees to participate. Each discussion was hosted by two Executive Committee members, who would post comments and questions to initiate and facilitate discussion throughout the day. During the event, the team posted daily polling questions on the Company's intranet site, probing deeper into themes raised during the previous day's discussion. These questions were used to further analyze reactions to discussion topics.

EVALUATION

An in-depth, qualitative analysis was conducted on all Blog Blast entries, revealing 29 distinctive themes and 41 unique types of workplace behaviors. An analysis of the distribution of behaviors by value and by business group revealed insights into what employees say each value "should" and "should not look like" at The Coca-Cola Company (see Blog Blast '06 Results Global Report). This analysis enabled TCCC to identify specific behaviors associated with each value; and the behaviors are being embedded into business processes and procedures such as the Company's performance management process.

The 2,409 employee posts from more than 45 countries and the 136,862 employee page views demonstrate significant engagement. In fact, more than 30,000 page views were captured on the first day alone, exceeding participation rates in similar events hosted at two other Fortune 100 companies. Employee feedback about the discussion was overwhelmingly positive, and the event unleashed a tremendous amount of passion, energy and excitement for the Company and the Manifesto for Growth, which continues to be fostered in follow-up internal communication activities.

One of the key measures for this initiative was to inspire employees' passion and commitment to the Company's values. A positive impact can be seen in the Employee Insights Survey results indicating significant improvements in the following key categories:

	2005 Employee Insights Survey Results	2006 Employee Insights Survey Results	% Change
Employee Engagement	74%	79%	+5%
Diversity and Fairness	69%	77%	+8%
Communication and Awareness	65%	75%	+10%
Performance Management	68%	76%	+8%
Leadership	54%	64%	+10%

"Blog Blast '06" provided a forum for a worldwide conversation about TCCC's values and culture, but it also provided an opportunity to understand what employees think the Company needs to do to achieve the ultimate goal of sustainable growth. TCCC recognizes that much work is still needed, however this initiative contributed significantly to the Company's vision of driving long-term sustainable growth by accelerating the transformation of the organization's culture. Ultimately, the Company's success is truly measured by its shareholders, and in that area it continues to deliver, with a share price that increased approximately 20% in 2006 and exceeding Wall Street estimates eight quarters in a row.

Appendix D

Effective Media Engagement

Media engagement deals with the various philosophical and practical ways an organization interacts with the news media. Sometimes this is called **media training** or **interview training**, though "engagement" suggests much more than merely practicing certain techniques. Rather, it involves a mindset through which an organization effectively and energetically engages the media as part of its overall efforts toward advancing its mission and promoting its bottom-line goals.

What follows is an approach drawn from various actual media-interview training programs and crisis-communication consultations developed by the author, who has provided such training in both corporate and nonprofit settings. The principles themselves are straightforward and are drawn from standard approaches toward effective engagement with the media.

Reputation. The first part of effective media engagement focuses on reputation. This section is presented as a discussion-starter with the participation of both top- and mid-level management of organizations as well as their senior support staff. It is important, for example, not only to help a program director or corporate vice president be effective in communicating on behalf of the organization but for administrative assistance to help create an environment that gives priority to opportunities presented through the media. This section seeks to provide insight into the role of the news media in molding the organization's reputation with various important constituent groups. Its aim is to help organizational leaders better understand both the benefits that a healthy relationship with the news media offers and the role they can play in enhancing that relationship.

Credibility. The second section is presented as a hands-on coaching of individuals likely to find themselves in front of cameras and microphones. It flows from three professional observations:

1. The media will report on an organization in good times and bad, with or without organizational involvement, though the organization can impact that reporting positively or negatively.
2. By becoming more competent in communicating through the news media, spokespersons can extend the organization's message and foster public support for its mission.
3. Every interview offers the organization an opportunity to increase its credibility and enhance its reputation.

Crisis. Effective media engagement reaches its advanced stage with concepts for organizational administrators who need to communicate in times of crisis. The premise is that, while a certain amount of crisis is inevitable within any organizations, their consequences can be controlled. Indeed, organizations can turn a crisis into an opportunity to enhance its credibility and its position vis-à-vis its many publics. The objectives of this section are directed toward public relations managers and other organizational executives:

- To increase awareness and understanding of both the complexity of crises as well as the opportunities for successfully managing them.
- To increase confidence that they can effectively manage crisis situations.
- To enhance their crises management skills.

Reputation

The dictionary defines *reputation* as "honor, credit, recognition or esteem given to a person or organization." Reputation lies at the heart of strategic communication. Effective engagement of news media requires a solid appreciation of the role that reputation plays in the life of an organization.

Structurally, this section presents a series of professional observations, followed by points for discussion. It is meant to be used in a group setting, with a public relations professional guiding organizational executives through an active discussion of how reputation affects their organization and how they might impact that process.

Reputation and Performance

Reputation involves perception. The reputation of an organization is the estimation by which it is commonly held, whether favorable or unfavorable. Reputation is based both on what people know about us and what they feel about us based on that knowledge.

Reputation should reflect performance. Ideally, what people think of the organization's performance will mirror its actual performance. More often, however, there is a distortion between our performance (what we do and how well we do it) and their perception (what people know and think about what we do).

> ### *Discussion Points*
>
> How important is your organization's reputation to your job? Is your job unaffected by your organization's reputation?

Reputation as a Strategic Tool

A good reputation has practical value. In general, a positive reputation can give an organization a competitive advantage that others cannot easily match. What is your organization's reputation? Answer this carefully, based not on wishful thinking but on an honest assessment of how others perceive you.

A good reputation is an insurance policy. Especially in times of trouble, your organization's good reputation can maintain credibility and goodwill. These, in turn, give supporters reasons to continue their trust, defer criticism, balance the picture, and generally maintain their support.

> ### *Discussion Points*
>
> Does your organization have the ability to shape its reputation? To what extent is this possible?

Reputation Management

Every organization can enhance its reputation. Reputation is manageable. It can be molded and developed by the way we actively and strategically interact with important groups of stakeholders. Reputation management involves research, strategic planning, deliberate implementation of that plan, and continual monitoring and evaluation.

Every organization can also jeopardize its reputation. Reputation will suffer if, through misjudgment or neglect, an organization fails to remain credible or responsive with important groups or if it does not communicate accurate and positive information about ourselves.

> ### *Discussion Point*
>
> How important do you think the news media are in developing your organization's reputation?

Reputation and News Media

The news media help shape an organization's reputation. Newspapers, radio, and television offer opportunities for organizations to proactively present messages that strengthen their reputation and promote their mission. The media also provide opportunities to respond to media inquiries, presenting positive messages, and minimizing negative impressions.

Organizations risk their good reputation by not responding to media inquiries. The media *will* report on your organization when they choose to. The issue is *to what extent* the organization will effectively and positively impact such reporting. If your voice is absent from the media, you give up the opportunity to talk with your publics, allowing others to interpret you to the community.

> ### *Discussion Point*
>
> What offices or entities within your organization should try to influence the organization's reputation?

Reputation as a Participant Activity

Your reputation is everybody's business. Public relations and similar offices may manage publicity and promotional activities that affect the organization's reputation. But ultimately, everyone associated with your organization can help or hurt its reputation. Consciously or not, everything said and done by management, employees, volunteers, even customers has an impact on the organization's reputation.

Your reputation is fragile. Like an old-growth forest ravaged by fire, a reputation can be destroyed in minutes. All associated with an organization must be continuously aware that what they do and say affect the reputation. Poor delivery of services and negative publicity easily lead to dissatisfied and angry consumers, the ultimate threat to reputation.

> ### Discussion Point
>
> How have recent events that have been reported in the news media affected your organization's reputation?

Headlines and Bottom Lines

News coverage can affect many different publics of an organization, often in unanticipated ways. Consider each of the following headlines. This exercise uses the examples of a nonprofit organization (a university), but the principles can apply to any other nonprofit, as well as a corporation, membership organization or government agency.

- Headline: "Low, Delayed Graduation Rates at Local University Cited in Report"
- Headline: "Coed Nabbed for Prostitution; Blames Snafu in Financial-Aid Office"
- Headline: "Local Student Charged with Arson, Attempted Murder for Firebombing Car of Fellow Student"
- Headline: "Local University Drops in Rankings of Top Colleges, Universities"
- Headline: "Local Professor Accused of Anti-Gay Harassment"
- Headline: "Dorm Fire Leaves 300 Homeless After Explosion by Student Cooking Drugs"

> ### Discussion Points
>
> Consider each of the above headlines from three different perspectives:
>
> 1. As the parent of a high school student considering attending this university, how does the headline affect your thoughts about the university? What is the likelihood that you and your child will want to be associated with this institution?
> 2. As a student or faculty member here, how does the headline affect your pride in being associated with this university? Do you have any concerns about what others think of you and your colleagues?
> 3. As director of public relations for the university, what alternative headline would you have preferred in this situation? What could your institution have done to warrant your preferred headline?

Media Relations

Media relations is the subset of public relations and marketing communication dealing with an organization's ongoing involvement with news media for the purpose of enhancing its reputation and promoting its mission.

Media Relations . . . from the Media Side

Reporters want news. News is information that is timely, accurate, and of significance to a particular audience. It may show subjects in a positive or negative light. In gathering news, reporters try to talk with many news sources: insiders, experts, and people involved in the issue. They expect access to public institutions such as the university. They try to report all sides without taking sides.

Reporters are skeptical. They see it as their mission to probe beneath the surface, to not take things at face value, and to seek out hidden agendas. They consider nothing to be none of their business. And if they catch someone doing something wrong and expose that, they see this as the rendering of public service.

Not all reporters are alike. Each medium of public communication has its own style of operating, and reporters have differing practices for interviewing:

- Newspaper reporters often work over the telephone. Their interviews may be either brief or in-depth. They may ask questions on side issues as well as the main topic, and they may quote extensively.
- Radio reporters usually do interviews in person, though they sometimes do brief telephone interviews to get a "sound bite."
- Television reporters interview their news sources on camera. A television reporter may talk with a news source on camera for five minutes or more and then use only one or two sentences during a newscast. Television reporters are interested in photogenic situations that are colorful, active, and interesting.
- Bloggers or Internet journalists often are independent agents who value their autonomy and often are advocates of a particular social or partisan perspective.

> ### *Discussion Point*
> What does your organization want from reporters?

Media Relations . . . from the Organization's Side

Your organization wants fair treatment. As the subject of a news report, it wants, needs, and deserves reporting that is fair and professional. This means expecting reporters to treat the organization with objectivity and neutrality. The organization also wants to be recognized as a contributing and respected member of its industry or profession and of its community.

Your organization benefits from a healthy relationship with the media. With fair and accurate reporting, your organization benefits by having a strong and respected voice in its industry or profession. Healthy media relations enables the organization to be recognized as a course of commentary about matters of interest to the community. It also gives the organization the opportunity to balance criticism. In short, healthy media relations can allow the organization to maximize "good news" and minimize "bad news."

> ### *Discussion Point*
>
> How can your organization use the news media to its advantage?

Media Relations . . . from Both Sides

Your organization communicates in two ways: proactively and reactively. Proactively, the organization provides story ideas and offers of interviews to reporters. It also disseminates news releases and fact sheets, and it presents speeches and news conferences. Reactively, the organization response to reporters' questions and allegations.

Reporters have many news sources. In gathering information for their stories, reporters contact many different organizations and individuals. They check the validity of their information and question the motivations of their sources. Here are some of the ways they might obtain information about your organization:

- Official sources such as the public relations office and organizational spokespersons, through information vehicles such as news releases and interviews.
- Publications such as an employee newsletter, member magazine, mailings and other semipublic publications, as well as information at your organization's website.
- Public records such as documents and statements involving regulatory agencies, as well as police and legal records.
- Unofficial sources such as employees, customers, and other persons willing to speak about (but not necessarily on behalf of) your organization. This includes people who may be misinformed or disgruntled.
- Rumor and scuttlebutt, hearsay and gossip.

> ### *Discussion Points*
>
> In what ways has your organization communicated with the media, both proactively and reactively? What sources of information have the media used in reporting on your organization?

Reputational Bumps and Bruises

Which puts the bigger dent in your organization's reputation? Consider the following.

- Inadequacy, or arrogance?
- Bad judgment, or dishonesty?

- Negative reports, or poor performance?
- Unpopular decisions, or unexplained actions?
- Being scrutinized, or being found unresponsive?

Twelve Principles of Effective Media Relations

1. A relationship is both inevitable and necessary between your organization and the media. The behavior of the organization will determine if this relationship is good or bad.
2. The organization should publicly speak with one voice in any situation, by designating and preparing a single spokesperson authorized to speak in the name of the organization.
3. The person closest to the situation should be the designated spokesperson, or at least should be in close communication with the spokesperson.
4. "No comment" is never an option. Every bona fide question should be answered.
5. The organization should look upon reporters as allies rather than as intruders or enemies.
6. The organization should consider itself accountable to its various publics: employees, volunteers, customers, donors, supporters, and the community. Further, it should view the news media as one of the vehicles available for communicating with these constituencies.
7. The organization should not expect to control the media's agenda or their assessment of what is newsworthy. But you can help add issues to that agenda.
8. Public relations professionals should always be "in the loop" in all newsworthy situations, especially those with negative potential.
9. Reporters should be accommodated with professional assistance such as parking permits and a functioning media room.
10. The organization should expect that it occasionally will "take a hit" in the media. The response should be to accept this, try to understand it, and get over it as quickly as possible. Lingering hostility to reporters never serves the organization's interests.
11. Media skepticism and scrutiny can be more bearable when the organization interacts with reporters in a timely manner and with openness, accuracy and candor.
12. Media coverage is considerably more credible than either advertising or the use of internal media such as brochures, publications and websites. Effective use of the news media gives the organization a believable voice in the community.

Points for Consideration

True or False? I shouldn't waste time talking with reporters who are already biased against my organization.

Consider this: If you want people to support you, first they have to understand you. Much of their impression about your organization comes through the media. Your time spent with reporters is not doing the reporter a favor; rather it is setting up a means of communication with your publics.

True or False? Reporters don't understand what I'm doing and they always get it wrong, so I should avoid them.

Consider this: You can direct the tone of an interview. Invest whatever time it takes to educate reporters about what you are doing. Prepare for the interview, perhaps by providing a glossary and background sheet if necessary. Explain the significance of your actions and opinions.

True or False? If I don't talk to reporters, I won't get into trouble.

Consider this: If you don't talk to reporters, people won't know how honest, competent, and effective you are.

True or False? It's a real compliment to hear that our organization is one of the best-kept secrets in our area or within our industry or profession.

Consider this: Being called a best-kept secret is an insult to everyone associated with your organization. It means that neither you nor your colleagues are doing enough to share information about your organization's achievements and boast about its successes.

Credibility

Effective media engagement involves an applied set of skills and practices to help organizational spokespeople. This section offers tips and techniques on various aspects of interviewing, from the standpoint of the person being interviewed.

Interview Settings

There are at least nine different ways that an organizational spokesperson or executive might be interviewed by the news media:

1. *Individual news interview.* This is the most common interview situation you are likely to face. You are being interviewed by a single reporter for print, radio, or television. The interview may take place in your office, in a studio, or in a remote location. Unless it is an ambush situation, you will have time to prepare for the news interview. Maintain eye contact and respond directly to the reporter. Ignore microphones and/or camera operators.
2. *Straight-to-the-camera interview.* You are being interviewed by a single television reporter who is doubling as the camera operator. Look directly at the camera, but visualize an individual member of your audience and speak to him.
3. *Telephone interview.* You are being interviewed over the telephone by a reporter. This is most commonly used by print reporters, who will either record your voice or simply take notes. It is used sometimes by radio reporters and only infrequently by television reporters. Maintain a professional demeanor and posture even though you cannot be seen. Maintain a professional control of your voice. Handle this interview as carefully as you would a face-to-face encounter. Always presume you are being taped throughout the entire telephone interview.
4. *News conference interview.* News conferences have three parts: You present a brief statement or announcement. You then distribute prepared printed materials to a gathering of reporters from various media. This is followed by a question-answer session with these reporters. News conferences generally are videotaped; on rare occasions, they may be broadcast live.
5. *Panel interview or debate.* You are one of two or more interviewees being questioned by reporters from various media. Panels and debates often are held before an audience and many are broadcast live. They often involve questions from a panel of interviewers

and/or from members of the audience. Before the interview, investigate the position of your co-panelists, and then frame your message with their positions in mind. Be prepared to fight for a fair share of time to present your message. Avoid shouting matches, but do not hesitate to differentiate your position from that of others.

6. *Call-in radio interview.* This is an increasingly popular format for live radio. You are interviewed in a radio studio by a host, and at some point during the interview you will respond to phone-in callers. Listen carefully to questions, and respond as personally as possible to each individual caller.
7. *Call-in television interview.* This is similar to the call-in format for live radio, except that you are being televised as you interact with the on-camera host and the phone-in callers.
8. *Videoconference interview.* This is a live format similar to a call-in interview, except that your audience can see you on a video monitor. Usually the audience gathers at remote sites, where they can telephone questions to you. As with a simple call-in interview, listen carefully to questions and respond in a personal tone.
9. *Online interview.* Sometimes distance prevents one of the above real-time interview formats, so reporters occasionally resort to providing a set of questions via e-mail. This gives the news source time to carefully weight the message, but make sure you don't become long-winded in responding to such questions.

If You Are Asked for an Interview

1. Make sure you understand the topic to be discussed.
2. Decide if you can do the interview. Do you have the basic information? Being available to reporters is more important than having every last detail on an issue, which would be more than you'd need anyhow. Being unavailable breeds suspicion among the organization's publics. It also ignores an opportunity to present your message, which will be accepted by somebody else, often a person with lesser qualifications to speak authoritatively.
3. Are you the appropriate person to speak on behalf of your organization? If not, try to suggest another news source. Don't put reporters off without good cause. But if you must decline the interview opportunity, tell them why.
4. Ask the reporter to identify the source of the information on which the interview will be based. If it is information with which you are unfamiliar, try to get a copy of the source material; usually the reporter will provide you with a copy or direct you to the source.
5. Ask about the nature, length, and eventual use of the interview. Find out if the interview will be taped or live.

Dress for Interview Success

Organizational spokespeople appearing on television need to dress appropriately. Generally this means wearing conservative professional attire that you would normally wear at work, avoiding fashion fads that might distract some viewers and detract from your effectiveness as a credible representative of your organization. Here are some reminders:

1. Avoid busy patterns such as narrow stripes, small checks, plaids, herringbone, and other clothing with tight repeating patterns. These can cause video pictures to flutter.
2. Avoid large and flashy items of jewelry, especially necklaces, earrings, and tie pins. Avoid clothing with large, shiny buttons.
3. Avoid extremes of black and white. Instead prefer medium and dark colors in place of black. Prefer light pastels in place of white. Ideal professional and television-friendly attire is a conservatively cut suit of gray or navy, with a shirt or blouse of pale blue, pink or beige, and a scarf or tie of a strong but not garish accent color.
4. Use medium colors. If you have light or medium skin tones, prefer medium and dark colors. People with darker skin tones may use medium or light colors. In any case, avoid strong or loud colors, especially bright reds, oranges, and purples except as accents (such as ties and scarves).
5. If the interview is to be conducted while you are seated, wear clothing that does not constrict your neck. Avoid clothing that bulks up around your chest and shoulders.
6. Just before the interview, make a final check for gaping buttons and mussed hair. Men should check for socks that are too short.
7. Don't worry about eyeglasses. If you normally wear glasses, wear them for the interview; to not wear them will probably make you uncomfortable and you will look unnatural to others. Let camera operators and lighting crews worry about eliminating any glare. Avoid wearing lenses that darken under bright lights.
8. Consider wearing distinctive professional clothing if you are to be interviewed in your work setting. A lab coat, for example, would be very appropriate for an on-site interview. Generally it is not a good idea to wear such clothing in a studio setting.

Interview Posture

Your posture will go a long way in helping you present a positive image during televised interviews. Here are a few reminders.

- Sit with your back straight, knees together, both feet on the floor. Avoid twitching or moving your legs and feet.
- Don't slouch into a comfortable position; on television, casual looks sloppy. Even in a radio or print interview, your posture will spill over into your voice.
- If you feel a need to reposition yourself, lean in toward the interviewer and/or camera. Never lean away.
- Place your hands in your lap or in the arms of the chair.
- Use your hands naturally, but avoid nervous movements. Don't drum your fingers.
- Maintain eye contact with the interviewer.

Interview Planning

Here is a threefold approach to interview planning. In the first part, consider the following points of planning, which relate specifically to the organization.

- *What:* State the issue clearly and concisely.
- *Significance:* Note the importance of the issue and its potential impact on your organization.

- *Who:* List individuals and groups involved.
- *When:* Indicate any relevant time factors (future focus is preferred).
- *Where:* Note any relevant locations or boundaries (try to focus on local situations).
- *Communication History:* Consider the nature and extent of your previous communication on this issue.
- *Credibility:* Consider how people perceive your organization's credibility on this issue.
- *Organizational Expectations:* Note what your organization wants from you regarding this situation.
- *Motivation:* Summarize your motivation for being involved in this issue.

In the second part of your planning, consider the following points as they relate to the media audience and the organization's publics.

- *Key Publics:* List those groups most notably affected on this issue.
- *Understanding the Publics:* Note the wants, interests, needs, and expectations of the key publics you have identified.
- *Benefits:* Summarize the benefits and advantages your organization offers each key public.
- *Media Interest:* Indicate why the media are (or could become) interested in this issue.
- *Media Expectations:* Note if the media want to or might interview you.
- *Opponents*: List any groups or individuals who are likely to oppose you on this issue.
- *Balance*: Indicate the nature and credibility of opposing perspectives.

Finally, conclude the planning by considering objectives and strategy.

- *Awareness Objectives*: Indicate the impact you hope to make about the publics' knowledge and understanding on this issue.
- *Acceptance Objectives*: Indicate the impact you hope to make about the publics' interest and attitudes on this issue.
- *Action Objectives*: Indicate the impact you hope to make about the publics' opinions and behavior around this issue.
- *Tone of Message*: Note appeals to authority, fear, or guilt, or appeals for confidence, responsibility, calm, caution, and the like.
- *Visuals*: Try to incorporate visual elements and interesting locations into your interview.
- *Power Words*: Identify any particularly powerful and memorable words or phrases that you might incorporate into your message.

Preparing for the Interview

1. Never try to "play it by ear."
2. Know yourself. Rely on your own expertise.
3. Know your audience.
4. Know what you want to say.
5. Know what impact you hope to make.
6. Anticipate questions a reporter may ask.

7. Think of an anecdote or example that can enhance your key message.
8. Rehearse out loud.
9. Practice with a tape recorder.
10. Immediately before the interview, take a few moments to focus yourself.
11. Relax, but not too much. A little anxiety can give you an energetic edge.

Be-Attitudes for Interview Success

1. *Be accurate.* There is almost nothing worse than making an error of fact.
2. *Be honest.* The one thing worse than an error of fact is a deliberate error of fact. Remember that the long-term credibility of both you and your organization is at stake.
3. *Be brief.* Use short words and simple sentences. Think in terms of two or three sentences to present your message, or just enough time for a quick answer to a few questions. For most questions, you should be able to give one-sentence responses. Practice these.
4. *Be interesting.* Use colorful and pithy language. Give brief anecdotes and easy-to-understand analogies so your audience can grasp your message.
5. *Be enthusiastic.* Even be passionate. State your case and give your opinions with excitement. Show you care about the issue.
6. *Be clear.* Avoid technical or scientific language that you might use around your colleagues. Remember that your audience probably doesn't understand your professional jargon.
7. *Be positive.* Instead of dwelling on accusations, tell your side of the story.

Interview Attitude

1. Remain confident. You are the expert the reporter has sought out. You represent your client or organization in public.
2. Remember your conviction. Let your audience know that you believe in your message. If you appear to be unsure or unconvinced, you aren't likely to persuade others. Let your enthusiasm show on your face and in your speech.
3. Try to be credible. Persuasive message sources are those who are perceived as being both expert and sincere, in touch with their audiences, and friendly and/or worthy of respect.
4. Display your motivation. The impression you leave with the audience will linger far after it has forgotten your words.
5. Speak clearly and distinctly in your normal voice. If you are a fast talker, try to slow down a bit.
6. Smile naturally as it comes to you, but don't overdo it. There are fine lines distinguishing a smile, a smirk, and a pretentious display of teeth.
7. Keep your cool. Don't shout; don't swear; don't attack the questioner (even if you are asked a truly malicious question). Never show anger, no matter how angry you may feel.
8. You are not on trial, nor are you obliged to "air dirty laundry" in public. In an interview, you have rights. One of them is the right to discontinue a line of questioning if the reporter persists in trying to draw you where you don't wish to go.

9. Remember that an interview has mutual benefits to both you and the reporter. You are helping the reporter do a job; the reporter is helping you communicate with your audience toward achieving your strategic objectives.

Communicating During the Interview

1. Note your common bond with the audience. Show that you share their concerns, and clearly explain the direct benefit for them.
2. Propose convenient action (if any) for the audience.
3. Develop a sound bite—a meaningful, succinct and easy-to-recall message that you want your audiences to remember. Aim for 15–20 seconds.
4. Stick to your key message. Don't ramble, and don't allow yourself to be sidetracked. The more you talk, the more opportunity you give a reporter to use peripheral comments instead of central information. State the key message in different ways; keep coming back to the main topic.
5. If, for good reason, you cannot comment, don't. But give the reason. Don't say "No comment" if you mean "I don't know" or "I can't/won't talk about it now." Realize that most people interpret "No comment" as meaning that you have something to hide.
6. Don't address the reporter by name. Instead, speak to the audience. Imagine one individual (not the reporter) who is representative of your target public and address your comments to that person.
7. Let the reporter worry about dead air. Take a few seconds to think before you respond to the question. Rephrase the question while you're thinking of the best answer.
8. Don't guess. Say "I don't know" or "I'll find out for you." (But try not to appear ill-prepared or uninformed.)
9. Signal your message. "The most important thing about this is . . ." or "Three things stand out here. One . . . . Two . . . . And finally . . . ."
10. Humanize statistics. Say "two out of three people" rather than "65% of the population." Avoid using numbers as much as possible.
11. "Off the record" is not an option. If you cannot answer a question publicly, don't try to answer at all. Don't put reporters in the awkward position of knowing information they cannot use.
12. Pay attention to body language and facial expressions. Your nonverbal actions should complement your words.
13. Don't be drawn into criticism of your opponents unless you strategically decide to do so.
14. Don't volunteer information unless it is something you really want to say.
15. Have notes with you as you wish. Glance at them, but don't read from them.

Problem Interviews

Most reporters you deal with will be professional. Expect this, and treat all reporters as professionals unless they prove otherwise. A professional, competent interviewer (1) has prepared and is familiar with the issue, (2) has a no-nonsense approach, and (3) is friendly without being overly familiar. Appreciate this, and be professional in return.

Occasionally you may get a dud. If you encounter problem interviews, consider the following responses.

- A *misinterpreter* who draws an unwarranted conclusion. *Response:* Refute the incorrect statement.
- A *paraphraser* who puts words into your mouth. *Response:* Restate your response slowly, word for word.
- A *mind reader* who presumes to know your thoughts before you speak. *Response:* Dispute the unwarranted insinuation and state your message clearly.
- An *unprepared reporter* who did not adequately get ready for this interview. *Response:* Suggest questions to support your message. This opportunity in disguise lets you give basic information. Keep things simple.
- A *bully* who attacks with charges and allegations. *Response:* Refute the charges as you are able, but do not repeat the accusations.
- A *machine-gunner* who strafes you with nonstop questions. *Response:* Pick the one you prefer to answer and ignore the others.
- An *interrupter* who cuts you off before you have finished responding. *Response:* Make sure you are being concise. If so, ignore the interruption and continue your previous response. Stick to your own agenda.
- An *extremist* who frames the issue only in polarized terms. *Response:* Point out the middle ground, and speak from that perspective.
- A *speculator* who asks you why so-and-so said such-and-such. *Response:* Avoid the temptation to guess. Don't try to explain the motives of another.
- A *false starter* who frames questions on a false foundation. *Response:* Clarify and restate the question. Then answer it.
- A *flatterer* who puts you off guard with compliments. *Response:* Repeat your main message. Don't be lulled into a false sense of security. A tough question may be lurking.
- A *trapper* who tries to pit your personal opinion against organizational policy. *Response:* Say what you can, but never speak "off the record." A news interview probably is not the best place for loyal dissent.

After the Interview

1. Review your performance. Note any misstatements, and assess what you learned from the interview.
2. Take note of how the reporter handles the information, but don't second-guess the writing or reporting. You may have told the story differently, but that wasn't your role.
3. Put it behind you. You can't take back anything you said, and it's unlikely you can add anything useful to what you did say.
4. If you truly have been misquoted and your organization misrepresented in a way that will have long-term negative consequences, speak first with your media relations person. If there is consensus to seek redress, contact the reporter and, if necessary, the editor or news director. Ask for a follow-up interview; settle for a clarification (but don't expect most audiences to read it).

Crisis Communication

This is the advanced stage of effective media engagement. It involves both strategy and technique, building on two assertions: (1) that crises are inevitable within any organization, and (2) that it is within an organization's ability to influence the direction of media coverage and thus the consequences of a crisis.

First, a definition. The dictionary defines *crisis* as "a turning point for better or worse; a decisive moment." It is interesting to note that the Chinese/Japanese character for *crisis* combines two concepts: "danger" and "opportunity." This is particularly fitting for public relations professionals seeking to guide their organization through times of crisis.

It is important to understand that a crisis is not a mere problem for an organization. Problems are irritating annoyances commonplace in business and organizational life. Problems often focus on individuals and on interpersonal conflict. They can be serious—such as the need to fire an employee or to report low sales to stockholders—but they seldom rise to the level of a crisis, based on the following definition.

A crisis is a major, unfortunate, sudden, and unpredicted event. A crisis:

- can interfere with and seriously disrupt and organization's activity.
- is likely to have a negative impact on the organization's "bottom line" or mission.
- threatens the reputation and other assets of the organization.
- demands quick reaction by the organization.
- generally escalates in intensity.
- occurs in a public environment. Even private businesses and nonprofit organizations cannot shield themselves from the expectation of being held accountable.
- invites outside scrutiny that can jeopardize the organization's reputation.

If handled properly, a crisis presents the organization with an opportunity to create a positive impression on its key publics. A crisis shows what an organization is made of, by making visible under adverse situations its values, priorities, and commitments. A crisis brings out the best . . . or the worst.

The Institute for Crisis Management (http://www.crisisexperts.com) defines *crisis* as "a significant business disruption that stimulates extensive news media coverage. The resulting public scrutiny will affect the organization's normal operations and also could have a political, legal, financial and governmental impact on its business." It distinguishes between a sudden crisis (a disruption of business that occurs without warning and is likely to generate negative news coverage) and a smoldering crisis (a business problem not generally known that may generate negative news coverage if and when it goes public).

Not surprisingly, not all crises are the same. Here are some different types of crises:

- *Disaster (violent):* A natural occurrence such as earthquake, flood, and the like with immediate damage. Example: A school destroyed by fire.
- *Disaster (nonviolent):* A natural occurrence such as drought, epidemic, and the like with delayed damage. Example: Farm crops destroyed by an early frost.
- *Accident (violent):* A mishap involving people or equipment, with immediate injury or death. Example: An accident caused by a company truck in which a pedestrian is killed.

- *Accident (nonviolent):* A mishap involving people or equipment, with immediate damage. Example: An accident caused by company truck in which parked cars are damaged.
- *Crime (violent):* A personal action violating legal standards causing injury or death. Example: A pharmaceutical employee sabotaging medicine with a poisonous substance.
- *Crime (nonviolent):* A personal action violating legal standards, with delayed damage. Example: A company executive stealing money from a employee pension fund.
- *Ethical/moral failing (nonviolent):* A personal action violating ethical or moral standards (though not necessarily legal standards), with either immediate or delayed damage. Example: A public relations practitioner intentionally lying in a news release about a company product, with resulting media coverage of the lie.
- *Mismanagement (nonviolent):* Bad professional judgment impacting an organization's operations and procedures, with either immediate or delayed damage. Example: A financial planner losing hundreds of thousands of dollars for clients because of poor investments.
- *Opposition (violent):* Negative impact by external or internal forces, including product tampering, terrorism, and the like, with immediate damage. Example: Rioting, with injuries occurring, at a political rally.
- *Opposition (nonviolent):* Negative impact by external or internal forces, including competition, protests, recalls, lawsuits, etc., with delayed or damage. Example: Heckling at a political rally by supporters of the opposition candidate.

The Institute for Crisis Management simplifies the above listing and identifies instead four basic types of business crises: (1) acts of God (storms, earthquakes, volcanic action, etc.); (2) mechanical problems (ruptured pipes, metal fatigue, etc.); (3) human errors (opening the wrong valve, miscommunication about what to do, etc.); and (4) management decisions/indecision (presuming that a problem is minor and that it will blow over).

The institute reports the following categories of organizational crises for the year 2005, noting that most crises are not the result of natural disaster or employee error but instead are caused by management decisions, actions, or inactions:

18%	White-collor crime
14%	Catastrophes
13%	Class-action lawsuits
9%	Casualty accidents
9%	Labor disputes
9%	Mismanagement
7%	Consumer activism
3%	Defects and recalls
3%	Discrimination
14%	Miscellaneous

Important in this and other schemes of categorizing crises is the observation that few crises are unpredictable. Crises resulting from fires, floods, and other natural occurrences are unusual, and even some of these are somewhat predictable, such as a school or manufacturing company built in a flood zone or a high-rise office tower built in an area prone to earthquakes.

Most crises, however, are the result of management error of some sort: safety checks improperly made, inadequate supervision of employees or others, deficient background checks on employees working with children or the infirm, unsatisfactory handling of consumer complaints, failure to apply laws dealing with discrimination or harassment—all management failings that could have been avoided.

The institute also monitors specific industries. It found, for example, that 60% of crises in the chemical industry were caused by management, 23% by employees, and 17% by other causes.

Principles for Crisis Communication

Crises are inevitable within every organization. You can minimize their occurrence but you can't prevent them entirely. Rather, your aim should be to exercise control in the way you manage the crisis, impacting on whether the outcome is positive or negative. Here are several principles for crisis communication:

The principle of existing relationships. In crisis situations, communicate with employees, volunteers, stockholders, donors, and other constituent groups, as well as with colleagues. Minimally, keep these publics informed, because their continued support will be important in your rebuilding process following the crisis. Ideally, enlist their assistance during the crisis to communicate credibly and effectively.

The principle of quick response. Become accessible to your publics as quickly as possible. The one-hour rule applies here; within one hour of learning about a crisis, the organization should have its first message available to its publics, particularly the media which generally are the most significant public in the early stages of a crisis.

The principle of full disclosure. Silence is not an acceptable response during a crisis. Without admitting fault, the organization should provide as much information as possible. The presumption should be that everything the organization knows should be made available, subject to specific justification for not releasing certain information.

The principle of one voice. A single spokesperson should represent the organization. If multiple spokespersons are needed, each should be aware of what the others are saying, and all should work from the same set of facts and the same coordinated message.

The principle of media-as-ally. In crisis situations, organizations are best advised to treat the news media as allies that provide opportunities for the organization to communicate with its key publics and constituents. In situations in which the media are intrusive and/or hostile to the organization, this often is because the organization has not been forthcoming in providing legitimate information to the media and its other publics. A good existing program of media relations can minimize media hostility.

The principle of recovery. The most pressing need in a crisis situation is for the organization to put the issue behind it and initiate a recovery program. Focus on repairing any damage to the organization's reputation and its relationship with important publics.

Crisis Strategy

During a crisis, every organization has a range of strategic responses available to it. Here is an overview of eight strategic responses to crisis. These strategies exist on a continuum between full responsibility and full blame. Note that some of the strategies may be used in combination. For a fuller treatment of these strategic options, review Step 5 of the planning process outlined in this book.

1. *Attack.* The organization confronts the person or group who claims that a crisis exists or who the organization accuses of causing the crisis, and threatens to use force or pressure against the person or group. Do not use this strategy to blame the messengers reporting the crisis. Use this strategy only when a strong case can be made that accusers have grossly overstated the organization's involvement in the crisis.
2. *Denial.* The organization states that no crisis exists and explains why there is no crisis. Or the organization denies that any culpability in a crisis that does exist. Use this strategy only when the organization can present a strong case that it did not cause the crisis.
3. *Excuse.* The organization tries to minimize responsibility for the crisis such as by denying any intention to do harm or claiming that it had no control over events that led to the crisis. Use this strategy, perhaps in conjunction with compassion, when a strong case can be made that the organization did not intentionally cause any harm.
4. *Justification.* The organization tries to minimize the perceived damage associated with the crisis or claims that it had no control over events that led to the crisis. Use this strategy, perhaps in conjunction with compassion, when a strong case can be made that the organization is not to blame.
5. *Ingratiation.* The organization takes action to cause its publics to like and side with the organization. Use this strategy when the crisis has been a nonviolent one and when the organization has not been culpable in the crisis.
6. *Corrective action.* The organization takes steps to contain the crisis, repair the damage, and/or prevent a recurrence. Use this strategy if the organization was in any way unprepared or negligent in preventing the crisis in the first place.
7. *Compassion.* The organization expresses regret, remorse, and/or concern without admitting guilt. Use this strategy when injury, death, or serious damage has occurred to express the humanity of the organization.
8. *Apology.* The organization takes full responsibility, asks forgiveness, and makes compensation or restitution. Use this strategy when the organization is at fault and when long-term rebuilding of relationships is more important than short-term stalling.

An organization's choice among various crisis strategies depends on several interdependent factors, including the following:

- *Severity of the crisis.* The more serious the crisis, the less likely that excuses or denials will be accepted without strong and compelling evidence. Also, the more severe the crisis, the harsher the public verdict will be against the organization.
- *Culpability of the organization.* If the organization is fully or even partly responsible for the crisis, this inevitably will be revealed. Crisis managers must be aware of the role the organization played in the evolution of the crisis.

- *Preventability of the crisis.* Crisis managers must be aware of the extent to which the crisis could have been prevented. Culpability can be mitigated if the organization tried to prevent or minimize the crisis before it struck.
- *Organizational reputation.* As in every aspect of public relations, the reputation of the organization prior to the crisis will play a major role in how the organization manages the crisis and recovers from it. The goodwill of the public is invaluable to an organization.

Crisis Messages

An organization's friends and supporters can tolerate error, but they will not tolerate lies or arrogance. Crisis communication must show that the organization values their support and that it will communicate honestly and respectfully. In addition to specific facts and attention to legal concerns, keep the following messages in mind:

- Reassure publics about key points, including safety and security, as well as likelihood of recurrence.
- Don't attempt to shift blame.
- Show concern and compassion for injury, death, and other loss.
- Stick to the facts.
- Avoid speculation. In particular, don't speculate as to the cause or fault for the crisis, nor the financial or other costs involved. While the crisis is going on, it is too early to accurately assess either cause or consequences, and particularly when life and safety are at stake, it is unseemly to speculate about cost.
- Be candid and honest.
- "No comment" isn't an option. It implies guilt or cover-up.
- If you can't comment, indicate why silence is necessary at this time and when you expect to have a comment.
- Don't minimize the situation. Never characterize a real emergency as a minor incident, and don't point out that other situations may have been worse.
- Balance the data content of your message with the symbolism and emotion it carries.
- Try to prevent any unauthorized statements from organizational personnel.
- Provide timely updates.
- Communicate with all publics, not only with the media.
- Try to time your communication program. Giving comment too early means you may not have adequate facts and could appear to be uninformed. Offering comment too late means that the media will release the facts first and you will appear to be hiding information.

Preparing for Crisis

Because crisis is an inevitable fact of life for every organization, preparedness is essential. Here are several aspects of preparing for crisis:

- *Establish a crisis management team.* Provide training for its members, establish organizational policy for use during a crisis, and conduct regular drills.
- *Develop a crisis management plan.* Include a series of "to do" lists. Also include an outline of both the chain of command and the chair of communication. To implement

these procedures, develop information materials such as telephone and e-mail contact lists, media lists, fact sheets, and related information.

- *Conduct regular crisis research.* Identify emerging issues with the potential for crisis. Investigate these issues and respond to them before they reach crisis stage. Even if they do emerge as crises, you will gain the support of your publics by showing that you tried to prevent or minimize them.
- *Pay attention to rumors.* Listen to "the word on the street," which can serve as part of the early-warning system within the organization.
- *Be prepared to communicate.* Create a plan for prompt communication with important publics and key constituents.
- *Try to avoid mistakes that lead to crises.*

The Flow of Information During a Crisis

Consider how each key public receives information during a crisis:

NEWS MEDIA

Public relations representative of the organization
Organizational spokesperson or other official
Police, fire, or other emergency scanners
Unauthorized "leaks"
Eyewitnesses or bystanders with knowledge
Bystanders with hearsay
Outside "experts"

EMPLOYEES, VOLUNTEERS, CLIENTS, STUDENTS, PATIENTS

Direct knowledge
Other employees, volunteers, clients, etc.
News reports
Organizational and other websites
E-mail and text messaging
Managers
Rumor

SUPPORTERS, DONORS, STOCKHOLDERS

News reports
E-mail
Letters
Organizational and other websites
Telephone contact
Newsletters
Rumor

COMMUNITY RESIDENTS, PUBLIC OFFICIALS

News reports
Organizational newsletters
Organizational and other websites
Rumor

Glossary

academic research type of research that generates theory, explores new interests and focuses on universal knowledge; also called *theoretical research, basic research* and *pure research*

acceptance objective second level of objectives, the affective or feeling component, dealing with levels of interest or attitude (compare with **awareness objective** and **action objective**)

accident (see **excuse**)

accounts theory that identifies various communication responses to manage relationship in the wake of rebuke or criticism

action objective third and final level of objectives, the conative or behavioral component, dealing with opinion (verbal action) or behavior (physical action)

action strategies category of proactive public relations that involves organizational performance, audience participation, special events, alliances and coalitions, sponsorships, and strategic philanthropy

active public stage of development in which a public recognizes that it shares an issue with an organization, perceives consequences as being relevant, and is organized to discuss or act

activism confrontational proactive public relations strategy focused mainly on persuasive communication and the advocacy model of public relations

activist type of opponent, similar to an advocate, but seeking change rather than focusing on discussion

actuality recording accompanying a news release and providing actual quotes or sound bites; may be cassette or digitized computer download

adaptation willingness and ability of an organization to make changes necessary to create harmony between itself and key publics

administrative research (see **applied research)**

advertising and promotional media category of communication tactics using controlled and paid media

advertising equivalency type of outputs evaluation focusing on the relative costs that a particular public relations message would carry if instead it had been an advertising message

advertising inserts inserts such as coupons or postcards in magazines

advertisorial type of print advertisement that features a series of consecutive pages dealing with a single theme or product/service line

advocate type of opponent that uses mainly vocal tactics against an organization because the advocate supports something else and because the organization appears to stand in the way of the advocate's goal

aerial advertising category of advertising associated with airplanes, including blimps, skywriting and airplane tows

after-only study type of research design that reviews a situation after a communication project has been implemented (compare with **before-after study**)

agenda-setting theory theory that identifies the relationship between the **media agenda** and **public agenda**

aggregate nonhomogenous assortment of individuals with little in common (see also **audience**)

alliance informal, loosely structured and often small working relationship among organizations (compare with **coalition**)

all-you-can-afford budgeting provides for public relations funding when the organization's financial condition is sound, but limits funding during lean times (compare with **unit-of-sales budgeting** and **percentage-of-sales budgeting**)

analogy persuasion technique and type of verbal evidence using familiar situations and allusions to help an audience understand new ideas

announcement releases type of news release, generally dealing with events, personnel, progress, bad news, programs or products (compare with **response releases** and **hometowner releases**)

annual report category of organizational media; type of progress report required by the Securities and Exchange Commission of American companies that issue stock

anonymity research term indicating that a respondent's identity project will not be known by anybody, including the researcher (compare with **confidentiality**)

ANR (see **audio news release**)

anti type of opponent that acts as a dissident on a global scale, being against seemingly everything associated with an organization

apathetic public stage of development in which a public is aware of an issue involving an organization but is nevertheless unconcerned about this issue or its potential consequences

apologetics systematic attempt to explain the reasonableness of religious faith and to refute opposing arguments. See also **homiletics**.

apologia formal defense that offers a compelling case for an organization's opinions, positions or actions

apology vocal commiseration strategy in which an organization admits sorrow and accepts blame

applied research type of research that deals with practical problems faced by organizations and guides effective resolution of such problems; also called *market research* or *administrative research*

arena poster billboardlike advertisements on walls and fences of sports arenas, entertainment centers or similar facilities

association (see **excuse**)

attack offensive response strategy of claiming that an accusation of wrongdoing is an attempt to impugn the organization's reputation by an accuser who is negligent or malicious

attractiveness aspect of persuasion that focuses on the message source's physical looks, demeanor, poise and presence

audience people who pay attention to a particular medium of communication (compare with **aggregate**)

audience feedback type of acceptance evaluation based on the voluntary reaction of an audience

audio news release news release written and produced specifically for radio stations, presented as an edited story package; abbreviated *ANR*

authority aspect of persuasion that focuses on an audience's acceptance of a message source's right to rule over or direct its actions

average term for usual or ordinary instance; statistically this can be a mean, median or mode

aware public stage of development in which a public recognizes that it shares an issue with an organization and perceives consequences as being relevant, but is not yet organized to discuss or act on the issue

awareness evaluation research focusing on the content of a message. Evaluation includes message exposure, message content, readability measures, and message recall

awareness objective first level of objectives, the cognitive or thinking component, dealing with levels of information, understanding and retention (compare with **acceptance objective** and **action objective**)

balance theory theory that identifies the tension caused by inconsistent information baseline study (see **benchmarking**)

baseline study (see **benchmarking**)

basic research (see **academic research**)

before-and-after study type of research design that reviews a situation before a communication project has been implemented, then investigates the situation after the project is completed; also called pretest/post-test (compare with **after-only study**)

benchmarking continuous and systematic research process of measuring an organization and its products or services against the best practices of strong competitors and recognized industry leaders, in order to improve the organization's performance; also called *baseline study*

benefit statement part of planning process that articulates a benefit or advantage that a product or service offers a public

billboard stationary outdoor advertising sign with changeable messages

biography type of feature release focusing on the background of a person

blame shifting see **denial**

bleed ad type of print advertisement that eliminates page borders and carries the image to the edge of the paper

blog short for web log, is an open-to-all website with usually maintained by an individual

bottom line a term that identifies an organization's mission or fundamental goal

brainstorming group-creativity technique consisting of two steps. *Divergence,* where a group surfaces a large number of ideas on how to solve a problem or answer a question, and *convergence,* where the list of ideas is pared down.

branding creation of a clear and consistent message for an organization

break-even point level of success required to offset the cost of the development and implementation of a strategic plan; the point beyond which profit begins accruing

breakout ad targeted approach to advertising in national publications, in which an advertiser buys space for copies distributed in a narrow geographic area or to a particular demographic group of subscribers

brochure category of organizational media; standalone publication dealing with a particular topic or issue and used for recruiting, product/service lines, membership and other purposes

B-roll (see **video B-roll**)

budget outline of financial and other resources within a strategic plan, including personnel, material, media costs, equipment and facilities, and administrative costs

bursting (see **flighting**)

bus sign advertising located on busses, including street-side, curb-side, front and back

cable crawl message scrolled across the bottom of a TV screen, often associated with news/weather announcements, sports scores, election returns and so on

campaign systematic set of public relations activities, each with a specific and finite purpose, sustained over a length of time and dealing with objectives associated with a particular issue (compare with **project** and **program**)

car card advertising placed above windows inside trains and busses

case study qualitative research technique based on the investigation of a single event, product or situation and looking at how an organization has handled it, undertaken for the purpose of understanding and learning from a real-life situation; also called case history or field research

casual research gathering of information haphazardly and informally

cell phones mobile phones that increasingly incorporate digital cameras and Internet capability

center spread type of print advertisement that features two facing pages

charisma aspect of persuasion that focuses on the magnetic appeal or personal charm of a message source; associated with **familiarity**, **likability**, **similarity** and **attractiveness**

civil disobedience type of activism that involves nonviolent, nonlegal activities, generally with a strong visual component

claim (see **proposition**)

clarity aspect of verbal communication dealing with the ease with which a message can be understood

classified ad type of advertisement common in newspapers featuring brief all-text messages

clipping service company that tracks publications and/or broadcasts and provides evidence that a public relations message has been used

closed-ended item format for survey questionnaire that provides for check-offs to predetermined response categories (compare with **open-ended item**)

cluster sampling probability sampling technique that first subdivides a large and heterogeneous population, breaking into smaller sections before drawing the final sampling; also called multistage sampling

coalition formal, structured relationship among organizations (compare with **alliance**)

cognitive dissonance theory theory that explores the role of psychological discomfort rooted in information that contradicts beliefs, values or attitudes

communication manager organizational decision maker, either a **tactical manager** or a **strategic manager**

communication outcome measured results of the implementation of tactics showing the level of achievement of goals and objectives

communication output tactic implemented during a communication campaign, such as fact sheets distributed or news conferences held

communication strategy part of an organization's inventory of proactive strategies focusing on publicity, newsworthy information and transparent communication

communication tactic menu of vehicle that an organization can use to present messages; four categories include **interpersonal communication**, **organizational media**, **news media**, and **advertising and promotional media**

communication technician organizational specialist in public relations and marketing communication who performs tasks directed by others

community calendar (see **event listing**)
comparison persuasion technique and type of verbal evidence highlighting the characteristics or value related to an issue
competence aspect of persuasion that focuses on the ability of a message source to remain calm under pressure and to be clear and dynamic in presenting the message
competitive parity approach to budgeting based on the cost of similar activity by major competitors
competitor public that is doing the same thing as an organization in the same area, thus competing head-to-head for the same resources
concern vocal commiseration strategy in which an organization expresses that it is not indifferent to a problem, without admitting guilt
concession diversionary response strategy by which an organization tries to rebuild its relationship with its publics by giving the public something it wants
condolence vocal commiseration strategy in which an organization expresses grief over someone's loss or misfortune, without admitting guilt
confidentiality research term indicating that the identity of a participant in a research project, though known to the researcher, will not be disclosed or linked to a particular response (compare with **anonymity**)
conflict resolution process of dialogue that involves making peace and restoring harmony, with communication as the primary tool
congruity theory theory that adds the aspect of measuring attitudes to consistency theories
conjecture proposition type of proposition stating that something probably exists, based on reasoned conclusion drawn from physical evidence
consensus building process of dialogue that identifies and then prevents or overcomes barriers between people and/or organizations
consistency theory family of theories dealing with the existence or lack of consistent information and the effect of this on message receivers
content analysis quantitative research technique based on the unobtrusive and after-the-fact analysis of a set of media artifacts such as a news cast, editorials, or articles on a particular topic
context (see **justification**)
contingency statement type of public relations writing in which an organization prepares written comment for various potential outcomes of a situation, releasing only that version appropriate to the outcome; also called **standby statement**
continuity approach to scheduling that presents a message at a consistent level throughout a time period
control aspect of persuasion that focuses on a message source's command over an audience and on the perceived willingness to exercise that power
controlled before-and-after study more sophisticated than **before-and-after study** as takes outside factors into consideration and involves two sample groups drawn from the same key public. One sample is the group to receive the message; the other is a control group that does not receive the message
controlled media media that allow the organization to determine various attributes (compare with **uncontrolled media**)
convenience sampling nonprobability sampling technique that draws subjects because they are readily available to a researcher

corporate video (see **nonbroadcast video**)

corrective action rectifying behavior strategy in which an organization takes steps to contain a problem, repair the damage and/or prevent its recurrence

cost-benefit analysis identifies the cost of implementing a tactic, then compares this cost to the estimated value of the expected results

cost per thousand standard measurement for expense of reaching media audiences, calculated not individually but rather as thousands; abbreviated *CPM*

CPM (see **cost per thousand**)

credibility aspect of persuasion that focuses on the power to inspire belief, demonstrated through expertise, status, competence and honesty

crisis management process by which an organization plans for, deals with, and tries to overcome out-of-control issues

customer type of public that receives the product or services of an organization, such as consumers, clients, patients, fans, parishioners, members and so forth

cybernetic model of communication theory that identifies a model for two-way communication, moving from sender to receiver and returning via feedback

daypart time period reflecting different audience demographics and usage patterns for television or radio, such as prime time and morning drive time

defamation legal situation in which language (1) is false, (2) is published or communicated to a third party, (3) identifies a person, (4) holds that person up to public hatred, contempt or ridicule, and (5) involves some measure of negligence and/or malice on the part of the communicator

demographic noise communication disruption caused by differences between message sender and receiver based on ethnicity, age, social status, and so on (see also **noise**)

demographics audience characteristics based on measurable physical criteria such as age, income, education, gender, geography, and so on (compare with **psychographics**)

denial defensive response strategy in which an organization refuses to accept blame by claiming innocence or mistaken identity or by shifting blame

deontological ethics approach to decision making rooted in a standard or moral code, suggesting that certain actions are, in and of themselves, good (compare with **teleological ethics** and **ethical relativism**)

dialogue model conceptual approach to communication that focuses on conscious interaction of two parties in communication for the purpose of mutual understanding

diffusion of innovations theory theory that identifies the role of opinion leaders as models in the process of mass adoption of news products or ideas

digital radio radio transmitted via satellite, therefore covering far larger areas than conventional terrestrial broadcasting; also called *subscription radio*

digital media category of organizational media focusing on computer-based electronic media vehicles, such as e-mail, Web sites, Intranets and so on

diorama (see **station poster**)

direct mail category of organizational print media featuring written messages disseminated to individual recipients

direct news material category of news media including information presented to the media in ready-to-use format, such as news releases or feature releases

direct observation type of action evaluation based on proof of audience activity, such as voting outcomes, attendance, sales and so on

disassociation diversionary response strategy that attempts to distance an organization from wrongdoing associated with it

display ad type of advertisement common in newspapers and magazines, featuring headlines, illustrations and copy blocks

disproportionate sampling approach to stratified sampling in which each demographic group is sized not according to its proportion in the population in order to compensate for its being a small proportion; also called *weighted sampling*

dissident type of opponent that combats an organization because of positions or actions taken by the organization

doublespeak words and phrases that are deliberately misleading and thus both dishonest and unethical attempts to obscure meaning, violating ethical standards (compare with **pretentious language**)

drawing conclusions presenting the evidence and then explicitly telling the audience how to interpret it

editorial conference formal meeting between news sources or organizational representatives with editors and editorial boards of newspapers in order to increase understanding between reporters and organizations and to elicit media support for the organization's agenda

electronic media media delivered primarily through electronic vehicles (compare with **print media**)

e-mail (short for **electronic mail**) type of organizational media using computers to transmit memos and letters

embarrassment offensive response strategy of trying to lessen an opponent's influence by using shame or humiliation

enabler type of public that serves as a regulator by setting the norms or standards for an organization, opinion leader, allies or the media

endorsement persuasion technique and type of verbal evidence using comments by people who espouse an organization's ideas

EPSEM sampling equal probability of sampling methods (see **probability sampling**)

ethical relativism approach to decision making suggesting that actions are ethical to the extent that they reflect particular social norms (compare with **deontological ethics** and **teleological ethics**)

ethos principle identified with Aristotle that focuses on the communication effectiveness based on the character of a speaker and on the common ground shared by speakers and audiences

event listing simple newspaper notice announcing upcoming events; also called *community calendar*

example persuasion technique and type of verbal evidence providing conclusions drawn from related instances

excuse defensive response strategy in which an organization tries to minimize its responsibility for harm or wrongdoing by citing provocation, lack of control, victimization or mere association

executive summary one- or two-page synopsis of a strategic plan or other report intended as an overview for executives and others who need general information but not details

existing relations strategic principle of crisis management that an organization should communicate with employees, volunteers, stockholders, community leaders, customers, and other groups with which it has an existing relationship in order to strengthen existing support

expertise aspect of persuasion that focuses on the degree to which a message source knows what he or she is talking about (compare with **competence**)

external impediment social, political or economic factor outside an organization that might limit the effectiveness of a public relations program (compare with **internal impediment**)

external media media that exist outside of an organization (compare with **internal media**)

extra name for additional feature within a spectacular billboard (see **spectacular**)

extrapolation research term indicating that the findings of a study of a sample can be presumed for the entire population

facilitator (see **moderator**)

fact sheet category of organizational media that presents information in bullet form

factual proposition type of proposition stating that something exists, based on provable evidence

false assumption error in logic featuring a conclusion that an audience may not accept

familiarity aspect of persuasion that focuses on the extent to which an audience already knows the message source

fanatic type of zealot opponent without social stabilizers

FAQ presentation of frequently asked questions about a particular issue or organization (see also **fact sheet**)

feature release media release focusing on background info (**history**, **biography**, **backgrounder**, **Q&A**, **service article**)

fear appeal persuasion technique and type of negative appeal based on anxiety and worry

field research (see **case study**)

final report (see **summative report**)

flyer category of organizational media; stand-alone publication meant to be read as a single unit

flighting approach to scheduling that presents a message in waves over a period of time; also called *bursting*

focus group qualitative research technique involving conversation among several participants, guided by a monitor and recorded for later analysis; less formally called **group interview**

Fog Index formula to calculate the level of reading difficulty for any piece of writing; also called *Gunning Readability Formula*

formal opinion leader opinion leader whose influence is based on structured authority role (compare with **informal opinion leader**)

formative research first phase of strategic planning process, dealing with gathering and analyzing information about the public relations situation, the organization, and its publics; also called **situation analysis**

front organization set up to appear to operate independently, when in fact they are controlled by another organization that wants to remain anonymous in the relationship

full disclosure strategic principle of crisis management that an organization should provide as much information as possible, without admitting fault or speculating about facts not yet known

full-cost budget inclusion within budgets of the value of all items, not only those to be purchased but also those inherent within an organization (such as personnel and overhead) and generated income (such as contributed goods or services, donations, grants and fees)

Gantt chart common type of flow chart listing tactics and associated tasks, with indication of the time needed for each task
gatekeeper media person (such as editor, producer or webmaster) who controls the flow of information in publications, newscasts and so on
geodemography research technique combining elements of demographics and census data
goal part of organizational strategy; statement rooted in organization's mission or vision, acknowledging an issue and sketching out how the organization hopes to see it settled
good intention (see **justification**)
grabbers (see **power words**)
group interview (see **focus group**)
guerrilla theater (see **street theater**)
guest editorial enhanced letter to the editor, often commissioned by a publication; also called an *op-ed piece* because it usually is positioned opposite the editorial page
guilt appeal persuasion technique and type of negative appeal based on shame
Gunning Readability Formula (see **Fog Index**)

halo effect phenomenon in which a message is likely to be believed mainly because the source is perceived as credible, charismatic and/or in a position of control over an audience
Hawthorne effect (see **placebo effect**)
hierarchy of needs theory of human motivation that identifies structured levels of human needs, with one needing to be met before another becomes relevant
history type of feature release focusing on the background or history of an organization
homiletics application of effective communication for preaching. See also **apologetics**.
hometowner type of news release focusing on announcements about people and disseminated to their home towns
honesty aspect of persuasion that focuses on the willingness and ability of a message source to provide full and accurate information, operating without bias
horns effect opposite of **halo effect**
house ad type of advertisement placed in performance programs and other publications associated with special events, often focusing simply on corporate identity
how-to piece (see **service article**)
humor appeal persuasion technique and type of positive emotional appeal based on comedy and amusement

idealism (see **justification**)
image restoration theory based on the presumption that, in the face of criticism, both people and organizations seek to maintain or rebuild a positive reputation
implementation report research report documenting how program tactics are carried out
in-depth interview (see **intensive interview**)
indirect news material category of news media including information presented for media guidance but not meant to be published or aired, such as announcements of news conferences

inflatable category of advertising using giant outdoor balloons or air-filled promotional items

infomercial program-length television advertisement often packaged as an interview, game show or educational program

informal opinion leader opinion leader whose influence is based on force of personality and circumstance (compare with **formal opinion leader**)

information exchange category of interpersonal communication tactics centering on opportunities for organizations and publics to meet face to face

information model conceptual approach to communication that focuses on the content and channels of communication

information-seeking publics people who have gone somewhat out of their way to interact with the organization

information subsidy information from public relations sources that editors use to help underwrite the cost of reporting news

ingratiation diversionary response strategy in which an organization tries to charm its publics or gives them something of little significance to the organization in an attempt to turn the spotlight away from criticism

inoculation theory theory that explores the role that persuasive information has on previously unchallenged beliefs and attitudes

innocence see **denial**

integrated communication conscious blending of the concepts and tools of both **public relations** and **marketing communication**

intensive interview qualitative research technique involving lengthy, detailed and systematic interview conducted with several respondents; also called *in-depth interview*

intercession process of using an influential go-between to link an organization and its public

intercessory public transitional public that serves as a bridge between an organization and other publics

internal impediment obstacles within an organization that might limit the effectiveness of a public relations program (compare with **external impediment**)

internal media media that exist within an organization (compare with **external media**)

internal video (see **nonbroadcast video**)

Internet a vast computer network linking smaller computer networks worldwide

interpersonal communication category of communication tactics offering face-to-face opportunities for personal involvement and interaction

interstitial ad computer advertising that insinuates itself on computer users without invitation; also called pop-up ad (compare with **superstitial ad**)

interview notes verbatim transcripts presented in a question-and-answer format, based on an interview that a public relations writer has done with an organizational news source

investigation rectifying behavior strategy in which an organization promises to examine a situation and then to act as the facts warrant

issue situation that presents a matter of concern to an organization; trend, event, development, or matter in dispute that may affect an organization

issues management process of monitoring and evaluating information by which an organization tries to anticipate emerging issues and respond to them before they get out of hand

judgment sampling (see **purposive sampling**)

judgmental assessment evaluation methodology based on hunches and personal experience

justification defensive response strategy in which an organization admits doing wrong but claims it was for a good reason, citing good intention, context, idealism or mitigation

key public (see **strategic public**)

lack of control (see **excuse**)
latent public stage of development in which a public shares an issue with an organization but is not yet aware of this fact
lead time amount of time it takes reporters and other media professions to gather and present stories
libel written or broadcast **defamation**
likability aspect of persuasion that focuses on the extent to which an audience admires what it knows about a message source or what it sees and hears when the source begins to communicate
Likert scale popular bipolar scale used in questionnaires to elicit response in categories such as "strongly agree," "agree," "disagree" and "strongly disagree"
listservs electronic mailing lists
limiter type of public that reduces or undermines the success of an organization, including competitors, opponents and hostile forces
logo type of nonverbal communication in which an image identifies an organization
logos principle identified with Aristotle that focuses on communication effectiveness based on rational appeal of messages
love appeal persuasion technique and type of positive emotional appeal based on aspects of love such as family, nostalgia, compassion, sympathy and so on

magazine category of news media; periodic publication featuring news, commentary and feature information
management by objectives process by which organizations plan their activities based on prior objectives rather than present opportunities; abbreviated MBO
manager (see **communication manager**)
margin of error (see **sampling error**)
market segment of a population including people with characteristics (age, income, lifestyle, and so on) that can help an organization achieve its consumer-oriented goals
market research (see **applied research**)
marketing communications management function that focuses on products and services that respond to the wants and needs of consumers, fostering an economic exchange between the organization and its consumers (compare with **public relations**)
mass media media that are accessible to most people and thus enjoy vast audiences (compare with **targeted media**)
mathematical theory of communication theory that identifies a model for one-way communication, moving from sender to receiver
MBO (see **management by objective**)
mean type of statistical average calculated by dividing a total by the number of elements (compare with **median** and **mode**)
media advisory type of indirect news material providing media gatekeepers with information about upcoming news opportunities; also called *media alert*

media agenda topics the media report on (compare with **public agenda**)
media alert (see **media advisory**)
media directory books and online resources providing information on media outlets
media impressions potential total audience of people who could have been exposed to a message presented in a particular medium
media kit collection of materials for reporters attending news conferences and other news-oriented events; includes news releases, biographies, photos, backgrounders, fact sheets and related material; less accurately also called press kit
media-as-ally strategic principle of crisis management that an organization should treat news media as an ally offering an opportunity to communicate with the organization's publics
median type of statistical average calculated from the middle number on a list (compare with **mean** and **mode**)
memo (short for memorandum) category of organizational media; brief written message, usually internal to an organization
message cost type of outputs evaluation focusing on the expense associated with the production of a particular message
message distribution type of outputs evaluation focusing on the frequency and manner of message dissemination
message exposure type of awareness evaluation based on the number of people in key purpose who were exposed to a message
message frequency number and pattern of messages presented to a particular public in a given period of time (compare with **message reach**)
message production type of outputs evaluation focusing on the number of messages written or produced
message recall type of awareness evaluation based on how frequently and accurately audiences remembered a previous advertising or public relations message
message reach number of different people who are exposed to a single message (compare with **message frequency**)
missionary self-righteous type of activist in support of a cause, often operating under the presumption of moral imperative
mistaken identity see **denial**
mitigation (see **justification**)
mobile billboard painted side of tractor-trailer or delivery trucks, often leased for advertising purposes
mode type of statistical average calculated as the most frequently occurring number (compare with **mean** and **median**)
moderator person who leads a focus group; also called facilitator
multistage sampling (see **cluster sampling**)

network placement use of television advertising at the network level, with distribution through all stations affiliated with the network (compare with **spot advertising**)
network radio same as network placement in reference to radio advertising
networking (see **intercession**)
news brief type of news releases presenting two or three paragraphs of information
news conference hybrid of speech and group interview used to announce important news to reporters
news fact sheet bulleted presentation of newsworthy information (compare with news release)

news interviews sessions in which journalists ask questions and public relations practitioners or organizational spokespersons respond

news media category of communication tactics using journalistic media

news release news-type article written by a public relations practitioner and presented to a newspaper or other publication or media outlet; meant to be used either verbatim or as background information (compare with **news fact sheet**)

newsletter category of organizational media; organizational publication combining the informative approach of newspapers with relationship-building features of mail

newspaper category of news media; periodic publication featuring objective news and information; various types include general-interest, trade, special-interest, special-audience, and organizational newspapers

niche aspect of an organization's internal environment focusing on the specialty or the unique function or role that makes the organization different from others

noise concept identifying potential interferences with message communication; may be **physical**, **psychological**, **semantic** or **demographic**

nonapology an insincere or halfhearted apology

nonbroadcast video category of organizational media using television technology for internal distribution; also called *corporate video* and *internal video.* Can also be posted on the Internet as *web video* or *streaming video*

nonprobability sampling a series of techniques for selecting samples of a population not based on the principle of probability; categories include **convenience**, **volunteer**, **purposive** and **snowball sampling**

nonpublic group that does not share any issues with an organization

nonpublic media media that are restricted in their coverage and their availability (compare with **public media**)

nonverbal communication communication occurring through actions and cues other than words (compare with **verbal communication**)

objective part of organizational strategy; statement emerging from an organization's goal, presented in clear and measurable terms, pointing toward particular levels of awareness, acceptance or action (compare with **goal**)

objective-based budgeting approach to budgeting based on established goals and objectives

obstacle public relations situation limiting the organization in realizing its mission (compare with **opportunity**)

one voice strategic principle of crisis management that a single, trained spokesperson or coordinated team of spokespersons should represent the organization

op-ed piece (see **guest editorial**)

open-ended item format for survey questionnaire that allows respondents to answer in their own words (compare with **closed-ended item**)

opinion leader individual with a particular influence on an organization's publics; opinion leaders may be **formal** or **informal**

opponent public that is against an organization

opportunity public relations situation offering a potential advantage to the organization or its publics (compare with **obstacle**)

order of presentation refers to how you decide to present information in an argument. You may present arguments in order of least to most important, or vice versa, depending on what point you want to make.
organizational media category of communication tactics using media that are published or produced by organizations, which control the message content as well as its timing, packaging and distribution
out-of-home advertising advertising venues designed to reach people in locations other than home or offices, including billboards, transit and aerial advertising
out-of-home video category of advertising featuring video in public locations such as sports arenas and concert halls
outputs evaluation evaluation methodology focusing on communication outputs

paint stationary outdoor advertising sign, also called painted bulletin, with relatively permanent message
paraphrase statements presented as an approximation or abbreviation of an original message from an information source
pathos principle identified with Aristotle that focuses on communication effectiveness based on emotional appeal of messages
pci (see **per column inch**)
percentage-of-sales budgeting drawn from the field of marketing, where some companies base their advertising budget on the previous year's profits.
per column inch basic unit of measure for print advertising; abbreviated *pci*
per-capita cost association of budgetary expenses with the number of people needed to cover the cost
performance aspect of an organization's internal environment focusing on the quality of the goods and services provided by the organization, as well as the viability of the causes and ideas it espouses
performance fee fee structure for public relations or advertising agency tying compensation to the achievement of stated objectives
personal involvement where an organization actively involves its publics and creates an environment rooted in two-way communication
persuasion model conceptual approach to communication that focuses on ethical attempts to influence people
PERT chart common type of flow chart using circles and arrows to visually display tasks associated with a strategic plan
physical noise communication disruption caused by use of inefficient communication channels
placebo effect research phenomenon in which change is noted but attributed not to the content of the campaign but rather to the mere fact that participants knew that a campaign was in progress and/or that they were being observed; also called Hawthorne effect
podcasts (a portmanteau for *iPod* and *broadcast*) are Internet-based audio feeds that allow users to listen to postings
policy proposition type of proposition identifying a new course of action and encouraging its adoption
polling (see **survey**)
popular media media that focus on information of interest to people in their personal lives (compare with **trade media**)

population research term indicating a large group of subjects that are of interest to a researcher
pop-up (see **interstitial ad**)
position statement type of opinion material used by organizations to analyze issues and present formal opinions on issues of public policy; variations include *position paragraph*; also called *white paper*
positioning process of managing how an organization distinguishes itself with a unique meaning in the mind of its publics
poster generic name for several kinds of outdoor stationary advertisements, including billboards, paints and spectaculars
power aspect of persuasion that focuses on the raw and recognized ability of a message source to dominate and to reward or punish
power words aspect of verbal communication dealing with strong and evocative language. Also called *grabbers*
provocation (see **excuse**)
prebuttal term linked to the notion of pre-emptive strike when bad news is inevitable, referring to the practice of an organization announcing its own bad news
press packet (see **media kit**)
pretentious language words and phrases that imply more than is warranted, thus risking misleading audiences and raising ethical issues (compare with **doublespeak**)
pretest/posttest (see **before-after** study)
primary research generation and analysis of new information to address a research question or problem (compare with **secondary research**)
print media media delivered primarily through print vehicles (compare with **electronic media**)
privacy legal right to be left alone
proactive strategy approach to organizational strategy that enables an organization to launch a communication program under the conditions and according to the timeline that seems to best fit the organization's interests (compare with **reactive strategy**)
probability the notion that every element in a population has an equal chance of being selected for a sample
probability sampling a series of techniques for selecting samples of a population based on the principle of probability; categories include **simple random**, **systematic**, **stratified** and **cluster sampling**; also called *EPSEM sampling*
producer type of public that provides input to an organization, including employees, volunteers, suppliers and financial backers
product integration company pays for a commercial product to be woven into a TV or movie story line
product placement a company can pay for their products to appear in TV programs or movies
program ongoing public relations activity dealing with several objectives associated with a goal; part of a continuing mission within the organization and focused on its relationship with a particular public (compare with **project** and **campaign**)
progress report research report monitoring program tactics at various key points during implementation period
project single and usually short-lived public relations activity designed to meet an objective (compare with **campaign** and **program**)

project fee fee structure for public relations or advertising agency featuring costs associated with specific tasks

propaganda debasement of persuasive communication associated with half-truths and hidden agendas

proportionate sampling approach to stratified sampling in which each demographic group is sized according to its proportion in the population

proposition primary idea in a speech, editorial, advertisement, television program or other communication vehicle; may be a **factual proposition**, **conjecture proposition**, **value proposition**, or **policy proposition**; also called *claim*

pseudo-event (see **staged activity**)

psychographics audience characteristics based on lifestyle characteristics and interests (compare with **demographics**)

psychological noise communication disruption caused by emotional distractions by the receiver

psychological type concept observing that people have different natural preferences in gathering and processing information, making decisions, and acting on those decisions (compare with **temperament**)

public group of people that shares a common interest vis-à-vis an organization, recognizes its significance, and sets out to do something about it

public agenda topics the citizenry or media audiences are interested in (compare with **media agenda**)

public media media that are generally accessible by everybody (compare with **nonpublic media**)

public relations management function that classically focuses on long-term patterns of interaction between an organization and all of its publics, both supportive and nonsupportive, seeking to enhance those relationships and thus generate mutual understanding, goodwill and support (compare with **marketing communication** and **integrated communication**)

public relations audit analysis of the strengths and weaknesses of the public relations concerns of an organization or client

public relations situation set of circumstances facing an organization, whether an **opportunity** or an **obstacle**

publicity aspect of communication strategy that involves the attention given by the news media to an organization

publicity stunt gimmick planned by an organization mainly to gain publicity, having little value beyond attention (compare with **staged activity**)

pulsing approach to scheduling that combines **continuity** and **flighting** approaches, resulting in a continuous base of messages augmented with intermittent bursts of greater communication activity

purdah (see **strategic silence**)

pure research (see **academic research**)

purposive sampling nonprobability sampling technique that includes subjects simply because they have a particular demographic characteristic (also called **judgment sampling**)

Q&A (see **question-and-answer piece**)

qualitative research type of research based on informal methodologies not capable of generating number-based information and conclusions

quantitative research type of research based on formal methodologies, generating number-based information and conclusions

query letter type of indirect news material inquiring whether editors or news directors would be interested in a particular article, particularly one contemplated by a freelance writer or producer

question-and-answer piece type of feature release written in question-and-answer format; also called *Q&A*

questionnaire instrument used in survey research that presents a series of questions/items and response choices

quick response strategic principle of crisis management that an organization should be as accessible to its publics as possible, aiming to end the crisis as soon as possible

quota sampling nonprobability sampling technique that begins with a selection of subjects based on demographic criteria, then continues with other nonprobability techniques

quotes statements presented as the verbatim words of an information source

random sampling (see **simple random sampling**)

Rank's model of persuasion model that identifies typical patterns used to compare one's own and opponent's arguments or positions

rating scale response technique used in survey questionnaires calling for respondents to rate the degree of their feeling or certainty about an item

reactive strategy approach to organizational strategy in which an organization responds to influences and opportunities from its environment (compare with **proactive strategy**)

readability level of reading difficulty

regret vocal commiseration strategy in which an organization admits sorrow and remorse for a situation, without directly admitting fault

reiteration internal repetition of main ideas within a persuasive message

relabeling diversionary response strategy that tries to distance an organization from criticism by offering an agreeable name to replace a negative label applied by others

relationship management goal type of goal focusing on how an organization connects with its publics

repentance rectifying behavior in which an organization demonstrates a change of heart and change in action, signaling full atonement and becoming an advocate for a new way of thinking and acting

reputation aspect of an organization's external environment dealing with how people evaluate the information they have about an organization

reputational management goal type of goal dealing with an organization's identity and perception

reputational priorities strategic principle of crisis management that an organization should set objectives to maintain and/or restore credibility, using a crisis as an opportunity to enhance its reputation

research formal program of information gathering (see academic research and applied research)

research design plan for program evaluation that outlines criteria for determination of what to evaluate, based on particular criteria related to objectives

response releases type of news release that deals with new or updated information, comments, public interest tie-ins, and speeches

response strategies category of reactive public relations
restitution rectifying behavior strategy in which an organization makes amends by compensating victims or restoring a situation to its earlier condition
retainer fee structure for public relations or advertising agency featuring fixed monthly rates paid in advance for a predetermined level of agency availability
rhetoric art of using words effectively in speaking and writing for the purpose of influencing, persuading or entertaining
risk management process of identifying, controlling and minimizing the impact of uncertain events on an organization
ROB (see **run of book**)
ROP (see **run of press**)
ROS (see **run of station**)
rotary paint type of outdoor advertising sign that can be moved from place to place
run of book indication that an advertisement can be placed anywhere within a magazine, compared to special placement; abbreviated *ROB*
run of press indication that an advertisement can be placed anywhere within a newspaper, compared to special placement; abbreviated *ROP*
run of station indication that an advertisement can be placed anywhere with a daily cycle for radio advertising, compared with placement on a particular program; abbreviated *ROS*

saliency degree to which information is perceived as being applicable or useful to an audience
same-as-before budgeting looking at how much an organization spent on a similar recent project and allowing the same budget for the new project
sampling research practice of first identifying a subset of a population that reflects and represents the larger body, then using this sample as the basis of study (see also **extrapolation**)
sampling error extent to which a research sample does not perfectly correspond with its population (also called *margin of error*)
satellite media tour type of news interview featuring a news source at one location and reporters linked via satellite television from various locations; abbreviated *SMT*
scrutiny aspect of persuasion that focuses on the ability of a message source to examine or investigate an audience and thus to pronounce blame, proclaim innocence, or grant forgiveness
secondary customer subgroup of customer public that uses the services of the organization's primary customers, such as graduate schools or businesses that receive a college's graduates
secondary research re-analyzing existing information obtained by previous researcher for a new and specific purpose (compare with **primary research**)
semantic differential scale type of rating scale asking respondents to select a point on a continuum between two opposing positions
semantic noise communication disruption caused by use of language not understood or appropriately interpreted by the receiver
service article type of feature release providing step-by-step directions and practical information; also called *how-to piece*
service mark words or phrases developed to be closely associated with specific organizations and protected by law for the use of those organizations

sex appeal persuasion technique and type of positive emotional appeal based on gender, nudity and sexuality
shadow constituency subgroup of customer public involving people who, though they do not have a direct link to the organization's products or services, can affect the perception of an organization by its publics
shelter poster advertising panels located in or on bus shelters
shock offensive response strategy of deliberately agitating the mind or emotions of publics through the use of surprise, disgust or other strong and unexpected stimulus
shovelware term for the posting of already-published articles from newspapers and magazines in their original print version
signage generic name for range of stationary outdoor signs promoting an organization and its facilities
SiLoBaTi+UnFa acronym identifying the major elements of newsworthy information: significance, local, balance, timely plus unusual and famous
similarity aspect of persuasion that focuses on the extent to which a message source resembles the audience
simple random sampling probability sampling technique exemplified by a lottery-type drawing
single-issue public may be active on all of the issues important to an organization, active only on some popular issues, or active on single and often controversial issues. See also *active public*
situation (see **public relations situation**)
situation analysis (see **formative research**)
situational ethics (see **ethical relativism**)
slander spoken **defamation**
slogan catchphrase developed as part of a communication program or campaign; also called *tagline* or *verbal logo*
SMT (see **satellite media tour**)
snipe billboard overlay that can update existing poster messages without the need to change the poster completely
snowball sampling nonprobability sampling technique that begins with a small group of individuals with certain demographic characteristics and continues with similar individuals they recommend; also called *sociosampling*
social judgment theory theory that observes that individuals accept or reject messages to the extent that they perceive the message as corresponding to their beliefs and attitudes
social media release (SMR) type of news release intended for **blogs**, **websites**, and other online uses
sociosampling (see **snowball sampling**)
special events category of interpersonal communication tactics centering on planned activities created by an organization for the purpose of interacting with its publics
spectacular type of billboard featuring an element beyond the standard rectangular surface, sometimes 3-D add-ons, use of lighting with a billboard, or other feature
sponsored news organizations use their expertise to present objective and credible information to their publics; also called *sponsored public affairs programming*
sponsorship proactive strategy of offering or supporting programs oriented toward community relations

spot advertising use of television advertising at the local level (compare with network placement)

spot radio same as spot advertising in reference to radio

staged activity activity developed or orchestrated by an organization to provide an opportunity to gain attention and acceptance of key publics; also called *pseudo-event* (compare with **publicity stunt**)

stage-of-life-cycle budgeting examination of the phases of development, knowing that start-up programs generally require more financial resources than maintenance programs (compare with **zero-based budgeting**)

standard error statistic used to describe **sampling error**

standby statement (see **contingency statement**)

station poster advertising panels located in subway, train and bus stations and in airport terminals; also called *diorama*

statistics persuasion technique and type of verbal evidence providing clear and hard-to-dispute facts to make a case

status aspect of persuasion that focuses on the social position or prestige of a message source

stereotype oversimplified shortcut to describe groups of people, based on common and repeated perceptions of who people are, how they act, and what they think and value

story idea memo type of indirect news material proving media gatekeepers with tips and ideas for feature articles; also called *tip sheet*

strategy organization's overall plan

strategic ambiguity refusal to be pinned down to a particular response, often by artfully dodging a question.

strategic communication planned communication campaigns associated with public relations or marketing communication, undertaken by an organization, usually for information or persuasive purposes

strategic inaction public relations response strategy of making no statement and taking no overt action, allowing a situation to fade

strategic manager organizational manager who makes decisions concerned with management, trends, issues, policies and corporate structure (compare with **tactical manager**)

strategic philanthropy proactive strategy in which businesses fund or otherwise support community relations gestures with an eye toward employees and customers

strategic public public with which an organization chooses to engage in communication and relationship (compare with **target public**)

strategic research systematic gathering of information about issues and publics that affect organizations (compare with **tactical research**)

strategic silence by not responding to criticism an organization may be able to shorten the life span of a crisis situation; also called *purdah*

strategy organization's overall plan, determining what it wants to achieve and how it wants to achieve it, offering direction in both proactive and reactive organizational activity and messages: theme, source, content and tone (compare with **tactic**)

stratified sampling probability sampling technique that first ranks elements according to demographic factors, then draws elements from each factor using **random** or **systematic sampling** techniques

streaming video (see **nonbroadcast video**)

street theater type of activism that focuses on dramatization in public places; also called **guerrilla theater**

structure the role public relations plays within the organization's administration

studio interview hybrid of interview and news conference, featuring a media interviewer or host questioning one or more guests or spokespersons

subscription radio (see **digital radio**)

summative report research report at conclusion of strategic program, reviewing the impact and outcome of the complete program; also called *final report*

superstitial ad computer advertising that insinuates itself onto computer screens to fill in time between moves from one site to another (compare with **interstitial ad**)

supporter public that currently or potentially can help an organization achieve its objectives

survey quantitative research technique based on a standard series of questions and yielding statistical results and conclusions; also called *polling* (compare with **questionnaire**)

SWOT analysis strategic planning tool analyzing an organization's strengths, weaknesses, opportunities and threats

symbol type of nonverbal communication in which visual representations point to realities beyond themselves

symbolic consensus tagline that acts as a rallying cry for supporters

symmetry theory theory that extends consistency theory to groups

systematic sampling probability sampling technique involving the selection of subjects spaced at equal intervals

tactic visible element of a strategic plan; specific vehicles of communication

tactical manager organizational manager who makes day-to-day decisions on practical and specific issues (compare with **strategic manager**)

tactical research gathering of information to guide the production and dissemination of messages (compare with **strategic research**)

tagline (see **slogan**)

target public term sometimes used as synonymous with strategic public but carrying the connotation that the public is an object of action by an organization rather than a partner in a relationship (compare with **strategic public**)

targeted media media that have narrow and homogeneous audiences (compare with **mass media**)

task management goal type of goal concerned with getting certain things accomplished

teleological ethics approach to decision making focused on the impact that actions have on people, rooted in the notion that good results come from good actions (compare with **deontological ethics** and **ethical relativism**)

temperament concept observing that people have different approaches and predispositions (compare with **psychological type**)

testimony persuasion technique and type of verbal evidence using comments by witnesses and by people who have used an organization's products or services

theoretical research (see **academic research**)

theory of accounts (see **accounts**)

theory of image restoration (see **image restoration**)

third-party endorsement concept referring to the added credibility that comes with the endorsement of an outside and unbiased agent, such as a reporter or editor
threat offensive response strategy involving the promise of harm toward an accuser
timeline implementation schedule for strategic plan
tip sheet (see **story idea memo**)
touch-sensitive computers touch-screen technology that allows user to input information without using a keyboard
trade media media that focus on information of interest to people in their professional lives (compare with **popular media**)
transit advertising category of advertising on vehicles, including bus signs and mobile billboards
transparent communication concept of proactive public relations strategy referring to open and observable activity by an organization that helps publics understand the organization and support its actions
triggering events activities that generate action among key publics
two-step flow of communication theory theory that identifies opinion leaders as a key link in the process of organizational communication with publics

uncontrolled media media that limit or eliminate an organization's ability to determine various attributes (compare with **controlled media**)
unique selling proposition special something that a product or service offers that is different from all the competition. A kind of niche statement that positions the product for the intended **market segment**.
unit-of-sales budgeting based not on dollars but on prior outcomes
unobtrusive research where the subjects in a study do not know they are being observed
unwarranted conclusion error in logic based on a deduction not supported by evidence

value proposition aspect of logical persuasive appeal arguing the virtue or merits of something
verbal communication communication occurring through written and spoken words (compare with **nonverbal communication**)
verbal logo (see **slogan**)
verbal evidence type of proof claim in a discussion or argument based not on physical evidence but rather on words and ideas
victimization (see **excuse**)
video B-roll sound bites and raw, unedited footage provided to television stations to use in news reports
videoconference television technology used to produce live informational or educational programs for remote audiences; also called teleconference
video news release news release written and produced specifically for television stations, presented as an edited story package; abbreviated *VNR*
virtual ads for examples, product billboards that appear in the background during a televised sporting event that are digitally inserted for the TV audience
virtue appeal persuasion technique and type of positive emotional appeal based on values that individuals and society hold in esteem
visibility aspect of an organization's external environment focusing on the degree to which its publics know about the organization, and the accuracy of that information

vlogs blogs that primarily consist of video
VNR (see **video news release**)
vocal activist type of opinion leader who is linked with a particular issue and/or who acts as an advocate for a cause
volunteer sampling nonprobability sampling technique that draws subjects who willingly offer themselves to be part of a study

wall mural type of outdoor advertising featuring the painted exterior of a building leased for advertising purposes; also called **wallscape**
web-only commercials video advertisements that are used only on the Internet
websites set of interconnected web pages, usually prepared and maintained as a collection of information by a person, group, or organization
web video (see **nonbroadcast video**)
weighted sampling (see **disproportionate sampling**)
what-if-not-funded analysis examines consequences of inaction and their effect on the organization's mission
white paper (see **position statement**)
wiki collaborative website where all users can edit and update content
word-of-mouth support effective type of communication relying on opinion leaders

zealot single-issue activist acting with missionary fervor
zero-based budgeting approach to budgeting based on current needs rather than past expenditures

Citations and Recommended Readings

Introduction

Austin, E. W., & Pinkleton, B. E. (2006). *Strategic public relations management: Planning and managing effective communication program* (2nd ed.). Mahwah, NJ: Erlbaum.

Blakeman, R. (2007). *Integrated marketing communication: Creative strategy from idea to implementation*. Lanham, MD: Rowman & Littlefield.

Botan, C. H. (1997). Ethics in strategic communication campaigns: The case for a new approach to public relations. *Journal of Business Communication, 34*(2), 188–202.

Botan, C. H., & Soto, F. (1998). A semiotic approach to the internal functioning of publics: Implications for strategic communication and public relations. *Public Relations Review, 24*(1), 21–44.

Burnett, J., & Moriarty, S. (1998). *Introduction to marketing communications: An integrated approach.* Upper Saddle River, NJ: Prentice Hall.

Caywood, C. L. (1995). *International handbook of public relations and corporate communications.* Hillsdale, NJ: Erlbaum.

Caywood, C. L. (1997). *The handbook of strategic public relations and integrated communications.* New York: McGraw-Hill.

Clow, K. E., & Baack, D. E. (2006). *Integrated advertising, promotion and marketing communications* (3rd ed.). Upper Saddle River, NJ: Prentice Hall.

Crifasi, S. C. (September 2000). Everything's coming up Rosie. *Public Relations Tactics, 7*(9).

Cutlip, S. M., Center, A. H., & Broom, G. M. (2005). *Effective public relations* (9th ed.). Upper Saddle River, NJ: Prentice Hall.

Goldman, J. (1984). *Public relations in the marketing mix: Introducing vulnerability relations.* Lincolnwood, IL: NTC Business.

Gray, R. (1998, June 11). PR does the business. *Marketing,* 24–26.

Gronstedt, A. (2000). *The customer century: Lessons from world class companies in integrated marketing and communications.* New York: Routledge.

Grunig, J. E. (Ed.). (1992). *Excellence in public relations and communication management.* Hillsdale, NJ: Erlbaum.

Grunig, J. E., & Hunt, T. (1984). *Managing public relations*. New York: Holt, Rinehart, & Winston.

Harris, T. L., & Whalen, P. T. (2006). *The marketer's guide to public relations in the 21st century.* Mason, OH: Thomson/South-Western Educational.

Harris, T. L. (2000). *Value added public relations: The secret weapon of integrated marketing.* Chicago: NTC Business.

Hendrix, J. (2006). *Public relations cases* (7th ed.). Belmont, CA: Wadsworth.

Hiebert, R. W. (2000, Fall). The customer century: Lessons from world class companies in integrated marketing and communications. *Public Relations Review, 26*(3), 381.

Holmes, P. (1998, September 28). With Bell's appointed, Y&R's commitment to integration now goes beyond lip service. *Inside PR, 5*(9), 2, 10.

Italian American stereotypes in U.S. advertising (Summer 2003). Washington, DC: Order of Sons of Italy in America.

Kelly, K. S. (2001). Stewardship: The fifth step in the public relations process. In R. I. Heath & G. M. Vasquez, eds., *Handbook of public relations* (pp. 279–290). Thousand Oaks, CA: Sage.

Kendall, R. (1997). *Public relations campaign strategies: Planning for implementation* (2nd ed.). New York: Addison-Wesley.

Kitchen, P. J., & Schultz, D. E. (1999). A multi-country comparison of the drive for IMC. *Journal of Advertising Research, 39*(7), 21–38.

Kotler, P., Roberto, N., & Lee, N. (2002). *Social marketing: Improving the quality of life* (2nd ed.). Thousand Oaks, CA: Sage.

Marston, J. E. (1963). *The nature of public relations*. New York: McGraw-Hill.

McElreath, M. (1997). *Managing systematic and ethical public relations campaigns* (2nd ed.). Madison, WI: Brown & Benchmark.

Miller, D. A., & Rose, P. B. (1994). Integrated communications: A look at reality instead of theory. *Public Relations Quarterly, 39*(11), 13–16.

Nemec, R. (1999). PR or advertising: Who's on top? *Communication World, 16*(3), 25–28.

Newsom, D., VanSlyke Turk, J., & Kruckeberg, D. (2006). *This is PR: The realities of public relations* (9th ed.). Belmont, CA: Wadsworth.

Ostrowski, H. (1999). Moving the measurement needle. *Public Relations Strategist, 5*(2), 37–39.

Parkinson, M., & Ekachai, D. G. (2005). *International and intercultural public relations: A campaign case approach.* Boston: Allyn & Bacon.

Ries, A., & Ries, G. (2002). *The fall of advertising and the rise of PR.* New York: HarperCollins.

Ross, B. I., & Richards, J. I. (Eds.). (2008). *Where shall I go to study advertising and public relations? Advertising and public relations programs in the United States colleges and universities.* Lubbock, TX: Advertising Education Publications.

Scheufele, D. A. (1999) Framing as a Theory of Media Effects. *Journal of Communication, 49*(4), 103–122.

Schultz, D. E., Tannenbaum, S. I., & Lauterborn, R. F. (1993). *Integrated marketing communications: Pulling it together and making it work.* Lincolnwood, IL: NTC Business.

Seitel, F. P. (2006). *The practice of public relations* (10th ed.). Upper Saddle River, NJ: Prentice Hall.

Sirgy, M. J. (2004). *Integrated marketing communications: A systems approach.* Upper Saddle River, NJ: Pewarson.

Wilcox, D. L., Ault, P. H., Agee, W. K., & Cameron, G. T. (2005). *Public relations: Strategies and tactics* (8th ed.). New York: Longman.

Wilson, L. (2000). *Strategic program planning for effective public relations campaigns* (3rd ed.). Dubuque, IA: Kendall-Hunt.

Zappala, J., & Carden, A. R. (2004). *Public relations worktext: A writing and planning resource.* Mahwah, NJ: Erlbaum.

Phase One

Aguilar, F. J. (1967). *Scanning the business environment.* New York: Macmillan.

Bakhsheshy, A. (2003). Chapter 5. Retrieved from http://www.business.utah.edu~mgtab

Boe, A. R. (1979). Fitting the corporation to the future. *Public Relations Quarterly, 24,* 4–6.

Chase, W. H. (1977). Public issue management: The new science. *Public Relations Journal, 33*(10), 25–26.

Cuddeford-Jones, M. (2002, March). Brand redemption and risk management: Morag Cuddeford-Jones asks if it is possible for brands to redeem themselves after a PR disaster. *Brand Strategy*, p. 10.

Dearing, J. W., & Rogers, E. M. (1996). *Communication concepts 6: Agenda-setting*. Thousand Oaks, CA: Sage.

Dewey, J. (1927). *The public and its problems*. Chicago: Swallow.

Esman, M. J. (1972). The elements of institution building. In J. W. Eaton (Ed.), *Institution building and development* (pp. 78–90). Beverly Hills, CA: Sage.

Evan,W. H. (1976). *Interorganizational relations*. New York: Penguin.

Ewing, R. P. (1997). Issues management: Managing trends through the issues life cycle. In C. C. Caywood (Ed.), *The handbook of strategic public relations and integrated communications* (pp. 173–188). New York: McGraw-Hill.

Finn, D. (1998). How ethical can we be? Retrieved from www.ruderfinn.com/persp/how_ethical.html

Grunig, J. E., & Hunt, T. (1984). *Managing public relations*. New York: Holt, Rinehart, & Winston.

Hart, R. (2006, April). Measuring success: How to 'sell' a communications audit to internal audiences. *Public Relations Tactics*, *13*(4).

Hedrick, T. E., Bickman, L., & Rog, D. J. (1993). *Applied social research methods; Vol. 32, Applied research design: A practical guide*. Newbury Park, CA: Sage.

Jackson, P. (Ed.). (1994). *Practical, actionable research for public relations purposes*. Exeter, NH: PR Publishing.

Jones, B. L., & Chase, W. H. (1979). Managing public policy issues. *Public Relations Review, 5,* 2–23.

Klein, P. (1999). Measure what matters. *Communication World, 16*(9), 32.

Lauzen, M. (1997). Understanding the relation between public relations and issues management. *Journal of Public Relations Research, 9*(1), 65–82.

Lazarsfeld, P. F., Berelson, B., & Gaudet, H. (1944). *The people's choice*. New York: Columbia University Press.

Ledingham, J. A. & Bruning, S. D. (2000). *Public Relations as relationship management: A relationship approach to the study and practice of public relations*. Mahwah NJ: Erlbaum.

Lippmann, W. (1922). *Public opinion*. New York: Macmillan.

Lukaszewski, J. E. (1997). Establishing individual and corporate crisis communication standards: The principles and protocols. *Public Relations Quarterly, 42,* 7–14.

Maslow, A. (1987). *Motivation and personality* (3rd ed.). Boston: Addison-Wesley.

Martin J. (2008, June 1). Miss Manners. Syndicated column.

Matera, F. R., & Artigue, R. J. (2000). *Public relations campaign and techniques: Building bridges into the 21st century.* Boston: Allyn & Bacon.

Mau, R. R., & Dennis, L. B. (1994). Companies ignore shadow constituencies at their peril. *Public Relations Journal, 50*(5), 10–11.

Morton, L. P. (2002a). Targeting Native Americans. *Public Relations Quarterly, 47*(1), 37.

Morton, L. P. (2002b). Targeting Generation Y. *Public Relations Quarterly, 47*(2), 46.

Opinion leaders. New study outlines how to reach them. (1992, October 5). *PR Reporter, 35*(38), 1–3.

Packard, V. (1964). *The hidden persuaders*. New York: Pocket Books.

Rawlins, B. L. (2006). *Prioritizing stakeholders for public relations*. New York: Institute for Public Relations Research.

Regester, M., & Larkin, J. (2005). *Risk issues and crisis management* (3rd ed.). London: Kogan Page.

Rogers, E. (1995). *The diffusion of innovations* (4th ed.). New York: Free Press.

Salmon, R., & De Linares, Y. (1999). *Competitive intelligence: Scanning the global environment.* Bucharest, Romania: Economica.

Sandman, P. (2003). Stakeholders. Retrieved from www.petersandman.com/col/stakeh.htm.

Schwartz, P., & Gibb, B. (1999). *When good companies do bad things: Responsibility and risk in an age of globalization*. New York: Wiley.

Phase Two

Associated Press. (1998, November 4). Store circular runs with m-i-s-t-a-k-e. *Journal Record* (Oklahoma City). Retrieved from http://findarticles.com/p/articles/mi_qn4182/is_/ai_n10123109?tag=art Body;col1

Barlow, W. G. (1995). *Establishing public relations objectives and assessing public relations results.* Gainesville, FL: Institute for Public Relations Research.

Barnhurst, K. G., & Mutz, D. (1997). American journalism and the decline in event-centered reporting. *Journal of Communication, 47*(4), 27–53.

Benjamin, J. (1997). *Principles, elements, and types of persuasion*. Fort Worth, TX: Harcourt Brace.

Benoit, W. L. (1995). *Accounts, excuses, and apologies: A theory of image restoration strategies*. SUNY Series in Speech Communication. Albany, NY: State University of New York Press.

Berlo, D. (1960). *The process of communication: An introduction to theory and practice*. San Francisco: Rinehart.

Botan, C. (1997). Ethics in strategic communication campaigns: The case for a new approach to public relations. *Journal of Business Communication, 34*(2), 188–202.

Bouchez, Colette. (n.d.). Hollywood takes action on health. Retrieved September 29, 2008 from http://men.webmd.com/features/hollywood-takes-action-on-health

Buber, M. (1947). *Between man and man.* London: Routledge & Kegan Paul. Reprinted in F. W. Matson & A. Montagu (Eds.). (1967). *The human dialogue: Perspectives on communication* New York: Free Press.

Burson-Marsteller Public Relations. (1998, May). Market Facts Omnibus: Knowledge Works. Retrieved from www.bm.com

Christians, C. G., Fackler, M., & Rotzoll, K. B. (2004). *Media ethics: Cases and moral reasoning* (7th ed.). New York: Longman.

Cody, M. J., & McLaughlin, M. L. (1985). Models for the sequential construction of accounting episodes: Situational and interactional constraints on message selection and evaluation. In R. L. Street & L. Capella (Eds.), *Sequence and pattern in communication behavior* (pp. 50–69). London: Edward Arnold.

Cody, M. J., & McLaughlin, M. L. (1990). Interpersonal accounting. In H. Giles & W. P. Robinson (Eds.), *Handbook of language and social psychology* (pp. 227–255). Chichester, England: Wiley.

Commentary: It's time to put the Valdez behind us (1999, March 29). *Business Week.*

Delwiche, A. (n.d.). Fear. Retrieved September 28, 2008 from http://www.propagandacritic.com/articles/ct.sa.fear.html

Edelman Change and Employee Engagement, in partnership with PeopleMetrics. (2006). New frontiers in employee communications. Retrieved September 28, 2008 from http://www.edelman.com/news/storycrafter/uploads/NewFrontiers2006_Finalpaper.pdf

Fearn-Banks, K. (2007). *Crisis communications: A casebook approach* (3rd ed.). Mahwah, NJ: Erlbaum.

Festinger, L. (1957). *A theory of cognitive dissonance*. Stanford, CA: Stanford University Press.

Fitzpatrick, K. R., & Rubin, M. S. (1995). Public relations vs. legal strategies in organizational crisis decisions. *Public Relations Review, 21*(1), 21–33.

Friedman, M. (2003). Objectives: The "weakest link" in public relations campaigns. *PR Insight*. Retrieved March 20, 2004, from www.internetprguide.com

Goffman, E. (1974). *Frame analysis: An essay on the organization of experience*. London: Harper & Row.

Gottschalk, J. A. (Ed.). (1993). *Crisis response: Inside stories in managing image under siege*. Detroit: Gale Research.

Hearit, K. M. (1994). Apologies and public relations crises at Chrysler, Toshiba, and Volvo. *Public Relations Review, 20*(2), 113–125.

Heath, R. L. (1997). *Strategic issues management: Organizations and public policy challenges*. Thousand Oaks, CA: Sage.

Heider, F. (1946). Attitudes and cognitive organization. *Psychological Review, 51,* 358–374.

Heider, F. (1958). *The psychology of interpersonal relations*. New York: Wiley.

Hon, L. C. (1998). Demonstrating effectiveness in public relations: Goals, objectives, and evaluation. *Journal of Public Relations Research, 10*(2), 103–135.

Infante, D. A., Rancer, A. S., & Womack, D. F. (2003). *Building communication theory* (4th ed.). Prospect Heights, IL: Waveland.

Iyengar, S., & Kinder, D. R. (1987). *News that Matters: Television and American opinion*. American Politics and Political Economy. Chicago: University of Chicago Press.

Jackson, P. (Ed.). (1997). Items of importance to practitioners. *PR Reporter, 40*(46), 3.

Jenkins, P. (2003). *The new anti-Catholicism: The last acceptable prejudice*. New York: Oxford University Press.

Johnston, D. D. (1994). *The art and science of persuasion*. Boston: McGraw-Hill.

"Juice-Poisoning Case Brings Guilty Plea and a Huge Fine." (1998, July 24). *New York Times*.

Keirsey, D., & Bates, M. (1984). *Please understand me.* Del Mar, CA: Prometheus Nemesis.

Kelly, J. A., St. Lawrence, J. S., Diaz, Y. E., Stevenson, L. Y., Hauth, A. C., Brasfield, T. L., et al. (1991). HIV risk behavior reduction following intervention with key opinion leaders of a population: An experimental community-level analysis. *American Journal of Public Health, 81,* 168–171.

Kelly, J. A., St. Lawrence, J. S., Stevenson, L. Y., Hauth, A. C., Kalichman, S. C., Diaz, Y. E., et al. (1992). Community AIDS/HIV risk reduction: The effects of endorsement by popular people in three cities. *American Journal of Public Health, 82,* 1483–1489.

Kotler, P., Roberto, N., & Lee, N. (2007). *Social marketing: Influencing behaviors for good* (3rd ed.). Thousand Oaks, CA: Sage.

Kowalski, R. M., & Erickson, J. R. (1997). Complaints and complaining: Functions, antecedents and consequences. *Psychological Bulletin, 119*(2), 179–196.

Larson, C. U. (2000). *Persuasion: Reception and responsibility* (9th ed.). Belmont, CA: Wadsworth.

Larson, R. J., Woloshin, S., Schwartz, L. M., & Welch, H. G. (2005, May 4). Celebrity Endorsements of Cancer Screening. *Journal of the National Cancer Institute, 97*(9), 693–695.

Lasswell, H. D. (1948). The structure and function of communication in society. In L. Bryson (Ed.), *The communication of ideas* (p. 34). New York: Harper.

Lee, F., Peterson, C., & Tiedens, L. (2004). Mea culpa: Predicting stock prices from organizational attributions. *Personality and Social Psychology Bulletin, 30*(12), 1636–1649.

Lipstein, B. (1985). An historical retrospective of copy research. *Journal of Advertising Research, 24*(6), 11–14.

The Lives We Touch. (1992). In J. A. Hendrix, *Public relations cases* (2nd ed.). Belmont, CA: Wadsworth.

Macdaid, G. P., McCaulley, M. H., & Kainz, R .I. (1986). *MBTI Atlas of Type Tables* (2 vols.). Gainesville, FL: Center for Applications in Psychological Type.

Marconi, J. (1996). *Image marketing: Using public perceptions to attain business objectives.* Lincolnwood, IL: NTC/Business.

Martin, J. (1999, May 10). Miss Manners. Syndicated column.

Martinelli, K. A., & Briggs, W. (1998, Winter). Integrating public relations and legal responses during a crisis: The case of Odwalla, Inc. *Public Relations Review, 20,* 443–460.

Martosko, D. (2005). *Holy cows: How PETA twists religion to push "animal rights."* Washington, DC: Center for Consumer Freedom.

McCombs, M. E., & Shaw, D. L. (1972). The agenda-setting function of mass media. *Public Opinion Quarterly, 36,* 176–187.

McGuire,W. J., & Papageorgis, D. (1961). The relative efficacy of various types of prior belief defense in producing immunity against persuasion. *Journal of Abnormal and Social Psychology, 62,* 327–337.

Miciak, A. R., & Shanklin, W. L. (1994). Choosing celebrity endorsers: The risks are real, but sports and entertainment spokespersons still burnish corporate images and sell brands. *Advertising Management, 3*(3), 51.

Minogue, S. (2003a, June 30). How can you get the most marketing value out of CSR? *Strategy,* 18.

Minogue, S. (2003b, June 30). Special report: Public relations. *Strategy,* 18.

Myers, I. B. (1987). *Introduction to type.* (Rev. A. L. Hammer.) Gainesville, FL: Center for Applications of Psychological Type.

Myers, I. B., & Myers, P. B. (1980). *Gifts differing: Understanding personality type.* Palo Alto, CA: Consulting Psychologists Press.

Nager, N. R., & Allen, T. H. (1984). *Public relations management by objectives.* Lanham, MD: University Press of America.

Newcomb, T.M. (1953). An approach to the study of communicative acts. *Psychological Review, 60,* 393–404.

Nyer, P. U. (1999). Cathartic complaining as a means of reducing consumer dissatisfaction. *Journal of Consumer Satisfaction, Dissatisfaction and Complaining Behavior, 12,* 15–25.

Nyer, P. U. (2000). An investigation into whether complaining can cause increased consumer satisfaction. *Journal of Consumer Marketing, 17*(1), 9–19.

Osgood, C. E., & Tannenbaum, P. H. (1955). The principle of congruity in the prediction of attitude change. *Psychological Review, 62,* 42–55.

Pfau, M., & Parrott, R. (2001). *Persuasive communication campaigns.* Boston: Pearson.

Pharma Opinion Leaders. (2003, November 11). *PR Newswire.*

Rank, H. (1976). Teaching about public persuasion. In D. Dieterich (Ed.), *Teaching and doublespeak* (pp. 3–19). Urbana, IL: NCTE.

Ray, M. (1973). Marketing communication and the hierarchy of effects. In P. Clarke (Ed.), *New models for communication research* (pp. 147–176). Newbury Park, CA: Sage.

Ries, A., & Trout, J. (2001). *Positioning: The battle for your mind.* New York: McGraw-Hill.

Rogers, E. (2003). *The diffusion of innovations* (5th ed.). New York: Free Press.

Roser, C., & Thompson, M. (1995). Fear appeals and the formation of active publics. *Journal of Communication, 45*(1),103–119.

Ross, R. S. (1994). *Understanding persuasion* (4th ed.). Englewood Cliffs, NJ: Prentice Hall.

Scheufele, D. (1999). Framing as a theory of media effects. *Journal of Communication, 49*(1), pp. 103–122.

Schramm, W. (1971). The nature of communication between humans. In W. Schramm & D. F. Roberts (Eds.), *The process and effects of mass communication*. Urbana,: University of Illinois Press.

Schreiber, A. L. (1994). *Lifestyle and event marketing: Building the new customer partnership*. New York: McGraw-Hill.

Seideman, T. (1997, May/June). Nonprofit prophets. *Reputation Management*, 46–53.

Shannon, C. E., & Weaver, W. (1949). *The mathematical theory of communication*. Urbana: University of Illinois Press.

Sherif, M., & Hovland, C. I. (1961). *Social judgment.* New Haven, CT: Yale University Press.

Sieberg, E. (1976). Confirming and disconfirming organizational communication. In J. L. Owen, P. A. Page, & G. I. Zimmerman (Eds.), *Communication in organizations.* St. Paul, MN: West.

Simons, H. W., Morreale, J., & Gronbeck, B. (2001). *Persuasion in society*. Thousand Oaks, CA: Sage.

Smith, R. D. (1993). Psychological type and public relations: Theory, research, and applications. *Journal of Public Relations Research, 5*(3), 177–199.

Smith, R. D. (2008). *Becoming a public relations writer* (3rd ed.). New York: Routledge.

Sperry, R. W. (1985). Consciousness, personal identity and the divided brain. In D. F. Benson & E. Zaidel (Eds.), *The dual brain: Hemispheric specialization in humans*. UCLA Forum in Medical Sciences, No. 26. New York: Guilford Press.

Stewart, C. J., Smith, C. A., & Denton, R. E. (2001). *Persuasion and social movements* (4th ed.). Prospect Heights, IL: Waveland.

Sugimoto, N. (1997). A Japan-U.S. comparison of apology styles. *Communication Research, 24*(4), 349–370.

Wiener, N. (1954). *The human use of human beings: Cybernetics and society* (2nd ed.). Boston: Houghton Mifflin.

Wild, C. (1993). *Corporate volunteer programs: Benefits to businesses. Report 1029*. New York: Conference Board.

Young, D. (1996). *Building your company's good name: How to create and protect the reputation your organization wants and deserves*. New York: American Management Association.

Phase Three

Amos, J. S. (1995). *Fundraising ideas: Over 225 money making events for community groups, with a resource directory*. Jefferson, NC: McFarland.

Brogan, K. S. (Ed.). (2007). *2008 writer's market*. Cincinnati, OH: Writer's Digest Books.

Brown, M. S. (Ed.). (2008). *Giving USA, 2008* (53rd ed.). Glenview, IL: Giving USA Foundation.

Bulldog Reporter and TEKgroup International, Inc. (2007, October). *2007 journalist survey on media relations practices*. Pompano Beach FL: Bulldog Reporter/TEKgroup International, Inc.

Cameron, G. T. (1994). Does publicity outperform advertising? An experimental test of the third-party endorsement. *Journal of Public Relations Research, 6*(3), 185–207.

Corder L., Deasy, M., & Thompson, J. (1999a, Spring). PR is to experience what marketing is to expectations. *Public Relations Quarterly, 44*(1), 23–26.

Corder L., Deasy, M., & Thompson, J. (1999b, May). Answering the age-old marketing question: What have you done for me lately? *Public Relations Tactics, 12*.

Curtain, P. A. (1999). Reevaluating public relations information subsidies: Market-driven journalism and agenda-building theory and practice. *Journal of Public Relations Research, 11*(1), 53–90.

Edelman Change and Employee Engagement, in partnership with PeopleMetrics. (2006). New frontiers in employee communications. Retrieved September 28, 2008 from http://www.edelman.com/news/storycrafter/uploads/NewFrontiers2006_Finalpaper.pdf

Gale Research. (2005). *Newsletters in print* (19th ed.). Detroit, MI: Gale.

Gillin, P. (2007). *New media, new influencers and implications for the public relations profession.* Retrieved September 28, 2008 from http://www.instituteforpr.org/files/uploads/NewInfluencer.pdf

Glass, S.A. (2001). *Approaching fundraising: Suggestions and insights for fundraising; No. 28, Summer 2000: New directions for philanthropic fundraising, sponsored by the Center on Philanthropy at Indiana University*. San Francisco: Jossey-Bass.

Harris Interactive. (2005, November). *Executive, congressional and consumer attitudes toward media, marketing and the public relations profession*. Rochester NY: Harris Interactive.

Harris Poll. (2001, May 18). *Presenting: The class of 2001: Millennium's first college grads are "connected, career-minded and confident"—way!* Rochester NY: Harris Interactive.

Hunt-Lowrance, K. (Ed.). (2007). *Gale directory of publications and broadcast media* (142nd ed.). Detroit, MI: Gale Research.

Kim, J. B. (1995). The cassette is in the mail. *Advertising Age, 68,* 51.

Krugman, H. E. (1972). Why three exposures may be enough. *Journal of Advertising Research, 12,* 11–28.

Lang, K., & Lang, G. E. (1983). *The battle for public opinion: The president, the press, and the polls during Watergate.* New York: Columbia University Press.

Lippy, C. H. (Ed.). (1986). *Religious periodicals of the United States: Academic and scholarly journals.* New York: Greenwood.

Maddux, D. (Ed.). (2008). *International yearbook 2008* (88th ed.). New York: Editor & Publisher.

McManus, J. (1994). *Market-driven journalism: Let the citizen beware?* Thousand Oaks, CA: Sage.

Middleberg, D., & Ross, S. S. (2001). *The Middleberg/Ross survey of media in the wired world, 2000.* New York: Middleberg Euro.

Moriarty, S., Mitchell, N., & Wells, W. D. (2007). *Advertising: Principles and practices* (8th ed.). Upper Saddle River, N.J.: Prentice Hall.

Newport, F., & Saad, L. (1998). A matter of trust: News sources Americans prefer. *American Journalism Review, 20*(6), 30–33.

Pew Research Center for the People and the Press. (2008, January 11). *Social networking and online videos take off; Internet's Broader Role in Campaign 2008: A survey conducted in association with the Pew Internet and American Life Project*. Washington, DC: Pew Research Center for the People and the Press.

Piirto, R. (1994). Why radio thrives. American Demographics*, 16*(5), 40ff.

Project for Excellence in Journalism. (2006). State of the News Media 2006. Retrieved September 25, 2008 from http://www.stateofthemedia.org/2006

Project for Excellence in Journalism. (2007). State of the News Media 2007. Retrieved September 25, 2008 from http://www.stateofthemedia.org/2007

Rules of engagement: Six tips for pitching the blogosphere—and finding the right blog for your client. (2005, April). *Ragan's Media Relations Report.*

Stenson, P. (1993). How (and why) corporate communicators use video. *Communication World, 10*(10), 14–15.

Survey shows radio use patterns. (1996). *PR News, 52*(15).

Tyson, C. B., & Snyder, L. B. (1999). The impact of direct mail video. *Public Relations Quarterly, 44*(1), 28–32.

Vanden Bergh, B. G., & Katz, H. E. (1999). *Advertising principles: Choice, challenge, change.* Lincolnwood, IL: NTC Business.

West Glen Communications. (2002, April). West Glen Communications releases new PSA survey. New York: West Glen Communications.

Wilcox, D. L., Cameron, G. T., Ault, P. H., & Agee, W. K. (2005). *Public relations: Strategies and tactics* (8th ed.). Boston: Allyn & Bacon.

Williams. W. (1994). *User friendly fund raising: A step-by-step guide to profitable special events.* Alexander, NC: WorldComm.

Phase Four

Bissland, J. H. (1990). Accountability gap: Evaluation practices show improvement. *Public Relations Review, 16*(2), 25–35.

Broom, G., & Dozier, D. (1990). *Using research in public relations: Applications to program management.* Englewood Cliffs, NJ: Prentice Hall.

Corder L., Deasy, M., & Thompson, J. (1999, May). Answering the age-old marketing question: What have you done for me lately? *Public Relations Tactics.*

Dozier, D. M. (1984). Program evaluation and the roles of practitioners. *Public Relations Review, 10*(2), 13–21.

Edelman Public Relations, Opinion Research Corporation, and Northwestern University. (1997, Aug. 25). Planning, goals and measurement (Corporate Communications Benchmark 1997, Section III). Cited in Written PR plans now common—but many not integrated. *PR Reporter,* 3–4.

Evaluation research on the rise, study finds. (1994). In P. Jackson (Ed.), *Practical, actionable research for public relations purposes.* Exeter, NH: PR Publishing.

Fischer, R. (1995). Control construct design in evaluating campaigns. *Public Relations Review, 21*(1), 45–58.

Gofton, K. (1999, April 12). The measure of PR: Measurement and evaluation of public relations campaigns. *Campaign,* S13 (1).

Hon, L. C. (1997). What have you done for me lately? Exploring effectiveness in public relations. *Journal of Public Relations Research, 9*(1), 1–30.

Hon, L. C. (1998). Demonstrating effectiveness in public relations: Goals, objectives, and evaluation. *Journal of Public Relations Research, 10*(2), 103–135.

Lindenmann, W. K. (1997a). Guidelines and standards for measuring and evaluating PR effectiveness. Retrieved from www.instituteforpr.com/pdf/2002_Guidelines_Standards_Book.pdf.

Lindenmann, W. K. (1997b). Setting minimum standards for measuring public relations effectiveness. *Public Relations Review, 213*(1), 391–408.

Peterson, Eric. (2007). How to measure visitor engagement, redux. Retrieved October 13, 2008, from http://blog.webanalyticsdemystified.com/weblog/2007/10/how-to-measure-visitor-engagement-redux.html

Rice, R., & Atkin, C. (2002). Communication campaigns: Theory, design, implementation, and evaluation, in J. Bryant and D. Zillmann (Eds.), *Media effects: Advances in theory and research.* (pp. 427–452). Hillsdale, NJ: Lawrence Erlbaum.

Rossi, P. H., Lipsey, M. W., & Freeman, H. E. (2003). *Evaluation: A systematic approach* (7th ed.). Newbury Park, CA: Sage.

Scoble, R. (2006). New audience metric needed: Engagement. Retrieved October 13, 2008, from http://scobleizer.com/2006/10/25/new-audience-metric-needed-engagement/

Tellis, G. J., & Ambler, T. (1998). *The Sage handbook of advertising.* Reading MA: Addison-Wesley.

Weiner, M. (1995, March). Put client "values" ahead of newsclips when measuring PR. *PR Services,* 48.

Wiener, N. (1954). *The human use of human beings: Cybernetics and society* (2nd ed.). Boston: Houghton Mifflin.

Xavier, R., Johnston, K., Petel, A., Watson, T., Simmons, P. (2005, September). Using evaluative techniques and performance claims to demonstrate public relations impact: An Australian Perspective. *Public Relations Review, 31*(3) pp. 417–424.

Appendixes

Ayles, C. B., & Bosworth, C. C. (2002, Summer). Campaign excellence: A survey of Silver Anvil award winners compares current PR practice with planning, campaign theory. *Public Relations Strategist.*

Babbie, E. (2006). *The practice of social research* (11th ed.). Belmont, CA: Wadsworth.

Clymer, A. (2001, July 22). The nation: Wrong number; the unbearable lightness of public opinion polls. *New York Times*.

Edmunds, H. (2000). *The focus group research handbook.* Lincolnwood, IL: NTC Business.

Fink, A. (2002a). *The survey kit: 2. How to ask survey questions.* (2nd ed.). Thousand Oaks, CA: Sage.

Fink, A. (2002b). *The survey kit: 6. How to sample in surveys.* (2nd ed.). Thousand Oaks, CA: Sage.

Fletcher, A. D., & Bowers, T. A. (1991). *Fundamentals of advertising research* (4th ed.). Belmont, CA: Wadsworth.

Haskins, J., & Kendrick, A. (1993). *Successful advertising research methods.* Lincolnwood, IL: NTC Business.

Lindenmann, W. K. (1977). Opinion research: How it works, how to use it. *Public Relations Journal, 1,* 13.

Mangione, T. W. (1995). *Mail surveys: Improving the quality.* Applied Social Research Methods Series No. 40. Thousand Oaks, CA: Sage.

Merton, R. K. (1987). The focused interview and focus groups: Continuities and discontinuities. *Public Opinion Quarterly, 51,* 550–566.

Morgan, D. L. (1997). *Focus groups as qualitative research* (2nd ed.). Qualitative Research Methods Series Vol. 16. Thousand Oaks, CA: Sage.

Rasinski, K. A. (1989). The effect of question wording on public support for government spending. *Public Opinion Quarterly, 53,* 388–396.

Rubenstein, S. M. (1995). *Surveying public opinion.* Belmont, CA: Wadsworth.

Seitel, F. P. (2006). *The practice of public relations* (10th ed.). Upper Saddle River, NJ: Prentice Hall.

Singletary, M. (1994). *Mass communication research.* White Plains, NY: Longman.

Waddell, H. (1995). Getting a straight answer: CSM scales all ask the wrong question: "How am I doing?" *Marketing Research, 7*(3), 5–8.

Wimmer, R. G., & Dominick, J. R. (2005). *Mass media research: An introduction* (8th ed.). Belmont, CA:Wadsworth.

Yin, R. K. (1994). *Case study research: Design and methods* (2nd ed.). Applied Social Research Methods Series No. 5. Thousand Oaks, CA: Sage.

Yin, R.K. (2002). *Case study research: Design and methods* (3rd ed.). Applied Social Research Methods Series No. 5. Thousand Oaks, CA: Sage.

Zeuschner, R. (2002). *Communicating today: The essentials.* Boston: Allyn & Bacon.

Index

N

O